THE
MAGDALEEN VAN WYK

COMPLETE
SOUTH AFRICAN
COOKBOOK

THE
MAGDALEEN VAN WYK
COMPLETE
SOUTH AFRICAN
COOKBOOK

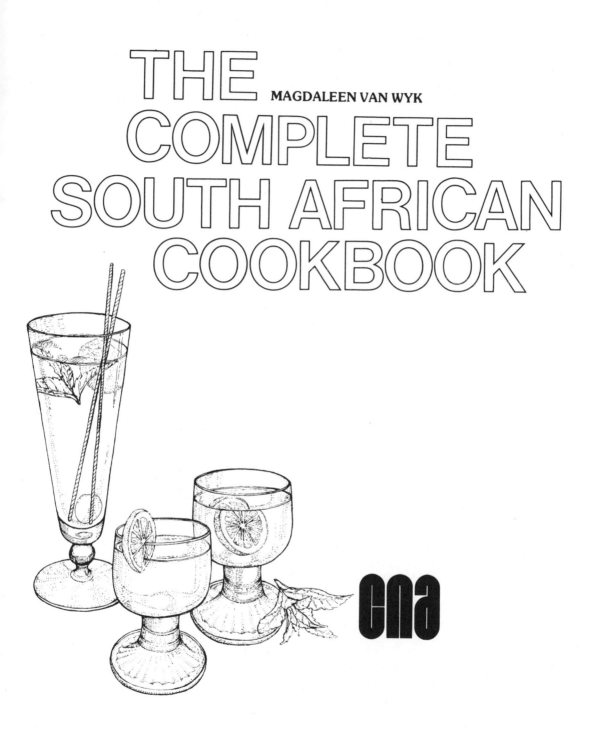

cna

CENTRAL NEWS AGENCY LTD
CNA Building, Laub Street, New Centre,
Johannesburg, 2001

Reg. No.: 01/02033/06

© Magdaleen van Wyk, Stellenbosch, 1980

First Edition 1980
Second Impression 1981
Third Impression 1984
Fourth Impression 1985
Fifth Impression 1986
Sixth Impression 1987
Seventh Impression 1988

Designed by Wim Reinders, Cape Town
Photoset by McManus Bros (Pty) Ltd, Cape Town
Lithographic reproduction colourplates by Hirt & Carter (Pty) Ltd,
Cape Town
Line sketches by Nicci Page, Cape Town
Photography by Lennart Osbeck, Cape Town
Printed and bound by National Book Printers, Goodwood

ISBN 0 620 04356 3

PREFACE

The idea for a book such as this has been at the back of my mind for a long time: one that would present the basic principles of cookery and that would cater for South African tastes. From the start I envisaged a comprehensive, up-to-date household companion that would meet the needs of beginners as well as experts, of traditionalists as well as of the adventurous, of vegetarians as well as of meat-eaters. In view of this, simplicity, economy and South African eating habits were my guide-lines in making the selection.

My initial selection ran to over a thousand recipes, and perhaps the most difficult task was to decide what to leave out. In the end I chose some 650 recipes, all of them tested and many of them firm favourites, and added many variations. I offer them here in the hope that this book will be both practical and exciting.

While my original idea seemed simple enough, its execution was so complex that without the help and advice of a great number of people, mine would have been an impossible task. But one person, above all others, deserves my special thanks: Pat Barton, who helped to weed out, check and recheck the ingredients, who undertook the demanding task of typing it all out and then read the proofs. At every step, she was there providing support and encouragement.

Magdaleen van Wyk
Stellenbosch, 1979

TABLE OF CONTENTS

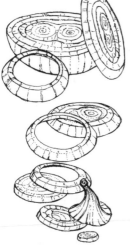

How to use this book

WEIGHTS AND MEASURES

Metrication of recipes

At first glance, to those of us who grew up in the age of imperial measures, metricised quantities for ingredients in recipes may look strange, but all that has changed is that the volume of liquids and dry ingredients is now expressed directly in units of volume (millilitres and litres) instead of by using special unit names such as teaspoon, tablespoon, cup and so on.

In this book, all liquids are given in millilitres (ml) and litres. Small quantities of dry ingredients are also given in millilitres and where this is done, the measures previously used are given in brackets: for instance 25 ml (2 tablespoons). Quantities of dry ingredients large enough to be weighed are given in grams.

How to weigh and measure

Use a reliable *kitchen scale* to weigh larger quantities of dry ingredients and such things as meat, fish and poultry.

Measuring cups for dry ingredients are now available in sets of four volumes: 25 millilitres, 50 millilitres, 100 millilitres and 250 millilitres. To measure dry ingredients with these measuring cups, scoop up a cupful, taking care not to press the contents tightly into the measure, then scrape the top with the edge of a knife to even it.

Measuring spoons with a level volume of 1 millilitre, 2 millilitres, 5 millilitres and 12,5 millilitres respectively are used to measure small quantities of both dry and liquid ingredients.

Use a transparent ovenproof glass or plastic *measuring cup,* graduated from 50 millilitres to 250 millilitres in 10 millilitre divisions, for measuring liquids *only.* Remember to read off the correct amount at eye-level, not from the top.

Approximate metric volume equivalents used in this book

¼ teaspoon	= 1 ml	1 tablespoon	= 12,5 ml
½ teaspoon	= 2 ml	2 tablespoons	= 25 ml
1 teaspoon	= 5 ml	3 tablespoons	= 37,5 ml
2 teaspoons	= 10 ml	4 tablespoons	= 50 ml
3 teaspoons	= 15 ml		
4 teaspoons	= 20 ml		

¼ cup	= 60 ml	1 cup	= 250 ml
½ cup	= 125 ml	2 cups	= 500 ml
¾ cup	= 190 ml	3 cups	= 750 ml

Note: Metric quantitites, both ml and g, are NOT exact equivalents of the imperial measurements but have been adjusted so that they can be gauged with the new kitchen measures.

Metric conversions for pressure cookers

100 kPa = 15 lbs pressure per square inch
70 kPa = 10 lbs pressure per square inch
35 kPa = 5 lbs pressure per square inch

Approximate mass and volume equivalents of recipe ingredients

Ingredient	Volume in ml													
	1	2	5	7	10	12,5	20	25	37,5	50	100	150	200	250
Breadcrumbs (dry)						6		12		25	50		100	120
Butter and margarine			5			10		20		50	90	140	180	230
Cheese; grated (Cheddar & sweetmilk)						5		10		20	40	60	80	100
Cheese; cottage & cream						12,5		25		50	100	150	200	250
Cheese; Gruyère & Roquefort						6		12		25	50	70	100	120
Cocoa			2		4	5		10		20	40	60	80	100
Coconut			1,5		3	5		8		15	30	50	70	80
Coffee (instant)			1,5		3	4		7		15	30	40	60	70
Cornflour					5	6		12	20	25	50	70	100	120
Curry powder	0,5	1	2,5		5	7		15		25	50	80	100	130
Flour; cake & bread					5	6		12	20	25	50	70	100	120
Gelatine	0,6	1	3		6	8	12	15		30				150
Milk powder (fat-free)			2,5	5	6	10			20			100		
Rice			3		8	10		20		40	80	120	160	200
Salt	1	2	5	8	11	15		30		60	110	170	220	280
Self-raising flour			3	4	5,5	7		15		30	60	90	110	140
Sugar; castor			4		8	10		20		40	80	125	170	210
Sugar; granulated, brown & yellow			4		8	10		20		40	80	120	160	200
Sugar; icing						7		15		25	50	80	100	130
Yeast; compressed	0,85	1,5	4		8	10	15			40				210

Mass in grams

Note: Reprinted with the permission of the South African Bureau of Standards.

Abbreviations and symbols

The following abbreviations and symbols are used in this book:

kg	=	kilogram	kPa	=	kilopascal
g	=	gram	kJ	=	kilojoules
mg	=	milligram	°C	=	degree Celsius
ml	=	millilitre	°F	=	degree Fahrenheit
cm	=	centimetre	min	=	minute(s)
mm	=	millimetre			

Note: *hour* and *litre* are not abbreviated.

Oven temperatures

°C	°F	Gas	Oven	°C	°F	Gas	Oven
100	200			200	400		Hot
120	250	¼ – ½	Very cool				
140	275			220	425	5	Very hot
150	300	1	Cool	230	450	6	Extremely hot
160	325	2	Moderately cool	240	475		
				260	500	7 to 8	
180	350	3	Moderate	280	550		
190	375	4	Moderately hot				

Position in oven

Position	Electricity		Gas	
	Temperature	Foods	Temperature	Foods
Near the top	Hot to very hot	Small cakes, sponge cakes, shallow tarts. Dishes that need quick browning.	Hot to very hot	Small cakes, sponge cakes, shallow tarts. Dishes that need quick browning.
Centre	Cooler	Large cakes, fruit pies, casseroles. All dishes that need a longer baking period.	Cooler	Large cakes, fruit pies, casseroles. All dishes that need a longer baking period.
Near the bottom	Hot to moderately hot	Small cakes, sponge cakes, shallow tarts. All dishes that need quick baking but not browning.	Cool (see note below)	Foods which need very slow baking.

Note:
- Read the instructions for your make of stove to find out which position in the oven will be right for a particular dish – the above is intended only as a general guide.
- Never over-pack a conventional oven, as uneven baking will result.
- Gas ovens that have a burner at the bottom will have the same temperature near the bottom as electric stoves.

13

Temperatures for deep-fat frying

Temperature at sea-level		Time it takes to brown a cube of bread, 2 cm x 2 cm	Fry at this temperature for:
°C	°F		
175-185	347-365	40-55 seconds	Raw food; food that is crumbed or coated with batter; dough and batter mixtures
185-190	365-374	30-40 seconds	Croquettes; small pieces of raw food; cooked food
195-200	383-400	20 seconds	Potato chips

Other useful temperatures

°C	°F	
−18	0	Storage of frozen goods
0	32	Freezing point at sea-level
1	33,8	Storage of fresh fish
2	35,6	Storage of fresh meat and poultry
5-7	41-44,6	Storage of other refrigerated goods
8-10	46-50	Storage of fresh vegetables
37	98,4	Proving temperature for goods made with yeast
76	168,8	Coagulation of eggs
100	212	Boiling point at sea-level
160	320	Sugar for glazing
170	338	Caramelisation of sugar

HOW TO USE THE RECIPES

1. Read the recipe through carefully, bearing in mind the following:
   - the 'preparation time' is the *estimated* time that it will take you to prepare the ingredients for cooking, e.g. chopping, dicing, grating, etc. It also includes the time that you will be *actively* involved – for example in making sauces – and may overlap with the cooking time.
   - the 'cooking time' is the *estimated* total cooking time for that dish, which may or may not include your active attendance.
   - kilojoule values are *approximate*.
   - the symbol (F) after the name of a dish indicates that it is suitable for freezing and (f) in the instructions indicates the point at which it should be frozen. General freezing instructions for each section are given in the lead-in.
   - the **note** gives important supplementary information and hints.
   - the **variations** give ideas for ringing the changes.

2. Make a brief timetable, listing the tasks and giving the order in which you have to perform them. These can be ticked off as they are completed.
3. Assemble all the ingredients, measuring or weighing them as meticulously as possible, before you start.
4. Get together all the equipment you will need and set the oven if you will be using it.
5. Prepare the dish, following the instructions carefully.

HERBS, SPICES AND SEASONINGS

Allspice The fruit of a West Indian tree, the flavour of which resembles a mixture of all spices, particularly cinnamon, nutmeg and cloves. Use for meat (stews, mince dishes), vegetables and in wine sauces, rich fruit or spice cakes.

Angelica An aromatic plant from Europe. The young, tender leaf stalks are candied and used in cakes and puddings, often for decoration.

Aniseed Grown in the Mediterranean areas, Switzerland and Germany, aniseed is used to flavour sweets, syrups, rusks and bread.

Basil An aromatic sweet herb from India, used with lamb and to flavour salads.

Bay leaves The leaves of the laurel tree, which have a very strong flavour and are used to flavour soups, stews, pickles, bobotie and fish dishes.

Capers The flower buds of the caper bush, which are dried and preserved in vinegar and brine and used with fish and seafood.

Caraway seeds The small dark-brown seeds of an aromatic plant grown in the European countries, used in baking (rusks, seed cakes) and liqueurs.

Chervil An aromatic herb whose leaves are used in soups and salads.

Chilli The small fruit pods of a pungent plant, used fresh or dried (cayenne pepper when ground), and having a very strong flavour. Used particularly to flavour meat dishes (chilli con carne), fish and vegetables.

Chives A plant resembling young spring onions, with a similar taste, used for salads, soups, sauces and dips.

Cinnamon The inner bark of the young wood of the cinnamon tree, which comes from tropical Asia. It is used in stick and ground form in cakes, pancakes, sweet fruit pies (apple tart) and sweet sauces.

Cloves The dried flower buds of the clove tree, grown in Zanzibar and the East Indies, which is used for meat (baked ham), in stews and chutneys.

Coriander The seed of the coriander plant, used in curry powder and with meat (boerewors, dried sausage and biltong).

Fennel Looks rather like a bulbous celery plant and has a flavour reminiscent of aniseed. Used with vegetables and in salads.

Garlic Bulbous plant with a pungent flavour, used in meat and fish dishes, or with salads and vegetables.

Ginger The root of a perennial reedlike plant, grown in tropical countries. Used fresh or dried and ground, the young roots may also be candied or preserved in syrup. Use in sweets, baking, and sweet and sour meat dishes.

Horseradish A long stem-type root plant, used either fresh, dried or pickled, but always minced; it is particularly tasty with roast meats (beef, lamb).

Mace Thin, red strips from the outer casing of the nutmeg, used in meat stews and rissoles, cream sauces for vegetables and in cakes and pastry to obtain a rich golden colour.

Marjoram An aromatic sweet herb used in soups, stews and stuffings.

Mint A plant which grows in temperate climates. The leaves are used to make a sauce for roast lamb, with vegetable dishes such as peas or garlic potatoes, and added to butter with lemon juice for serving with fish.

Mustard The seed of the mustard plant, dried and ground to a powder. Prepared and used as a condiment with beef, lamb, ham, pork, curries, stews and in soups.

Nutmeg The aromatic kernel of the fruit of the nutmeg tree, usually ground and used to flavour sweet dishes, puddings, cakes, and with vegetables (cabbage and beans).

Oreganum An aromatic herb used in soups, stews and salads, particularly when tomatoes are included.

Parsley An easily grown herb with a tart taste, used as a flavouring with meat and vegetables or as a garnish.

Pepper The dried berries of the pepper plant commonly used in ground form. *Black* pepper is the whole dried berry; *white* pepper is the ripe berry with the outer husk first removed and the berry then dried. These are used in a great variety of dishes (for example, pepper steak). *Green* pepper is picked green and canned.

Paprika Produced from dried and ground large red sweet peppers and used in meat dishes (Hungarian goulash), with vegetables and salads.

Poppy seed Deep blue seeds of the poppy, used in breads and cakes.

Rosemary The leaves of an evergreen plant used either fresh or dried with meat dishes (lamb), poultry, soups (tomato) and in the dressings for salads.

Saffron The orange-red stigmas of the purple autumn crocus which is used to impart flavour and a yellow colour to rice, stuffings and meat.

Sage The silver-white dried leaves of a shrub used with meat and in stuffings for meat and poultry.

Sorrel Similar to the summer spinach plant, it lends a distinctive flavour to soups.

Tarragon A perennial aromatic herb used with meat (veal) and in sauces, pickles and vinegar.

Thyme A small-leaved garden herb used with meat (lamb), vegetables, in sauces and soups.

Turmeric Part of the pepper plant which is dried and ground to a powder and used in curry powder, bobotie and curries to impart a yellow colour.

GLOSSARY OF TERMS USED IN THIS BOOK

Bain marie A method for keeping food at a certain temperature, for example, to keep sauces at simmering point. The utensil used to do so has the same name.

Bake To cook breads, cakes, pastry, etc. in dry heat in the oven. Meat cooked in this way is *roasted*.

Bake blind To bake a pastry shell before adding the filling in cases where the filling will prevent the base from puffing up and/or will make the sides collapse, or when the filling does not require baking (method p. 311).

Baste To spoon hot liquid or fat over meat, poultry or other food to moisten it while it is cooking.

Beat To mix briskly with a spoon, wire whisk, rotary beater or electric mixer to enfold air in a mixture and make it light and smooth.

Bind To thicken soups, sauces, batters etc. by blending the ingredients with eggs, flour, cream or other thickening agents.

Blanch To place in boiling water for a short while either to loosen the skins of fruit, vegetables or nuts, or to prepare fruit and vegetables for freezing, canning or preserving.

Blend To mix ingredients together thoroughly.

Blender An electric appliance used to mix the ingredients for pâtés, purées, etc.

Boil To cook in liquid at boiling point (100°C/212°F at sea-level).

Boil down To boil a liquid vigorously, uncovered, so that it becomes concentrated.

Boiling point The temperature at which bubbles continually rise to and break over the surface of a liquid.

Bouquet garni A bunch of fresh herbs, usually bay leaf, thyme and parsley, immersed in soups, stews and casseroles while they cook to impart extra flavour.

Broil See **Grill**

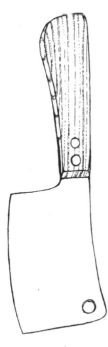

Braise To brown ingredients in a little oil or fat at a high temperature and then cook them in their own juices, with a little additional liquid, either over low heat, at boiling point or in the oven at 160°C (325°F) to 180°C (350°F).

Caramelise To melt sugar in a heavy-bottomed saucepan, stirring all the time, until it forms a golden brown syrup.

Casserole A baking dish with a fitting lid, made of glass, ceramic or unglazed earthenware (for example, Römertopf), used to cook stews. The name of the utensil is often given to the dish prepared in it; for example, chicken casserole.

Chill To place in the refrigerator until cold.

Chop To cut food into small pieces with a knife or food chopper.

Clarify (a) To clear a stock or bouillon (see p. 42); or (b) to 'clean' butter, oil or dripping (see p. 111).

Coat To cover food completely with a specific ingredient; for example, to coat meat in flour before frying it.

Coagulate To allow a mixture, for example crème caramel, to thicken or set.

Convection oven An oven using conventional dry heat to cook food, but fitted with a fan which blows hot air. The advantage is that an even temperature is maintained throughout the oven. It can be loaded to capacity and cooking times are approximately 10% to 15% shorter than in a conventional oven.

Cool To stand at room temperature until no longer warm to the touch.

Consistency The appearance and texture of a mixture.

Cream To soften and blend one ingredient or a mixture of ingredients until the soft consistency of cream is obtained.

Crockpot See **Slow cooker.**

17

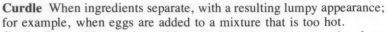

Curdle When ingredients separate, with a resulting lumpy appearance; for example, when eggs are added to a mixture that is too hot.

Cut in To combine dry ingredients and fat with two knives, using them like a pair of scissors.

Deep-fat frier (deep-frier) A saucepan with a loose frying-basket which can be lowered into deep fat or oil when frying food and lifted to rest on the rim to drain off the excess fat when the food is cooked.

Deep-fry To cook in deep, hot fat until crisp and golden.

Dice To cut into small, even cubes.

Dilute To make less concentrated by adding a liquid, such as water.

Double boiler A combination of two saucepans, one fitting inside the other, which is used to prepare food that requires gentle cooking over simmering water; for example, sauces and lemon curd.

Dredge To cover completely with a dry substance such as flour.

Dust To coat lightly, usually with sugar or flour.

Electric deep-frier A thermostatically controlled deep-frier.

Electric frying-pan A thermostatically controlled frying-pan, which is extremely versatile: it can be used to grill steaks, make stews or bake scones and cakes. It is easy to clean and extremely economical to use.

Electric mixer An electric appliance used to mix, blend and beat which – in the larger models – has additional aids such as a shredder, mincer, liquidiser, etc.

Fermentation The chemical change that occurs when yeast is added; for example, in wine-making.

Flake To divide into small pieces with a fork.

Flan A special round baking tin, usually shallow and sometimes with fluted sides. It is lined with dough or pastry which is then either baked blind to form a case for fillings or baked with the filling. The resulting pie or tart is also termed a flan.

Fold in To lightly incorporate ingredients, that have already been beaten until light and fluffy, one into the other.

Fry To cook in a little fat or oil in a frying-pan (shallow frying). See also **Deep-fry.**

Glaze To brush with syrup or egg before or while baking to give a shine to meats, scones, fruit tarts, etc.

Grease To rub lightly with butter, margarine, fat or oil.

Grill To cook by direct heat either on the rack of a roasting pan in the oven, in a frying-pan or over hot coals.

Knead To mix ingredients with the hands until they have the desired consistency.

Lard To insert strips of bacon or fat (lardons) into lean meat such as venison with the purpose of adding flavour and moisture.

Liquidiser An electric appliance which is used to reduce fruits, vegetables etc. to a pulp or purée.

Marinade A highly-flavoured and seasoned mixture in which tougher or fibrous foods are soaked to make them more tender before cooking.

Marinate To coat with or dip in a marinade.

Microwave cooking A revolutionary cooking method, which greatly reduces cooking time. Microwaves are used to cook the food by activating the individual food particles and thus create heat. The microwave oven is particularly useful for thawing frozen food and heating left-overs.

Oven roast To cook meat or poultry by dry heat in the oven.

Parboil To pre-cook or cook partially.

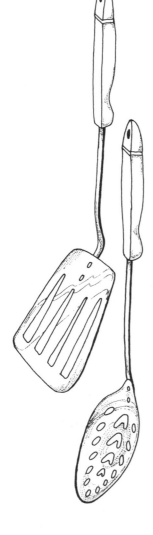

Poach To cook gently in a very little simmering liquid. The poaching liquid is often used to make a sauce to serve with the dish.

Prove To allow to rise in a warm place; term used where leavening agent has been added to the mixture.

Purée To press through a fine sieve or whirl in a liquidiser to obtain a soft, smooth, creamy mixture.

Ramekin A small earthenware dish for cooking individual portions.

Rise The change that takes place while cakes, bread, pastry etc. are baking, usually because a leavening agent has been added.

Roast To cook meat and poultry by direct heat, either over the open coals or in the oven.

Roux The combination of a fat, usually butter, and flour over a low heat as the first step to making a sauce (see p. 177).

Roll out To roll dough with a rolling pin until it is the desired shape and thickness.

Rub in To mix butter, margarine or other fat and flour together with the fingertips until the mixture resembles breadcrumbs; for example, when making scones or short pastry.

Sauté To fry lightly in a little oil or fat, shaking the pan often to ensure that the food is browned evenly.

Scald To heat milk to just below boiling point, usually in a double boiler, to prevent scorching.

Score To make evenly spaced cuts in meat, fat or other foods with a knife, either to allow flavouring to penetrate or to prevent the skin from bursting.

Sear To brown the surface of meat quickly over high heat to seal in the juices.

Season To add salt and pepper.

Shallow frying See **Fry.**

Sift To put food through a sieve.

Simmer To cook steadily in liquid at just below boiling point, with tiny bubbles rising occasionally to the surface.

Slotted spoon A metal spoon with evenly spaced cuts in the bowl, which is used to skim stocks, soups and gravies or to drain food deep-fried in fat or oil.

Slow cooker A thermostatically controlled electric cooker, generally used for soups, stews and other dishes that require long, slow simmering.

Soufflé dish A large or small straight-sided round dish used to make hot or cold soufflés. It is usually ceramic or made of ovenproof glass.

Spatula A flat flexible implement with a handle, used to loosen food, turn omelettes, etc. Wooden or plastic spatulas are used with non-stick frying-pans.

Sponging The fermenting of yeast with flour.

Steam To cook food in vapour over boiling water.

Steep To allow food to stand in a hot liquid to extract the colour or flavour.

Stew To cook food in liquid at, or just below, boiling point. This method is generally used when ingredients are tough or hard.

Strain To remove solid particles from a liquid by pouring it through a fine-mesh strainer or sieve.

Stir To mix with a circular motion until all the ingredients are blended well.

Stir fry To fry quickly in a very hot pan, tossing all the time; for example, preparing chow mein and chop suey.

Toss To turn vigorously, so that the food is completely coated; for example, when stir frying vegetables.

Whip To beat vigorously, in order to thicken.

Whisk To beat rapidly with a wire whisk, rotary beater or electric mixer to incorporate air; for example, egg whites.

MENU-PLANNING

Good nutrition is the basis of good health and the old adage 'we are what we eat' is largely true. Because the body has only a limited capacity for storing nutrients except for what it stores as fat, it needs most nutrients daily, in balanced amounts, throughout our lifespan although not all people need these nutrients in the same quantities. Growing children and pregnant women, for example, need more of some nutrients than other people.

One would think that these individual needs would create problems in menu-planning, but fortunately it is possible to satisfy all the requirements of each person by selecting a balanced diet from readily available foods. All the essential nutrients are provided by a diet composed of meats, fish, legumes, milk and dairy products, eggs, fruit and vegetables, cereals and whole grain products.

As foods are used (burned or oxidised) in the body, so they provide *energy* which makes possible our daily activities as well as the vital functions such as respiration, cardiovascular activity and the maintenance of muscle tone. The energy value of foods is expressed in kilojoules (calories).

Only three nutrients yield energy when oxidised: carbohydrates, fats and protein. Carbohydrates and protein yield 17 kJ (4 calories) per gram and fats yield 37 kJ (9 calories) per gram. Foods differ in kilojoule value because the amount of carbohydrates, protein, fats and water they contain differs. For example, water contains no kilojoules, therefore foods that contain a high proportion of water, such as lettuce, spinach and tomatoes are low in kilojoules.

Depending on age, size, sex, and what they do, individuals differ in their energy needs, but regardless of what they eat, excess kilojoules are converted into fat by the body and stored. To lose weight you must eat fewer kilojoules than the body needs, thereby forcing it to find energy by burning the stored fat.

Proteins are essential in the diet of all age groups for the building and repair of body tissues and to produce many biological substances, including some hormones and enzymes. They are especially important during periods when new tissues are being formed, such as growth, pregnancy and recovery from illness. The body does not store much protein and it needs to be replenished daily.

Food proteins differ in composition and, although everybody needs all proteins for rebuilding of tissues, some foods are particularly good sources of proteins for body building and growth; for example milk, meat, eggs, fish, nuts and soybeans.

Carbohydrates include all starches and sugars. *Sugars* are present in such foods as sweets, honey, marmalade, jam, cakes, fruits and some vegetables. *Starches* occur in flour and all flour products as well as in some vegetables, for example potatoes and pumpkin. Unrefined starches – whole grain cereals and breads made from whole grain flours – add fibre to the diet as well as essential vitamins and minerals.

Fats are important for the production of energy and for the absorption of fat-soluble vitamins. They are found in butter, cream, oil and lard as well as the fat in meat and oil in fish.

Most foods contain at least some of the essential minerals, which are used for vital processes: iron, for instance is necessary for blood formation, and calcium for strong bones and teeth. Good sources of iron are liver, red meat, eggs and spinach, and an adequate supply of calcium is ensured by milk and all dairy products, in conjunction with vitamin D. Other essential minerals are phosphorus, iodine, magnesium and potassium.

Vitamins, essential to health and well-being, are divided into two groups on the basis of solubility: those that are fat-soluble and those that are water-soluble.

Vitamin	Food sources
Water-soluble: vitamin C (Ascorbic acid)	citrus fruits, guavas, tomatoes, potatoes, strawberries, cantaloupe, broccoli
vitamin B complex e.g. thiamin, riboflavin, niacin	whole grains, yeast, legumes, nuts, vegetables, fruits
Fat-soluble: vitamin A	yellow vegetables such as carrots, pumpkin, spinach, yellow fruit
vitamin D	fish oils, margarine, sunlight

Note: The properties of water solubility should be considered when cooking vegetables and fruits (see Cooking methods p. 198).

DAILY NUTRITIONAL REQUIREMENTS

Foods	Recommended daily intake	Portion sizes
Group 1 Foods rich in calcium: Milk, skimmed milk powder, yoghurt, buttermilk	Children – 500 ml Adults – 400 ml Pregnant and lactating women – 650 ml	
Cheese, cream cheese, cottage cheese	30 g	

Foods	Recommended daily intake	Portion sizes
Group 2 Foods rich in protein: Meat (lamb, beef, mutton, pork, venison, etc.), offal, poultry, fish	2 or more portions	Children up to 2 years: 30 g Other children and adults: 90 – 110 g, cooked weight
eggs legumes, nuts		1 (All ages) 30 g (Older children and adults)
Group 3 Foods rich in vitamins and minerals:	Choose 4 portions altogether	
Vitamin C: (raw) Guavas, pawpaw, mango, citrus fruits, strawberries, pineapple, tomatoes, cabbage, broccoli, lettuce	Choose at least 1 portion from this group	Children up to 2 years: 30 g Other children and adults: 1 fruit; 125 ml juice or 100 g vegetables
Vitamin A: Yellow peaches, apricots, pawpaw, mango, carrots, pumpkin, peas, green beans, avocado pear	Choose at least 1 portion from this group	Children up to 2 years: 30 g Other children and adults: 1 fruit; 125 ml juice or 100 g vegetables
Other vitamins and minerals: Apples, bananas, peaches, grapes, potatoes, cauliflower, onions, raisins, dried fruit, etc.	1 portion after choosing vitamin A and C sources	
Group 4 Foods rich in Carbohydrates, B – complex vitamins and minerals: Bread, rusks, cake, cereals, rice, noodles (choose the whole-grain varieties)	Choose 4 or more portions	For babies and other children, choose portions in line with their energy requirements Adults: 1 slice bread or cake 100 g cereals 100 g rice or noodles
Group 5 Foods rich in fats: Butter, margarine, oil, cream	15 g or more of one of these sources	For babies and other children, choose portions in line with their energy requirements

From information contained in *Science Writes the Menu* (2nd edition), issued by the Department of Health, Pretoria.

To plan a satisfying and attractive meal, it is important to keep several factors in mind:

● **Nutritional balance:** Consider the guide to daily nutritional needs when planning a menu. Remember not to serve more than one starch per meal and to serve a fresh vegetable or fruit at least once, and preferably twice daily. It is better to eat fruit and vegetables as a source of carbohydrate than to eat too many cakes, sweets and puddings.

● **Colour:** Because we use all our senses when we eat food, a pleasant colour combination of the different foods on the plate will stimulate the appetite. Garnishes such as parsley and fresh herbs add colour to the foods, but remember that the colours should complement each other.

● **Texture:** Vary the texture of food in one course as well as between different courses: for example, croûtons or parsley add texture to soup, and alternating cooked food with a crisp salad or serving a smooth dessert after a meal filled with raw and coarse textured foods makes the meal more interesting.

- **Flavours:** Vary bland foods with strongly-flavoured ones, but do not use too many strong flavours at the same meal. Do not serve more than one kind of curry, for example, or more than one course with the same main ingredient – both tomato soup and tomato bredie, for instance.
- **Vary the method of preparation:** Do not serve too many foods prepared in the same way at one meal: have roast foods with a fresh salad and stewed fruit for dessert, for example.
- **Alternate hot and cold courses.**

The wise shopper

Always	**Never**
plans the menu beforehand, makes a list of what to buy and sticks to it;	buys indiscriminately, on impulse or when hungry;
knows the prices of foods bought regularly;	buys the same foodstuffs irrespective of price;
checks the mass and price of different brands to buy the best value;	buys the first brand she sees, irrespective of whether it is good value for money or not;
knows the grading of meats and other foodstuffs and buys according to the quality required;	buys grades unsuitable for what she plans to make;
takes advantage of special offers, but is practical about it;	buys in bulk if she does not have sufficient storage space or only uses small quantities;
buys vegetables and fruits that are in season and therefore cheaper;	buys those vegetables and fruits that are not readily available and are therefore expensive.

HORS D'OEUVRES

Hors d'oeuvres, the first course on the menu, prepare the diner's palate for the meal that is to follow and for this reason, the choice should complement the rest of the meal. If the main course is filling, such as a roast or pasta, start with something light and cool, like a grapefruit cocktail or a mousse. Variety is also important so do not serve a liver pâté as an hors d'oeuvre when you are having liver or kidneys as the main course or, if you have something fruity as an hors d'oeuvre, do not choose fruit as a dessert.

An hors d'oeuvre may be simple or elaborate – the choice is yours – but it should always be fresh, not too filling and attractively presented. It is not an exaggeration to say that an hors d'oeuvre should please the eye as much as it should tempt the palate. A beautifully presented and carefully chosen hors d'oeuvre whets the appetite and sets the tone for an entire meal.

- Always serve fruit and fruit juices chilled in glasses. Fruit juice, in particular, must remain chilled so it is best to serve it either in tall glasses half-filled with ice cubes or perhaps in frosted wine glasses, each standing on a bed of crushed ice in a shallow bowl. To achieve a frosted effect on the glasses, dip the rims first in water or egg white and then in castor sugar. Fruit cups look appetising served in scooped-out melon or pineapple halves, and a sprig of mint on top enhances the flavour.
- Serve pâté and cold fish dishes with a garnish. Seafood cocktails, presented on shredded lettuce in glass bowls, look most attractive and keep their freshness and crispness if, just before serving, each bowl is stood in a larger bowl filled with crushed ice.
- For a change, hors d'oeuvres more usually served from one large dish can be served in individual portions: make small soufflés in ramekins for each person instead of one large soufflé and serve pâté individually moulded in small dishes.
- Have a finger bowl of warm water with a slice of lemon or rose petals floating in it at each place setting if you are serving an hors d'oeuvre that is to be eaten with the fingers.

1 Canapé spreads

1. Flaked crayfish or prawns, mixed with horseradish, chopped chives and sour cream.
2. Liver pâté topped with paprika, nutmeg and chopped black olives.
3. Ground almonds, cream cheese and smoked cheese mixed together.
4. Minced chicken, mixed with chopped sweet pickles, a pinch of curry powder and mayonnaise.
5. Tuna, flaked and mixed with sour cream and chutney.

24

6. Minced shrimps or prawns mixed with French dressing and chopped fresh dill.
7. Blue cheese mixed with cream cheese, sherry and chopped mint.
8. Minced turkey mixed with finely chopped walnuts, desiccated coconut and mayonnaise.
9. Chopped ham mixed with minced pickled onions and sliced, stuffed green olives.
10. Grated Parmesan cheese mixed with yoghurt and finely chopped chives.
11. Sliced fried chipolatas topped with minced mushrooms and tomato sauce.
12. Minced cucumber mixed with finely chopped hard-boiled egg and sour cream.
13. Rounds of French bread spread with a little mayonnaise, topped with shrimps and surrounded with a border of black caviar.

2 Appetizer tray (Hors d'oeuvres variées)

Cherry tomatoes (Serves 12)
Cut the tops off 18 small or cherry tomatoes, and remove the pulp. Combine flaked canned tuna, mayonnaise, tomato pulp and chopped chives to a stiff consistency and fill the tomato shells with it.

Cucumber slices (Serves 12)
Peel 2 medium cucumbers, cut off 5 cm from each end and scoop out the seeds. Mix finely chopped ham and minced pineapple and pack the mixture tightly into the cucumber shells. Chill in the refrigerator for 1 hour. Cut into 2,5 cm slices and serve.

Blaauwkrantz mushrooms (Serves 12)
Wash and wipe dry 12 large brown mushroom caps. Soften and cream the Blaauwkrantz cheese and fill the mushroom caps with it.

Stuffed celery (Serves 12)
Wash 3 celery stalks and cut each into 4 equal lengths. Mix cream cheese and a little curry powder and stuff the lengths of celery with it.

Avocados
Toss diced avocado pear in mayonnaise with finely chopped walnuts and a little lemon juice.

Smoked salmon
Toss coarsely chopped smoked salmon with finely chopped parsley and lemon juice.

Pickled ham
Toss finely chopped ham with finely chopped gherkins and capers in a vinaigrette dressing (recipe 408).

Smoked sausages
Thinly sliced salami, garlic sausage, teewurst and other smoked sausages, topped with capers.

Beetroot and apples
Toss beetroot cubes and apple cubes in a vinaigrette dressing (recipe 408) and top with finely chopped chives.

Radishes

Toss crisp, fresh radishes in melted butter and salt.

New potatoes

Toss boiled new potatoes in Sauce Aioli (p.187) with finely chopped parsley and chives.

Broad beans

Toss canned broad beans in vinaigrette dressing (recipe 408) with raw sliced onions, finely chopped parsley and garlic.

Shrimps

Boil and shell shrimps, then toss them in vinaigrette dressing (recipe 408) with grated lemon rind and finely chopped green pepper.

Note: When greasing pans or moulds, use butter for hot dishes and oil for cold, because butter stiffens and sticks when chilled.

---

3 Greek appetizers (Meze)

Arrange the following on a large platter:
Black olives
Feta cheese wedges
Stuffed eggs (recipe follows)
Pickled mushrooms (recipe follows)
Taramasalata (recipe follows)

Stuffed eggs

12 hard-boiled eggs, shelled	**25 ml vinegar**
125 ml (½ cup) cooked beetroot, minced	**65 ml mayonnaise**
20 ml (4 teaspoons) capers, minced	**salt and pepper**
37,5 ml (3 tablespoons) parsley, chopped	Garnish:
	whole capers

1. Halve the eggs and remove and set aside the yolks. Cut a thin slice from the end of each half so that it will stand on end.
2. In a small bowl, combine the egg yolks with the rest of the ingredients, except the whole capers, and beat until smooth.
3. Spoon the mixture into the halved egg whites and top each with a whole caper.

Pickled mushrooms

450 g small mushrooms	**2 bay leaves**
65 ml salad oil	**pinch oreganum**
37,5 ml lemon juice	**2 ml (½ teaspoon) salt**
1 clove garlic, halved	**pinch black pepper**

1. Remove the stems from the mushrooms. Dry the caps with a paper towel and place them in a jar.
2. Combine the remaining ingredients in a saucepan and bring to the boil. Remove from the stove and allow to cool.
3. Pour the mixture over the mushrooms in the jar, cover and refrigerate for at least 2 days, shaking occasionally.
4. To serve, pour off the liquid and place the mushrooms on the serving dish.

Taramasalata (F)

220 g red caviar (tarama)
1 onion, minced
juice of 2 lemons
5 slices white bread, crusts removed

hot water
250 ml olive oil
Garnish:
olives
chopped parsley

1. Liquidise the caviar, onion and lemon juice in a blender.
2. Dip the bread in hot water, squeeze dry and break into small pieces. Add to the caviar mixture, blending well.
3. Add the olive oil and whirl in the blender until there is no visible oil left (f).
4. Garnish with chopped parsley and olives, and serve with crusty French bread.

Note: These quantities will serve 12 people.

---

4 Antipasto

Serves 6; kJ per portion 400; Prep time 30 min.

170 g canned white meat tuna, flaked and combined with 60 g boiled rice, a little oil, vinegar and 1 ml (¼ teaspoon) each of salt and pepper
8 flat fillets of anchovies
8 rolled anchovies
120 g raw button mushrooms
pickled beetroot, diced

8 pickled onions
3 hard-boiled eggs, sliced
1 green pepper, seeded and diced
4 tomatoes, thinly sliced
8 sardines
6 green olives
6 black olives
120 g cooked chicken, diced

1. Arrange the tuna mixture and the other ingredients in rows on a long, oblong serving dish.
2. Serve at once.

---

5 Stuffed tomatoes

4 large tomatoes
60 g Cheddar cheese, grated
2 hard-boiled eggs, finely chopped
2 young carrots, finely grated
2 ml (½ teaspoon) salt
2 ml (½ teaspoon) pepper
a little mayonnaise
shredded lettuce
Garnish:
finely chopped parsley

Serves 4; kJ per portion 300; Prep time 20 min.

1. Halve the tomatoes and scoop out the pulp.
2. Combine the pulp with the carrots, cheese, eggs and half the salt and pepper. Stir in a little mayonnaise.
3. Sprinkle the inside of the tomato cases with the remaining salt and pepper, then pile the pulp mixture into them.
4. Line an oblong serving dish with lettuce and place the tomato cases on top. Sprinkle with the parsley and serve.

---

6 Egg mayonnaise

4 hard-boiled eggs, shelled and halved lengthwise
75 ml mayonnaise
pinch crushed red peppers or chillis
2 ml (½ teaspoon) salt
2 ml (½ teaspoon) pepper
Garnish:
lemon wedges

Serves 4; kJ per portion 510; Prep time 15 min.

1. Shake the mayonnaise, chillis, salt and pepper in a screw-top jar.
2. Place 2 egg halves, cut side down, on each of 4 plates, pour a little of the mayonnaise over them and serve with a lemon wedge.

Note: If the mayonnaise is too thick, dilute it with a few drops of lemon juice.

27

250 g baked ham, thinly sliced
50 ml (4 tablespoons) parsley,
finely chopped
Filling:
500 g cooked chicken, minced
50 ml (4 tablespoons) canned
pineapple, finely chopped
65 ml mayonnaise
125 ml double cream
2 ml (½ teaspoon) curry
powder
1 ml (¼ teaspoon) black
pepper
2 ml (½ teaspoon) salt

7 Ham cones

Serves 4;   kJ per portion 750;   Prep time 20 min.

1. Cut each slice of ham diagonally into two triangles. Roll into cones and set aside.
2. Combine the filling ingredients in a bowl.
3. Spoon some of the filling into each ham cone.
4. Place the chopped parsley on a plate and dip the top of each cone into the parsley, coating it well.
5. Place all the cones on a large serving dish and serve at once.

---

250 g cooked chicken, minced
120 g cooked ham, minced
1 small onion, finely chopped
15 cm piece cucumber, peeled
and grated
12,5 ml (1 tablespoon) butter
or margarine
25 ml (2 tablespoons) flour
10 ml mint sauce
12,5 ml (1 tablespoon)
powdered gelatine
150 ml single cream, whipped
25 ml water; 375 ml milk
1 ml (¼ teaspoon) salt
1 ml (¼ teaspoon) pepper
Garnish:
sliced cucumber

8 Chicken and ham mousse

Serves 4-6;   kJ per portion 850;   Prep time 30 min;   Cooking time 10 min.

1. In a large saucepan, sauté the onion in the butter or margarine until tender but not brown, then stir in the flour and cook for 1 minute, stirring all the time.
2. Remove the saucepan from the stove and gradually stir in the milk.
3. Return the saucepan to the stove and bring to the boil, stirring.
4. Boil for 1 minute, then remove from the stove.
5. Stir in the grated cucumber, chicken, ham, mint sauce and seasoning.
6. In a large bowl, dissolve the gelatine in the water over a pan of hot water.
7. Stir in the chicken mixture and allow to cool slightly.
8. Stir in the cream, then pour the mixture into a serving dish or a wet mould to set.
9. When set, either garnish with sliced cucumber and serve, or turn out of the mould before garnishing.

Note: The mould can be sprayed with a non-stick spray instead of being rinsed with water.

---

400 g canned salmon, drained
2 egg yolks, beaten
250 ml (1 cup) celery, coarsely
chopped
125 ml (½ cup) cucumber,
seeded and puréed
5 ml (1 teaspoon) powdered
horseradish
125 ml vinegar
65 ml cold water; 12,5 ml milk
190 ml whipped cream
12,5 ml (1 tablespoon)
powdered gelatine
25 ml (2 tablespoons) sugar
5 ml (1 teaspoon) prepared
mustard
5 ml (1 teaspoon) salt

9 Salmon mousse

Serves 8;   kJ per portion 1 050;   Prep time 1 hour;   Cooking time 15 min.

1. Soften the gelatine in the cold water. Set aside.
2. Mix the sugar, salt and mustard together in a bowl.
3. Place this mixture in the top half of a double boiler, and stir in the vinegar and egg yolks. Cook over boiling water until thick, stirring all the time.
4. Remove from the stove and add the gelatine, stirring until dissolved.
5. Combine the horseradish powder and the milk in a small bowl and stir into the gelatine mixture. Chill until the mixture begins to thicken.
6. Stir in the salmon, celery and cucumber, then fold in the whipped cream. Turn into individual ramekins or moulds and chill until firm.
7. Serve either in the dishes or unmoulded, with a green salad.

Variations:
1. Use canned light meat tuna instead of the salmon.
2. Use canned crabmeat instead of the salmon.
3. Use minced smoked oysters instead of the salmon.

400 g (2 small tins) salmon
2 eggs, hard-boiled
12,5 g onion, finely chopped
250 ml mayonnaise
250 ml whipped cream
150 ml cold water; tabasco
sauce
cochineal
1 envelope gelatine
Garnish:
Sliced cucumber, fresh dill or
chervil

10 Simple salmon mousse

Serves 8;   kJ per portion 1 000;   Prep time 45 min.

1. Combine thoroughly the fish, eggs and onion.
2. Dissolve the gelatine in the cold water and then place over a pot of hot water.
3. Allow the dissolved gelatine to cool, then add it to the fish mixture and stir in the mayonnaise.
4. Add 3 drops cochineal and 3 drops tabasco sauce and blend well to give the salmon a uniform delicate pink colour.
5. Lightly grease a mould and fold the salmon mixture into it, then place in the refrigerator for 2 to 2½ hours, or till needed.
6. To serve, turn the mousse out of its mould onto a bed of crisp lettuce. Garnish with thinly sliced cucumber, or sprays of fresh dill or chervil.

Note: If you have difficulty turning the salmon mousse out of its mould you can immerse the mould in hot water for a moment or give the base of the mould a few sharp taps with the butt of a knife.

---

150 g smoked snoek, flaked
250 g homogenised skimmed
milk cheese
25 ml (2 tablespoons) butter or
margarine
10 ml (2 teaspoons) onion,
minced
10 ml (2 teaspoons) powdered
gelatine
125 ml very hot water
1 ml (¼ teaspoon) freshly
ground black pepper
Garnish:
cucumber slices
watercress

11 Snoek mousse

Serves 4;   kJ per portion 750;   Prep time 30 min;   Cooking time 5 min.

1. Melt the butter or margarine in a small frying-pan and sauté the onion until tender but not brown.
2. Combine the onion, flaked snoek and cheese in a large bowl.
3. Dissolve the gelatine in hot water, then beat it into the snoek and cheese mixture. Stir in the pepper.
4. Pour the mixture into a 500 g loaf tin, rinsed with cold water, and stand in a cool place until the mousse has set.
5. Turn the mousse out onto a serving dish and garnish with cucumber slices and watercress. Serve at once.

Note: The mousse can also be set in a fish mould. Spray the mould well with a non-stick spray to make it easier to turn out.

---

500 g chicken livers
250 g fresh mushrooms, finely
chopped
1 large green pepper, seeded
and finely chopped
1 small onion, finely chopped
200 g butter, margarine or
225 ml oil
125 ml dry white wine or
sherry
1 clove garlic, minced
1 ml (¼ teaspoon) dill seeds
4 drops hot pepper sauce
5 ml (1 teaspoon) salt

12 Chicken liver pâté with wine   (F)

Makes 750 ml; kJ per portion 600; Prep time 30 min; Cooking time 15 min.

1. Melt 62,5 ml (5 tablespoons) of the butter, margarine or oil in a frying-pan and sauté the liver, mushrooms, green pepper and onion in it for 5 minutes.
2. Add the wine or sherry, garlic, dill seeds, salt and hot pepper sauce and simmer, covered, until the chicken livers and mushrooms are very tender, about 10 minutes. Remove from the stove.
3. Allow the mixture to cool slightly, then place in a blender with the rest of the butter, margarine or oil and blend until smooth.
4. Pack the pâté tightly in an earthernware crock and chill for at least 3 hours before use (f).

Variation: Use smooth skimmed milk cheese instead of the butter or margarine and the wine or sherry. Then use oil to sauté the livers, mushrooms, green pepper and onion.

Note: The flavours of the pâté blend better if it is left for a day or two before use.

29

13 Roquefort mousse

500 g Roquefort cheese, crumbled
250 ml single cream
375 ml double cream, beaten until thick but not stiff
25 ml (2 tablespoons) powdered gelatine, dissolved in 50 ml hot water
10 ml vegetable oil
2 ml (½ teaspoon) ground cinnamon
Garnish:
finely chopped parsley

Serves 4-6; kJ per portion 750; Prep time 45 min.

1. Grease 8 individual serving dishes with the oil and set them upside down on absorbent paper to drain.
2. With the back of a wooden spoon rub the cheese through a fine sieve into an ovenproof dish.
3. Gradually add the single cream, beating all the time.
4. Place the bowl over a saucepan half-filled with hot water, add the cinnamon and stir until the mixture is smooth and creamy. Remove the bowl from the saucepan, allow to cool for 10 minutes, then chill for 1 hour.
5. Remove the cheese mixture from the refrigerator and with a metal spoon fold in the double cream and dissolved gelatine.
6. Spoon equal amounts of the cheese mixture into the serving dishes and chill until the mousse is firm, about 1 hour.
7. Just before serving, remove the dishes from the refrigerator and run a knife around the edge of each mousse. Turn out onto plates and serve at once, garnished with chopped parsley.

Variation: Use Blaauwkrantz or Gorgonzola cheese instead of Roquefort.

Note:
- This mousse may be served as a savoury after the meal instead of dessert.
- Dishes may be sprayed with a non-stick spray instead of being greased.

14 Chopped liver

350 g chicken livers
3 hard-boiled eggs
1 medium onion, finely chopped
chicken fat
5 ml (1 teaspoon) salt
1 ml (¼ teaspoon) black pepper
Garnish:
egg worked through a sieve
sliced, pickled cucumber

Serves 6; kJ per portion 500; Prep time 30 min; Cooking time 10 min.

1. Melt the chicken fat in a frying-pan and sauté the chicken livers in it until tender but not completely cooked. Remove from the pan.
2. Sauté the onion in the remaining chicken fat until transparent.
3. Finely mince the livers, onion and two of the hard-boiled eggs. Place in a bowl.
4. Add a little chicken fat to give the mixture a smoother texture and then season with salt and pepper. Spread on a platter and then garnish with pickled cucumber and the remaining hard-boiled egg, finely sieved.

15 Sardine pâté (F)

240 g canned sardines, drained and mashed
85 g cream cheese, softened
1 hard-boiled egg, mashed
12,5 ml (1 tablespoon) minced onion
2 ml (½ teaspoon) lemon rind, grated
25 ml double cream
12,5 ml to 25 ml lemon juice
1 ml (¼ teaspoon) garlic salt
Garnish:
tomato slices
green pepper, finely chopped
parsley sprigs

Serves 4; kJ per portion 1 150; Prep time 25 min.

1. In a large bowl, beat together the sardines, cream cheese, lemon rind, onion and egg.
2. Add 12,5 ml of the lemon juice and all the cream, stirring constantly until a smooth consistency is obtained. Add more lemon juice if necessary.
3. Season with garlic salt (f) and serve at once, garnished with tomato slices, green pepper and parsley.

16 Pâté Provençale (F)

1 kg lean pork, minced
1 kg veal, minced
500 g pork liver, minced with 6 cloves garlic
500 g fresh spek, diced
3 eggs; bacon rashers
100 ml brandy
5 ml (1 teaspoon) dried basil
12,5 ml (1 tablespoon) salt
5 ml (1 teaspoon) black pepper
Garnish:
chopped green and red pepper

Makes ± 2 ½ kg; kJ per portion 800; Prep time 45 min; Cooking time 2 ½ hours

1. Combine the minced pork, veal, liver and garlic, and diced spek in a large bowl.
2. Beat the eggs, brandy, basil, salt and pepper together in another bowl.
3. Add to the meat mixture and blend well.
4. Press the pâté into a straight-sided casserole and top with a few rashers of bacon.
5. Cover the pâté with a sheet of foil and bake in the oven at 160°C (325°F) until done, 2 to 2½ hours, removing the foil after the first hour.
6. Remove from the oven and cool for 30 minutes, then cover with a plate or board, weigh down with a heavy object and chill for at least 2 hours (f).
7. When ready to serve, turn out on a platter and garnish with chopped red and green peppers. Serve cut in slices.

17 Haddock pâté (F)

125 g smoked haddock, cooked, boned and flaked
12,5 ml (1 tablespoon) onion, finely grated
125 g butter or margarine
5 ml lemon juice
1 ml (¼ teaspoon) curry powder
pinch chilli powder
sprinkling black pepper
Garnish:
finely chopped chives

Serves 4; kJ per portion 650; Prep time 10 min.

1. Place the fish, butter or margarine and pepper in a bowl and blend well.
2. Stir in the lemon juice, curry powder, chilli powder and onion. Place in an electric blender and blend until smooth.
3. Place the pâté in a small bowl, cover and chill for at least 2 hours (f).
4. Before serving, sprinkle the top with chopped chives and serve at once with triangles of toast or slices of fresh wholewheat bread.

Variation: 100 ml thick cream and 25 ml (2 tablespoons) butter may be used instead of 125 g butter or margarine.

Note: Wrap very well for freezing. To serve, thaw in the refrigerator for 6 hours, blend well, adding a little cream if the mixture appears dry.

18 Snoek pâté (F)

1 kg smoked snoek, flaked and bones removed
300 ml dry white wine
150 g butter or margarine
grated rind and juice of 1 lemon
250 ml whipped cream
dash vodka (optional)
freshly ground black pepper

Serves 25-30; kJ per portion 700; Prep time 20 min.

1. Combine the snoek, wine and butter or margarine in an electric blender until a smooth paste is formed, adding a little of each at a time and blending thoroughly after each addition. Stir in the lemon rind, pepper and vodka.
2. Fold in the whipped cream.
3. Transfer to an earthenware crock and chill for 2 to 3 hours before use (f).
4. Serve with Melba toast (recipe 435) or fresh wholewheat bread.

Note: Snoek pâté freezes very well. Divide into smaller quantities, wrap well or place in plastic containers with tight-fitting lids, and freeze. Before serving, thaw for 6 hours in the refrigerator and blend well.

16 canned asparagus spears, drained
Welsh Rarebit mix (recipe 423)

19 Savoury asparagus

Serves 4; kJ per portion 600; Prep time 25 min; Cooking time 10 min.

1. Place 4 asparagus spears on each of 4 individual serving dishes.
2. Top each with Welsh Rarebit mixture and place under the grill until the cheese starts to sizzle. Serve immediately.

Variations:
1. Use slices of Cheddar or other strong cheese instead of the Welsh Rarebit mix. Continue with step 2.
2. Use cheese sauce (p. 180) instead of the Welsh Rarebit mix. Top the asparagus spears with the sauce and heat in the oven at 180 °C (350 °F) for 10 minutes.

---

1 large aubergine, cut in 4 thick slices
1 medium tomato, coarsely chopped
1 large onion, finely chopped
5 ml (1 teaspoon) mixed dried herbs
125 ml (½ cup) Cheddar cheese, grated
1 ml (¼ teaspoon) garlic salt
few grains freshly ground black pepper
oil for frying

20 Aubergine hors d'oeuvre

Serves 4; kJ per portion 280; Prep time 20 min; Cooking time 20 min.

1. Sprinkle the aubergine slices with salt and leave to draw for 30 minutes. Rinse with cold water and drain on absorbent paper.
2. Heat a little oil in a frying-pan and fry the aubergine slices on both sides until lightly browned. Drain on absorbent paper and keep warm.
3. Meanwhile, heat a little oil in another frying-pan. Add the tomatoes, onion, mixed herbs, garlic salt and pepper and sauté until the onion is transparent.
4. Place the aubergine slices on a baking sheet, top each with a quarter of the onion and tomato mixture and a little grated cheese and bake in the oven at 180 °C (350 °F) until the aubergine is soft and the cheese melts, 10 to 15 minutes. Serve hot.

Crust:
250 g rich shortcrust pastry (recipe 565)
Filling:
180 g rindless bacon, finely chopped
2 eggs; 1 egg white
100 ml milk
65 ml single cream
180 g Cheddar cheese, grated
1 tomato, sliced
6 large mushrooms, thinly sliced
2 ml (½ teaspoon) salt
2 ml (½ teaspoon) pepper
chopped parsley

21 Quiche Lorraine   (F)

Serves 6; kJ per portion 1 100; Prep time 35 min; Cooking time 40 min.

1. Roll out the dough to a thickness of 3 mm and line a well-greased 20 cm quiche pan.
2. Make the filling. Beat the eggs, egg white, milk and cream together in a bowl. Stir in the salt, pepper, bacon, cheese and most of the parsley.
3. Pour the filling into the crust, add the mushrooms and layer the tomato slices on top of the filling. Sprinkle with the rest of the parsley.
4. Bake for 10 minutes at 220 °C (425 °F) then lower the heat to 180 °C (350 °F) and bake a further 10 minutes (f). Serve hot.

Note: After freezing, thaw in the refrigerator for 6 hours, then heat in the oven at 180 °C (350 °F) for 15 minutes. Note, however, that the filling might become slightly watery.

250 g chicken livers, halved
1 ml (¼ teaspoon) baking
powder
125 ml (½ cup) flour
25 ml soy sauce
12,5 ml sherry
85 ml water
2 ml (½ teaspoon) salt
dash pepper; oil for frying

22 Deep-fried chicken livers

Serves 4;   kJ per portion 800;   Prep time 35 min;   Cooking time 30 min.

1. Combine the sherry and soy sauce in a jug.
2. Place the chicken livers in a shallow dish, pour the sherry mixture over them and marinate for 30 minutes.
3. Meanwhile, combine the flour, water, baking powder, salt and pepper in a bowl to form a batter.
4. Heat the oil in a deep-frying pan. Dip each piece of chicken liver separately in the batter and fry them in the oil until golden brown.
5. Remove liver from the pan as it is done, drain on absorbent paper and keep warm.
6. When all the liver has been fried, serve on toothpicks.

Pastry:
350 g sifted flour
130 g butter or margarine
1 ml (¼ teaspoon) salt
water to bind
Filling:
300 ml thick Béchamel sauce
(p. 179)
1 thick slice baked ham, diced
120 g Gruyère or Cheddar
cheese, grated
1 egg yolk
1 ml (¼ teaspoon) salt
1 ml (¼ teaspoon) pepper

23 Ham and cheese turnovers

Serves 4;   kJ per portion 550;   Prep time 1 hour + 2 hours for dough to stand;   Cooking time 20 min.

1. To make the pastry, place the sifted flour in a mixing bowl and make a well in the centre.
2. Cut up the butter or margarine and place in the well together with the salt. Work in with the fingertips, adding just enough water to make a smooth dough. Set aside for at least 2 hours before use.
3. Meanwhile, make the filling. Prepare the Béchamel sauce and remove it from the stove.
4. Stir in the grated cheese and diced ham and season with salt and pepper.
5. Roll the pastry out thinly on a floured surface and cut out 12 rounds, 6 cm in diameter. Moisten the edges with water.
6. Place 12,5 ml (1 tablespoon) of the ham and cheese mixture on half of each round, fold the pastry over to form a halfmoon and press the edges together firmly.
7. Mix the egg yolk with 5 ml water and brush each turnover with the egg mixture.
8. Place the turnovers on a baking sheet and bake in the oven at 200 °C (400 °F) for 12 minutes. Serve very hot.

Variations:

1. Use 225 g canned creamed mushrooms instead of the ham, Béchamel sauce and cheese.
2. Use 225 g finely chopped canned asparagus instead of the ham and cheese.

Note: Any pastry that remains can be wrapped in plastic and frozen or stored in the refrigerator for up to 5 days.

Summer soups: Jellied Consommé (recipe 82), Quick Cold Pea Soup (recipe 83), Vichyssoise (recipe 84) and Gazpacho (recipe 86).

24 Mushroom vol-au-vents

4 large baked vol-au-vent cases (recipe 575)
Filling:
500 g canned creamed mushrooms
125 ml (½ cup) Cheddar cheese, grated
1 small onion, finely chopped
2 ml (½ teaspoon) salt
2 ml (½ teaspoon) pepper
oil for frying
milk or single cream if necessary

Serves 4; kJ per portion 900; Prep time 20 min; Cooking time 10 min.

1. Heat the oil in a frying-pan and sauté the onion in it until transparent.
2. Add the creamed mushrooms, cheese, salt and pepper. Simmer over low heat until the sauce starts to bubble, but do not allow it to boil. Add a little milk or single cream if the mixture is too thick.
3. Spoon the mushroom mixture into the vol-au-vent cases and serve at once.

Variations:
1. Instead of canned mushrooms, use 500 ml Béchamel sauce (p. 179) and add 100 g sautéed sliced fresh mushrooms.
2. Use 500 ml Béchamel sauce (p. 179) and 100 g canned asparagus pieces instead of the canned mushrooms.

25 Texas onion toast

4 slices bread
2 large onions, thinly sliced
grated Parmesan cheese
olive oil

Serves 4; kJ per portion 670; Prep time 15 min; Cooking time 5 min.

1. Place the slices of bread on a shallow grilling pan and drizzle olive oil over them Brown them on one side under the grill.
2. Turn the slices of bread over and top the untoasted sides with the sliced onion. Drizzle a little more oil over the onion and brown the toast under the grill.
3. Sprinkle the onion-topped toast with grated Parmesan cheese and return to the grill for a few seconds. Serve at once.

26 Sardine salad

450 g canned sardines in oil
1 medium onion, finely chopped
4 medium tomatoes, finely chopped
12 black olives, finely chopped
4 large, firm lemons
12,5 ml oil; 25 ml vinegar
Garnish:
sliced olives; parsley sprigs

Serves 4; kJ per portion 600; Prep time 20 min.

1. Cut the tops off the lemons, leaving the stalk end intact. Scoop out the pulp, discarding pith, membranes and pips, and set the shells aside. Chop the flesh very finely and place in a bowl.
2. Place the sardines in the bowl and add the chopped onion. Mash the sardines and combine thoroughly with the lemon pulp and onion.
3. Place a layer of chopped tomato at the bottom of each lemon case and top with a little oil, vinegar and chopped olives.
4. Fill each lemon case with the sardine mixture and serve topped with parsley sprigs and sliced olives.

27 Soused herrings

6 small herrings, cleaned and filleted
1 medium onion, thinly sliced, in rings
145 ml malt vinegar
145 ml cold water; 1 bay leaf
6 peppercorns; 3 whole allspice
1 whole chilli

Serves 6; kJ per portion 300; Prep time 15 min; Cooking time 1 hr

1. Lay the fillets of fish on a flat surface and scatter a few of the onion rings over each. Roll them up and secure with toothpicks.
2. Lay the rolled fillets in a flat ovenproof dish. Scatter the rest of the onion rings on top of them, as well as the bay leaf, peppercorns, allspice and whole chilli.
3. Combine the vinegar and water in a jug and pour it over the fish.
4. Cover the dish with foil and bake on the centre shelf of the oven at 160°C (325°F) for 1 hour.
5. Leave the herrings to cool overnight in their liquid before serving.

10 salt herring fillets
10 pickled gherkins
2 large onions, thinly sliced, in rings
375 ml white wine vinegar
375 ml water; 6 peppercorns
3 juniper berries (optional)
12,5 ml (1 tablespoon) mustard seed
3 whole allspice; 1 bay leaf
25 ml (2 tablespoons) mustard powder
12,5 ml (1 tablespoon) capers

28 Rollmops

Serves 4;   kJ per portion 300;   Prep time 20 min;   Cooking time 10 min.

1. Place the herring fillets in a large bowl and pour over enough water to cover. Chill for 12 hours. Drain the fillets, rinse with cold water and pat dry with absorbent paper.
2. Place the vinegar, water, peppercorns, juniper berries, mustard seed, allspice and the bay leaf in a large saucepan; cover, bring to the boil quickly. Reduce the heat to low and simmer, uncovered, for 10 minutes. Set aside to cool.
3. Lay the herring fillets out flat on a wooden board, skin sides down. Spread a little mustard powder over each and sprinkle with some of the capers.
4. Place a gherkin at the widest end of each fillet and roll up, securing with a toothpick. Set aside.
5. Place a third of the onion rings in the bottom of a large, deep dish and arrange half the rollmops on top. Repeat these layers, then place the remainder of the onion rings on top.
6. Pour the vinegar and spice mixture over the rollmops through a fine sieve and discard the contents of the sieve.
7. Cover the dish with aluminium foil and leave in the refrigerator for 1 week before serving.

Note: Prepared Bismarck herrings can also be used: Start at step 2 and leave the rollmops to marinate for 4 days only.

---

120 g cooked, shelled prawns, shrimps or diced crayfish flesh
lettuce
Dressing:
50 ml mayonnaise
12,5 ml tomato purée or sauce
5 ml Worcester sauce
25 ml double cream
2 ml (½ teaspoon) salt
2 ml (½ teaspoon) pepper
Garnish:
lemon slices

29 Seafood cocktail

Serves 4;   kJ per portion 700;   Prep time 20 min.

1. Shred the lettuce very finely and use to line 4 seafood glasses.
2. Combine the ingredients for the dressing in a bowl, then toss the prawns, shrimps or diced crayfish in it.
3. Spoon the fish mixture into the serving glasses and serve with lemon slices.

Variations:

1. Add 100 g diced mushrooms, raw or sautéed, to the seafood mixture.
2. Add 50 ml (4 tablespoons) capers to the seafood mixture.

Note: Any firm-fleshed white fish such as monkfish makes a tasty alternative to seafood.

---

120 g cream cheese
120 g cooked, shelled prawns
2 red-skinned apples
60 g toasted almonds, finely chopped
150 ml mayonnaise
juice of 1 lemon
25 ml (2 tablespoons) parsley, finely chopped
2 ml (½ teaspoon) salt
2 ml (½ teaspoon) pepper
lettuce

30 Apple and prawn cocktail

Serves 4;   kJ per portion 700;   Prep time 15 min.

1. Mould the cream cheese into small balls and coat with the nuts. Chill for 1 hour.
2. Blend the mayonnaise, parsley, salt and pepper and pass through a fine sieve or liquidise. Chill for 1 hour.
3. Core and slice apples thinly. Toss the prawns and sliced apple in the lemon juice and arrange on a bed of lettuce in 4 individual bowls.
4. Top with the cream cheese balls and pour a little mayonnaise over each. Serve at once.

500 g raw shrimps, shelled
2 eggs, beaten
3 slices canned pineapple, diced
125 ml (½ cup) flour
125 ml (½ cup) sugar
12,5 ml (1 tablespoon) cornflour
milk, if necessary
65 ml pineapple juice
75 ml vinegar; 10 ml soy sauce
1 ml (¼ teaspoon) salt
oil for deep-frying

31 Sweet and sour shrimps (F)

Serves 4; kJ per portion 1 400; Prep time 30 min; Cooking time 15 min.

1. Combine the eggs, flour and salt in a bowl to form a batter. If the consistency is too thick, stir in a little milk.
2. Heat the oil in a deep-frying pan, dip the shrimps in the batter and then fry them in the oil until they are golden brown, about 3 minutes. Drain on absorbent paper and keep warm on a heated serving dish.
3. Place the pineapple cubes, sugar, cornflour, pineapple juice, vinegar and soy sauce in a small saucepan. Simmer over low heat, stirring constantly, until the sauce has thickened.
4. Pour the sweet and sour sauce over the shrimps (f) and serve at once.

---

12 large brown mushroom caps
37,5 ml (3 tablespoons) butter or margarine, melted
12 thin slices toast, buttered and cut into rounds
12 anchovy fillets
65 ml sour cream
Garnish:
chopped parsley

32 Anchovied mushrooms

Serves 6; kJ per portion 900; Prep time 20 min; Cooking time 10 min.

1. Brush the mushroom caps on both sides with the melted butter or margarine, place them on a shallow grilling pan and grill until just tender, approximately 10 minutes.
2. Meanwhile, chop the anchovy fillets finely and combine them in a bowl with the sour cream and a little of the chopped parsley.
3. Place a grilled mushroom cap on each round of toast, top with a spoonful of the anchovy and cream mixture and garnish with a sprig of parsley. Serve at once.

---

500 g monkfish fillets, skinned
125 ml (½ cup) ham, minced
225 g spinach, cooked and minced
1 egg; 250 ml (1 cup) flour
125 ml water; 25 ml soy sauce
½ clove garlic, minced
2 ml (½ teaspoon) sesame seeds
12,5 ml ginger root, finely shredded
oil for frying
Garnish:
lemon slices

33 Stuffed fish rolls

Serves 4; kJ per portion 1 500; Prep time 35 min; Cooking time 15 min.

1. Combine the soy sauce and ginger in a shallow dish and dip the fish fillets in it, coating them completely.
2. Mix the ham, garlic and spinach together in a bowl.
3. Spread some of the ham mixture onto each fish fillet and roll it up, fastening with a toothpick.
4. In a large bowl, combine the egg, flour and water to form a batter.
5. Dip each fillet in the batter, then in the sesame seeds.
6. Heat the oil in a deep-frier and fry the fillets in it until golden brown all over, approximately 4 to 5 minutes. Serve at once with slices of lemon.

Variation: Use sole fillets instead of monkfish fillets.

290 g canned mussels in brine or fresh mussels
250 g tomatoes, skinned, seeded and finely chopped
120 g Gouda cheese, grated
1 ml (¼ teaspoon) salt

34   Mussel hors d'oeuvre

Serves 4;   kJ per portion 410;   Prep time 20 min;   Cooking time 10 min.

1. Place the mussels and brine in a large saucepan over medium heat until nearly boiling. Drain and place the mussels in a serving dish.
2. Combine the tomatoes, cheese and salt in a bowl and spread this mixture over the mussels.
3. Brown under the grill until the cheese melts, about 10 minutes, and serve at once.

Note: If using fresh mussels, clean (method p. 85), remove from shells and heat in a large saucepan with 10 ml (2 teaspoons) butter or margarine and 2 ml (½ teaspoon) salt for 10 minutes. Continue with step 2 and 3.

---

1 can snails and shells for serving
120 g butter or margarine
1 ml Worcester sauce
1 ml lemon juice
10 ml (2 teaspoons) garlic, finely chopped
10 ml (2 teaspoons) parsley, finely chopped
1 ml (¼ teaspoon) salt
1 ml (¼ teaspoon) pepper

35   Escargots

Serves 2;   kJ per portion 800;   Prep time 25 min;   Cooking time 15 min.

1. Drain the snails and rinse them well under cold running water.
2. In a small bowl, cream together the butter or margarine and the parsley, garlic, Worcester sauce, lemon juice, salt and pepper.
3. Place a little of this mixture in each shell, insert a snail and more of the mixture.
4. Place the shells in a casserole and bake in the oven at 220°C (425°F) until the butter or margarine begins to sizzle, 10 to 15 minutes.
5. Serve immediately with wafer-thin slices of brown bread.

Note: Cans of snails and the shells to serve them in are available at delicatessens and speciality grocery stores.

Crust:
500 g cheese shortcrust pastry (recipe 565)
Filling:
500 ml (2 cups) smoked snoek, flaked
3 hard-boiled eggs, finely chopped
125 ml (½ cup) Cheddar cheese, grated
1 raw egg; 250 ml milk
12,5 ml Worcester sauce
12,5 ml (1 tablespoon) parsley, finely chopped

36   Snoek pie   (F)

Serves 8;   kJ per portion 1 300;   Prep time 30 min;   Cooking time 30 min.

1. Make the pastry as directed and press it into a pie dish. Set aside.
2. Combine the snoek and hard-boiled eggs in a bowl.
3. Beat together the milk, egg and Worcester sauce and fold into the snoek mixture. Stir in the parsley.
4. Spoon the filling into the pie shell and bake in the oven at 180°C (350°F) for 30 minutes (f).
5. Sprinkle with the grated cheese and serve hot.

Variations:
1. Use Blaauwkrantz cheese instead of Cheddar cheese.
2. Make individual pies, but bake them for 15 instead of 30 minutes.

Note: To serve after freezing, heat in the oven at 160°C (325°F) for 45 minutes to 1 hour.

**4 firm, ripe eating pears,
peeled, halved and cored**
Dressing:
**120 g cream cheese
25 ml medium cream sherry
25 ml lemon juice
125 ml (½ cup) walnuts,
coarsely chopped
1 ml (¼ teaspoon) salt
1 ml (¼ teaspoon) pepper**
Garnish:
lettuce; watercress

37   Pears with cream cheese

Serves 4;   kJ per portion 740;   Prep time 20 min.

1. Blend the cream cheese, sherry, lemon juice, salt and pepper in a blender until smooth and thick.
2. Stir in the chopped walnuts.
3. Place 2 pear halves on a bed of lettuce on each of 4 plates, pour over the cream cheese sauce and serve at once, garnished with watercress.

**2 grapefruit
25 ml (2 tablespoons) butter or
margarine
25 ml (2 tablespoons) brown
sugar
2 ml (½ teaspoon) ground
cinnamon
25 ml medium sherry**

38   Hot grapefruit cocktail

Serves 4;   kJ per portion 350;   Prep time 20 min;   Cooking time 5 min.

1. Halve the grapefruit and, using a sharp knife, loosen the segments from the skin and from the centre so that they are easy to remove.
2. Pour sherry over each of the grapefruit halves and allow them to stand for an hour.
3. Blend the sugar and cinnamon.
4. Spread a little of the butter or margarine on top of each grapefruit half, then sprinkle generously with the sugar and cinnamon mixture.
5. Place under the grill until the topping is bubbling hot, about 4 minutes. Serve at once.

**1 large or 2 small honeydew
melons, diced or in balls
75 ml (6 tablespoons)
preserved ginger, finely diced
12,5 ml sherry or van der Hum
liqueur
a little honey**
Garnish:
sprigs of mint

39   Melon and ginger cocktail

Serves 4;   kJ per portion 400;   Prep time 20 min.

1. Combine the melon and ginger in a bowl.
2. Spoon the mixture into 4 glasses and drizzle a little honey and sherry or van der Hum over each.
3. Chill for 1 hour, then serve garnished with a sprig of mint.

**2 large honeydew melons,
peeled, seeded and cut in thin
slices
450 g prosciutto, Parma ham
or very thinly sliced lean baked
ham
10 lemon wedges
sprinkling black pepper**
Garnish:
shredded lettuce

40   Melon with prosciutto

Serves 10;   kJ per portion 580;   Prep time 15 min.

1. Place 2 or 3 slices of melon on each of 10 plates and top with 2 paper-thin slices of prosciutto, Parma ham or lean baked ham. Sprinkle with a few grains of black pepper.
2. Serve with shredded lettuce and lemon wedges.

Variations:
1. Serve peeled ripe figs with the ham instead of melon.
2. Serve grapefruit segments with the ham instead of melon.
3. Serve halved canned or fresh yellow peaches with the ham instead of melon.

41 Ham and fig hors d'oeuvre

8 large, ripe figs, peeled
8 very thin slices baked ham,
cut in strips
Dressing:
2 egg yolks
2 ml (½ teaspoon) prepared
mustard
1 ml (¼ teaspoon) sugar
12,5 ml lemon juice
140 ml olive oil
25 ml boiling water
1 ml (¼ teaspoon) salt
sprinkling black pepper

Serves 8; kJ per portion 700; Prep time 15 min.

1. Roll strips of ham around the figs and secure them with toothpicks.
2. Place the egg yolks, sugar, mustard, salt and pepper in a bowl. Whisk in the lemon juice and beat until the egg yolks thicken slightly.
3. Add the oil very gradually and beat until the dressing is very thick. Add the boiling water, beating all the time.
4. Place the figs on an oblong serving dish and top each with a little of the dressing. Serve at once.

Variations:

1. Use cored halved pears instead of the figs.
2. Use halved yellow peaches instead of the figs.
3. Use avocado slices instead of the figs. Sprinkle the avocado slices with a little lemon juice to prevent them from browning.

42 Avocado Ritz

2 ripe avocado pears, halved
and stoned
120 g cooked prawns, shelled
juice of 1 lemon
1 ml (¼ teaspoon) salt
1 ml (¼ teaspoon) pepper
seafood dressing (p. 187)
Garnish:
lemon slices

Serves 4; kJ per portion 850; Prep time 20 min.

1. Sprinkle the avocado halves with the lemon juice to prevent discolouring.
2. Combine the prawns, salt and pepper and spoon into the avocado halves.
3. Prepare the dressing as directed and pour a little over each avocado half.
4. Serve at once, garnished with slices of lemon.

Variations:

1. Use cooked shrimps or crayfish or flaked, canned tuna or crab meat instead of the prawns.
2. Use cooked, diced chicken and a blue cheese dressing (recipe 410) instead of the prawns and seafood dressing.
3. Use black caviar instead of the prawns and seafood dressing.

43 Avocado and grapefruit cocktail

3 grapefruit, halved and
segments and juice reserved
2 ripe avocados, peeled and
diced
50 ml French dressing
(recipe 408)
Garnish:
mint sprigs

Serves 4; kJ per portion 600; Prep time 20 min.

1. Toss the grapefruit segments, diced avocado and grapefruit juice in a bowl. Chill thoroughly.
2. Spoon the mixture into 4 individual serving dishes with a little of the juice.
3. Add 12,5 ml French dressing to each dish and serve, garnished with a sprig of mint.

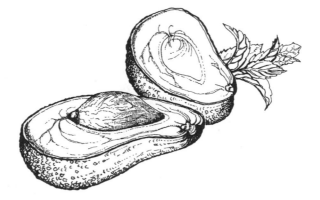

SOUPS

Soup is one of the oldest, most nutritious, varied and international of dishes. Nearly every country has its special soup – borscht in Russia, avgolemono soupa in Greece, egg petal soup in China and onion soup in France – and indeed stock, the cooking liquid of most soups, is an almost universal element in the major cuisines of the world.

Soups may be classified broadly into two categories: clear soups and thick soups.

Clear soups, which include consommés and bouillons, are prepared from stock flavoured with various meats, poultry, game, fish, vegetables, herbs and seasonings. *Consommés* are clarified (see p. 42), have a transparent appearance and vary in colour from pale amber to deep brown. They are usually served with accompaniments and garnishes. *Bouillons* are strained but not clarified and can be served either plain or with garnishes. They are the basis for many meat soups.

Thick soups are prepared from cut vegetables simmered in various stocks, often with meat, fish or poultry added. They are thickened by adding flour, rice flour, cornflour, barley, sago, tapioca, or similar substances. Thick soups may be further classified into purées, veloutés, cream soups and bisques.

Purées differ from other thick soups in that the ingredients form the sole thickening agent. They are usually made from fresh or dried vegetables such as peas, beans and lentils, though meat, poultry and fish soups may be puréed as well. The soup ingredients are usually rubbed through a sieve or whirled in a blender when cooked to form a thick, smooth cream or purée, and then returned to the saucepan and brought back just to the boil. Milk, cream or a beaten egg may be added where a richer soup is desired.

Veloutés are prepared from a white sauce base (p. 181) diluted with the appropriate stock flavour and simmered with vegetables, meat, poultry, game or fish. These soups are always strained through a fine sieve and a mixture of egg yolk and cream added just before serving. They have the consistency of single cream and are always garnished.

Cream soups contain similar ingredients and have a similar consistency to purée-based soups, but cream or a mixture of cream and milk is added just before serving. Cream soups often have a Béchamel sauce (p. 179) base with the puréed cooked ingredients and stock added.

Bisques are made from raw shellfish, vegetables, fish stock, herbs and seasoning. They may be either thickened or strained through a fine sieve, and wine, cream or milk may be added.

40

SOUP VEGETABLES

Almost all vegetables are suitable for soup, but onions, carrots, celery and leeks are the most usual for they impart a rich flavour and aroma. Sauté them in a little butter before adding them to the stock to enhance the taste.

STOCK

The basis of most soups is stock – the liquid flavoured by the juices of various ingredients extracted during long, slow cooking. In the past, when meals were prepared for many people every day, the left-over scraps and bones bolstered the contents of the ever-simmering stockpot. This not only yielded delicious soups but was also a vital ingredient in sauces, gravies and meat dishes.

Today few housewives maintain a stockpot: people tend to eat more simply and leave out soup at the start of a meal, and the rising cost of fuel has made it generally uneconomical to keep the stockpot simmering. Nowadays, if stock is required, it usually has to be prepared specially. To save time, stock cubes or powder dissolved in boiling water and canned bouillon often provide the basis for soups.

The first essential for making your own stock is a large, deep, heavy-bottomed saucepan – about 6 litre capacity – with a lid. The basic ingredients are meat, poultry or fish and their trimmings, bones, vegetables, water and seasoning. The method for extracting all the nutriment and flavour – simmering the ingredients in water – is the same for all kinds of stock, but the result depends on the quality and kind of ingredients used and how long the stock is cooked.

The basic stocks are:

Meat stock (Bouillon) is made from raw meat trimmings, bones, vegetables, water and seasoning (recipe 44).

Brown stock, also a meat stock, is made from beef, beef bones, vegetables, water and seasoning, sometimes with veal or chicken added. The meat and bones are browned in hot fat before the water is added. Brown stock is used mainly for consommés or for glazing meat.

White stock is made from veal trimmings, bones, vegetables, water and seasoning. Chicken and chicken bones are sometimes added, and an excellent stock for white soups is the water in which chicken, veal, rabbit or mutton has been boiled (recipe 47).

Game stock is made from game or game bones and trimmings, vegetables, water and seasoning (recipe 48). Meat stock is frequently the basis for game soups.

Vegetable stock, used for vegetarian soups and dishes, is made from vegetables, water and seasoning (recipe 49). Many vegetable soups have meat stock as their basis.

Fish stock is made from the bones and trimmings of fish, vegetables, water and seasoning. Adding the flesh of fish and shellfish trimmings enhances the flavour. Fish stock should not be simmered for longer than 1 hour, as boiling it longer sometimes gives the stock a bitter taste) (recipe 90).

Skimming. As most soups and stocks throw up a lot of frothy scum on the surface as they boil, they should be skimmed if you want them to have a fresh, clear, clean taste and colour. Dip a soup ladle or slotted spoon in cold water and shake it dry, then dip it straight down into the stock or soup, just below the surface, and skim off any froth that has accumulated at the sides of the saucepan. Skim, rinsing the ladle or spoon frequently, until the surface is clear. This process may have to be repeated a few times before the soup or stock is completely free of scum.

Removing fat. When soup or stock has finished cooking, a thin film of fat may form on the surface. To remove this fat, skim as described above, or run an absorbent paper towel lightly over the surface. An easy way to remove fat is to cool the soup or stock in the refrigerator and then to lift off the hardened fat. It is best not to remove the fat until just before use, however, as it helps to preserve the soup or stock by keeping out the air.

Straining. All stocks and some soups need straining, either to remove certain ingredients from them or to make them smooth. Use a fine sieve or fine-mesh strainer to allow the soup or stock to pass through and keep back the unwanted elements. If a soup is too thick to pass through easily, use the back of a wooden spoon to force it through. A damp muslin cloth should be used to strain soups such as consommé, which must be completely clear.

Clarifying. Consommés must be clarified to give them their characteristically clear appearance. To clarify soup, add the well-washed broken shell and slightly beaten white of 1 egg for every litre of meat stock. Heat the stock slowly, stirring occasionally, until it boils. Boil for 2 minutes, then remove from the stove and leave undisturbed in a warm place for 20 minutes. Strain once or twice through a double layer of cheesecloth.

Thickening. Soups may be thickened with vegetable purées, a *roux* made of flour with butter or margarine, milk and egg or cream and egg. Soups made from vegetables such as peas, beans, lentils and potatoes do not require additional thickening, but those made from the more watery vegetables such as celery, lettuce and carrots need a thickening agent to make them cohere. While vegetable purées can be stirred directly into hot stock, the other thickening agents must be added with more care. If a mixture of beaten egg and milk or cream is added directly to the soup, it will curdle. To avoid this, a little of the hot stock should first be stirred separately into the beaten egg and the resultant mixture then stirred into the soup. After eggs and cream have been added to the soup, it should not be boiled again but merely reheated.

POINTS TO NOTE ABOUT MAKING STOCK

1. Shin of beef makes the best meat stock because it produces a good jelly, but neck can also be used. There should be more bone than meat and very little fat. When making meat stock for a clear soup, veal and chicken are often added to impart extra flavour.
2. Ham or a ham bone may be added to white stock for extra flavour.

3. The proportion of water to the other ingredients should be 2 to 1. Other liquids, such as the water in which meat or vegetables have been cooked, may be used instead of plain water, but the water used to boil cabbage should not be used as it imparts a sour taste. The water in which potatoes have been cooked should also be avoided as it makes the stock cloudy.
4. When preparing stock, vegetables should be used sparingly to avoid overpowering the flavour of the meat, chicken or fish. Vegetables should never be left in the stock overnight as this makes it sour.
5. Thickened sauces, rice, ground pepper and bread should not be used to make stock as they will make it cloudy.
6. Stock is always brought to the boil slowly and then simmered for several hours to obtain the most flavour. The saucepan is usually covered to prevent excessive loss by evaporation, but when the stock must be concentrated, it is simmered uncovered.
7. Stock should always be made the day before it is to be used because simmering for a long time gives the best results.
8. Vegetables, spices, herbs, salt and pepper are added to the stock during the last hour of cooking.
9. The meat and bones used to make stock should not be thrown away, as they can be used to make a second stock. Fresh water is added, but no seasoning, as second stock is used specifically for those soups, stews and sauces which have a distinctive flavour of their own and do not require a strongly flavoured stock.
10. Stock may be stored in the refrigerator for up to 2 weeks, but must then be boiled again before using. It is generally better, however, to store stock by freezing it

FREEZING SOUPS

Most soups freeze well, without losing taste or texture, if they are stored for no longer than 4 to 6 months in the freezer.

To freeze soups
1. Cool the soup thoroughly.
2. Pour it into freezer foil bags, rigid polythene containers or a plastic bag placed inside a rigid container from which the bag can be removed after the soup has frozen. Make sure that the container is airtight. Bouillon or other meat soups can be frozen in ice trays, which makes it easy to control portions.
3. Leave 2 cm to 3 cm head space in the container, because liquids expand as they freeze.
4. Seal the container and label it with all the relevant information: type of soup, date of freezing, amount.

Note: Cream soups should be frozen before the cream or egg yolk is added.

To serve frozen soups

1. Frozen soup may be heated immediately or thawed and then heated:
   a. Place the frozen soup in a saucepan and simmer, covered, over low heat, stirring occasionally to blend well.

   or

   b. Thaw the frozen soup in the refrigerator for 8 hours or outside the refrigerator for 2 hours, then heat as above.
2. Heat frozen *cream soups* slowly in a covered saucepan, then add the thickening agent as described in the recipe.
3. Thaw *cold soups* in the refrigerator for 8 hours, stir to blend and serve. To serve thick soup really cold, add ice cubes just before serving.
4. Add croûtons or other garnishes just before serving.

Note: Thaw only the required amount of soup as soups should not be refrozen once they have been thawed.

Consult the section on Sauces (p. 177) for hints on making *roux*-based soups and correcting soups that 'go wrong'.

Note: Soups which are too salty may be corrected by adding either a raw potato – which will absorb the excess salt – or a little sugar.

BASIC STOCKS AND MEAT SOUPS

44   Meat stock (Bouillon)   (F)

Makes 1,5 litres;   kJ per portion 120;   Prep time 20 min;
Cooking time 4-5 hours

1 kg shin or neck of beef
25 ml (2 tablespoons) butter or fat
1,5 litres cold water
10 ml (2 teaspoons) salt
3 each of carrots, turnips, leeks, celery stalks, onions
5 peppercorns
3 cloves
1 bouquet garni (3 sprigs parsley, 1 sprig thyme, 1 bay leaf)

1. Cut the meat off the bone and cut into small pieces. Chop the bones into smaller pieces, too.
2. Melt the butter or fat in a large saucepan and brown the meat.
3. Add the salt, peppercorns, cloves and water. Cover and allow to simmer for 3 to 4 hours, skimming when necessary (method p. 42).
4. Chop the vegetables coarsely, add to the stock with the bouquet garni and simmer for another hour. Top up with water. Strain through a fine sieve and cool.
5. Remove the layer of fat that forms on top, and strain again if necessary (f).

Note:
● A pressure cooker may be used to speed up the process: place all the ingredients at the same time in the pressure cooker and add water, taking care that the cooker is no more than two-thirds full. Close the cooker, then heat slowly to build up pressure. Keep at 50 kPa for 35 to 45 minutes. Let the pressure drop to 0 before opening the cooker. Strain and cool stock, then proceed with step 5.

- Meat stock may be kept in the refrigerator for some time. Do not remove the layer of fat if it is to be kept without freezing, because the fat forms an airtight layer and so helps to preserve the stock.
- Meat stock can also be frozen in freezer-trays and the cubes stored in the freezer for later use. Remove the layer of fat before freezing.
- If the meat stock is to be used immediately, skim off the fat with a slotted spoon. Use an ice cube tied in cheesecloth to remove any remaining fat.
- Meat stock may be served with accompaniments or used as a base for various other soups.

---

2 kg chicken or turkey
2 leeks, sliced
4 carrots, peeled and sliced
1 onion, sliced
2 stalks soup celery, chopped
3 litres water
bouquet garni (parsley, thyme and bay leaf)
1 clove garlic, crushed
2 cloves
6 peppercorns
10 ml (2 teaspoons) salt

45   Chicken stock   (F)

Makes 3 litres;   kJ per portion 90;   Prep time 30 min; Cooking time 3 hours

1. Place the chicken or turkey, all spices and herbs and the water in a large saucepan. Bring slowly to the boil then simmer, covered, for 1 to 1½ hours, skimming the scum from the surface when necessary.
2. Add the vegetables and continue simmering until the chicken is tender, 1½ to 2 hours.
3. Skim the fat from the surface.
4. Strain the stock through a fine sieve. Cool and store in the refrigerator until needed (f).

---

1 kg meat and bone of lamb, veal, mutton, chicken, or fish
1,5 litres cold water
2 cloves; 4 peppercorns
3 carrots; 2 leeks
1 bouquet garni (parsley, 1 sprig thyme, 1 bay leaf)
1 clove garlic
5 ml (1 teaspoon) salt

46   Consommé   (F)

Makes 1,5 litres;   kJ per portion 120;   Prep time 20 min; Cooking time 3 hours

1. Trim meat of excess fat, break the bones and cut meat into small pieces. Place in a large saucepan.
2. Add the water, salt, peppercorns and cloves and bring slowly to the boil. Simmer for at least 1 hour with the water barely bubbling and skim the scum from the surface frequently.
3. Add the leeks, carrots, bouquet garni and garlic and simmer for another 1½ to 2 hours.
4. Strain, leave until cold, remove the layer of fat and clarify (method p. 42) (f).

1,5 kg veal knuckle, boned
1 small ham bone
1 carrot, peeled
1 turnip; 1 onion
1 leek; 1 stalk celery
1 bouquet garni (parsley, 1 sprig thyme, 1 bay leaf)
3,375 litres water
2 to 4 cloves
8 white peppercorns
12,5 ml (1 tablespoon) salt

47   White stock (F)

Makes 3 litres;   kJ per portion 120;   Prep time 30 min; Cooking time 3 hours

1. Trim the meat of excess fat and dice it. Chop the bones into smaller pieces.
2. Place the meat, bones, ham bone and water in a saucepan and slowly bring to the boil. Simmer, covered, for 1 to 1½ hours, skimming the scum from the surface often.
3. Add the vegetables, bouquet garni, cloves, peppercorns and salt. Continue simmering until the meat is tender, 1½ to 2 hours, skimming occasionally.
4. Remove the fat from the surface and add more salt if necessary.
5. Strain the stock through a fine sieve or cheesecloth stretched tightly over a colander. Cool and store in the refrigerator until needed (f).

48 Game stock (F)

Makes 3,5 litres; kJ per portion 140; Prep time 30 min; Cooking time 4 hours

1 kg venison, cubed and the bones chopped
500 g beef shin or neck, boned and the meat diced
85 g bacon, diced
2 carrots, peeled and diced
1 large turnip, diced
1 onion, diced
2 stalks celery, diced
3 tomatoes, sliced
3 mushrooms, thinly sliced
3,75 litres water
bouquet garni (3 sprigs parsley, 1 sprig thyme, 1 bay leaf)
6 peppercorns; 4 cloves
12,5 ml (1 tablespoon) salt

1. Chop the bones into smaller pieces.
2. Sauté the diced bacon in a large, heavy-bottomed saucepan over low heat until the fat begins to melt.
3. Add the venison, beef and bones and sauté in the bacon fat until lightly browned.
4. Add the water and bring slowly to the boil.
5. Add the salt, skim well and simmer for 1 hour, skimming occasionally. Add the vegetables, peppercorns, cloves and bouquet garni and simmer for a further 3 hours.
6. Strain the stock through a fine sieve. Cool and store in the refrigerator until needed (f).

49 Vegetable stock (F)

Makes 2 litres; kJ per portion 110; Prep time 20 min; Cooking time 2 hours 45 min.

6 large carrots, peeled and diced
2 turnips, peeled and diced
1 onion, coarsely chopped
2 large leeks, coarsely chopped
4 stalks celery, finely chopped
60 g dried beans, soaked overnight
25 ml (2 tablespoons) butter or margarine
25 ml olive oil
2,25 litres water or liquid in which vegetables were boiled
bouquet garni (3 sprigs parsley, 1 sprig thyme, 1 bay leaf)
5 ml (1 teaspoon) sugar
10 ml (2 teaspoons) salt
freshly ground black pepper

1. Melt the butter or margarine in a large saucepan, add the olive oil and sauté all the vegetables – except the beans – in it, stirring all the time, until they change colour, 10 to 15 minutes.
2. Add 250 ml water or vegetable liquid and simmer until all the liquid has been absorbed.
3. Add the beans and the remaining water or vegetable liquid, mixing well, and bring to the boil.
4. Skim the stock, then add the bouquet garni, sugar, salt and freshly ground black pepper and simmer, covered, for 2 to 2½ hours.
5. Strain the stock through a fine sieve. Cool and store in the refrigerator until needed (f).

Note: Any clean, fresh vegetables and their trimmings are suitable for vegetable stock.

50 Clear tomato soup (F)

Serves 4-6; kJ per portion 300; Prep time 20 min; Cooking time 20 min.

1 kg tomatoes, coarsely chopped
½ small raw beetroot
1 stalk celery, finely chopped
1 small onion, finely chopped
dash Worcester sauce
5 ml lemon juice
1 litre water or white stock
2 ml (½ teaspoon) sugar
2 bay leaves
5 ml (1 teaspoon) salt
2 ml (½ teaspoon) pepper

1. Place all the ingredients in a large saucepan and cook over a medium heat until the tomatoes are very soft, about 15 minutes.
2. Remove the beetroot and bay leaves.
3. Rub the soup through a sieve or purée in a blender (f).
4. Reheat and serve with tiny meat rissoles, or serve cold with a dollop of yoghurt as garnish.

150 g cooked chicken, diced
2 carrots, peeled and diced
2 stalks celery, finely chopped
3 spring onions, finely chopped
150 g mushrooms, thinly sliced
50 g raw egg noodles
1,5 litres chicken stock
5 ml (1 teaspoon) salt
2 ml (½ teaspoon) pepper

51 Chicken noodle soup (F)

Serves 4-6;   kJ per portion 300;   Prep time 20 min;   Cooking time 30 min.

1. Bring the stock to the boil in a large saucepan.
2. Add the carrots, celery, spring onions, salt and pepper and simmer, covered, for 15 minutes.
3. With a wooden spoon stir in the mushrooms and noodles.
4. Add the chicken and simmer a further 10 minutes (f). Serve at once.

500 g dried haricot or sugar
beans, soaked in water
overnight, covered
25 ml (2 tablespoons) rindless
bacon, finely chopped
1 onion, finely chopped
1 small cabbage, finely
shredded
4 leeks, finely sliced
4 baby marrows, diced
2 cloves garlic, crushed
4 stalks table celery, diced
4 carrots, diced
2 tomatoes, skinned and diced
1,5 litres boiling water
1 sprig fresh rosemary or a
pinch dried rosemary
pinch dried basil; 1 bay leaf
12,5 ml (1 tablespoon) parsley,
finely chopped
75 ml oil
125 ml (½ cup) raw elbow
macaroni
12,5 ml (1 tablespoon) salt
pinch freshly ground black
pepper
Garnish:
grated Parmesan cheese

52 Minestrone (F)

Serves 10-12;   kJ per portion 430;   Prep time 20 min;   Cooking time 2 hours

1. In a saucepan, cook the beans in the water in which they were soaked until tender, 1 to 1½ hours.
2. Cool the beans slightly, then press half through a sieve or liquidise in a blender to form a purée. Drain the remaining beans and set aside.
3. Heat the oil in a large saucepan and gently sauté the garlic, onion, celery, carrots, rosemary and bacon until golden brown.
4. Add the tomatoes and sauté a few minutes longer, adding a little sugar if necessary.
5. Add the cabbage, leeks, baby marrows, basil, bay leaf, parsley, salt and pepper.
6. Add the whole and puréed beans together with the boiling water.
7. Add the macaroni and simmer, covered, until the macaroni is tender, about 50 minutes (f).
8. Serve garnished with Parmesan cheese.

Note: The soup may also be frozen before the macaroni is added. To serve, thaw the soup at room temperature for 2 hours, reheat over low heat and continue with steps 7 and 8.

680 g mutton, diced
1 small onion, finely chopped
1 small leek, diced
1 small cabbage, shredded
1 small carrot, finely chopped
250 ml (1 cup) raw peas,
shelled
1 stalk celery, finely chopped
5 ml (1 teaspoon) parsley,
finely chopped
12,5 ml (1 tablespoon) barley,
washed thoroughly
2 litres cold water
5 ml (1 teaspoon) salt
2 ml (½ teaspoon) pepper

53 Scotch broth (F)

Serves 3-4;   kJ per portion 240;   Prep time 15 min;   Cooking time 3 hours

1. Simmer the meat in a large saucepan together with the water and 5 ml (1 teaspoon) salt until the meat is tender, about 2 hours.
2. Add the vegetables and barley to the broth and simmer a further hour.
3. Strain the broth and return it to the saucepan.
4. Cut the meat into smaller pieces still and return, together with the vegetables, to the saucepan (f).
5. Bring to the boil, lower the heat and simmer for 5 minutes. Serve at once.

---

4 large onions, finely sliced
25 ml oil
10 ml (2 teaspoons) flour
2 litres chicken stock or
vegetable stock
12,5 ml lemon juice
2 cloves garlic, crushed
37,5 ml (3 tablespoons)
parsley, finely chopped
pinch dried thyme
pinch dried tarragon
6 slices French bread
5 ml (1 teaspoon) salt
pinch freshly ground black
pepper
Garnish:
125 ml (½ cup) cheese, grated
chopped parsley

54 French onion soup (F)

Serves 4-6;   kJ per portion 450;   Prep time 20 min;   Cooking time 1 hour

1. Heat the oil in a large saucepan and sauté the onions in it until tender.
2. Sprinkle the flour, salt and pepper over the onions and add the garlic, parsley, thyme, tarragon and lemon juice, stirring gently.
3. Add the chicken or vegetable stock gradually, stirring all the time.
4. Simmer, uncovered, until the soup has been reduced to 1,5 litres, about 1 hour (f).
5. Place a slice of French bread in the bottom of each soup bowl; fill bowls with soup and serve at once, garnished with parsley and grated cheese.

---

100 g lean pork, shredded
1 green onion, thinly sliced
1 cucumber, peeled and diced
1 egg, lightly beaten
5 ml (1 teaspoon) cornflour
1,5 litres chicken stock
25 ml oil; 5 ml sherry
5 ml soy sauce
pinch monosodium glutamate
5 ml (1 teaspoon) salt
2 ml (½ teaspoon) pepper

55 Egg petal soup with cucumbers (F)

Serves 4;   kJ per portion 150;   Prep time 15 min;   Cooking time 15 min.

1. Combine the sherry, cornflour and soy sauce in a bowl and mix thoroughly with the pork.
2. Heat the oil in a deep saucepan and quickly brown the pork mixture in it.
3. Add the chicken stock and simmer, covered, for 10 minutes.
4. Add the onion, cucumber and monosodium glutamate. Season with the salt and pepper and simmer a further 5 minutes (f).
5. Bring the soup to a fast boil and gradually add the beaten egg, stirring constantly. Serve at once.

Note: To ensure that the egg will cook in shreds, turn off the stove the minute you start adding it.

56 Oxtail soup (F)

1 oxtail
12,5 ml (1 tablespoon) butter or dripping
3 carrots, diced
1 large onion, finely chopped
1 turnip, thinly sliced
2 tomatoes, skinned and finely chopped
37,5 ml (3 tablespoons) table celery, finely chopped
2 litres water
250 ml sherry (optional)
125 ml (½ cup) flour
1 bouquet garni (parsley, thyme and a bay leaf)
3 peppercorns; 2 cloves
5 ml (1 teaspoon) salt
1 ml (¼ teaspoon) cayenne pepper

Serves 6; kJ per portion 350; Prep time 15 min; Cooking time 3 ¼ hours

1. Wash the oxtail thoroughly and separate it at the joints.
2. Melt the butter or dripping in a heavy saucepan. Add the meat and onion and fry until golden brown.
3. Add the remaining vegetables, the peppercorns, cloves, water and bouquet garni and simmer, covered, for 3 hours.
4. Remove the meat when it is tender and strip it from the bones.
5. Remove the bouquet garni and strain the soup, reserving the stock.
6. Purée the vegetables by pressing through a fine sieve or liquidising in a blender, add to the stock and return the saucepan to the stove.
7. Mix the flour with a little water, add to the soup and stir until thickened.
8. Add the sherry, if desired, and season with salt and cayenne pepper.
9. Add the meat (f) and serve at once.

57 Kidney soup (F)

Serves 6; kJ per portion 350; Prep time 15 min; Cooking time 3 ¼ hours

Follow the recipe for oxtail soup, using 340 g diced kidneys instead of the oxtail.

58 Goulash soup (F)

400 g stewing steak, cubed
2 frankfurters, thickly sliced
2 medium onions, finely chopped
1 medium carrot, thinly sliced
450 g canned tomatoes and juice
or fresh tomatoes, skinned
250 ml (1 cup) canned sauerkraut, drained
1,5 litres beef stock
125 ml sour cream
oil for frying
5 ml (1 teaspoon) paprika
5 ml (1 teaspoon) salt

Serves 5-6; kJ per portion 940; Prep time 30 min; Cooking time 2 ½ hours

1. Heat a little oil in a saucepan and sauté the onion until soft.
2. Add the steak and fry on both sides until brown.
3. Add the paprika and salt and stir over medium heat for 1 to 2 minutes.
4. Add the carrot, the tomatoes and their juice and the beef stock. Simmer, covered, for 2 hours.
5. Rinse the sauerkraut in cold water, drain well and add to the saucepan with the frankfurters (f). Cover and simmer for 15 minutes.
6. Stir in the sour cream and simmer a further minute. Serve at once.

59 Cucumber and pork soup (F)

250 g pork fillet, cut in thin strips
2 medium cucumbers, peeled and thinly sliced
1,125 litres chicken stock
12,5 ml soy sauce
5 ml (1 teaspoon) salt

Serves 6; kJ per portion 150; Prep time 5 min; Cooking time 15 min.

1. Combine the stock, salt, soy sauce and pork in a large saucepan, bring to the boil for 10 minutes.
2. Add the cucumbers and bring back to the boil for 3 minutes (f). Serve at once.

125 g liver, minced
1 onion, finely chopped
6 thin slices stale white bread
1 egg
1 litre beef stock
75 ml lukewarm milk
12,5 ml vegetable oil
25 ml (2 tablespoons) parsley,
finely chopped
grated rind of ½ lemon
pinch dried marjoram
pinch white pepper
5 ml (1 teaspoon) salt
Garnish:
chopped chives

60   Soup with liver dumplings   (F)

Serves 4;   kJ per portion 540;   Prep time 5 min;   Cooking time 30 min.

1. Place the bread in a large bowl, sprinkle with a little of the salt and pour the lukewarm milk over it to soften.
2. In a frying-pan, heat the oil and sauté the onion until transparent, then add the parsley.
3. Add the onion mixture, liver, egg, pepper, marjoram, lemon rind and the remaining salt to the bread and combine. Form the mixture into large dumplings.
4. Bring the stock to boil in a saucepan. Add the liver dumplings and simmer, covered, for 15 to 20 minutes (f). Serve at once.

---

100 g salt pork, diced
1 small onion, finely chopped
25 ml (2 tablespoons) green
pepper, seeded and finely
chopped
2 medium potatoes, diced
250 ml (1 cup) celery, diced
250 ml (1 cup) cooked whole
kernel corn
1 pimento, finely chopped
(fresh or canned)
10 ml (2 teaspoons) flour
375 ml boiling water
410 g can undiluted
evaporated milk
2 ml (½ teaspoon) salt
dash pepper

61   Corn chowder

Serves 4;   kJ per portion 500;   Prep time 20 min;   Cooking time 30 min.

1. Fry the pork slowly in a large saucepan until crisp. Remove the pork and pour off all but 25 ml (2 tablespoons) of the fat. Reserve 10 ml (2 teaspoons) of the poured-off fat.
2. Add the onion and the green pepper to the 25 ml (2 tablespoons) fat in the saucepan and sauté for 2 to 3 minutes.
3. Add the potatoes, celery, water, corn, salt and pepper. Bring to the boil and simmer, covered, until the potato is tender, about 15 minutes.
4. Blend the milk and reserved pork fat into the flour, stir the mixture into the soup and bring to the boil, stirring continuously.
5. Stir in the pimento and bits of pork and serve immediately.

---

bones of left-over venison,
chopped or any left-over meat
or bones of game bird
2 cloves; ½ bay leaf; 1 onion
125 ml (½ cup) celery, coarsely
chopped
1 carrot, coarsely chopped
1 turnip, thinly sliced
65 ml sherry; 2 litres water
5 ml (1 teaspoon) salt
2 ml (½ teaspoon) pepper
1 thick slice brown bread,
cubed

62   Venison soup   (F)

Serves 6;   kJ per portion 360;   Prep time 30 min;   Cooking time 3 hours

1. Place the bones, cloves, bay leaf and vegetables in a large saucepan and cover with the water. Simmer, covered, for 3 hours.
2. Strain the soup through a fine sieve and season with salt and pepper (f).
3. Add the sherry to the soup and serve at once over cubes of brown bread.

63 Cockaleekie (F)

1,75 litres white stock
half a small chicken, jointed
3 leeks, parboiled
12,5 ml (1 tablespoon) cooked
rice
25 ml (2 tablespoons) butter or
margarine
bouquet garni (parsley, thyme
and a bay leaf)
5 ml (1 teaspoon) salt
2 ml (½ teaspoon) pepper

Serves 5 - 6; kJ per portion 300; Prep time 5 min; Cooking time 2 hours

1. Melt the butter or margarine in a large saucepan and brown the chicken ·
   pieces.
2. Pour off the fat and add the stock.
3. Bring the soup to boiling point over low heat, removing the scum as it rises.
4. Strain the soup after it has boiled for about 30 minutes. Return it to the
   saucepan and add the leeks, herbs and diced chicken. Simmer gently for
   about 1 hour, then remove the bouquet garni.
5. Skim off any excess fat that remains, then add the rice, salt and pepper (f).
   Serve immediately.

64 Mulligatawny soup (F)

125 ml (½ cup) cooked
chicken, diced
125 ml (½ cup) onion, diced
1 carrot, diced
2 stalks celery, finely chopped
1 Granny Smith apple, diced
125 ml (½ cup) boiled rice
62,5 ml (5 tablespoons) butter
or margarine
15 ml (3 teaspoons) flour
1 litre chicken stock
125 ml cream, heated
10 ml (2 teaspoons) curry
powder
pinch dried thyme
5 ml (1 teaspoon) salt
2 ml (½ teaspoon) pepper

Serves 4-6; kJ per portion 800; Prep time 10 min; Cooking time 50 min.

1. Melt the butter or margarine in a large saucepan and sauté the onion, carrot
   and celery in it until lightly browned.
2. Remove from the stove and stir in the flour and curry powder until well
   blended. Return the saucepan to the stove and cook for 3 minutes, stirring all
   the time.
3. Add the chicken stock and simmer, covered, for 30 minutes.
4. Add the apple, rice, chicken, salt, pepper and thyme and simmer for a
   further 15 minutes (f).
5. Stir in the hot cream and serve immediately.

THICKENED AND CREAM SOUPS

65 Pea soup (F)

250 ml (1 cup) dried split peas
2 pork shanks
2-4 smoked pork sausages,
skinned and thickly sliced
4 medium leeks, thickly sliced
125 ml (½ cup) celery, finely
chopped
2 litres water
10 ml (2 teaspoons) salt
freshly ground black pepper

Serves 8; kJ per portion 670; Prep time 20 min; Cooking time 3 ½ hours

1. Soak the peas overnight in the water. Transfer to a large saucepan.
2. Add the pork shanks and bring slowly to the boil, then simmer, covered, for
   3 hours. Add more water if the liquid boils away too quickly.
3. Add the leeks, celery and salt and simmer, covered, for about 30 minutes.
4. Remove the bones, cut the meat into small pieces and return the meat to the
   soup.
5. Add the sausages to the soup and bring to the boil (f).
6. Serve the soup in warm bowls, making sure that each serving has some meat
   and sausage.

Note: Pea soup is very good garnished with croûtons, grated cheddar cheese,
fresh cream or yoghurt.

750 g mutton or pork shanks
or 1 ham bone with some meat
3 rashers bacon, finely
chopped
500 ml (2 cups) lentils
1 medium onion, finely
chopped
2 celery stalks, finely chopped
1 carrot, thinly sliced
25 ml (2 tablespoons) butter or
margarine
25 ml (2 tablespoons) flour
(optional)
2 litres cold water
12,5 ml (1 tablespoon) salt
2 ml (½ teaspoon) pepper

66 Lentil soup (F)

Serves 8; kJ per portion 650; Prep time 20 min; Cooking time 2 ½ hours

1. Place the meat or bones, bacon and the water in a large saucepan. Bring to the boil and simmer, covered, until the meat is tender; 2 hours for pork shanks and 1 hour for the ham bone.
2. Melt the butter or margarine in a frying-pan and sauté the carrot, onion and celery in it for 3 minutes.
3. When the meat is tender, add the sautéed vegetables and lentils to the saucepan and simmer, uncovered, for 20 to 30 minutes, skimming the soup if necessary.
4. Remove the meat and bones from the saucepan, cut the meat into small pieces and set aside. Discard the bone, fat and gristle.
5. Rub the remaining contents of the saucepan through a fine sieve or liquidise in a blender to form a purée.
6. Return the puréed soup and the meat to the saucepan, add the salt and pepper and bring to the boil (f). Serve at once.

Note:
- The soup may be thickened with flour mixed with a little cold water if it is too thin.
- If the soup is too thick, add a little meat stock.

67 Bean soup

Serves 8; kJ per portion 650; Prep time 20 min; Cooking time 2 ½ hours

Follow the recipe for lentil soup, using instead of the lentils 450 g kidney or sugar beans, soaked overnight in water and drained.

225 g cooked spinach, finely
chopped
50 g raw pasta rings
2 egg yolks, beaten
1 litre meat stock
5 ml (1 teaspoon) salt
Garnish:
25 ml (2 tablespoons) grated
Parmesan cheese, sprinkled on
4 slices of buttered, toasted
bread

68 Spinach soup (F)

Serves 4; kJ per portion 800; Prep time 15 min; Cooking time 30 min.

1. Bring the stock to the boil in a large saucepan. Add the pasta rings and simmer gently for 7 minutes.
2. Add the spinach and salt and simmer for a further 7 minutes.
3. Bring to the boil, then remove from the stove (f).
4. Beat a little of the hot soup into the egg yolks and then stir the egg mixture into the soup.
5. Serve immediately, topped with squares of cheese-toasted bread.

2,25 litres chicken stock
125 ml (½ cup) raw spaghetti,
broken into very short lengths
2 eggs; juice of 1 lemon
5 ml (1 teaspoon) salt
2 ml (½ teaspoon) pepper

69 Egg-lemon soup (Avgolemono soupa)

Serves 6; kJ per portion 650; Prep time 15 min; Cooking time 25 min.

1. Bring the stock to the boil in a large saucepan.
2. Add the spaghetti, cover, and simmer until it is tender, 15 to 20 minutes.
3. Add the salt and pepper.
4. Beat the eggs in a bowl and add the lemon juice. Gradually add a little of the hot soup to the eggs, while continuing to beat.
5. Stir the egg mixture into the soup, cover and let stand for 5 minutes off the stove. Serve at once.

500 g Jerusalem artichokes
2 medium onions, thinly sliced
1 stalk celery, thinly sliced
25 ml (2 tablespoons) butter or
margarine
1 litre water; 500 ml milk
12,5 ml vinegar
5 ml (1 teaspoon) salt
2 ml (½ teaspoon) pepper

70 Artichoke soup (F)

Serves 4;   kJ per portion 600;   Prep time 20 min;   Cooking time 1 ½ hours

1. Wash the artichokes in water to which the vinegar has been added, then pare and slice.
2. Heat the butter or margarine in a large saucepan and sauté the vegetables in it until soft but not brown, 10 to 15 minutes.
3. Add the water and boil, covered, until the vegetables are tender.
4. Rub the soup through a fine sieve or liquidise in a blender to make a purée (f).
5. Return the purée to the saucepan, add the milk and season with salt and pepper. Bring to the boil and serve immediately.

---

500 g carrots, coarsely grated
4 medium potatoes, diced
1 onion, finely chopped
25 ml (2 tablespoons)
margarine
10 ml (2 teaspoons) butter
1,75 litres chicken stock
10 ml (2 teaspoons) parsley,
finely chopped
5 ml (1 teaspoon) sugar
5 ml (1 teaspoon) salt

71 Classic carrot soup (F)

Serves 6;   kJ per portion 800;   Prep time 15 min;   Cooking time 20 min.

1. Place the carrots, potatoes, onion and margarine in a saucepan. Cover and simmer over very low heat for 10 minutes.
2. Stir in the salt, sugar and stock. Simmer, covered, until the carrots and potatoes are very tender.
3. Purée the soup by forcing it through a coarse sieve or liquidising in a blender (f).
4. Return the purée to the saucepan, adding a little water if it is too thick.
5. Reheat to just boiling, then stir in the butter and parsley and simmer a further 2 minutes. Serve at once.

---

100 g ham, boiled and cubed
500 g brisket, boiled and cubed
120 g frankfurters, finely
chopped
60 g onions, finely chopped
750 g beetroot, peeled and cut
in strips
250 g cabbage, finely chopped
2 tomatoes, peeled, seeded and
chopped
25 ml (2 tablespoons) butter or
margarine
2 litres beef stock
37,5 ml red wine vinegar
250 ml sour cream
4 sprigs parsley and 1 bay leaf
tied together
60 ml (¼ cup) dill or parsley,
finely chopped
5 ml (1 teaspoon) sugar
5 ml (1 teaspoon) salt
dash black pepper
Garnish:
finely chopped fresh dill or
parsley

72 Beetroot soup (Borshch Moskovskaia) (F)

Serves 6;   kJ per portion 1 100;   Prep time 30 min;   Cooking time 1 ½ hours

1. Melt the butter or margarine in a large saucepan, add the onions and sauté them until they are soft but not brown, stirring frequently.
2. Stir in the uncooked beetroot, then add the wine vinegar, sugar, chopped tomatoes, salt and black pepper.
3. Pour in 75 ml of the stock, and simmer, covered, for 50 minutes.
4. Pour the rest of the stock into the saucepan and add the chopped cabbage. Bring to the boil, then stir in the meat.
5. Submerge the tied parsley and bay leaf in the soup, add a little salt and simmer, covered, for 30 minutes.
6. Transfer the soup to a large tureen and sprinkle with fresh dill or parsley (f).
7. Serve with a bowl of sour cream as an accompaniment, to be added by the diners.

Note: To speed up cooking time, use cooked or pickled beetroot. Simmer for 15 minutes instead of 50 minutes (step 3), then continue with steps 4 to 7.

4 firm heads of lettuce,
coarsely diced (approx. 2 kg)
750 ml chicken stock
750 ml Béchamel sauce or
medium white sauce (p. 179)
60 g butter or margarine
125 ml double cream
25 ml dry sherry

73   Cream of lettuce soup   (F)

Serves 8;   kJ per portion 820;   Prep time 20 min;   Cooking time 45 min.

1. Melt the butter or margarine in a heavy saucepan over medium heat. Add the lettuce and turn over with a spoon to coat it evenly. Simmer for 3 minutes.
2. Blend the Béchamel or white sauce thoroughly with the stock, pour over the lettuce, stirring constantly, and boil, uncovered, for 10 minutes.
3. Purée the soup in a blender or rub it through a sieve. Return to the saucepan and heat again to just boiling (f).
4. Add the cream and sherry and serve at once.

Note: Lettuce soup goes well with croûtons.

---

74   Cream of celery soup   (F)

Serves 8;   kJ per portion 820;   Prep time 20 min;   Cooking time 45 min.

Follow the recipe for cream of lettuce soup (recipe 73) but substitute the white part of two cooked heads of celery for the lettuce. Begin at step 2.

---

75   Cream of broccoli soup   (F)

Serves 8;   kJ per portion 820;   Prep time 20 min;   Cooking time 45 min.

Follow the recipe for cream of lettuce soup (recipe 73) but substitute 750 g cooked broccoli for the lettuce. Begin at step 2.

---

250 g potatoes, thickly sliced
1 small onion, thinly sliced
50 g butter or margarine
750 ml chicken stock
25 ml single cream
5 ml (1 teaspoon)
mixed dried herbs
5 ml (1 teaspoon) salt
2 ml (½ teaspoon) pepper

76   Herbed potato soup

Serves 6;   kJ per portion 800;   Prep time 20 min;   Cooking time 15 min.

1. Melt the butter or margarine in a large saucepan and sauté the potatoes, onion and herbs in it until the onions are transparent, about 5 minutes.
2. Place the sautéed herbs and vegetables in an electric blender with 250 ml of the stock and blend for 45 seconds.
3. Return the blended mixture to the saucepan together with the rest of the stock, salt and pepper.
4. Bring to the boil, stirring occasionally, and simmer, covered, for 5 to 10 minutes.
5. Remove the soup from the stove and stir in the cream. Serve at once.

---

3 large cucumbers, peeled and
finely chopped
1 litre chicken stock
25 ml (2 tablespoons) flour
90 g butter or margarine
2 egg yolks, slightly beaten
200 ml double cream
2 medium onions, finely
chopped
5 ml (1 teaspoon) salt
2 ml (½ teaspoon) pepper
Garnish:
25 ml (2 tablespoons) finely
chopped fresh parsley or chives

77   Cucumber bisque

Serves 6;   kJ per portion 900;   Prep time 40 min;   Cooking time 40 min.

1. Heat 60 g of the butter or margarine in a heavy saucepan, add the onions and three-quarters of the chopped cucumbers and sauté until the vegetables are transparent, about 5 minutes.
2. Add the chicken stock and bring to the boil. Lower the heat and simmer, uncovered, until the cucumber is tender, about 20 minutes.
3. Strain the soup through a coarse sieve, forcing the vegetables through with a wooden spoon.
4. Melt the remaining butter or margarine (30 g) in the saucepan, and stir in the flour, blending well. Pour in the puréed soup, beating well with a whisk.
5. Over medium heat bring to the boil, whisking constantly, until the soup has thickened slightly, about 4 minutes.
6. Combine the egg yolks with the cream in a small bowl.

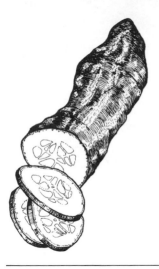

7. Add 125 ml of the soup to the egg and cream mixture, beating constantly with the whisk.
8. Slowly pour this warmed mixture back into the soup, still beating with the whisk. Simmer over low heat for 5 minutes, but do not let the soup boil.
9. Just before serving, stir in the remaining raw diced cucumber. Season with the salt and pepper, and sprinkle with chopped parsley or chives.

Note:
- This soup is delicious served chilled. Do not add the raw cucumber and herbs until ready to serve. A spoonful of whipped cream added to each portion just before serving the soup enhances the flavour.
- Remove the saucepan from the stove when adding the flour to ensure that a smooth paste (*roux*) is obtained. Return the saucepan to the stove and pour in the puréed soup, stirring all the time. Continue with step 5.

---

4 carrots, diced
250 ml (1 cup) fresh green peas
1 small head cauliflower, broken into flowerets
2 new potatoes, diced
250 g green beans, thinly sliced
4 small radishes, halved
100 g fresh spinach, finely chopped
1 litre cold water
25 ml (2 tablespoons) butter or margarine
25 ml (2 tablespoons) flour
250 ml milk; 1 egg yolk
60 ml double cream
250 g cooked shrimps, shelled
10 ml (2 teaspoons) salt
dash pepper
Garnish:
25 ml (2 tablespoons) parsley, finely chopped

78 Finnish summer vegetable soup (Kesakeitto)

Serves 6; kJ per portion 820; Prep time 30 min; Cooking time 20 min.

1. Place all the vegetables except the spinach in a large saucepan, cover with the cold water and add the salt. Bring to the boil and boil, uncovered, until the vegetables are just tender, about 5 minutes.
2. Add the spinach and boil for another 5 minutes.
3. Remove the saucepan from the stove and strain the liquid through a fine sieve into a bowl. Set aside. Place the vegetables in another bowl and set aside.
4. Melt the butter or margarine in a saucepan and stir in the flour, blending till smooth.
5. Slowly pour in the stock, beating briskly. Beat in the milk.
6. Combine the egg yolk and cream in a small bowl.
7. Whisk 250 ml of the hot stock into the egg mixture, a little at a time.
8. Slowly whisk the egg mixture back into the soup.
9. Add the reserved vegetables to the soup and simmer.
10. Add the shrimps and simmer, covered, for 3 to 5 minutes. Adjust the seasoning, adding more salt and pepper if necessary, and serve at once, sprinkled with parsley.

---

1 litre beer (lager)
125 ml (½ cup) sugar
4 egg yolks
50 ml sour cream
2 ml (½ teaspoon) ground cinnamon
1 ml (¼ teaspoon) salt
freshly ground black pepper

79 Beer soup

Serves 4; kJ per portion 1 200; Prep time 15 min; Cooking time 20 min.

1. Heat the beer and sugar in a saucepan, stirring constantly. Remove from the stove when all the sugar has dissolved.
2. Beat the egg yolks in a small bowl, then beat in the sour cream, a little at a time.
3. Add a little of the hot beer to the egg and cream mixture, stirring all the time with the whisk, then whisk into the rest of the beer in the saucepan.
4. Return to the stove and simmer over low heat, stirring constantly, until the soup thickens slightly. Do not let it boil or it may curdle.
5. Stir in the salt and cinnamon and serve at once, garnished with a little freshly ground black pepper.

500 g frozen broccoli
3 ripe avocados
1 litre chicken stock
juice of 1 lemon
125 ml double cream
5 ml (1 teaspoon) onion, minced
5 ml (1 teaspoon) salt
pinch freshly ground black pepper

80   Cream of avocado and broccoli soup

Serves 4-6;   kJ per portion 1 140;   Prep time 20 min;   Cooking time 10 min.

1. Prepare the broccoli as directed on the packet and remove the stalks.
2. Peel the avocados, remove the stones and mash the flesh.
3. Combine the broccoli stalks, mashed avacados, stock and lemon juice and liquidise in a blender or pass through a fine sieve to make a purée.
4. Add the cream, onion, broccoli heads, salt and pepper to the purée; place in a saucepan and heat to just below boiling point. Serve immediately.

---

500 g (2 cups) cooked pumpkin
25 ml (2 tablespoons) onion, finely chopped
12,5 ml (1 tablespoon) butter or margarine
500 ml chicken stock
500 ml milk; 5 ml lemon juice
50 ml double cream
1 ml (¼ teaspoon) ground cloves
2 ml (½ teaspoon) sugar
2 ml (½ teaspoon) salt
Garnish:
croûtons

81   Pumpkin soup   (F)

Serves 6;   kJ per portion 1 000;   Prep time 40 min;   Cooking time 20 min.

1. Melt the butter or margarine in a heavy saucepan and sauté the onion until transparent but not brown.
2. Add the cooked pumpkin, chicken stock, milk, lemon juice, ground cloves, sugar and salt but not the cream and simmer, covered, for 15 minutes, stirring occasionally.
3. Purée the soup by forcing it through a fine sieve or, if a coarser consistency is desired, stir well with a wooden spoon (f).
4. Stir in the cream and heat well, but do not boil. Serve hot with croûtons.

Note: To serve the soup cold, chill for at least 2 hours and serve garnished with a thin slice of peeled orange instead of the croûtons.

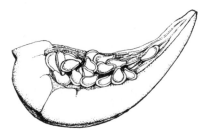

COLD SOUPS

82   Jellied consommé

Serves 6;   kJ per portion 160;   Prep time 10 min.

1. Use the basic consommé recipe (recipe 46). Adding 1 calf's foot to the other meat and bones when making the stock will result in a firmer jelly. Do not dilute the basic stock.
2. Flavour when still slightly warm with one of the following for every 1 litre consommé:
   100 ml dry sherry
   100 ml port wine
    50 ml lemon juice
   100 ml white wine
3. Allow the consommé to set in a shallow pan. Chill for 4 hours. Break into pieces with a fork just before serving, and serve in glass bowls.
4. Garnish each serving with finely chopped parsley, slices of stuffed olive, a slice of lemon or a dollop of sour cream.

250 g frozen peas, preferably
petits pois
125 ml double cream
50 ml plain yoghurt
25 ml medium cream sherry
250 ml cold chicken or
vegetable stock
2 ml onion juice (optional)
freshly ground black pepper
Garnish:
sprigs of fresh mint

83   Quick cold pea soup

Serves 4;   kJ per portion 600;   Prep time 10 min.

1. Place the slightly thawed peas in a liquidiser or blender with the sherry and blend to combine completely.
2. Add the cream, stock, yoghurt, onion juice and black pepper and mix lightly.
3. Transfer to a serving dish and chill well. Serve cold with sprigs of mint.

360 g onions, thinly sliced
2 large potatoes, thickly sliced
1 celery head, thinly sliced
50 g butter or margarine
1 litre vegetable stock
125 ml double cream
pinch ground nutmeg
5 ml (1 teaspoon) salt
2 ml (½ teaspoon) pepper

84   Vichyssoise   (F)

Serves 4;   kJ per portion 680;   Prep time 20 min;   Cooking time 40 min.

1. Melt the butter or margarine in a large saucepan and sauté the onions until soft.
2. Add half the celery and sauté for a further 2 to 3 minutes.
3. Add the potato slices and stock. Season with salt, pepper and nutmeg and bring to the boil. Simmer, covered, until the vegetables are soft.
4. Cool the soup slightly and force it through a fine sieve or liquidise in a blender to form a purée. Chill for at least 1 hour.
5. Poach the remaining celery in a little water until just tender, about 5 minutes. Drain the celery and allow it to cool, then stir it into the soup (f).
6. Stir in the cream and chill before serving.

Variation: Use plain yoghurt instead of the cream.

Note: To serve soup that has been frozen, allow it to thaw completely, then stir briskly to blend well, add more salt and pepper if necessary and continue with step 6.

1 kg ripe tomatoes, skinned
125 ml (½ cup) cooked ham,
diced
125 ml (½ cup) cucumber,
diced
25 ml (2 tablespoons) celery,
diced
juice and grated rind
of ½ lemon
4 drops tabasco sauce
100 ml double cream
12,5 ml (1 tablespoon) sugar
10 ml (2 teaspoons) salt

85   Chilled summer tomato soup

Serves 4;   kJ per portion 430;   Prep time 15 min.

1. Liquidise the tomatoes in a blender or pass them through a fine sieve to form a purée.
2. Chill for at least 1 hour before serving, then add all the other ingredients and stir well. Serve at once.

Note: To skin tomatoes easily, pour boiling water over them, leave for 1 minute, then peel off the skin.

1 kg fresh ripe tomatoes,
skinned and coarsely chopped
1 small cucumber, peeled and
finely chopped
1 green pepper, seeded and
finely chopped
½ onion, finely chopped
1 stalk celery, finely chopped
1 clove garlic, crushed
25 ml tomato purée
125 ml cold water
50 ml olive oil
25 ml white wine vinegar
2 slices white bread without
crusts
10 ml (2 teaspoons) salt
freshly ground black pepper

86   Gazpacho

Serves 6;   kJ per portion 600;   Prep time 30 min.

1. Place all the ingredients in a blender and blend until the mixture is smooth and thick.
2. Chill for 2 hours before serving, then serve with all or a few of the following: croûtons; chopped cucumber; chopped tomato; chopped onion or spring onion; black olives; chopped chives or parsley.

---

1 avocado pear, peeled and
pitted
750 ml chicken stock, cooled
25 ml (2 tablespoons) spring
onions, finely chopped
125 ml plain yoghurt
2 ml (½ teaspoon) salt
dash pepper
Garnish:
finely chopped chives

87   Avocado bisque

Serves 4;   kJ per portion 900;   Prep time 10 min.

1. Purée all the ingredients, except the yoghurt and chives, in a blender.
2. In a large bowl, beat the yoghurt until it is smooth.
3. Add the purée, stirring well.
4. Cover the soup and refrigerate for at least 2 hours before serving. Serve topped with chopped chives.

---

1 medium-sized cucumber
500 ml plain yoghurt
12,5 ml strained lemon juice
5 ml olive oil
5 ml (1 teaspoon) fresh mint
leaves, finely chopped
2 ml (½ teaspoon) fresh dill,
finely chopped
5 ml (1 teaspoon) salt

88   Cold yoghurt and cucumber soup

Serves 4;   kJ per portion 800;   Prep time 10 min.

1. Peel the cucumber, slice it lengthways, then scoop out and discard the seeds. Grate the cucumber coarsely.
2. In a deep bowl, stir the yoghurt with a whisk until it is completely smooth. Using the whisk, gently beat in the grated cucumber and all the other ingredients.
3. Chill the soup for at least 1 hour and serve in chilled soup bowls.

---

450 g soft pears, peeled, cored
and thinly sliced
3 fresh peaches, skinned and
stones retained
10 ml (2 teaspoons) cornflour
750 ml water
rind and juice of 2 lemons
125 ml sour cream
85 to 115 g sugar
5 to 10 ml (1 to 2 teaspoons)
ground cinnamon
Garnish:
lemon slices
watercress

89   Summer fruit soup   (F)

Serve 4-5;   kJ per portion 900;   Prep time 15 min;   Cooking time 25-30 min.

1. Place the fruit in a large saucepan with the water and lemon rind and simmer, covered, until the fruit is soft.
2. Pass the fruit through a coarse sieve and return the purée to the saucepan.
3   Mix the cornflour with the lemon juice to a smooth paste. Stir the paste gradually into the soup and heat until thickened, stirring continuously.
4. Gradually add the cinnamon and sugar to taste, stirring often. Chill for at least 2 hours (f).
5. Serve garnished with lemon slices and watercress, and with the sour cream as an accompaniment.

1 kg whole white fish, entrails and fins removed, washed and cut in pieces
1 carrot, peeled; 1 onion, peeled
1,5 litres water
bouquet garni (1 sprig parsley, 1 bay leaf)
1 clove
2 white peppercorns
5 to 10 ml (1 to 2 teaspoons) salt

90   Fish stock   (F)

Makes 1,5 litres; kJ per portion 105;   Prep time 20 min;   Cooking time 1 hour

1. Place the fish in a large saucepan together with the water.
2. Bring to the boil, uncovered, skimming the scum off the surface before the stock boils.
3. Add the vegetables, clove, bouquet garni, salt and peppercorns and simmer, covered, until the fish is tender.
4. Strain the stock through a fine sieve. Cool and store in the refrigerator until needed (f).

Note: Shellfish trimmings may be added for extra flavour.

---

2 to 3 kg fish, filleted and cut in small pieces
1 to 2 whole cooked crayfish, shelled and the flesh finely chopped
250 ml (1 cup) cooked prawns, shelled and the flesh finely chopped
2 large onions, finely chopped
2 cloves garlic, crushed
4 tomatoes, skinned and finely chopped
2 litres fish stock
250 ml cooking oil
dry white wine to taste
37,5 ml (3 tablespoons) parsley, finely chopped
2 ml (½ teaspoon) each of dried thyme, basil, oreganum and rosemary
2 bay leaves; pinch saffron
2 ml (½ teaspoon) celery salt
10 ml (2 teaspoons) salt
pinch freshly ground black pepper

91   Bouillabaisse   (F)

Serves 4-6;   kJ per portion 1 500;   Prep time 30 min;   Cooking time 45 min.

1. Heat the oil in a saucepan and sauté the onions and parsley until the onions are soft.
2. Add the garlic, herbs, bay leaf and tomatoes and simmer, uncovered, for 10 to 15 minutes.
3. Add the fish stock, wine, saffron, celery salt, salt and pepper and simmer a further 10 to 15 minutes.
4. Add the fish, crayfish and prawns and simmer, covered, until the fish is cooked (f).
5. Serve immediately with garlic bread spread with rouille (see below).

Note: Use at least 5 kinds of fish and shellfish for the best result.

Rouille
2 to 4 cloves garlic; 1 thin slice bread, soaked in fish stock
25 ml oil; 12,5 ml mayonnaise
5 ml (1 teaspoon) cayenne pepper; 10 ml (2 teaspoons) paprika

1. Crush the garlic with the cayenne pepper and paprika.
2. Mix to a paste with the rest of the ingredients.

92 Curried snoek soup (F)

2 large snoek heads
2 large onions, thinly sliced
125 ml (½ cup) table celery, thinly sliced
2 medium potatoes, diced
1 or 2 chillis, seeded and finely chopped
25 ml (2 tablespoons) soft butter or oil
125 ml (½ cup) flour
small piece green ginger, crushed
3 cloves garlic, finely chopped
5 ml (1 teaspoon) turmeric
12,5 ml (1 tablespoon) curry powder
1,5 litres water
10 ml (2 teaspoons) salt

Serves 4-6;   kJ per portion 1 200;   Prep time 35 min;   Cooking time 45 min.

1. Wash the snoek heads and cut them in half, leaving on some of the flesh behind the neck.
2. Heat the butter or oil in a large saucepan and sauté the onions until transparent. Add the ginger, garlic, celery and potatoes.
3. Remove the saucepan from the stove, blend in the flour to form a smooth paste and return the saucepan to the stove.
4. Add the salt and water, stirring all the time, and simmer, covered, for 10 minutes.
5. Mix the turmeric and curry powder to a smooth paste with a little water and add to the soup, together with the chillis, stirring constantly.
6. Add the fish heads to the soup and simmer, covered, until the flesh is cooked, adding more water if necessary.
7. Remove the fish bones (f) and serve at once.

93 Clam chowder

580 g canned clams, drained and the liquid reserved
60 ml (¼ cup) pork, diced
2 onions, finely chopped
500 ml (2 cups) raw potato, diced
25 ml (2 tablespoons) butter or margarine
500 ml boiling water
500 ml milk, scalded
250 ml evaporated milk
5 ml (1 teaspoon) salt
2 ml (½ teaspoon) pepper

Serves 8;   kJ per portion 1 000;   Prep time 15 min;   Cooking time 15 min.

1. Fry the pork in a large saucepan until crisp. Remove and set aside.
2. Add the onions to the fat in the saucepan and fry them until they are tender but not brown.
3. Add the potato, salt, pepper, clam liquid and the boiling water and simmer, covered, for 10 minutes.
4. Add the clams and simmer for a further 5 minutes. Stir in the scalded and the evaporated milk and the butter or margarine, blending well.
5. Chill the soup for a few hours to ripen, then reheat but do not allow to boil. Serve at once.

94 Cream of mussel soup

1 litre (4 cups) mussels
1 onion; 250 ml water
500 ml thin white sauce (p. 179 and table on p. 180)
12,5 ml vinegar
12,5 ml dry white wine
1 small bunch parsley, tied with string
5 ml (1 teaspoon) salt
2 ml (½ teaspoon) pepper

Serves 6-8;   kJ per portion 900;   Prep time 30 min;   Cooking time 45 min.

1. Scrub the mussels well, discarding those that are open and will not close when tapped sharply.
2. Place the mussels in a saucepan with the water, onion, salt, pepper and the parsley. Place over low heat until the mussels open, discarding any that do not.
3. Remove the beard and weedy growths from the mussels and strain the stock through a fine sieve.
4. Make the white sauce in a large saucepan and add the mussel stock, vinegar, wine and more salt and pepper, if necessary.
5. Now add the mussels, shelled or in the shells, and heat gently but do not boil. Serve at once.

60

150 g cooked perlemoen, sliced
5 ml (1 teaspoon) cornflour
5 ml soy sauce; 5 ml dry sherry
500 ml chicken stock or fish
stock
5 ml (1 teaspoon) salt
1 ml (¼ teaspoon) pepper
Garnish:
finely chopped parsley

95 Perlemoen soup (F)

Serves 4; kJ per portion 900; Prep time 15 min + 30 min for marinating; Cooking time 10 min.

1. In a large, flat dish, mix the cornflour to a smooth paste with the soy sauce and sherry.
2. Marinate the perlemoen slices in the mixture for about 30 minutes, turning occasionally.
3. Bring the chicken or fish stock to the boil in a large saucepan.
4. Add the perlemoen slices and the marinade to the saucepan and simmer, uncovered, for 5 minutes. Add the salt and pepper (f).
5. Serve at once, sprinkled with chopped parsley.

Note: Thaw frozen soup and stir to blend before heating.

2 small whole crayfish, cooked
450 g fish trimmings (head,
skin, bones, etc)
25 ml (2 tablespoons) butter or
margarine
50 ml (4 tablespoons) flour
1 carrot, diced
1 onion, finely sliced
2 stalks soup celery, finely
chopped
pinch dried mixed herbs
1 litre water
250 ml dry white wine
12,5 ml double cream
12,5 ml (1 tablespoon) salt
2 ml (½ teaspoon) pepper

96 Crayfish soup (F)

Serves 4-6;   kJ per portion 900;   Prep time 30 min;   Cooking time 50 min.

1. Remove the meat and coral from the crayfish, dice and set aside.
2. Crush the shells and place them in a saucepan together with the fish trimmings, vegetables, salt, pepper, herbs and water. Cover and boil for 40 minutes, then strain the stock through a fine sieve, discarding the shells and fish trimmings.
3. Melt the butter or margarine in a saucepan, remove from the stove and stir in the flour to form a smooth paste. Return the saucepan to the stove. Stirring constantly, add as much stock as is necessary to make a thick, creamy soup (f).
4. Just before serving, stir in the wine, cream and the diced crayfish.

Note: Freeze the diced crayfish and the soup separately. To serve, place the soup over low heat, then add the frozen diced crayfish and heat but do not allow to boil. Add the wine and cream and serve at once.

GARNISHES AND ACCOMPANIMENTS TO SOUPS

Garnishes or accompaniments greatly enhance the appearance and taste of a soup – particularly instant and canned soups, which can be transformed so that they become tastier and more interesting. All soups should be garnished just before serving.

The following give that extra 'something' to soups:
● Add chopped chives, parsley or raw vegetables such as grated carrot, sliced avocado, chopped onion, sliced green pepper, cauliflower flowerets and fresh herbs. Where a recipe calls for dried herbs, use fresh – if available – for they will give the soup an aromatic lift.

- Crisp bacon: remove the rind, cut the bacon into small pieces and fry until crisp. This is delicious sprinkled on bean, tomato or potato soups.
- Crisp fried onion rings for flavour and texture.
- Grated Cheddar, Parmesan or blue cheeses can change the character of a soup dramatically.
- Serve crushed ice in cold soups.
- Add a dollop of yoghurt, cream or sour cream just before serving.

---

cake flour
2 ml (½ teaspoon) salt
1 egg, slightly beaten

97   Noodles

kJ per portion 500;   Prep time 20 min;   Cooking time 15 min.

1. Stir the salt and enough flour into the egg to form a very stiff dough.
2. Knead well and roll out very thinly. Leave for 20 minutes.
3. Cut into narrow strips with a sharp knife or in small shapes with a pastry cutter.
4. Boil in the soup for 15 minutes.

---

250 ml (1 cup) cake flour
5 ml (1 teaspoon) baking powder
12,5 ml (1 tablespoon) soft butter or oil
125 ml milk or 1 egg mixed with 50 ml milk
2 ml (½ teaspoon) salt

98   Dumplings

kJ per portion 560;   Prep time 15 min;   Cooking time 15 min.

1. Sift the dry ingredients together into a bowl and cut in the butter or oil with a knife.
2. Mix with the egg or egg and milk to make a stiff batter.
3. Place teaspoonfuls in the boiling soup 15 minutes before serving and boil, covered, for the rest of the cooking time.

Variations:

1. Use a mixture of 125 ml (½ cup) cake flour and 125 ml (½ cup) wholewheat flour instead of 250 ml (1 cup) cake flour.
2. Substitute sour cream or yoghurt for the butter or oil.

Note: Use the batter immediately as the dumplings may be heavy and lumpy if the batter is allowed to stand.

99   Croûtons

kJ per portion 370;   Prep time 15 min;   Cooking time 1 min.

1. Cut day-old white bread in 10 mm thick slices and remove crusts.
2. Spread with butter and bake in the oven at 180°C (350°F) until light brown all over.
3. Cut into 10 mm cubes and serve in soup.

Variations:

1. Cut day-old white bread in 1 cm cubes. Deep-fry in oil and drain well.
2. Cut slices of unbuttered toast into cubes.
3. Cut slices of white bread into strips, sprinkle with grated cheddar cheese and paprika, and bake in the oven at 200°C (400°F) until crisp and brown. Cut into cubes.
4. Cut slices of white bread into strips, spread thickly with butter mixed with 5 ml (1 teaspoon) mixed herbs and bake in the oven at 200°C (400°F) until crisp and brown. Cut into cubes.

FISH AND SEAFOODS

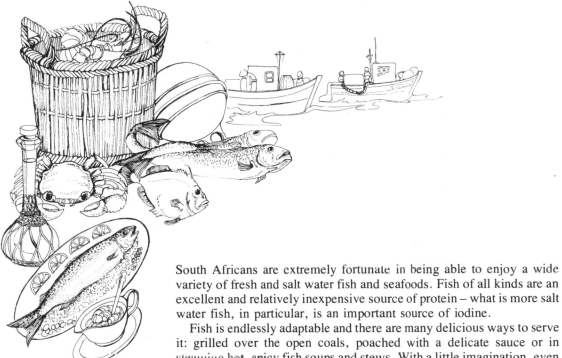

South Africans are extremely fortunate in being able to enjoy a wide variety of fresh and salt water fish and seafoods. Fish of all kinds are an excellent and relatively inexpensive source of protein – what is more salt water fish, in particular, is an important source of iodine.

Fish is endlessly adaptable and there are many delicious ways to serve it: grilled over the open coals, poached with a delicate sauce or in steaming hot, spicy fish soups and stews. With a little imagination, even the beginner is able to prepare fish and seafood dishes that are a gourmet's delight.

Salt water fish may be classified as *white, moderately fat* and *fat*. The following are the more common South African varieties:

	Kind	Appearance and taste	Cooking method
White fish Less oily because the fat is stored in the liver	Haddock (Smoked hake)	Smoked, pale yellow in colour and tends to lose flavour quickly. Sold in fillets, usually frozen.	Poach, kedgerees, pies, casseroles.
	Hake (Stockfish, Cape Whiting)	Tender, white, flaky fish with few bones and a delicate flavour. Sold fresh or frozen, as fillets or portions.	Poach, fry, grill, bake, use in soup and in casseroles.
	Kingklip	Flesh is particularly firm, white and moist.	Fry, bake, deep-fry, grill, stew, casserole, pickle.
Moderately fat fish Fairly oily; fat stored throughout the body	Kabeljou (Kob)	Firm flesh and excellent taste.	Bake, fry, grill, boil, smoke, pickle
	Silverfish	Very tasty, tender fish. Fishermen consider the head a delicacy.	Grill, bake, mince, stuff
	Sole	Flat fish; very tasty with firm, white flesh.	Grill, bake with sauce, fry.

	Kind	Appearance and taste	Cooking method
Fat fish Very oily; fat stored throughout the body	Anchovy	Very oily fish with excellent taste. Usually available canned.	If available fresh, grill over hot coals.
	Angelfish	Firm, white flesh.	Fry, grill, poach, smoke.
	Elf(Shad)	Very tasty fish with firm, white flesh.	Grill, fry, poach.
	Galjoen (Blackfish)	Moist fish with a layer of fat just under the skin. Strong, distinctive flavour.	Grill over open coals.
	Geelbek (Cape Salmon)	Firm white flesh with rather oily skin. Younger fish very tender. Often canned.	Grill, bake whole, fry.
	Harder (Mullet)	Very oily fish with dull white flesh; rich and tasty.	Grill, fry, bake, salt, smoke. Salted and dried haarders called *bokkoms*.
	Hottentot (Copper or Bronze Bream)	Soft, juicy white flesh with a delicious and distinctive flavour.	Steam, poach.
	Kippers (smoked herring)	Very oily fish sold whole or filleted.	Poach, grill, use in pâtés and mousses.
	Maasbanker	Oily fish with dark and very tasty flesh.	Bake, curries, pickle, smoke, grill.
	Mackerel	Oily flesh, but can be very moist, delicate and tasty if cooked when really fresh. Often sold canned.	Grill, bake.
	Monkfish	Sweet flavour and succulent, firm white flesh. Sold in steaks.	Steam, fry, grill, bake, salads.
	Pilchards	Soft, oily fish with a rich, tasty flesh. Usually canned because it doesn't keep well.	If available fresh, grill over hot coals.
	Seventy-four	Firm flesh and excellent taste.	Any cooking method.
	Snoek	Large fish with very firm, oily flesh. Sold whole or in fillets; salted, fresh, smoked or dried.	Grill, fry, bake, use in stews, curries and soups.
	Steenbras	Young fish has tender white flesh, but the older fish is too coarse for good eating.	Grill, fry, bake, poach.
	Stumpnose	Soft white flesh with a sweet flavour.	Grill, fry, bake whole.
	Tuna	Solid, packed flesh, dark red in colour. Very oily and rich taste. Sold in steaks.	Grill, bake.
	Yellowtail (Albacore)	Oily fish, often sold canned.	Steam, grill, fry, pickle.

The *freshwater* fish available in South Africa include trout, carp, bass, bream (kurper), barbel, eel and yellowfish. Most freshwater fish are best grilled over the open coals immediately after being caught, or deep-fried until crisp. The most versatile is trout, which may be prepared in a number of ways.

64 Kob Creole (recipe 100), a delectable mixture of flavours and textures.

Seafoods are popular, if expensive, in South Africa. They may be divided into *Molluscs* and *Crustaceans:*

	Appearance and taste	Cooking method
Molluscs Octopus, squid calamari	Tentacles only are used and are sold fresh or frozen.	Soups, stews, deep-fried in batter.
Oysters	Sold in the shell.	Raw, smoked, grill, stews.
Mussels	Must be really fresh. Have a very distinctive flavour.	Risottos, stews, boil, grill, fry, soups.
Perlemoen (Abalone)	Rather tough but flavoursome flesh which must be carefully prepared.	Stews, soups, rissoles.
Alikreukel (Giant Periwinkle)	Flesh tough and must be correctly prepared.	Stews, soups, curries.
Clams	Available canned in brine or smoked.	Stews, casseroles, soups.
Crustaceans Crabs	Pinkish white and brown flesh with sweet taste.	Mousses, salads, grill, stews, casseroles.
Crayfish (Rock Lobster)	Sweet, firm white flesh, should be eaten as fresh as possible.	Grill, boil, salads, curries, soups, casseroles.
Langoustines (King Prawns)	Usually sold frozen or ready-cooked, flesh similar to crayfish.	Grill, soups, curries, casseroles, salads, deep-fry.
Prawns and Shrimps	Flesh similar to crayfish, but very much smaller. Sold frozen or ready-cooked.	Grill, soups, curries, casseroles, salads, deep-fry.

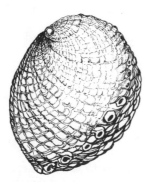

Selecting fresh and frozen fish and seafoods

Fish and seafoods may be purchased either fresh or frozen, but because they spoil easily, extreme care should be taken in selecting and handling them.

Fresh fish should always:
- have a clean smell.
- have full, lustrous and slightly protruding eyes; never dull, sunken eyes.
- have bright red gills.
- have flesh that is firm to the touch and leaves no depression when pressed lightly with the fingertips.
- have firm flesh along the backbone; if it is soft, this is a reliable indication that the fish is no longer fresh.
- have a shiny, moist appearance; never look dull and dry.

Crayfish is freshest when bought live from a tank. Live crayfish should move their legs and the tail should curl under the body. To check that it is fresh, pull back the tail and release it; if the crayfish is fresh, the tail will recoil immediately. Cooked fresh crayfish and prawns should have a clean smell.

Uncooked frozen *crayfish* has a greyish-brown shell and the underside of the tail should be translucent and firm.

Frozen or unfrozen *cooked crayfish* should have a bright red shell and firm, white flesh. If the flesh is soft and jelly-like, it has spoiled.

Oyster, mussel and *clam* shells should still be closed. If they are open, it is a sign that the creature inside is dead and that it might be poisonous.

Note:
- Make sure that you know, and adhere to, the regulations regarding the size, amount and time of year when seafoods may be legally caught.
- Calculate on 220 g raw fish with bones and 180 g filleted fish per person.
- When buying a whole fish, for example kabeljou, galjoen or roman, allow 1,25 kg for 4 people.

Fish and seafoods bought *frozen* should always:
- be bought from a reputable dealer.
- be frozen hard.
- have a wrapping that is neither loose nor moist.

Scaling and cleaning fish
1. Before working with fish, wash your hands in cold water and rub them with a slice of lemon – this will prevent their absorbing a fishy smell. Rinse your hands in cold water again when you have finished preparing the fish.
2. Insert a small, sharp, pointed knife into the opening under the gills and cut along the belly towards the tail. Remove the entrails and rinse the inside of the fish under cold running water.
3. Place the fish on a wooden board covered with a sheet of paper, hold it firmly by the tail and scrape the scales off, working from the tail towards the head. Use the blunt edge of the knife to avoid damaging the skin.
4. Rinse the fish under cold water, and if desired, remove the head and tail.

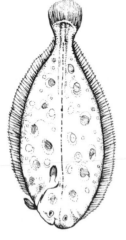

Skinning and filleting fish
1. Cut a strip of the skin off along the backbone, using a pair of scissors.
2. Cut the skin away around the gills.
3. Pull the skin off by hand, starting at the tail end. If the flesh tears, use a knife to hold the flesh down.
4. To remove the bones, insert a sharp knife close to the backbone at the tail end and cut, as close as possible to the backbone, in the direction of the head in order to separate the flesh from one side of the backbone. Follow the same procedure on the other side.
5. Small bones can be removed by hand.
6. To skin soles, first make a slit at the head and at the tail end of the fish. Grasp the skin firmly at the tail end and pull it off in one swift motion. Repeat on the other side. Now grasp the row of bones along the edge of the sole and rip off the whole row, from tail to head.

Note:

- Keep the bones, head and skin to make fish stock.
- It is easier to skin and fillet fish if it is very cold.
- If fish is to be pickled, it is not necessary to remove the small bones as these will soften in the acidity of the curry sauce.

Storing fresh and frozen fish

Because fish spoils so easily it is generally better to use fresh fish immediately or to freeze it for later use. It should be loosely packed if stored in the refrigerator but, as the fish smell soon permeates all other foodstuffs in its proximity, fish should be used as soon as possible – under no circumstances should it be stored for longer than 36 hours in the refrigerator without freezing.

Freezing fish

1. Gut the fish and discard the entrails. Wash out the body cavity thoroughly with cold water.
2. Cut off the head and tail and cut the fish into serving portions.
3. Wrap each serving portion in plastic or aluminium foil, making sure that the flesh is covered completely to avoid the possibility of freeze burn.
4. Label each package, stating type of fish, quantity and date, and freeze at −18 °C (0 °F) in the freezer.

Note:

- Fresh fish may be frozen whole after removing the head, tail and entrails.
- Crayfish, prawns and shrimps may be frozen either raw or cooked.
- Perlemoen must be removed from the shells and cleaned before freezing.
- Alikreukel should be cooked before freezing.
- Fish and seafoods bought frozen should also be labelled and then stored in the freezer at −18 °C (0 °F).
- Fish should be frozen immediately after it is caught, so unless you can be sure that shop-bought fish is absolutely fresh, it is usually safer to buy commercially frozen fish.

Preparing and cooking frozen fish and seafoods

Most frozen fish should be thawed before cooking. Generally speaking, it is sufficient to thaw *whole* fish for 8 to 10 hours in the refrigerator or 5 hours at room temperature and *fish pieces* for 1 hour in the refrigerator.

Frozen *fish fillets, crumbed fish* or *fish sticks* can be cooked directly from the frozen state, but remember that if it is deep-fried, frozen fish will make the temperature of the oil decrease quickly. Care should therefore be taken to maintain the correct temperature.

Frozen *crayfish* or *prawns* should be boiled either frozen or immediately after thawing.

Frozen *perlemoen* should be thawed completely before being cooked.

Note: All thawed raw fish and seafoods should be used as soon as possible. If too much has been thawed, the excess cannot be refrozen although if desired it can be cooked and then frozen.

67

To keep raw fish fillets fresh and odourless, rinse them in fresh lemon juice and water, then dry thoroughly, wrap and refrigerate.

Most of the basic cooking methods are well-suited to fish, but the main point is not to overcook it as fish dries out quickly, thus losing its delicate flavour.

Steaming

This is an excellent way to prepare a delicate fish or fish cut into thin fillets.
1. Sprinkle the cleaned fish with salt and lemon juice or vinegar, allowing 5 ml (1 teaspoon) salt per kilogram of fish. Dot with butter.
2. Using boiling water, half-fill the bottom of a double boiler or a saucepan large enough to support a plate or suspend a wire basket above the water.
3. Place the fish on the plate or in the wire basket. The fish can also be wrapped in aluminium foil before placing it in the container above the boiling water.
4. Cover tightly with the lid and allow the water to boil briskly so that the fish is enveloped in steam. Steam until done, usually 10 to 20 minutes. To test whether the fish is ready, prick it with a fork; if done, the flesh will flake easily.
5. Steamed fish can be served either with a sauce or plain with chopped parsley and butter sauce.

Poaching

To poach fish, it is simmered in a little liquid at just below boiling point, so that it retains its delicate flavour.
1. Use sufficient cold liquid – water, wine, fish stock or a mixture of milk and stock – to barely cover the fish in a shallow saucepan.
2. If using white fish, season with salt and a little pepper; do not season if using smoked fish. Heat slowly, covered, but do not allow to boil.
3. Allow 5 to 8 minutes cooking time for thin fillets such as sole and 10 minutes for thicker fillets.
4. Lift the fish out of the poaching liquid with a slotted spoon and keep warm while making the sauce.

Note:
● Fish may be poached either on top of the stove or in the oven.
● Keep the temperature constant at 80 °C (180 °F) if cooking on top of the stove and at 150 °C (300 °F) if poaching in the oven.

100 Kob Creole

500 g kob, cleaned
1 onion, peeled and finely chopped
1 green pepper, seeded and sliced
120 g mushrooms, sliced
400 g tomatoes, skinned and chopped
62,5 ml (5 tablespoons) butter or margarine
25 ml tomato sauce
mashed potato for the decorative border

Serves 4;   kJ per portion 1 310;   Prep time 45 min;   Cooking time 50 min.

1. Wash the fish and place it in a large saucepan. Cover with water and simmer, covered, over low heat until done, about 15 minutes.
2. Meanwhile, melt the butter or margarine in a saucepan and sauté the onion and green pepper until tender, about 7 minutes.
3. Add the mushrooms and sauté for a further 3 minutes.
4. Stir in the tomatoes and tomato sauce and simmer, covered, for 30 minutes. Add salt and pepper.
5. Pipe the potato around the edge of an oval serving dish. Drain the kob and place it in the centre, then pour the sauce over the fish. Serve at once.

---

101 Gefilte fish

1 kg white fish, filleted (reserve bones, head and skin if desired)
1 egg; 2 small onions
3 or 4 medium carrots
1 thick slice white bread (without crusts)
5 ml butter or margarine
10 ml water
5 ml (1 teaspoon) chopped parsley (optional)
25 ml (2 tablespoons) ground almonds
5 ml (1 teaspoon) sugar
12,5 ml (1 tablespoon) salt
5 ml (1 teaspoon) pepper
Garnish:
slices of the cooked carrot

Serves 8;   kJ per portion 980;   Prep time 30 min;   Cooking time 1½ hours

1. Mince the fish, 1 carrot, 1 onion and the parsley.
2. Break the bread into smallish pieces and add it with the egg and salt to the minced fish, now stir to blend well. Add the pepper, sugar, butter or margarine and water and stir in.
3. You should now have a fairly stiff but easily malleable mixture. With dampened hands, shape the fish into balls slightly bigger than golf balls.
4. Now fill a large saucepan with enough water to cover the gefilte fish when it is added. Before placing the fish in the pot, put in the remaining onion, sliced carrots and a sprig of parsley – for extra flavour add the large fish bones, heads and skins of the filleted fish. Bring this mixture to the boil.
5. Using a slotted spoon, gently lower the fishballs into the stock and lower the heat. Simmer the gefilte fish, covered, for about 1½ hours.
6. Once cooked, remove the fishballs from the stock and arrange on a large, flat dish. To garnish, place a slice of the cooked carrot on top of each fishball and pour over the strained stock. Allow to cool in the refrigerator; after a time the stock will gel to form a tasty aspic.

Note: Traditionally, a combination of two or three varieties of white fish may be minced together to give gefilte fish a more distinctive flavour.

---

102 Fish in yoghurt sauce

500 g hake fillets, skinned
2 large onions, cut in thick slices
a little water
125 ml plain yoghurt
2 ml (½ teaspoon) dried mixed herbs
5 ml (1 teaspoon) salt
2 ml (½ teaspoon) pepper

Serves 4;   kJ per portion 1 360;   Prep time 25 min;   Cooking time 15 min.

1. Place the hake in a large frying-pan with a little water and sprinkle with salt and pepper. Add the slices of onion and sprinkle them with the mixed herbs.
2. Cover the frying-pan with a lid or with foil and steam over medium heat until the fish is tender, about 10 minutes.
3. Remove the lid or foil and reduce the heat to low. Push the fish to one side and add the yoghurt to the onions, stirring constantly. Simmer for 2 minutes.
4. Transfer the fish to a serving dish, decorate on top with the onions and pour over the sauce. Serve hot.

Variations:
1. Add cooked peas or mixed vegetables to make the dish more substantial.
2. Use sour cream instead of the yoghurt.

103 Pearl balls in sweet and sour sauce (F)

170 g white fish, filleted, skinned and minced
37,5 ml (3 tablespoons) parboiled long-grain rice
5 ml soy sauce; 1 egg, beaten
1 ml (¼ teaspoon) garlic salt
2 ml (½ teaspoon) salt
2 ml (½ teaspoon) pepper
Sweet and sour sauce (recipe 324)

Serves 4; kJ per portion 1 600; Prep time 45 min; Cooking time 20 min.

1. Spread the parboiled rice evenly on absorbent paper to dry thoroughly.
2. Combine the fish, soy sauce, a little flour, the garlic salt, salt and pepper. Add sufficient beaten egg to bind and with floured hands form into 12 balls. Roll each ball in the rice – making sure that it is completely coated – and press the rice grains firmly into the balls.
3. Place pearl balls well apart in a colander lined with absorbent paper and steam, covered, over a saucepan of boiling water until the rice is tender, about 20 minutes.
4. Prepare the sauce as directed (recipe 324).
5. Place the pearl balls on a heated serving dish and serve at once with the piquant sauce (f).

104 Poached steenbras in lemon sauce

1 kg steenbras, filleted, skinned and sliced
fish stock (recipe 90)
10 ml (2 teaspoons) salt
5 ml (1 teaspoon) pepper
Sauce:
grated rind and juice of 2 lemons
2 egg yolks, beaten
5 ml (1 teaspoon) cornflour

Serves 6; kJ per portion 1 010; Prep time 30 min; Cooking time 30 min.

1. Sprinkle the fish slices with the salt and pepper.
2. Make the fish stock as directed (recipe 90) and poach the fish slices in it
3. Combine the sauce ingredients in a bowl and beat in a little of the hot stock. Stir the mixture into the remaining hot stock in the saucepan.
4. Bring the sauce to the boil and continue boiling rapidly, uncovered, until it is reduced to approximately 400 ml. Stir occasionally.
5. Serve the fish at once with the sauce.

105 Poached soles in mushroom sauce

3 large soles, filleted
white wine to cover
350 ml mushroom sauce (p. 180)
5 ml (1 teaspoon) salt
2 ml (½ teaspoon) pepper

Serves 3; kJ per portion 1 100; Prep time 45 min; Cooking time 20 min.

1. Season the soles with salt and pepper.
2. Poach them in white wine as described on p. 68.
3. Prepare the mushroom sauce (p. 180).
4. Place the soles on a large heatproof dish, pour over the sauce and place under the grill until the sauce is golden brown but not boiling. Serve at once.

106 Sole Mornay

6 small soles, filleted, rolled and secured with a skewer
375 ml (1½ cups) thick Mornay sauce (p.180)
125 ml (½ cup) Cheddar cheese, grated
250 ml dry white wine
1 bouquet garni (parsley, thyme, bay leaf)
10 ml (2 teaspoons) salt
5 ml (1 teaspoon) pepper

Serves 4; kJ per portion 1 100; Prep time 40 min; Cooking time 20 min.

1. Season soles with salt and pepper.
2. In a large saucepan, poach the soles in the wine, to which a bouquet garni has been added, for 10 minutes.
3. Carefully remove the soles and place on a serving dish, keeping them warm. Remove the bouquet garni.
4. Boil the poaching liquid briskly to reduce it to 125 ml and add to the Mornay sauce (p. 180), beating to blend well.
5. Pour the Mornay sauce over the soles, sprinkle with the grated cheese and bake in the oven at 220°C (425°F) until the cheese is lightly browned. Serve at once.

6 serving portions kingklip, filleted
60 g butter or margarine
200 ml white wine
7 ml (1½ teaspoons) salt
2 ml (½ teaspoon) pepper
Sauce:
125 g canned shrimps, drained
125 g canned mushroom pieces, drained
50 ml (4 tablespoons) celery, coarsely chopped
1 small onion, studded with 3 cloves
50 ml (4 tablespoons) stuffed olives, coarsely chopped
25 ml (2 tablespoons) parsley, finely chopped
50 ml (4 tablespoons) butter or margarine
50 ml (4 tablespoons) flour
500 ml milk
5 ml Worcester sauce
½ bay leaf; sprinkling salt
pinch pepper
Garnish:
finely chopped parsley
sliced stuffed olives

107 Poached kingklip in shrimp sauce

Serves 6;   kJ per portion 1 340;   Prep time 30 min;   Cooking time 20 min.

1. Place the kingklip in a shallow ovenproof dish, season with salt and pepper and dot with the butter or margarine.
2. Add the white wine and bake in the oven at 160 °C (325 °F) until the fish flakes easily.
3. Meanwhile, make the sauce. Melt the butter or margarine in a saucepan and stir in the flour, a little at a time, to make a smooth paste. Cook, stirring, for 1 minute.
4. Heat the milk with the onion and bay leaf in another saucepan and allow to stand for 30 minutes. Strain through a fine sieve.
5. Add the strained milk to the butter and flour mixture and heat, stirring all the time, until the mixture is thick and smooth.
6. Remove from the stove and stir in the shrimps, mushrooms, celery, olives, parsley and Worcester sauce. Return to the stove and heat through, adding salt and pepper if necessary.
7. Place the cooked kingklip on a heated serving dish. Pour the sauce over the fish and place under the grill for 2 minutes. Serve at once, garnished with sliced olives and chopped parsley.

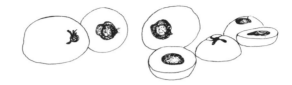

Add a little lemon juice to the water when boiling fish and the flesh will stay white.

Fishy odour on cooking utensils can be removed by soaking them in strong tea.

Before you start cleaning fish, rub salt into your fingers and they won't slip.

To scale fish more easily, dip it in boiling water for a minute before scraping.

2 medium barbel
2 fresh anchovies
2 small onions, thinly sliced
warm water; salted water
25 ml vinegar
juice of 1 lemon
bouquet garni (parsley, thyme, bay leaf)
grated mace; grated nutmeg
12,5 ml (1 tablespoon) salt

108 Poached barbel in anchovy sauce   (F)

Serves 4;   kJ per portion 1 020;   Prep time 45 min;   Cooking time 45 min.

1. Soak the barbel in salted water for 3 hours. Drain.
2. Place the barbel in a large saucepan with the salt and warm water to cover. Simmer, covered, until done. Remove the fish and set aside.
3. Combine 500 ml of the cooking liquid with the anchovies, onions, vinegar, lemon juice, bouquet garni, a little mace and nutmeg in a saucepan and simmer for 15 minutes. Strain through a fine sieve and return the strained liquid to the saucepan.
4. Add the fish to the sauce (f) in the saucepan and simmer but do not allow it to boil. Transfer to a heated serving dish and serve at once.

BAKED FISH

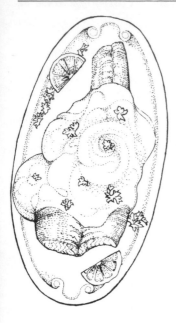

Baking is a dry heat cooking method and, since fish dries out more quickly than meat, special care must be taken to ensure that baked fish does not become hard and dry.

1. Season the fish with salt and pepper and place in a greased or ungreased casserole. If using an ungreased dish, dot the fish with butter or margarine.
2. Bake, covered, in the oven at 200 °C (400 °F) for 25 to 30 minutes, depending on the size of the fish. Test the fish to see if it is done by flaking it with a fork.
3. Remove the lid from the dish for the last 5 minutes of the baking time to allow the fish to brown. Serve hot.

Note:
- This method works very well for stuffed fish, but you must allow extra time for the stuffing to cook through.
- To ensure that it does not dry out, fish can also be wrapped in greased foil before baking or brushed with a marinade.
- Baked fish is delicious when served with a sauce.

---

500 g cooked white fish, flaked
250 g cooked potatoes, mashed
25 ml (2 tablespoons) butter or margarine, melted
3 eggs, separated
125 ml (½ cup) Cheddar cheese, finely grated
50 ml milk
10 ml (2 teaspoons) parsley, finely chopped
5 ml (1 teaspoon) salt
2 ml (½ teaspoon) pepper

109   Fish with cheese sauce

Serves 4;   kJ per portion 1 710;   Prep time 20 min;   Cooking time 30 min.

1. Combine the flaked fish, potatoes, melted butter or margarine, 2 egg yolks and milk in a bowl.
2. Place in a shallow ovenproof dish and bake in the oven at 190 °C (375 °F) for 20 minutes.
3. Meanwhile, whisk the egg whites until very stiff but not dry. Beat the remaining egg yolk and fold the egg whites into it, together with the grated cheese, parsley, salt and pepper.
4. Spread the egg and cheese mixture over the fish and return to the oven immediately. Bake until the top is brown, about 10 minutes. Serve at once.

---

12 kipper fillets, skinned and cut in strips
6 large parboiled potatoes, cubed
3 large onions, thinly sliced
85 g butter or margarine, melted
5 ml (1 teaspoon) pepper

110   Kipper bake   (F)

Serves 6;   kJ per portion 1 210;   Prep time 25 min;   Cooking time 1 hour 10 min.

1. Mix the kippers and onions and season with half the pepper.
2. Place half the potato cubes in a greased casserole and season with the remaining pepper.
3. Pour over a little of the melted butter or margarine, then cover with the kipper and onion mixture.
4. Place the rest of the cubed potatoes around the edges of the dish. Brush the remaining melted butter or margarine over the ingredients, making sure that the potatoes are covered.
5. Bake in the centre of the oven at 180 °C (350 °F) until golden brown, about 1 hour (f). Serve at once.

500 g cooked haddock, flaked
2 eggs
grated cheese
120 g vermicelli, cooked
300 ml white sauce (p. 179)
25 ml mayonnaise
5 ml prepared mustard

111 Haddock savoury

Serves 6;   kJ per portion 1 110;   Prep time 20 min;   Cooking time 10 min.

1. Combine the haddock and vermicelli in a greased ovenproof dish.
2. Make two hollows in the mixture and drop in the raw eggs.
3. Mix the mayonnaise and mustard into the white sauce (p. 179) and pour over the haddock mixture.
4. Sprinkle with the grated cheese and bake in the oven at 180°C (350°F) until the eggs have set, about 10 minutes. Serve hot.

Note: More eggs may be used, if desired.

---

1 kg geelbek, entrails and backbone removed
25 ml (2 tablespoons) butter or margarine
30 g dry breadcrumbs
10 ml (2 teaspoons) salt
5 ml (1 teaspoon) pepper
Stuffing:
375 ml (1½ cups) fresh white breadcrumbs
1 egg, beaten
5 ml (1 teaspoon) onion, minced
12,5 ml (1 tablespoon) parsley, finely chopped
2 ml (½ teaspoon) salt
freshly ground black pepper

112 Stuffed geelbek

Serves 4;   kJ per portion 1 040;   Prep time 15 min;   Cooking time 1 hour

1. Sprinkle the fish, inside and out, with salt and pepper.
2. Combine the ingredients for the stuffing in a bowl. Stuff the cavity and tie string around the fish so that the stuffing is securely covered with flesh to prevent it from spilling out while the fish is baking.
3. Place the stuffed fish in an ovenproof dish, sprinkle with dry breadcrumbs and dot with butter or margarine.
4. Bake in the oven at 180°C (350°F) for 40 minutes to 1 hour (f). Serve with butter sauce (recipe 317) or parsley sauce (recipe p. 181).

Variations:
1. Use sage and onion stuffing (recipe 306) instead of parsley stuffing.
2. Use raisin and walnut stuffing (recipe 313) in place of the parsley stuffing.

---

1 herring, soaked in cold water to extract salt and drained
1 sweetbread, boiled and cut in 12 pieces
1 egg, beaten
breadcrumbs seasoned with salt and pepper
butter
12 oyster shells

113 Mock oysters

Serves 1-2;   kJ per portion 1 200;   Prep time 15 min;   Cooking time 10 min.

1. Mince the herring finely and divide into 12 portions. Place each portion in an oyster shell.
2. Dip each piece of sweetbread in the beaten egg and then coat with breadcrumbs. Place one on top of each portion of herring in the oyster shells.
3. Sprinkle more seasoned breadcrumbs over the filling in each shell and dab with butter.
4. Bake in the oven at 180°C (350°F) until the butter sizzles and the breadcrumbs are brown. Serve at once.

Remove the skin of yellowtail before steaming, grilling, frying or pickling.

130 g canned mackerel, drained, boned and flaked
2 large eggs, separated
62,5 ml (5 tablespoons) butter or margarine
100 ml (²/₅ cup) flour
300 ml milk
grated rind and juice of ½ lemon
5 ml (1 teaspoon) salt
2 ml (½ teaspoon) pepper

114 Mackerel soufflé

Serves 4; kJ per portion 1 005; Prep time 45 min; Cooking time 45 min.

1. Melt the butter or magarine in a saucepan over medium heat. Remove from the stove and stir in the flour to form a smooth paste. Gradually stir in the milk, blending well.
2. When the sauce is smooth, return the pan to the stove and bring to the boil, stirring all the time. Add the salt and pepper, and remove from the stove once more.
3. Now stir the mackerel into the sauce together with the egg yolks, lemon rind and juice.
4. Whisk the egg whites in a bowl until they are just stiff and fold them with a metal spoon quickly and carefully into the sauce.
5. Turn the mixture into a 1 litre soufflé dish and bake in the centre of the oven at 190 °C (375 °F) until the soufflé is well risen and golden brown, about 35 minutes. Serve at once.

FISH CASSEROLES AND STEWS

Fish and seafoods make excellent stews and casseroles. The basic method is the same as that described on p. 133.

1,5 kg carp, scales, entrails, head and tail removed
3 onions, finely chopped
3 carrots, peeled and thinly sliced
170 g bacon rashers
6 anchovies, finely chopped
62,5 ml (5 tablespoons) butter or margarine
25 ml (2 tablespoons) flour
375 ml dry red wine
375 ml cold water
5 ml lemon juice
salted water to cover
25 ml vinegar
2 cloves garlic, finely chopped
12,5 ml (1 tablespoon) parsley, finely chopped
12,5 ml (1 tablespoon) sweet basil, finely chopped
1 sprig thyme
10 ml (2 teaspoons) salt
5 ml (1 teaspoon) pepper

115 Braised carp (F)

Serves 6; kJ per portion 1 600; Prep time 45 min. + soaking time; Cooking time 1 hour 20 min.

1. Wash the carp well and soak in the salted water and vinegar for 2 hours. Drain.
2. Place the bacon strips, vegetables, garlic, herbs and anchovies in a heavy-bottomed saucepan.
3. Season the fish with salt and pepper and place on top of this mixture. Cook, covered, over low heat for 10 minutes.
4. Add 125 ml red wine and simmer, uncovered, until the wine cooks away. Add the rest of the wine and the cold water. Cover and simmer for a further hour, basting often.
5. When the fish is done, lift it gently out of the liquid and place it on a serving dish.
6. Purée the vegetables by passing them through a fine sieve or liquidising in a blender. Add to liquid.
7. Melt the butter or margarine in a small saucepan, remove from the stove and blend in the flour. Return to the stove.
8. Gradually add the hot puréed vegetables, stirring all the time, and bring to the boil for 5 minutes.
9. Add the lemon juice and a little butter, if necessary, and pour over the fish (f). Serve at once.

116 Skate with savoury rice

2 wings of skate (about 900 g),
cut in smaller pieces
1 large onion, finely sliced
1 large green pepper, seeded
and finely sliced
4 large tomatoes, skinned and
coarsely chopped
150 g raw rice
25 ml (2 tablespoons) butter or
margarine
25 ml (2 tablespoons) flour
375 ml chicken stock
1 clove garlic, finely chopped
5 ml (1 teaspoon) salt
1 ml (¼ teaspoon) pepper
freshly ground black pepper
10 ml oil for frying
Garnish:
finely chopped parsley

Serves 4-6; kJ per portion 1 920; Prep time 20 min; Cooking time 5 min.

1. Dust the skate with the flour and season with salt and pepper.
2. Melt the butter or margarine in a large frying-pan and sauté the garlic, onion and green pepper until the onion is transparent but not brown.
3. Stir in the rice and chicken stock and simmer, covered, over medium heat until all the liquid has been absorbed and the rice is tender, stirring occasionally.
4. Stir in the tomatoes and season well with black pepper.
5. Heat the oil in a frying-pan and brown the fish quickly on both sides. Drain on absorbent paper.
6. Pile the rice mixture in the centre of a serving dish and arrange the fish around it. Serve at once, garnished with chopped parsley.

117 Paprika fish

1 kg firm white fish, skinned,
filleted and cut into 2 steaks
2 rashers rindless bacon,
coarsely chopped
250 g canned whole kernel
corn
25 ml (2 tablespoons) flour
62,5 ml (5 tablespoons) butter
or margarine
25 ml oil
150 ml dry white wine or water
250 ml sour cream
7 ml (1½ teaspoons) paprika
5 ml (1 teaspoon) salt

Serves 4; kJ per portion 1 400; Prep time 1 hour; Cooking time 40 min.

1. Clean the fish then dredge in a mixture of 12,5 ml (1 tablespoon) flour, the salt and 1 ml (¼ teaspoon) paprika.
2. Heat the oil and butter or margarine in a large frying-pan. Add the fish and brown lightly on both sides. Remove fish from pan and set aside.
3. Add the bacon to the frying-pan and fry until the fat starts to melt.
4. Remove from the stove, stir in the rest of the flour, blending well, and return to the stove. Add the corn, the remaining paprika and the wine or water. Bring to the boil, stirring all the time.
5. Reduce the heat and place the fish steaks on top of the corn. Simmer, covered, over low heat for 20 minutes.
6. Pour the cream over the fish and heat, but do not allow to boil.
7. Sprinkle with paprika and serve.

118 Kedgeree

400 g smoked haddock or
kippers
200 g raw long-grain rice
3 hard-boiled eggs, shelled and
coarsely chopped
62,5 ml (5 tablespoons) butter
or margarine
50 ml water
50 ml milk
12,5 ml (1 tablespoon) parsley,
finely chopped
2 ml (½ teaspoon) black
pepper

Serves 6; kJ per portion 1 003; Prep time 30 min; Cooking time 25 min.

1. Wipe the haddock, place it in a shallow pan and pour over the water and milk. Add the butter or margarine and pepper and gently simmer over low heat, covered, until tender, about 10 minutes.
2. Meanwhile, cook the rice. Drain it in a colander then run hot water through the grains to separate them and remove any excess starch.
3. Remove the fish from the pan, reserving the liquor. Remove the skin and bones and flake the fish.
4. In a large bowl, mix the rice with the fish and some of the reserved liquor. Stir the eggs and chopped parsley into the rice and fish mixture and turn into a serving dish. Serve immediately.

Note: Do not add too much of the reserved liquor as the kedgeree will then be too mushy.

119 Herbed fish fillets (F)

500 g white fish fillets
12,5 ml vegetable oil
125 ml white wine
1 clove garlic
2 ml (½ teaspoon) fresh thyme,
finely chopped
2 ml (½ teaspoon) fresh basil,
finely chopped
flour
5 ml (1 teaspoon) salt
2 ml (½ teaspoon) pepper

Serves 4;   kJ per portion 780;   Prep time 30 min;   Cooking time 20 min.

1. Dust the fish fillets with flour and season with the salt and pepper.
2. Heat the oil in a large frying-pan and sauté the thyme, basil and garlic lightly. Do not allow to brown.
3. Add the fish fillets to the frying-pan and fry on both sides until golden brown.
4. Now add the white wine and simmer until the fish is tender (f). Serve at once.

120 Snoek curry

1 kg unsalted snoek, sliced
1 large onion, finely chopped
5 ml tomato paste
2 cloves garlic, finely chopped
10 ml (2 teaspoons) flour
oil for frying
juice of ½ lemon
250 ml water
85 ml vinegar
20 ml (4 teaspoons) sugar
12,5 ml (1 tablespoon) apricot
jam
2 whole allspice
1 bay leaf
12,5 ml (1 tablespoon) curry
powder
5 ml (1 teaspoon) turmeric
5 ml (1 teaspoon) salt
2 ml (½ teaspoon) pepper

Serves 4;   kJ per portion 1 000;   Prep time 45 min;   Cooking time 20 min.

1. Season the slices of snoek with the salt and pepper and sprinkle with the lemon juice. Set aside.
2. Heat a little oil in a saucepan and sauté the onion and garlic until lightly browned. Add the curry and turmeric and mix well.
3. Sprinkle the flour over the mixture and stir in, blending well.
4. Add the water and bring to the boil, stirring all the time.
5. Reduce the heat to low and add the snoek, allspice, bay leaf and tomato paste. Simmer, covered, for 15 minutes.
6. Mix together the vinegar, sugar and apricot jam and add to the fish. Simmer another 5 to 7 minutes, stirring occasionally.
7. Add more salt and pepper if necessary and serve at once on a bed of boiled rice.

121 Pickled fish

1 kg yellowtail or kingklip,
skinned, filleted, sliced and
dipped in flour
2 medium onions, finely
chopped
2 red chillis, finely chopped
2 pieces root ginger, finely
chopped
125 g desiccated coconut
25 ml (2 tablespoons) smooth
apricot jam
12,5 ml (1 tablespoon) flour
375 ml chicken stock
50 ml salad oil
1 clove garlic, finely chopped
10 ml (2 teaspoons) turmeric
salt to taste

Serves 4;   kJ per portion 1 600;   Prep time 45 min;   Cooking time 20 min.

1. Boil the stock in a saucepan, then pour it over the coconut in a bowl and allow to stand for 30 minutes. Drain off and reserve any liquid.
2. Heat half the oil in a frying-pan and sauté the onion, ginger, garlic and chillis in it until lightly browned, about 5 minutes.
3. Add the jam, flour and liquid from the coconut, season well with salt and simmer over low heat for 20 minutes.
4. Meanwhile, heat the remaining oil in another frying-pan and fry the slices of fish on both sides until lightly browned and tender. Transfer to a deep casserole.
5. Pour over the hot curry mixture and leave to stand overnight, then chill.

Note: Chilled pickled fish will keep for about 2 weeks in the refrigerator. Store in a dish with a tight-fitting lid.

1 kg snoek, whole
1 large onion, cut in thick slices
2 large potatoes, thinly sliced
2 medium tomatoes, quartered
500 ml (2 cups) boiled rice
3 cloves garlic, finely chopped
2 allspice
1 bay leaf
25 ml cooking oil
12,5 ml (1 tablespoon) butter
or margarine
10 ml (2 teaspoons) salt
2 ml (½ teaspoon) pepper
water

122 Gesmoorde snoek (F)

Serves 6; kJ per portion 1 600; Prep time 45 min; Cooking time 25 min.

1. Place the snoek in a large saucepan with enough cold water to cover, the allspice, bay leaf and a slice of onion. Simmer, covered, over low heat until tender.
2. Remove the fish from the water and allow to cool, then remove the skin and bones and flake the flesh.
3. Heat the oil and butter or margarine in a saucepan and sauté the garlic for 1 minute. Chop the rest of the onion finely and add to the garlic. Sauté until the onion is transparent.
4. Add the potato to the garlic and onion mixture and sauté until the potato starts to soften, stirring often.
5. Add the tomatoes and simmer, covered, until the vegetables are tender.
6. Add the flaked snoek to the vegetables in the saucepan, shake well to mix the ingredients thoroughly and simmer until the fish is heated through and the flavours blended, about 10 minutes.
7. Add the salt and pepper and mix well (f). Serve on a bed of hot boiled rice.

Variations:

1. Use smoked instead of fresh snoek. Flake snoek, remove the skin and bones and continue from step 3.
2. Salted snoek can also be used. Soak the fish in cold water for 1 hour before cooking and do not add extra salt. Drain and use fresh water to cook the fish.

---

1 kg firm white fish, cut into portions
3 medium onions, sliced in thin rings
5 medium potatoes, peeled and thinly sliced
375 ml (1½ cups) parboiled rice
250 ml buttermilk
juice of 1 lemon
10 ml oil
10 ml (2 teaspoons) green ginger and garlic pounded together
10 ml (2 teaspoons) curry powder
5 ml (1 teaspoon) turmeric
5 ml (1 teaspoon) cumin seeds
5 ml (1 teaspoon) ground coriander
5 ml (1 teaspoon) saffron (if available) dissolved in 125 ml boiling water
5 ml (1 teaspoon) salt

123 Fish buriyani (F)

Serves 6; kJ per portion 1 600; Prep time 45 min; Cooking time 1 hour

1. Wash the fish well and pat dry with absorbent paper.
2. Combine the lemon juice, oil and buttermilk in a bowl.
3. Mix the garlic and ginger, curry powder, salt, turmeric, cumin seeds and coriander well and add to the buttermilk mixture. Brush the fish portions with this mixture.
4. Heat a little oil in a large frying-pan and fry the fish until done. Set aside, keeping warm.
5. Add a little more oil to the frying-pan and sauté the onions until soft. Remove and keep warm.
6. Fry the potato slices in the same oil, then remove and arrange in a layer in a large, heavy saucepan. Sprinkle with salt and a little of the oil from the frying-pan.
7. Arrange a layer of onions on top of the potatoes, place a layer of fish on top of the onions and finish with a layer of rice, seasoning each layer with salt and sprinkling with a little of the oil.
8. Pour the saffron dissolved in water over the top and steam over low heat until the rice is tender and fluffy, approximately 30 min (f). Serve at once with lemon wedges.

Note: Test that the fish is done by piercing it with a fork. If the flesh flakes easily, the fish is cooked.

340 g cooked white fish,
skinned and boned
62,5 ml (5 tablespoons) butter
or margarine
1 large onion, coarsely
chopped
2 large eggs
1 thick slice white bread, crusts
removed
300 ml milk
juice of 1 lemon
10 ml (2 teaspoons) curry
powder
25 ml (2 tablespoons) seedless
raisins
25 ml (2 tablespoons) blanched
almonds, finely chopped
2 bay leaves
5 ml (1 teaspoon) salt
1 ml (¼ teaspoon) pepper

124 Fish bobotie (F)

Serves 4; kJ per portion 1 000; Prep time 45 min; Cooking time 35 min.

1. Flake the fish and place it in a bowl.
2. In a separate bowl, soak the bread in the milk.
3. Melt the butter or margarine in a frying-pan and sauté the onion until light honey-coloured.
4. Add the onion, almonds, raisins, curry powder, lemon juice, salt and pepper to the fish and mix well.
5. Squeeze the milk from the bread and reserve it. Add the bread to the fish and combine thoroughly.
6. Beat the eggs, add the milk and beat again until well-blended.
7. Pour the fish mixture into a greased ovenware dish, pour the egg and milk mixture over it and place the bay leaves on top.
8. Bake in the oven at 190 °C (375 °F) until the egg and milk mixture has set, about 35 minutes (f). Serve hot with boiled rice.

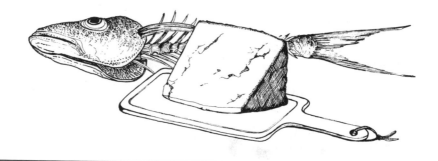

500 g white fish
500 g mashed potatoes
25 ml (2 tablespoons)
margarine
62,5 ml (5 tablespoons) flour
85 g Cheddar cheese, grated
300 ml milk
2 ml (½ teaspoon) salt
2 ml (½ teaspoon) pepper

125 Fish pie

Serves 4; kJ per portion 1 300; Prep time 45 min; Cooking time 40 min.

1. Poach the fish in the milk over medium heat for 20 minutes. Drain, reserving the liquor. Remove the skin and bones and flake the fish.
2. Line the bottom of a greased 1 litre casserole with the potatoes.
3. Melt the margarine in a small saucepan, remove from the stove and stir in the flour to make a smooth paste. Gradually stir in the reserved liquor, blending well. Return the saucepan to the stove and bring to the boil, stirring all the time.
4. Gradually add half the cheese, stirring constantly, then season with salt and pepper and stir in the flaked fish.
5. Pour the mixture over the potatoes, sprinkle with the remaining cheese and place under the grill until the topping is golden brown. Serve at once, garnished with slices of lemon.

Galjoen must be bled immediately it leaves the water; the arteries under the neck must be severed and the fish rinsed in clear water to prevent the flesh discolouring.

500 g hake fillets, cubed
25 ml (2 tablespoons) butter or
margarine
25 ml (2 tablespoons) flour
250 ml milk
2 ml (½ teaspoon) mustard
powder
12,5 ml (1 tablespoon) parsley,
chopped
5 ml (1 teaspoon) salt
2 ml (½ teaspoon) pepper
Topping:
500 ml (2 cups) self-raising
flour
125 ml (½ cup) Cheddar
cheese, grated
62,5 ml (5 tablespoons) butter
or margarine
125 ml milk
2 ml (½ teaspoon) salt
egg or milk to glaze

126   Fish and cheese cobbler

Serves 6;   kJ per portion 1 890;   Prep time 30 min;   Cooking time 30 min.

1. Melt the butter or margarine in a saucepan and stir in the flour, blending well. Cook, stirring, for 2 minutes without browning.
2. Gradually add the milk and bring to the boil for 2 minutes, stirring all the time.
3. Remove from the stove and stir in the salt and pepper, mustard powder, parsley and fish. Transfer to a 1 litre casserole.
4. Prepare the topping. Place the flour and salt in a mixing bowl. Add the butter or margarine and with the fingers rub into the flour until the mixture resembles fine breadcrumbs.
5. Stir in the milk and mix to form a soft dough. Turn out on a floured board and knead lightly.
6. Roll out to an oblong 40 cm × 15 cm and sprinkle with cheese to within 2,5 cm of the edge. Brush the edges with water and roll up loosely like a Swiss roll. Cut into 12 slices and place, cut side down, on a floured board. Flatten each scone slightly and place, slightly overlapping one another, on top of the fish.
7. Brush the scones with egg or milk and bake in the centre of the oven at 200 °C (400 °F) until the scone topping is golden brown, about 25 minutes. Serve at once with mashed potatoes and green vegetables.

Allow grilled kingklip to stand for 10 minutes before serving.

250 g kabeljou, filleted,
skinned and cut in 5 cm pieces
250 g hake, filleted, skinned
and cut in 5 cm pieces
250 g yellowtail, filleted,
skinned and cut in 5 cm pieces
100 g prawns, cooked and
shelled
125 g canned mussels, drained
125 g canned asparagus salad
cuts, drained and liquid
reserved
250 g mushrooms, thinly sliced
125 g canned whole baby
carrots, drained
1 large onion, finely chopped
62,5 ml sour cream, mixed
with asparagus liquid to make
up 100 ml
1 egg, beaten
Parmesan cheese, grated
10 ml (2 teaspoons) dried
tarragon
garlic salt
black pepper

127   Seafood casserole   (F)

Serves 6;   kJ per portion 1 650;   Prep time 25 min;   Cooking time 30 min.

1. Place the kabeljou pieces in a large casserole. Add a few mushrooms, asparagus pieces, half of the onion and baby carrots and sprinkle with some of the tarragon, garlic salt and black pepper.
2. Place the prawns on top.
3. Place the hake fillets on top of the prawns and add some more of the mushrooms, asparagus pieces, onion and baby carrots and sprinkle with tarragon, garlic salt and black pepper.
4. Cover with a layer of mussels.
5. Place the yellowtail pieces on top of the mussels and add the rest of the mushrooms, asparagus pieces, onion and baby carrots. Sprinkle with the remainder of the tarragon, a little garlic salt and black pepper.
6. Combine the sour cream mixture and the egg and pour over. Top with grated Parmesan cheese.
7. Bake, covered, in the oven at 180 °C (350 °F) for 30 minutes (f). Serve at once on a bed of boiled rice.

Note:
- Use milk in place of the sour cream if you want the casserole to be less rich.
- For a really distinctive flavour, use a packet of thick white onion soup mix instead of the sour cream. Mix it with 100 ml of the asparagus juice.

200 g canned light meat tuna, flaked
120 g Swiss or Cheddar cheese, grated
4 eggs, beaten
8 slices crustless white bread, buttered and cubed
2 slices crustless white bread, buttered and cut into triangles
425 ml milk
2 ml Worcester sauce
1 ml (¼ teaspoon) paprika
5 ml (1 teaspoon) salt
1 ml (¼ teaspoon) cayenne pepper

128 Tuna and cheese casserole (F)

Serves 6;   kJ per portion 1 200;   Prep time 20 min;   Cooking time 1 hour

1. Place alternate layers of bread cubes, grated cheese and flaked tuna in a greased casserole, ending with tuna.
2. Combine the eggs, milk, salt, paprika, Worcester sauce and cayenne pepper thoroughly and pour carefully over the tuna mixture.
3. Stand the triangles of bread around the edge of the casserole and bake in the oven at 180°C (350°F) for 1 hour (f). Serve hot.

GRILLED FISH

Several of the oilier kinds of fish are excellent for grilling, either over hot coals or in the oven. Fish can be grilled whole, in fillets or as sosaties (kebabs).

1. Sprinkle the fish with salt, pepper and lemon juice. Dot with butter or brush with marinade.
2. Pack the pieces of fish in the griller and place it approximately 300 mm above the coals or, if grilling in the oven, 100 to 120 mm below the upper element.
3. Grill very slowly, brushing frequently with butter or lemon juice.
4. When done on one side, turn and grill on the other.
5. Allow the following times for grilling:
   Fish steaks or sosaties; 10 to 15 minutes
   Whole small fish, e.g. harders; 20 minutes
   Whole large fish, e.g. snoek; 30 to 35 minutes.
6. Grilled fish is delicious when accompanied by a sauce.

Note:
- Do not remove the skin if grilling the fish whole. Score the skin diagonally across the sides in a few places.
- Fish can also be grilled in foil but, as it then tends to look as if it has been steamed, open the foil 5 to 10 minutes before done, brush with a little oil and brown.

129 Grilled whole snoek (F)

1 whole snoek, entrails removed
melted butter or margarine
lemon juice
15 ml (3 teaspoons) salt
5 ml (1 teaspoon) pepper

*Serves 8-10;   kJ per portion 1 000;   prep time 15 min;
Cooking time 40 min.*

1. Wash the snoek well. Brush the outside with melted butter or margarine. Season, inside and out, with salt and pepper and sprinkle a little lemon juice inside.
2. Wrap the snoek securely in a large sheet of greased foil and place under the grill or over hot coals until the fish is tender, 30 to 40 minutes (f). Serve hot.

Note: The snoek can be grilled without wrapping, but remember to brush frequently with melted butter while grilling. When cooking over coals, grill the fish low over the coals for 3 minutes on each side, then raise the griller to 300 mm above the coals and grill for a further 15 minutes on either side.

130 Fish kebabs

1,5 kg steenbras, skinned, filleted and cubed
12 brown mushroom caps
6 thick wedges onion
6 cherry tomatoes
juice of 1 lemon
10 ml wine vinegar
250 ml cooking oil
1 ml (¼ teaspoon) each of dried thyme, sweet basil and rosemary
6 bay leaves or lemon leaves, halved
7 ml (1½ teaspoons) salt
2 ml (½ teaspoon) pepper

*Serves 6;   kJ per portion 900;   Prep time 30 min. + marinating time;
Cooking time 15 min.*

1. Combine the vinegar, onion wedges, lemon juice, oil, herbs, salt and pepper in a bowl.
2. Add the pieces of fish and the bay leaves or lemon leaves and marinate for 30 minutes.
3. Remove the pieces of fish from the marinade, drain them on absorbent paper and reserve the marinade.
4. Thread the ingredients onto 6 skewers in the following order: tomato, fish, ½ bay leaf (or lemon leaf), fish, onion, fish, mushroom cap.
5. Place the skewers in a greased shallow oven dish. Spoon 25 ml of the marinade over the kebabs and cover the dish with aluminium foil, dull side out. Bake in the oven at 200°C (400°F) for 10 minutes.
6. Remove the foil and place the kebabs under the preheated grill.
7. Grill on all sides, basting frequently with the marinade, until crisp and brown.
8. Remove from the grill, add more salt and pepper if necessary and serve immediately with a salad.

Note: Instead of baking the kebabs in the oven, grill over live coals, about 300 mm above the heat, for 10 minutes, basting and turning frequently to ensure that they are cooked evenly.

Elf should be cleaned and prepared as soon after catching as possible.

Fat white worms and tiny grey-black worms are sometimes found in hake (stockfish). If the white one is present, it is harmless and may be removed, and the fish eaten but if the black one is present the fish should not be eaten.

Fried fish is always popular, and ideally it should be crisp and tasty. It is therefore important to use the correct utensils. Use a wire basket to deep-fry fish in oil or fat and use a fish slice to remove fish fried in shallow fat from the frying-pan.

1. Prepare and clean the fish, then cut it into portions 20 to 30 mm thick. Dry each portion with absorbent paper, then sprinkle on both sides with salt and pepper.
2. Coat the fish with dry breadcrumbs, flour or a batter (see below).
3. Heat the oil or fat to 180°C (350°F) in the frying-pan or deep-frier.
4. Place the fish in the frying-pan or deep-frier. If frying in shallow fat in the frying-pan, turn once after 5 to 10 minutes – depending on the thickness of the fillet – then fry for a further 5 minutes. If deep-frying, fry thin fillets for 3 minutes and thick fillets (about 30 mm thick), for 5 minutes.
5. Lift the fish out of the oil or fat and hold suspended for about 1 minute to allow the excess to drip off. Place on a plate lined with absorbent paper.
6. Serve hot with lemon slices or with your favourite sauce.

Note:
- Always use a good quality oil or fat, with a high burning point.
- Fat or oil may be used again, but remember to strain it before storage to remove the food particles.
- Never overload the frying-pan or deep-frier; the pieces of fish should not touch one another.
- Dry each fish portion completely to avoid spluttering when placing the fish in the hot oil or fat.
- The temperature of the oil or fat must be kept constant.
- If it is necessary to keep fried fish portions warm while frying the rest, do not cover tightly or the crisp surface will turn soft and mushy.

Coatings and batters for fried fish: (Sufficient for 4 pieces of fish)

Flour coating	Batter 1	Batter 2
30 g flour seasoned with 2 ml (½ teaspoon) salt and 1 ml (¼ teaspoon) pepper 1. Dry the fish well, then dredge well in flour and continue from step 3 in basic recipe above.	120 g flour 2 ml (½ teaspoon) baking powder 250 ml water OR 125 ml milk mixed with 125 ml water	120 g flour 2 ml (½ teaspoon) salt 1 ml (¼ teaspoon) pepper 2 ml (½ teaspoon) baking powder 1 egg, slightly beaten 250 ml milk 5 ml oil
Variations: 1. Use 60 g seasoned dry breadcrumbs instead of the flour. 2. Dip the fish in milk, then roll in seasoned dry breadcrumbs.	1. Mix the ingredients to form a thin batter. 2. Dip the fish in the batter and continue with step 3 in basic recipe above	1. Combine the dry ingredients and stir in the milk. 2. Beat in the oil until a smooth batter is obtained. 3. Dip the fish in the batter and continue with step 3 in basic recipe above.

4 medium soles, trimmed and cleaned
flour
100 g butter
juice of 1 lemon
12,5 ml (1 tablespoon) parsley, finely chopped
7 ml (1½ teaspoons) salt
2 ml (½ teaspoon) pepper

131   Sole meunière

Serves 4;   kJ per portion 1 440;   Prep time 20 min;   Cooking time 10 min.

1. Wash and dry the soles thoroughly, season with salt and pepper and coat lightly with flour.
2. Melt the butter in a large frying-pan and sauté the soles in it for 5 minutes on each side.
3. Transfer the soles to a heated serving dish and pour the butter over them. Serve at once, sprinkled with lemon juice and garnished with parsley.

Variation: Trout cooked this way is delicious.

---

750 g cooked white fish or raw minced fish
1 onion, parboiled
1 slice white bread, crusts removed and soaked in a little milk
1 egg, beaten
25 ml (2 tablespoons) parsley, finely chopped
5 ml (1 teaspoon) salt
2 ml (½ teaspoon) pepper
oil for frying
Garnish:
lemon wedges

132   Fish cakes   (F)

Serves 4;   kJ per portion 1 399;   Prep time 30 min;   Cooking time 10 min.

1. Mince together the onion, fish, parsley and soaked bread.
2. Add the beaten egg, salt and pepper and mix well. Form into patties about 2 cm thick, and dust with a little flour (f).
3. Heat the oil in a large frying-pan and fry the fish cakes until brown all over. Remove the fish cakes and drain on absorbent paper. Serve hot with wedges of lemon.

Variations:
1. Instead of the cooked white fish and bread soaked in milk, use 450 g canned pilchards in tomato sauce, thickened with a little plain flour and 1 egg to a fairly stiff consistency.
2. Add 2 to 3 drops anchovy essence to the mixture.
3. Use grated apple instead of the breadcrumbs.
4. Use canned salmon or tuna instead of the white fish.
5. Use crumbled cornflakes or allbran flakes instead of the breadcrumbs.
6. Add 12,5 ml (1 tablespoon) curry powder and 10 ml fruit chutney to the mixture.

---

4 trout
100 g butter
37,5 ml (3 tablespoons) flour
150 ml milk
25 g flaked almonds
5 ml (1 teaspoon) salt
Garnish:
tomato wedges
lemon wedges
parsley sprigs

133   Trout with almonds

Serves 4;   kJ per portion 1 100;   Prep time 20 min;   Cooking time 12 min.

1. Marinate the trout in the milk and salt for 10 minutes, then remove the fish and dredge in the flour.
2. Melt 75 g butter in a frying-pan and fry the trout over medium heat for 6 minutes on each side. Remove trout and place on a heated serving dish. Keep warm.
3. Add the remaining butter to the pan and fry the flaked almonds until they are golden brown. Scatter them over the trout and serve at once, garnished with tomato and lemon wedges and sprigs of parsley.

450 g snoek roes
1 egg, beaten
salted water
1 ml (¼ teaspoon) cayenne
pepper
2 ml (½ teaspoon) salt
1 ml (¼ teaspoon) pepper
oil for frying

134   Fried snoek roes

Serves 4;   kJ per portion 800;   Prep time 30 min;   Cooking time 15 min.

1. Wash the roes thoroughly and boil them in salted water in a saucepan. Drain and allow to cool.
2. Cut the roes into portions and season with cayenne pepper, pepper and salt.
3. Heat the oil in a frying-pan.
4. Dip the roes in the beaten egg and fry in the oil, turning once or twice, until golden brown. Serve hot.

---

2 filleted harders, dredged in
flour seasoned with salt and
pepper
1 small onion, coarsely
chopped
85 g mushrooms, coarsely
chopped
2 large tomatoes, skinned and
seeded
35 ml vegetable oil
37,5 ml (3 tablespoons) butter
or margarine
65 ml wine vinegar
1 large clove garlic, coarsely
chopped
25 ml (2 tablespoons) parsley,
finely chopped
5 ml (1 teaspoon) salt
2 ml (½ teaspoon) pepper

135   Fried harders with mushrooms and tomatoes

Serves 4;   kJ per portion 1 480;   Prep time 30 min;   Cooking time 15 min.

1. Heat 25 ml of the oil and 12,5 ml (1 tablespoon) of the butter or margarine in a frying-pan and place the fish fillets in it, skin side uppermost.
2. Fry the fillets on both sides until crisp and brown. Remove from the pan and keep hot on a serving dish.
3. Wipe the frying-pan out with a cloth and return it to the stove.
4. Heat 10 ml oil and 12,5 ml (1 tablespoon) butter or margarine in the pan and sauté the onion and garlic until the onion is transparent but not brown, about 2 minutes.
5. Add the mushrooms and cook, covered, for 5 minutes.
6. Add the wine vinegar and season with salt and pepper. Pour the mushroom mixture over the fish fillets.
7. Cut the tomatoes into 6 slices each. Melt the remaining butter or margarine in a small frying-pan and fry the tomatoes for 1 minute on either side.
8. Place the slices of tomato around the fillets and serve at once.

Variation: Serve with fried bananas or fried pineapple rings instead of the tomatoes.

Note: Mackerel may also be used for this dish.

SEAFOODS

Oysters

Allow 6 oysters per person.
1. Using a brush, scrub the shell until completely clean. Rinse under cold running water.
2. Insert a sharp-pointed knife between the two shells at the back of the oyster and cut around the edge until the strong muscles which hold the shell together have been severed.
3. The oysters may either be removed from the shells, cooked in their own juice and put back in the washed half shells or served raw in the half shell on a bed of crushed ice and garnished with slices of lemon.

Note: Do not flavour oysters too strongly as this overpowers their delicate taste.

> Fresh black mussels can be kept overnight in a bucket of water to which a handful of sea salt has been added.

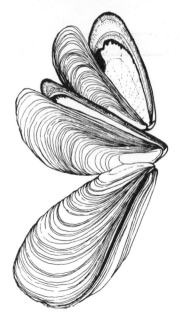

Mussels

Allow at least 12 mussels per person.
1. Collect the mussels at low tide. Soak them in water for 1½ hours, discarding those that float or open.
2. Using a small knife, scrape off the head by which the mussels were attached to the rocks, then scrub the shells thoroughly to remove all the sand.
3. The mussels can now be opened and served raw in the same way as oysters, or cooked:
   ● Place the cleaned mussels in a wire basket and suspend the basket over boiling water in a saucepan, taking care not to let the water touch the mussels. Steam, covered, until the shells open, about 10 minutes. Discard any mussels that have not opened.
   ● Place the mussels in a saucepan of cold water, bring to the boil and simmer for 10 to 15 minutes.
   ● Place the mussels in a saucepan, cover with cold water and dry white wine then add sliced onion, a bay leaf and peppercorns and simmer for 10 minutes.
4. Mussels may be served in the shells immediately after cooking or removed from the shells, fried for 2 minutes in a butter and garlic sauce (recipe 328), then served with wholewheat bread.

---

12 to 18 mussels per person
200 ml white wine
Sauce:
2 cloves garlic, crushed
62,5 ml (5 tablespoons) butter
25 ml (2 tablespoons) parsley, finely chopped
25 ml (2 tablespoons) Parmesan cheese, grated
pinch salt

136   Grilled mussels in garlic butter sauce

Serves 4;   kJ per portion 610;   Prep time 30 min;   Cooking time 10 min.

1. Clean the mussels as described above (steps 1 and 2).
2. Place them in a shallow saucepan with the wine and cover. Shake over high heat until the shells open, about 5 minutes.
3. Remove the empty half shells from each mussel and discard any mussels that have not opened. Place the remaining mussels in their half shells into fireproof ramekins. Strain the cooking liquor and set aside.
4. Work the garlic into the butter with the herbs, salt and cheese and spread a little over each mussel. Sprinkle each with a little of the cooking liquor and place under the grill until the sauce has melted and browned slightly. Serve at once.

Note: Clams, oysters and scallops can also be served in this way.

---

425 g canned mussels
1 medium onion, coarsely chopped
375 ml (1½ cups) tomatoes, coarsely chopped
250 ml (1 cup) raw rice
25 ml (2 tablespoons) butter or margarine
25 ml olive oil or sunflower oil
water
2 ml (½ teaspoon) dried oreganum
5 ml (1 teaspoon) salt
2 ml (½ teaspoon) pepper

137   Mussel pilaff   (F)

Serves 6;   kJ per portion 1 200;   Prep time 30 min;   Cooking time 35 min.

1. Melt the butter or margarine in a large saucepan, then add the oil and heat.
2. Add the onion and sauté until golden brown.
3. Drain the mussels, reserving the liquid. Add enough water to the liquid to make 375 ml.
4. Add the mussels, liquid, rice, chopped tomatoes and oreganum to the saucepan and simmer, covered, until the rice is tender, about 30 minutes (f). Serve at once.

Variation: Use canned clams or oysters instead of the mussels.

Perlemoen *(Abalone)*

1. With a sharp, strong knife remove the perlemoen from the shell.
2. Trim the perlemoen, then scrub the flat dark side vigorously with a hard brush or pot scourer.
3. Beat the cleaned perlemoen with a mallet – this is of the utmost importance because if it is not done thoroughly, the perlemoen will be tough when cooked. To make beating easier, first cut into steaks.
4. The perlemoen may now either be prepared as steaks or diced or minced before cooking.

---

6 to 8 perlemoen
250 ml water
125 ml dry white wine
25 ml (2 tablespoons) butter or margarine
boiled rice
Sauce:
liquid from the cooked perlemoen
25 ml white wine
50 ml (4 tablespoons) dry breadcrumbs
1 ml (¼ teaspoon) grated nutmeg
salt and pepper
Garnish:
lemon wedges

138 Perlemoen in its own sauce (F)

Serves 6-8;   kJ per portion 1 010;   Prep time 30 min;   Cooking time 25 min.

1. Clean the perlemoen as described above (steps 1 to 4).
2. Steam the perlemoen in 125 ml white wine and the water in a pressure cooker for 15 minutes, or simmer in a covered saucepan until tender when tested with a skewer, about 1 hour (f). Cube the perlemoen.
3. Melt the butter or margarine in a frying-pan and sauté the perlemoen in it until lightly browned all over, about 5 minutes.
4. Add the perlemoen liquid, white wine, breadcrumbs and nutmeg and season well with salt and pepper. Simmer, uncovered, for 5 more minutes.
5. Serve on a bed of cooked rice, with lemon wedges.

Variations:

1. Instead of cubing the perlemoen after it has been tenderised, mince it and serve it as described above.
2. Instead of serving the perlemoen in this sauce, mince it when tender and form into rissoles. Fry until golden brown all over, about 5 minutes on each side.
3. Place whole perlemoen in a tightly closed casserole with no water, and bake overnight in the oven at 100 °C (200 °F) to tenderise.

Note: Do not use water or salt when cleaning the fish as this will make it tough.

---

500 g minced perlemoen and 25 ml of the cooking liquid
250 ml condensed cream of chicken soup
125 ml (½ cup) green pepper, seeded and minced
Parmesan cheese, grated
soft breadcrumbs
250 ml (1 cup) herb-seasoned croûtons, crumbled (recipe 99)
Worcester sauce
hot pepper sauce
5 ml (1 teaspoon) curry powder
2 ml (½ teaspoon) salt
1 ml (¼ teaspoon) pepper

139 Perlemoen coquille

Serves 6;   kJ per portion 1 010;   Prep time 30 min;   Cooking time 15 min.

1. Combine the perlemoen, reserved liquid, chicken soup, crumbled croûtons, green pepper, curry powder, a little Worcester sauce, a little hot pepper sauce, salt and pepper in a saucepan.
2. Simmer over moderate heat, stirring occasionally, for 5 minutes.
3. Spoon mixture into 6 ramekins and sprinkle each with grated Parmesan cheese and breadcrumbs.
4. Bake in the oven at 180 °C (350 °F) for 10 minutes and serve at once.

86

Alikreukel (Giant Periwinkles)

1. Place the alikreukel in a saucepan, cover with cold water and boil in the shell for approximately 20 minutes.
2. Remove the flesh from the shell with a long pin, cut off the flat disc from the one end and the intestines from the other.
3. Wash very well under running cold water to remove all the sand.
4. Mince the cooked flesh.

---

48 alikreukel
4 large onions, thinly sliced
4 small potatoes, diced
3 large tomatoes, thickly sliced
12,5 ml oil
2 cloves garlic, finely chopped
2 bay leaves
4 whole allspice
2 ml (½ teaspoon) salt
1 ml (¼ teaspoon) pepper

140   Gesmoorde alikreukel   (F)

Serves 4;   kJ per portion 1 100;   Prep time 45 min;   Cooking time 20 min.

1. Prepare the alikreukel as described above (steps 1 to 3). Set aside.
2. Heat the oil in a large saucepan and sauté the onions in it until golden brown.
3. Add the tomatoes, garlic, salt, pepper, allspice, bay leaves and potatoes and stir well. Simmer, covered, over low heat for 15 minutes.
4. Add the alikreukel and simmer until the potatoes are cooked, about 10 minutes (f). Serve at once.

Variation: Omit the tomatoes and add 3 finely sliced carrots, and a little water to prevent burning.

---

72 alikreukel
1 large onion, thinly sliced
4 large potatoes, thinly sliced
125 ml vinegar
500 ml water
10 ml (2 teaspoons) sugar
12,5 ml (1 tablespoon) curry powder
5 ml (1 teaspoon) turmeric
2 cloves garlic, finely chopped
3 whole allspice
1 bay leaf
10 ml (2 teaspoons) salt
5 ml (1 teaspoon) pepper
oil for frying

141   Curried alikreukel   (F)

Serves 6; kJ per portion 1 350; Prep time 30 min; Cooking time 25–30 min.

1. Prepare the alikreukel as described above (steps 1 to 3). Set aside.
2. Heat the oil in a large saucepan and sauté the onion and garlic until light brown.
3. Stir in the curry powder, turmeric, salt, pepper, vinegar, sugar, allspice, bay leaf and water and simmer for 5 minutes.
4. Add the potatoes and simmer, covered, for 10 minutes.
5. Add the alikreukel and simmer, covered, for a further 10 minutes (f). Serve hot with rice.

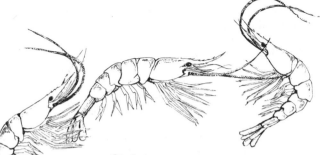

Shrimps

Shrimps are generally used in seafood dishes with mayonnaise or in casseroles. Allow 500 g unshelled and 250 g shelled shrimps per person.

1. Boil frozen or thawed shrimps, unshelled, in 1 litre water, to which 10 ml (2 teaspoons) salt has been added.
2. Boil until the shells are bright red, about 15 minutes.
3. Cool, shell, and remove the black vein from the back.

500 ml (2 cups) cooked shrimp,
shelled
230 g butter or margarine,
melted
2 ml (½ teaspoon) ground
mace
1 ml (¼ teaspoon) grated
nutmeg
2 ml (½ teaspoon) salt
1 ml (¼ teaspoon) pepper
Garnish:
lettuce leaves
parsley sprigs

142   Potted shrimp

Serves 4;   kJ per portion 800;   Prep time 15 min.

1. Chop the shrimps finely and combine with the spices in a bowl. Season with salt and pepper.
2. Fill 4 ramekins with the shrimp mixture and pour over the melted butter or margarine to cover. Chill in the refrigerator for at least 4 hours.
3. Unmould onto lettuce leaves and garnish with the sprigs of parsley. Serve with thin slices of buttered rye or wholewheat bread.

---

500 ml (2 cups) cooked shrimp,
coarsely chopped
4 eggs, slightly beaten
480 g canned creamstyle
sweetcorn
37,5 ml (3 tablespoons) butter
or margarine, melted
250 ml single cream
2 ml hot pepper sauce
1 ml (¼ teaspoon) ground
mace
7 ml (1½ teaspoons) salt

143   Shrimp and corn casserole

Serves 6;   kJ per portion 1 310;   Prep time 15 min;   Cooking time 40 min.

1. Combine all the ingredients thoroughly in a bowl and turn into a 2 litre casserole.
2. Bake in the oven at 150°C (300°F) until set, about 40 minutes. Serve at once with a green salad.

---

600 g cooked shrimps, shelled
6 hard-boiled eggs, shelled and
halved
1 medium onion, coarsely
chopped
1 medium green apple, peeled
and diced
37,5 ml (3 tablespoons) flour
62,5 ml (5 tablespoons) butter
or margarine
60 g desiccated coconut
25 ml black treacle
juice of 1 lemon
425 ml boiling water
25 ml tomato purée
12,5 ml (1 tablespoon) curry
powder
5 ml (1 teaspoon) salt
1 ml (¼ teaspoon) pepper

144   Shrimp curry   (F)

Serves 6;   kJ per portion 1 100;   Prep time 45 min;   Cooking time 30 min.

1. Pour the boiling water over the coconut in a bowl. Leave until cold, then strain and reserve the liquid.
2. Melt the butter or margarine in a large saucepan and sauté the onion and apple until golden brown.
3. Stir in the flour and curry powder and simmer for 1 minute, stirring all the time. Remove from the stove and gradually stir in the coconut liquid.
4. Return to the stove and bring to the boil, stirring all the time, then add the tomato purée, lemon juice and black treacle.
5. Season with salt and pepper and simmer, covered, for 10 to 15 minutes.
6. Add the shrimps (f) and hard-boiled eggs and simmer a further 10 to 15 minutes. Serve with boiled rice and side dishes of: yoghurt and fresh cucumber; diced cooked potato and chopped green pepper sprinkled with paprika; sliced tomato with onion rings; and peanuts and bananas sprinkled with lemon juice.

Variation: Use prawns instead of the shrimps and 50 ml apricot purée instead of the tomato purée.

Note: Do not add the eggs before freezing. To serve, thaw then heat, add the eggs and continue with the rest of step 6.

Prawns

Allow 6 large or 10 small prawns per person.

Prawns may be boiled like shrimps or grilled over coals or in the oven; they are also delicious fried in butter.

● When grilling prawns over the open fire, keep them at least 300 mm above the coals. Brush with butter or with butter and garlic sauce (recipe 328), and grill for 4 minutes on each side.

● To fry in butter, melt the butter in a frying-pan, then add the prawns and fry for 2 to 3 minutes on each side. Serve on rice with garlic butter or a lemon butter sauce (recipe 328).

Note: Thaw frozen prawns before cooking if they are to be shelled.

---

18 large cooked prawns, shelled
batter 1 or 2 (p. 82)
oil for deep-frying
Garnish:
lemon wedges
parsley sprigs

145　Fried scampi

Serves 4;　kJ per portion 1 210;　Prep time 30 min;　Cooking time 5-6 min.

1. Make the batter as directed.
2. Heat the oil in a deep-frier to a temperature where a 2,5 cm cube of bread dropped into it browns within 1 minute.
3. Dip the prawns in the batter, coating completely, then deep-fry them in the oil until crisp. Remove from the oil and drain on absorbent paper.
4. Serve at once, garnished with lemon wedges and sprigs of parsley.

---

1 kg raw prawns, shelled
250 g mushrooms
2 medium green peppers,
seeded and cut in 2,5 cm pieces
500 g small onions
90 ml soy sauce
125 ml salad oil
125 ml dry white wine
2 ml (½ teaspoon) celery salt

146　Prawn kebabs

Serves 6;　kJ per portion 1 600;　Prep time 30 min. + marinating time;　Cooking time 5 min.

1. Place the prawns, mushrooms, green pepper and onions in a bowl.
2. Mix the oil, wine, soy sauce and celery salt thoroughly and pour over the contents of the bowl. Cover and marinate in the refrigerator for 8 hours.
3. Thread the prawns alternately with the onions, mushrooms and green pepper onto skewers.
4. Grill under the griller or over hot coals for 5 minutes, rotating the skewers. Serve hot.

Variation: Use cooked crayfish instead of the prawns.

---

400 g cooked prawns, shelled
1 small onion, finely chopped
25 ml (2 tablespoons) flour
seasoned with
5 ml (1 teaspoon) paprika
12,5 ml (1 tablespoon) butter, melted
12,5 ml oil
12,5 ml brandy
200 ml seasoned chicken stock
50 ml dry white wine
10 ml tomato purée
50 ml double cream
2 ml (½ teaspoon) sugar

147　Prawns paprika

Serves 2;　kJ per portion 1 620;　Prep time 20 min;　Cooking time 10 min.

1. Toss the prawns in the seasoned flour and set aside.
2. Heat the butter and oil in a large frying-pan and sauté the onion until soft.
3. Add the prawns and toss over low heat until well mixed and heated through.
4. Add the brandy and ignite. When the flame dies down, add the chicken stock, white wine, sugar and tomato purée and simmer, covered, over low heat until the sauce thickens, 3 to 4 minutes.
5. Stir in the cream and simmer, stirring, for 2 minutes. Serve on yellow rice.

12 large cooked prawns, shelled
sweet and sour sauce (recipe 324)
oil for frying

148   Sweet and sour prawns

Serves 2;   kJ per portion 1 610;   Prep time 30 min. + 30 min. marinating time;   Cooking time 5 min.

1. Make the sauce as directed in recipe 324 and marinate the prawns in it for 30 minutes.
2. Heat the oil in a frying-pan. Remove the prawns from the marinade and fry them in the oil for 3 minutes.
3. Pour the remaining marinade over the prawns and simmer for a further 2 minutes. Serve at once.

Variation: Use 500 g shrimps or 500 g crayfish or crab meat in place of the prawns.

Langoustines

They may be prepared in the same ways as prawns, but should be cooked for 1 to 2 minutes longer.

Crayfish (Rock Lobster)

Allow 1 whole crayfish or crayfish tail per person.

1. Plunge the live crayfish, head first, into a large saucepan three-quarters filled with boiling salted water. Some people prefer to use sea water.
2. Boil, covered, until the crayfish shell is bright red, 10 to 15 minutes. If using uncooked frozen crayfish, plunge into the boiling water, bring back to the boil and boil for 10 minutes.
3. Remove the tail by pulling it out of the body cavity.
4. Cut the soft cartilage with a pair of scissors; then remove the flesh, dice it and replace it in the shells.

Note:

- If only the tails are used, do not discard the claws; remove the flesh and keep for use in a seafood cocktail.
- The creamy green part and the liver, as well as the eggs found in the female, are edible. The spongy part between the flesh and the shell, however, is not.
- If still in the shell, use crayfish, prawns and langoustines on the same day as they are thawed or cooked.
- Crayfish removed from the shell will keep for up to 24 hours in the refrigerator.
- Remember to provide finger bowls when crayfish is served whole.

149 Crayfish mayonnaise

750 g cooked crayfish meat, cubed
mayonnaise (p. 186) or seafood mayonnaise (p. 187)
Garnish:
1 hard-boiled egg, shelled and sliced
3 anchovy fillets, cut in thin strips
4 stuffed green olives, thinly sliced
capers
lettuce leaves

Serves 4;   kJ per portion 1 100;   Prep time 20 min.

1. Wash and dry the lettuce and line a large salad bowl.
2. Heap the crayfish pieces on top of the lettuce and pour the mayonnaise over it.
3. Garnish with strips of anchovy, egg slices, sliced green olives and capers and serve at once.

Variation: Serve in the shell of the tails instead of in a bowl.

Note: This can be served as a light main course for 4 or as an hors d'oeuvre for 8.

150 Grilled crayfish

2 cooked crayfish
25 ml (2 tablespoons) butter, melted
lemon juice mixed with melted butter
1 ml (¼ teaspoon) salt
1 ml (¼ teaspoon) pepper
Garnish:
finely chopped parsley

Serves 2;   kJ per portion 900;   Prep time 20 min;   Cooking time 10 min.

1. With a sharp knife, split each crayfish down the centre of its underside, removing the black vein from the tail and the sac from beneath the head.
2. Brush each half with melted butter and place on an oiled grid.
3. Place under the grill, 100 mm away from the direct heat. Grill, brushing continually with melted butter, until the meat is white and opaque, about 10 minutes.
4. Season with salt and pepper and serve at once with the lemon juice mixture and parsley sprinkled over the tails.

151 Crayfish thermidor

2 large live crayfish
25 ml oil
Sauce:
1 medium onion, finely chopped
85 g Gruyère, Parmesan or Cheddar cheese, grated
250 ml (1 cup) mushrooms, thinly sliced
fine dry breadcrumbs
25 ml (2 tablespoons) butter or margarine
200 ml Béchamel sauce (p. 179)
175 ml dry white wine
185 ml single cream
12,5 ml dry sherry
5 ml (1 teaspoon) mustard powder
1 ml (¼ teaspoon) paprika
1 ml (¼ teaspoon) cayenne pepper

Serves 2;   kJ per portion 1 700;   Prep time 1 hour;   Cooking time 30 min.

1. Cut the live crayfish down the centre of the underside with a sharp knife and remove the vein from the tail and the sac under the head. Crack the large claws.
2. Heat the oil in a large frying-pan and place the crayfish, shell side up, in the hot oil. Fry for 3 to 4 minutes, turn and cook, covered, over low heat for 15 minutes. Remove the flesh from the tail and claws, taking care to leave the shell intact, and keep the shells and flesh warm.
3. Make the sauce. Sauté the onion in the oil until transparent, then add the mushrooms and sauté a further 3 minutes.
4. Add the wine and boil, uncovered, until the liquid is reduced to half. Remove from the stove.
5. Stir in the cream and the Béchamel sauce (p. 179), a little at a time, then stir in the cayenne pepper, mustard powder, paprika and sherry.
6. Return to the stove, bring to the boil and continue boiling, uncovered and stirring all the time, until the sauce is smooth and thick.
7. Stir in the grated cheese and simmer until the cheese has melted, stirring constantly.
8. Chop the crayfish meat coarsely and stir it into the sauce.
9. Spoon the mixture into the shells, dot with butter or margarine and sprinkle with fine breadcrumbs. Place under the grill until the topping is brown. Serve at once.

152 Curried crayfish (F)

1 large cooked crayfish
1 large onion, coarsely chopped
2 tomatoes, seeded and skinned
1 green apple, cored and grated
12,5 ml (1 tablespoon) apricot jam
85 g butter or margarine
12,5 ml (1 tablespoon) flour
250 ml fish stock (recipe 90)
50 ml dry white wine
2 ml lemon juice
10 ml tomato paste
1 small clove garlic, finely chopped
12,5 ml (1 tablespoon) curry powder

Serves 4;   kJ per portion 1 308;   Prep time 30 min;   Cooking time 30 min.

1. Split the crayfish as described in the recipe for grilled crayfish (recipe 150). Remove all the flesh and cut into large pieces. Discard the shell, reserving the coral and the liver. Crack the claws and remove the flesh. Set the flesh aside.
2. Melt the butter or margarine in a large saucepan and sauté the onion and garlic until the onion is transparent.
3. Add the curry powder, stirring well.
4. Remove from the stove, stir in the flour and blend well. Return to the stove.
5. Add the tomatoes, tomato paste, stock, wine, lemon juice, apple and apricot jam and mix well.
6. Bring to the boil, stirring continuously, then lower heat and simmer, covered, for 15 minutes.
7. Add the crayfish flesh, coral and liver and simmer, covered, until the crayfish is heated through, about 10 minutes (f). Serve on a bed of boiled rice.

Crabs

Allow 1 large crab per person.
1. Boil the crab in salted water for 5 to 20 minutes, depending on the size.
2. The shell will turn red when it is cooked. Remove from the saucepan and cool completely.
3. Twist off the legs and claws and extract the pinkish meat.
4. Lay the crab on its back and prise the white body meat out of the shell. Discard the grey feathery fingers below the claw joints and scoop out the brownish meat. Clean and lightly oil the shell.
5. Mix the brownish meat with fine, fresh breadcrumbs and a sprinkling of salt and pepper. Line the shell with this mixture.
6. Flake the white and pinkish meat and pile in the centre of the shell. Sprinkle with salt and pepper and a little lemon juice and top with a sprig of parsley.

153 Devilled crab

500 g cooked crab meat
12,5 ml (1 tablespoon) onion, finely chopped
25 ml (2 tablespoons) green pepper, seeded and finely chopped
100 g buttered fresh breadcrumbs
125 ml double cream
12,5 ml prepared French mustard
2 ml Worcester sauce
25 ml brandy
few drops tabasco sauce
12,5 ml (1 tablespoon) parsley, finely chopped
2 ml (½ teaspoon) salt
2 ml (½ teaspoon) pepper
1 ml (¼ teaspoon) cayenne pepper

Serves 4;   kJ per portion 1 000;   Prep time 30 min;   Cooking time 20 min.

1. Combine the crab meat, half the breadcrumbs, the onion, green pepper, parsley, Worcester sauce, brandy, salt, pepper and cayenne in a bowl.
2. Mix the mustard and cream together and stir into the crab mixture.
3. Add the tabasco, a drop at a time, tasting after each addition to check that it is not too hot.
4. Pile the mixture into scallop shells or a greased ovenproof dish and sprinkle with the remaining breadcrumbs.
5. Bake in the oven at 200 °C (400 °F) until well-browned, about 20 minutes. Serve at once.

Variation: Use cooked, diced crayfish flesh instead of the crab meat.

154   Deep-fried squid

1 kg squid, sliced
batter 1 or 2 (p. 82)
oil for deep-frying

Serves 8;   kJ per portion 1 210;   Prep time 15 min;   Cooking time 5 min.

1. Heat oil to approximately 180°C (350°F).
2. Dip squid rings in the batter and deep-fry until golden.
3. Drain well and serve with rice, garnished with lemon.

155   Braised squid   (F)

1,25 kg squid, cubed
4 medium tomatoes, skinned
and seeded
juice of 1 lemon
65 ml olive oil
125 ml dry sherry
3 cloves garlic, coarsely
chopped
10 ml (2 teaspoons) parsley,
finely chopped
1 ml (¼ teaspoon) oreganum
1 ml (¼ teaspoon) sweet basil
5 ml (1 teaspoon) salt
2 ml (½ teaspoon) pepper

Serves 6;   kJ per portion 1 010;   Prep time 30 min;   Cooking time 45 min.

1. Wash the cubed squid well, sprinkle with lemon juice and set aside for 10 minutes.
2. Heat the oil in a saucepan and sauté the garlic in it for 1 minute.
3. Add the squid and sauté for 10 minutes.
4. Add the sherry and shake the saucepan gently for a minute to allow the squid cubes to absorb the sherry.
5. Add the tomatoes and half the parsley, the oreganum, sweet basil, salt and pepper and simmer, covered, until the squid is tender, about 30 minutes (f). Serve sprinkled with the rest of the parsley.

Note: Squid and octopus are available frozen from supermarkets.

156   Paella   (F)

4 cooked chicken joints, diced
8 large cooked prawns, shelled
1 small cooked crayfish,
shelled and diced
6 cooked mussels, shelled
6 cooked mussels, in their
shells
12 smoked oysters
120 g raw rice
250 g frozen peas
12 black olives
2 medium tomatoes, skinned
and diced
1 large onion, finely sliced
1 red pepper, seeded and finely
chopped
1 clove garlic, finely chopped
1 chicken stock cube, dissolved
in 600 ml water
25 ml olive oil
600 ml water
pinch saffron or turmeric
5 ml (1 teaspoon) salt
2 ml (½ teaspoon) pepper

Serves 6;   kJ per portion 1 710;   Prep time 45 min;   Cooking time 45 min.

1. Heat the oil in a large frying-pan. Add the chicken, red pepper, onion and garlic and fry until golden.
2. Add the water and simmer for 15 minutes.
3. Add the tomatoes, rice, water with the stock cube dissolved in it, salt and pepper and simmer for 5 minutes. Stir in the saffron or turmeric.
4. Arrange the crayfish, prawns, mussels, smoked oysters, olives and peas on top of this mixture and continue simmering until the rice has absorbed most of the liquid, 15 to 20 minutes (f). Serve immediately.

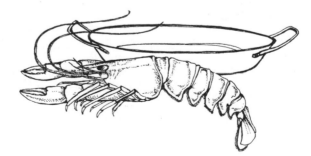

10 pancakes, 20 cm in diameter (recipe 547)
Filling:
125 ml (½ cup) cooked shrimps, shelled
125 ml (½ cup) cooked monkfish, flaked
2 hard-boiled eggs, shelled and coarsely chopped
62,5 ml (5 tablespoons) butter or margarine
37,5 ml (3 tablespoons) flour
375 ml milk
25 ml dry sherry
1 ml (¼ teaspoon) grated nutmeg
1 ml (¼ teaspoon) cayenne pepper
2 ml (½ teaspoon) salt
Topping:
25 ml (2 tablespoons) Parmesan cheese, grated

157 Seafood pancakes

Serves 5;   kJ per portion 1 100;   Prep time 1 hour;   Cooking time 30 min.

1. Melt 37,5 ml (3 tablespoons) of the butter or margarine in a saucepan over moderate heat.
2. Stir in the flour, salt, cayenne pepper and nutmeg, stirring until the mixture is bubbly.
3. Gradually add the milk and continue stirring until the sauce is thick and smooth.
4. Blend in the sherry, shrimps, monkfish and eggs. Remove from the heat.
5. Fill each pancake (recipe 547) with 25 ml (2 tablespoons) of the mixture. Roll up and place closely together, seam side down, in a greased shallow baking dish.
6. Spoon the mixture that is left over the pancakes.
7. Melt the remaining butter or margarine over high heat and drizzle over the pancakes.
8. Sprinkle the pancakes with the grated Parmesan cheese and bake in the oven at 180°C (350°F) until the filling bubbles, about 15 minutes. Serve at once.

MEAT, POULTRY AND GAME

Meat, an important source of body-building protein, has always held pride of place in the South African diet. The earliest settlers at the Cape found a ready source of food in the abundance of game, cattle and sheep, and South Africans have been big meat eaters ever since. The meat most often used is beef, veal, mutton, lamb, pork, venison and poultry.

Judging the quality of meat

The characteristics of a truly succulent meat dish are its tenderness, juiciness and flavour, and these depend entirely on the quality of meat used in its preparation. How tender meat will be depends to a large extent on the quantity and nature of the connective tissue and, to a lesser extent, on how much fat is present in the muscle. A general rule is that the younger the animal, the more tender the meat.

The quality of any kind of meat can be determined primarily by examining:

- the overall appearance of the carcass or the cut of meat. The best cut has the largest proportion of meat to bone.
- the colour, thickness, degree of hardness or softness and the even distribution of fat over the carcass – described as the 'finish'.

Points to consider when buying meat

Type	Flesh	Fat	Bones	Carcass	Other
Beef	Bright cherry red, firm and finely grained.	White or creamy white in the young animal. Deep yellow in the older animal.			If there is a high degree of fat in the muscle tissue (marbling), the meat is particularly tasty and juicy. Beef should be well-hung; at least 8 days' ripening at the butcher.
Veal	Pale pink, finely grained and smooth.	Thin outer covering of fat. No marbling.	Large in proportion to the amount of meat. Cut surfaces are red and porous.		
Mutton	Darker red than lamb.	White and brittle.	Much harder than lamb		Meat from animal more than 3 years old is stringy and tough. An overlarge carcass with too much fat is a sure sign that the animal is old.
Lamb	Light red and finely grained.	White or creamy white in the young animal.	Soft and porous.	Evenly fleshed and even covering of fat.	
Pork	Light pink, firm and finely grained. Lean parts of young animal are a light greyish-pink.	Not more than 15% fat.			Bacon and ham should be dry to the touch with a clean, sweet smell. Any curing mould that has formed should be dry.

95

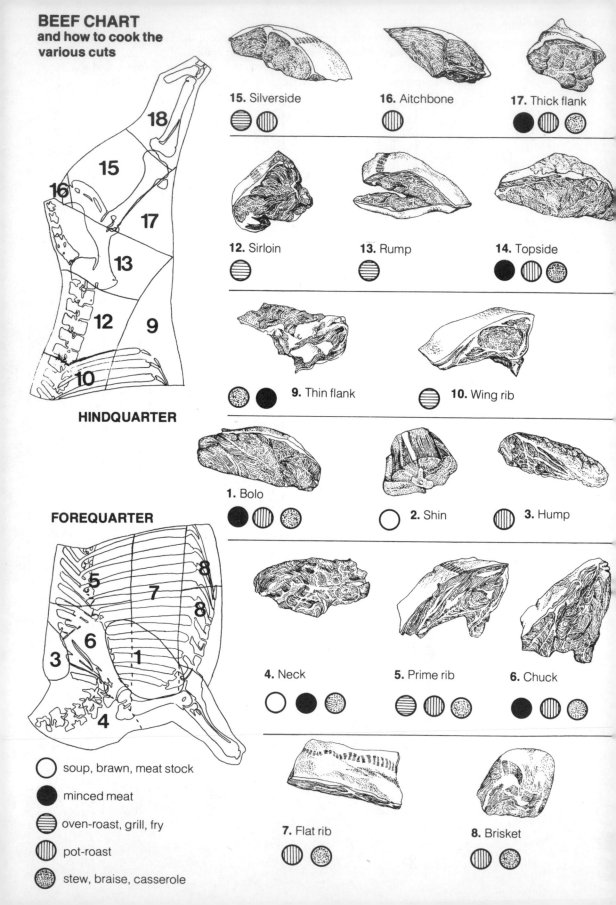

BEEF CHART
and how to cook the various cuts

18
15
16
17
13
12
9
10

HINDQUARTER

FOREQUARTER

5
8
7
8
6
3
1
4

15. Silverside

16. Aitchbone

17. Thick flank

12. Sirloin

13. Rump

14. Topside

9. Thin flank

10. Wing rib

1. Bolo

2. Shin

3. Hump

4. Neck

5. Prime rib

6. Chuck

7. Flat rib

8. Brisket

⭕ soup, brawn, meat stock

⚫ minced meat

⊜ oven-roast, grill, fry

⦀ pot-roast

▦ stew, braise, casserole

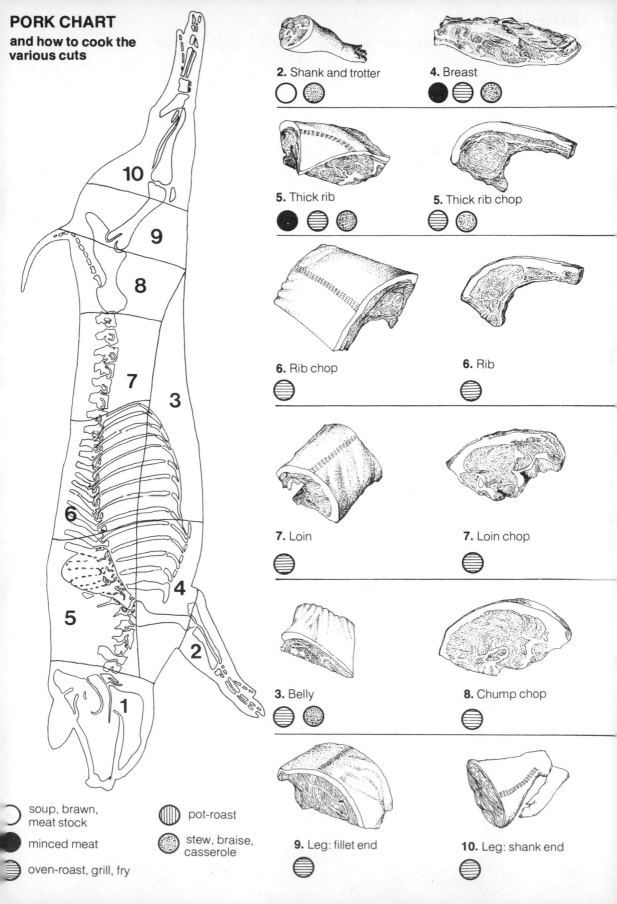

PORK CHART
and how to cook the various cuts

10
9
8
7
6
5
3
4
2
1

2. Shank and trotter

4. Breast

5. Thick rib

5. Thick rib chop

6. Rib chop

6. Rib

7. Loin

7. Loin chop

3. Belly

8. Chump chop

9. Leg: fillet end

10. Leg: shank end

soup, brawn, meat stock

minced meat

oven-roast, grill, fry

pot-roast

stew, braise, casserole

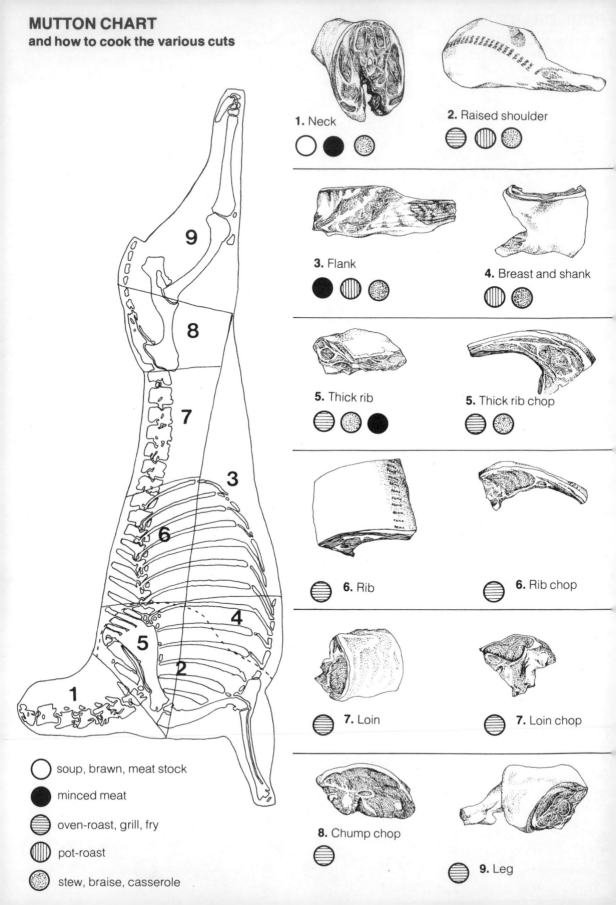

MUTTON CHART
and how to cook the various cuts

1. Neck

2. Raised shoulder

3. Flank

4. Breast and shank

5. Thick rib

5. Thick rib chop

6. Rib

6. Rib chop

7. Loin

7. Loin chop

8. Chump chop

9. Leg

○ soup, brawn, meat stock

● minced meat

⊜ oven-roast, grill, fry

⦀ pot-roast

⊛ stew, braise, casserole

POULTRY

The broad term 'poultry' – domestic birds specially bred for the table – includes the different varieties of chicken, turkey, duck, goose and muscovy duck. Guinea-fowl are also classified as poultry, but the colour and flavour are similar to that of pheasant and they are usually considered to be – and prepared like – game birds.

Whereas in the past *chicken* was a luxury and a sign of social status, new breeding and marketing techniques have made it an everyday commodity. Chicken is versatile and easy to prepare, which probably accounts for its popularity: it can be grilled, braised, fried, roasted, curried, served in wine or with a cream sauce or mouth-watering stuffing.

Turkey is usually associated with festive occasions in this country, particularly with Christmas. It is usually roasted, but can be temptingly served as a casserole or fricassée.

Not seen on supermarket shelves in South Africa as often as chicken, *ducks* and ducklings make the most delicious roasts, stews and casseroles. French cuisine has long celebrated the duck, which forms the basis of many of the classic dishes.

Goose has a stronger flavour than turkey and may even taste oily sometimes, but correctly prepared it is a most delectable bird. It is at its best roasted, in which case a bird of less than a year old is ideal. Because goose is fatty and can be indigestible if roasted in its own fat, it should always be set on a trivet in the roasting pan so that the fat can drip off.

Quality, selection and purchasing

Chickens are sold farm-fresh (hung and prepared on a poultry farm and usually sold whole), chilled (air-chilled and available whole and oven-ready, halved or in portions) and frozen (whole and oven-ready, halved or in portions). Frozen chickens take in water and are generally weighed after they have been frozen, which makes them less economical because you are also paying for the water.

Dressed chickens are classified for marketing as:
Chickster: 6 to 8 weeks old, 350 to 625 g
Chicken: 8 to 9 weeks old, 625 to 900 g
Boiler: any age, 900 g and over

Turkeys may be sold oven-ready or frozen and are generally sold whole. *Ducks*, if available, are sold chilled or frozen and usually whole. *Geese* are seldom readily available through retail outlets.

Jointing poultry

Turkeys, ducks and geese are generally cooked whole, but chickens are frequently cut into portions. A good-sized chicken should yield at least 10 portions.

Points to consider when selecting poultry

	Flesh	Bone	Skin	Carcass	Other
Chicken	Plump, firm white breast.	End of breast bone soft and flexible; if firm it is and older bird. Breast should be broad.	White or cream, un-broken; if thick and coarse it is an older bird. Blue discoloration indicates deterioration in quality. Boiling fowl has a slightly yellow tinge to its skin.	Legs should be bright yellow with firm claws.	Long hairs on the skin indicate an older bird. The longer a bird is left after killing and before preparing it for cooking, the stronger the flavour will be.
Turkey	Plump, well-formed breast.		Unbroken, white to slightly bluish.	Legs small in pro-portion to size of bird.	Must have a clean, fresh smell.
Duck and goose	Young bird has a well-formed breast. Ducks should have soft, white flesh and smell fresh.		Unbroken and no sign of stickiness.	Legs should be firm.	Young birds are tastier. Goose has a slightly 'gamey' flavour.

Note: Allow 250 to 300 g dressed mass (with bone) or 500 g live mass per serving.

1. If necessary, singe a dressed chicken over a clear flame to remove all the remaining down.
2. With poultry scissors or a heavy knife remove the legs by cutting through the skin and flesh between the leg and the body. Twist the leg backwards until the joint snaps, then cut the tendons. Separate the drumstick from the thigh at the knee joint.
3. Cut the wings from the body by cutting through the skin and flesh. Twist the wing backwards until the joint snaps, then cut the tendons.
4. Cut the body in half through the rib cage so that the breast is separated from the back. Cut lengthwise through the breastbone, then halve the breast lengthwise.
5. Cut the back into two portions.

Stuffing and trussing poultry

Chickens and other poultry are usually trussed for roasting to keep the legs and wings close to the body and thus prevent their drying out and becoming tough.
1. Sprinkle the inside of the dressed poultry with 10 ml lemon juice and season with 10 ml (2 teaspoons) salt for every 1 kg of meat.
2. Fill the crop and body cavity with the stuffing, but be careful not to stuff too tightly as the stuffing expands during cooking and may burst the skin or overflow.
3. Secure the openings with skewers or sew them up with a needle and thread.
4. Tie the ends of the drumsticks and the tail-end together with string.
5. Lift and twist the wings so that they lie flat across the back.
The bird is now ready for roasting.

Carving a chicken, duck, goose or turkey

1. Place the bird on its back with the legs to the right if you are right-handed or to the left if you are left-handed.
2. With a fork held in the left or right hand secure the bird firmly over the breastbone.
3. Remove the legs with a knife and separate them into drumstick and thigh. Carve the legs of a turkey or goose into slices.
4. Carve down the middle of the flesh on either side of the breast bone as far as the wing joints and remove the wings.
5. Carve the breast meat into thin slices.

Note: Always serve a piece of white and a piece of dark meat.

GAME

The term 'game' includes venison, rabbit, hare and game birds such as pheasant, guinea-fowl and pigeons.

The meat of many kinds of antelope *(venison)* can be made into the most succulent roasts, stews and casseroles. Game meat is very lean and many cuts, for instance the steaks, chops and saddle, have virtually no fat at all. Therefore these cuts must be larded with fat or bacon when they are prepared for cooking (recipe 167).

The tender cuts of younger animals, such as springbok raised for the market, need not be marinated, but the tougher cuts or venison from older and bigger animals should be marinated to tenderise the meat and enhance the flavour (recipes 167, 169, 170). Although it is better to lard venison before it is marinated, this can also be done afterwards. The marinating period varies from 12 hours to several days, depending on the toughness of the cut, but this period can be shortened to no more than 12 hours by injecting the marinade into the meat with a hypodermic syringe.

Many famous continental dishes are based on *rabbit* and *hare*. The meat is fine-textured, lightly gamey and resembles chicken in texture, but has less fat. Most wild rabbits should be marinated before cooking (recipe 231). A rabbit will serve 3 to 4 people and a hare 6 to 8.

Game birds are cleaned and jointed in much the same way as poultry (see p. 99). Generally speaking, most game birds are much leaner than chicken, so pork, bacon or fat should be added when they are cooking. Stuffing can provide internal basting, so long as it is fat and moist enough, but if the bird is very small, avoid using stuffing which would take too long to cook and result in the bird drying out on the outside. Birds that are not stuffed should be greased well inside the body cavity with oil or melted butter.

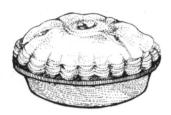

The flesh of game birds makes an excellent, though strongly flavoured, filling for pies (recipe 592). If the meat is too strongly flavoured for your taste, it can be combined with venison, pork or poultry.

STORAGE

Meat can be stored in the refrigerator for immediate use or in the freezer for later use.

Storing fresh meat in the refrigerator

1. Store meat as soon as possible after buying in the meat compartment or any other part of the refrigerator, *except* in the tray under the freezer – if the meat is placed in an area that is too cold, it will get freeze burn.
2. Wrap the meat loosely in wax paper, not in plastic or anything airtight, to allow for good air circulation.
3. Remove or loosen the wrapping from prepacked meat, except for meat that has been vacuum packed.
4. Steaks, chops and small roasts can be kept in the refrigerator for approximately 3 days and larger roasts for 1 to 2 days longer. Use ground, cubed or processed meats with 24 hours to obtain the best results.

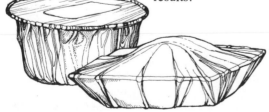

Freezing meat

Freezing fresh or prepared and cooked meat is a very simple and effective method of food preservation. If the meat is correctly wrapped and frozen at the right temperature, the nutritional value, appearance and taste will not be adversely affected. It is generally safer to freeze cooked meat rather than to keep it in the refrigerator for longer than 4 to 5 days. Remember always to freeze food and store it at a temperature of $-18\,°C$ (0 °F).

Freezing raw meat

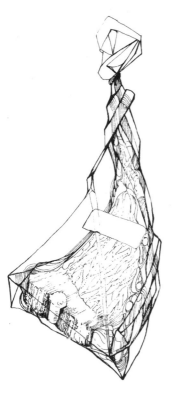

1. Cut meat as desired for cooking, e.g. chops, steaks, etc. This makes frozen meat easier to handle as once it has frozen it is very difficult to cut off smaller pieces.
2. If you so require, remove the bone, fat and gristle before freezing.
3. Freeze chops and mincemeat in batches ready for cooking. Chops, steaks or hamburger patties may be frozen with plastic sheets in between them to make it easy to remove single chops or patties. All meat frozen like this – except steak served rare – can be cooked without thawing.
4. Cuts such as the shoulder or ribs will take up less space and be easier to use if they are first boned and then frozen.
5. Stuffings may be added to poultry or boned cuts of meat before freezing, but do not use stuffings containing fresh fruit, vegetables or hard-boiled eggs as these do not freeze well. Larded legs of venison may also be frozen, but remember that larded and stuffed meat should be used within 2 or 3 months as certain spices change their flavour if they are frozen for too long.
6. The wrapping and packaging of meat for freezing makes all the difference to the result:
   (a) as little air as possible should remain in the package;
   (b) the wrapping should be thin enough to facilitate fast freezing but strong enough not to be easily punctured or torn; and
   (c) the packages should fit well into the freezer for optimum use of space.
7. Label all packages with the relevant information, i.e. type of meat, amount and date of freezing.

Note: Do not open the freezer too often as the temperature should be kept as stable as possible.

Freezing cooked meat

Cooked meat and meat dishes are frozen in the same way as raw meat, but the following must be remembered:
1. Cool cooked meat before freezing it. If it is hot when placed in the freezer, it may cause already-frozen food to thaw partially and thus spoil.
2. Leave 2 cm headspace to allow for expansion when freezing a cooked dish containing a lot of liquid.
3. When freezing a meat pie, cool the meat before adding it to the unbaked pastry shell.
4. Freeze roasted meat in one piece and slice it when thawed and just before serving. If sliced before it is frozen, the meat will dry out.

Note:

● Any meat which has a large proportion of fat on it will keep in the freezer for a short period only before the fat becomes rancid. Veal, beef, lean turkey and game freeze well, but pork, goose and larded cuts do not.

● Ham or cured meat should not be packed in foil for freezing as the curing mixture could react chemically to the foil and make holes in it.

● Meat should never be refrozen after it has been thawed. If too much raw meat is thawed, it is better first to cook what is left over and then freeze it.

● It is better not to use the ice compartment of a refrigerator for freezing meat, but if it has to be used, do not store meat in it for longer than 2 months as the temperature fluctuates more in the refrigerator than it does in a freezer.

● Meat bought ready-frozen should be placed in the freezer as soon as possible.

● Do not place too much food in the freezer to be frozen at one time as it takes time for the freezer to reach the correct freezing temperature again.

● Freezing cannot improve the quality of poor meat; always buy the best quality meat for freezing and follow the freezing rules meticulously for the best results.

Thawing and cooking frozen meat

Most meat dishes, with the exception of rare steak or roast beef, can be heated slowly from the frozen state without thawing; add at least a quarter of the original cooking time given in the recipe to the total cooking time to ensure that the dish will be done. Given sufficient time, however, it is generally better to thaw frozen meat before cooking it.

1. Remove meat from freezer and leave, in its original wrapping, in the refrigerator overnight – the rule of thumb is to calculate 8 to 9 hours per 500 g. To speed up the thawing process, thaw in the refrigerator overnight, then thaw at room temperature for the last 2 hours. If in a hurry, thaw at room temperature for 6 to 8 hours **but** remember not to leave meat outside the freezer for too long before use and **never** to thaw meat in hot water as too much of the blood and juices will be lost.

2. If meat is cooked directly from the frozen state make sure that big roasts – especially pork – are heated to the required internal temperatures: start the roast at 135 to 150°C (275 to 300°F) and calculate 40 to 45 minutes roasting time for every 500 g.

3. The sauce or gravy in cooked casserole dishes may separate or become watery when thawed. If this happens, add an extra thickener such as flour, cornflour or gravy powder **or** stir well to blend thoroughly (see p. 177). To avoid this problem altogether, make the sauce when the dish is to be served, not before freezing. This applies particularly to sauces that have eggs or cream in them, as it is the addition of these ingredients that makes a sauce separate when thawed.

4. Taste cooked dishes that have been frozen and add more salt and pepper if necessary.
5. Always heat casseroles to boiling point after freezing – freezing cannot kill bacteria, only inhibit it.
6. Grill meat that has been frozen in a very hot pan so that the meat browns quickly before it has a chance to thaw and draw water into the pan. Thicker cuts grilled in the pan should also be browned quickly, and the heat then lowered for the rest of the cooking time.

Storing poultry

Whether purchased fresh, chilled or frozen, chicken and other poultry should be treated as a perishable commodity. Prepacked fresh and chilled birds should be unwrapped and stored, lightly covered, in the refrigerator for not longer than 3 days. Frozen poultry should be stored in the freezer at −18 °C (0 °F) or lower until required. Allow frozen poultry to thaw in the refrigerator for at least 24 hours or at room temperature for 7 to 8 hours before use. A microwave oven can also be used to thaw frozen poultry; instructions are usually given with the oven.

Note: The giblets are often enclosed in a packet inside frozen birds; these should be removed before cooking.

Suggested periods for storing frozen meat at − 18 °C (0 °F)

Kind	Period	Kind	Period
beef, mutton, venison (raw and unseasoned)	10 months – 1 year	chicken, guinea-fowl (raw and unseasoned)	10 months – 1 year
pork, veal, mince (raw)	4-6 months	turkey (raw)	6 months
sweetbreads, kidneys, liver (raw)	4 months	goose and duck (raw)	4-5 months
sausage, cured raw meat and cold meats (processed)	2 months	cooked meat and meat dishes	2-3 months
meat frozen in ice compartment of refrigerator	2 months		
prepared meat (raw): larded, stuffed, marinated	2-3 months		

Note: Storing meat or meat dishes longer than these recommended periods will not necessarily result in 'bad meat' or food poisoning, but it will affect the quality.

PRESERVING MEAT

Ham is made by treating the leg or shoulder of pork with salt or brine *(curing)*. Ham and various other meats such as topside, bolo, tongue, hump or silverside may also be smoked, which preserves the meat and gives it a distinctive flavour.

Dry salt curing

Use the basic salt or brine mixture given for pickling (see below), but leave out the water. Allow 60 g of the mixture for every 1 kg of meat and calculate 3 days' curing time for every 500 g of meat; for example, 3 kg of meat should be cured for 6 days.

1. Mix the ingredients together thoroughly, rub the mixture into the meat and leave in the refrigerator for 2 days.
2. Rub more of the salt mixture into the meat every 2 days until the total curing time is up; for example, 3 kg of meat will have the salt mixture rubbed into it 3 times in all.

Note: The dry salt method is no longer favoured as it results in too great a loss of moisture and mass.

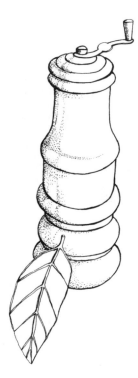

Pickling

Ingredients:

Meat	2-12 kg	25 kg	50 kg
Water	4,5 litres	9 litres	18 litres
Salt	1 kg	2 kg	4 kg
Saltpetre	20 g	45 g	90 g
Brown sugar	90 g	180 g	360 g
Bicarbonate of soda	30 g	60 g	120 g

Spices can be added according to taste; for instance, for 25 kg meat:

24 bay leaves
24 whole pimentos
12 peppercorns
2 sticks cinnamon
30 g mustard powder
3 to 6 cloves garlic

or 15 g black pepper
24 bay leaves
24 whole pimentos
62,5 ml (5 tablespoons) ground ginger
3 to 6 cloves garlic

Note: Salt preserves the meat, and saltpetre gives cured meat its pink colour and prevents bacterial decay.

1. Boil the water in a large saucepan, allow it to cool and transfer it to a large plastic, wooden, enamel or earthenware container. Add all the other ingredients and stir well.
2. Add the meat, making sure that the brine covers it completely. Press the meat down with a heavy object, such as a bowl filled with water or a clean, heavy stone.
3. Meat cuts up to 3 cm thickness should be ready in 14 days; thicker cuts should be left for a few days longer. Hams up to 6 kg should be left in the brine mixture for 4 to 6 days per kg, with a maximum of 18 to 21

days, and hams 6 kg and more should be left in the brine for 4 days per kg, with a maximum of 21 to 25 days. To test if it is pickled, pierce the ham with a sharp knife: it should be pink right through if the brine has reached the centre of the meat. If it is still grey inside, it is not ready.

4. After 5 days in the brine, the hams should be carefully examined. If there are any signs of scum or slime the meat should be removed, washed in cold water, scrubbed and placed in fresh brine. Even if there are not signs of mould, meat should be repacked at least once a week.

5. At the end of the curing period the hams should be scrubbed and washed in hot water, then soaked in cold water for 4 to 6 hours and dried thoroughly. The hams may now be smoked if desired.

Note:
● Never use a metal container for curing as the metal may react with the salt mixture.
● To shorten the curing time the brine mixture may be injected into the meat with a special brine needle. Inject approximately one quarter of the brine mixture into the meat. Leave the meat in the rest of the brine, allowing 1 day for every 1,5 kg meat.
● Store ham in a cool, dry place or freeze it.
● Paint the ham with smoke essence to obtain a golden colour and good flavour.

Biltong

Biltong is usually made from venison, beef or ostrich meat – normally during the cool, dry months. The tender cuts, such as fillet, rump and sirloin, should be used.

For every 25 kg meat, allow:
1,25 kg good quality fine salt
250 ml (1 cup) brown sugar
50 ml (4 tablespoons) bicarbonate of soda
20 ml (4 teaspoons) saltpetre (optional)
25 ml (2 tablespoons) pepper
100 g coarsely ground coriander

Note: The sugar keeps the biltong moist and the soda makes the meat tender.

1. After the animal has been skinned, with a sharp knife cut along the natural dividing lines of the muscles down the length of the whole leg or a large portion of it.

2. Cut the pieces into strips 5 to 7 cm thick, if possible with some fat on each strip.

3. Mix the salt, sugar, bicarbonate of soda, saltpetre and coriander together. Rub the mixture into the strips of meat.

4. Layer the meat, larger pieces at the bottom, in a wooden, earthenware, plastic or enamel container – never use iron or metal because the salt may react with it. Sprinkle a little vinegar over each layer.

5. Leave in a cool place for 24 to 48 hours, depending on how thick the meat is and how salty you want it to be.

6. Dip the biltong in a mixture of 500 ml vinegar and 5 litres warm water. This makes it shiny and dark.

107

7. Dry the pieces and hang them up on s-shaped hooks or pieces of string, about 5 cm apart, so that the air can circulate freely around them. Leave for 2 to 3 weeks, depending on how tender the meat is.

Note:
- Do not cut the strips of meat more than 2 cm thick if the weather is not really cool.
- Biltong should be dried in a cool, dry, airy place, protected from flies and dust.
- In humid areas, biltong should be dried in a drying chamber.
- To store in humid conditions, freeze biltong and only thaw enough for immediate use.

Dried sausage

Sausage for drying is made as follows:
3 kg beef
500 g mutton tail fat
20 ml (4 teaspoons) salt
2 ml (½ teaspoon) pepper
50 ml (4 tablespoons) ground roasted coriander
2 ml (½ teaspoon) ground allspice
2 ml (½ teaspoon) ground cloves
25 ml vinegar
85 g sausage casing

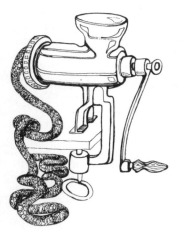

1. Season the meat with salt, pepper and spices.
2. Mince all the ingredients together coarsely and fill casings loosely with the mixture.
3. Hang up to dry in a cold, dry place, ensuring that the sausages are protected from flies and dust. Makes 3,5 kg.

Boerewors

Make *boerewors* as follows:
1,5 kg beef
1,5 kg pork
500 g pork siding (spek) cut in 7 mm cubes
25 ml (2 tablespoons) salt
5 ml (1 teaspoon) pepper
50 ml (4 tablespoons) coriander
2 ml (½ teaspoon) grated nutmeg
1 ml (¼ teaspoon) ground cloves
2 ml (½ teaspoon) ground dried thyme
2 ml (½ teaspoon) ground allspice
125 ml vinegar
1 clove garlic, crushed
50 ml Worcester sauce
85 g sausage casing

1. Roast the coriander until light brown, then grind and mix it with all the other spices, salt and pepper.
2. Mince the meat coarsely and mix very lightly with all the other ingredients.
3. Fill the casings not too firmly with the meat mixture.

Note:
- Do not knead the meat, otherwise the sausage will be too firm.
- Use good quality meat without sinews and membranes.
- Make sure that the cubes of siding are evenly distributed.
- Sausage freezes very well, provided that it is made from fresh meat.
- Other kinds of meat may be used, for example, veal, pork, lamb, venison.

COOKING METHODS

The cooking method depends on the kind of meat, its quality and the cut. Tender cuts may be cooked by dry heat methods, while tougher cuts require long, slow cooking in moist heat to make them tender. Consult the charts on p.96 to 98 to find out which methods suit which cuts.

Dry heat
There are three methods:
1. roasting with the addition of little or no liquid or fat;
2. grilling or broiling, either in the oven, over red-hot coals, in an electric griller or in a heavy grilling or frying-pan, with as little fat as possible added; and
3. pan frying in deep or shallow fat.

ROASTING

Oven roasting
All meat can be roasted in a little liquid, covered, in the oven. Tender cuts, however, can be roasted uncovered and without any extra moisture.

Roasting meat, covered, with added liquid

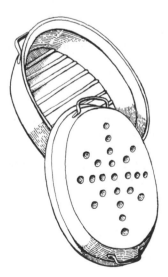

1. Clean meat with a damp cloth, dry it and trim off any excess fat. Meat can be roasted in one piece, or deboned and rolled with a filling.
2. Season the meat with a mixture of 50 ml (4 tablespoons) flour; 10 ml (2 teaspoons) salt and 2 ml (½ teaspoon) pepper for every 1 kg of meat. 1 ml (¼ teaspoon) mustard powder, peppercorns, bay leaves and various other spices and herbs can also be added (see recipe section). Rub the seasoning into the meat.n 1 Place the meat, fat side up, in a deep, heavy pan with a lid. Heavy-duty aluminium foil can also be used to seal the pan tightly, **but** remember that the meat must not touch the lid or the foil, as it will stick.
3. Add fat or oil to the meat: 100 ml (²⁄₅ cup) for a 2 kg piece of meat or, if the meat is exceptionally lean, as in the case of venison, add 125 ml (½ cup). Fat meat, such as pork, and well-larded cuts do not require extra fat or oil.
4. For a 2 kg piece of meat, add 50 to 75 ml water, stock, wine, beer or fruit juice.
5. Cover and roast in the oven at 190°C (375°F) for 30 minutes. Lower the heat to 160°C (325°F) for the rest of the roasting time (see table p. 111).
6. Baste occasionally with fat, or add more liquid if necessary.
7. For a crisp appearance, remove the lid or open the foil for the last 15 minutes of the roasting time.

Note:
- For really tender cuts, higher roasting temperatures may be used: 220 °C (425 °F) for 15 minutes, then lower the heat to 180 °C (350 °F) for the rest of the roasting time.
- Ask your butcher to debone meat if you want to roll it before roasting.

Roasting meat, uncovered, without added liquid

1. Prepare and season the meat as described above.
2. Place the meat, fat side up, in a shallow roasting pan. Boned cuts should be placed on a rack in the pan. If you have a meat thermometer, insert it into the thickest part of the muscle to control the cooking time. Spread fat or oil over lean meat, as described in the previous method.
3. Roast, uncovered, in the oven at 190 °C (375 °F) for 30 minutes, then lower the heat to 160 °C (325 °F) for the rest of the roasting time. (see table p.111)
4. Baste meat every 15 to 20 minutes with the dripping and with extra fat or oil, if necessary.

Note: Use only tender prime cuts for this method.

Other roasting methods

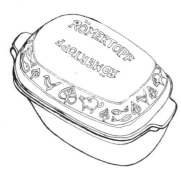

1. *Cooking bags*. Place the meat in the bag and secure. Roast at 190 °C (375 °F) for 30 minutes, then at 160 °C (325 °F) for the rest of the roasting time (see table p.111). The meat will brown through the bag, but to give a crisp finish, open the bag for the last 15 minutes of the roasting time. Meat will roast better if 20 ml (4 teaspoons) flour is added to the cooking bag and the meat shaken in it to dust well. If holes are made in the bag to allow the steam to escape, the roast will brown crisply without having to open the bag for the last 15 minutes of the roasting time.
2. *Unglazed pottery (Römertopf)*. Prepare dish according to instructions so that no moisture or extra fat need be added, but the lid must fit tightly. Roast at 190 °C (375 °F) for 30 minutes, then at 160 °C (325 °F) for the rest of the roasting period (see table p.111).
3. *Foil*. Cut a piece of heavy-duty foil large enough to wrap around the meat. Grease the shiny side of the foil lightly with butter or fat and wrap tightly around the meat, dull side out. The meat will be kept moist and juicy, but to give a crisp finish, open foil and brown for the last 15 minutes of the roasting time. Allow an extra 15 or 20 minutes total roasting time for the heat to penetrate through the foil, or increase the oven temperature to 200 °C (400 °F) for the entire roasting time.
4. *Pressure cooker*. Tougher meat can be steamed in a pressure cooker for 35 minutes at high pressure (100 kPa), then roasted in the oven at 190 °C (375 °F) for 15 minutes to obtain a crisp finish.
5. *Rotisserie*. Pre-heat the oven to 190 °C (375 °F). Spear the meat onto the spit and place in the oven. Roast for 30 minutes, then lower the heat to 160 °C (325 °F) for the rest of the roasting time. Baste the meat often with the dripping.

Reasons for an unsatisfactory result
- If the meat is hard and dry on the outside, the oven was initially too hot, or too little or too much fat was used.
- If the meat is tough, the wrong roasting method was used for that specific cut or grade of meat.

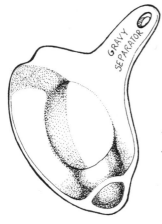

To clarify dripping

Dripping, the fat and juices released when meat is roasting, is used to make gravies, sauces and so on. It usually contains particles of food which can spoil when stored and make the dripping unusable. These must therefore be removed before the dripping is either stored or used. Place the dripping in a large saucepan and cover with cold water. Bring slowly to the boil and continue boiling, uncovered, for 15 minutes. Cool slightly, then pour through a thin muslin cloth or a fine sieve into a bowl. Leave until the dripping has set and can be lifted from the brown residue at the bottom. Store the dripping in a container and use as needed.

Roasting times

Cut	Time	Oven temperature	Serve with
Beef: Sirloin Ribs Aitchbone Topside Rump Fillet	Rare to medium: 10 to 15 min per 500 g plus 15 min Well-done: 20 min per 500 g plus 20 min	190 °C (375 °F) for 30 min, then 160 °C (325 °F) for the rest of time	Yorkshire pudding horseradish sauce mustard gravy fruit sauce wine sauce
Mutton or Lamb: Leg Loin Shoulder Rib	20 to 30 min per 500 g plus 15 min	190 °C (375 °F) for 30 min then 160 °C (325 °F) for the rest of the time	herb sauce mint sauce gravy rolled with fruit stuffing
Pork, Veal or Venison: Leg Loin Rib	35 to 40 min per 500 g plus 30 minutes.	190 °C (375 °F) for 30 minutes then 160 °C (325 °F) for the rest of the time	stuffings apple sauce gravy fruit jelly fruit

Note:
- Pork must always be well-done.
- The internal temperatures on a meat thermometer are:
  Rare: 57 °C (135 °F)
  Medium: 68 °C (155 °F)
  Well-done: 94 °C (170 °F)

Roasting times – Poultry

Kind	kg	Period per kg		Oven temperature
		Stuffed	Unstuffed	
Duck, goose and chicken	1,5 to 2 kg	allow 80 min	60 to 80 min	190 °C (375 °F) for 30 min then 160 °C) (325 °F) for the rest of the time
	2,5 to 3 kg	allow 80 min	50 to 60 min	
Turkey	3 to 5 kg	allow 60 min	50 to 60 min	190 °C (375 °F) for 30 min then 160 °C (325 °F) for the rest of the time
	5,5 to 6 kg	allow 60 min	50 min	
	6,5 kg and over	allow 60 min	40 min	

111

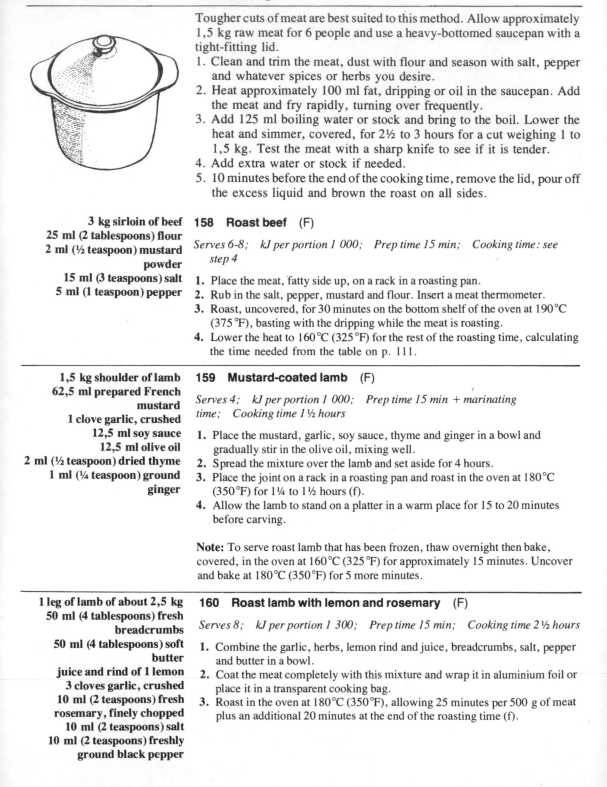

Tougher cuts of meat are best suited to this method. Allow approximately 1,5 kg raw meat for 6 people and use a heavy-bottomed saucepan with a tight-fitting lid.

1. Clean and trim the meat, dust with flour and season with salt, pepper and whatever spices or herbs you desire.
2. Heat approximately 100 ml fat, dripping or oil in the saucepan. Add the meat and fry rapidly, turning over frequently.
3. Add 125 ml boiling water or stock and bring to the boil. Lower the heat and simmer, covered, for 2½ to 3 hours for a cut weighing 1 to 1,5 kg. Test the meat with a sharp knife to see if it is tender.
4. Add extra water or stock if needed.
5. 10 minutes before the end of the cooking time, remove the lid, pour off the excess liquid and brown the roast on all sides.

---

3 kg sirloin of beef
25 ml (2 tablespoons) flour
2 ml (½ teaspoon) mustard powder
15 ml (3 teaspoons) salt
5 ml (1 teaspoon) pepper

158   Roast beef   (F)

Serves 6-8;   kJ per portion 1 000;   Prep time 15 min;   Cooking time: see step 4

1. Place the meat, fatty side up, on a rack in a roasting pan.
2. Rub in the salt, pepper, mustard and flour. Insert a meat thermometer.
3. Roast, uncovered, for 30 minutes on the bottom shelf of the oven at 190°C (375°F), basting with the dripping while the meat is roasting.
4. Lower the heat to 160°C (325°F) for the rest of the roasting time, calculating the time needed from the table on p. 111.

1,5 kg shoulder of lamb
62,5 ml prepared French mustard
1 clove garlic, crushed
12,5 ml soy sauce
12,5 ml olive oil
2 ml (½ teaspoon) dried thyme
1 ml (¼ teaspoon) ground ginger

159   Mustard-coated lamb   (F)

Serves 4;   kJ per portion 1 000;   Prep time 15 min + marinating time;   Cooking time 1½ hours

1. Place the mustard, garlic, soy sauce, thyme and ginger in a bowl and gradually stir in the olive oil, mixing well.
2. Spread the mixture over the lamb and set aside for 4 hours.
3. Place the joint on a rack in a roasting pan and roast in the oven at 180°C (350°F) for 1¼ to 1½ hours (f).
4. Allow the lamb to stand on a platter in a warm place for 15 to 20 minutes before carving.

Note: To serve roast lamb that has been frozen, thaw overnight then bake, covered, in the oven at 160°C (325°F) for approximately 15 minutes. Uncover and bake at 180°C (350°F) for 5 more minutes.

---

1 leg of lamb of about 2,5 kg
50 ml (4 tablespoons) fresh breadcrumbs
50 ml (4 tablespoons) soft butter
juice and rind of 1 lemon
3 cloves garlic, crushed
10 ml (2 teaspoons) fresh rosemary, finely chopped
10 ml (2 teaspoons) salt
10 ml (2 teaspoons) freshly ground black pepper

160   Roast lamb with lemon and rosemary   (F)

Serves 8;   kJ per portion 1 300;   Prep time 15 min;   Cooking time 2½ hours

1. Combine the garlic, herbs, lemon rind and juice, breadcrumbs, salt, pepper and butter in a bowl.
2. Coat the meat completely with this mixture and wrap it in aluminium foil or place it in a transparent cooking bag.
3. Roast in the oven at 180°C (350°F), allowing 25 minutes per 500 g of meat plus an additional 20 minutes at the end of the roasting time (f).

2 breasts of lamb, boned and trimmed
bread stuffing (recipe 307)
1 egg, beaten
2 red peppers, seeded and finely chopped
1 onion, grated
225 g canned apricots, drained and coarsely chopped
37,5 ml honey, melted
12,5 ml (1 tablespoon) salt
5 ml (1 teaspoon) pepper
melted butter or margarine

161 Noisettes of lamb

Serves 6; kJ per portion 1 300; Prep time 20 min; Cooking time 2¾ hours

1. Spread the breast of lamb out flat and season with salt and pepper.
2. Combine the bread stuffing (recipe 307), beaten egg, apricots, red peppers and onion in a small bowl and spread evenly over the lamb breasts.
3. Roll the lamb up, tying it securely with string at regular intervals. Cut each breast into three rolls (noisettes) and brush each with melted butter or margarine.
4. Roast on a baking tray in the oven at 180°C (350°F) for 1 hour. Brush the noisettes with melted honey and roast for a further 1¾ hours.
5. Serve at once on a bed of vegetables.

---

1 suckling pig
250 g butter or fat
500 ml boiling water
15 ml (3 teaspoons) salt
5 ml (1 teaspoon) pepper

162 Roast suckling pig

Serves 20-30; kJ per portion 960; Prep time 20 min; Cooking time: see step 5.

1. Clean and weigh suckling pig to calculate cooking time (see step 5).
2. Make four skin-deep incisions 7 cm long on both sides of, and at right angles to, the backbone.
3. Place the pig on the rack of the roasting pan and season with salt and pepper. Spread with butter or fat.
4. Add the boiling water to the roasting pan, cover the pig with foil or well-oiled brown paper. Cover the ears and feet with an extra layer of foil to prevent burning.
5. Roast for 15 minutes in the oven at 240°C (450°F), then lower the heat to 150°C (300°F) for the rest of the roasting time. Calculate 50 minutes roasting time for every 500 g meat (a meat thermometer should register 100°C (180°F) internal temperature).
6. Remove foil or paper after 2½ hours and spread thick cream or a mixture of honey and ginger, or apricot jam and brown sugar, over the skin. Roast, uncovered, for the rest of the roasting time.
7. Serve the pig whole on a large platter with an apple in its mouth.

Note: The abdominal cavity of the pig may be filled with raw apples, which will cook slowly with the meat and impart a delicious flavour.

1,5 kg pork spareribs, washed and trimmed
1 clove garlic, crushed
125 ml soy sauce
25 ml honey
12,5 ml sherry

163 Pork spareribs

Serves 4; kJ per portion 1 100; Prep time 15 min + marinating time; Cooking time 40-45 min.

1. Place the spareribs in a shallow baking dish.
2. Combine the soy sauce, honey, sherry and garlic in a bowl, then pour the mixture over the spareribs. Marinate for 1 hour, turn over and marinate for a further hour. Drain, reserving the marinade.
3. Replace the spareribs in the baking dish and roast in the oven at 180°C (350°F) for 20 minutes on each side, basting with the marinade every 10 minutes.
4. Brown the ribs on both sides under the grill and serve immediately.

Variation: Serve with a sweet and sour sauce (recipe 324) and fruit kebabs (recipe 164).

164 Crispy roast pork with fruit kebabs (F)

1,5 kg loin of pork, chined and
rind scored into diamonds
12,5 ml oil
sprigs of fresh rosemary
garlic salt (optional)
salt and pepper
Fruit kebabs:
12 cubes canned pineapple
1 small orange, peeled and cut
into 12 pieces
12 canned cherries, stoned
12 black or white grapes,
seeded
Gravy:
25 ml (2 tablespoons) flour
250 ml meat stock
12,5 ml sherry
Garnish:
1 bunch watercress
sprigs of fresh rosemary

Serves 6;   kJ per portion 1 500;   Prep time 50 min;   Cooking time 2 hours

1. Wipe the joint with a clean, damp cloth. Sprinkle with garlic salt, salt and pepper.
2. Brush the rind with oil and rub in more salt. Insert a few sprigs of rosemary in the pork rind and flesh.
3. Tie the joint neatly with string and place on the rack in a roasting pan. Leave at room temperature for 1 hour, then roast, without basting, in the middle of the oven at 190 °C (375 °F) until the meat is cooked through and the crackling crisp and golden, about 2 hours (f).
4. Meanwhile, thread the fruit onto 12 wooden skewers. Sprinkle with a little salt.
5. Add the fruit kebabs to the roasting pan 5 minutes before the meat is ready to serve.
6. Lift the joint onto a hot platter and remove the string. Drain the fruit kebabs and arrange around the roast. Keep it warm while making the gravy.
7. Pour off all but 25 ml of the fat in the roasting pan. Sprinkle in the flour and cook, stirring, on top of the stove for 1 minute.
8. Blend in the stock and bring to the boil, stirring all the time. Boil for 3 minutes, then strain through a fine sieve into a saucepan, add the sherry and a little salt and pepper if necessary. Reheat and pour into a warmed sauceboat.
9. Arrange extra sprigs of rosemary and the watercress around the meat and serve at once.

165 Baked glazed ham (F)

1 ham or gammon, about 5 kg
10 cloves
5 peppercorns
200 g brown sugar
250 ml apricot juice
25 ml lemon juice, ginger
syrup, honey or apricot jam
10 ml (2 teaspoons) ground
ginger
5 ml (1 teaspoon) mustard
powder
1 bay leaf
125 ml (½ cup) preserved
ginger, finely chopped
or 250 ml (1 cup) pineapple
rings
or 250 ml (1 cup) canned
apricot halves
or 125 ml (½ cup) glacé
cherries

Serves 20-25;   kJ per portion 1 100;   Prep time 30 min;   Cooking time 3½-4 hours.

1. Scrub ham and, if necessary, soak in cold water to remove salt. Dry the meat, coat it with mustard powder and place on a large sheet of aluminium foil. Add the bay leaf and peppercorns.
2. Wrap the foil loosely around the ham and place, fat side up, in a roasting pan.
3. Bake in the oven at 160 °C (325 °F), calculating the baking period as follows:
   Less than 5 kg . . . 40 to 50 min per kg
   More than 5 kg . . . 35 to 40 min per kg
4. Remove the ham from the oven 45 minutes before the end of the baking period, remove foil and peel off the skin, leaving the layer of fat intact (f).
5. Score the fat side of the ham by making criss-cross cuts 5 mm deep and about 20 mm apart to form a diamond pattern on the surface.
6. Spread with lemon juice, ginger syrup, apricot jam or honey. Sprinkle brown sugar over the ham and pour apricot juice over it. Brown in the oven for the rest of the baking time.
7. To serve, decorate ham with cloves and pineapple rings, preserved ginger, glacé cherries or apricot halves.

Note:
● To serve frozen ham, thaw completely, heat through and continue with steps 5, 6 and 7.
● Salty hams must be soaked; those that are not too salty need not be.
● To save time, boil the ham in water, then glaze it in the oven.

Turn a whole chicken that is being browned by inserting a spoon in the end cavity.

166　Fruity gammon

6 gammon steaks or Kasseler chops
1 large onion, finely chopped
2 large oranges
75 ml (6 tablespoons) fruit mincemeat
62,5 ml (5 tablespoons) butter or margarine
2 ml (½ teaspoon) mustard powder
2 ml (½ teaspoon) pepper
Garnish:
1 large orange

Serves 6;　kJ per portion 1 200;　Prep time 20 min;　Cooking time 35-40 min.

1. Cut the rind from the gammon with a pair of scissors and snip the edges of the meat at 2 cm intervals to prevent the meat from curling as it cooks.
2. Grease a large roasting pan with half the butter or margarine and lay the meat in it.
3. Melt the rest of the butter or margarine in a small saucepan and sauté the onion until soft.
4. Remove the pan from the stove and add the grated rind and juice of 2 oranges, the mustard powder, fruit mincemeat and pepper. Pour the mixture over the meat.
5. Bake, uncovered, on a shelf above the centre of the oven at 180°C (350°F) until tender, about 35 minutes. Peel and slice the remaining orange and garnish.

167　Oven-roasted venison　(F)

1 leg of venison, approximately 2 to 2,5 kg
250 g lardons (strips of spek) for every kg meat
37,5 ml (3 tablespoons) fat or 200 g bacon strips
25 ml (2 tablespoons) flour
Marinade:
250 ml vinegar or a mixture of 125 ml vinegar and 125 ml dry red wine
2 bay leaves
25 ml (2 tablespoons) brown sugar
2 ml (½ teaspoon) ground coriander
2 ml (½ teaspoon) mustard powder
5 ml (1 teaspoon) salt
1 ml (¼ teaspoon) pepper

Serves 8-10;　kJ per portion 1 000;　Prep time 30 min + marinating time;　Cooking time 2-2½ hours

1. Clean and trim venison. Using a sharp knife, make deep vertical slits in the meat about 20 mm apart and stuff each slit with a lardon 6 mm × 5 cm (f).
2. Combine the vinegar or the vinegar and wine with all the seasonings and marinate the venison in it for 2 to 3 days, turning it twice daily.
3. Remove the meat from the marinade, rub with flour and place on the rack of the roasting pan.
4. Spread fat over the surface of the meat or layer with bacon strips.
5. Roast in the oven at 140° to 160°C (275°F to 325°F), calculating the roasting time at 50 to 60 minutes for each kg of meat.
6. Baste every 30 minutes with the pan drippings. Increase the heat to 200°C (400°F) to brown the meat 5 minutes before serving (f). Serve with quince jelly or any fresh, dried, preserved or stewed fruit.

Note:
● Venison can be frozen after larding or after it has been roasted. To serve roasted meat after freezing, thaw completely then heat in the oven at 150°C (300°F) for about 1 hour. Reheating at too high a temperature will dry the meat out.
● Venison can also be roasted wrapped in foil. Roast in the oven at 160°C (325°F), calculating the roasting time as outlined in step 5. To allow meat to brown, the foil should be opened for the last 30 minutes of the cooking time.

168　Roast stuffed pigeons　(F)

8 pigeons
50 ml (4 tablespoons) lard or margarine
5 ml (1 teaspoon) salt
2 ml (½ teaspoon) pepper
Stuffing:
2 hard-boiled eggs
1 egg, raw
50 ml (4 tablespoons) butter
1 slice fresh bread, crumbled
12,5 ml (1 tablespoon) parsley, finely chopped
5 ml (1 teaspoon) salt
2 ml (½ teaspoon) pepper

Serves 8;　kJ per portion 1 100;　Prep time 20 min;　Cooking time 1½ hours

1. First make the stuffing. Chop the hard-boiled eggs and blend them with the breadcrumbs, butter, parsley, salt and pepper. Mix in the raw egg to bind.
2. Lightly season the pigeons inside and out and stuff them. Secure with skewers.
3. Cover the pigeons with lard or margarine and roast in the oven at 180°C (350°F) for 1¼ hours, basting often (f). Serve at once.

Note: To serve after freezing, heat still frozen and covered or wrapped in aluminium foil, in the oven at 180°C (350°F) for approximately 30 minutes. The stuffing must be heated through.

3 kg saddle of venison, about
60 cm in length
200 g streaky bacon, rind
removed
37,5 ml (3 tablespoons) apricot
jam
25 ml fruit chutney
500 g canned apricot halves
37,5 ml medium sherry
2 to 4 cloves garlic,
thinly sliced
5 ml (1 teaspoon) mixed dried
herbs
10 ml (2 teaspoons) salt
freshly ground black pepper

169 Saddle of venison with apricots (F)

Serves 8-10; kJ per portion 1 200; Prep time 20 min; Cooking time 40-60 min.

1. Make slits in the saddle using a sharp knife, and stuff the incisions with slivers of garlic.
2. Season with the salt, pepper and herbs, then cut the saddle loose from the backbone, leaving the meat attached to the ribs.
3. In a bowl combine the apricot jam, chutney and sherry and rub the mixture into the meat.
4. Place bacon rashers over the saddle and bake, uncovered, in the oven at 160°C (325°F) for 40 to 60 minutes (f). Serve with canned apricot halves.

Note: Wrap still frozen meat in foil and heat in the oven at 180°C (350°F) for approximately 20 minutes. Open foil for the last 5 minutes to brown the meat.

Use tongs to turn steaks or pieces of meat that are being browned; never prick meat as piercing lets the juices escape and makes the meat dry.

Meat that has to be sautéed will not stick to the pan if the pan is heated before the butter or oil is added.

Never carve a sizeable piece of meat or poultry directly it comes out of the oven – give a big roast or turkey at least 20 minutes to set into itself and it will be much easier to slice.

---

1 leg of venison, 2 to 2,5 kg
250 g lardons (strips of spek)
1 onion, thinly sliced
25 ml (2 tablespoons) flour
25 ml (2 tablespoons) fat or oil
25 ml (2 tablespoons) brown
sugar
100 g seedless raisins
500 ml vinegar
250 ml dry red wine
50 ml medium sherry
(optional)
50 ml (4 tablespoons) apricot
jam
2 cloves garlic, cut into thin
slivers
2 ml (½ teaspoon) ground
ginger
1 bay leaf
6 cloves
25 ml (2 tablespoons) salt
2 ml (½ teaspoon) pepper

170 Pot roast leg of venison

Serves 6-8; kJ per portion 1 100; Prep time 30 min + marinating time; Cooking time 2-3 hours

1. Marinate the lardons for 45 minutes in a mixture of 125 ml of the vinegar, 5 ml (1 teaspoon) of the salt and 5 ml (1 teaspoon) of the sugar.
2. With a sharp-pointed knife, pierce holes in the leg of venison and stuff each incision with a raisin, a sliver of garlic and a marinated lardon.
3. Rub the rest of the salt and sugar, and the pepper and ground ginger into the meat.
4. Place the meat in an earthenware or glass container together with the onion slices, bay leaf and the rest of the vinegar and red wine.
5. Marinate for 2 to 3 days, turning the venison twice daily.
6. Then heat the fat or oil in a heavy saucepan and brown the meat.
7. Add the cloves and 250 ml water and simmer until tender, 2 to 3 hours.
8. Make a paste with the flour, apricot jam and sherry (if desired) and baste the meat with it. Roast for a further 5 minutes. Serve with stewed dried fruit, quinces or apples.

171 Duck à l'orange (F)

1,75 to 2 kg duck, trussed
1 veal knuckle, sawn in pieces
100 g butter or margarine
5 oranges
275 ml chicken stock
150 ml dry white wine
10 ml (2 teaspoons) salt
5 ml (1 teaspoon) pepper
125 ml water

Serves 4-6; kJ per portion 1 300;   Prep time 20 min;   Cooking time 2-3 hours

1. Melt the butter or margarine in a large saucepan and brown the duck over medium heat.
2. Season with salt and pepper. Add the chicken stock, wine and veal bones and simmer, covered, for 2 hours.
3. Remove the duck from the saucepan (f), set aside and keep warm.
4. Strain the sauce through a fine sieve, then return it to the saucepan.
5. Cut the rind of 2 of the oranges into thin strips; set aside peeled oranges. Boil rind in the water for 2 minutes. Drain well.
6. Add the boiled orange rind and the juice of the 2 peeled oranges to the sauce and mix well. Boil for 2 minutes (f).
7. Meanwhile, place the duck on a large serving dish, and garnish with slices of the remaining 3 oranges.
8. Pour the sauce over the duck. Serve with boiled rice.

Note: Freeze the duck and sauce separately. To serve after freezing, thaw and heat the meat and sauce, then continue with steps 7 and 8.

172 Oven-roasted poultry (F)

1 turkey, goose, duck or chicken
25 ml (2 tablespoons) flour
25 ml (2 tablespoons) butter or fat
12,5 ml lemon juice
stuffing (recipes 302 to 314)
10 ml (2 teaspoons) salt for every kg of meat
2 ml (½ teaspoon) pepper for every kg of meat

Serves 10;   kJ per portion 980;   Prep time 30 min;   Cooking time 2-3 hours

1. If necessary, singe off the down and stubble. Clean body cavity thoroughly.
2. Stuff body cavity with a stuffing of your choice. Sew up openings or secure with skewers.
3. Rub bird with lemon juice, salt and pepper.
4. Spread with butter or fat and dredge in flour.
5. Pour a little water into the roasting pan, add the bird and roast, covered, in the oven at 160°C (325°F), basting frequently.
6. Uncover and brown bird for the last 15 minutes of the roasting time (f).

Note:
- Cooked poultry freezes very well. Reheat still frozen bird at a low heat to prevent drying out, and baste frequently with butter or oil.
- It is generally better not to freeze a cooked stuffed bird.
- Do not stuff a bird too tightly as stuffing expands as it cooks and may split the skin.
- Lean birds must be basted frequently.

GRILLING AND FRYING

Grilling (Broiling)

Use tender, prime cuts and grill over hot coals, under the grilling element of an oven or on a gas griller. Allow approximately 180 g raw meat, without bone, and 220 g raw meat, with bone, per person.

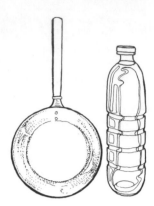

Grilling over hot coals

1. Let the fire burn until all the flames die down and only the hot coals remain. Use only dry wood of a type that will yield good hot coals, such as rooi els, vines or mealie stalks.
2. Sterilize the griller by placing it on the fire for 10 minutes.
3. Clean, trim and season the meat with salt and pepper according to taste. Pack the meat onto the griller, secure and place it 7 cm above the coals. Splash a little water on the fire to extinguish any flames.
4. If desired, baste the meat with a marinade (recipes 295 to 300) or oil while it grills.
5. Grill meat on both sides, then test with a small, sharp knife to see if it is done to taste (see grilling times below) and remove from the coals. Serve immediately.

Note: If the meat cannot be served at once, place it in a dish, cover loosely with a lid and keep warm, either in the oven at 100 °C (200 °F) or in a warming drawer. Do not cover the dish tightly, as the meat might lose its crisp, brown texture.

Grilling in an oven

1. Clean, trim and season the meat with salt and pepper.
2. Preheat the grilling element. Place the meat on the rack of the roasting pan and place the pan in the oven, approximately 6 to 8 cm below the grilling element. If the meat is very thick, place the pan 2 to 3 cm lower.
3. When done on one side, turn the meat and grill it on the other side. If the meat is lean, baste it with oil or a marinade as it grills.
4. Serve immediately when done to taste (see grilling times below).

Pan grilling

1. Use either a heavy frying-pan, greased with a little fat, or a pan with a non-stick finish. Heat a non-stick pan until your palm feels very hot if you hold your hand 8 cm above it, and a greased pan until the fat begins to sizzle.
2. Season the meat with salt and pepper and place it in the pan. Grill the meat to taste on one side, then turn it to grill on the other side:
   for rare steak: brown on both sides and serve
   for medium steak: grill for 2 to 3 minutes on each side
   for well-done steak: grill for 2 to 3 minutes on each side, then lower the heat and grill for a further 4 to 5 minutes on each side.
3. Serve immediately.

Pan frying

Prime cuts and the tenderest cuts only should be used for pan frying. Tougher cuts should be minced and made into hamburgers or rissoles before frying.

Shallow fat frying

1. Heat a little fat or oil in a heavy frying-pan until it appears hazy. The oil or melted fat should be between 0,5 cm and 1,5 cm deep.
2. Trim, clean and season the meat with salt and pepper. Fry quickly on both sides and, if the meat is to be well-done, lower the heat and continue frying until done to taste (see grilling table p. 118).
3. Drain the fried meat well on absorbent paper or crumpled brown paper, and serve as soon as possible.

Note:

- If there is so much meat that it has to be fried in batches, heat more oil or fat before frying the next batch.
- Remove all the gristle, crumbs and other particles of the previous batch from the frying-pan before heating the oil or fat for the next.

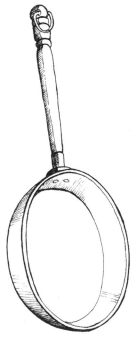

Deep-fat frying

1. Half-fill a deep frying-pan or special deep-frier with oil or melted fat. Heat to 180°C (350°F) for raw meat or 190°C (375°F) for cooked meat. To obtain the best results, use an oil thermometer to check that the temperature is correct – under no circumstances should the hot fat start smoking (smoking point).
2. To prepare the meat for deep-frying, wipe with a damp cloth and dry thoroughly, then season with salt and pepper and either dust with flour or dip in a batter (p. 82).
3. Lower the meat into the oil, frying only one or two pieces at a time, as frying too much at once will cool the oil too rapidly. If using a frying-pan, fry the meat on one side, then turn it with a fork and fry on the other. In a deep-frier, the whole surface of the meat will be done at once.
4. When fried to taste, lift the meat out of the fat or oil, allow the excess to drain off and place the meat on absorbent paper towels to drain completely. Serve at once.

Note:

- For the best results, the hot fat must be kept at a constant temperature.
- It is best to use a vegetable oil or fat because it will neither burn rapidly nor absorb all the odours of the food that is being fried in it.
- If you do not have an oil thermometer, test the temperature of the oil by placing a cube of white bread in it. If it turns brown in 40 to 55 seconds, the temperature will be approximately 175°C to 185°C (347°F to 365°F); if it turns brown in 30 to 40 seconds the temperature will be approximately 185°C to 190°C (365°F to 374°F); and if it turns brown in 20 seconds the temperature is about 195°C to 200°C (383°F to 400°F).
- If you want to re-use the oil, cool it, pour it through a fine sieve or through muslin into a clean container to remove the residue food particles.

4 pieces rump or fillet steak
5 ml (1 teaspoon) salt
2 ml (½ teaspoon) black
pepper

173   Grilled steak

Serves 4;   kJ per portion 1 100;   Prep time 10 min;   Cooking time 5-10 min.

1. Season the steaks on both sides with salt and pepper.
2. Grill as described on p. 118. Serve at once with a sauce or a savoury butter (recipes p. 175) and salad.

---

4 fillet steaks, 2,5 cm thick
4 thick slices white bread, cut
into rounds
50 g butter or margarine
12,5 ml oil
5 ml (1 teaspoon) salt
freshly ground black pepper
Sauce:
50 ml meat stock
50 ml old brown sherry
Garnish:
4 slices liver pâté
4 truffles or grilled black
mushroom caps

174   Tournedos

Serves 4;   kJ per portion 1 200;   Prep time 15 min;   Cooking time 10-15 min.

1. Season steaks with salt and pepper.
2. Heat the butter or margarine and the oil in a large frying-pan and fry the rounds of bread in it until they are crisp and golden brown.
3. Shape the steaks into rounds, securing the circular shape with string so that the fillet retains its shape while cooking. Fry the steaks in the frying-pan until done to taste (see p. 118). Remove the string and place each steak on a round of the fried bread. Arrange on a serving dish and keep warm.
4. Stir the stock and sherry into the residue in the pan and stir to blend well.
5. Pour a little of the sauce over each steak and the rest around them. Serve at once, topped with liver pâté and truffles or mushrooms.

Variations:

1. Top with fried tomatoes and crisply fried onion rings instead of liver pâté and truffles or mushrooms.
2. Use chasseur sauce (p. 185) instead of the brown sherry sauce.
3. Serve on slices of fried aubergine instead of fried bread.

---

1 kg rump steak, 5 cm thick
100 g canned smoked oysters
or clams
lemon juice
50 ml (4 tablespoons) butter or
margarine
5 ml (1 teaspoon) salt
freshly ground black pepper

175   Carpetbag steak

Serves 4;   kJ per portion 1 210;   Prep time 15 min;   Cooking time 10-15 min.

1. Cut a deep pocket into the side of the steak and sprinkle inside with salt and pepper.
2. Sprinkle the smoked oysters or clams with a little lemon juice and stuff them into the opening in the steak. Close the slit with small skewers.
3. Spread one side of the steak with half the butter or margarine and place under the griller for 5 to 6 minutes. Turn the steak over, spread with the remaining butter or margarine and grill for a further 5 to 6 minutes. Slice into 4 or 8 slices and serve immediately.

Variation: Stuff the steak with shredded sharp-flavoured processed cheese mixed with minced ham instead of the smoked oysters or clams.

Note: The steak may be fried in margarine or butter instead of being grilled. Cut the meat into 4 thick steaks. Make a slit in each steak, fill with the oysters or clams and close the slits with skewers. Melt butter or margarine in a frying-pan and fry the steaks to taste (see p. 118).

4 pieces rump or fillet steak
25 ml (2 tablespoons) black
peppercorns
25 ml (2 tablespoons) butter or
margarine
125 ml meat stock
25 ml brandy
5 ml (1 teaspoon) salt
oil for frying
Garnish:
finely chopped parsley

176 Pepper steak

Serves 4; kJ per portion 1 010; Prep time 10-15 min + marinating time; Cooking time 5-10 min.

1. Crush the peppercorns coarsely and with the palm of the hand press some into each side of the steaks. Allow to stand for 1 hour.
2. Pour a thin film of oil into a heavy frying-pan and heat. Now add the steaks and fry until done to taste (see p. 118).
3. Sprinkle the steaks with salt and remove from the pan. Place on a heated serving dish and set aside; keep warm.
4. Warm the brandy in a small saucepan, set it alight and pour brandy into the frying-pan, shaking the pan until the flames die down.
5. Stir in the stock and bring to the boil. Remove the pan from the stove and stir in the butter or margarine, a little at a time, until well blended. Pour over the steaks and serve at once, garnished with chopped parsley.

Variation: If available, use green peppercorns instead of the black.

---

500 g topside beef, thinly sliced
into pieces 10 cm × 8 cm
1 onion, thinly sliced
1 carrot, thinly sliced
62,5 ml (5 tablespoons) lard or
oil
62,5 ml (5 tablespoons) flour
425 ml meat stock
1 bay leaf
5 ml (1 teaspoon) salt
2 ml (½ teaspoon) pepper
Stuffing:
250 ml (1 cup) fresh
breadcrumbs
37,5 ml (3 tablespoons) lard or
margarine
5 ml (1 teaspoon) lemon rind,
grated
2 rashers bacon, finely
chopped
1 egg
milk to mix
5 ml (1 teaspoon) dried thyme
12,5 ml (1 tablespoon) parsley,
finely chopped
5 ml (1 teaspoon) salt
2 ml (½ teaspoon) pepper

177 Beef olives (F)

Serves 4; kJ per portion 1 490; Prep time 20 min; Cooking time 2-2½ hours

1. Combine all the stuffing ingredients thoroughly in a bowl. Set aside.
2. Beat the beef to flatten, spread some of the stuffing on each slice and roll up into sausage shapes, securing them with thick cotton or fine string.
3. In a large frying-pan, heat the lard or oil and brown the onion and beef olives.
4. Add the carrot, salt and pepper and bay leaf.
5. Stir a little stock into the flour, then add the rest of the stock and stir into the mixture in the frying-pan. Cook until the sauce thickens, stirring all the time, then simmer, covered, until the meat is tender (f).
6. Remove the string and serve at once with mashed potatoes and vegetables.

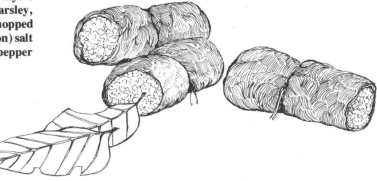

4 thin fillets of veal
125 ml (½ cup) flour mixed
with 5 ml (1 teaspoon) salt and
2 ml (½ teaspoon) pepper
1 egg, lightly beaten
125 g butter or margarine
125 ml (½ cup) breadcrumbs
Garnish:
lemon slices
sliced hard-boiled egg
rolled anchovy fillets

178 Wiener schnitzel

Serves 4;   kJ per portion 1 280;   Prep time 15 min;   Cooking time 8-12 min.

1. Dredge the veal schnitzels in the seasoned flour, dip them in the beaten egg and then in the breadcrumbs, covering completely.
2. In a large frying-pan, melt the butter or margarine and fry the veal quickly on both sides until golden brown and crisp.
3. Lower the heat and fry for a few minutes more, to ensure that the veal is tender. Garnish each schnitzel with a slice of hard-boiled egg topped with a rolled anchovy, and serve with slices of lemon and mashed potato.

---

4 large, thin fillets of veal
125 ml (½ cup) flour
1 egg, lightly beaten
115 g butter or margarine
125 ml (½ cup) dry
breadcrumbs
5 ml (1 teaspoon) salt
2 ml (½ teaspoon) pepper
Filling:
4 slices processed Gruyère
cheese
4 slices lean ham

179   Veal cordon bleu

Serves 4;   kJ per portion 1 310;   Prep time 20 min;   Cooking time 15 min.

1. Place a slice of cheese and ham on each fillet and fold over to make a sandwich. Secure with skewers.
2. Mix together the flour, salt and pepper in a flat dish, then dredge the folded veal in the flour, dip in the egg and coat in breadcrumbs.
3. Melt the butter or margarine in a large frying-pan and fry the veal quickly on either side until golden brown and crisp.
4. Lower the heat and fry for another 5 to 10 minutes, to ensure that the veal is cooked through and the cheese melted. Serve at once.

Variations:

1. Use 125 ml (½cup) shredded salami and 125 ml (½ cup) grated Cheddar cheese instead of the Gruyère cheese and ham.
2. Use 125 ml (½ cup) shredded cooked chicken breasts and 125 ml (½ cup) grated blue cheese instead of the Gruyère cheese and ham.
3. Use 125 ml (½ cup) crisply fried, crumbled bacon instead of the ham.

---

1 lamb of about 15 kg
salt and pepper
Marinade:
500 ml oil
100 ml lemon juice
3 cloves garlic, crushed
10 ml (2 teaspoons) fresh
thyme, finely chopped

180   Whole barbecued lamb

Serves 40-60;   kJ per portion 980;   Prep time 45 min;   Cooking time 5-7 hours

1. Combine the marinade ingredients in a bowl.
2. Split the ribs from below and flatten the lamb carcass.
3. Season well with salt and pepper and pass the spit through carcass lengthwise. Place over hot coals and grill, revolving frequently.
4. Baste lamb constantly with the marinade as it grills.
5. Cut into serving portions when done and serve at once, sprinkled with salt and pepper.

Note:

- Allow 250 to 400 g carcass mass per person.
- Allow 15 minutes grilling time per 500 g.
- Test to see if the meat is done by piercing the flesh with a sharp knife or skewer. The juices should not be pink.
- The coals must be kept hot. Make a fire alongside the grilling lamb as a source of hot coals.

122

181 Crumbed lamb

2 large lamb breasts
1 egg, beaten
1 bay leaf
2 sprigs parsley
1 sprig thyme
250 ml (1 cup) seasoned fine dry breadcrumbs
750 ml (3 cups) boiled rice
salted water
oil for frying
Garnish:
12,5 ml (1 tablespoon) capers
lemon wedges

Serves 4; kJ per portion 1 100; Prep time 20 min; Cooking time 1 hour

1. Place the lamb breasts in a large saucepan of salted water. Add the bay leaf, parsley and thyme and bring to the boil. Simmer, covered, until the meat is just tender, about 45 minutes.
2. Now place the breasts on a board, cover with foil and flatten them with heavy weights. Leave to cool.
3. Remove and discard the bones and cut the meat into 4 cm wide strips.
4. Dip the strips in beaten egg and then in breadcrumbs, using the fingertips to press the crumbs into the meat.
5. Heat the oil in a frying-pan and fry the strips of meat until crisp and brown.
6. Arrange the lamb on a bed of boiled rice and garnish with capers and lemon wedges.

Variation: Serve on a bed of cooked green ribbon noodles instead of rice.

182 Sosaties (F)

1 kg leg of lamb, cut in 2,5 cm cubes
125 g mutton fat, cubed
250 g dried apricots
3 onions, thickly sliced
75 ml (6 tablespoons) smooth apricot jam
25 ml (2 tablespoons) brown sugar
3 cloves garlic
2 bay leaves
25 ml (2 tablespoons) curry powder
25 ml wine vinegar
12,5 ml (1 tablespoon) salt
5 ml (1 teaspoon) pepper
oil for frying

Serves 6-8; kJ per portion 1 080; Prep time 30 min + marinating time; Cooking time 15 min.

1. Heat the oil in a frying-pan and sauté the onion rings for 1 to 2 minutes, taking care to ensure that the rings remain intact, then remove them from the pan and drain well on absorbent paper.
2. Combine the apricot jam, vinegar, sugar, bay leaves, garlic, salt, pepper and curry powder in a bowl and add the onion rings.
3. Place the meat cubes in this mixture (f) and marinate for 24 hours in a cool place, turning 2 or 3 times.
4. Soak the apricots in a little water until plump.
5. Remove the meat from the marinade and thread on the skewers alternately with the mutton fat, apricots and onion.
6. Grill the sosaties, turning several times.
7. Place the marinade in a saucepan and heat to almost boiling. Serve the sosaties and sauce separately, with crumbly mealie pap, baked potatoes or freshly baked bread and butter as accompaniments.

Note: The sosatie meat may be frozen raw in the marinade for 1 month. To prepare after freezing, thaw, remove meat from the marinade and continue with steps 4 to 7.

183 Braised pork chops

6 pork chops, bones removed
2 green onions, finely chopped
12,5 ml oil
85 ml soy sauce
12,5 ml (1 tablespoon) sugar
6 whole peppercorns
Marinade:
37,5 ml soy sauce
25 ml sherry
½ clove garlic, minced
3 slices fresh ginger root, minced

Serves 4; kJ per portion 1 100; Prep time 15 min + marinating time; Cooking time 40 min.

1. Combine the marinade ingredients in a large flat dish and marinate the pork chops in it for 30 minutes.
2. Heat the vegetable oil in a large frying-pan and fry the chops in it, turning once to brown on both sides.
3. Combine the green onions, soy sauce, sugar and whole peppercorns and pour over the chops.
4. Cover the pan and simmer for 30 minutes. Serve at once.

4 lamb chump or loin chops
a little oil
Bercy butter (p. 175)
5 ml (1 teaspoon) salt
2 ml (½ teaspoon) pepper

184 Baked lamb chops

Serves 4; kJ per portion 880; Prep time 10 min; Cooking time 50 min.

1. Snip the fat around the edge of each chop and place chops in a greased baking dish.
2. Brush the chops with oil and sprinkle with salt and pepper.
3. Bake, covered, in the oven at 180°C (350°F) for 40 minutes, turning once.
4. Spread Bercy butter (p. 175) over each of the chops and bake, uncovered, for a further 10 minutes. Serve at once.

Variations:

1. Brown the chops on both sides in oil, then place them in an ovenproof dish. Spread a little tomato sauce over each, sprinkle with salt and pepper and top each with a slice of lemon, a slice of onion, chopped tomato and crumbled dried basil. Bake for 2 minutes, then top with shredded Cheddar or Gruyère cheese and bake until the cheese melts.
2. Prepare chops as above (step 1). Mix together 10 ml Worcester sauce and 120 g crumbled Blaauwkrantz cheese and spread a little on each chop. Pour 125 ml meat stock around the chops and bake, uncovered, for 45 minutes.
3. Top the chops with chutney or sweet and sour sauce (recipe 324) instead of the Bercy butter.

---

6 lamb loin chops
1 large onion, thinly sliced
18 prunes
15 ml (3 teaspoons) cornflour
150 ml dry red wine
200 ml meat stock
4 whole cloves
2,5 cm stick of cinnamon
10 ml (2 teaspoons) salt
5 ml (1 teaspoon) pepper
oil for frying

185 Lamb chops with prunes

Serves 6; kJ per portion 980; Prep time 20 min; Cooking time 45 min.

1. Heat the oil in a large saucepan and sauté the chops on both sides over low heat.
2. Pour the oil off and arrange the onion slices on top of the chops. Sprinkle with the salt and pepper.
3. Add the prunes, wine, stock, cloves and cinnamon and simmer, covered, until the chops are tender, about 40 minutes. Add a little more wine or stock if necessary.
4. Remove the chops and prunes to a heated serving dish and keep them warm.
5. Mix the cornflour with a little water and stir it into the sauce in the saucepan. Bring to the boil, then simmer for 1 to 2 minutes to thicken, stirring all the time.
6. Spoon the sauce over the chops and serve at once.

Variation: Use dried apricots or pear halves instead of the prunes.

---

1 pig, up to 18 kg, head and
feet intact
spicy stuffing such as raisin
and walnut stuffing (recipe
313) or apricot, celery and
walnut stuffing (recipe 314)
salt and pepper
Marinade:
500 ml oil combined with
100 ml lemon juice

186 Barbecued pig

Serves 50-70; kJ per portion 1 100; Prep time 30 min; Cooking time 7-9 hours

1. Make a slit in the belly but do not cut through the ribs.
2. Fill the abdominal cavity loosely with the stuffing and sew up the opening. Tie string around the pig to prevent the cavity from bursting open during grilling.
3. Cover the head and feet with aluminium foil, shiny side innermost, to prevent them from burning.
4. Push a spit through the pig and rest the ends on poles so that the pig is suspended above the hot coals.

5. Rotate the pig constantly while grilling; slowly when the fire is cooler and quickly when the fire is hot.
6. Baste the pig constantly with the marinade as it grills.
7. Test whether the pig is done: cut a small slit in the thick part of the leg. If a pink juice oozes out, the meat is not yet ready. When done, the skin should be crisp and brown, but not burnt.
8. To serve, remove the spit, foil and all the string. Remove the legs and shoulders and slice the meat at the table. Sprinkle with salt and pepper. Serve meat and stuffing together.

Note:
- Coals must be red hot but should not flame. Make a reserve fire for additional hot coals to replenish those over which the pig is grilling.
- Depending on the size of the pig and the heat of the fire, the pig will take 7 to 9 hours to cook.

---

1 kg lean pork, cut in 5 cm cubes
6 skewers
Marinade:
250 ml (1 cup) salted peanuts, crushed or sprinkle nuts
25 ml (2 teaspoons) ground coriander
2 cloves garlic
5 ml (1 teaspoon) crushed red pepper
250 ml (1 cup) onion, thinly sliced
25 ml (2 tablespoons) brown sugar
60 ml lemon juice
60 ml soy sauce
2 ml (½ teaspoon) pepper
115 g butter or margarine, melted
125 ml meat stock (recipe 44)

187 Indonesian pork skewers (Saté)

Serves 4-6; kJ per portion 1 280; Prep time 15 min + marinating time; Cooking time 30 min.

1. Combine all the marinade ingredients except the butter or margarine and stock in an electric blender, to form a fine purée.
2. Transfer the marinade to a saucepan and bring to the boil. Add the melted butter or margarine and stock and remove from the stove. Cool.
3. Place the pork cubes in a shallow dish and pour the cooled marinade over it. Marinate for at least 3 hours, turning every now and then.
4. Thread the pork on skewers and grill slowly over the coals or under the grill until evenly browned, 25 to 30 minutes.
5. Heat left-over marinade to just boiling and pour over the meat immediately before serving.

---

4 pork chops or Kasseler rib chops
450 g canned cherries, pitted
50 ml (4 tablespoons) almonds, slivered
6 whole cloves
lard or butter
12,5 ml vinegar
5 ml (1 teaspoon) salt
2 ml (½ teaspoon) pepper

188 Pork chops with cherries

Serves 4; kJ per portion 1 100; Prep time 15 min; Cooking time 30 min.

1. Brown the pork chops in a little lard or butter in a large frying-pan. Season with salt and pepper.
2. Combine the cherries and their syrup, the almonds, cloves and vinegar in a bowl.
3. Pour this mixture over the pork chops and simmer, covered, for 30 minutes. Serve hot.

Variations:
1. Use 450 g finely chopped preserved ginger and syrup instead of the cherries.
2. Use 450 g canned loganberries and their syrup instead of the cherries.
3. Use 450 g stewed quinces instead of the cherries.
4. Use 450 g canned mandarin oranges and their syrup instead of the cherries and finely chopped walnuts or salted peanuts instead of the almonds.

125

250 g veal sweetbread, cleaned, blanched and cut into 4 pieces
4 large pieces calf's liver
1 aubergine, thickly sliced
8 cauliflower flowerets, boiled in salted water for 2 minutes
2 baby marrows, thickly sliced
5 ml (1 teaspoon) salt
oil for frying
Batter:
120 g plain flour
150 ml tepid water
white of 1 large egg
25 ml olive oil
5 ml (1 teaspoon) salt
Garnish:
1 lemon, quartered
parsley sprigs

189   Mixed sweetbread fry   (Fritto misto)

Serves 4;   kJ per portion 1 300;   Prep time 45 min;   Cooking time 30 min.

1. Sprinkle the aubergine slices with salt and leave to draw for 30 min in a colander, then rinse and pat dry.
2. Meanwhile, make the batter. Sift the flour and salt into a basin, then stir in the water and oil to form a smooth, fairly stiff batter. Beat well and leave in a cold place for 1 hour.
3. Then whisk the egg white until foamy and fold it lightly into the batter.
4. Heat the oil in a large frying-pan to a temperature at which a 2 cm cube of bread dropped in it turns golden in 45 seconds.
5. Sprinkle the sweetbread and liver with salt, dip the pieces in batter and fry in the oil until cooked through and golden brown.
6. Repeat the procedure for the vegetables, cooking them in batches and allowing the oil to regain the correct temperature before cooking the next batch.
7. As the pieces are cooked, drain them on crumpled absorbent paper and keep hot.
8. When the various components have been cooked, arrange them separately on a large heated serving dish. Serve at once, garnished with wedges of lemon and parsley sprigs.

---

340 g lamb's liver, trimmed and cut in 5 cm cubes
6 rashers rindless streaky bacon, halved and rolled up
3 medium onions, quartered or 12 small onions
oil for brushing
5 ml (1 teaspoon) salt
2 ml (½ teaspoon) pepper

190   Liver and bacon kebabs

Serves 4;   kJ per portion 980;   Prep time 15 min;   Cooking time 10 min.

1. Preheat the grill to 180°C (375°F).
2. Thread the liver, bacon and onion alternately onto 4 metal skewers.
3. Place the skewers in the grill pan. Brush them with oil and sprinkle with salt and pepper.
4. Place under the grill for 10 minutes, turning often and basting now and then with the pan juices. Serve at once.

Variations:
1. Use kidneys instead of liver.
2. Add 3 button mushrooms to each skewer.

---

9 lambs' kidneys, skinned, cored and halved
120 g onion, finely chopped
12,5 ml (1 tablespoon) flour
25 ml (2 tablespoons) butter or margarine
150 ml chicken stock
2 ml prepared mustard
5 ml fruit chutney
12,5 ml tomato purée
10 ml (2 teaspoons) salt
5 ml (1 teaspoon) pepper

191   Devilled kidneys   (F)

Serves 4;   kJ per portion 980;   Prep time 20 min;   Cooking time 15 min.

1. Melt the butter or margarine in a large frying-pan and sauté the onion until lightly browned.
2. Toss the kidneys in the flour, season with salt and pepper, add to the pan and fry quickly for 2 to 3 minutes to seal in the juices.
3. Stir in the chopped onion, chicken stock, mustard, tomatoe purée and chutney and bring to the boil slowly, stirring. Simmer, uncovered, for 10 minutes, stirring occasionally (f).
4. Transfer to a hot serving dish and serve at once with boiled rice or noodles.

192 Country grilled venison chops

6 venison chops
50 ml oil
15 ml lemon juice
80 ml medium cream sherry
125 ml (½ cup) quince jelly or
cranberry jelly
1 clove garlic, crushed
2 ml (½ teaspoon) dried thyme
5 ml (1 teaspoon) salt
freshly ground black pepper

Serves 6; kJ per portion 1 200; Prep time 20 min + marinating time; Cooking time 20 min.

1. Combine the garlic, thyme, oil and lemon juice in a bowl and marinate the chops for 2 hours.
2. Now season the chops with salt and pepper and grill over hot coals or under the griller until done, approximately 15 minutes.
3. Sprinkle the chops with sherry just before they are ready and serve immediately with quince or cranberry jelly.

193 Venison steaks in cream

8 young, tender venison steaks
3 medium onions,
finely chopped
200 g mushrooms,
finely chopped
50 ml (4 tablespoons) butter
10 ml lemon juice
5 ml Worcester sauce
100 ml dry red wine
250 ml single cream
250 ml sour cream
25 ml (2 tablespoons) parsley,
finely chopped
10 ml (2 teaspoons) salt
freshly ground black pepper

Serves 8; kJ per portion 1 500; Prep time 15 min; Cooking time 20 min.

1. Melt the butter in the grilling pan and grill the steaks to taste (see p. 118). Remove from pan and keep warm.
2. Add the onions and mushrooms to the pan and sauté until the onion is transparent. Add the wine, lemon juice, Worcester sauce, salt, pepper and meat and simmer for 5 minutes.
3. Stir in single cream, sour cream and parsley. Heat to just below boiling point. Serve immediately.

194 Chicken chasseur (F)

2 kg chicken joints
25 ml (2 tablespoons) finely
chopped fresh parsley, chervil
and tarragon
or 12,5 ml (1 tablespoon) of the
dried herbs
400 g mushrooms,
finely chopped
25 ml tomato paste
25 ml (2 tablespoons) butter or
margarine
25 ml oil
25 ml brandy
150 ml dry white wine
300 ml chicken stock
10 ml (2 teaspoons) salt
2 ml (½ teaspoon) pepper

Serves 6; kJ per portion 1 100; Prep time 15 min; Cooking time 1 hour

1. Heat the butter and oil together in a large, heavy-bottomed frying-pan and brown the chicken pieces lightly on both sides.
2. Spoon the brandy over the chicken and ignite. When the flames die down, add the wine and chicken stock.
3. Season with salt and pepper, then add the chopped herbs and cook over medium heat for 20 minutes.
4. Stir in the tomato paste and mushrooms and reduce the heat to low. Cook a further 15 minutes (f). Serve hot.

Note:
- Left-over cooked chicken may be used. Add all the ingredients, except the brandy. Omit the chicken stock. Pour over the brandy, ignite, and simmer for 15 minutes when the flames die down.
- To serve after freezing, heat gently on top of the stove for approximately 10 minutes.

2 young chickens, halved
or 4 poussins
100 g butter or margarine
2 egg yolks, lightly beaten with
150 ml double cream
25 ml brandy or peach brandy
2 ml (½ teaspoon) dried
rosemary
5 ml (1 teaspoon) salt
5 ml (1 teaspoon) pepper

195   Chicken flambé

Serves 4;   kJ per portion 1 480;   Prep time 20 min;   Cooking time 40 min.

1. Heat half the butter or margarine in a frying-pan and brown the chicken, turning occasionally, until golden.
2. Season with the salt, pepper and rosemary, then turn down the heat and simmer, covered, for 30 minutes.
3. Pour the brandy over the chicken and ignite. When the flames have died down, gradually stir in the beaten egg and cream mixture.
4. Add the remaining butter or margarine, a little at a time, stirring continuously. Add more salt and pepper if necessary and serve immediately.

Note: Do not allow the sauce to boil, as it will curdle.

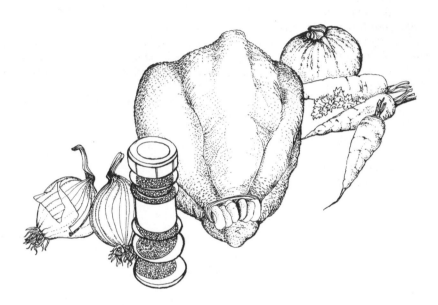

breasts of 2 small, young
chickens, boned and halved
125 g butter, cut in 4 pieces
2 eggs, beaten
200 ml (⁴⁄₅ cup) crisp
breadcrumbs
10 ml (2 teaspoons) salt
2 ml (½ teaspoon) pepper
olive or vegetable oil for frying

196   Chicken Kiev

Serves 4;   kJ per portion 1 380;   Prep time 20 min;   Cooking time 20 min.

1. Season the chicken breasts with salt and pepper.
2. Place a lump of butter on each portion of chicken and roll it up firmly, securing with a toothpick or small skewer.
3. Now coat each portion first in beaten egg and then in breadcrumbs.
4. Heat the oil in a large frying-pan and fry the chicken portions until golden brown. Drain well on absorbent paper. Serve immediately with cooked vegetables or salad.

Saddle of Venison with Apricots (recipe 169) is a delicious combination of slightly tart fruit and oven-roasted meat.

197 Chinese fried chicken with vegetables (Chao chi ting)

4 raw chicken breasts, diced
2 carrots, diced
1 red pepper, seeded and diced
1 green pepper, seeded and diced
4 stalks celery, diced
small can bean sprouts, drained
8 water chestnuts, diced
6 cm slice bamboo shoot, diced
120 g mushrooms, thinly sliced
37,5 ml chicken stock
12,5 ml soy sauce
37,5 ml oil
boiling salted water

Serves 4;   kJ per portion 1 100;   Prep time 25 min;   Cooking time 20 min.

1. In a small saucepan, simmer the carrots in boiling, salted water until just tender.
2. Heat the oil in a frying-pan and toss the cubed chicken in it for a few minutes.
3. Add the red and green peppers and the celery and toss for a few minutes more.
4. Continue frying the chicken and peppers until the chicken is tender, stirring frequently to avoid sticking.
5. Now add the carrots, mushrooms, bean sprouts, water chestnuts, diced bamboo shoot, chicken stock and soy sauce, and stir fry briskly.
6. Serve at once on a bed of boiled rice.

198 Chicken Maryland

4 chicken joints
1 egg, beaten
25 ml (2 tablespoons) flour, seasoned with
5 ml (1 teaspoon) salt and
5 ml (1 teaspoon) pepper
125 ml (½ cup) dry breadcrumbs
62,5 ml (5 tablespoons) butter or margarine
50 ml cooking oil
Sweetcorn fritters:
200 g canned whole corn kernels, drained
1 large egg, beaten
200 ml (⁴/₅ cup) self-raising flour
25 ml milk
5 ml (1 teaspoon) salt
2 ml (½ teaspoon) pepper
Other accompaniments:
2 large bananas, peeled and halved lengthways
6 rashers rindless streaky bacon
2 large tomatoes, thickly sliced

Serves 4;   kJ per portion 1 900;   Prep time 1 hour;   Cooking time 1 hour

1. Dust the chicken joints with the seasoned flour, then dip them first in the beaten egg and then in the breadcrumbs, making sure that the joints are completely coated.
2. Melt the butter or margarine in a large frying-pan over low heat, then add the oil and increase heat.
3. Add the chicken joints and fry until tender and golden brown, about 30 minutes. Set aside and keep warm.
4. Strain the fat used for cooking the chicken and, once clear, return to the frying-pan. Heat once more.
5. In a large bowl mix together all the ingredients for the fritters.
6. Drop teaspoonsful of the fritter mixture into the hot fat in the frying-pan and brown on both sides. Drain on absorbent paper and set aside, keeping warm.
7. Roll up the bacon rashers and fry until quite crisp, then add the banana slices and sauté until cooked through and lightly browned all over.
8. Arrange the chicken joints on a heated serving dish with the sweetcorn fritters, bacon rolls and bananas. Slip a slice of tomato between each fritter and serve immediately.

Always dramatic, this Chicken Flambé is made with cream, brandy and herbs (recipe 195).

Batter:
170 g flour
2 eggs
100 g butter or margarine
425 ml milk
pinch salt
Filling:
62,5 ml (5 tablespoons) raw rice
300 g cooked chicken, finely chopped
2 hard-boiled eggs, finely chopped
680 g spinach, cooked and finely chopped
1 egg
5 ml (1 teaspoon) salt
5 ml (1 teaspoon) pepper
Coating:
2 eggs, beaten with a little water
200 ml ($^4/_5$ cup) crisp breadcrumbs
fat for frying
Garnish:
lemon wedges

199 Chicken rolls (Piroshki)

Serves 6;   kJ per portion 1 800;   Prep time 25 min;   Cooking time 30 min.

1. Combine all the batter ingredients, except the butter or margarine, in a bowl.
2. Heat the butter or margarine in a frying-pan, pour a thin layer of batter in the pan and fry for 2 minutes on either side, then place on a heated plate. Repeat until all the batter has been used.
3. Boil the rice in salted water in a saucepan until tender.
4. Now combine the chicken, hard-boiled eggs, rice, 37,5 ml (3 tablespoons) of the spinach, the salt and pepper in a bowl. Stir in the fresh egg to bind.
5. Place a little of the filling on each pancake and roll it up firmly.
6. Dip each roll in the beaten egg and water, then in the breadcrumbs.
7. Melt the fat in a large frying-pan and fry the rolls, turning occasionally, until crisp and golden all over.
8. Meanwhile, reheat the spinach with a knob of butter in a small saucepan, then spoon onto a heated serving dish.
9. Place the chicken rolls on top and serve at once, garnished with lemon wedges.

Note: Other meat, such as minced lamb, beef or venison, can be used in place of chicken.

---

pancake batter to make 12 paperthin pancakes (recipe 547)
Filling:
360 g cooked chicken, cubed
2 stalks celery, cut into thin strips
3 medium boiled potatoes, diced
37,5 ml (3 tablespoons) canned whole kernel corn, drained
25 ml (2 tablespoons) butter or margarine
150 ml milk
50 ml single cream or top of milk
2 ml (½ teaspoon) salt
2 ml (½ teaspoon) pepper
Garnish:
tomato wedges
black olives

200 Chicken pancakes (F)

Serves 4;   kJ per portion 1 780;   Prep time 25 min;   Cooking time 30 min.

1. Make the batter as directed (recipe 547) and set aside while making the filling.
2. In a small saucepan, simmer the celery in the milk until tender, about 15 minutes.
3. Add the butter or margarine, a little at a time, and blend well.
4. Stir in the chicken, corn and potatoes and simmer, covered, until hot.
5. Season with salt and pepper, then gradually stir in the cream, blending well. Set aside, keeping hot.
6. Make the pancakes as directed (recipe 547).
7. Fill each pancake with some of the filling, roll up and serve at once, garnished with tomato wedges and black olives.

Note:
- Freeze pancakes and filling separately. Cool the pancakes completely, then place one on top of the other with sheets of plastic wrap or butter paper in between them. Wrap and freeze.
- To serve after freezing, remove the plastic wrap and interleaving plastic sheets and heat in the oven at 100 °C (200 °F) or on a plate, covered, over a saucepan of boiling water. Heat the filling and proceed with step 7.

130

350 g cooked turkey, cut into 16 pieces
1 green pepper, seeded and cut into 12 pieces
12 button mushrooms
1 medium onion, quartered
8 rashers rindless streaky bacon, halved
4 bay leaves, halved
12,5 ml cooking oil
25 ml tomato purée
12,5 ml Worcester sauce
2 ml prepared mild mustard
2 ml (½ teaspoon) salt

201   Turkey kebabs

Serves 4;   kJ per portion 1 200;   Prep time 10 min + marinating time;   Cooking time 10 min.

1. Mix the oil, tomato purée, Worcester sauce, bay leaves, mustard and salt in a bowl.
2. Add the meat and leave to marinate for 30 minutes.
3. Boil the peppers and mushrooms in a little water in a small saucepan for 1 minute. Drain well and set aside.
4. Wrap bacon around each piece of marinated turkey meat and thread the turkey, green pepper, mushrooms and onion alternately onto 4 skewers.
5. Place the kebabs on a grilling tray under a pre-heated grill for about 10 minutes, turning once. Serve straight from the oven on a bed of mashed potatoes.

Note:
Turkey kebabs can also be grilled over hot coals.

Moist heat

The following methods apply where meat is cooked by means of moist heat: boiling, braising, stewing, potroasting (method p. 112) and pressure cooking.

PRESSURE COOKING

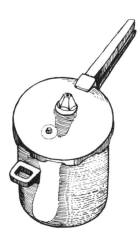

Using a pressure cooker cuts the cooking time to a third or a quarter of that normally required. The vegetables can be cooked with the meat – a further time-saver – and the pressure cooker is therefore particularly useful to the busy housewife. Usually, only the tougher cuts of meat are prepared in a pressure cooker because the quicker cooking has a tenderising effect. Provided that it is not overcooked, meat prepared in this way can be very tasty. The main disadvantage of this method is that the meat shrinks considerably.

1. Clean and trim the meat and season with salt, pepper, flour and the desired spices or herbs. Brown the meat in hot fat.
2. Add all the other ingredients except the vegetables, as these need a far shorter cooking time and should therefore be added towards the end of the cooking period.
3. Add approximately 125 ml water, cover tightly and steam as directed for the specific time required for that cut and mass of meat (consult the instructions provided with the pressure cooker for this information).

BOILING

Only salted or cured meats such as bacon, ham, gammon, brisket, silverside of beef and ox tongue are boiled. They must always be boiled gently, over low heat; *never* briskly as this robs the meat of its flavour.

1. Unless it is only lightly salted, soak the meat in cold water for 3 hours, or overnight, before cooking. Drain.
2. Place the meat in a large saucepan with a lid. Cover the meat with fresh cold water and add peppercorns, bay leaves and mustard powder.
3. Bring the water to the boil, cover the saucepan and reduce the heat to low so that the meat will simmer slowly. If you let it boil too vigorously, the meat will fall apart when you serve it.
4. For all the cuts mentioned above, allowing 30 minutes for every 500 g of meat plus 30 minutes should be ample.

2,25 kg brisket
700 g salt pork
1 marrow bone
10 medium onions
9 leeks, well washed
10 carrots, thickly sliced
8 small turnips, peeled
1 medium cabbage, cut in sixths
4 whole cloves
1 bay leaf
5 ml (1 teaspoon) dried thyme
2 or 3 sprigs parsley
5 ml (1 teaspoon) salt
pinch black pepper
water

202   Pot au feu

Serves 8;   kJ per portion 1 110;   Prep time 30 min;   Cooking time 2½ hours

1. Place the brisket, salt pork, marrow bone, 2 of the onions stuck with the cloves, 3 leeks, 2 carrots and the herbs in a large, heavy saucepan. Add sufficient water to cover the meat by about 5 cm.
2. Bring to the boil and continue boiling rapidly for 5 minutes. Skim the top to remove any scum that forms. Add salt and pepper when clear. Lower the heat and simmer, covered, until the meat is tender, 2 to 2½ hours. Remove all the meat and keep warm.
3. Add the remaining vegetables, except the cabbage, to the saucepan and simmer until just tender. Add the cabbage and simmer for a further 10 minutes.
4. Slice the pork and beef and arrange on a heated serving dish. Surround the meat with the vegetables and garnish with the marrow from the marrow bone. Serve the sauce separately.

1,5 kg ready-salted ox tongue
1 medium onion
6 peppercorns
1 bay leaf
5 ml (1 teaspoon) mustard powder
water

203   Pressed tongue   (F)

Serves 10-12;   kJ per portion 860;   Prep time 10 min + soaking time;   Cooking time 3 hours

1. Place the tongue in a large basin, cover with water and soak for 3 to 4 hours.
2. Transfer the tongue to a large saucepan, add the onion, peppercorns, mustard powder, bay leaf and fresh cold water to cover.
3. Bring slowly to the boil then reduce the heat to low and simmer, covered, for 2½ to 3 hours.
4. Leave the tongue to cool slightly in the liquid, then transfer it carefully to a board. Remove any small bones and gristle that may adhere, then peel off the outer skin.
5. Ease the tongue, tightly curled, into a small round cake tin; it must fit tightly to ensure a good shape.
6. Lay a small plate on top of the tongue, fitting inside the rim of the cake tin, and weight it down with a heavy object. Enough liquid will be pressed out of the meat to surround it and set into a jelly when cold.
7. Leave overnight in a cool place to set (f). Turn out onto a serving dish.

Variation: Serve hot, sliced, with raisin sauce (recipe 333) or mustard sauce (recipe 318).

Note: Follow the same method, up to step 4, for any cooked tongue dish.

1 kg silverside, salted or
unsalted
1 large onion, studded with 4
or 5 cloves
2 carrots, peeled and
quartered
1 medium onion, coarsely
chopped
62,5 ml (5 tablespoons) flour
a little butter
1 bay leaf
5 ml (1 teaspoon) mustard
powder
sprig parsley
water to cover
3 peppercorns and 5 ml
(1 teaspoon) salt for
unsalted meat
Garnish:
1 large apple, sliced and fried
in butter

204 Boiled silverside (F)

*Serves 6;   kJ per portion 980;   Prep time 30 min + soaking time;   Cooking
time 1½-2 hours*

1. If salted, soak the joint in cold water for several hours, then place it in a large
   saucepan, cover with fresh cold water and bring to the boil. Simmer for 1
   hour, then change the water. If unsalted, simply cover the meat with cold
   water and add the salt, peppercorns and mustard powder.
2. Add the onion studded with cloves, carrots, bay leaf and parsley; bring to the
   boil and simmer over medium heat, calculating 35 to 40 minutes for every
   500 g meat.
3. Heat a little butter in a small frying-pan and sauté the chopped onion until
   golden brown.
4. Sprinkle the flour over the onions and simmer, stirring, for 3 minutes.
5. Gradually add 280 ml of the stock from the simmering beef, stirring
   constantly. Simmer for 20 minutes, stirring now and then.
6. When the meat is done (f), slice it thinly, cover with the onion sauce and
   serve immediately, garnished with the slices of fried apple.

Note: Freeze the meat (in one piece) and the sauce separately. To serve after
freezing, wrap the meat in foil and heat in the oven at 160°C (325°F) for
approximately 30 minutes, reheat the sauce, then continue with step 6.

1,5 kg thin mutton rib
12,5 ml (1 tablespoon) brown
sugar
250 g (1 cup) coarse salt
2 ml (½ teaspoon) saltpetre
cold water to cover
lemon juice

205 Salted rib

*Serves 6-8;   kJ per portion 1 000;   Prep time 15 min + soaking & boiling
time;   Cooking time 30 min.*

1. Combine the sugar, salt and saltpetre and rub into the surface of the meat.
   Place the meat in an earthenware bowl and leave in the refrigerator for 2
   days, then hang the meat in a cool dry place until it is dry.
2. Place the ribs in a large saucepan and cover them with cold water.
3. Simmer, covered, for 2 to 2½ hours, then remove the ribs from the water
   and drain in a sieve or colander.
4. Grill the ribs over hot coals until done to taste then sprinkle with lemon juice
   and serve.

STEWING AND BRAISING

These two terms are often interchanged although there is a technical
difference between the two: when braising, the meat is first browned in
fat or oil, which enhances the flavour of the dish; when stewing, the meat
is not browned first. Otherwise the methods are very similar. A casserole
is not a cooking method but the container in which a stew or braise is
cooked in the oven. It is served directly from the dish in which it was
cooked.
1. Cut the meat into uniform cubes or pieces, 3 to 4 cm in size. Season
   with flour, salt and pepper.

2. If braising, brown the meat in a little hot fat or oil in a heavy frying-pan or saucepan.
3. Add sufficient hot water or stock to the saucepan to just cover the meat. Add any other ingredients – spices, seasonings, bouquet garni, green peppers, garlic, vinegar, onions and so on – which require the same cooking time as the meat.
4. Cover the saucepan and simmer over low heat until the meat is tender. Never boil a stew rapidly; slow cooking will make the meat more tender and flavoursome. Add extra hot water or stock if the stew or braise becomes too dry.
5. Vegetables should never be over-cooked, so add them when there is just enough time left of the total cooking period to ensure that they will add the most flavour to the stew but not cook away (see p. 200 to 204 for cooking times of particular vegetables).
6. If desired, the gravy may be thickened by adding, for every 2 litres of liquid, approximately 12,5 ml (1 tablespoon) flour or cornflour; 12,5 ml (1 tablespoon) flour mixed to a paste with 12,5 ml (1 tablespoon) melted butter; or 1 to 2 egg yolks mixed with 125 ml milk or cream.

Note:

- Stewing recipes may also be adapted for casseroles and vice versa. Always allow a little extra liquid when using a casserole recipe for stewing on top of the stove where more liquid is lost by evaporation, and allow less liquid or thicken the gravy a little more if adapting a stew recipe for baking in the oven. Allow more time for cooking a stewing recipe in the oven: e.g. if a dish must be stewed on top of the stove for 2 hours, allow 2¼ to 2½ hours for cooking in the oven at 160 °C (325 °F).
- If dumplings are included, make sure that there is sufficient liquid in which to cook them.

450 g beef, cubed
450 g pork, cubed
800 g canned tomato purée
250 ml (1 cup) onion, finely chopped
3 large cloves garlic, crushed
125 ml (½ cup) pitted ripe olives
25 ml (2 tablespoons) lard or bacon fat
5 ml (1 teaspoon) chilli powder
10 ml (2 teaspoons) dried oreganum
2 ml (½ teaspoon) cumin seeds
10 ml (2 teaspoons) salt

206   Chilli con carne   (F)

Serves 6;   kJ per portion 920;   Prep time 40 min;   Cooking time 1 hour

1. Sauté the garlic and onion in the lard in a large saucepan until the onion is transparent.
2. Add the meat and brown.
3. Add the tomato purée, chilli powder, dried oreganum, cumin seeds and salt but not the olives and simmer until the meat is tender, 45 minutes to 1 hour.
4. Now add the olives and simmer until they are heated through (f). Serve at once.

Variations:

1. Add 250 g to 300 g drained, canned butterbeans when you add the meat.
2. Add 250 g to 300 g cooked soya beans or sugar beans when you add the meat.

134

450 g lean beef, cubed
450 g veal, cubed
280 ml tomato pulp
450 g onions, thinly sliced
450 g potatoes, thickly sliced
62,5 ml (5 tablespoons) butter
or margarine
10 ml (2 teaspoons) paprika
5 ml (1 teaspoon) salt
Garnish:
finely chopped parsley

207   Hungarian goulash   (F)

Serves 4;   kJ per portion 1 210;   Prep time 30 min;   Cooking time 1 ½ hours

1. Melt the butter or margarine in a large saucepan. Add the meat and onions and fry until the onions are pale gold.
2. Add the seasoning and tomato pulp and simmer, covered, for 30 minutes.
3. Add the sliced potatoes and simmer until the meat and potatoes are very tender, 1 to 1½ hours (f).
4. Transfer to a large serving dish and serve at once, garnished with chopped parsley.

Note: Heat frozen goulash very gently to avoid burning the potatoes.

---

680 g sirloin steak, cut in
10 cm strips
2 small white onions, finely
chopped
500 g fresh mushrooms, finely
sliced
62,5 ml (5 tablespoons) butter
or margarine
100 ml double cream
100 ml sour cream
25 ml sherry (optional)
pinch paprika
pinch cayenne pepper
5 ml (1 teaspoon) salt

208   Beef stroganoff   (F)

Serves 4-6;   kJ per portion 1 410;   Prep time 15 min;   Cooking time 15 min.

1. Melt 50 ml (4 tablespoons) of the butter or margarine in a frying-pan and sauté the steak for 5 minutes. Season with the salt, cayenne pepper and paprika.
2. Meanwhile, melt the rest of the butter or margarine in a small saucepan and sauté the onions and mushrooms until just tender. Stir in the sherry, if desired.
3. Add the meat (f), then stir in the cream and sour cream. Simmer until the cream is hot, but do not allow to boil.
4. Add more cayenne pepper if necessary and serve at once.

Variation: Use stewing steak instead of sirloin. Brown the meat in the butter or margarine and stew until tender, about 1½ hours, adding a little water when necessary. Continue with steps 2, 3 and 4.

Note: Freeze before adding the cream and sour cream. To serve after freezing, heat gently and continue as directed in the rest of step 3 and in step 4.

1,5 kg oxtail, cut into joints
1 clove garlic, crushed
1 small onion, thinly sliced
1 carrot, thinly sliced
20 ml (4 teaspoons) flour
12,5 ml (1 tablespoon) butter
or margarine
250 to 500 ml boiling water
1 bay leaf
4 cloves
10 ml (2 teaspoons) salt
5 ml (1 teaspoon) pepper

209   Oxtail stew   (F)

Serves 4-6;   kJ per portion 1 030;   Prep time 30 min;   Cooking time 4 hours

1. Trim the oxtail and wash thoroughly.
2. Place it in a heavy saucepan; add the spices, salt, pepper, garlic and 250 ml water. Simmer for 3 to 4 hours, adding more boiling water if necessary.
3. When 2 hours of the cooking time have elapsed, add the carrot and onion.
4. When the meat is done, remove the cloves and bay leaf and skim off as much fat as possible.
5. To make the gravy, melt the butter or margarine in a frying-pan; stir in the flour and cook over gentle heat until it browns.
6. Add to the meat and stir until the gravy thickens.
7. Cook for another 15 minutes (f) and serve immediately.

680 g stewing veal, cubed and
tossed in flour
1 medium onion, thinly sliced
225 g carrots, thinly sliced
1 small cooking apple, thinly
sliced
60 g prunes, soaked and pitted
37,5 ml (3 tablespoons)
almonds, coarsely chopped
25 ml (2 tablespoons) butter or
margarine
25 ml tomato sauce
300 to 425 ml water
5 ml (1 teaspoon) salt
2 ml (½ teaspoon) pepper

210   Country braise   (F)

Serves 4;   kJ per portion 1 308;   Prep time 20 min;   Cooking time 1 hour 40 min.

1. Melt the butter or margarine in a large frying-pan and sauté the onion, carrots and apple until lightly browned. Remove from the pan and keep warm.
2. Add the veal to the frying-pan, sprinkle with the salt and pepper and fry gently for 5 minutes.
3. Return the vegetables and apple to the pan, add 300 ml water and the tomato sauce and bring to the boil.
4. Reduce the heat and simmer, covered, for 1½ hours, adding more water if necessary.
5. Add the prunes when 1 hour of the cooking time has elapsed (f).
6. Just before serving, stir in the almonds.

Note: To serve stew after freezing, thaw and simmer gently over low heat, then continue with step 6.

1,4 kg shoulder or leg of veal,
cubed
1 large onion, stuck with
2 cloves
1 carrot
24 large brown mushroom caps
18 small white onions
62,5 ml (5 tablespoons) flour
62,5 ml (5 tablespoons) butter
or margarine
5 ml (1 teaspoon) butter or
margarine
2 egg yolks
125 ml single cream
10 ml lemon juice
125 ml dry white wine
boiling water
1 clove garlic
1 ml (¼ teaspoon) dried thyme
10 ml (2 teaspoons) salt

211   French veal stew (Blanquette de veau)

Serves 8;   kJ per portion 1 210;   Prep time 30 min;   Cooking time 2½ hours

1. Place the veal, the onion stuck with cloves, garlic, carrot, thyme and 9 ml (1¾ teaspoons) of the salt in a large saucepan. Add boiling water to cover and simmer, with the lid on, for 1½ hours.
2. Remove the meat, set aside and keep warm. Boil the stock, uncovered, until reduced to 375 ml.
3. Place the mushrooms, white wine and half the lemon juice in a small saucepan and boil until the mushrooms are just tender, about 5 minutes.
4. In another saucepan, poach the small onions in a little boiling water until just tender, about 5 minutes. Drain, reserving the water, then season the onions with the remaining 1 ml (¼ teaspoon) salt and dot with 5 ml (1 teaspoon) butter or margarine. Set aside and keep warm.
5. Add the cooking liquid from the mushrooms and onions to the stock.
6. Melt the rest of the butter or margarine in a small saucepan. Remove from the stove and stir in the flour to make a smooth paste. Add a little of the stock, stirring to blend well.
7. Return the saucepan to the stove and add the rest of the stock gradually, stirring all the time. Simmer over low heat, stirring constantly, until the sauce is thick and smooth.
8. Beat the egg yolks and cream together in a bowl. Pour a little of the hot sauce into the bowl, beat well, then gradually add the egg yolk mixture to the sauce in the saucepan, stirring all the time. Stir in the remaining lemon juice and remove from the stove.
9. Place the meat on a heated serving dish, surround with the onions and mushroom caps and pour over the sauce. Serve at once with boiled rice.

212 Tarragon veal casserole (F)

1 kg stewing veal, cubed
8 large mushrooms, thinly sliced
1 large onion, finely chopped
5 baby marrows, cut into 2 cm thick slices
50 ml (4 tablespoons) butter or margarine
15 ml (3 teaspoons) flour
250 ml dry white wine
125 ml chicken stock
1 bay leaf
2 ml (½ teaspoon) dried tarragon
5 ml (1 teaspoon) salt
2 ml (½ teaspoon) pepper

Serves 6; kJ per portion 910; Prep time 30 min; Cooking time 1 ½ hours

1. Place the veal in a large casserole, together with the onion, mushrooms and baby marrows.
2. Pour over the white wine and chicken stock, and season with salt and pepper.
3. Gently mix in the dried tarragon and the bay leaf.
4. Bake, covered, in the oven at 180 °C (350 °F) for 30 minutes.
5. Stir the casserole, then bake, covered, for a further 45 minutes.
6. Melt the butter or margarine in a small saucepan; remove from the stove and stir in the flour to make a smooth paste.
7. Add to the casserole bit by bit, allowing each spoonful to melt before stirring to blend. Return the casserole to the oven and bake, covered, for a further 15 minutes (f). Serve immediately.

Note: When re-heating the casserole, stir once to blend the sauce.

213 Basic bredie (F)

1 kg fat mutton, cubed
2 large onions, thinly sliced
vegetable and appropriate flavourings (see below)
400 g potatoes, diced
2 chillis or 1 green pepper, seeded and finely chopped
10 ml (2 teaspoons) salt
25 ml oil

Serves 4-6; kJ per portion ± 1 400; Prep time 25 min; Cooking time 1 ½-2 hours

1. Heat the oil in a large saucepan and sauté the onions until transparent.
2. Add the meat and brown quickly to seal in the juices.
3. Add the potatoes, salt and chillis or green pepper, the vegetable of your choice and appropriate flavourings (see below) and simmer, covered, until the meat and potatoes are tender. Add a little water if the bredie becomes too dry (f). Serve with boiled rice.

Tomato bredie: Add 1 kg tomatoes, skinned and coarsely chopped; 5 ml (1 teaspoon) sugar and 2 ml (½ teaspoon) dried thyme.

Pumpkin bredie: Add 2,5 kg diced pumpkin, 2 cm piece green ginger and a few sticks of cinnamon.

Cabbage bredie: Add 1 head cabbage, shredded; 250 ml (1 cup) finely chopped celery and grated nutmeg.

Cauliflower bredie: Add 1 head cauliflower, broken into flowerets; 250 ml (1 cup) finely chopped celery and grated nutmeg.

214 Green bean bredie (F)

500 g neck of mutton, chopped
1 kg green beans, thinly sliced
2 large potatoes, diced
½ large green pepper, seeded and finely chopped
2 large onions, diced
250 ml water
5 ml (1 teaspoon) sugar
5 ml (1 teaspoon) salt
oil for frying

Serves 6; kJ per portion 1 400; Prep time 25 min; Cooking time 2 hours

1. In a large saucepan, heat the oil and sauté the onions and green pepper until the onions are transparent.
2. Add the meat and brown evenly.
3. Add the water and simmer until the meat is almost done, about 1¾ hours. Add the beans, salt and sugar and continue simmering until the beans are just tender, adding more water if necessary.
4. Add the potatoes and simmer until they too are tender (f). Serve with boiled rice and cucumber salad.

Note: To serve bredie after freezing, thaw and heat well but do not boil.

1,5 kg thick rib of mutton, cubed
2 litres waterblommetjies, picked when flowers are open
2 medium onions, finely chopped
1 large sour apple, thinly sliced
450 g potatoes, thinly sliced
250 ml water
250 ml dry white wine
5 ml (1 teaspoon) sugar
12,5 ml (1 tablespoon) salt
2 ml (½ teaspoon) pepper
oil for frying

215 Waterblommetjie bredie (F)

Serves 4-6; kJ per portion 1 210; Prep time 30 min; Cooking time 1½-2 hours.

1. Pick the flowers from the stems and remove the hard parts. Soak the flowers overnight in salted water, drain and wash thoroughly under running water to remove sand.
2. Place the waterblommetjies in a saucepan with fresh cold water to cover and bring to the boil quickly, then drain.
3. Heat the oil in a large saucepan and sauté the onions until golden brown.
4. Season the meat with salt, pepper and sugar and add to the saucepan.
5. Add all the wine, potatoes, apple and water and simmer, covered, until the meat is tender, 1½ to 2 hours. Add more boiling water if needed (f). Serve at once with boiled rice.

Note: Do not allow the bredie to boil when reheating after it has been frozen.

---

1 kg middle neck of mutton, trimmed and cut in pieces
1 large onion, thinly sliced
100 g shallots, thinly sliced
1 kg potatoes, thickly sliced
500 ml boiling water
25 ml tomato sauce
10 ml (2 teaspoons) parsley, finely chopped
10 ml (2 teaspoons) salt
5 ml (1 teaspoon) pepper
Garnish:
finely chopped parsley

216 Irish stew (F)

Serves 4-6; kJ per portion 1 400; Prep time 30 min; Cooking time 2 hours

1. Place a layer of sliced potatoes in the bottom of a large casserole. Cover it with a layer of meat, dust with a little salt and pepper, sprinkle with parsley and over that place a layer of shallots and onions.
2. Continue layering in this way, ending with a layer of potatoes.
3. Stir the tomato sauce into the boiling water and add gradually to the casserole.
4. Cover and bake in the oven at 180°C (350°F) until the contents begin to simmer.
5. Lower the heat to 160°C (325°F) and simmer, covered, for a further 1½ hours (f). Serve at once, sprinkled with finely chopped parsley.

Note: Thaw, then heat, covered, over low heat for approximately 15 minutes.

---

1 shoulder lamb, boned and excess fat removed
100 ml (²/₅ cup) yellow split peas
1 medium onion, finely chopped
2 large Granny Smith apples, peeled, cored and cubed
5 ml (1 teaspoon) ground cinnamon
pinch grated nutmeg
25 ml lemon juice
10 ml (2 teaspoons) salt
5 ml (1 teaspoon) black pepper
oil for frying
water
butter or margarine

217 Lamb and pea stew

Serves 5; kJ per portion 1 210; Prep time 20 min + soaking time; Cooking time 2 hours

1. Soak the peas in water overnight. Drain and boil gently in fresh water to cover in a saucepan for 1 hour. Drain and set the peas aside.
2. Heat the oil in a large saucepan over low heat and brown the lamb.
3. Add the onion, sauté for 3 to 4 minutes, then drain off all the oil.
4. Add the split peas, cinnamon, nutmeg, salt and black pepper and enough water to cover. Simmer, with the lid on, until the meat is tender, about 1½ hours. Add a little more water if necessary.
5. Meanwhile, melt a little butter or margarine in a frying-pan and sauté the apple cubes until lightly coloured.
6. When the meat is tender, add the apple cubes and lemon juice and simmer for another 5 minutes. Serve hot on a bed of boiled rice.

Variation: Use quinces instead of apples.

2 kg stewing mutton, boned and cubed
250 ml (1 cup) ripe tomatoes, skinned, juice squeezed out and coarsely chopped
1 onion, finely chopped
250 ml (1 cup) apples, finely chopped
8 potatoes, diced
37,5 ml (3 tablespoons) sultanas
50 ml fruit chutney
2 cloves garlic, finely chopped
10 ml (2 teaspoons) sugar
20 ml (4 teaspoons) curry powder
10 ml (2 teaspoons) turmeric
10 ml (2 teaspoons) ground coriander
10 ml (2 teaspoons) ground ginger
4 lemon leaves, bruised to release flavour
10 ml (2 teaspoons) salt
5 ml (1 teaspoon) pepper
oil for frying
water

218   Mutton curry   (F)

Serves 8;   kJ per portion 1 010;   Prep time 30 min;   Cooking time 1 ½ hours

1. Heat the oil in a large saucepan and brown the mutton.
2. In a bowl, combine the curry powder, turmeric, coriander, ginger, sugar, salt, pepper, sultanas, apple and chutney.
3. Add this to the saucepan, mixing well, then add the bruised lemon leaves, garlic, onion and tomatoes.
4. Simmer, covered, until the meat is almost tender, about 1¼ hours, adding a little water if the curry becomes too dry.
5. Add the potatoes and cook a further 30 minutes, adding more water if necessary (f).
6. Add more salt and pepper, if necessary, then serve on boiled rice, accompanied by fried bananas rolled in coconut, diced pineapple, and cucumber and onion salad (recipe 399).

Note: Stir the sauce once to blend when heating the frozen curry.

1,25 kg stewing lamb, cubed
2 large onions, thinly sliced
4 canned anchovy fillets, soaked in milk for 30 minutes
15 ml (3 teaspoons) flour
5 ml (1 teaspoon) grated lemon rind
12,5 ml oil
325 ml chicken stock
12,5 ml (1 tablespoon) parsley, finely chopped
2 ml (½ teaspoon) dried fennel
10 ml (2 teaspoons) salt
freshly ground black pepper
White beans
250 g haricot beans, soaked in water for 30 minutes and drained
2 cloves garlic, crushed
1 large tomato, skinned and coarsely chopped
12,5 ml oil
5 ml (1 teaspoon) salt
2 ml (½ teaspoon) pepper
water

219   Tuscan lamb stew   (F)

Serves 5;   kJ per portion 1 710;   Prep time 30 min;   Cooking time 1 ½ hours

1. Place the beans in a saucepan, cover with fresh water and simmer, covered, for 30 minutes.
2. Meanwhile, season the meat with the salt. Heat the oil in a large saucepan and sauté the meat until evenly browned. Remove from saucepan and set aside.
3. Add the onions to the saucepan and sauté until soft and transparent. Sprinkle the flour over the onions and cook for 1 minute.
4. Stir in the stock, scraping the juices from the bottom of the saucepan to mix well.
5. Return the meat to the saucepan and simmer, covered, for 40 minutes.
6. Chop the anchovies and stir them into the meat mixture with the fennel, parsley, lemon rind and black pepper. Continue simmering, covered, until the meat is tender, adding more stock if the stew becomes too dry (f).
7. While the stew is cooking, continue preparing the beans. Add the garlic, tomato, salt and pepper and simmer until tender.
8. Drain the excess liquid from the beans and stir in the cooking oil (f). Serve the stew hot with the beans.

Note: Freeze the lamb and beans separately. To serve after freezing, heat separately over low heat for approximately 10 minutes and serve.

139

220 Marinated lamb chops

8 lamb chops
grated rind and juice of
1 orange
1 onion, thinly sliced
12,5 ml (1 tablespoon) brown
sugar
37,5 ml oil
37,5 ml dry white wine or
sherry
10 ml (2 teaspoons) cornflour
25 ml (2 tablespoons) fresh
mixed herbs
10 ml (2 teaspoons) salt
2 ml (½ teaspoon) pepper
Garnish:
lemon wedges

Serves 8; kJ per portion 990; Prep time 15 min + marinating time; Cooking time 45 min.

1. Combine the grated rind and juice of the orange, the sugar, herbs, onion, salt and pepper, oil and wine or sherry in a small bowl.
2. Place the chops in a flat dish, pour the marinade over them and leave for 12 hours in the refrigerator, turning once.
3. Place the chops on a baking dish, pour the marinade over and bake in the oven at 190°C (375°F) for 40 minutes.
4. Remove the chops from the baking dish, place them on a heated serving platter and keep warm.
5. Stir the cornflour into the pan juices and mix thoroughly to thicken.
6. Pour the sauce over the chops and serve at once, garnished with lemon wedges.

Variations:

1. Marinate in curry marinade (recipe 295) instead of the herb marinade.
2. Instead of the herb marinade, marinate in 125 ml red wine to which 3 sticks of cinnamon and 4 whole cloves have been added.

221 Lancashire hot pot (F)

1 kg middle neck of lamb,
chopped and excess fat
removed
2 lambs' kidneys, skinned,
cored and thinly sliced
800 g potatoes, thickly sliced
340 g onions, thickly sliced
275 ml meat stock
a little butter or margarine
5 ml (1 teaspoon) curry
powder
10 ml (2 teaspoons) salt
5 ml (1 teaspoon) pepper

Serves 5-6; kJ per portion 1 490; Prep time 25 min; Cooking time 2¼ – 2½ hours

1. Place a layer of meat in a 2,5 litre casserole. Lay some of the kidney slices over the lamb and season with a little salt, pepper and curry powder.
2. Arrange a layer of sliced onions and some potatoes on top of the kidneys, then season once more with salt, pepper and curry powder.
3. Continue layering the ingredients until they have all been used, ending with a layer of potato slices.
4. Carefully pour in the stock and dot the surface with butter or margarine.
5. Bake, uncovered, in the centre of the oven at 180°C (350°F) for 2¼ to 2½ hours (f). Serve hot.

Note: To serve after freezing, thaw and reheat, covered, in the oven at 160°C (325°F) for approximately 20 minutes.

222 Lamb casserole with herb dumplings

750 g neck of lamb, cubed
10 small onions
2 apples, cored and
thinly sliced
62,5 ml (5 tablespoons) flour
25 ml oil
150 ml cider or apple juice
300 ml meat stock
5 ml (1 teaspoon) salt
2 ml (½ teaspoon) pepper
fat for frying
herb dumplings (recipe 303)

Serves 6; kJ per portion 1 460; Prep time 1 hour; Cooking time 2 hours

1. Melt the fat in a large casserole on top of the stove and brown the meat quickly to seal in the juices.
2. Heat the oil in a large frying-pan and sauté the onions until transparent, then transfer them to the casserole.
3. Stir the flour into the oil that remains in the frying-pan, a little at a time, and cook for 1 minute, stirring constantly.
4. Gradually add the cider or apple juice and the meat stock, stirring all the time, and simmer until the sauce thickens.
5. Pour the hot sauce over the meat and onions in the casserole, add the salt and pepper and arrange the apple on top.
6. Bake in the oven at 160°C (325°F) for 1¾ to 2 hours.
7. Meanwhile, make the dumplings as directed (recipe 303). Place them in the casserole for the last 30 minutes of the baking time. Serve hot.

140

1 kg lamb rib, trimmed of
excess fat and cubed
2 onions, finely chopped
425 g tomatoes, skinned
30 g desiccated coconut
37,5 ml fruit chutney
25 ml (2 tablespoons) flour
250 ml beef stock
25 ml oil
1 finely crumbled bay leaf
2 ml (½ teaspoon) ground
cinnamon
5 ml (1 teaspoon) ground
coriander
2 ml (½ teaspoon) ground
cumin
2 cloves garlic, crushed
20 ml (4 teaspoons) curry
powder
5 ml (1 teaspoon) turmeric
5 ml (1 teaspoon) sugar
10 ml (2 teaspoons) salt
freshly ground black pepper

223 Lamb curry (F)

Serves 6;   kJ per portion 1 510;   Prep time 30 min;   Cooking time 1 ¾ hours

1. In a large saucepan, fry the onions in the oil until soft.
2. Add the bay leaf, cinnamon, coriander, cumin, garlic, curry powder, flour and turmeric and simmer for a few minutes, stirring with a wooden spoon.
3. Add the meat and a little more oil, if necessary, and brown the meat lightly.
4. Add all the remaining ingredients except the coconut and mix thoroughly.
5. Transfer the curry to a large casserole and bake, covered, in the oven at 150°C (300°F) for 1½ hours.
6. Add the coconut and bake a further 15 minutes (f).
7. Serve at once with boiled rice and various side-dishes.

Note: Thaw frozen curry, then reheat, covered, either over low heat or in the oven at 160°C (325°F) for approximately 25 minutes.

When browning meat cubes, do not allow the pieces to touch each other while they cook, or they will stew – meat needs air around it to seal in the juices. Brown a few cubes at a time.

250 g fat pork, diced
250 g fat pork, thickly sliced
450 g haricot beans
3 large onions, thinly sliced
25 ml (2 tablespoons) bacon fat
12,5 ml (1 tablespoon) black
treacle
25 ml (2 tablespoons) sugar
850 ml boiling water
10 ml (2 teaspoons) salt

224 Boston baked beans

Serves 8;   kJ per portion 1 910;   Prep time 45 min + soaking time;
Cooking time 7 hours

1. Soak the beans overnight in cold water; drain thoroughly and place in a large saucepan. Add sufficient cold water to cover and simmer over low heat until the beans begin to soften, about 2 hours.
2. Drain the beans through a colander and leave to stand for about 10 minutes to make sure that they are dry.
3. Place a layer of diced pork in the bottom of a large, deep casserole.
4. Heat the bacon fat in a frying-pan and toss the onions in it until lightly browned; blend with the beans and place on top of the diced pork in the casserole.
5. In a small bowl, blend the sugar, treacle and salt with the boiling water and pour over the beans.
6. Place the slices of pork on top of the beans and simmer over medium heat, covered, for 5 hours, adding more water if necessary.
7. Remove the top layer of pork before serving; cut it into pieces and add to each helping.

1 kg lean pork, cubed
2 large green peppers, seeded
and cubed
25 ml (2 tablespoons) green
onions, thinly sliced
2 large tomatoes, cut in small
wedges
500 ml (2 cups) pineapple
chunks
100 ml (^{2}/$_5$ cup) cornflour
1 clove garlic, minced
2 ml (½ teaspoon) ground
ginger
125 ml soy sauce
75 ml water
pinch monosodium glutamate
oil for deep-frying
Sweet and sour sauce:
250 ml pineapple juice
125 ml white vinegar
60 ml tomato purée
200 ml (^{4}/$_5$ cup) caramel
brown sugar
12,5 ml Worcester sauce
dash hot pepper sauce
Garnish:
chopped parsley

225 Sweet and sour pork

Serves 6; kJ per portion 1 720; Prep time 30 min + marinating time; Cooking time 15 min.

1. Place the pork in a flat dish.
2. Combine the soy sauce, ginger, monosodium glutamate and garlic in a bowl. Pour the mixture over the pork and marinate for 30 minutes, stirring occasionally.
3. Remove the pork from the marinade, dredge it in 75 ml (6 tablespoons) of the cornflour and fry, a few pieces at a time, in very hot oil until crisp and brown, 8 to 10 minutes. Drain on absorbent paper and keep warm.
4. Combine the ingredients for the sauce in a large frying-pan; bring to the boil and simmer for a few seconds.
5. Add the green peppers and onions to the sauce and boil over high heat for 1 minute.
6. Stir in the tomato, pineapple and the fried pork.
7. Mix the remainder of the cornflour with water in a small bowl and then add to the mixture. Cook, stirring, until the sauce is hot and has thickened, about 1 minute.
8. Turn the mixture onto a heated serving dish and serve at once, garnished with parsley.

Note: Although sweet and sour pork can be frozen, this is not recommended as the pork will lose its crispness.

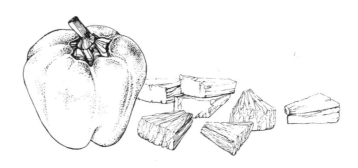

1 kg smoked pork or bacon
450 g canned sauerkraut,
drained
2 raw potatoes, grated
500 ml water
5 ml (1 teaspoon) sugar
pinch salt

226 Eisbein and sauerkraut

Serves 6; kJ per portion 1 310; Prep time 15 min; Cooking time ± 3 hours

1. Wash the meat well, place it in a large saucepan and add the water. Bring quickly to the boil, covered.
2. Lower the heat and simmer the meat for 1½ hours.
3. Add the sauerkraut and simmer another hour.
4. Add the grated potatoes and bring to the boil, then reduce the heat and simmer, covered, for 20 minutes.
5. Stir in the salt and sugar and serve at once.

340 g gammon, cubed
3 small leeks, finely chopped
4 medium carrots, thinly sliced
220 g broad beans
220 g runner beans,
thinly sliced
4 radishes, thinly sliced
3 tomatoes, cubed
½ red pepper, thinly sliced
1 green pepper, seeded and
coarsely chopped
110 g cabbage, shredded
25 ml (2 tablespoons) lard
500 ml meat stock
freshly ground black pepper

227 Garden casserole

Serves 4;   kJ per portion 1 400;   Prep time 20 min;   Cooking time 1 hour

1. Melt the lard in a large frying-pan and sauté the leeks in it for a few minutes.
2. Add the cubed gammon, stock and pepper and simmer for 30 minutes.
3. Add the vegetables and simmer until the meat and vegetables are tender, about 30 minutes. Serve at once.

Note: Leftover cooked ham or gammon can also be used. Simmer the vegetables in the stock for 20 minutes and add the cubed meat 10 minutes before serving.

---

500 g belly pork, diced
500 g stewing mutton or lamb,
diced
1 ham bone
3 frankfurters, thinly sliced
500 g haricot beans
6 small onions
25 ml tomato purée
white breadcrumbs
37,5 ml (3 tablespoons) brown
sugar
12,5 ml (1 tablespoon) black
treacle
62,5 ml (5 tablespoons) lard
1,2 litres meat stock
1 clove garlic, crushed
bouquet garni (parsley, thyme,
bay leaf)
10 ml (2 teaspoons) salt
5 ml (1 teaspoon) pepper

228 Cassoulet (F)

Serves 7-8;   kJ per portion 1 910;   Prep time 45 min + soaking time;   Cooking time 5 hours

1. Soak the beans overnight in cold water. Drain.
2. Place the beans in a saucepan with the ham bone, sugar and treacle; cover with the stock and simmer, covered, for 2 hours.
3. Melt the lard in a frying-pan and lightly brown the pork and lamb or mutton in it, then add the garlic, onions, tomato purée, bouquet garni and the salt and pepper. Simmer for a few minutes. Remove the bouquet garni.
4. Drain the beans and reserve the stock.
5. Place a layer of beans in a deep casserole and add a layer of the meat mixture.
6. Continue making these layers, ending with a layer of beans.
7. Cover the beans with some of the reserved stock and bake, covered, in the centre of the oven at 160°C (325°F) for 3 hours, adding more stock if necessary.
8. When 2 hours of the cooking time have elapsed, add the sliced frankfurters, cover with breadcrumbs and continue baking, uncovered (f). Serve immediately.

Note: To serve after freezing, thaw and heat, covered, in the oven at 160°C (325°F) for approximately 20 minutes.

---

1 large pheasant, cleaned and
trussed
1 large onion, quartered
75 ml (6 tablespoons) butter or
margarine
juice of ½ lemon
250 ml double cream
12,5 ml (1 tablespoon) paprika
10 ml (2 teaspoons) salt
5 ml (1 teaspoon) pepper

229 Pheasant in cream

Serves 4;   kJ per portion 1 200;   Prep time 15 min;   Cooking time 45 min.

1. Melt the butter or margarine in a large casserole, add the pheasant and onion and braise, covered, over medium heat for 30 minutes.
2. Stir in the cream, lemon juice and paprika, season with salt and pepper and simmer over very low heat until the pheasant is tender, about 15 minutes. Serve immediately.

Note: The cooking time will be longer if the pheasant is an older bird.

750 g venison, cubed
8 carrots, thinly sliced
120 g mushrooms, thickly sliced
75 g fat or lard
100 ml ($^2/_5$ cup) flour
12,5 ml Worcester sauce
600 ml stout
2 ml (½ teaspoon) dried mixed herbs
5 ml (1 teaspoon) salt
2 ml (½ teaspoon) pepper

230   Venison stew   (F)

Serves 4;   kJ per portion 1 300;   Prep time 30 min + marinating time; Cooking time 2½ hours

1. Marinate the venison in half the stout for 1 to 2 hours.
2. Melt the fat or lard in a large frying-pan, stir in the flour and simmer for 2 to 3 minutes, stirring all the time.
3. Blend in the rest of the stout, bring to the boil and continue boiling, stirring, until the mixture thickens.
4. Add the meat, marinating liquid, herbs, carrots, Worcester sauce, salt and pepper, and mix well.
5. Pour the mixture into a deep casserole and bake, covered, in the oven at 160 °C (325 °F) for 2 hours.
6. Stir in the mushrooms and bake, covered, for a further 25 minutes (f). Serve hot.

Note:
- This stew can be prepared on top of the stove as well. Follow the recipe up to step 4. Simmer for 1½ hours, then stir in the mushrooms and simmer for a further 20 minutes.
- To serve after freezing, thaw stew and then heat, covered, either in the oven at 160 °C (325 °F) for 30 minutes or on top of the stove for 15 minutes.

---

1 hare or rabbit, skinned and cut into portions, as much blood as possible reserved
3 onions, thinly sliced
2 carrots, thinly sliced
25 ml (2 tablespoons) quince jelly
25 ml (2 tablespoons) apple jelly
62,5 ml (5 tablespoons) butter or margarine
125 ml (½ cup) flour
little lemon juice
1,2 litres water
25 ml port
bouquet garni (parsley, thyme, bay leaf)
10 ml (2 teaspoons) salt
5 ml (1 teaspoon) pepper
Garnish:
tiny meat balls
croûtons (recipe 99)
glacé cherries
parsley sprigs

231   Jugged hare or rabbit   (F)

Serves 6;   kJ per portion 1 400;   Prep time 45 min + marinating time; Cooking time 3½ hours

1. Soak the hare or rabbit joints in cold water for a few minutes, then drain and dry. Place the joints on a flat dish and sprinkle with salt and pepper. Pour over the port and place a few slices of onion on top of the meat. Marinate for 1 hour.
2. Melt the butter or margarine in a large saucepan and fry the remaining onions and the carrots in it for 1 minute, then stir in the flour a little at a time. Blend in the water, then add the hare or rabbit's liver and simmer, covered, for 30 to 40 minutes.
3. Stir in the blood, jellies, marinade and lemon juice then force the mixture through a sieve or whirl in a blender until smooth. Return to the saucepan.
4. Add the hare or rabbit and bouquet garni and simmer over low heat, covered, for 3 hours.
5. Remove the bouquet garni (f) and serve at once garnished with tiny meat balls, croûtons, cherries and parsley sprigs.

Note: To serve rabbit or hare after freezing, thaw completely and then heat gently, covered, for approximately 20 minutes. Continue with step 5.

144

1 rabbit, washed in cold water
to which a little vinegar has
been added, then diced
120 g fat bacon, finely chopped
1 large onion, finely chopped
220 g mixed carrots, leeks and
turnips, diced
62,5 ml (5 tablespoons) flour
150 ml milk
550 ml water
5 ml Worcester sauce
5 ml (1 teaspoon) curry
powder
5 ml (1 teaspoon) salt
2 ml (½ teaspoon) pepper
Garnish:
finely chopped parsley

232 Devilled rabbit (F)

Serves 4;   kJ per portion 1 200;   Prep time 20 min;   Cooking time 1½ hours

1. Sauté the bacon in a large saucepan with the onion, carrots, leeks, turnips, rabbit, curry powder and Worcester sauce for 2 to 3 minutes.
2. Add the water and bring to the boil. Season with the salt and pepper and reduce the heat to low. Simmer, covered, until the rabbit is tender, about 1½ hours.
3. Blend the milk and flour in a small bowl, then stir into the mixture, a little at a time. Bring to the boil, stirring continuously, and cook until the sauce is smooth and thick (f).
4. Add more salt and pepper if necessary and serve at once, garnished with chopped parsley.

Note: To serve rabbit after freezing, thaw and heat, covered, over low heat for approximately 15 minutes.

---

1 large guinea-fowl
170 g bacon or ham, diced
4 smoked sausages
170 g prunes, soaked overnight
and stones removed
1 small cabbage, shredded
1 large onion, finely sliced
25 ml (2 tablespoons) fat or
lard
62,5 ml (5 tablespoons) flour,
seasoned with
5 ml (1 teaspoon) salt and
5 ml (1 teaspoon) pepper
125 ml red wine

233 Guinea-fowl casserole

Serves 4;   kJ per portion 1 300;   Prep time 25 min;   Cooking time 2¼ hours

1. Roll the fowl in the seasoned flour.
2. Melt the fat or lard in a large frying-pan and fry the fowl in it, turning occasionally, until golden brown all over. Remove from the pan.
3. Add the onion and bacon or ham to the frying-pan and sauté for 5 minutes.
4. Mix in the cabbage, and place half the mixture in the bottom of a large casserole.
5. Place the fowl and some of the prunes on top of this layer, then cover with the remaining cabbage mixture, the rest of the prunes and the red wine. Arrange the smoked sausages on top.
6. Bake in the oven at 180°C (350°F), covered, for 2 hours.
7. Carve the fowl, arrange the slices on a heated serving dish and arrange the prunes, cabbage mixture and sausages around it. Serve at once.

Note: The skin of the guinea-fowl is extremely tough and is best removed before cooking.

---

680 g lambs' liver, cut in thick
slices
4 rashers lean rindless bacon,
diced
1 large onion, thinly sliced
450 g tomatoes, skinned and
thickly sliced
680 g cooking apples, peeled,
cored and thinly sliced
300 ml beef stock
1 ml (¼ teaspoon) salt
1 ml (¼ teaspoon) pepper

234 Liver and bacon hotpot (F)

Serves 4;   kJ per portion 1 310;   Prep time 15 min;   Cooking time 1½ hours

1. Line the bottom of a deep casserole with a third of the apple and onion slices.
2. Top with half the liver slices, half the chopped bacon and half the tomato slices. Season with salt and pepper.
3. Repeat these layers once, then top with the remaining onion and apple slices. Carefully pour over the stock.
4. Place the casserole on the centre shelf of the oven and bake at 180°C (350°F), covered, until the liver is tender, about 1½ hours (f). Serve hot.

Note: Do not freeze for longer than 1 month. To serve after freezing, thaw and then heat for approximately 20 minutes in the oven at 160°C (325°F).

500 g tripe, cleaned and trimmed
1 large onion, thinly sliced
60 g mushrooms, thinly sliced
200 g canned or fresh, skinned tomatoes
225 g small potatoes, peeled
25 ml (2 tablespoons) lard or margarine
15 ml (3 teaspoons) cornflour
150 ml each milk and water, mixed together
50 ml dry cider or apple juice
12,5 ml Worcester sauce
1 bay leaf
pinch ground nutmeg
5 ml (1 teaspoon) salt
2 ml (½ teaspoon) pepper

235 Tripe and onions (F)

Serves 4;   kJ per portion 1 510;   Prep time 20 min;   Cooking time 2 hours

1. Place the diluted milk and salt in a saucepan and add the tripe. Bring to the boil, then reduce the heat to low and simmer, covered, for 1 hour. Remove the tripe from the liquid and, when cool enough to handle, cut it into 2 cm wide strips. Discard the liquid.
2. Melt the lard or margarine in a large saucepan and sauté the onion until transparent. Add the mushrooms and sauté until tender.
3. Stir in the tomatoes, potatoes, cider or apple juice, bay leaf, nutmeg, Worcester sauce, pepper and tripe and bring to the boil.
4. Reduce the heat to low and simmer, covered, until the tripe is tender and the potatoes are cooked, about 1 hour.
5. Mix the cornflour with a little water to make a smooth paste. Add a little of the hot liquid from the tripe, stirring all the time, ensuring that there are no lumps.
6. Stir this into the mixture in the saucepan and bring to the boil, stirring gently until thickened (f).
7. Transfer the stew to a heated serving dish and serve at once.

Note: To serve after freezing, thaw and then heat over high heat for approximately 15 minutes.

---

4 medium lamb's hearts, washed, cored and cut into strips
120 g bacon, diced
25 ml (2 tablespoons) flour
100 g butter or margarine
1 ml (¼ teaspoon) mustard powder
5 ml (1 teaspoon) salt
5 ml (1 teaspoon) pepper
Sauce:
3 stalks celery, diced
3 onions, thinly sliced
2 potatoes, diced
3 skinned tomatoes, diced
300 ml stock
2 bay leaves
sprig parsley

236 Braised heart (F)

Serves 4;   kJ per portion 1 010;   Prep time 20 min;   Cooking time 1 ½ hours

1. In a flat dish, combine the flour, salt, pepper and mustard. Coat the strips of heart in this mixture.
2. In a large frying-pan, melt half the butter or margarine and fry the strips of heart for a few minutes, then remove them from the pan.
3. Add the diced bacon to the frying-pan and sauté until the fat starts to run, then remove.
4. Melt the remaining butter or margarine in the frying-pan, then add the onions, celery and potatoes and sauté until the onions are transparent.
5. Add the bay leaves, parsley and tomatoes to the frying-pan and gradually add the stock, stirring all the time.
6. Place the fried strips of heart and bacon on top of the vegetables and simmer, covered, for 1½ hours.
7. Remove the strips of heart and bacon (f), place them on a heated serving dish and keep warm.
8. Purée the vegetables and stock by forcing through a sieve or blending in a blender (f), then reheat.
9. Spoon the vegetable purée around the heart and bacon and serve at once.

Note: Freeze the meat and puréed vegetables separately. To serve, thaw, heat separately and continue with step 9.

146

12 sheep's trotters
4 cloves
12 whole allspice
12 peppercorns
12,5 ml (1 tablespoon) coriander
4 bay leaves
250 ml vinegar
110 g lime dissolved in 9 litres boiling water
cold water
10 ml (2 teaspoons) salt

237   Brawn   (F)

Serves 8;   kJ per portion 890;   Prep time 20 min + soaking time;   Cooking time 2½-3 hours

1. Dip the trotters in the boiling lime water and scrape them clean. Chop along the cleft of the trotters up to the first joint, removing the glands and the hard skin over the toe. Soak in a basin of salted water for 1 hour.
2. Chop up the trotters and cover with cold water in a heavy saucepan; then simmer over low heat until the meat is tender. Remove all the bones.
3. Tie all the spices in a muslin bag and add to the meat.
4. Add the vinegar and salt and simmer, covered, for 1 hour.
5. Pour into a large dish, or small dishes, cool and then chill until set (f).

Variations:

1. Add small pieces of cooked meat such as chicken, tongue, etc.
2. Curry the brawn by adding 12,5 ml (1 tablespoon) curry powder, 12,5 ml (1 tablespoon) sugar and the grated rind of 1 lemon to the vinegar before adding it to the brawn.

Note: To freeze, wrap well or freeze in plastic containers. Thaw in the refrigerator before serving.

500 g kidneys, skinned, cored and coarsely chopped
120 g mushrooms, thinly sliced
37,5 ml (3 tablespoons) sultanas
37,5 ml (3 tablespoons) almonds, finely chopped
340 g raw long-grained rice
12,5 ml (1 tablespoon) plum or quince jam
12,5 ml (1 tablespoon) cornflour
25 ml (2 tablespoons) butter or margarine
10 ml double cream
425 ml chicken stock
12,5 ml vinegar
5 ml (1 teaspoon) salt
2 ml (½ teaspoon) pepper
Garnish:
tomato quarters
mushroom slices
chopped parsley

238   Kidneys shiraz   (Γ)

Serves 6;   kJ per portion 1 510;   Prep time 20 min;   Cooking time 45 min.

1. Melt the butter or margarine in a large saucepan, add the kidneys, stock and vinegar and simmer, covered, for 30 minutes.
2. Meanwhile, boil the rice in salted water in a small saucepan until tender.
3. Add the plum or quince jam, chopped almonds, sultanas, mushrooms, salt and pepper to the kidney mixture.
4. In a small bowl, mix the cornflour to a smooth paste with a little water, then blend it into the kidney mixture, a little at a time. Simmer, covered, for 15 minutes (f).
5. Stir the cream into the kidney mixture.
6. Drain the rice and pack firmly into a wet ring mould. Turn out the rice onto a heated serving dish.
7. Fill the centre of the rice ring with the kidney mixture. Garnish with the tomato, mushroom slices and parsley and serve.

Note:

- Rinse the ring mould out with warm water to prevent the rice sticking when turning out.
- Freeze the kidneys and rice separately. To serve after freezing, thaw, then heat the kidneys in a saucepan and stir in the cream. Continue with steps 6 and 7.

147

239 Chicken in honey-lemon sauce

4 chicken joints
60 g butter or margarine
37,5 ml (3 tablespoons)
parsley, finely chopped
50 ml (4 tablespoons) clear
honey
juice of 1 lemon
2 sprigs lemon thyme, finely
chopped
5 ml (1 teaspoon) salt
freshly ground black pepper
Garnish:
lemon slices
parsley sprigs

Serves 4;   kJ per portion 1 200;   Prep time 45 min;   Cooking time 30 min.

1. Melt the butter or margarine in a large frying-pan over low heat and sauté the chicken, turning occasionally, until lightly browned all over, about 20 minutes.
2. Add the lemon, thyme, parsley, honey, lemon juice, salt and pepper.
3. Turn up the heat to medium and cook for a further 2 minutes, basting the chicken occasionally with the sauce.
4. Remove the chicken and place on a heated serving dish; keep warm.
5. Increase the heat and simmer, uncovered, until the sauce is reduced by a quarter.
6. Pour the sauce over the chicken joints and serve at once, garnished with lemon slices and parsley.

240 Chicken Provençale   (F)

1,5 kg chicken, jointed
4 large tomatoes, skinned and
coarsely chopped
50 g pitted black olives
37,5 ml olive oil
150 ml dry white wine
1 clove garlic
2 ml (½ teaspoon) dried basil
5 ml (1 teaspoon) salt
5 ml (1 teaspoon) pepper

Serves 6;   kJ per portion 1 280   Prep time 25 min;   Cooking time 30 min.

1. Heat the oil in a deep frying-pan and sauté the chicken portions in it, turning occasionally, until they are golden brown all over.
2. Add the white wine, garlic, tomatoes, black olives, basil, salt and pepper and simmer, uncovered, until the chicken is tender, 20 to 25 minutes (f). Serve at once.

Note: Thaw and then heat, covered, over low heat for approximately 15 minutes.

241 Chicken with asparagus   (F)

4 chicken breasts, skinned and
boned
1 large onion, quartered
1 small carrot, quartered
37,5 ml (3 tablespoons) butter
or margarine
62,5 ml (5 tablespoons) flour
300 g canned asparagus spears
or cooked fresh asparagus
water to cover
12,5 ml dry vermouth
bouquet garni (thyme, parsley
and bay leaf)
5 ml (1 teaspoon) salt
2 ml (½ teaspoon) pepper
Garnish:
sliced stuffed green olives
lemon slices twisted into
butterfly shapes

Serves 4;   kJ per portion 1 100;   Prep time 45 min;   Cooking time 40 min.

1. In a shallow saucepan place the chicken breasts, carrot, onion, bouquet garni, salt, pepper and enough water to cover.
2. Bring to simmering point over low heat and continue simmering, covered, until the chicken is tender, about 30 minutes.
3. Place the chicken on a heated serving dish and keep warm. Reserve 300 ml of the chicken stock.
4. Melt the butter or margarine in a small saucepan, remove from the stove and stir in the flour, blending well. Return to the stove and cook for 1 minute, stirring continuously.
5. Stir in the vermouth, then gradually add the reserved chicken stock. Bring to the boil and boil for 3 minutes, stirring continuously. Add more salt and pepper if necessary and pour the sauce over the chicken breasts (f).
6. In a small saucepan, heat the asparagus spears in their canning liquid until the liquid bubbles, then drain and arrange the spears around the chicken. Serve at once, garnished with the sliced olives and lemon butterflies.

Note: If using fresh asparagus, cook them just before serving.

1,5 kg chicken pieces
1 medium onion, finely
chopped
60 g mushrooms, thinly sliced
230 g tomato purée
1 clove garlic, minced
60 ml oil
125 ml dry red wine
5 ml (1 teaspoon) crushed
dried oreganum
2 ml (½ teaspoon) crushed
dried thyme
5 ml (1 teaspoon) salt
2 ml (½ teaspoon) pepper

242 Chicken cacciatora (F)

Serves 4;   kJ per portion 1 210;   Prep time 15 min;   Cooking time 2 hours

1. Heat the oil in a large frying-pan and brown the chicken evenly in it.
2. Drain and place in a large, heavy-bottomed saucepan.
3. Add the onion, mushrooms, tomato purée, garlic, oreganum, thyme, salt, pepper and wine and simmer, covered, over very low heat until the chicken is cooked, about 1¼ hours (f). Serve at once on a bed of cooked spaghetti or rice.

Note:

- Chicken cacciatora can also be baked, covered, in the oven at 180°C (350°F) for 1½ hours.
- To serve after freezing, thaw completely and heat in the oven at 180°C (350°F) for approximately 20 minutes.

Make meatballs that are even in size by using an ice-cream scoop.

---

6 chicken thighs
12,5 ml (1 tablespoon) onion,
grated
100 g canned mandarin
oranges (naartjies), drained
250 ml (1 cup) green or black
grapes, seeded
62,5 ml (5 tablespoons) flour,
seasoned with 2 ml
(½ teaspoon) paprika and
2 ml (½ teaspoon) salt
12,5 ml (1 tablespoon)
cornflour
25 ml (2 tablespoons) butter or
margarine
1 chicken stock cube, crumbled
and dissolved in 425 ml hot
water
1 bay leaf
25 ml lemon juice
Herb Rice:
375 ml (1½ cups) hot, cooked
rice
12,5 ml (1 tablespoon) butter
or margarine
12,5 ml (1 tablespoon) parsley,
finely chopped
2 ml (½ teaspoon) dried
rosemary
2 ml (½ teaspoon) dried basil
1 ml (¼ teaspoon) salt

243 Chicken with mandarin oranges and grapes

Serves 6;   kJ per portion 1 400;   Prep time 30 min;   Cooking time 40 min.

1. Combine the cooked rice with the butter or margarine, parsley, rosemary, basil and salt in a large bowl. Toss lightly to mix thoroughly, then set aside; keep warm.
2. Dip the chicken into the seasoned flour, coating well.
3. Melt the 25 ml (2 tablespoons) butter or margarine in a large frying-pan and brown the chicken thighs over low heat for 20 minutes.
4. Stir in the chicken stock, onion, lemon juice and bay leaf; bring to the boil.
5. Pile the rice on a heated deep serving dish, place the chicken pieces on top and set aside; keep it warm.
6. Mix the cornflour with a little cold water, and stir into the liquid in the frying-pan.
7. Bring to the boil, stirring constantly, and cook until the sauce is thick, about 3 minutes.
8. Stir in the mandarin orange sections and the grapes, reserving a few of each for garnish.
9. Heat the sauce until it bubbles and spoon over the chicken.
10. Serve at once, garnished with the reserved mandarin segments and grapes.

2 chickens, approximately
1,5 kg each, cut into portions
8 hard-boiled eggs, thinly
sliced
12 medium onions, finely
chopped
12 medium potatoes, cubed
600 g raw rice
250 ml (1 cup) red lentils
12,5 ml (1 tablespoon) chillis,
finely chopped
3 tomatoes, skinned and
coarsely chopped
125 ml lemon juice
375 ml oil
salted boiling water
12,5 ml (1 tablespoon) ground
coriander
5 ml (1 teaspoon) saffron
2 sticks cinnamon
4 bay leaves
10 cardamom seeds
5 ml (1 teaspoon) cumin seeds
12,5 ml (1 tablespoon)
turmeric
8 cloves garlic
2 pieces fresh root ginger,
crushed
10 ml (2 teaspoons) salt
black peppercorns

244 Breyani (F)

Serves 10; kJ per portion 1 810; Prep time 45 min; Cooking time 2½ hours

1. Heat the oil in a frying-pan and brown the onion. Remove the onion and set aside.
2. Add the potatoes to the frying-pan and sauté until lightly browned. Remove the potatoes, drain on absorbent paper and set aside.
3. Boil the rice in salted, boiling water in a saucepan. Cook until the rice is almost tender but still firm. Add more salt if necessary.
4. In another saucepan, boil the lentils for a few minutes in 500 ml salted water, then drain thoroughly.
5. Combine the rice, a quarter of the fried onion and the lentils in a bowl.
6. Rub salt into the chicken pieces and place them in a large mixing bowl.
7. Combine the herbs, spices, lemon juice, tomatoes, chillis, salt, peppercorns, the rest of the fried onion, the garlic, and the ginger in a bowl. Pour over the chicken and leave for 15 minutes.
8. Invert a heavy dinnerplate in a large saucepan so that it covers the bottom completely. Arrange the ingredients on top of the plate in the following order:
   half the browned potatoes, sprinkled with 5 ml oil
   chicken pieces and sauce
   hard-boiled eggs
   rice and lentil mixture
   the rest of the oil sprinkled over the contents of the saucepan.
9. Cover with a tight-fitting lid and simmer for 1½ to 2 hours (f).
10. Serve at once on a large serving dish with apple salad, banana slices dipped in lemon juice, tomato wedges, desiccated coconut and chutney.

Note:
- To retain all the flavour, do not open the saucepan during cooking.
- To serve frozen Breyani, thaw and then heat, covered, in the oven at 160 °C (325 °F) for approximately 30 minutes.

1,5 kg chicken, cut in pieces
2 medium onions, finely
chopped
125 ml (½ cup) raisins
125 ml (½ cup) desiccated
coconut
12,5 ml (1 tablespoon)
cornflour
25 ml oil
25 ml (2 tablespoons) butter,
melted
500 ml chicken stock
125 ml single cream
12,5 ml brandy
25 ml (2 tablespoons) curry
powder
10 ml (2 teaspoons) turmeric
10 ml (2 teaspoons) ground
coriander
pinch cinnamon
pinch sugar
10 ml (2 teaspoons) salt

245 Chicken curry (F)

Serves 6; kJ per portion 1 250; Prep time 20 min; Cooking time 1¼ hours

1. Fry the chicken pieces and onions in the oil and butter in a large saucepan until golden brown.
2. Combine the stock, salt, curry powder, turmeric, coriander, raisins, coconut, sugar and cinnamon in a bowl.
3. Transfer the chicken, onion and pan juices to a large casserole and then pour the curry mixture over.
4. Bake, covered, in the oven at 160 °C (325 °F) until tender, about 1 hour.
5. Mix together the cream, cornflour and brandy in a small saucepan and simmer over medium heat, stirring all the time until thickened.
6. Pour the sauce over the chicken (f) and serve with boiled rice.

Note:
- Leftover cooked chicken can also be used. Fry the chicken and onion in the oil and butter until the onion is transparent, then continue with step 2.
- To serve curry that has been frozen, thaw and then heat in the oven at 180 °C (350 °F), covered, for approximately 20 minutes.

4 chicken joints, cooked, skinned and coarsely chopped
120 g mushrooms, thinly sliced
1 green pepper, seeded and thinly sliced
62,5 ml (5 tablespoons) butter or margarine
12,5 ml (1 tablespoon) flour
2 egg yolks
275 ml chicken stock
150 ml milk
150 ml single cream
5 ml (1 teaspoon) salt
freshly ground black pepper

246   Chicken à la king   (F)

Serves 4;   kJ per portion 1 380;   Prep time 25 min;   Cooking time 20 min.

1. Melt the butter or margarine in a large frying-pan and sauté the green pepper in it until soft, about 5 minutes.
2. Add the mushrooms and sauté until tender.
3. Remove the frying-pan from the stove, blend in the flour and then gradually stir in first the chicken stock and then the milk.
4. Return the frying-pan to the stove and bring the mixture to the boil, stirring continuously until thickened.
5. Add salt and pepper and the pieces of chicken and heat through, about 10 minutes (f).
6. Beat the cream and egg yolks lightly in a bowl, stir some of the hot sauce into it, then stir the mixture into the sauce and heat, but do not boil. Serve immediately with boiled rice.

Note: Freeze before adding the cream and egg yolks. To serve, thaw, heat and continue with step 6.

1,75 to 2 kg duck, cleaned and trussed
juice of ½ grapefruit
½ grapefruit, peeled and segmented
75 ml (6 tablespoons) butter or margarine
275 ml chicken stock
20 ml brandy
150 ml sherry, heated
5 ml (1 teaspoon) salt
5 ml (1 teaspoon) pepper

247   Duck with grapefruit

Serves 6;   kJ per portion 1 310;   Prep time 30 min;   Cooking time 1 ½ hours

1. Melt the butter or margarine in a large, deep saucepan and sauté the duck, turning occasionally, until well browned.
2. Pour the brandy over the duck and ignite. When the flame dies, add the stock, heated sherry and grapefruit juice. Season with salt and pepper.
3. Simmer, covered, until the duck is tender, 45 minutes to 1 hour.
4. Add the grapefruit segments to the sauce 5 minutes before the duck is ready to serve. Serve hot.

Note: If preferred, thicken the sauce with 12,5 ml (1 tablespoon) cornflour made into a paste with a little water and gradually stirred into the sauce.

1,75 to 2 kg duck, cleaned and trussed
1 kg apples, peeled and cored
37,5 ml (3 tablespoons) seedless raisins
75 ml (6 tablespoons) butter or margarine
300 ml white muscadel
20 ml calvados (optional)
5 ml (1 teaspoon) salt
5 ml (1 teaspoon) pepper

248   Braised duck with apples

Serves 6;   kJ per portion 1 210;   Prep time 30 min;   Cooking time 1 ½ hours

1. Soak the raisins in cold water for 30 minutes.
2. Melt half the butter or margarine in a deep casserole and sauté the duck in it over low heat, turning occasionally until evenly browned, about 15 minutes.
3. Add the muscadel, raisins and salt and pepper.
4. Braise in the oven at 200 °C (400 °F) until tender, about 45 minutes, basting every now and then.
5. Remove the excess fat from the sauce, add more salt and pepper if necessary and add the calvados, if desired.
6. Meanwhile, cut all but two of the apples into slices and sauté them in the rest of the butter or margarine in a frying-pan until lightly browned.
7. Wrap the other two apples in foil and bake in the oven with the duck.
8. Place the duck on a serving dish, decorate with the apple slices and place a baked apple at each end. Strain the sauce through a fine sieve and pour it over the duck. Serve at once.

151

6 chicken joints
8 small onions
3 stalks celery, finely chopped
1 lemon, thinly sliced
180 g carrots, thinly sliced
120 g green peas
125 ml (½ cup) flour, seasoned
with 5 ml (1 teaspoon) salt and
5 ml (1 teaspoon) pepper
62,5 ml (5 tablespoons) butter
or margarine
1 bay leaf
150 ml sour cream
500 ml water
Garnish:
finely chopped parsley

249 Country chicken casserole (F)

Serves 6;   kJ per portion 1 210;   Prep time 30 min;   Cooking time 45 min.

1. Coat the chicken pieces in the seasoned flour. Reserve the excess flour.
2. Melt the butter or margarine in a large frying-pan and fry the chicken until golden brown, then place in a large, deep casserole.
3. Add the onions and celery to the frying-pan and sauté until the onions are transparent. Add to the chicken pieces in the casserole.
4. Stir the remaining flour into the butter or margarine in the frying-pan, then gradually stir in the water. Bring to the boil and continue boiling until thickened, stirring constantly.
5. Pour the sauce over the chicken, then add the lemon and bay leaf.
6. Bake in the oven at 180 °C (350 °F), covered, until the chicken is tender, about 1 hour.
7. Meanwhile, boil the carrots and peas in salted water in a saucepan. Drain and add to the casserole.
8. Remove the lemon slices and bay leaf from the casserole (f) and stir in the sour cream. Serve garnished with chopped parsley.

Variation: Add herb dumplings (recipe 303) to the casserole 30 minutes before serving.

Note: To serve casserole that has been frozen thaw overnight in the refrigerator, then heat in the oven at 180 °C (350 °F) for approximately 20 minutes. Continue with step 8.

2 kg duck
4 medium onions, finely
chopped
250 g raw rice
50 ml (4 tablespoons) rindless
streaky bacon, finely chopped
12,5 ml (1 tablespoon) butter
or margarine
125 ml oil
1 litre boiling water
5 ml (1 teaspoon) salt
freshly ground black pepper

250 Portuguese baked duck (F)

Serves 4;   kJ per portion 1 200;   Prep time 20 min;   Cooking time 1½ hours

1. Heat the oil and butter or margarine in a deep, heavy saucepan and sauté the onions and bacon in it until the onions are transparent.
2. Add the duck and sauté, turning it so that it browns all over. Sprinkle with the salt and pepper and simmer over low heat, tightly covered, until the duck is tender, about 1 hour.
3. Remove the duck, cut it into portions (f) and keep them warm.
4. Add the rice to the saucepan together with the water and simmer for 10 minutes. Transfer the mixture to a baking dish (f).
5. Arrange the pieces of duck on top and bake in the oven at 180 °C (350 °F) until the rice is tender and the duck well-browned, approximately 10 minutes. Serve hot.

Note: Freeze the meat and rice separately. To serve after freezing, thaw and continue with steps 5 and 6, but bake for 20 minutes instead of 10 minutes.

500 g topside mince
1 medium onion, finely
chopped
1 green pepper, blanched,
seeded and finely chopped
250 ml (1 cup) tomatoes, finely
chopped
250 ml (1 cup) dry
breadcrumbs
1 egg and an equal quantity of
water
5 ml prepared mustard or
Worcester sauce
10 ml (2 teaspoons) salt
2 ml (½ teaspoon) pepper

251 Meat loaf (F)

Serves 4-6; kJ per portion 1 010; Prep time 15 min; Cooking time 50 min.

1. Mix the mince, onion, green pepper and tomato in a large bowl. Add the remaining ingredients and stir well.
2. Place the mixture in a greased loaf tin and bake at 180 °C (350 °F) for 45 to 50 minutes.
3. When cooked, loosen the loaf from the sides of the tin and turn out to cool (f). Serve hot or cold.

Note: Freeze wrapped in foil. To serve hot after freezing, thaw and heat, still wrapped, in the oven at 160 °C (325 °F) for approximately 25 minutes. To serve cold, thaw in the refrigerator.

Loaf:
500 g minced beef
1 medium onion, finely
chopped
2 large eggs
500 ml (2 cups) fresh white
breadcrumbs
12,5 ml (1 tablespoon) parsley,
finely chopped
5 ml (1 teaspoon) salt
2 ml (½ teaspoon) pepper
Stuffing:
2 rashers rindless streaky
bacon, diced
30 g Cheddar cheese, grated
1 hard-boiled egg, finely
chopped

252 Stuffed meat loaf

Serves 4-6; kJ per portion 1 200; Prep time 20 min; Cooking time 1 ¾ hours

1. In a large bowl, mix the minced beef with all the other loaf ingredients. Turn half of the mixture into a greased loaf tin.
2. Mix the stuffing ingredients in another bowl, then spread the mixture evenly on top of the mince in the tin
3. Spoon the remaining mince over the stuffing.
4. Cover the loaf tin with foil and bake on the centre shelf of the oven at 180 °C (350 °F) for 1 ¾ hours.
5. When cooked, loosen the loaf from the sides of the tin and turn out to cool. Serve cold with salads.

350 g cooked topside mince
1 medium onion, finely
chopped
2 tomatoes, skinned and
coarsely chopped
500 g mashed potato
25 ml (2 tablespoons) lard
25 ml (2 tablespoons) butter or
margarine
5 ml (1 teaspoon) dried mixed
herbs
150 ml meat stock
5 ml (1 teaspoon) salt
2 ml (½ teaspoon) pepper

253 Shepherd's pie (F)

Serves 4; kJ per portion 1 300; Prep time 45 min; Cooking time 30 – 45 min.

1. Heat the lard in a large frying-pan and sauté the onion in it until lightly browned, 3 to 4 minutes.
2. Add the tomatoes and mince and heat through, about 3 minutes.
3. Add the herbs, salt, pepper and stock, stirring well (f).
4. Place the meat mixture in a deep casserole and cover with the mashed potato. Dot small pieces of butter or margarine on top of the mashed potato.
5. Bake in the centre of the oven at 180 °C (350 °F) until the top is crisp and brown. Serve.

Note: Freeze the meat only. To serve, thaw meat and continue with steps 4 and 5.

153

254 Basic boiled meatballs with variations (F)

1,5 kg beef, minced
1 medium onion, finely chopped
1 thick slice bread, soaked in 125 ml water
1 litre beef stock
1 egg, beaten
flour
12,5 ml (1 tablespoon) parsley, finely chopped
2 ml (½ teaspoon) grated nutmeg
10 ml (2 teaspoons) salt
pinch pepper

Serves 4;   kJ per portion 1 010;   Prep time 45 min;   Cooking time 30 min.

1. Squeeze the water out of the bread. Combine the bread, meat, onion, egg, parsley, nutmeg, salt and pepper in a large bowl. Shape the mixture into balls about the size of golf balls.
2. Bring the stock to the boil and then reduce heat to simmering point.
3. Lower the meat balls carefully into the liquid, cover, and bring back to the boil. Continue simmering for 45 minutes or until the meatballs are tender and cooked through.
4. If desired, thicken the cooking liquid with a little flour or a packet of cream soup such as mushroom or onion. Lift out the meatballs and keep them warm while you thicken the gravy.
5. Pour the gravy over the meatballs (f) and serve hot.

Variations:

1. To make meatballs in a rich tomato sauce; add 1 can of tomato paste, 2 ml (½ teaspoon) mustard powder, 10 ml (2 teaspoons) sugar and a little cornflour stirred into cold water.
2. To make curried meatballs: add 1 stick of cinnamon, 12,5 ml (1 tablespoon) chutney, vinegar, sugar and salt to taste along with 25 ml (2 tablespoons) commercial brand curry powder mixed as directed on the package.

Hamburgers
See Quick meat dishes, p. 162 to 165

Add as much water as the mixture will hold to ensure that your mince dishes are light.

255 Salisbury steaks (F)

1 kg minced beef
250 ml (1 cup) mushrooms, thinly sliced
100 ml (²/₅ cup) dry breadcrumbs
2 eggs, lightly beaten
25 ml (2 tablespoons) flour
37,5 ml (3 tablespoons) butter or margarine
25 ml oil
250 ml beef stock
water
5 ml (1 teaspoon) salt
2 ml (½ teaspoon) pepper
Garnish:
chopped parsley

Serves 6;   kJ per portion 1 210;   Prep time 45 min;   Cooking time 15 min.

1. Mix the mince, eggs, salt and pepper together in a bowl, then shape the mixture into 6 oval steaks 1 cm thick and 10 cm long. Dredge the steaks in breadcrumbs, pressing the crumbs firmly into both sides of each steak, then chill them in the refrigerator.
2. Melt 25 ml (2 tablespoons) of the butter or margarine in a large frying-pan and sauté the mushrooms in it, stirring occasionally, until golden brown. Remove from the pan.
3. Heat the remaining butter or margarine and the oil in the frying-pan and fry the steaks, about 2 minutes on either side, then place them on a heated serving dish.
4. Stir the stock into the juices in the frying-pan.
5. Blend the flour with a little cold water to form a smooth paste, then stir gradually into the mixture in the frying-pan. Bring to the boil, stirring, and cook until thick and smooth.
6. Stir in the mushrooms, then add the steaks and simmer in the sauce for 3 to 5 minutes (f). Serve at once, garnished with the parsley.

256 Bobotie (F)

1 kg minced beef or mutton
1 medium onion, finely chopped
125 ml (½ cup) seedless raisins (optional)
125 ml (½ cup) blanched almonds (optional)
12,5 ml (1 tablespoon) apricot jam
12,5 ml fruit chutney
1 slice white bread
10 ml (2 teaspoons) butter or oil
3 eggs
250 ml milk
25 ml lemon juice
10 ml (2 teaspoons) curry powder
5 ml (1 teaspoon) turmeric
2 lemon or bay leaves
10 ml (2 teaspoons) salt

Serves 8;   kJ per portion 1 210;   Prep time 30 min;   Cooking time 50 min.

1. Soak the bread in 125 ml milk, squeeze to remove the milk and mix the bread with the minced beef. Mix in all the other ingredients except the butter or oil, eggs, milk and leaves.
2. Melt the butter or heat the oil in a frying-pan and brown the meat mixture lightly in it. Turn out into a casserole (f).
3. Beat the eggs and the rest of milk together and pour over the meat. Garnish with the leaves.
4. Bake in the oven at 180°C (350°F) until set, about 50 minutes.

Note: Bobotie freezes very well. To serve, thaw and continue with steps 3 and 4.

---

257 Picadillo (F)

500 g topside mince
1 large onion, finely chopped
2 large tomatoes, skinned and coarsely chopped
1 green pepper, seeded and coarsely chopped
25 ml (2 tablespoons) raisins
6 stuffed green olives
1 clove garlic, crushed
oil for frying
125 ml dry red wine
1 ml (¼ teaspoon) dried thyme
1 ml (¼ teaspoon) dried oreganum
5 ml (1 teaspoon) salt
2 ml (½ teaspoon) pepper

Serves 6;   kJ per portion 1 200;   Prep time 15 min;   Cooking time 35 min.

1. Heat the oil in a large frying-pan and brown the meat in it over low heat, stirring occasionally.
2. Add the onion and garlic and sauté until the meat is well-browned. Pour off the excess fat.
3. Stir in the raisins, herbs, tomatoes and wine and season with salt and pepper.
4. Increase the heat, bring the mixture to the boil, then turn down the heat to low and simmer for 20 minutes.
5. Stir in the green pepper and olives, and simmer a further 10 minutes (f). Serve immediately.

Note: Thaw and heat, covered, over low heat for approximately 15 minutes.

---

258 Herbed beef ring (F)

750 g topside mince
1 large onion, grated
125 ml (½ cup) soft breadcrumbs
1 egg, lightly beaten
12,5 ml (1 tablespoon) Parmesan cheese, grated
125 ml tomato purée
5 ml (1 teaspoon) dried oreganum
25 ml (2 tablespoons) parsley, finely chopped
7 ml (1½ teaspoons) salt
2 ml (½ teaspoon) pepper

Serves 6;   kJ per portion 1 080;   Prep time 30 min;   Cooking time 1 hour

1. Combine the mince, onion, cheese and breadcrumbs in a bowl.
2. Stir in the egg, tomato purée, herbs, salt and pepper and mix well.
3. Pack the mixture firmly into a lightly oiled ring mould, then turn out into a shallow baking dish and bake in the oven at 180°C (350°F) for 1 hour.
4. Remove from the oven, allow to cool for 5 minutes (f), then serve, sliced.

Note: Freeze the beef ring in the mould, turn out when frozen and wrap well. To serve after freezing, replace in an oiled ring mould and reheat. To serve cold, thaw in the refrigerator.

400 g spaghetti
25 ml (2 tablespoons) butter
grated Parmesan cheese
boiling salted water
Sauce:
250 g minced beef
60 g streaky bacon, derinded
and finely chopped
1 medium onion, finely
chopped
1 medium carrot, finely
chopped
1 stalk celery, finely chopped
12,5 ml (1 tablespoon) butter
or margarine
40 ml tomato purée
25 ml double cream (optional)
50 ml dry white wine (optional)
200 ml water
pinch grated nutmeg
5 ml (1 teaspoon) salt
2 ml (½ teaspoon) pepper

259 Spaghetti Bolognaise (F)

Serves 4;   kJ per portion 1 700;   Prep time 45 min;   Cooking time 1 hour

1. First make the sauce: melt the butter or margarine in a large saucepan, add the onion, carrot, celery and bacon and fry until tender and the onion is golden brown, about 10 minutes.
2. Add the meat and sauté, stirring, until lightly browned. Add the wine, if desired, and boil briskly until the wine has almost evaporated.
3. Stir in the tomato purée, water, salt, pepper and nutmeg and simmer, covered, over very low heat for about 45 minutes, stirring occasionally (f).
4. Stir in the cream, if desired, and add more salt and pepper if necessary.
5. 15 minutes before serving, boil the spaghetti in plenty of boiling, salted water until just tender.
6. Drain the spaghetti completely and place it in a heated serving dish dotted with the butter, then add 25 ml (2 tablespoons) of the sauce and 12,5 ml (1 tablespoon) Parmesan cheese and toss lightly with two forks until the spaghetti is well coated.
7. Pour the remaining sauce on top and serve hot, sprinkled with grated Parmesan cheese.

Note: Meat sauce freezes very well. To use after freezing, heat from the frozen state over medium heat and continue with steps 5, 6 and 7.

---

500 g minced beef
1 medium onion, grated
125 ml (½ cup) fresh white
breadcrumbs
12 cannelloni tubes or
pancakes (recipe 547)
25 ml (2 tablespoons)
Parmesan cheese, grated
1 egg, lightly beaten
12,5 ml (1 tablespoon) parsley,
finely chopped
pinch dried oreganum
5 ml (1 teaspoon) salt
2 ml (½ teaspoon) pepper
oil for frying
Sauce:
1 small onion, grated
375 ml water
230 g tomato paste
oil for frying
2 ml (½ teaspoon) salt
1 ml (¼ teaspoon) pepper
Garnish:
grated Parmesan cheese

260 Cannelloni (F)

Serves 6;   kJ per portion 1 700;   Prep time 1 hour;   Cooking time 1 hour

1. Combine the mince, onion, salt and pepper in a large bowl.
2. Heat a little oil in a large frying-pan and brown the meat mixture lightly in it.
3. Pour the excess fat from the pan, then stir in the oreganum, breadcrumbs, 25 ml Parmesan cheese, parsley and the beaten egg. Simmer for 4 to 5 minutes.
4. Meanwhile, cook the cannelloni tubes in boiling salted water for 10 minutes, then drain thoroughly.
5. Carefully stuff each tube or pancake with some of the meat mixture. Arrange the tubes in a single layer in a greased, shallow ovenproof dish.
6. Make the sauce. Heat a little oil in a frying-pan and sauté the onion in it until soft, then add the salt, pepper, tomato paste and water, stirring all the time.
7. Bring to the boil and pour over the cannelloni in the ovenproof dish (f).
8. Dust the top of the sauce with plenty of grated Parmesan cheese and bake in the oven at 180 °C (350 °F) for 35 minutes. Serve immediately.

Note:
• To serve after freezing, thaw, add the Parmesan cheese and bake, uncovered, in the oven at 180 °C (350 °F) for approximately 45 minutes.
• If cannelloni tubes are not available, use pancakes (recipe 547). Place some of the filling in the centre of each pancake, roll up and continue with the rest of step 5.

Bolognaise sauce (recipe 259)
120 g raw wide ribbon noodles,
spinach flavoured
250 ml Béchamel sauce
(p. 179)
37,5 ml double cream
60 g Parmesan cheese, grated

261 Lasagne verdi (F)

Serves 4;   kJ per portion 1 700;   Prep time 45 min;   Cooking time 45 min.

1. Prepare the meat sauce first, as for Spaghetti Bolognaise (recipe 259).
2. Boil the noodles in a saucepan with plenty of boiling, salted water until tender. Drain carefully and lay the noodles flat on a cloth.
3. Meanwhile, make the Béchamel sauce and stir in the cream.
4. Grease a flat ovenproof dish 20 × 15 × 5 cm and place alternate layers of meat sauce, overlapping noodles, Béchamel sauce and a sprinkling of Parmesan cheese, ending with a smooth layer of Béchamel sauce and a thick coating of Parmesan cheese (f).
5. Bake in the oven at 180°C (350°F), uncovered, until the top browns, 25 to 30 minutes. Serve hot.

Variation: Use 250 g cottage cheese instead of the Béchamel sauce and cream.

Note: To serve after freezing, thaw and bake, uncovered, in the oven at 180°C (350°F) for approximately 45 minutes. Add more cheese if required.

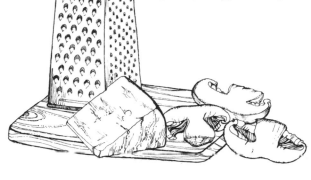

500 g cooked lamb, minced
1 large aubergine, thickly
sliced
1 small onion, finely chopped
250 g mushrooms, thinly sliced
250 g tomatoes, thickly sliced
1 egg yolk
37,5 ml (3 tablespoons) butter
or margarine
125 ml (½ cup) Cheddar
cheese, grated
1 small can tomato purée
1 clove garlic, crushed
300 ml thick Béchamel sauce
(p. 179)
5 ml (1 teaspoon) dried mixed
herbs
5 ml (1 teaspoon) salt
2 ml (½ teaspoon) pepper

262 Moussaka (F)

Serves 6;   kJ per portion 1 680;   Prep time 30 min;   Cooking time 30 min.

1. Heat 12,5 ml (1 tablespoon) of the butter or margarine in a large frying-pan and sauté the onion in it until transparent.
2. Add the meat and sauté for a few minutes, shaking the pan now and then, then set aside.
3. Season with salt and pepper and stir in the tomato purée. Turn into a heated casserole and keep warm.
4. Heat the remaining butter or margarine in a frying-pan and sauté the aubergine slices for 5 to 7 minutes. Arrange on top of the meat in the casserole.
5. Place the tomatoes and mushrooms on top and sprinkle with the garlic and mixed herbs.
6. Prepare the Béchamel sauce, then beat the egg yolk into it and pour the mixture over the contents of the casserole.
7. Sprinkle grated cheese over the sauce and bake in the oven at 200°C (400°F) until well-browned, about 30 minutes (f). Serve immediately.

Note: To serve frozen Moussaka, thaw in the refrigerator overnight then heat, covered, in the oven at 160°C (325°F) for approximately 30 minutes. Remove the cover, add more grated cheese and heat a further 5 minutes.

750 g minced beef
1 medium onion, finely minced
200 ml (⁴/₅ cup) dry breadcrumbs
2 eggs
37,5 ml (3 tablespoons) butter, margarine or oil
125 ml water
1 ml (¼ teaspoon) ground allspice
5 ml (1 teaspoon) salt
1 ml (¼ teaspoon) pepper

263 Basic frikkadel (F)

Makes 40;   kJ per portion 1 100;   Prep time 30 min;   Cooking time 15 min.

1. Heat 12,5 ml (1 tablespoon) of the butter, margarine or oil in a frying-pan and sauté the onion in it until lightly browned.
2. Combine the mince, breadcrumbs, water, eggs, salt, pepper, allspice and onion in a large bowl and form into medium-sized balls.
3. Melt the remaining butter or margarine or heat the oil in the frying-pan and brown the rissoles in it in batches, turning occasionally to brown evenly all over. Remove rissoles when cooked through and keep warm (f). Serve hot or cold.

Variations:
1. Make curry sauce (p. 182) and add when the rissoles have browned. Simmer until the rissoles have cooked through (f) and serve hot.
2. Use 1 grated Granny Smith apple or All-bran flakes instead of the breadcrumbs.

Note:
- Rissoles freeze well and can be kept for up to 3 months in the freezer.
- This recipe can also be used as a basic mix for hamburgers.

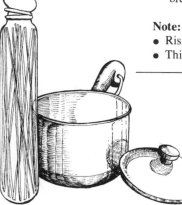

500 g topside mince
4 slices white bread, crusts removed
1 small onion, finely chopped
400 g tomatoes, skinned and coarsely chopped
1 large egg
25 ml (2 tablespoons) lard
25 ml (2 tablespoons) flour
125 ml milk
dash Worcester sauce
175 ml sour cream
5 ml (1 teaspoon) dried mixed herbs
5 ml (1 teaspoon) salt
2 ml (½ teaspoon) pepper

264 Rissoles in sour cream sauce (F)

Serves 4-6;   kJ per portion 1 500;   Prep time 20 min;   Cooking time 35 min.

1. Break the bread into small pieces and place in a bowl. Stir in the egg, milk, onion, herbs, salt and pepper and allow the bread to absorb the liquid.
2. Beat the mixture until it is smooth, then stir in the topside, blending well.
3. Make 24 rissoles, rolling them with lightly floured hands.
4. Melt the lard in a large frying-pan, add the rissoles in batches and fry them until they are golden brown all over. Remove the rissoles from the pan as they are browned, set aside and keep warm.
5. Stir the flour into the fat remaining in the frying-pan, a little at a time, then add the tomatoes and the Worcester sauce. Bring the sauce to the boil, stirring continuously, and add more salt and pepper if necessary.
6. Return the rissoles to the pan and simmer, covered, for 10 minutes (f).
7. Stir the sour cream in carefully and continue simmering until the rissoles are cooked through, about 5 minutes. Serve on a bed of cooked spaghetti or brown rice.

Note:
- Freeze the rissoles in the sauce, wrapping the container well.
- To serve after freezing, thaw and heat gently on top of the stove for about 10 minutes, then continue with step 7.

265 Swedish rissoles (F)

750 g minced beef
250 ml (1 cup) mashed potatoes
125 ml (½ cup) cooked beetroot, diced
1 small onion, grated
1 egg, lightly beaten
125 ml evaporated milk
1 ml (¼ teaspoon) dried basil
7 ml (1½ teaspoons) salt
1 ml (¼ teaspoon) pepper
oil for frying

Serves 6; kJ per portion 1 100; Prep time 15 min; Cooking time 10 min.

1. Combine the meat, onion, potatoes, basil and beetroot in a bowl.
2. Stir the evaporated milk into the beaten egg and add to the meat mixture, blending well.
3. Season with salt and pepper, then with lightly floured hands form the mixture into 6 rissoles.
4. Heat a little oil in a frying-pan and fry the rissoles until browned and cooked through, turning once (f). Serve hot.

Note: To serve after freezing, thaw and heat, covered, in the oven at 160 °C (325 °F) for approximately 20 minutes.

266 Yoghurt rissoles

500 g minced beef
250 ml (1 cup) onion, grated
62,5 ml (5 tablespoons) flour
50 ml (4 tablespoons) butter or margarine
250 ml plain yoghurt
2 ml (½ teaspoon) ground ginger
7 ml (1½ teaspoons) turmeric
7 ml (1½ teaspoons) ground coriander
pinch saffron
7 ml (1½ teaspoons) salt
2 ml (½ teaspoon) black pepper

Serves 6; kJ per portion 1 280; Prep time 20 min; Cooking time 20 min.

1. In a bowl, combine the mince, onion, salt, ginger, saffron, turmeric, coriander, pepper and half the yoghurt. Roll the mixture into sausage shapes.
2. Dip the rolls in the remaining yoghurt and then in the flour, coating well.
3. Melt the butter or margarine in a large frying-pan and fry the rolls in it, turning occasionally, until well-browned.
4. Serve with baked potatoes and a green salad.

267 Sweet and sour meatballs (F)

350 g minced beef
250 ml (1 cup) fresh breadcrumbs
1 egg
37,5 ml oil
5 ml (1 teaspoon) salt
2 ml (½ teaspoon) pepper
Sauce:
1 carrot, cut into long strips
2 stalks celery, thinly sliced
1 leek, thinly sliced
1 onion, finely chopped
60 g mushrooms, quartered
7 ml (1½ teaspoons) cornflour
10 ml (2 teaspoons) brown or white sugar
10 ml tomato sauce
10 ml soy sauce
150 ml water
12,5 ml vinegar

Serves 4-6; kJ per portion 1 300; Prep time 15 min; Cooking time 45 min.

1. Prepare and fry rissoles as for recipe 263. Set aside while making the sauce.
2. Add the onion, carrot, leek, celery and mushrooms to the frying-pan and fry over low heat until the onions are transparent.
3. Combine the cornflour and sugar in a bowl and gradually stir in the water.
4. Add the tomato sauce, vinegar and soy sauce, blending well. Stir into the mixture in the frying-pan.
5. Return the rissoles to the pan, add a little more salt and pepper if necessary and simmer, covered, for 30 minutes (f). Serve at once with noodles or mashed potatoes.

Variations: Use the sweet and sour sauce given in recipe 324.

Note: To serve after freezing, thaw and heat, covered, over low heat for approximately 15 minutes or in the oven at 160 °C (325 °F) for about 20 minutes. Stir the sauce to blend well before serving.

500 g minced beef
250 ml (1 cup) fresh white breadcrumbs
425 g canned or fresh tomatoes, skinned
25 ml (2 tablespoons) flour
12,5 ml tomato sauce
25 ml oil
dash Worcester sauce
5 ml (1 teaspoon) dried mixed herbs
5 ml (1 teaspoon) salt
2 ml (½ teaspoon) pepper
250 g uncooked spaghetti
boiling salted water

268 Spaghetti meatballs (F)

Serves 4;   kJ per portion 1 600;   Prep time 10 min;   Cooking time 25 min.

1. Combine the minced beef, herbs, tomato sauce, breadcrumbs and half the salt and pepper in a bowl.
2. Divide the mixture into 12 portions and with lightly floured hands form each into a rissole.
3. Heat the oil in a large frying-pan and brown the rissoles in it quickly, turning once. Remove the rissoles from the pan and set aside, keeping warm.
4. Remove the frying-pan from the stove and sprinkle the flour over the oil. Stir in the tomatoes, Worcester sauce and the rest of the salt and pepper. Return the frying-pan to the stove. Return the rissoles to the pan.
5. Bring the sauce to the boil, stirring continuously, then reduce the heat and simmer, covered, until the rissoles are cooked, about 20 minutes (f).
6. Meanwhile, place the spaghetti in a saucepan of boiling, salted water and boil until tender, about 15 minutes. Drain, then run hot water through the strands and toss them in a little oil to prevent sticking.
7. Turn the spaghetti onto a heated serving dish, spoon the rissoles and sauce on top and serve at once, topped with grated Parmesan cheese.

Note:
- Do not freeze the spaghetti – prepare it just before use.
- To serve after freezing, reheat the meatballs and sauce, covered, over medium heat for approximately 15 minutes, then continue with steps 6 and 7.

QUICK MEAT DISHES

600 g canned corned beef
250 ml (1 cup) onion, finely chopped
450 g cooked potatoes, diced
25 ml (2 tablespoons) butter or margarine
2 ml tabasco sauce
125 ml beef stock
Garnish:
25 ml (2 tablespoons) parsley, coarsely chopped

269 Corned beef hash

Serves 6;   kJ per portion 1 080;   Prep time 20 min;   Cooking time 15 min.

1. Combine the corned beef, potato, onion, stock and tabasco sauce in a large bowl.
2. Melt the butter or margarine in a large frying-pan, spread the mixture evenly over the bottom of the pan and fry over low heat until browned on one side.
3. Fold in half and serve at once, garnished with parsley.

Variations:
1. Add 25 ml fruit chutney to the mixture.
2. Sprinkle grated Cheddar cheese over the hash, fold in half and serve.

450 g cold cooked beef, shredded
450 g cold mashed potatoes
450 g cooked cabbage, finely chopped
25 ml (2 tablespoons) butter or margarine
2 ml (½ teaspoon) salt
2 ml (½ teaspoon) pepper

270 Bubble and squeak

Serves 3;   kJ per portion 1 100;   Prep time 20 min;   Cooking time 10 min.

1. Melt the butter or margarine in a large frying-pan, add the potatoes and cabbage and fry until the potato begins to brown, stirring continuously.
2. Stir in the shredded meat, salt and pepper.
3. Fry for a few more minutes and serve.

Simple to make, spectacular to serve, Roast Pork with Fruit Kebabs (recipe 164) is accompanied by deep-fried cauliflower (recipe 342), buttered carrots and onions (recipe 340) and green beans.

450 g pork sausages
340 g cooking apples, cored and thinly sliced
450 g canned sauerkraut, drained

271 Sausages and sauerkraut

Serves 4; kJ per portion 980; Prep time 10 min; Cooking time 40 min.

1. Place the sauerkraut and apples in a deep casserole and top with the sausages.
2. Bake, covered, in the oven at 200 °C (400 °F) for 40 minutes.
3. Remove the lid when 30 minutes of the cooking time have elapsed and brown the sausages. Serve hot.

450 g pork or beef sausages, skinned
120 g flour
1 egg
12,5 ml oil
250 ml milk
2 ml (½ teaspoon) baking powder
pinch salt

272 Toad-in-the-hole

Serves 4-6; kJ per portion 1 200; Prep time 15 min; Cooking time 35 min.

1. Sift the flour and baking powder into a large bowl and make a well in the centre. Break the egg into the well and stir lightly with a fork.
2. Add the milk gradually, stirring all the time to form a smooth batter. Stir in the salt and allow to stand for 30 minutes.
3. Place the sausages in a shallow flame-proof dish, with the oil, and fry on top of the stove for 5 minutes.
4. Pour the batter over the sausages and bake in the oven at 220 °C (425 °F) for 30 minutes. Serve at once.

500 g chipolata sausages
60 g rindless streaky bacon, diced
2 medium onions, thinly sliced
110 g button mushrooms, thinly sliced
250 g canned baked beans
12,5 ml tomato purée
25 ml (2 tablespoons) lard
62,5 ml (5 tablespoons) flour
250 ml beef stock
Garnish:
finely chopped parsley

273 Chipolata stew

Serves 4; kJ per portion 1 600; Prep time 15 min; Cooking time 30 min.

1. In a large frying-pan, melt the lard and fry the sausages over low heat, turning often, until lightly browned, about 10 minutes. Remove from the pan and keep warm.
2. Sauté the onions in the fat until transparent, then add the bacon and sauté for 3 minutes.
3. Add the flour gradually, stirring all the time.
4. Add the mushrooms, tomato purée and stock, stirring constantly to blend.
5. Stir in the baked beans, then return the sausages to the pan and simmer, covered, for 10 to 15 minutes. Transfer the mixture to a heated serving dish and serve at once, garnished with chopped parsley.

250 g frankfurters, halved
250 g canned or fresh ripe tomatoes, skinned
2 stalks celery, coarsely chopped
1 large onion, finely chopped
250 g cooked long-grained rice
12,5 ml (1 tablespoon) parsley, finely chopped
25 ml olive oil
2 ml (½ teaspoon) salt
2 ml (½ teaspoon) pepper
Garnish:
50 ml (4 tablespoons) Parmesan cheese, grated

274 Jambalaya

Serves 4; kJ per portion 1 400; Prep time 20 min; Cooking time 25 min.

1. Heat the oil in a large frying-pan and gently sauté the onion and celery until the onion is golden brown.
2. Stir in the rice, then add the frankfurters, tomatoes, parsley, salt and pepper and heat gently until very hot. Serve at once, garnished with the grated Parmesan cheese.

Traditional fare, Mutton Curry (recipe 218) with fruity accompaniments.

275 Hamburgers

500 g minced beef
1 egg
12,5 ml (1 tablespoon) dry breadcrumbs
1 small onion, finely chopped
1 clove garlic, minced
5 ml (1 teaspoon) salt
1 ml (¼ teaspoon) pepper
4 round rolls, halved, toasted and buttered
oil for frying
Garnish:
4 thick slices tomato
4 thick slices onion
4 lettuce leaves

Serves 4; kJ per portion 1 400; Prep time 15 min; Cooking time 10 min.

1. In a bowl combine the minced beef , egg, breadcrumbs, onion, garlic, salt and pepper. Form into 4 large patties.
2. Heat the oil in a large frying-pan and fry the patties in it for 4 minutes on each side.
3. Place a lettuce leaf on each of 4 halves of hamburger roll, top with a cooked pattie, an onion ring, a slice of tomato and another half roll. Serve immediately.

Variations:

1. Use 1 small apple, grated, instead of the breadcrumbs.
2. Add 25 ml (2 tablespoons) chutney to the mixture.
3. Use cornflakes or All-bran flakes instead of the breadcrumbs.
4. Spread a little mustard on the hamburger rolls and add sliced gherkin to the tomato-lettuce-onion combination.

Note: If your hamburgers are heavy, add water – as much as the mixture will hold.

276 Cheeseburgers

4 meat patties (recipe 275)
50 ml (4 tablespoons) strong Cheddar cheese, grated, or 4 slices strong processed cheese
4 round rolls, halved and buttered
Garnish:
lettuce leaves

Serves 4; kJ per portion 1 500; Prep time 15 min; Cooking time 15 min.

1. Prepare the meat patties as directed.
2. Place a pattie on each of 4 halves of roll, top each with 12,5 ml (1 tablespoon) grated cheese or 1 slice processed cheese and grill until the cheese melts.
3. Top each cheeseburger with a lettuce leaf and the other half of each roll and serve.

Variations:

1. Add 1 thick slice of cooked ham to each hamburger before adding the cheese.
2. Add 1 fried egg to each hamburger before adding the cheese.
3. Top the cheese with crumbled, crisply fried bacon.
4. Use blue cheese instead of Cheddar cheese.

277 Blaauwkrantz-stuffed hamburgers

500 g minced beef
125 ml (½ cup) Blaauwkrantz cheese, crumbled
5 ml (1 teaspoon) onion, grated
25 ml double cream
2 ml (½ teaspoon) salt
pinch pepper
4 round rolls, halved, toasted and buttered
12,5 ml oil
Garnish:
4 thick slices tomato

Serves 4; kJ per portion 1 500; Prep time 20 min; Cooking time 10 min.

1. Combine the Blaauwkrantz cheese, cream and onion in a bowl.
2. Flatten the meat evenly on wax paper to 1 cm thickness and, with a sharp knife that has been dipped in cold water, cut into eight 7 cm squares.
3. Spread the cheese mixture evenly to within 1 cm of the edges of 4 of the squares. Top each square with one of the remaining squares, crimp the edges together firmly and shape into rounds. Sprinkle with salt and pepper.
4. Heat the oil in a large frying-pan and fry the rounds in it for 5 minutes on either side.
5. Place the rounds on the bottom halves of the rolls, garnish with tomato slices and top with the other halves of the rolls. Serve at once.

162

278 Nut burgers

500 g minced beef
125 ml (½ cup) walnuts, finely chopped
25 ml (2 tablespoons) green onion, minced
1 egg
25 ml soy sauce
pinch salt
pinch pepper
4 round sesame rolls, halved, toasted and buttered
oil for frying
Garnish:
½ cucumber, finely sliced
125 ml sour cream
50 ml (4 tablespoons) green onions, finely chopped

Serves 4;   kJ per portion 1 500;   Prep time 10 min;   Cooking time 10 min.

1. In a bowl combine the mince, walnuts, green onion, egg, soy sauce, salt and pepper. Form the mixture into 4 large patties.
2. Heat the oil in a large frying-pan and fry the patties over medium heat for 4 minutes on each side.
3. Place the patties on the bottom halves of the rolls and top with sliced cucumber, sour cream, green onions and the other half of the roll. Serve at once.

Variation: Use pecans, cashews or hazelnuts instead of the walnuts.

---

279 Ham and beef burgers

500 g minced beef
125 ml (½ cup) cooked ham, finely diced
12,5 ml prepared German mustard
2 ml (½ teaspoon) salt
1 ml (¼ teaspoon) pepper
4 muffins, halved, toasted and buttered
oil for frying
Garnish:
4 thick slices tomato
20 ml (4 teaspoons) sweet pickle relish

Serves 4;   kJ per portion 1 400;   Prep time 10 min;   Cooking time 8 min.

1. Combine the minced beef, ham, mustard, salt and pepper in a bowl. Form into 4 large patties.
2. Heat the oil in a large frying-pan and fry the patties over medium heat for 4 minutes on either side.
3. Place the patties on the bottom halves of the muffins, top each with a thick slice of tomato, 5 ml (1 teaspoon) pickle relish and the other half of the muffin. Serve immediately.

Variation: Use 125 ml (½ cup) minced salami instead of the ham.

---

280 Roman hamburgers

500 g minced beef
50 ml (4 tablespoons) parsley, finely chopped
50 ml (4 tablespoons) Parmesan cheese, grated
1 egg
12,5 ml (1 tablespoon) dry breadcrumbs
1 clove garlic, minced
2 ml (½ teaspoon) oreganum
5 ml (1 teaspoon) salt
1 ml (¼ teaspoon) pepper
4 wedges French bread, toasted and buttered
oil for frying
Garnish:
2 canned pimento (red Spanish sweet pepper) cut in strips
shredded Mozzarella or Cheddar cheese

Serves 4;   kJ per portion 1 580;   Prep time 15 min;   Cooking time 15 min.

1. In a bowl, combine the minced beef, parsley, Parmesan cheese, garlic, egg, breadcrumbs, oreganum, salt and pepper. Form into 4 large patties.
2. Heat the oil in a large frying-pan and fry the patties in it for 4 minutes on each side.
3. Place a pattie on each wedge of French bread, criss-cross a few strips of pimiento on top and sprinkle with shredded Mozzarella or Cheddar cheese. Brown under the grill until the cheese melts. Serve immediately.

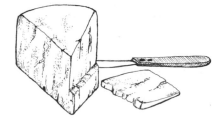

500 g minced beef
340 g mushrooms, finely
chopped
1 large onion, finely chopped
37,5 ml sour cream
37,5 ml oil
1 ml (¼ teaspoon) dried basil
5 ml (1 teaspoon) salt
pinch pepper
4 round rolls, halved, toasted
and buttered
oil for frying
Garnish:
finely chopped parsley

281   Mushroom-stuffed hamburgers   (F)

Serves 4;   kJ per portion 1 400;   Prep time 20 min;   Cooking time 10 min.

1. Heat the 37,5 ml oil in a large frying-pan. Sauté the mushrooms and onion in it for 6 to 8 minutes over medium heat, stirring frequently.
2. Combine the sautéed mushrooms, sour cream, basil and half the salt in a bowl.
3. Flatten the meat evenly on wax paper to 1 cm thickness and cut into eight 7 cm squares with a sharp knife that has been dipped in cold water.
4. Spread the mushroom mixture evenly to within 1 cm of the edges of 4 of the squares. Top each square with one of the remaining squares, crimp the edges together firmly and shape into rounds. Sprinkle with the remaining salt and the pepper (f).
5. Heat a little oil in a large frying-pan and fry the meat rounds in it for 5 minutes on either side over medium heat (f).
6. Place the patties on the bottom halves of the rolls, garnish each with chopped parsley and top with the other half of the roll. Serve immediately.

Note:
- Hamburgers can be frozen either fried or raw.
- Freeze the meat patties and hamburger rolls separately.
- To serve after freezing, heat 10 ml (2 teaspoons) butter or margarine in a frying-pan and fry patties in it for 5 minutes on either side. Heat rolls in oven at 180°C (350°F), for 5 minutes. Continue with step 6.

500 g minced beef
8 rashers bacon, rinds cut off
1 small onion, finely chopped
2 ml (½ teaspoon) salt
1 ml (¼ teaspoon) pepper
4 round sesame rolls, halved,
toasted and buttered
Garnish:
4 bacon curls
1 gherkin, sliced lengthwise
into four pieces
4 lettuce leaves

282   Bacon burgers

Serves 4;   kJ per portion 1 400;   Prep time 20 min;   Cooking time 15 min.

1. Fry the bacon in a large frying-pan until limp. Remove 4 pieces, roll them up and fasten each with a wooden toothpick. Return them to the frying-pan. Fry all the bacon until crisp, then remove the curled up bacon rolls and set aside as a garnish. Remove the toothpicks.
2. Remove the other rashers of bacon, crumble them finely, and in a small bowl combine with the meat, onion, salt and pepper. Form the mixture into 4 large patties.
3. Pour off all but 12,5 ml (1 tablespoon) of the bacon fat and fry the patties over medium heat for 4 minutes on either side.
4. Place a lettuce leaf on each of 4 halves of the toasted sesame rolls, place a pattie on each half, top with the sliced gherkin, a bacon curl and the other half of the roll. Serve at once.

283 Vegetable burgers

500 g minced beef
125 ml (½ cup) carrot, finely shredded
125 ml (½ cup) celery, finely minced
12,5 ml (1 tablespoon) bottled horseradish
1 egg
80 ml (¹/₃ cup) wheatgerm
62,5 ml tomato sauce
2 ml (½ teaspoon) mustard powder
5 ml (1 teaspoon) salt
1 ml (¼ teaspoon) pepper
6 round wholewheat rolls, halved, toasted and buttered
12,5 ml oil
Garnish:
6 radish slices

Serves 6;   kJ per portion 1 300;   Prep time 25 min;   Cooking time 10 min.

1. Combine the minced beef, carrot, celery, wheatgerm, tomato sauce, egg, horseradish, mustard, salt and pepper in a bowl. Shape into 6 large patties.
2. Heat the oil in a large frying-pan and fry the patties for 5 minutes on each side.
3. Place the patties on the bottom halves of the rolls, garnish each with sliced radish and top with the other half of the roll. Serve at once.

284 Chilli burgers

500 g minced beef
125 ml (½ cup) tomato, diced
25 ml (2 tablespoons) green onion, finely chopped
25 ml (2 tablespoons) green pepper, seeded and finely chopped
2 canned hot red peppers, finely chopped
12,5 ml (1 tablespoon) dry breadcrumbs
1 egg
2 ml (½ teaspoon) chilli powder
1 ml (¼ teaspoon) oreganum
7 ml (1½ teaspoons) salt
pinch pepper
2 round rolls, halved and buttered
oil for frying
Garnish:
4 lettuce leaves

Serves 4;   kJ per portion 1 500;   Prep time 20 min;   Cooking time 10 min.

1. Combine the mince, 1 canned red pepper, the breadcrumbs, egg, 5 ml (1 teaspoon) of the salt, the pepper and chilli powder in a bowl. Shape the mixture into 4 large patties.
2. Heat the oil in a frying-pan and fry the patties over high heat for 4 minutes on each side.
3. Meanwhile, combine the tomato, green onion, green pepper, the remaining hot red pepper, oreganum and the rest of the salt in a bowl.
4. When the patties are done, place a lettuce leaf on each of the roll halves, place a pattie on top and spoon over some of the tomato mixture. Serve immediately.

285 Liver fritters (F)

500 g calf's liver, trimmed and cubed
1 medium onion, thinly sliced
2 eggs, beaten
12,5 ml vinegar or lemon juice
5 ml (1 teaspoon) parsley, finely chopped
5 ml (1 teaspoon) salt
1 ml (¼ teaspoon) pepper
oil for frying

Serves 4-6;   kJ per portion 1 100;   Prep time 20 min;   Cooking time 10 min.

1. Mince the onion and liver together and place in a large bowl.
2. Add the eggs, vinegar or lemon juice, parsley, salt and pepper and mix well.
3. Heat the oil in a frying-pan. Drop tablespoonfuls of the mixture in the oil and brown on both sides (f).
4. Serve very hot with mashed potato and peas.

Note:
- Do not freeze for longer than 1 month.
- To serve after freezing thaw and heat, covered, in the oven at 160°C (325°F) for approximately 20 minutes.

286 Brains with mushrooms

2 sets calf or lamb brains, washed, skinned and cubed
250 g mushrooms, thinly sliced
soft breadcrumbs
Cheddar cheese, grated
62,5 ml (5 tablespoons) butter or margarine
62,5 ml (5 tablespoons) flour
250 ml chicken stock
125 ml unsweetened evaporated milk
1 ml (¼ teaspoon) grated nutmeg
1 ml (¼ teaspoon) cayenne pepper
5 ml (1 teaspoon) salt

Serves 6;   kJ per portion 880;   Prep time 15 min;   Cooking time 35 min.

1. Melt the butter or margarine in a large saucepan and sauté the mushrooms in it over low heat for 2 minutes. Remove the mushrooms and keep warm.
2. Add the flour to the pan, a little at a time, and cook for 2 minutes, stirring constantly.
3. Combine the stock and evaporated milk gradually by stirring. Add the nutmeg, cayenne pepper and salt and cook over medium heat until the mixture comes to the boil.
4. Add the mushrooms and brains, mixing well.
5. Turn the mixture into a greased ovenproof dish, then sprinkle with breadcrumbs and a layer of grated cheese.
6. Bake in the oven at 180°C (350°F) until the top is lightly browned, about 30 minutes. Serve immediately.

287 Pork casserole

500 ml (2 cups) cooked pork, diced
2 rashers bacon
1 large onion, finely chopped
410 g canned condensed tomato soup
640 g cooked lima beans
125 ml water
125 ml (½ cup) buttered soft breadcrumbs

Serves 4-6;   kJ per portion 1 610;   Prep time 10 min;   Cooking time 20 min.

1. Fry the bacon in a large frying-pan until crisp; drain and crumble.
2. Brown the onion in the bacon fat, then add the remaining ingredients except the breadcrumbs and mix thoroughly.
3. Transfer the mixture to a large casserole, sprinkle with breadcrumbs and bake in the oven at 220°C (425°F) until the crumbs are browned, about 15 minutes. Serve at once.

288 Ham and asparagus rolls

8 thin slices lean ham
24 canned asparagus spears (liquid reserved)
Sauce:
25 ml (2 tablespoons) butter or margarine
62,5 ml (5 tablespoons) flour
110 g Cheddar cheese, grated
275 ml milk
50 ml liquid from the can of asparagus
2 ml (½ teaspoon) salt
2 ml (½ teaspoon) pepper
2 small tomatoes, halved
Garnish:
finely chopped parsley

Serves 4;   kJ per portion 1 100;   Prep time 10 min;   Cooking time 10 min.

1. Place 3 asparagus spears in the centre of each slice of ham and roll it up. Place rolls in a shallow casserole.
2. Melt the butter or margarine in a small saucepan, remove from the heat and stir in the flour to make a smooth paste. Return saucepan to the stove and cook for 3 minutes, stirring all the time.
3. Gradually add the milk and then the asparagus liquid, stirring constantly. Bring to the boil and, stirring, boil until thickened.
4. Mix in the cheese, salt and pepper and pour the sauce over the rolls. Arrange the halved tomatoes around the rolls.
5. Bake in the oven at 180°C (350°F) until the cheese browns, 5 to 10 minutes. Serve at once, garnished with parsley.

360 g cooked chicken, minced
600 ml Béchamel sauce
(recipe p. 179)
2 egg yolks
5 egg whites, stiffly beaten but
not dry
5 ml (1 teaspoon) dried
tarragon leaves
5 ml (1 teaspoon) salt
2 ml (½ teaspoon) pepper

289   Chicken soufflé

Serves 5;   kJ per portion 1 200;   Prep time 45 min;   Cooking time 35 min.

1. Make the Béchamel sauce in a large saucepan; add the chicken and tarragon and season with salt and pepper.
2. Remove the saucepan from the stove and stir in the egg yolks, mixing thoroughly.
3. Fold the beaten egg whites carefully into the chicken sauce, adjust seasoning if necessary, and pour into a greased soufflé dish.
4. Bake in the oven at 180°C (350°F) for approximately 25 minutes, until the soufflé is well risen and firm to the touch. Serve immediately.

Variation: For a ham soufflé replace the cooked chicken with the same amount of cooked minced ham.

---

800 g chicken livers, thinly
sliced
4 rashers bacon, rinds
removed, diced
1 large onion, finely chopped
300 g raw rice
700 ml hot chicken stock
50 ml sherry
25 ml soy sauce
25 ml (2 tablespoons) butter or
margarine
25 ml oil
2 ml (½ teaspoon) dried thyme
12,5 ml (1 tablespoon) parsley,
finely chopped
5 ml (1 teaspoon) salt
5 ml (1 teaspoon) pepper

290   Chicken liver risotto

Serves 6;   kJ per portion 1 410;   Prep time 15 min;   Cooking time 30 min.

1. In a large frying-pan, heat the butter or margarine and oil and sauté the onion and bacon until the onion is soft.
2. Add the rice and chicken livers and fry for a few minutes, tossing with a fork.
3. Add the chicken stock, sherry and thyme and simmer, covered, until all the stock has been absorbed, about 25 minutes.
4. Mix in the parsley and soy sauce and cook for a further 5 minutes. Add more salt and pepper if necessary and serve at once.

Note: Leftover rice may be used. Fry the onion, bacon and livers, then add the sherry, thyme, parsley, salt and pepper. Add the rice and simmer, tossing with a fork, until all the liquid has been absorbed.

---

375 ml (1½ cups) cooked
turkey, diced
85 g canned or fresh
mushrooms, finely chopped
125 ml (½ cup) onion, finely
chopped
12,5 ml (1 tablespoon) butter
or margarine
250 ml medium white sauce
(p. 179)
125 ml (½ cup) Cheddar
cheese, grated
37,5 ml (3 tablespoons) stuffed
green olives, thinly sliced
125 ml (½ cup) cream
crackers, crushed
12,5 ml lemon juice
12,5 ml (1 tablespoon) butter
or margarine, melted
500 ml (2 cups) cooked
macaroni

291   Turkey au gratin

Serves 4;   kJ per portion 1 800;   Prep time 20 min;   Cooking time 1 hour

1. Melt the butter or margarine in a frying-pan and sauté the onion in it until tender.
2. Prepare the white sauce, then combine it with the onion, turkey, mushrooms, cheese, olives and lemon juice in a large bowl.
3. Fold in the macaroni and transfer the mixture to a 1,5 litre casserole.
4. Combine the cracker crumbs with the melted butter or margarine in a bowl and sprinkle over the casserole.
5. Bake, uncovered, in the oven at 180°C (350°F) until heated through, about 50 minutes. Serve at once.

250 g cold cooked chicken, cubed
120 g mushrooms, thinly sliced
120 g frozen peas
25 ml (2 tablespoons) butter or margarine
62,5 ml (5 tablespoons) flour
300 ml milk
60 g canned anchovy fillets
5 ml (1 teaspoon) salt
2 ml (½ teaspoon) pepper

292 Chicken fricassée

Serves 4;   kJ per portion 1 200;   Prep time 30 min;   Cooking time 20 min.

1. Melt the butter or margarine in a large frying-pan, add the mushrooms and sauté until tender.
2. Remove the pan from the stove, stir in the flour and gradually blend in the milk.
3. Return the frying-pan to the stove, bring to the boil and boil, stirring all the time, until the sauce thickens.
4. Stir in the chicken cubes and the peas and simmer, stirring occasionally, until the ingredients are heated through, 5 to 10 minutes.
5. Add salt and pepper, then transfer the fricassée to a heated serving dish and serve decorated with the anchovy fillets arranged in a lattice pattern.

---

750 g cooked turkey meat, finely chopped
225 g cooked pork, minced
1 onion, finely chopped
50 g canned mushrooms, thinly sliced
120 g canned asparagus tips, drained and finely chopped
2 egg yolks
50 g (4 tablespoons) flour
25 ml oil
600 ml stock
juice of 1 lemon
50 ml single cream
1 clove garlic, crushed
2 ml (½ teaspoon) salt
2 ml (½ teaspoon) pepper

293 Turkey fricassée

Serves 4-6;   kJ per portion 1 580;   Prep time 15 min;   Cooking time 10 min.

1. Heat the oil in a large frying-pan and fry the onion in it until soft but not browned.
2. Add the flour and cook for 1 to 2 minutes without browning, stirring continuously.
3. Gradually stir in the stock, bring to the boil, then add the mushrooms, garlic and turkey meat.
4. Form the pork into small balls and add to the pan.
5. Stir in the lemon juice and salt and pepper; simmer for 5 minutes.
6. Add the asparagus and heat through, about 5 minutes.
7. In a small bowl, beat the egg yolks and cream together, then add to the turkey mixture, a little at a time. Heat through, but do not boil. Add more salt and pepper if necessary and spoon the mixture into a heated serving dish. Serve at once with rice and peas.

Variations:
1. Use cooked chicken or duck instead of turkey.
2. Use left-over venison and minced cooked Kasseler rib chops instead of the pork.

---

400 g cooked turkey, coarsely chopped
1 green pepper, seeded and finely chopped
100 g mushrooms, thinly sliced
2 medium tomatoes, thinly sliced
200 g raw rice
1 medium onion, finely chopped
a little butter
500 ml chicken stock
5 ml (1 teaspoon) salt
2 ml (½ teaspoon) pepper
Garnish:
chopped parsley

294 Turkey with fried rice

Serves 4;   kJ per portion 1 680;   Prep time 10 min;   Cooking time 25 min.

1. Melt the butter in a large frying-pan and sauté the onion and green pepper until tender.
2. Add the rice and sauté for 2 minutes more, then stir in the chicken stock, cover, and simmer for 10 minutes.
3. Stir in the turkey, mushrooms and tomatoes, season with salt and pepper and simmer for another 10 minutes. Serve at once.

Variation: Use cooked chicken or duck instead of the turkey.

12,5 ml (1 tablespoon) curry powder
12,5 ml (1 tablespoon) flour
12,5 ml (1 tablespoon) brown sugar
2 ml (½ teaspoon) mustard powder
2 bay leaves or lemon leaves
4 peppercorns
2 onions, thinly sliced
1 green pepper, seeded and thinly sliced
1 clove garlic, crushed
125 ml (½ cup) dried apricots
12,5 ml vinegar
250 ml water
10 ml (2 teaspoons) salt

295   Curry marinade or sauce   (F)

Makes 250 ml;   Prep time 15 min;   Cooking time 10 min.

1. Combine all the ingredients except the vinegar, water, onion, green pepper and apricots in a saucepan.
2. Add the vinegar and the water to the dry ingredients, mixing well. Add the onion, green pepper and apricots.
3. Simmer over medium heat, stirring all the time, until the sauce thickens.
4. Remove from the stove and cool (f) to use as a marinade or use hot as a sauce for meat.

Note:
● Curry sauce is an excellent marinade for pork chops. Leave chops in the marinade for 24 hours. Remove and grill over live coals. Heat the marinade and serve with the chops as a sauce.
● After freezing, heat slowly if using the mixture as a sauce; thaw completely if using it as a marinade. Do not freeze for longer than 4 weeks, as the spices might change the flavour if frozen for longer.

1 onion, finely chopped
2 cloves garlic, crushed
25 ml chutney
25 ml tomato sauce
25 ml Worcester sauce
5 ml prepared mustard
5 ml (1 teaspoon) brown sugar
12,5 ml brown vinegar
5 ml (1 teaspoon) salt
freshly ground black pepper

296   Marinade for steak

Prep time 10 min.

1. Mix all the ingredients together.
2. Pour over the meat and leave for 6 hours, turning twice.

Note: Sufficient for 700 g fillet or rump steak

1 onion, finely chopped
2 cloves garlic, crushed
12,5 ml honey
25 ml chutney
50 ml tomato sauce
25 ml Worcester sauce
12,5 ml lemon juice
5 ml (1 teaspoon) paprika
50 ml oil
5 ml (1 teaspoon) Aromat or Fondor

297   Marinade for chicken

Prep time 10 min.

1. Mix all the ingredients.
2. Marinate the chicken pieces in it for 4 hours, turning occasionally.

Note:
● Grill the chicken over a deep slow fire, not over flames, and baste it with the remaining marinade as it cooks.
● Sufficient for 1,4 kg chicken pieces.

2 onions, grated
4 cloves garlic, crushed
10 ml (2 teaspoons) fresh thyme, finely chopped
5 ml (1 teaspoon) dried rosemary
125 ml olive oil
25 ml lemon juice
10 ml (2 teaspoons) Aromat or Fondor
pinch freshly ground black pepper

298   Herb marinade

Prep time 5 min.

1. Combine all the ingredients in a bowl.
2. Marinate meat in it for 24 hours.

Note:
● Sufficient for 1 boned leg of lamb.
● Barbecue the lamb over live coals, basting with the marinade as it cooks.

1 carrot, finely chopped
1 onion, finely chopped
1 shallot, finely chopped
150 ml oil
125 ml wine vinegar
800 ml dry white wine
1 whole clove
1 bay leaf
2 sprigs thyme or 2 ml
(½ teaspoon) dried thyme
5 ml (1 teaspoon) salt

299   White wine marinade for rabbit

Makes 1 litre;   Prep time 10 min;   Cooking time 45 min.

1. Heat the oil in a saucepan over very low heat.
2. Add the vegetables, herbs and spices and brown lightly, stirring frequently with a wooden spoon.
3. Add the vinegar and wine and simmer for 45 minutes.
4. Cool completely, then marinate the rabbit in it for 12 hours.

---

1 small onion, grated
25 ml oil
12,5 ml lemon juice
2 ml (½ teaspoon) dried marjoram
2 ml (½ teaspoon) dried thyme
1 large clove garlic, crushed
12,5 ml soy sauce
a few grindings black pepper

300   Marinade for grilled lamb chops

Prep time 10 min.

1. Shake all the ingredients together in a screw-top jar until completely blended.
2. Pour over the lamb chops and leave for 4 hours, turning twice.

Note: Sufficient for 700 to 800 g chops.

---

125 g plain flour
1 large egg
150 ml milk
150 ml water
25 ml hot dripping from roast
pinch salt

301   Yorkshire pudding

Serves 4-6;   kJ per portion 290;   Prep time 30 min;   Cooking time 30 min.

1. Sift the flour and salt into a mixing bowl and make a hollow in the centre. Break the egg into the hollow and add the milk.
2. Using a wooden spoon and mixing from the centre, gradually incorporate the flour into the liquid. Add a little of the water and continue beating until the batter is smooth and shiny. Stir in the rest of the water.
3. Spoon a little dripping into each cup of a patty tin. Fill each one with batter.
4. Bake on the top shelf of the oven at 200°C (400°F) until golden brown and well-risen, about 25 minutes. Serve at once with the roast.

Note: Do not overfill the patty tin cups as the puddings may overflow as they rise.

---

1 litre (4 cups) fresh white breadcrumbs
85 g seedless raisins
finely grated rind and juice of 1 orange
rind of 1 lemon, finely grated
2 eggs, beaten
50 ml (4 tablespoons) butter or margarine, cubed
2 ml (½ teaspoon) salt
2 ml (½ teaspoon) freshly ground black pepper
50 ml (4 tablespoons) parsley, finely chopped

302   Orange and raisin stuffing

Prep time 10 min.

1. Combine the breadcrumbs, salt, pepper, lemon and orange rind in a bowl.
2. Add the butter or margarine and rub it in until it is well distributed through the mixture.
3. Stir in the raisins and parsley and bind the mixture with the orange juice and beaten eggs.

Note: Sufficient to stuff a 5 kg turkey.

125 g self-raising flour
60 g suet
5 ml (1 teaspoon) dried mixed herbs
2 ml (½ teaspoon) salt
water to mix

303 Herb dumplings

Serves 4-5;   kJ per portion 290;   Prep time 30 min;   Cooking time 15-20 min.

1. Sift the flour and salt into a basin.
2. Cut in the suet with a knife, blend in the herbs and stir in enough water to bind. The dough should be soft enough to form into balls.
3. Divide into 8 to 10 portions and, with floured hands, roll into balls (dumplings).
4. Check that the liquid in the stew or casserole is boiling, then add the dumplings.
5. Cook the dumplings for at least 15 minutes, making sure that the liquid boils steadily until the dumplings are cooked.

Variations:

1. Add 10 ml (2 teaspoons) finely chopped parsley or chives instead of the mixed herbs.
2. Add 10 ml (2 teaspoons) finely chopped salami or crumbled, crisply fried bacon instead of the mixed herbs.

Note: These dumplings are an excellent accompaniment to boiled beef, chicken, bacon, stews and casseroles.

50 g oatmeal
1 small onion, finely chopped
5 ml (1 teaspoon) dried mixed herbs
25 ml (2 tablespoons) prepared shredded suet
12,5 ml cold water
5 ml (1 teaspoon) salt

304 Oatmeal stuffing

Prep time 10 min.

1. Mix the oatmeal, suet, onion, salt and herbs in a large bowl.
2. Stir in the water, mixing well to bind the mixture.

Note: Sufficient to stuff 1 chicken.

500 ml (2 cups) fresh white breadcrumbs
85 g shredded suet
125 g mushrooms, finely chopped
25 ml (2 tablespoons) fresh parsley, finely chopped
1 medium onion, finely chopped
grated rind and juice of 1 lemon
1 large egg
5 ml (1 teaspoon) Aromat or Fondor
2 ml (½ teaspoon) pepper

305 Mushroom stuffing

Prep time 10 min.

1. Mix the breadcrumbs and suet in a bowl.
2. Stir in the mushrooms, parsley, onion, Aromat or Fondor, pepper, lemon juice and rind.
3. Bind the ingredients with the egg and pack the stuffing into the meat.

Note: Sufficient to stuff 1 chicken or 1 leg of lamb.

500 ml (2 cups) fresh white
breadcrumbs
60 g prepared shredded suet
1 medium onion, finely
chopped
12,5 ml (1 tablespoon) fresh
sage, finely chopped or
10 ml (2 teaspoons) dried sage
1 large egg
12,5 ml milk
5 ml (1 teaspoon) salt
2 ml (½ teaspoon) pepper
boiling, salted water

306   Sage and onion stuffing

Prep time 10 min;   Cooking time 5 min.

1. In a bowl, mix together the breadcrumbs and suet. Season with the salt and pepper.
2. Blanch the chopped onion in boiling, salted water for 2 to 3 minutes, then drain well and stir into the breadcrumb mixture. Stir in the sage.
3. Beat the egg and milk together in another bowl. Add to the dry ingredients to bind them, and pack the stuffing into the meat.

Note:
● Raw onion can also be used.
● This is sufficient to stuff a chicken or a leg of lamb.

---

500 ml (2 cups) dry white
breadcrumbs
12,5 ml (1 tablespoon) onion,
finely chopped
1 egg (optional)
5 ml (1 teaspoon) parsley,
finely chopped
25 ml (2 tablespoons) butter or
margarine
125 ml milk
2 ml (½ teaspoon) dried thyme
2 ml (½ teaspoon) celery salt
5 ml (1 teaspoon) salt
pinch pepper

307   Bread stuffing

Prep time 15 min;   Cooking time 10 min.

1. Melt the butter or margarine in a small frying-pan and brown the onion in it.
2. Add the onion to the other ingredients (except the egg) in a small bowl and mix well.
3. If necessary, bind the mixture with the egg.

Note:
● Sufficient to stuff 1 chicken.
● Make 1½ times the quantity to stuff a turkey.

---

500 ml (2 cups) prunes, stoned,
soaked and finely chopped
1 large onion, finely chopped
6 rashers bacon, diced
500 ml (2 cups) fresh white
breadcrumbs
50 ml hot meat stock
5 ml (1 teaspoon) salt
pinch pepper

308   Prune and bacon stuffing

Prep time 15 min;   Cooking time 15 min.

1. Fry the bacon until crisp.
2. Add the onion and fry until transparent but not brown.
3. Combine the onion and bacon mixture with all the other ingredients in a bowl and use as a stuffing for venison.

Note: Sufficient for 1 leg of venison or venison roll.

---

450 g chestnuts
450 ml chicken stock
170 g ham, finely chopped
100 g butter or margarine
2 bay leaves
water
2 ml (½ teaspoon) salt
2 ml (½ teaspoon) pepper

309   Chestnut stuffing

Prep time 15 min;   Cooking time 25 min.

1. Slit the skins of the chestnuts and boil steadily in a saucepan with water to cover for 5 to 10 minutes. Lift the chestnuts out; remove the shells and inner skins.
2. Place the stock, shelled chestnuts and bay leaves in a saucepan and simmer for 15 to 20 minutes.
3. Remove the chestnuts from the stock and chop them finely. Discard the bay leaves.
4. Combine the chestnuts, ham, and butter or margarine in a bowl and season with the salt and pepper.

Note: Sufficient to stuff 1 chicken.

310 Forcemeat stuffing

250 g pork or beef sausage meat
125 ml (½ cup) fresh breadcrumbs
12,5 ml (1 tablespoon) parsley, finely chopped
1 egg
pinch dried mixed herbs
5 ml (1 teaspoon) salt
2 ml (½ teaspoon) pepper

Prep time 10 min.

Combine all the ingredients in a bowl.

Note:
- Sufficient to stuff 1 chicken.
- The stuffing can also be used to make forcemeat balls as accompaniments to poultry and roasts.

311 Ham and horseradish stuffing

170 g uncooked ham or bacon, minced
375 ml (1½ cups) fresh breadcrumbs
1 green pepper, seeded and finely chopped
10 ml (2 teaspoons) horseradish, grated
1 egg
50 ml (4 tablespoons) shredded suet
2 ml (½ teaspoon) salt
2 ml (½ teaspoon) pepper

Prep time 10 min.

Combine all the ingredients in a bowl.

Note: Sufficient for 1 chicken.

312 Rosemary butter stuffing

100 g butter
1 medium onion, finely chopped
500 ml (2 cups) fresh breadcrumbs
1 egg
12,5 ml (1 tablespoon) fresh rosemary, finely chopped
2 ml (½ teaspoon) salt
2 ml (½ teaspoon) pepper

Prep time 15 min;   Cooking time 4 min.

1. Heat the butter in a frying-pan and toss the breadcrumbs in it until crisp.
2. Add the onion, egg, rosemary, salt and pepper and mix well.

Note: Sufficient to stuff 1 chicken or to serve 6 people if used as a garnish with veal.

313 Raisin and walnut stuffing

125 ml (½ cup) seedless raisins, finely chopped
125 ml (½ cup) walnuts, finely chopped
300 g fresh breadcrumbs
125 g butter or margarine, melted
25 ml (2 tablespoons) parsley, finely chopped
2 ml (½ teaspoon) dried thyme
pinch dried mace
2 ml (½ teaspoon) salt, Aromat or Fondor
pinch lemon pepper

Prep time 10 min.

1. Combine the spices in a bowl, add the breadcrumbs and mix thoroughly.
2. Stir in the melted butter or margarine, then add the nuts, raisins and parsley and blend well.
3. If the mixture is too dry, moisten with a little milk.

Note:
- Sufficient for 1 chicken.
- 7 slices of crustless bread, crumbled, will make 300 g fresh breadcrumbs.

173

125 g dried apricots, soaked
overnight in water
225 g walnuts, finely chopped
2 celery stalks, thinly sliced
37,5 ml (3 tablespoons) butter
or margarine
4 medium onions, finely
chopped
375 ml (1½ cups) fresh
breadcrumbs
25 ml (2 tablespoons) parsley,
finely chopped
5 ml (1 teaspoon) salt
2 ml (½ teaspoon) pepper

314   Apricot, celery and walnut stuffing

Prep time 15 min;   Cooking time 5 min.

1. Drain the apricots and chop finely.
2. Melt the butter or margarine in a frying-pan and sauté the onions in it until transparent.
3. Add the celery, apricots and walnuts and cook over high heat, stirring continuously, for 4 minutes.
4. Place the mixture in a bowl and allow to cool.
5. Add the parsley and breadcrumbs, blending well, and season with salt and pepper.

Note: Sufficient for 1 turkey.

12,5 ml (1 tablespoon) flour
500 ml water
dripping from the roast

315   Gravy

Prep time 10 min;   Cooking time 10 min.

1. After the roast has been removed, drain almost all the dripping from the roasting pan, leaving about 25 ml.
2. Stir the flour into the dripping in the pan and cook gently over low heat until lightly browned.
3. Remove the pan from the stove and gradually blend in the water.
4. When the gravy is smooth, return the pan to the stove and bring to the boil, stirring all the time.
5. Add salt and pepper if necessary and pour the gravy into a sauceboat for serving.

---

giblets (neck, gizzard, heart,
liver) from duck or chicken
50 ml (4 tablespoons) flour
dripping from pan in which
poultry was roasted
12,5 ml (1 tablespoon) parsley,
finely chopped
5 ml (1 teaspoon) salt
2 ml (½ teaspoon) pepper
salted water

316   Giblet gravy

Makes 500 ml;   Prep time 20 min;   Cooking time 3 hours

1. Boil the neck, gizzard and heart in salted water until tender, about 2 hours.
2. Add the liver and boil a further 15 minutes.
3. Drain the stock and make it up to 500 ml with water if necessary.
4. Dice the meat, discarding the gristle and bone.
5. Heat the dripping in a saucepan, stir in the flour and cook until foamy.
6. Gradually stir in the stock and cook, stirring continuously, until the gravy thickens, about 3 minutes.
7. Stir in the diced giblets and parsley, season with salt and pepper and serve with the roast poultry.

SAVOURY BUTTERS TO SERVE WITH GRILLED MEAT AND FISH

Basic Method
1. Cream 50 g salted or unsalted butter until soft and oily.
2. Combine well with the other ingredients.
3. Chill for 2 hours.
4. Shape into pats with waxproof paper or foil.

Variations

Kind	Add to 50 g butter	Method	Serve with
Anchovy	5 ml lemon juice; 3 anchovy fillets, drained and finely chopped	Basic	Grilled steak Grilled veal
Garlic	1 to 2 cloves garlic, crushed; 5 ml (1 teaspoon) parsley, finely chopped; 5 ml lemon juice	Basic	Grilled steak Spread on French bread, heat in oven and serve with grilled meat or fish
Bercy	2 spring onions, finely chopped; 10 ml dry white wine; 10 ml (2 teaspoons) parsley, finely chopped	1. Simmer spring onions in the wine until 5 ml remain. Cool. 2. Continue with basic.	Grilled steak Grilled lamb chops
Crayfish	50 g crayfish shells and cooked trimmings, pounded in a mortar until fine	1. Blend the crayfish with the butter. 2. Place in a small saucepan standing in a larger pan of hot water, allowing the butter to melt slowly. 3. Pour the mixture through a muslin cloth secured over a basin of iced water. 4. Twist the cloth to squeeze all the butter out. The butter will solidify in the iced water. 5. Spoon the butter out of the water and dry on a muslin cloth.	Seafood stews, casseroles and soups
Curry	5 ml (1 teaspoon) onion, finely chopped; oil for frying; 5 ml (1 teaspoon) curry powder; 2 ml (½ teaspoon) turmeric; 2 ml (½ teaspoon) ground ginger; 10 ml lemon juice	1. Sauté onion in a little oil for 1 minute. 2. Add curry powder, turmeric and ginger and cook for 2 minutes, stirring continuously. 3. Continue with basic.	Grilled pork Grilled lamb chops
Mustard	5 ml prepared French mustard; 5 ml lemon juice	Basic	Grilled steak, gammon, pork chops, lamb chops
Maitre d'hotel	5 ml (1 teaspoon) parsley, finely chopped; 5 ml lemon juice	Basic	Grilled steak
Paprika	5 ml (1 teaspoon) onion, grated; 5 ml (1 teaspoon) paprika; 5 ml white vinegar	Basic	Grilled veal chops, ham, grilled gammon

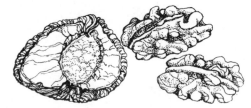

176

SAUCES

In the sauce lies the secret of many a famous dish, yet sauces derive from but a few basic methods which, once mastered, allow for almost endless variety.

A sauce is perhaps best described as a liquid which has been thickened by adding one or a combination of the following: a *roux* (see below), a starch (e.g. flour, cornflour or arrowroot), egg yolks or a *beurre manié* (see p. 178). But this is only the starting point, for to this thickened base one can add any of hundreds of ingredients, either alone or in a combination. Sauce-making is creative and, if imaginatively applied, subtly enhances the flavour, appearance and succulence of almost any dish.

Making a roux

A *roux*-based sauce is made by blending flour into an equal quantity of a melted fat such as butter, margarine or oil, and then adding a liquid.

Melt the fat in a heavy-bottomed saucepan over low heat. Then blend the flour into it and cook the resulting paste *(roux)* to one of three stages: a light yellow colour for a white *roux* (white sauce); a light fawn colour for a blond *roux* (velouté sauce); or a light brown for a brown *roux* (brown sauce). To prevent burning, stir the *roux* continuously with a wooden spoon or wire whisk as it cooks. Once the *roux* is ready, add the liquid a little at a time and stir continuously to avoid lumps, and combine well. Remove the *roux* from the stove and allow it to cool slightly. With a wooden spoon or a wire whisk, work at any lumps that remain. When smooth, return the sauce to the stove and, stirring all the time, heat it gently until thick and creamy.

Note:
- It is important to stir the *roux* and the sauce at all times to prevent lumps forming.
- The *roux* must never be cooked at too high a temperature or too quickly.

Thickening a sauce with a starch

The starch, such as flour, cornflour or arrowroot, must first be mixed to a paste with *cold* water, stock or milk. Heat the rest and add a little of this to the cold paste, stirring all the time. Add the warm mixture to the hot liquid. Then heat slowly, stirring, until the sauce thickens.

Although white flour and cornflour may form the basis for both sweet and savoury sauces, a white *roux*-based sauce is more commonly used for savoury sauces and cornflour for sweet sauces. Cornflour is only used for savoury sauces when a slightly viscous, shiny consistency is required, for example, when making sweet and sour sauce.

Note:
- The cornflour paste may be stirred directly into a cold liquid and then heated.
- Use cornflour to thicken fruit sauces because it clarifies when cooked.

Using egg yolks to make a sauce

Egg yolks combined with cream, butter or oil thicken both cold sauces, for example mayonnaise, and hot ones such as Hollandaise sauce. If you need to incorporate beaten egg yolks into a hot liquid, a little of the hot liquid must be stirred into them separately first and the resulting mixture then added gradually to the rest of the hot liquid in the saucepan while being stirred continuously. The sauce is then heated and stirred until it reaches the desired thickness.

Beurre manié

A *beurre manié* consists of two parts of butter to one of flour, mixed to a smooth paste. It is added gradually to a boiling liquid, which is stirred all the time, and the sauce is brought back to the boil and then removed from the stove immediately.

Note:
- To make a perfect sauce, always use the correct utensils: a wooden spoon, a whisk or rotary beater for stirring and a heavy-bottomed saucepan just large enough to hold the sauce. If eggs are to be added to the sauce, use a double-boiler rather than a saucepan. If preparing a brown *roux*-based sauce, a fine-mesh strainer is essential, as these sauces often have to be strained.
- Use only the best quality ingredients to achieve the best results.

BASIC SAUCES

The basic **white** sauces of classic French cuisine are Béchamel and Velouté. There are four basic **brown** sauces – simple brown sauce, *jus lié*, *Espagnole* sauce and *demi-glace* – and two basic **emulsion** sauces: mayonnaise and Hollandaise sauce.

White sauces

White and brown *roux*-based sauces are made in basically the same way, with the proportion of fat and flour to the liquid depending on the consistency of the sauce required (see p. 180). The liquid is usually milk, or a mixture of milk and vegetable, white, chicken or fish stock.

The classic Béchamel sauce differs from the simple basic white sauce in that the liquid (milk) used to make a Béchamel sauce is flavoured first with shallots, carrots, celery, mace and peppercorns, which makes for a much tastier result.

Velouté sauce is a richer version of Béchamel – a well-flavoured stock is used and egg yolks and cream are added. Velouté sauces are always made to a consistency that allows the sauce to coat the food.

Simple white sauce

1. Bring the milk to simmering point.
2. Meanwhile, melt the butter in a heavy-based saucepan over low heat and remove from the stove.
3. Add the flour and stir to blend well. Return to the stove and cook for 2 minutes, stirring all the time. Remove from the stove.
4. Gradually add the liquid to the *roux,* stirring all the time.
5. Return to the stove and simmer over low heat for 5 minutes, stirring frequently. Season with salt and pepper.

Béchamel sauce

1. First prepare the liquid: place 1 small carrot, ½ onion, 1 celery stalk, mace, peppercorns and 250 ml milk in a heavy-based saucepan.
2. Bring the milk to simmering point over low heat. Remove from the stove, cover and leave for 30 minutes.
3. Strain the liquid through a fine sieve and discard the vegetables.
4. Continue as for white sauce, from step 2.

Note:
- If time permits, prepare a Béchamel rather than a simple white sauce; it has a far superior flavour.
- Do not allow the *roux* to colour while it is cooking.
- Using a lukewarm liquid will ensure that the sauce blends better.
- A sauce made with 250 ml liquid and 25 g each of fat and flour is enough to serve 4 people.

300 g powdered skimmed milk
120 g flour
250 g vegetable fat
5 ml (1 teaspoon) salt

White sauce mix

1. Sift the powdered milk, salt and flour together, mixing very well.
2. Grate the vegetable fat and rub into the dry milk and flour mix.
3. Store in plastic containers in the freezer or refrigerator until needed.
4. To make up:

Thin white sauce – 40 g mix to 200 ml cold water, salt and pepper
Medium white sauce – 60 g mix to 200 ml cold water, salt and pepper
Thick white sauce – 80 g mix to 200 ml cold water, salt and pepper

Method:
1. Mix the sauce mix with a little of the water to form a paste.
2. Add the rest of the water and heat gently, stirring all the time. Boil for 3 minutes until smooth and thick.

Note:
- Skimmed milk scalds easily, so keep the heat low.
- The sauce may be used as a base: add cheese, cream or herbs as desired.

Consistencies for Béchamel sauce

Consistency	Amount of flour and butter	Amount of Liquid	Uses
Thin (Pouring) Sauce
At boiling point this sauce should be thick enough to glaze the back of a wooden spoon.	15 g of each	250 ml	Basis for soups and for sauces
Medium (Coating) Sauce
This sauce should be thick enough to coat the back of a wooden spoon at boiling point.	25 g of each	250 ml	For coating foods
Thick (Panada) Sauce
This sauce should be very thick at boiling point.	50 g of each	250 ml	Basis for soufflés and croquettes

Variations of the basic white and Béchamel sauces

Sauce	Additions	Method	Serve with
Anchovy
250 ml Béchamel sauce	5 ml anchovy essence or 3 crushed anchovy fillets.	Stir in just before serving.	Poached or steamed fish.
Caper
250 ml Béchamel sauce	20 ml (4 teaspoons) capers;
5 ml lemon juice.	Use half milk and half fish or vegetable stock for the liquid when making the basic sauce. Stir in capers and lemon juice just before serving.	Lamb, fish or cured meat such as ham.
Celery
250 ml Béchamel sauce	3 celery stalks;
10 ml lemon juice.	Chop celery, steam for 20 minutes, purée. Stir in just before serving.	Chicken, ham, fish.
Cheese
250 ml white sauce	50 g Cheddar cheese;
2 ml (½ teaspoon) mustard powder.	Grate cheese, mix with mustard and stir in just before serving.	Fish, vegetables, pasta, eggs, meat.
Mornay
250 ml Béchamel sauce	50 g Gruyère or Parmesan cheese;
1 egg yolk and
50 ml cream (optional)	Grate cheese, stir in just before serving (beat egg yolk and cream together; add carefully to sauce if desired).	Fish, pasta, chicken, vegetables.
Mushroom
250 ml Béchamel sauce	50 g fresh or canned mushrooms;
10 g butter.	Melt butter, sauté sliced mushrooms. Stir in just before serving. Use equal quantities milk and vegetable stock for the liquid when making the basic sauce.	Chicken, fish, veal.

Sauce	Additions	Method	Serve with
Mustard 250 ml white sauce	5 ml (1 teaspoon) mustard powder; 5 ml lemon juice.	Stir into white sauce just before serving.	Fish, veal.
Onion 250 ml Béchamel sauce	3 medium onions, finely chopped; 10 ml onion essence.	Sauté onion in a little oil till transparent, add to sauce with onion essence.	Fish, lamb veal.
Herb 250 ml Béchamel sauce	10 ml (2 teaspoons) tarragon; 10 ml (2 teaspoons) parsley; 10 ml (2 teaspoons) chervil.	Chop herbs finely, stir into sauce with 20 ml wine and 50 ml cream.	Fish, veal, vegetables.
Parsley 250 ml Béchamel sauce	10 ml (2 teaspoons) finely chopped parsley; 5 ml lemon juice.	Stir into sauce.	Fish, vegetables.
Aurore 250 ml Béchamel sauce	25 ml tomato concentrate.	Stir in just before serving.	Vegetables.
Nantua 250 ml Béchamel sauce	25 ml (2 tablespoons) crayfish butter (p. 175)	Stir in and serve.	Seafood.

25 g butter
25 g flour
250 ml hot chicken, white, fish
or vegetable stock
mushroom peelings or stems
(optional)
2 ml lemon juice
2 ml (½ teaspoon) salt
1 egg yolk (optional)
30 ml double cream (optional)

Velouté sauce

Makes 250 ml; kJ per portion 300; Prep time 15 min; Cooking time 10 min.

1. Melt the butter in a saucepan over low heat, remove from the stove and stir in the flour. Return to the stove.
2. Cook over low heat, stirring continuously to make a white *roux,* approximately 3 minutes.
3. Remove from the stove and gradually add hot but not boiling stock, stirring all the time. Add the mushrooms if desired.
4. Return to the stove, bring to the boil, then simmer for 10 minutes. Strain through a fine sieve and season with the salt and lemon juice.
5. For a richer sauce, add the egg yolk and cream: Whisk the egg yolk and cream together in a bowl. Add 25 ml of the hot sauce to the egg mixture, whisking all the time. Pour the egg sauce mixture into the saucepan in a thin stream, whisking continuously.
6. Return the saucepan to the stove, bring to boiling point and serve immediately.

Note:
- The mushrooms are optional, but give extra flavour. Use 3 to 4 mushrooms for every 250 ml stock.
- Use butter rather than margarine for a richer taste.
- Do not allow a Velouté sauce to boil after adding the egg and cream.

Variations of Velouté sauce

Sauce	Additions	Method	Serve with
Curry 250 ml Velouté sauce	5 ml (1 teaspoon) curry powder.	Add the curry powder to the stock.	Lamb, ham, pork.
Bercy 250 ml Velouté sauce (with egg and cream and fish stock)	50 ml white wine; 2 shallots, finely chopped; 1 sprig parsley, finely chopped; 25 g butter.	Simmer shallots in wine for 10 minutes; stir into sauce with butter and parsley.	Fish, sole.
Chivry 250 ml Velouté sauce (made with chicken stock)	250 ml (1 cup) spinach leaves; 2-3 sprigs each of tarragon, chervil and chives.	Boil the spinach and herbs for 5 minutes, purée with enough cooking liquid to give 15 ml purée. Stir into sauce.	Fish, chicken.
Garlic 250 ml Velouté sauce	1 garlic clove, crushed; bouquet garni; 4 peppercorns.	Add to sauce and strain before adding eggs and cream.	Eggs, vegetables, poultry.
Polonaise 250 ml Velouté sauce (made with chicken stock)	75 ml sour cream, or plain yoghurt; 5 ml (1 teaspoon) grated horseradish or horseradish sauce; 5 ml (1 teaspoon) chopped fennel; 5 ml lemon juice.	Stir all ingredients into sauce and serve.	Grilled lamb, steaks.
Suprême 250 ml Velouté sauce (made with chicken stock)	Replace the egg yolk and cream with 3 egg yolks and 150 ml double cream		Breast of chicken, ham.

Note: Other spices, herbs and vegetables, such as asparagus, mushrooms and paprika, can be added to Velouté sauce.

When things go wrong with a white, Béchamel or Velouté sauce

Fault	Cause	Solution
Sauce is lumpy	Fat too hot when flour was added. *Roux* not cooked sufficiently. Liquid added too quickly and not stirred enough.	Force the hot sauce through a coarse sieve into a clean saucepan, or blend in a liquidiser at high speed for 1 to 2 minutes. Reheat over low heat, stirring vigorously.

Fault	Cause	Solution
Sauce has raw taste or looks dull	Starch insufficiently cooked.	Continue cooking.
Greasy sauce, where fat and flour separate	Too much fat. *Roux* overcooked.	Remove saucepan from the stove and soak up the surface fat with absorbent paper towels.
Sauce is too thick	Proportions of flour and fat are wrong. Sauce allowed to evaporate during cooking.	Beat in more hot milk or stock, a little at a time, and add more salt and pepper if necessary.
Sauce is too thin	Proportions of ingredients are wrong. *Roux* either over- or undercooked.	Boil rapidly over high heat, stirring all the time, until the consistency is right.

Brown sauces

The basic brown sauces – simple brown sauce, *jus lié,* Espagnole sauce and *demi-glace* – are normally associated with meat and game, but also go well with vegetables, or can be used to bind fillings for pies, casseroles and stews. Although all four of the basic sauces can be used to make a great variety of sauces, Espagnole sauce and *demi-glace* are used most often.

1 carrot, finely chopped
1 onion, finely chopped
20 g dripping or 25 ml oil or
12,5 ml oil and 15 g butter
20 g flour
400 ml meat stock
5 ml (1 teaspoon) salt
5 ml (1 teaspoon) pepper

Simple brown sauce

Makes 250 ml; kJ per portion 150; Prep time 15 min; Cooking time 1 hour

1. Melt the dripping, oil, or oil and butter in a saucepan over low heat.
2. Add the vegetables and cook gently until they begin to brown, about 7 minutes.
3. Remove from the stove and stir in the flour smoothly.
4. Return to the stove and cook, still stirring, until a brown *roux* is obtained, 5 to 7 minutes.
5. Remove from the stove and gradually add the stock, stirring all the time.
6. Bring to the boil, then reduce the heat and simmer, half-covered, for 45 minutes.
7. Strain through a fine sieve and season with the salt and pepper.

Note:
- The vegetables must cook gently, not brown.
- The *roux* must be cooked slowly, otherwise it might burn and give the sauce a bitter taste.
- The stock must be cool or slightly warm, never hot.
- The sauce must be simmered very slowly and half-covered to obtain the best results.
- If the sauce becomes too thick, dilute it with a little extra stock, water, wine or sherry.
- If the sauce is too thin, boil it rapidly, uncovered, for a few minutes.

183

Jus lié

25 ml cold beef stock
220 ml hot beef stock
15 g cornflour
2 ml (½ teaspoon) salt
2 ml (½ teaspoon) pepper

Makes 250 ml; kJ per portion 180;   Prep time 10 min;   Cooking time 5 min.

1. Mix the cornflour and the cold stock in a basin to form a smooth paste. Remove the hot stock from the stove.
2. Stir the paste into the hot stock, return to the stove and bring to the boil. Reduce the heat and simmer for 3 minutes.
3. Season with the salt and pepper and serve.

Note: Use only the best quality stock.

Espagnole sauce   (F)

1 carrot, finely chopped
1 onion, finely chopped
1 stalk celery, finely chopped
25 g mushroom stalks, finely chopped
1 leek, finely chopped
50 g rindless streaky bacon, diced
50 g dripping or 25 g butter and 12,5 ml oil
50 g flour
700 ml beef stock
1 bouquet garni
4 peppercorns
250 g tomatoes, skinned and coarsely chopped or 10 ml tomato purée
5 ml (1 teaspoon) salt
freshly ground pepper

Makes 500 ml; kJ per portion 200;   Prep time 45 min;   Cooking time 1½ hour

1. Melt the dripping or oil and butter in a heavy-based saucepan and add the bacon. Sauté for 2 minutes.
2. Add all the vegetables and sauté until they begin to change colour.
3. Remove the saucepan from the stove and stir in the flour, a little at a time. Return to the stove and cook, stirring continuously, until a brown *roux* is obtained, 5 to 10 minutes.
4. Remove from the stove, and add the stock gradually, stirring all the time.
5. Return to the stove and bring to the boil, stirring continuously. Add the bouquet garni and the peppercorns and simmer for 30 minutes, skimming (method p. 42) every now and then.
6. Add the tomatoes or purée and simmer, half-covered, for a further 45 minutes.
7. Strain the sauce through a coarse sieve, pressing all the juices from the vegetables until only a dry pulp remains. Discard the pulp (f).
8. Reheat, season with salt and pepper and serve.

Note:
- This sauce freezes well.
- Use the sauce as it is or as a basis for other sauces.

Demi-glace sauce

250 ml Espagnole sauce
150 ml jellied beef stock (recipe 82)

Makes 250 ml; kJ per portion 200; Prep time 10 min; Cooking time 30 min.

1. Combine the Espagnole sauce and the stock and pour into a heavy-based saucepan.
2. Simmer, half-covered, until the sauce is reduced to 250 ml, about 30 minutes.
3. Add salt and pepper, if necessary, and serve.

Note:
- The flavour of the stock used is very important – use only the best.
- If a brown sauce must be reduced in quantity, add only a very little salt beforehand and season just before serving.

Additions to Espagnole sauce and Demi-glace

- *Vegetables* sautéed in butter or simmered in wine before being added to the sauce.
- *Fruit* juice or lemon, orange or tangerine rind may be added. Fruit jellies such as quince, apple or gooseberry added to brown sauces make a delicious accompaniment to pork, ham and game.
- *Alcohol and wine.* Sweet or dry red or white wine, brandy and liqueurs can add zest to a sauce, but be careful not to add too much – they should complement, not overpower, the food with which they are to be served.
- Specially flavoured *vinegars,* such as tarragon vinegar, can give individuality to a sauce.
- Simmer *mustard, herbs or spices* in the sauce or stir in just before serving.
- Add *cream, truffles* or chopped, cooked *chicken livers* just before serving.

Classic brown roux-based sauces

Sauce	Additions	Method	Serve with
Bigarade 250 ml Espagnole sauce	50 g chopped shallots; 25 ml (2 tablespoons) butter; 2 Seville oranges; 150 ml red wine; 12,5 ml (1 tablespoon) redcurrant or quince jelly.	Sauté shallots in butter. Peel 1 orange, cut peel in strips. Squeeze citrus juice. Combine all ingredients in a saucepan, simmer for 8 minutes. Add to sauce, simmer for 5 minutes.	Duck.
Bourguignonne 250 ml Espagnole sauce	25 g chopped shallots; 12,5 ml (1 tablespoon) butter; 500 ml red wine; bouquet garni.	Sauté shallots in the butter, add all other ingredients, simmer for 30 minutes, uncovered, till reduced to 150 ml. Add sauce, simmer for 5 minutes. Strain and serve.	Red meat, poultry.
Chasseur 250 ml Espagnole sauce	30 ml (6 teaspoons) butter; 100 g thinly sliced mushrooms; 60 g chopped shallots; 175 ml dry white wine; 100 g tomatoes, skinned and finel chopped or 12,5 ml tomato purée, 12,5 ml (1 tablespoon) finely chopped parsley.	Sauté shallots in butter, add mushrooms, simmer for 2 minutes Add wine; simmer, uncovered, for 10 minutes. Add the tomatoes, simmer for 10 minutes Add sauce, heat through, add parsley and serve.	Steaks, rabbit, lamb.
Fines herbes 250 ml *demi-glace* sauce	5 ml (1 teaspoon) each of tarragon, chervil, chives, parsley and lemon juice; 180 ml dry white wine.	Bring wine to boiling point, add herbs, simmer for 10 minutes – add sauce. Strain and serve. (If desired the herbs may be left in the sauce.)	Eggs, fish, veal.
Madère 250 ml *demi-glace* sauce	125 ml Madeira wine.	Simmer wine for 5 minutes, add sauce, simmer another 5 minutes.	Veal, game, beef.
Lyonnaise 250 ml simple brown sauce	100 ml dry white wine; 50 g finely chopped onion; 10 ml (2 teaspoons) butter 1 sprig parsley	Sauté onions in butter, add wine, boil for 5 minutes. Add sauce, heat through, add parsley.	Venison, chicken.

Emulsion sauces

An emulsion sauce is one in which the ingredients are beaten together until totally blended. If they are not beaten sufficiently, they will separate. There are two basic emulsion sauces: mayonnaise, where the egg yolks are combined with oil and seasoning without cooking; and the Hollandaise sauces, where the egg yolks and butter are cooked gently together.

5 ml (1 teaspoon) mustard powder
5 ml (1 teaspoon) salt
5 ml (1 teaspoon) sugar
1 ml (¼ teaspoon) cayenne pepper
2 egg yolks, well-beaten
25 ml lemon juice
25 ml vinegar
250 ml olive oil or salad oil

Mayonnaise

Makes 300 ml;   kJ per portion 350;   Prep time 20 min.

1. Combine the dry ingredients thoroughly in a bowl.
2. Add the egg yolks to the dry ingredients and mix well.
3. Beat in 12,5 ml each of the lemon juice and vinegar.
4. Add the oil drop by drop, beating all the time, until all the oil has been added and absorbed. The mayonnaise should be thick and creamy and should hold its shape.
5. Add the rest of the lemon juice and the vinegar and whisk well.

Note:
- Use *fresh,* cool, but not cold, ingredients. Remove eggs from the refrigerator a few hours before the mayonnaise is to be made.
- The most important point to remember about making mayonnaise is that the ingredients must be beaten *all* the time.
- If the mayonnaise curdles – a result of adding the oil too rapidly – immediately add a few drops of cold water, beating all the time. If this is unsuccessful, you have to start again; either (a) beat a fresh egg yolk in a clean bowl, slowly pour the curdled mixture onto the beaten yolk, beating continuously. If the mayonnaise becomes too thick, beat in a few drops of lemon juice or vinegar; or (b) beat 12,5 ml of the curdled mayonnaise into 5 ml prepared mustard, then gradually add the rest of the curdled mixture, beating all the time.
- For a light yellow mayonnaise, use white vinegar. If a darker coloured mayonnaise is required, use red vinegar. Tarragon vinegar or any other herbed vinegar adds a specially distinctive taste to the mayonnaise.
- Store for 2 to 3 weeks in the refrigerator, but do not freeze.

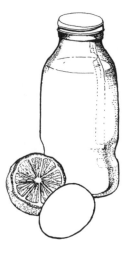

5 ml (1 teaspoon) mustard powder
5 ml (1 teaspoon) salt
5 ml (1 teaspoon) sugar
1 ml (¼ teaspoon) cayenne pepper
2 whole eggs, at room temperature
25 ml lemon juice
25 ml vinegar
250 ml olive or salad oil

Mayonnaise – liquidiser method

Makes 300 ml;   kJ per portion 450;   Prep time 10 min.

1. Place the eggs and the dry ingredients in the liquidiser jug. Blend for 4 seconds.
2. Reduce the speed to moderate and add the oil in a thin, steady stream. Blend until thick and creamy, then add the lemon juice and vinegar and blend.

Note: If your blender does not blend a small batch successfully, double the quantities.

300 ml mayonnaise
37,5 ml tomato sauce
37,5 ml double cream
12,5 ml brandy
juice of ½ lemon
2 ml (½ teaspoon) salt
2 ml (½ teaspoon) pepper

Seafood sauce

Makes 370 ml; kJ per portion 450; Prep time 10 min.

1. Combine the mayonnaise with the lemon juice, salt and pepper.
2. Add the tomato sauce, stirring constantly.
3. Add the cream, still stirring, then stir in the brandy. Add more salt and pepper if necessary. Chill for at least 1 hour before use. Pour over seafood cocktail.

Variations of mayonnaise

Sauce	Additions	Method	Serve with
Chantilly basic mayonnaise made with 250 ml oil	juice of ½ lemon; 50 ml single cream.	Whip cream, season with lemon juice and fold into mayonnaise.	Asparagus.
Rémoulade basic mayonnaise made with 250 ml oil	12,5 ml (1 tablespoon) finely chopped parsley, tarragon, chervil or basil; 5 ml (1 teaspoon) finely chopped capers; 5 ml (1 teaspoon) mustard powder; 1 finely chopped gherkin; 1 clove garlic; 2 ml anchovy essence.	Crush garlic, mix with all the other ingredients and fold into mayonnaise.	Fish, cold pork or ham, prawns, crayfish.
Aioli basic mayonnaise made with 250 ml oil	3 to 4 cloves garlic.	Omit mustard, vinegar and lemon juice from basic mayonnaise. Crush garlic to very smooth paste. Work into egg yolks before adding oil. Add lemon juice, salt and pepper to taste.	Steamed vegetables, hard-boiled eggs, boiled beef, fish soups, poached fish.
Mayonnaise verte basic mayonnaise made with 250 ml oil	40 ml (8 teaspoons) frozen chopped spinach; 125 ml (½ cup) watercress; 12,5 ml (1 tablespoon) parsley.	Place all ingredients in a saucepan, simmer slowly for 5 minutes. Purée. Fold into mayonnaise.	Cold salmon or trout.
Tartare basic mayonnaise made with 250 ml oil	2 hard-boiled egg yolks; 1 raw egg yolk; 5 ml (1 teaspoon) each of finely chopped chives, parsley and capers; 1 small pickled gherkin, finely chopped.	Sieve hard-boiled egg yolks and make mayonnaise with hard-boiled egg yolks mixed with raw egg yolk. Fold remaining ingredients into the finished sauce.	Fried or grilled fish, cold beef, cold chicken.

250 g butter, softened and cubed
4 egg yolks
25 ml lemon juice
200 ml boiling water
2 ml (½ teaspoon) salt
2 ml (½ teaspoon) pepper

Hollandaise sauce

Makes 275 ml; kJ per portion 650; Prep time 20 min; Cooking time 10 min.

1. Whisk the egg yolks with 20 ml lukewarm water in the top of a double-boiler. Place over simmering water in the bottom half of the double-boiler.
2. Add the butter bit by bit, beating all the time. Do not allow to boil.
3. Add the boiling water gradually, still beating.
4. Season with the salt, pepper and lemon juice, continue beating, and use at once.

Note: For a thicker sauce, use less water or an extra egg yolk.

Variations:

1. *Mousseline:* Fold 50 ml whipped cream into the finished sauce and serve with grilled salmon, asparagus, artichoke hearts, broccoli or lamb cutlets.
2. *Maltaise:* Use the juice and finely grated rind of a Seville orange instead of the lemon juice and serve with fried scampi, soles, broccoli or asparagus.
3. *Divine:* Reduce 25 ml sherry and 25 ml whipped cream to 12,5 ml liquid over high heat and stir into finished sauce. Serve with chicken or sole.

Note:

- Beat egg yolks for at least 3 minutes as they must thicken before you continue with the sauce.
- Eggs must be at room temperature.
- It is important to beat the eggs and the butter slowly so that they will form an emulsion.
- Use only the best ingredients available. Although the purists prescribe unsalted butter, ordinary butter will do. Margarine should not be used.
- For a thicker sauce, use less water or add an extra egg yolk.

Note: Use the egg whites in a soufflé or omelette.

120 g soft butter, cut in pieces
37,5 ml wine or tarragon vinegar
2 egg yolks
20 ml (4 teaspoons) parsley, finely chopped
20 ml (4 teaspoons) fresh tarragon, finely chopped or
10 ml (2 teaspoons) dried tarragon
12,5 ml hot water
5 ml lemon juice
5 ml (1 teaspoon) salt

Béarnaise sauce

Makes 200 ml; kJ per portion 500; Prep time 20 min; Cooking time 10 min.

1. Place the parsley and tarragon in the top of a double-boiler together with the wine or tarragon vinegar and boil over direct heat until the liquid is reduced to approximately 30 ml.
2. Remove from the stove and whisk in the egg yolks and hot water. Place the top of the double-boiler over simmering water in the bottom half.
3. Add the butter, bit by bit, stirring all the time. Do not allow the sauce to boil.
4. Season with salt and a little lemon juice and use immediately.

Note:

- If the sauce separates, remove from the heat and briskly whisk in 5 ml lukewarm water, then continue with step 4.
- Serve with grilled meat or fish.

When things go wrong
Acting quickly can usually save a Hollandaise or Béarnaise sauce

Fault	Cause	Solution
Sauce thickens too quickly and goes lumpy before all the butter has been added.	Sauce too hot.	Plunge the base of the saucepan or top half of double-boiler into a basin full of cold water. Leave for 1 minute then whisk the egg yolks vigorously until barely warm when tested with the fingertip. Reduce the heat of the stove and continue making the sauce.
Sauce begins to curdle.	Sauce too hot.	Remove from stove *immediately* and beat in 5 to 10 ml very cold water. Slightly reduce the heat of the stove and continue. If the curdling has gone too far, however, the sauce cannot be rescued.
Sauce separates into egg yolk and melted butter.	Sauce too hot. Proportions incorrect.	Remove saucepan from the stove and pour mixture into a bowl. Rinse out saucepan, place a fresh egg yolk in it and whisk. Gradually add the separated mixture, beating all the time over low heat.
Sauce does not thicken.	Butter added too quickly.	Rinse out a clean bowl with hot water and place 12,5 ml of the unthickened sauce and 5 ml strained lemon juice in it. Whisk until creamy, then gradually whisk in the rest of the unthickened sauce.
Sauce is too thick.	Proportions incorrect.	Remove from the stove and beat in 12,5 ml to 25 ml single cream, milk or hot water.

STORING SAUCES

Extreme care must be taken when storing sauces or any dish containing a sauce for longer than a day or two.

Egg-based sauces can be stored in the refrigerator for a maximum of 3 days, except mayonnaise which may be stored for longer. They are not suitable for freezing, as there is the danger that they may separate when thawed and reheated.

White sauces can be kept in an airtight container in the refrigerator for a week. They are suitable for freezing, but must first be thawed before reheating. Reheat over low heat – preferably in the top of a double-boiler – stirring all the time to prevent lumpiness and separating.

189

The *basic roux* can be made in large quantities, wrapped in plastic or foil and refrigerated or frozen. To make the sauce, heat the liquid and add the *roux* as described on p. 177, whisking all the time until the sauce thickens. Allow the following quantities:

25 g roux to 250 ml liquid for a thin (pouring) sauce;
50 g roux to 250 ml liquid for a medium (coating) sauce; and
100 g roux to 250 ml liquid for a thick (panada) sauce.

Dry white sauce mix (p. 179) can be stored in the refrigerator for up to 2 months, or in the freezer for up to 6 months.

Note: Recipes for sweet sauces may be found in the chapter on desserts.

Never boil a sauce with egg yolks added to it as it will separate. Reheat an egg yolk – based sauce gradually after hot stock has been added. Heat to just below boiling point.

To prevent curdling, first add some of the hot liquid separately to the beaten egg yolks to heat the mixture slightly before it is added to the hot liquid.

If an egg-based sauce is whisked continuously until it thickens, the result will be light and fluffy.

Serve a dish containing a hot egg-based sauce immediately.

If the sauce separates, whisk 12,5 ml warm water into an egg yolk and gradually add it to the separated sauce over low heat, whisking all time.

100 g butter
25 ml (2 tablespoons) flour
2 egg yolks
5 ml double cream
lemon juice
150 ml salted, boiling water

317 Butter sauce

Makes 200 ml; kJ per portion 300; Prep time 15 min; Cooking time 10 min.

1. Melt 12,5 ml (1 tablespoon) butter in a heavy-bottomed saucepan over low heat.
2. Stir in the flour and add the salted, boiling water, whisking briskly all the time. Bring to the boil.
3. Combine the egg yolks, cream and a little lemon juice in a small bowl. Pour the mixture into the saucepan and mix well. Heat, but do not allow the sauce to boil.
4. Strain the sauce through a fine sieve into a bowl.
5. Beat the remaining butter into the sauce bit by bit. Use immediately.

Note: Butter sauce is delicious served over grilled fish.

318 Mustard sauce

30 ml (6 teaspoons) mustard powder
75 ml (6 tablespoons) sugar
12,5 ml (1 tablespoon) flour
250 ml red vinegar
4 eggs
5 ml (1 teaspoon) salt
5 ml (1 teaspoon) pepper

*Makes 300 ml;   kJ per portion 200;   Prep time 10 min;
Cooking time 10 min.*

1. Beat 62,5 ml (5 tablespoons) of the sugar and the eggs together in a saucepan.
2. Combine the remaining sugar with the mustard powder, flour, salt and pepper.
3. Add the vinegar to the sugar and mustard and stir into the egg mixture in the saucepan.
4. Heat slowly, stirring continuously. When sauce thickens, remove from the stove immediately. Serve with ham, tongue or beef.

Note: Mustard sauce may be kept in the refrigerator in a tightly closed container for 6 to 7 days.

319 Mustard dill sauce

37,5 ml (3 tablespoons) butter or margarine
25 ml (2 tablespoons) flour
5 ml anchovy essence
10 ml vinegar
250 ml milk
2 ml (½ teaspoon) mustard powder
2 ml (½ teaspoon) fresh dill, finely chopped

Makes 320 ml; kJ per portion 450; Prep time 20 min; Cooking time 10 min.

1. Combine the mustard powder, anchovy essence and vinegar to form a smooth paste.
2. Melt the butter or margarine in a small saucepan. Sprinkle over the flour and stir to blend smoothly.
3. Gradually add the milk, stirring all the time over medium heat until the mixture boils. Simmer for 2 minutes, stirring continuously.
4. Stir in the mustard mixture and dill and bring back to the boil. Serve with grilled white fish.

320 Asparagus sauce

250 ml (1 cup) canned asparagus, drained and finely chopped
1 egg yolk
25 ml (2 tablespoons) flour
25 ml (2 tablespoons) butter
125 ml single cream
12,5 ml oil
250 ml milk
125 ml chicken stock
juice of 1 lemon
5 ml (1 teaspoon) salt
2 ml (½ teaspoon) pepper

Makes 400 ml; kJ per portion 350; Prep time 30 min; Cooking time 15 min.

1. Heat the butter and oil in a frying-pan. Gradually add the flour and stir until smooth. Remove from the stove.
2. Combine the milk, chicken stock and lemon juice in a jug and add to the pan, stirring until smooth and creamy. Season with salt and pepper. Add asparagus and cook another 5 minutes, stirring all the time.
3. Beat the egg yolk with the cream in a small bowl and add to the pan. Return the pan to the stove. Heat until just boiling, stirring all the time.
4. Serve with roast chicken.

Use hot but not boiling liquid for a *roux*-based sauce to save time.

If both the *roux* and the liquid are hot, it will prevent the sauce becoming lumpy.

321 Tomato sauce (F)

1,5 kg tomatoes, skinned,
quartered and seeded
6 medium onions, finely
chopped
170 g fat salt pork, washed in
warm water and diced
50 ml (4 tablespoons) parsley,
finely chopped
10 ml (2 teaspoons) sugar
37,5 ml oil
5 ml (1 teaspoon) salt
5 ml (1 teaspoon) pepper

Makes 250 – 300 ml;   kJ per portion 320;   Prep time 20 min;   Cooking time 1 hour 10 min.

1. Simmer the tomatoes in a large, shallow pan over low heat until soft and mushy.
2. Meanwhile, heat the oil in a frying-pan and sauté the diced pork, onions and parsley in it over low heat for 20 minutes.
3. Add the cooked tomatoes, sugar, salt and pepper and simmer, covered, for 45 minutes (f).

Note: If the sauce is too thick, add a little boiling water.

322 Barbecue sauce (F)

½ small onion, finely chopped
1 clove garlic, finely chopped
1 sprig parsley, finely chopped
25 ml wine vinegar
25 ml oil
5 ml Worcester sauce
145 ml tomato sauce
freshly ground black pepper

Makes 200 ml;   kJ per portion 200;   Prep time 10 min.

1. Place all the ingredients in a large screw-top jar, cover and shake vigorously until well blended.
2. Leave for 24 hours, shaking occasionally (f).

Note:
- Use as a baste.
- Do not freeze for longer than 3 to 4 weeks.

323 Piquant sauce (F)

1 shallot or ½ small onion, finely
chopped
25 ml (2 tablespoons) pickles,
finely chopped
62,5 ml (5 tablespoons) flour
37,5 ml (3 tablespoons) butter
50 ml red wine vinegar
300 ml stock
5 ml (1 teaspoon) sugar
5 ml (1 teaspoon) salt
5 ml (1 teaspoon) pepper

Makes 400 ml; kJ per portion 250; Prep time 25 min; Cooking time 10 min.

1. Heat the shallot or onion, sugar and vinegar in a small saucepan, uncovered, until the vinegar is reduced by half.
2. Melt the butter in another saucepan and remove from the stove. Stir in the flour, a little at a time, to make a smooth paste. Return to the stove and cook, stirring, until the mixture turns brown.
3. Add the stock gradually and stir over low heat until the mixture thickens. Stir in the salt and pepper.
4. Add the vinegar mixture and stir over low heat until the sauce thickens.
5. Strain the sauce through a fine sieve into a sauceboat and stir in the pickles (f). Serve with roast or grilled meat or grilled fish.

Note: Do not freeze for longer than 6 weeks.

324 Sweet and sour sauce

10 ml (2 teaspoons) cornflour
85 g canned pineapple, finely
chopped
60 g onions, finely chopped
25 ml vinegar
5 ml tomato purée
7 ml soy sauce
300 ml liquid (cold water and
juice of pineapple)
25 ml oil
20 ml (4 teaspoons) sugar

Makes 400 ml; kJ per portion 350; Prep time 20 min; Cooking time 5-10 min.

1. Combine the vinegar, sugar, tomato purée, cornflour, soy sauce and the liquid in a saucepan and bring to the boil. Cook until the mixture thickens.
2. Add the oil and continue boiling for 1 to 2 minutes.
3. Stir in the pineapple and onion, blending well. Use immediately.

250 g mushrooms, finely chopped
125 ml (½ cup) onion, grated
12,5 ml (1 tablespoon) flour
25 ml (2 tablespoons) butter
25 ml oil
375 ml meat stock
125 ml dry red wine
1 clove garlic, minced
2 ml (½ teaspoon) salt
2 ml (½ teaspoon) paprika

325 Wine sauce (F)

Makes 600 ml; kJ per portion 250; Prep time 30 min; Cooking time 20 min.

1. Heat half the butter and oil in a frying-pan and sauté the mushrooms in it until tender.
2. Heat the remaining butter and oil in a saucepan and sauté the onion and garlic until the onions are transparent.
3. Add the meat stock and wine to the onion mixture and simmer, covered, for 15 minutes.
4. Mix the flour to a smooth paste with a little cold water and stir into the onion mixture. Simmer, stirring all the time, until the sauce thickens.
5. Remove from the stove and stir in the mushrooms.
6. Season with salt and paprika (f) and serve hot with roast beef.

---

1 medium onion, grated
1 small chilli, finely chopped
12,5 ml (1 tablespoon) cornflour
375 ml chicken or fish stock
25 ml (2 tablespoons) butter

326 Peri peri sauce (F)

Makes 400 ml; kJ per portion 220; Prep time 20 min; Cooking time 30 min.

1. Melt the butter in a saucepan, add the cornflour and stir until smooth.
2. Combine the onion, chilli and chicken or fish stock in a small bowl and add to the butter and cornflour mixture.
3. Simmer over low heat, stirring continuously, until thickened (f).
4. Add the sauce to the meat or fish and simmer for 15 to 30 minutes.

Note: Use chicken stock for chicken and fish stock for seafoods.

---

125 ml water
200 ml soy sauce
2 cloves garlic, minced
5 ml (1 teaspoon) ground ginger
12,5 ml (1 tablespoon) brown sugar

327 Teriyaki sauce (F)

Makes 325 ml; kJ per portion 200;   Prep time 10 min.

1. Combine all the ingredients thoroughly (f).
2. Pour over meat rissoles in a flat baking dish and bake in the oven at 150 °C (300 °F) for 45 minutes, basting frequently.

Note: This sauce is also very good with grilled steak.

---

100 g butter
2 cloves garlic, crushed
2 ml (½ teaspoon) salt

328 Garlic butter sauce

Makes 125 ml; kJ per portion 200; Prep time 5 min; Cooking time 5 min.

1. Melt the butter over low heat.
2. Add the garlic and salt, shake or stir well and serve immediately with grilled seafood.

Variation: *Lemon butter sauce:* Substitute 5 ml lemon juice for the garlic.

Note: Left-over sauce can be used for garlic bread or frozen for later use.

250 ml fruit chutney
25 ml port
25 ml red vinegar
2 ml tabasco sauce

329   Monkeygland sauce (F)

Makes 300 ml;   kJ per portion 400;   Prep time 10 min;   Cooking time 5 min.

1. Combine all the ingredients in a small saucepan.
2. Heat to boiling point, stirring occasionally (f).
3. Serve at once with grilled steak.

---

50 ml (4 tablespoons)
horseradish, grated
2 ml (½ teaspoon) mustard
powder
10 ml vinegar
5 ml (1 teaspoon) castor sugar
150 ml double cream
2 ml (½ teaspoon) salt
2 ml (½ teaspoon) pepper

330   Horseradish sauce   (F)

Makes 200 ml;   kJ per portion 250;   Prep time 15 min.

1. Mix the horseradish, mustard powder, salt, pepper, vinegar and sugar in a bowl.
2. In another bowl, whip the cream lightly until it just begins to hold its shape, then stir in the other ingredients (f).
3. Turn the sauce into a small bowl for serving with hare, rabbit, pork, beef or trout.

---

handful of mint leaves,
removed from the main stalks
5 ml (1 teaspoon) granulated
sugar
25 ml boiling water
vinegar

331   Mint sauce   (F)

Makes 50 ml;   kJ per portion 50;   Prep time 10 min.

1. Place the mint leaves on a chopping board, sprinkle with the sugar and chop very finely with a sharp knife.
2. Place the chopped mint in a sauceboat and stir in the boiling water. Add vinegar to taste (f). Serve with roast lamb.

Note: This sauce may be stored in a small jar in the refrigerator until required.

---

10 ml (2 teaspoons) orange
rind, grated
12,5 ml (1 tablespoon) glacé
ginger, grated
25 ml (2 tablespoons) butter
25 ml (2 tablespoons) cornflour
62,5 ml (5 tablespoons) sugar
250 ml orange juice
65 ml white vinegar
65 ml water
37,5 ml soy sauce
65 ml sherry

332   Orange sauce

Makes 500 ml; kJ per portion 400; Prep time 20 min; Cooking time 15 min.

1. Melt the butter in a saucepan and stir in the orange juice, vinegar, sherry and sugar.
2. Mix the cornflour to a smooth paste with the water, then stir in the soy sauce.
3. Add to the mixture in the saucepan and bring to the boil.
4. Stir in the grated orange rind and ginger and continue simmering, stirring constantly, until the sauce thickens. This sauce is good with roast pork ribs.

125 ml (½ cup) brown sugar
5 ml (1 teaspoon) mustard powder
12,5 ml (1 tablespoon) flour
125 ml (½ cup) seedless raisins
2 ml (½ teaspoon) grated lemon rind
375 ml water
25 ml lemon juice
25 ml vinegar

333   Raisin sauce   (F)

Makes 450 ml;   kJ per portion 500;   Prep time 10 min;   Cooking time 10 min.

1. Combine the flour, sugar and mustard powder in a saucepan.
2. Add the rest of the ingredients and stir well.
3. Heat over low heat, stirring constantly, until the sauce thickens.
4. Cook a further 3 to 5 minutes (f) and serve with brisket, ham or tongue.

---

500 g cooking apples
25 ml water
sugar to taste, if required

334   Apple sauce   (F)

Makes 250 ml; kJ per portion 250; Prep time 20 min; Cooking time 20 min.

1. Wash and chop the apples coarsely.
2. Place the apples in a saucepan with the water and simmer, covered, until they are soft and pulpy, about 20 minutes.
3. Purée the apples by rubbing them through a coarse sieve or blending in a blender, then stir in the sugar to taste (f).
4. Turn into a small dish for serving with roast pork or gammon.

Variation: For a spicy apple sauce, add 5 ml (1 teaspoon) ground mixed spices, 2 ml (½ teaspoon) dried rosemary and 2 ml (½ teaspoon) ground ginger to the pulp. Do not purée.

---

2 shallots or 1 small onion, finely chopped
rind of 1 lemon, cut into thin strips
rind of 1 orange, cut into thin strips
62,5 ml (5 tablespoons) redcurrant jelly
juice of ½ lemon
juice of 1 orange
20 ml water
50 ml port
5 ml prepared French mustard
2 ml (½ teaspoon) ground ginger
1 ml (¼ teaspoon) cayenne pepper

335   Cumberland sauce   (F)

Makes 250 ml; kJ per portion 350; Prep time 30 min; Cooking time 15 min.

1. Place the shallots or onion with the water in a small saucepan and simmer, covered, for 3 minutes.
2. Boil the lemon and orange rind strips in a little water in a saucepan for 10 minutes. Drain well.
3. Heat the redcurrant jelly in a small saucepan, and when it has melted, add the shallots or onion, lemon and orange rinds, lemon juice, orange juice, port, mustard, ground ginger and cayenne pepper. Mix thoroughly (f) and use immediately with venison or other game.

Variation: Use quince or apple jelly in place of the redcurrant jelly.

For many of us, cooked vegetables conjure up visions of limp, unappetising looking – and tasting – additions to a meal that had to be eaten because 'vegetables are good for you'. Packed with vitamins and minerals, vegetables *are* good for us, and if they are properly prepared and carefully cooked, they can be really delicious.

Selecting vegetables

1. Use fresh vegetables in season. Choose frozen or canned vegetables when the fresh vegetables are not available or if time is at a premium.
2. Always select fresh vegetables which are crisp and firm, not wilted or bruised. Cauliflower, cabbage or lettuce should be firm and the leaves of green vegetables should never be yellow or dry.
3. Root vegetables should be firm and with as few surface blemishes as possible.
4. Canned vegetables are a useful standby. Once the can has been opened, however, the vegetables should be stored in the refrigerator and used within 3 to 4 days.
5. When buying frozen vegetables, make sure that they are hard-frozen, not soft and mushy. If they are not to be used immediately, store them in your own freezer as soon as possible.

Storing vegetables

Consult the tables on p. 200 to 204 for the best way to store vegetables.

Preparing vegetables for cooking or salads

The following general points can be made. For more specific instructions, consult the tables on p. 200 to 204 and the section on salads (p. 223 to 234).

1. Prepare vegetables just before cooking or serving.
2. Do not leave vegetables to soak in water for a long time as nutrients will be lost.
3. Wash and shake salad greens well in a salad shaker, sieve or strainer. Pat dry carefully.
4. If it is necessary to prepare vegetables or salads beforehand, store them in airtight containers in the refrigerator until required.
5. Wash lettuce, cauliflower, broccoli and other green vegetables in cold water, leave in cold salted water for 30 minutes, rinse and use immediately.
6. Scrub carrots, potatoes and sweet potatoes thoroughly with a brush, then peel or scrape thinly. Very young vegetables may be cooked in the skins; they will be tastier and more nutritious.

Cooking methods

Boiling

1. Use the minimum amount of water: only 3 to 3,5 cm in the saucepan for green vegetables and just enough to cover for root vegetables.
2. Bring the water to the boil before adding the vegetables. Add salt to the water in which tender, young vegetables and green vegetables are to be boiled. Boil mature vegetables and harder varieties until tender *before* adding any salt.
3. Bring back to the boil as quickly as possible after adding the vegetables – vegetables should boil continuously but not too rapidly – and continue boiling, covered, until tender.

Drain boiled vegetables thoroughly as soon as cooked and save the water for gravies, health drinks or stocks.

Never allow vegetables to boil until too soft; they will lose flavour, vitamins and minerals and are liable to become a nasty, soggy, waterlogged mess.

Note:
- Vegetables should be boiled covered as this shortens the cooking period and ensures that green vegetables do not turn yellow.
- Boil vegetables only until tender; the more lightly cooked the more flavoursome and nutritious.
- Do not add bicarbonate of soda when boiling vegetables as this will destroy the vitamins.
- Boil spinach and tomatoes without any water.
- Reserve the water in which vegetables have been boiled for sauces or to add to soups.

Steaming
1. Season vegetables lightly with salt and place in a steamer or colander. Suspend this container over a pan of boiling water.
2. Steam, covered or uncovered, until tender but still crisp.

Note:
- Steaming is particularly suited to green, leafy vegetables.
- Steaming vegetables in cooking bags retains the flavour and crispness.
- Use the microwave oven to cook vegetables. Place in cooking bags, pierce them in a few places and cook for the length of time specified in the instructions given with the oven.

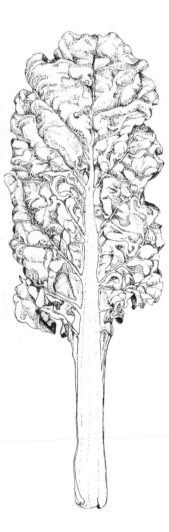

Pressure cooking
Cooking periods will be shortened if a pressure cooker is used, but remember that the loss of vitamins will be in direct proportion to the temperature and the length of the cooking period.
1. Heat quickly so that the vegetables will reach the desired pressure of 50 kPa as soon as possible.
2. Follow the directions and recommendations given with the cooker for length of cooking time.
3. At the end of the cooking time hold the pressure cooker under slowly running cold water to cool off rapidly.

Baking
1. Bake potatoes, sweet potatoes and pumpkin in the skin at 180 °C (350 °F) for 1 hour. The vegetables may be wrapped in foil or baked without wrapping (recipe 354).
2. To roast vegetables: heat about 5 cm fat or oil in a roasting pan. Add the vegetables and spoon the oil or fat over them. Roast for 30 to 45 minutes, depending on how crisp you want them.

Note:
- Potatoes or onions may be parboiled for 15 minutes before roasting. Roast for only 15 to 20 minutes.
- Vegetables may also be roasted with the meat. Add when just sufficient roasting time remains to ensure that they will be done at the same time as the meat (see table on p. 203).
- Vegetables particularly suited to roasting are potatoes, onions and carrots.

Frying

Most vegetables may be deep or shallow fried, depending on the type. If deep-fried, they are coated in batter first – the only exception is potato chips.

Shallow frying

This method is particularly suited to making vegetable fritters and to such vegetables as tomatoes, onions, aubergines and mushrooms.
1. Heat 1 cm deep oil or fat in a pan.
2. Prepare the vegetables, dry well and add to the fat.
3. Shake the pan or turn the vegetables with a lifter. Fry till done.
4. Lift vegetables out onto absorbent paper to drain. Serve immediately.

Stir-frying

This Chinese method has delicious results. Besides being used for vegetables, it is also the method used to make Chow Mein and Chop Suey.
1. Cut all vegetables into regular shapes: carrots and parsnips into 'matchsticks', onions and cabbage coarsely chopped, cauliflower and broccoli in small flowerets and so on. Wash and dry well.
2. Heat a wok or heavy skillet until your palm feels very hot if held 8 cm above it. Add oil to the depth of 5 mm in the pan.
3. Add the vegetables and fry, shaking the pan all the time and turning the vegetables with a fish slice or chopsticks. Fry for 2 to 4 minutes. Serve immediately.

Deep-fat frying

1. Prepare the vegetables and dry them well. Dip in batter, if desired.
2. Heat oil or fat in a saucepan or deep-fat frier to 190 °C to 200 °C (375 °F to 400 °F) – at this temperature, a 2,5 cm cube of bread dropped into the fat or oil takes 1 minute to turn pale golden.
3. Place the vegetables in a basket and lower into the oil. Fry until crisp.
4. Lift out and drain on absorbent paper.

Note:

- Do not add too many vegetables to the oil at once.
- Make sure that the oil remains at the desired temperature.
- Only use clean oil of the best possible quality.

Grilling

Grilling is particularly suited to tomatoes, aubergines, mushrooms and onions.
1. Prepare the vegetables and dry well.
2. Place them on the rack of the grilling pan, drizzle with a little oil or melted butter and place under the grilling element, turning once, until tender.

Vegetable	Storage	To Prepare	To Cook	Cooking Time
Artichoke, globe	Refrigerator for 4 days, unwashed and wrapped in plastic	Wash, cut away green stalk to the level of the leaves	Cook in boiling salted water. Serve with melted butter, cream sauce or vinaigrette sauce	30 minutes
Artichoke, Jerusalem	Dry cool place, unwrapped: 1 week	Scrub or peel. Soak in cold water with lemon juice for 30 minutes. Cut off long ends and peel under water	Cook in boiling salted water. Serve with cheese sauce, melted butter or Béchamel sauce (p. 179)	30 minutes
Asparagus	Wrapped, unwashed, in refrigerator: 2 days	Wash, cut 2 cm off thick white base of the stalk, tie in a bundle with string	Steam or boil upright bundle, with tips uppermost, in salted water in a deep saucepan. Serve cold with mayonnaise, hot with cheese sauce, grated cheese, vinaigrette sauce or Hollandaise sauce (p. 188)	20 minutes
Aubergine	In refrigerator, unwrapped: 4 to 5 days; out of refrigerator, unwrapped: 2 to 3 days	Remove the stalk, slice (with or without peeling). Soak in salted water for 30 minutes, or salt slices and allow to draw for 30 minutes	Dip in egg and crumbs and fry in shallow fat. Bake in a casserole. Stuff and bake	5 to 10 minutes 30 minutes 45 minutes
Avocado pear	Ripen in a dark, warm cupboard. When ripe, store in the refrigerator for 4 to 5 days. After cutting, sprinkle with lemon juice to prevent discolouring	Peel, halve and remove stone	Use in salads, patés, dips, soups and mousses	
Baby marrows	Cool, well-ventilated place: 2 days. Wrapped, in refrigerator: 4 days	Top and tail and slice	Boil in salted water Steam Use in casseroles	4 to 5 minutes 15 minutes

Vegetable	Storage	To Prepare	To Cook	Cooking Time
Bean sprouts	Wash and store in the refrigerator in an airtight container: 4 days		Use in salads	
Beans, green	Wrapped, in refrigerator: 3 days Frozen	Wash, string, french cut; when young, use whole	Boil in salted water Steam Serve with melted butter or finely chopped almonds Boil in salted water	15 minutes 20 minutes 10 minutes
Beans, lima	Frozen		Boil in salted water. Serve with knobs of butter	15 minutes
Beetroot	Unwrapped, in refrigerator: 1 week; or in a cool place: 3 days	Wash well, cut off greens	Boil whole in salted water or boil in pressure cooker to reduce cooking time. Serve cold, sliced, as a salad	2 to 4 hours
Broccoli	Wrapped, in refrigerator: 2 days	Wash well and trim Chopped	Boil in very little salted water Steam Serve with cheese sauce, grated cheese, herb croûtons (recipe 99) or Hollandaise Sauce Stir-fry	7 to 10 minutes 15 minutes 3 minutes
Brussels sprouts	Wrapped, in refrigerator: 2 days	Wash well, cut stem ends, remove outer yellow leaves if present	Boil in salted water Steam Serve with cheese sauce, melted butter or buttered crumbs	10 minutes 12 minutes
Cabbage, white or savoy	Wrapped, in refrigerator: 4 days; in cool place: 1 day	Remove outer leaves, wash. Slice or cook whole	Boil in salted water Steam: shredded whole Stir-fry Raw in salads	5 minutes 10 to 12 minutes 15 minutes 3 minutes
Carrots	Wrapped, in refrigerator: 7 days; in cool place: 2 days	Cut off greens, wash and scrape. Slice if desired. Cut in matchsticks	Boil in salted water Steam young carrots whole Stir-fry Roast whole or sliced, with the meat	15 to 20 minutes 20 minutes 3 minutes 45 to 60 minutes

Vegetable	Storage	To Prepare	To Cook	Cooking Time
Cauliflower	Wrapped, in refrigerator: 5 days	Cut off outer leaves and stalk. Wash well. Cut or use whole. Cut into flowerets	Boil in salted water: whole cut Steam: whole Stir-fry	15 to 20 minutes 10 minutes 25 to 30 minutes 3 minutes
Celeriac	Wrapped, in refrigerator: 3 days	Cut off top leaves, wash. Dice, cut in strips or use whole matchsticks	Boil in salted water Serve with cheese sauce, cream sauce, butter or grated cheese Steam: strips Stir-fry	15 minutes 12 minutes 3 minutes
Celery	Stand in a jug of water in the refrigerator	Cut off leaves	Boil in salted water Serve with melted butter or grated cheese Use in soups Use raw in salads	5 minutes
Chicory (Endive)	Wrapped, in refrigerator: 4 days	Wash, cut in pieces or use whole	Boil in salted water: whole Serve with white sauce or cheese sauce Use raw in salads	15 minutes (do not overcook)
Cucumber	Wrapped, in refrigerator: 4 days		Serve raw, sliced, in salads Serve grated in salads	
Leeks	Wrapped, in refrigerator: 3 days	Cut off roots and remove green tops 10 cm from white stem. Split lengthwise to within 7 cm of base. Fan layers under clean cold water to wash away grit	Boil in salted water: whole chopped Steam: whole chopped Serve with Béchamel sauce or grated cheese	15 to 20 minutes 5 to 10 minutes 20 minutes 10 minutes
Lettuce	Wrapped, in refrigerator: 3 days; or in crisper	Separate into leaves, wash in salted water and drain in a colander. Use whole leaves or break into bite-sized pieces	Serve raw in salads	
Mealies (Corn)	Wrapped (without leaves) or unwrapped (with leaves) in refrigerator: 4 to 6 days	Remove outer leaves and silky threads	Boil in salted water Serve with knobs of butter	15 to 30 minutes

Vegetable	Storage	To Prepare	To Cook	Cooking Time
Mushrooms	Dry, in plastic bag in refrigerator: 2 days or unwrapped: 1 day	Wipe skins clean and trim stalks level with caps	Fry in butter Grill large black mushrooms and serve with garlic butter sauce (recipe 328) Use raw in salads	5 minutes 5 minutes
Onions	Unwrapped in cool, dry, well-ventilated place: indefinitely	Peel and leave whole or slice	Boil in salted water: whole chopped Roast: whole (see p. 198) Fry in shallow fat Break into rings, dip in batter and deep-fry Stuffed and baked	15 to 20 minutes 5 to 10 minutes 45 to 50 minutes 5 minutes 5 minutes 20 minutes
Parsnips	Wrapped, in refrigerator: 7 days; in cool place: 4 days	Trim stalk and root. Peel and cook whole or diced	Boil in a little salted water: whole chopped Serve with melted butter and sprinkled with caraway seeds Roast with the meat	20 minutes 10 to 15 minutes 45 to 60 minutes
Peas	Fresh, in pods: 4 days Frozen	Shell fresh peas just before cooking	Boil in salted water Steam Serve with a knob of butter, finely chopped fresh mint or mint sauce (recipe 331) Boil in salted water	10 to 15 minutes 15 to 20 minutes 5 minutes
Peppers, green	Wrapped, in refrigerator: 4 days; unwrapped: 2 days	Cut off stalks, remove pith and seeds	Cut in strips and shallow fry in butter or oil Stir-fry Stuff and bake (recipe 349) Serve raw in salads	5 minutes 5 minutes 15 minutes
Potatoes	Cool, dry, well-ventilated place	Wash and scrub new potatoes and boil in jackets Old potatoes for baking treated the same. Peel and quarter for roasting Cut in sticks for deep-frying	Boiled in salted water: whole cut Serve with melted butter Serve boiled potatoes mashed with milk or cream, butter, salt and pepper Bake in foil over open fire Bake in oven (recipe 354) Roasting (see p. 198) Deep-fry in hot oil	15 to 20 minutes 15 minutes 1½ hours 40 to 70 minutes 40 to 70 minutes 5 minutes

203

Vegetable	Storage	To Prepare	To Cook	Cooking Time
Pumpkin	Cool, dry, well-ventilated place	Peel, remove pips and cube	Steam: chopped Stew (recipe 356)	15 minutes
Radishes	Cut off greens and store in airtight container in refrigerator: 7 days	Cut off stalks and slice or leave whole. Wash well in salted water	Serve raw in salads	
Soybeans	Store dried beans in dry, well-sealed jars	Wash well under running water	Soak in water overnight. Rinse, drain and boil in salted water	10 minutes
Spinach	Store in refrigerator, stems in a pitcher of cold water	Trim stalks. Rinse in running water and drain in a colander. Chop finely if boiling or puréeing	Boil without water Steam Serve with a knob of butter or with cheese sauce	8 minutes 12 to 15 minutes
Squash and Marrow	Cool, dry place	Cut off stalks, remove pips and chop or halve	Boil in salted water	15 minutes
Sweet potatoes	Cool, dry, well-ventilated place	Wipe with a damp cloth and leave whole if baking. Peel and cube if stewing	Bake in the oven at 200°C (400°F) and serve with butter Stew (recipe 361)	60 minutes
Tomatoes	Half-ripe in cool, well-ventilated place until ripe; ripe in refrigerator: 3 to 4 days	Remove stalks, wipe skin clean with damp cloth and halve horizontally or cut in thick slices. Leave whole	Shallow fry Grill, topped with chopped fresh herbs Stuff and bake Serve raw in salads	5 minutes 10 minutes
Turnips	Cool, dry, well-ventilated place; wrapped, in refrigerator: 7 days	Trim stalks and root. Peel and chop or leave whole	Boil in salted water: whole chopped Bake, grated, with knobs of butter in oven at 200°C (400°F)	20 to 30 minutes 10 minutes 10 minutes

Note:
- Do not store green vegetables in the refrigerator at a temperature which is too cold: the leaves might freeze.
- Always dry vegetables completely before storing.
- 'Wrapped' means wrapped in plastic.

204

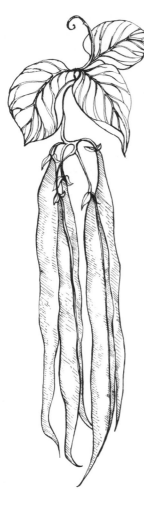

Most vegetables freeze very well, provided that they are excellent quality: fresh, young and frozen as soon as possible after picking. Unfortunately, vegetables which are to be eaten raw – lettuce, cucumber, etc. – cannot be frozen.

Preparation
Prepare each vegetable according to type (table p. 200 to 204), but try not to handle them too much as excessive bruising could become a source of bacteria.

Blanching
Vegetables should be blanched before freezing because this destroys 90% to 100% of the bacteria. They may be either steam or water blanched, but it is best to steam blanch cut green beans, peas and similar vegetables to retain as many vitamins as possible.

Note:
- Use a large wire-mesh basket and a large saucepan.
- Have enough ice-cold water ready to cool the vegetables.

Water blanching
1. Heat at least 5 litres of water in a saucepan: bring to the boil and keep boiling.
2. Place the vegetables in the wire-mesh basket – not more than 1 litre (4 cups) at a time.
3. Lower into the boiling water, cover saucepan with a tight-fitting lid and blanch for as long as required (see table below).
4. Remove the basket from the saucepan and place in the ice-cold water immediately. Leave for 3 to 5 minutes.

Steam blanching
1. Use a large saucepan with a lid and a basket or strainer which will fit the saucepan so that its base is suspended 60 to 80 mm above the level of the boiling water.
2. Place a single layer of vegetables in the strainer, position it in the saucepan and cover.
3. Blanch for as long as required (see table below).
4. Immerse in cold water immediately and leave for 3 to 5 minutes.

Blanching times

Vegetable	Time in minutes	
	Steam	Water
Green beans, peas, celery, asparagus tips	4	2
Spinach, broccoli	—	2
Brussels sprouts	5	4
Cauliflower (add 50 ml lemon juice to water)	—	3
Carrots: whole	—	8
cut	—	4
Green mealies on the cob	6-9	4-7
Mushrooms (rinse with an ascorbic acid solution to prevent discolouring)	—	1
Pumpkin	—	4-5
Potatoes: chips (blanch for 1 minute in hot oil)		

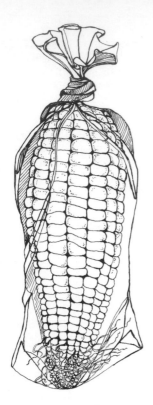

Packing and freezing

1. Remove the vegetables from the cold water.
2. Pack into plastic bags in quantities ready for use.
3. Make sure that there is no air in the packages.
4. Label and freeze immediately at −18°C (0°F).

Note:

- As oblong shapes fit better in the freezer, place a plastic bag in a rigid plastic container, fill with vegetables and freeze. When hard, remove the bag from the container and store the plastic containing the vegetables in the freezer.
- Heavy duty foil may be used instead of plastic bags, but remember to fold securely to exclude all air.

Storage time at − 18 °C (0 °F):

8 months	14 to 16 months	24 months
Asparagus tips Beans Brussels sprouts Broccoli Green mealies on the cob Mushrooms Potato chips	Cauliflower Peas Spinach	Green mealies Carrots Pumpkin

---

VEGETABLES AND VEGETARIAN DISHES

4 medium aubergines
2 onions, finely chopped
6 ripe tomatoes, seeded and
coarsely chopped
4 whole cherry tomatoes
oil for frying
2 cloves garlic, finely chopped
25 ml (2 tablespoons) parsley,
finely chopped
5 ml (1 teaspoon) sugar
5 ml (1 teaspoon) salt
black pepper

336 Stuffed aubergines

Serves 4;   kJ per portion 410;   Prep time 20 min;   Cooking time 1 hour

1. Trim the aubergines and cut them in half lengthwise. Scoop out some of the flesh, leaving a 1 cm thick shell.
2. Make 4 shallow lengthwise incisions in the flesh of each aubergine shell and salt the incisions. Leave for 20 minutes to draw.
3. Rinse the aubergines and squeeze them dry.
4. Heat a little oil in a large frying-pan and sauté the shells in it until soft and pliable. Remove and keep warm. Reserve the oil.
5. Heat a little oil in another frying-pan and sauté the onions in it until transparent.
6. Add the garlic, parsley, chopped tomatoes and sauté for 2 minutes, stirring occasionally. Allow to cool.
7. Place the aubergine shells, cut side up, in a shallow casserole and fill with the onion and tomato mixture. Spoon any leftover mixture around the shells.
8. Cut the cherry tomatoes in half and place on top of the stuffing. Sprinkle with the sugar, salt and black pepper.
9. Pour the reserved oil over each stuffed aubergine and add a little water to the casserole.
10. Bake in the oven at 160°C (325°F) for 1 hour. Serve at once.

Note: Use the scooped out flesh for another dish.

450 g canned baby beets, drained and liquid reserved
25 ml (2 tablespoons) butter or margarine
12,5 ml (1 tablespoon) cornflour
37,5 ml lemon juice or vinegar
25 ml (2 tablespoons) sugar or clear honey
2 ml (½ teaspoon) salt
2 ml (½ teaspoon) black pepper

337 Harvard baby beets

Serves 4; kJ per portion 210; Prep time 30 min; Cooking time 20 min.

1. Slice the beets evenly.
2. Combine the cornflour and 150 ml of the reserved beet juice in a saucepan. Add the vinegar or lemon juice, sugar or honey, salt and pepper.
3. Bring to the boil and, stirring constantly, boil until thickened.
4. Add the sliced beets and bring back to the boil.
5. Reduce the heat to medium, add the butter or margarine and simmer until it has melted. Add more lemon juice or vinegar, salt and pepper if desired. Transfer to a heated serving dish and serve at once.

Note: Harvard beets are an excellent accompaniment to egg dishes.

---

3 large baby marrows, halved
150 ml ($^3/_5$ cup) fresh breadcrumbs
1 ml (¼ teaspoon) dried rosemary
1 ml (¼ teaspoon) dried marjoram
1 ml (¼ teaspoon) dried oreganum
1 ml (¼ teaspoon) dried sage
water
Garnish:
25 ml (2 tablespoons) Parmesan cheese, grated

338 Stuffed baby marrows

Serves 6; kJ per portion 250; Prep time 20 min; Cooking time 15 min.

1. Steam the baby marrow halves for 5 minutes in a little water in a covered saucepan.
2. Scoop out enough of the centres to make 150 ml ($^3/_5$ cup), chop the flesh finely and combine with the breadcrumbs, rosemary, marjoram, oreganum and sage. Stuff the marrow shells with this mixture.
3. Place the shells in a greased baking dish and bake in the oven at 180 °C (350 °F) for 10 minutes. Sprinkle with the Parmesan cheese and serve at once.

Variation: Omit the rosemary, marjoram, oreganum, sage and Parmesan cheese. Sauté 25 ml (2 tablespoons) minced onion in a little oil until transparent. Add the chopped baby marrow flesh and sauté for 5 minutes. Combine with 30 ml (6 teaspoons) finely chopped almonds, 50 ml (4 tablespoons) breadcrumbs, 30 ml double cream, 50 ml (4 tablespoons) grated Cheddar cheese, 1 ml (¼ teaspoon) mixed herbs and a sprinkling of salt and pepper to form a stiff mixture. Stuff the marrows and top each with 10 ml (2 teaspoons) grated Cheddar cheese. Place in the greased baking dish and bake in the oven at 200 °C (400 °F) until the topping bubbles, about 20 minutes. Serve at once.

---

680 g small carrots, peeled
62,5 ml (5 tablespoons) butter or margarine
12,5 ml (1 tablespoon) brown sugar
7 ml (1½ teaspoons) aniseed
5 ml (1 teaspoon) salt
2 ml (½ teaspoon) pepper

339 Carrots with aniseed

Serves 4; kJ per portion 390; Prep time 20 min; Cooking time 15 min.

1. Melt the butter or margarine in a large saucepan over medium heat.
2. Stir in the sugar, aniseed, salt and pepper when the foam subsides.
3. Add the carrots and stir so that they are completely coated with the butter mixture.
4. Reduce the heat to low and simmer, covered, until the carrots are tender, about 15 minutes.
5. Turn the carrots and sauce into a heated serving dish and serve at once.

Variations:
1. When making glazed carrots, leave out the aniseed.
2. Use caraway or sesame seeds instead of the aniseed.

1 kg carrots, peeled and
quartered lengthwise
2 large onions, thinly sliced
85 g butter
75 ml oil
75 ml water
5 ml (1 teaspoon) salt
Garnish:
finely chopped parsley

340 Buttered carrots and onions

Serves 4;   kJ per portion 310;   Prep time 15 min;   Cooking time 30 min.

1. Cut the carrot strips into 5 cm pieces and sprinkle with the salt.
2. Heat the oil in a frying-pan and sauté the onions until transparent but not brown.
3. Add the carrots and the water and simmer, covered, over medium heat until the carrots are just tender, about 30 minutes.
4. Remove the vegetables with a slotted spoon and place in a heated serving dish.
5. Dot with butter and serve at once, garnished with chopped parsley.

---

1 medium cauliflower
boiling water
salt
Sauce:
25 ml (2 tablespoons) butter or
margarine
62,5 ml (5 tablespoons) flour
85 g Cheddar cheese, grated
300 ml milk
2 ml prepared French mustard
2 ml (½ teaspoon) salt
2 ml (½ teaspoon) pepper

341 Cauliflower cheese

Serves 4;   kJ per portion 410;   Prep time 15 min;   Cooking time 35 min.

1. In a large saucepan, boil the cauliflower in salted water to cover until just tender, about 20 minutes.
2. Melt the butter or margarine over low heat, remove from the stove and stir in the flour to form a smooth paste. Return to the stove for 1 minute, stirring all the time.
3. Remove from the stove and stir in the cold milk, blending well. Return to the stove and bring to the boil. Simmer, stirring all the time, until smooth then season with the salt and pepper. Stir the cheese and mustard into the hot sauce.
4. Place the cauliflower in a heated serving dish and coat it with the sauce. Place under the grill until golden brown on top. Serve at once.

Variations:

1. Use 750 g broccoli instead of the cauliflower and boil in salted water for 15 minutes. Proceed with step 2.
2. Use 750 g spinach instead of the cauliflower. Boil in salted water for 10 minutes, chop finely and proceed with step 2.
3. Use 750 g leeks instead of the cauliflower and boil in salted water for 15 minutes, drain, then proceed with step 2.

Vegetables with a high water content – cucumber, aubergines, mushrooms – are better cooked by another method than boiling or steaming.

1 large cauliflower, broken
into flowerets and boiled in
salted water for 10 minutes
250 ml (1 cup) dry
breadcrumbs
2 eggs, beaten with
5 ml (1 teaspoon) grated
nutmeg
oil for deep-frying

342 Deep-fried cauliflower

Serves 4;   kJ per portion 380;   Prep time 30 min;   Cooking time 5 min.

1. Dip the cold flowerets first in the egg mixture and then in the breadcrumbs and place them on a sheet of greaseproof paper. Chill for 10 minutes.
2. Heat the oil in a large saucepan or deep-frier to 180°C (350°F) – a 2 cm cube of stale bread dropped in the oil should turn brown in 50 seconds.
3. Drop the cauliflower flowerets into the oil, a few at a time, and fry them until golden brown, about 5 minutes. Remove with a slotted spoon and drain on absorbent paper, then keep warm while frying the other flowerets. Serve very hot.

343 Cucumber with dill

750 g cucumber, peeled and halved lengthwise
5 ml (1 teaspoon) cornflour
juice of ½ lemon
250 ml plain yoghurt
37,5 ml (3 tablespoons) butter or margarine
2 ml (½ teaspoon) sugar
50 ml (4 tablespoons) fresh dill, finely chopped
5 ml (1 teaspoon) salt

Serves 4; kJ per portion 350; Prep time 30 min; Cooking time 20 min.

1. Remove the seeds from the halved cucumbers and rinse the shells well, then cut them into bite-sized pieces.
2. Place the cucumbers in a saucepan with the salt, lemon juice, yoghurt, sugar and 25 ml (2 tablespoons) of the butter or margarine. Simmer, covered, for 10 minutes. Stir in the dill.
3. Combine the remaining butter or margarine with the cornflour to form a smooth paste and stir into the cucumber mixture. Simmer, stirring all the time, until thickened. Transfer to a heated serving dish and serve at once.

Variation: Use fresh tarragon in place of the dill.

344 Grilled endive

4 heads endive, trimmed and outer leaves removed
100 g butter or margarine
12,5 ml lemon juice
5 ml (1 teaspoon) salt
2 ml (½ teaspoon) black pepper
water

Serves 4; kJ per portion 250; Prep time 20 min; Cooking time 15 min.

1. Boil the endives in water for 10 minutes, then drain well. Squeeze out the excess moisture when cool enough to handle.
2. Melt the butter or margarine in a small saucepan over low heat and remove from the stove.
3. Place the endives in a shallow casserole and pour over the melted butter or margarine and the lemon juice, coating well. Season with the salt and black pepper.
4. Place the dish under the grill until the endives are crisp all over, turning occasionally. Serve immediately.

345 Mushrooms in white wine

750 g mushrooms, washed and trimmed
62,5 ml (5 tablespoons) butter or margarine
25 ml oil
juice and grated rind of 1 lemon
300 ml dry white wine
2 ml (½ teaspoon) salt
2 ml (½ teaspoon) pepper
Garnish:
chopped parsley

Serves 6; kJ per portion 280, Prep time 10 min; Cooking time 25 min.

1. Heat the butter or margarine and oil in a large frying-pan and toss the mushrooms in it until tender but not too brown.
2. Add the lemon rind, lemon juice, wine, salt and pepper and simmer, uncovered, for 20 minutes, turning often.
3. Transfer to a heated serving dish and serve at once, garnished with the parsley.

346 Parsnips in cider

8 parsnips, peeled, cored and quartered lengthwise
75 ml (6 tablespoons) butter or margarine, softened
50 ml (4 tablespoons) brown sugar
165 ml cider or apple juice
water

Serves 4; kJ per portion 380; Prep time 10 min; Cooking time 45 min.

1. Boil the parsnips in water to cover until just tender. Drain and transfer to a greased casserole.
2. Combine the rest of the ingredients thoroughly in a bowl and spread over the parsnips in the casserole.
3. Bake in the oven at 200 °C (400 °F) for 20 minutes, basting occasionally. Serve hot.

48 pickling onions
50 ml (4 tablespoons) butter or margarine
450 ml single cream
12,5 ml (1 tablespoon) flour
8 cloves
5 ml (1 teaspoon) sugar
boiling salted water
5 ml (1 teaspoon) salt
2 ml (½ teaspoon) black pepper
Garnish:
grated Parmesan cheese

347 Creamed onions

Serves 8; kJ per portion 350; Prep time 45 min; Cooking time 40 min.

1. Boil the onions, uncovered, in a saucepan with salted water to cover until almost tender. Drain and rinse in cold water.
2. Melt 37,5 ml (3 tablespoons) of the butter or margarine in a frying-pan. Stick the cloves into 8 of the onions and add all the onions to the melted butter or margarine.
3. Sprinkle with the sugar and sauté over low heat, shaking the pan frequently, until the onions are golden brown.
4. Transfer the onions and juices to a shallow casserole and season with the salt and black pepper.
5. Melt the rest of the butter or margarine in a small saucepan. Add the flour gradually, stirring until smooth.
6. Add the cream, stirring constantly until the sauce thickens. Pour the sauce over the onions and sprinkle with grated Parmesan cheese.
7. Bake in the oven at 190°C (375°F) for 20 minutes. Serve at once.

Delicate vegetables that lose their shape or become waterlogged easily – asparagus, cauliflower, broccoli, chicory, leeks, marrows – are better steamed than boiled.

750 ml (3 cups) fresh peas, shelled
62,5 ml (5 tablespoons) butter or margarine
1 ml (¼ teaspoon) grated lemon peel
12,5 ml lemon juice
25 ml (2 tablespoons) fresh mint, finely chopped
water

348 Peas with lemon-mint sauce

Serves 6; kJ per portion 310; Prep time 10 min; Cooking time 5 min.

1. Steam the peas in a little water in a large saucepan for 5 minutes.
2. Stir in the remaining ingredients, transfer to a heated serving dish and serve hot.

Variations:
1. Add 6 cooked baby carrots, thinly sliced.
2. Add 10 parboiled pickling onions.

Note: Frozen or canned peas may be used.

349 Stuffed green peppers

Serves 6; kJ per portion 520; Prep time 30 min; Cooking time 45 min.

Filling 1:

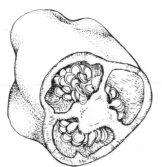

6 medium green peppers, tops cut off and seeded
250 ml (1 cup) pitted black olives, coarsely chopped
500 ml (2 cups) fresh breadcrumbs (white or wholewheat)

1 small onion, finely chopped
250 ml (1 cup) Cheddar cheese, grated
1 egg
250 ml milk
butter or margarine

1. Combine the filling ingredients, except the butter or margarine, and stuff the green peppers with the mixture. Place the green peppers in a greased casserole and dot each with a little butter or margarine.
2. Bake in the oven at 180°C (350°F) for 45 minutes and serve hot.

210

Filling 2:

2 medium onions, finely
chopped
2 cloves garlic, finely chopped
120 g mushrooms, thinly sliced
1 large apple, peeled, cored
and finely chopped
250 ml (1 cup) fresh brown
breadcrumbs

170 g canned sweetcorn
25 ml (2 tablespoons) butter or
margarine
2 ml (½ teaspoon) paprika
2 ml (½ teaspoon) black
pepper
5 ml (1 teaspoon) salt

1. Melt the butter or margarine in a frying-pan and sauté the onions and garlic
   in it for 5 minutes. Add the mushrooms and sauté for a further 3 minutes,
   stirring occasionally. Stir in the breadcrumbs, sweetcorn, apple, salt, pepper
   and paprika and sauté for 1 minute. Stuff the green peppers with the mixture,
   and place in a greased casserole. Dot each with butter or margarine.
2. Bake in the oven at 180°C (350°F) for 45 minutes. Serve hot.

Filling 3:

250 ml (1 cup) cooked brown
rice
1 small onion, minced
25 ml (2 tablespoons) parsley,
finely chopped

1 ml (¼ teaspoon) dried thyme
1 ml (¼ teaspoon) dried sage
50 ml olive oil
500 ml tomato purée

1. Sauté the onion in a little of the olive oil, then combine with all the
   ingredients except the remaining olive oil and the tomato purée.
2. Stuff the peppers with this mixture and place them in a greased casserole.
   Combine the remaining olive oil and the tomato purée and pour over the
   green peppers. Bake in the oven at 180°C (350°F) for 45 minutes and serve
   hot.

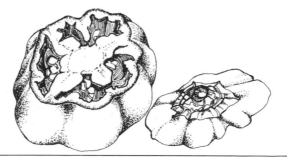

---

500 g new potatoes, thinly
sliced
75 ml (6 tablespoons) Gruyère
cheese, grated
25 ml (2 tablespoons)
Parmesan cheese, grated
butter or margarine
cold water
150 ml single cream
300 ml milk
5 ml (1 teaspoon) salt
2 ml (½ teaspoon) black
pepper

350 Potatoes baked in cream and cheese

Serves 4;   kJ per portion 420;   Prep time 20 min;   Cooking time 50 min.

1. Soak the potatoes in cold water for 2 to 3 minutes. Drain and place them in a
   small saucepan.
2. Add the milk, salt and black pepper and poach on top of the stove until half
   done, about 20 minutes. Drain.
3. Place the potatoes in a greased shallow casserole. Pour over the cream and
   sprinkle with the grated cheeses.
4. Dot with butter or margarine and bake in the oven at 180°C (350°F) until
   done, about 30 minutes. Place a sheet of foil over the dish if the potatoes
   become too brown. Serve hot, straight from the oven.

750 g potatoes, boiled in their jackets in salted water for 10 minutes
1 medium onion, grated
37,5 ml oil
2 ml (½ teaspoon) salt
2 ml (½ teaspoon) pepper

351   Rosti

Serves 4;   kJ per portion 500;   Prep time 25 min;   Cooking time 20 min.

1. Allow the potatoes to cool, then peel and grate them coarsely.
2. Heat the oil in a small frying-pan and sauté the onion until soft.
3. Add the potatoes, salt and pepper and spread evenly to form a thick cake.
4. Fry the cake over low heat for about 10 minutes, lifting it carefully from time to time to check that the bottom does not become too brown.
5. Turn the rosti onto a plate. Add a little more oil to the pan, if necessary, reheat it and replace the rosti in the pan, cooked side uppermost.
6. Continue frying the rosti over low heat for a further 10 minutes, checking occasionally to ensure that it does not become too brown underneath.
7. Turn the rosti onto a serving dish, cut into serving portions and serve immediately, either on its own or with a meat dish.

1 kg small new potatoes, peeled
2 small onions or 4 shallots, finely chopped
50 ml olive oil
lemon juice to taste
1 clove garlic, finely chopped
12,5 ml (1 tablespoon) parsley, finely chopped
12,5 ml (1 tablespoon) chervil, finely chopped
12,5 ml (1 tablespoon) chives, finely chopped
5 ml (1 teaspoon) salt
2 ml (½ teaspoon) black pepper

352   Herbed new potatoes

Serves 4;   kJ per portion 480;   Prep time 10 min;   Cooking time 20 min.

1. Place the whole potatoes in a frying-pan with the olive oil, parsley, chervil, chives, onions or shallots and garlic.
2. Season to taste with lemon juice, add the salt and black pepper and sauté until the potatoes are cooked through and golden brown all over, 15 to 20 minutes.
3. Transfer to a heated serving dish and serve immediately.

Test boiled potatoes with a skewer, not with a fork, to see if they are done – too many holes in them will make them absorb too much water.

3 large boiled onions
500 g boiled potatoes
2 eggs, well beaten
25 ml (2 tablespoons) fresh breadcrumbs
25 ml (2 tablespoons) butter or margarine, melted
37,5 ml (3 tablespoons) Parmesan cheese, grated
150 ml milk
grated nutmeg
5 ml (1 teaspoon) salt
2 ml (½ teaspoon) pepper

353   Potato and onion bake

Serves 6;   kJ per portion 610;   Prep time 30 min;   Cooking time 45 min.

1. Liquidise the onions and potatoes in a blender.
2. Add the milk, grated cheese and eggs and beat until the mixture is soft and creamy.
3. Season to taste with nutmeg, add the salt and pepper. Place in casserole, then sprinkle with the breadcrumbs and melted butter or margarine.
4. Bake in the oven at 160°C (325°F) for 45 minutes. Serve at once.

4 large potatoes, scrubbed and dried
Filling:
4 eggs, lightly beaten
12,5 ml (1 tablespoon) butter or margarine
50 ml double cream
12,5 ml (1 tablespoon) chives, finely chopped
1 ml (¼ teaspoon) grated nutmeg
5 ml (1 teaspoon) salt
1 ml (¼ teaspoon) black pepper

354   Stuffed baked potatoes

Serves 4; kJ per portion 520; Prep time 20 min; Cooking time 1 hr 40 min.

1. Prick the potatoes lightly with a fork, then place them on the centre shelf of the oven at 190 °C (375 °F) and bake for 1½ hours.
2. Remove the potatoes from the oven. Cut a cross in the top of each, and squeeze gently to open. Scoop out the flesh, leaving a 1 cm thick shell, and place the scooped-out flesh in a bowl.
3. Add the butter or margarine to the flesh and mash thoroughly. Add the chives, salt, pepper and nutmeg, mixing well.
4. Stir in the cream and beat until well-blended, then beat in the eggs, one at a time.
5. Stuff each potato shell with filling and place in a baking dish. Return to the oven and bake until the filling is lightly browned, about 10 minutes. Serve at once.

Variations:
1. Use sour cream instead of double cream.
2. Omit the eggs and chives and use 4 rashers of rindless bacon, crisply fried and crumbled and 2 ml (½ teaspoon) chopped parsley.
3. Omit the eggs and use 125 ml (½ cup) grated Cheddar cheese or blue cheese.
4. Combine the scooped-out potato flesh with the following: 225 g canned sweetcorn, 37,5 ml (3 tablespoons) chopped walnuts, 5 ml (1 teaspoon) salt and 2 ml (½ teaspoon) white pepper. Continue with step 5.

---

500 ml (2 cups) cooked pumpkin, mashed
1 egg, beaten
62,5 ml (5 tablespoons) flour
10 ml (2 teaspoons) baking powder
1 ml (¼ teaspoon) salt
butter, margarine or oil
Garnish:
sugar mixed with cinnamon
lemon slices

355   Pumpkin fritters

Serves 4;   kJ per portion 400;   Prep time 30 min;   Cooking time 5 min each

1. Combine the pumpkin, flour, baking powder and salt to form a soft batter.
2. Add the egg and beat well.
3. Heat the butter, margarine or oil in a frying-pan until it sizzles.
4. Drop spoonfuls of the batter in the fat and fry the fritters on both sides until golden brown.
5. Remove and keep warm. Serve hot, sprinkled with sugar and cinnamon and garnished with slices of lemon.

1,5 kg pumpkin, peeled, seeded and cut into smallish chunks
140 g butter or margarine
375 ml water
3 sticks cinnamon
500 ml (2 cups) brown sugar or 400 ml honey
5 ml (1 teaspoon) salt

356   Stewed pumpkin with cinnamon

Serves 5;   kJ per portion 750;   Prep time 30 min;   Cooking time 1 hour

1. Wash the chunks of pumpkin in lightly salted water, then place in a heavy-bottomed saucepan.
2. Add the remaining ingredients to the saucepan and allow to simmer over medium heat until the water has boiled away.
3. Now remove the cinnamon sticks and mash the pumpkin with a fork or rotary beater until it is smooth. Return to the saucepan and allow to heat through – you may add more butter if desired. Serve piping hot.

Variation: Do not mash the pumpkin chunks but at stage 3 add more butter, turn the heat up and allow the pumpkin to brown. Serve immediately.

Sprinkle lemon juice on the flat surfaces of halved onions and your eyes will not water when you chop them.

Use kitchen scissors to cut parsley.

357 Pumpkin goulash

250 g onions, finely chopped
1 kg pumpkin, peeled and cut in 1 cm cubes
12,5 ml (1 tablespoon) flour
62,5 ml (5 tablespoons) butter or margarine
25 ml oil
150 ml water
150 ml sour cream
10 ml (2 teaspoons) caraway seeds
12,5 ml (1 tablespoon) paprika
10 ml (2 teaspoons) salt
Garnish:
chopped chives *or* spring onions

Serves 4; kJ per portion 510; Prep time 30 min; Cooking time 30 min.

1. Heat the oil and butter or margarine in a large saucepan over low heat and sauté the onions in it until golden brown.
2. Stir in the pumpkin and paprika, then add the water and salt and simmer, covered, until the pumpkin is just soft, about 20 minutes.
3. Combine the flour and caraway seeds with 50 ml water to form a smooth paste. Stir into the pumpkin mixture and simmer, stirring, until the mixture thickens.
4. Remove from the stove and stir in the sour cream. Transfer to a heated serving dish and serve at once, garnished with the chives or spring onions.

Variations:
1. Use 1 kg sliced potato instead of the pumpkin.
2. Use 1 kg diced marrow instead of the pumpkin.

358 Basic risotto (F)

250 ml (1 cup) raw long-grained rice
1 large onion, finely chopped
125 ml (½ cup) Cheddar cheese, grated
500 ml water *or* vegetable stock
1 clove garlic, minced or crushed
2 ml (½ teaspoon) dried rosemary
37,5 ml (3 tablespoons) parsley, finely chopped
1 ml (¼ teaspoon) saffron
oil for frying

Serves 6; kJ per portion 400; Prep time 15 min; Cooking time 20 min.

1. Heat a little oil in a large frying-pan and sauté the rice, onion and garlic in it until golden brown.
2. Add 250 ml of the water or stock then sprinkle with the herbs and saffron, mixing well.
3. Simmer over medium heat, adding more water or stock as the mixture dries out. Stir occasionally.
4. When all the liquid has been absorbed and the rice is tender (f), add the cheese and mix well. Continue simmering until the cheese starts to melt. Serve at once.

Variations:
1. Add 125 g mushrooms, coarsely chopped and 125 g walnuts or pecan nuts, finely chopped, with the herbs.
2. Add 125 g canned baby peas, ½ green pepper, seeded and coarsely chopped and 125 g dried apricots, soaked for 1 hour in a little red wine and then chopped, with the herbs.
3. Add 125 g raisins, soaked in hot water for 1 hour and 125 g cashew nuts, finely chopped, with the herbs.

Note: Risotto may be reheated straight from the frozen state, over low heat.

214

250 ml (1 cup) raw long-grained rice, washed thoroughly
125 ml (½ cup) seedless raisins
12,5 ml (1 tablespoon) butter or margarine
1 litre boiling water
25 ml (2 tablespoons) yellow sugar
10 ml (2 teaspoons) turmeric
1 stick cinnamon
5 ml (1 teaspoon) salt

359   Yellow rice with raisins   (F)

Serves 4;   kJ per portion 410;   Prep time 15 min;   Cooking time 1 ½ hours

1. Add the rice, turmeric, cinnamon and salt to the water in a large saucepan and boil briskly for 20 minutes.
2. Drain the rice through a colander, stir in the raisins and steam in the colander over boiling water for 1 hour.
3. Transfer to a serving dish and remove the cinnamon. Stir in the butter or margarine and sugar (f) and serve at once.

---

2 kg spinach
37,5 ml (3 tablespoons) butter
100 ml double cream
10 ml (2 teaspoons) salt
2 ml (½ teaspoon) freshly ground black pepper
3 litres water

360   Creamed spinach

Serves 6;   kJ per portion 680;   Prep time 10 min;   Cooking time ± 15 min.

1. Wash the spinach very well under cold water and then remove the leaves from the tough central stalks.
2. Put the spinach leaves in a saucepan and allow them to cook for about 5 minutes. Then remove spinach from saucepan, place in a colander and rinse well under cold water, allowing all excess water to drain away.
3. Now place the spinach in a heavy saucepan over medium heat. Add the butter, pepper and salt and heat until the butter is completely melted and, using a wooden spoon, blend well into the spinach.
4. At this stage add half the cream and stir into the spinach until the mixture is well blended. Now empty into a bowl and, using an electric blender or rotary beater, beat the creamed spinach until it is smooth and thick.
5. Return the mixture to the saucepan and heat through. To serve, spoon the spinach into a serving dish or bowl and surround with the remaining cream which should be heated. You may also pour the hot cream over the spinach. Serve immediately as an accompaniment to meat, fish or as part of a vegetarian meal.

Variation: For a special occasion you can add 2 ml (½ teaspoon) freshly ground nutmeg and a squeeze of lemon juice to the spinach at step 3. Then spoon the creamed spinach into an ovenproof dish and sprinkle with about 50 ml (4 tablespoons) grated Parmesan cheese. Now pour over the remaining cream and place the dish under the grill until the cheese has melted and browned and the cream is gently bubbling.

1,5 kg sweet potatoes, peeled and sliced
140 g butter or margarine
375 ml water
dried naartjie peel
3 sticks cinnamon
500 ml (2 cups) brown sugar or honey
cardamom seeds
5 ml (1 teaspoon) salt

361   Stewed sweet potatoes

Serves 6;   kJ per portion 900;   Prep time 30 min;   Cooking time 1 hour

1. Wash the sweet potato slices in a little salted water, then arrange them in a heavy-bottomed saucepan. Add the other ingredients and simmer, uncovered, until the water boils away.
2. Increase the heat to high and continue stewing until the potatoes are brown.
3. Remove the cinnamon sticks and naartjie peel and serve at once.

Variation: Use 1,5 kg pumpkin instead of the sweet potato.

6 large cooked sweet potatoes, halved lengthwise
125 ml clear honey, melted
65 ml oil
juice of 1 lemon
1 ml (¼ teaspoon) ground mace

362 Sweet potatoes baked in honey

Serves 6;   kJ per portion 650;   Prep time 15 min;   Cooking time 30 min.

1. Arrange the sweet potatoes in a greased casserole.
2. Combine the remaining ingredients in a bowl and pour the mixture over the potatoes.
3. Bake in the oven at 180°C (350°F) for 30 minutes, basting occasionally with the juices. Serve at once.

---

90 g cooked spinach, puréed
3 egg yolks
5 egg whites
125 ml (½ cup) Cheddar cheese, grated
25 ml (2 tablespoons) dry breadcrumbs
12,5 ml (1 tablespoon) flour
12,5 ml (1 tablespoon) butter or margarine
150 ml milk
1 ml (¼ teaspoon) grated nutmeg
2 ml (½ teaspoon) salt
1 ml (¼ teaspoon) pepper

363 Spinach soufflé

Serves 4;   kJ per portion 620;   Prep time 1 hour;   Cooking time 45 min.

1. Sprinkle a greased 1 litre soufflé dish with the breadcrumbs, using the fingertips to press the crumbs to the bottom and sides.
2. Melt the butter or margarine in a saucepan over medium heat, then remove from the stove.
3. Add the flour, stirring with a wooden spoon to make a smooth paste. Gradually add the milk, stirring all the time. Return to the stove and simmer over low heat, stirring, until the sauce is thick and smooth, about 3 minutes.
4. Stir in the puréed spinach and remove from the stove.
5. Add the egg yolks, one at a time, beating constantly.
6. Gradually beat in the grated cheese, then stir in the salt, pepper and nutmeg.
7. Beat the egg whites in a bowl until they are stiff but not dry, then with a metal spoon fold them carefully into the spinach mixture.
8. Spoon the mixture into the soufflé dish and bake in the oven at 190°C (375°F) until puffed up and lightly browned, 20 to 25 minutes. Remove from the oven and serve immediately.

Variations:
1. Use puréed cooked asparagus instead of spinach.
2. Use puréed cooked broccoli instead of spinach.

---

680 g small turnips, peeled and quartered
1 small onion, thinly sliced
85 ml (⅓ cup) fine dry breadcrumbs
62,5 ml (5 tablespoons) Cheddar cheese, grated
25 ml (2 tablespoons) butter or margarine, softened
1,25 litres water
100 ml sour cream
5 ml (1 teaspoon) paprika
10 ml (2 teaspoons) salt
5 ml (1 teaspoon) black pepper

364 Turnips with sour cream

Serves 6;   kJ per portion 510;   Prep time 30 min;   Cooking time 35 min.

1. Place the turnips, onion, water and 5 ml (1 teaspoon) of the salt in a large saucepan and bring to the boil quickly.
2. Reduce the heat to medium and simmer, covered, until the turnips are tender, about 25 minutes. Drain the vegetables in a colander.
3. Add the remaining salt, pepper and paprika to the vegetables and mash.
4. Stir in the sour cream and blend well. Transfer to a baking dish greased with half the butter or margarine.
5. With the fingertips rub together the remaining butter or margarine, the breadcrumbs and the cheese. Sprinkle on top of the turnip mixture.
6. Place under the grill until the topping browns, about 10 minutes. Serve immediately.

6 large tomatoes, cut into 1,5 cm thick slices
25 ml (2 tablespoons) spring onions, finely chopped
250 ml (1 cup) fresh breadcrumbs
125 ml (½ cup) Parmesan cheese, grated
25 ml olive oil
1 ml (¼ teaspoon) dried oreganum
1 ml (¼ teaspoon) dried basil
1 ml (¼ teaspoon) salt
1 ml (¼ teaspoon) pepper

365　Herbed tomatoes

Serves 6;　kJ per portion 380;　Prep time 20 min;　Cooking time 5 min.

1. Combine the breadcrumbs, onion, herbs, salt and pepper in a bowl.
2. Dip the slices of tomato in the crumb mixture, coating well.
3. Pour the oil into a shallow baking dish, making sure that the bottom is evenly coated.
4. Arrange the tomato slices in the pan and place under the grill for 3 minutes.
5. Sprinkle the Parmesan cheese over the tomato slices and grill until the cheese melts. Serve at once.

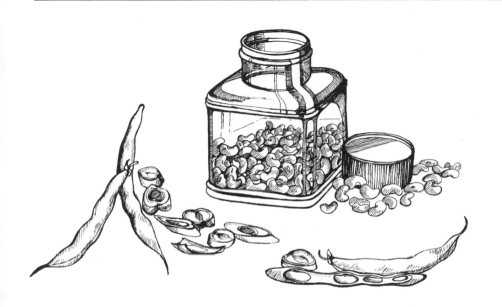

250 ml (1 cup) fresh or frozen lima beans
250 ml (1 cup) green beans, coarsely chopped
250 ml (1 cup) cooked sugar beans
375 ml (1½ cups) canned whole kernel corn, drained
1 onion, coarsely chopped
25 ml (2 tablespoons) butter or margarine
250 ml water
125 ml evaporated milk or single cream
5 ml (1 teaspoon) salt
2 ml (½ teaspoon) pepper

366　Succotash

Serves 4;　kJ per portion 540;　Prep time 30 min;　Cooking time 25 min.

1. Melt the butter or margarine in a large saucepan and sauté the onion in it for 3 minutes.
2. Add the water, lima beans, green beans, sugar beans, salt and pepper.
3. Bring to the boil and simmer, covered, until the vegetables are almost tender, about 15 minutes.
4. Add the corn and simmer, uncovered, until the water has almost evaporated, about 3 minutes.
5. Add the evaporated milk or cream and simmer until hot, adding more salt and pepper if necessary. Serve immediately.

217

250 g raw rice
3 large onions, finely chopped
3 large tomatoes, skinned and
coarsely chopped
120 g cucumber, peeled and
finely diced
3 stalks celery, finely chopped
1 large green pepper, seeded
and thinly sliced
50 ml olive oil
1 ml (¼ teaspoon) saffron *or*
turmeric soaked in 600 ml hot
water
1 large clove garlic, crushed
with 5 ml (1 teaspoon) salt
5 ml (1 teaspoon) grated
lemon rind
12,5 ml (1 tablespoon) parsley,
finely chopped
12,5 ml (1 tablespoon) fresh
thyme, finely chopped
170 g Cheddar cheese, grated
120 g salted cashew nuts
5 ml (1 teaspoon) salt
2 ml (½ teaspoon) pepper
Garnish:
6 black olives, stoned
thin strips of red pepper

367 Vegetarian paella

Serves 4;   kJ per portion 620;   Prep time 45 min;   Cooking time 30 min.

1. Heat the oil in a heavy-bottomed frying-pan and fry the rice until it turns pale yellow.
2. Add the onions, garlic and salt and sauté a further 3 minutes.
3. Add the tomatoes and the water and saffron mixture. Simmer, covered, for 15 minutes.
4. Stir in the cucumber and celery and simmer a further 5 minutes.
5. Stir in the green pepper and simmer until the rice is just tender and all the liquid has been absorbed, about 5 minutes. Add more hot water if the mixture is too dry.
6. Remove from the stove and stir in the parsley, thyme, lemon rind and nuts, adding more salt and pepper if necessary.
7. Turn the mixture into a casserole and garnish with the olives and red pepper strips.
8. Sprinkle the cheese on top and place under the grill until the cheese bubbles and the topping is brown. Serve at once.

1 medium onion, minced
1 green chilli, minced
680 g mixed vegetables, thickly
sliced (e.g. carrots, beans,
aubergines, turnips,
cauliflower, green peppers,
potatoes)
250 ml (1 cup) fresh coconut
flesh, puréed with 190 ml
water in a blender
50 ml oil
5 cm piece fresh root ginger,
peeled and minced
2 cloves garlic, quartered
lengthwise
7 ml (1½ teaspoons) turmeric
12,5 ml (1 tablespoon) ground
coriander
5 ml (1 teaspoon) mustard
seeds
5 ml (1 teaspoon) salt

368 Vegetable curry

Serves 4;   kJ per portion 590;   Prep time 30 min;   Cooking time 35 min.

1. Heat the oil in a large saucepan and sauté the mustard seeds, ginger and garlic for half a minute.
2. Reduce the heat to low and add the onion and green chilli. Sauté until the onion is golden brown.
3. Add the turmeric and ground coriander and sauté for another minute.
4. Add the vegetables and mix well.
5. Stir in the salt and coconut purée, adding a little water if the mixture is too dry. Simmer, covered, until the vegetables are tender, about 30 minutes.
6. Transfer to a warmed serving dish and serve at once.

120 g dried apricots, soaked in water overnight, drained and coarsely chopped
120 g dried prunes, soaked in water overnight, drained, stoned and coarsely chopped
120 g dried apple slices, soaked in water overnight, drained and coarsely chopped
125 ml (½ cup) seedless raisins, soaked in water for 30 minutes
125 ml (½ cup) almond slivers
1 medium cucumber, thinly sliced
60 g canned pineapple chunks, drained and finely chopped
250 ml (1 cup) fresh coconut puréed with 190 ml water in a blender
115 g butter or margarine
325 ml vegetable stock
5 ml (1 teaspoon) ground cloves
2 ml (½ teaspoon) ground ginger
5 ml (1 teaspoon) ground cardamom
2 ml (½ teaspoon) ground cumin
2 ml (½ teaspoon) mustard powder
1 ml (¼ teaspoon) hot chilli powder
12,5 ml (1 tablespoon) grated lemon rind

369   Fruit curry   (F)

Serves 4;   kJ per portion 900;   Prep time 45 min;   Cooking time 35 min.

1. Melt the butter or margarine in a large saucepan and sauté the apricots, prunes, apples, raisins, almonds, cucumber and pineapple in it for 5 minutes, stirring often.
2. Combine the cloves, ginger, cardamom, cumin, mustard, chilli powder and lemon rind in a small bowl.
3. Add the spices to the fruit in the saucepan and mix well.
4. Stir in the vegetable stock, increase the heat to high and bring to the boil. Reduce the heat to low and simmer, partly covered, for 15 minutes, stirring occasionally.
5. Stir in the coconut and simmer a further 15 minutes. Transfer to a heated serving dish and serve at once on a bed of rice (f).

Note:
- Fruit curry will keep for up to 2 months in the freezer. Omit the almonds.
- To serve after freezing, thaw and heat gently and add the almonds just before serving.

1 small onion, finely chopped
2 stalks celery, coarsely chopped
½ cauliflower, broken into flowerets
1 medium carrot, thinly sliced
250 g cabbage, shredded
25 ml oil
2,5 cm piece fresh ginger, coarsely chopped
2 ml (½ teaspoon) salt
Garnish:
5 ml (1 teaspoon) toasted sesame seeds

370   Chinese vegetables

Serves 4;   kJ per portion 320;   Prep time 30 min;   Cooking time 5 min.

1. Heat the oil in a heavy-bottomed frying-pan and stir-fry the onion, celery and carrot over high heat for 1 minute.
2. Add the cabbage, cauliflower, salt and ginger and continue stir-frying for 4 minutes, shaking occasionally. Serve at once, garnished with sesame seeds.

Variation: Use green and red peppers, swedes and sprouts instead of the celery and cabbage.

Soak limp carrots in ice water to freshen them.

Dip tomatoes in flour before frying to keep them whole.

Add a pinch of sugar when cooking tomatoes to eliminate sourness and bring out the flavour.

Plunge tomatoes into boiling water and they will be easy to skin.

371   Vegetable kebabs

1 large aubergine, trimmed and cut in 1 cm cubes
6 medium tomatoes, quartered
250 g button mushrooms, trimmed
2 green peppers, seeded and cut in large pieces
1 clove garlic, crushed
37,5 ml oil
2 ml (½ teaspoon) salt
sprinkling black pepper

Serves 6;   kJ per portion 290;   Prep time 20 min;   Cooking time 10 min.

1. Combine the garlic with the oil, salt and a little pepper in a bowl.
2. Thread the vegetables onto 6 skewers and brush well with the oil mixture.
3. Place the skewers on the grid of the grill pan and grill until the vegetables are tender, turning often and basting 2 or 3 times with the oil mixture. Serve at once.

Note:
● The kebabs may also be grilled over hot coals.
● Before making the kebabs, the aubergine should be cut into thick slices and salted. Allow to draw for 20 minutes, then fry lightly on both sides in oil. Cut into cubes.

372   Ratatouille

1 medium aubergine, thickly sliced
3 baby marrows, thinly sliced
3 large, firm tomatoes, thinly sliced
1 large onion, thickly sliced
200 g mushrooms, thinly sliced
75 ml olive or vegetable oil
3 cloves garlic, finely chopped
2 ml (½ teaspoon) dried oreganum
2 ml (½ teaspoon) dried thyme
5 ml (1 teaspoon) salt
2 ml (½ teaspoon) freshly ground black pepper
Garnish:
grated Parmesan cheese

Serves 4-6;   kJ per portion 480;   Prep time 35 min;   Cooking time 1 hour 10 min.

1. Sprinkle the aubergine with salt and leave to draw for 30 minutes. Rinse and pat dry.
2. Heat the oil in a large frying-pan and sauté the aubergine and baby marrow slices until lightly browned. Place in a greased casserole.
3. Layer the tomatoes, onion and mushrooms over the aubergines and baby marrows, sprinkling each layer with garlic, thyme and oreganum.
4. Sprinkle the salt and pepper over the top layer, and top with a thick layer of grated Parmesan cheese.
5. Bake in the oven at 180°C (350°F), uncovered, for 1 hour. Serve hot.

Variations:
1. Use 2 large gem squash, pips removed and coarsely chopped, and ½ a seeded and coarsely chopped green pepper instead of the tomato and baby marrows.
2. Serve each portion with a lightly fried egg.

Note: Ratatouille may also be stewed on top of the stove. It will take approximately 30 minutes to cook.

250 ml (1 cup) cooked tiny beetroot
250 ml (1 cup) cooked green beans, cut thickly
250 ml (1 cup) cooked carrots, thinly sliced
12,5 ml tarragon vinegar
25 ml oil
2 ml (½ teaspoon) salt
2 ml (½ teaspoon) pepper

373 Vegetables vinaigrette

Serves 12; kJ per portion 320; Prep time 10 min.

1. Arrange the vegetables on a serving dish and sprinkle with the vinegar, oil, salt and pepper.
2. Chill in the refrigerator for at least 1 hour before serving.

Variation: Cooked artichokes, asparagus, broccoli, cauliflower, celeriac, leeks, tiny green onions and peas are also delicious in vinaigrette sauce.

---

1 large onion, finely chopped
120 g mushrooms, coarsely chopped
1 green pepper, seeded and finely chopped
3 eggs
25 ml (2 tablespoons) butter or margarine
120 g fresh brown breadcrumbs
200 g Cheddar cheese, grated
1 ml (¼ teaspoon) mixed dried herbs
5 ml (1 teaspoon) salt
2 ml (½ teaspoon) pepper

374 Mushroom roast (F)

Serves 4; kJ per portion 520; Prep time 30 min; Cooking time 50 min.

1. Melt the butter or margarine in a large frying-pan and sauté the onion and green pepper in it over low heat until the onion is transparent but not browned.
2. Add the mushrooms and continue sautécing a further 2 minutes.
3. Remove from the stove and stir in all the remaining ingredients except the cheese and mixed herbs, blending well.
4. Press the mixture into a greased loaf tin and sprinkle with the cheese and mixed herbs.
5. Bake in the oven at 180 °C (350 °F) for 45 minutes (f).
6. Turn out onto a heated serving dish and serve at once with new potatoes and tomato sauce.

---

60 g walnuts, finely chopped
60 g cashew nuts, finely chopped
120 g brazil nuts, finely chopped
1 small onion, finely sliced
3 small tomatoes, skinned and finely sliced
2 eggs
12,5 ml (1 tablespoon) butter or margarine
25 ml (2 tablespoons) wheatgerm
5 ml (1 teaspoon) mixed dried herbs
5 ml (1 teaspoon) salt
2 ml (½ teaspoon) pepper

375 Nut roast

Serves 4; kJ per portion 710; Prep time 45 min; Cooking time 45 min.

1. Heat the butter or margarine in a small frying-pan and sauté the onion in it until translucent but not brown.
2. Combine the onion and all the other ingredients thoroughly in a bowl, then pack into a greased oblong casserole.
3. Brush the top of the loaf with a little melted butter or margarine and bake on the top shelf of the oven at 180 °C (350 °F) until brown, about 40 minutes. Serve hot or cold.

1 large onion, finely chopped
225 g carrots, finely chopped
225 g turnips, peeled and
finely chopped
2 stalks celery, finely chopped
125 ml (½ cup) Cheddar
cheese, grated
500 ml (2 cups) wholewheat,
soaked overnight in water and
drained
250 ml (1 cup) soya flour
70 ml oil
2 ml (½ teaspoon) dried thyme
2 ml (½ teaspoon) salt
1 ml (¼ teaspoon) black
pepper

376   Wholewheat and vegetable roast   (F)

Serves 6;   kJ per portion 780;   Prep time 30 min + soaking time;   Cooking time 45 min.

1. Heat 65 ml of the oil in a large frying-pan and sauté the onion in it until soft but not brown, about 7 minutes. Stir occasionally.
2. Stir in the carrots, turnips, celery and continue sautéeing, stirring occasionally, until the vegetables are just tender, about 15 minutes.
3. Transfer the vegetables to a large bowl and combine with the wholewheat, soya flour, thyme, salt and pepper, blending well to form a sticky batter.
4. Spoon the batter into a loaf tin greased with the remaining oil and sprinkle the cheese on top.
5. Bake in the oven at 200 °C (400 °F) for 45 minutes (f). Turn the roast out onto a heated serving dish and cool slightly before serving.

---

1 medium onion, finely
chopped
180 g brazil nuts, finely
chopped
60 g cashew nuts, finely
chopped
250 g fresh brown
breadcrumbs
60 g desiccated coconut
12,5 ml (1 tablespoon)
mushroom soup
mix powder
25 ml (2 tablespoons) milk
powder
10 ml (2 teaspoons) Marmite
150 ml water
75 ml oil
1 egg
5 ml (1 teaspoon) dried thyme
5 ml (1 teaspoon) salt

377   Nut rissoles

Serves 6;   kJ per portion 680;   Prep time 45 min;   Cooking time 40 min.

1. Heat 25 ml of the oil in a large frying-pan and sauté the onion until lightly browned.
2. Stir in the mushroom soup mix and salt and blend.
3. Stir in the Marmite and the water and bring to the boil. Boil, stirring constantly, until the sauce thickens. Remove from the stove.
4. Stir in the nuts, brown breadcrumbs, thyme, milk powder and the egg. Allow to stand for 30 minutes.
5. With wet hands, shape the mixture into 6 large patties. Roll the patties in the coconut and flatten them slightly.
6. Heat the remaining oil in a frying-pan and fry the patties in it, turning once, until browned on both sides. Reduce the heat to low and fry for a further 7 minutes. Serve at once, garnished with finely chopped parsley, and with side dishes of sautéed mushrooms and tomatoes.

SALADS AND SALAD DRESSINGS

Until fairly recently, salads were regarded as no more than an accompaniment to cold meats for a light lunch. Fortunately, the nutritional value of salads – most salad vegetables are rich in vitamins, minerals and fibre – is now recognised and they are beginning to figure more and more prominently in our diet.

Salads are extremely versatile: they can be served as hors d'oeuvres, as an accompaniment to the main meal, after the main course in the French manner or as a meal in themselves. Whichever way you serve them, their success will depend largely on the ingenuity of the cook.

Buying and storing salad ingredients

As salads should always be as fresh as possible, it is essential to buy the best and freshest vegetables and fruits available.

- Vegetables should have a bright colour and be crisp and firm. Avoid bruised or limp fruit and vegetables with dead or brown leaves.
- Shop around until you find a store with a regular supply of fresh produce.
- Store fruit and vegetables correctly once you get home, to ensure that they stay fresh. Use the table on p. 200 to 204 as a guide.

Points to note when making a salad

1. All the ingredients must be cold, crisp and fresh. If boiled vegetables are to be used, they should be steamed lightly and cooled well before being added to the salad.
2. Use only the best quality ingredients – poor quality cannot be disguised by elaborate sauces and dressings.
3. Wash lettuce leaves and salad vegetables thoroughly under running water, then in salt water. Drain well in a colander or sieve.
4. Do not store lettuce or any leafy vegetable damp – it will yellow.
5. To crisp lettuce, place it in a bowl of slightly sweetened water and leave in the refrigerator for 1 hour, or store in a special plastic salad crisper.
6. Always use a sharp knife, but remember not to cut salad greens too small. Lettuce leaves should never be cut, but broken with the fingers into bite-sized pieces.
7. Combine salad ingredients lightly with two forks to avoid bruising or mushiness.
8. A natural-looking, fresh salad is always more attractive than one that is over-decorated. Remember, too, that all garnishes must be edible.

223

9. The salad dressing should always complement the salad. If you are not sure that it does, serve the dressing separately. If you are dressing the salad, toss it lightly just before serving.
10. The only exceptions to the previous point are cooked vegetables such as beans, mushrooms or potatoes. These, as well as cooked meat or fish, will improve in flavour if covered with the dressing half an hour or more before the meal.
11. The salad should complement the main course: for example do not serve both an egg aspic and salmon mousse, for they both contain gelatine. Also do not serve separately the same vegetables that have been used in the salad.
12. Serve the salad in an attractive container: wood, glass or ceramic will enhance its appearance. Remember not to wash or soak wooden salad bowls in hot water; wash them quickly and dry them very well. Rub the bowl and wooden salad servers with a little salad oil after cleaning which will ensure that they do not warp.

SALADS

378 Egg mayonnaise

4 hard-boiled eggs, shelled and halved lengthwise
125 ml mayonnaise (p. 186)
5 ml (1 teaspoon) dried mixed herbs
Garnish:
paprika
sprigs of parsley

Serves 4; kJ per portion 640; Prep time 10 min.

1. Place the eggs cut side down on an oblong, shallow serving dish.
2. Stir the mixed herbs into the mayonnaise to blend well, and pour over the eggs.
3. Sprinkle with a little paprika and serve garnished with sprigs of parsley.

379 Chicken salad

500 g cooked chicken, cubed
120 g Gruyère cheese, diced
4 stalks celery, coarsely chopped
1 lettuce, washed and separated into leaves
125 ml mayonnaise (p. 186)
12,5 ml lemon juice
10 ml oil
1 clove garlic, crushed
2 ml (½ teaspoon) grated lemon rind
1 ml (¼ teaspoon) paprika
2 ml (½ teaspoon) salt
2 ml (½ teaspoon) pepper
Garnish:
2 hard-boiled eggs, shelled and sliced
4 stuffed green olives, sliced
4 black olives

Serves 4; kJ per portion 810; Prep time 20 min.

1. Mix the crushed garlic and the oil and toss the pieces of chicken in this.
2. In a large bowl, combine the cheese and chicken.
3. Blend the mayonnaise, lemon juice, lemon rind, paprika, salt and pepper in another bowl.
4. Arrange the lettuce leaves on individual salad plates and pile the chicken and cheese mixture on them with the celery on top.
5. Coat with the mayonnaise and garnish with the sliced hard-boiled eggs, stuffed olives and black olives. Chill well before serving.

Variations:
1. Mix 120 g canned tuna, flaked, with the chicken instead of the cheese.
2. Use strips of red and green pepper instead of the celery.
3. Use chopped canned asparagus and raisins soaked in hot water for 15 minutes instead of the celery.

A tasty and colourful combination of vegetables and gammon in Garden Casserole (recipe 227).

500 ml (2 cups) Granny Smith
apples, cored and diced
250 ml (1 cup) celery, coarsely
chopped
125 ml (½ cup) pecans or
walnuts
125 ml (½ cup) seedless raisins
juice of ½ lemon
mayonnaise or sour cream
lettuce
Garnish:
lemon wedges

380   Waldorf salad

Serves 6;   kJ per portion 940;   Prep time 20 min.

1. Toss the diced apple in lemon juice to prevent its discolouring.
2. Combine the apple and celery in a bowl, then add the nuts and raisins and toss well.
3. Add just enough mayonnaise or sour cream to bind, then toss once more.
4. Serve on a bed of lettuce, garnished with lemon wedges.

---

1 one-minute coddled egg
2 heads cos lettuce, broken into
large pieces
4 slices toast, cut into 2,5 cm
squares
50 ml (4 tablespoons)
Parmesan cheese, grated
juice of 1 lemon
25 ml garlic oil (see below)
7 ml Worcester sauce
75 ml French dressing
(recipe 408)
freshly ground black pepper

381   Caesar salad

Serves 4;   kJ per portion 490;   Prep time 20 min.

1. Wash and dry the lettuce.
2. In a small bowl, combine the lemon juice, garlic oil, Worcester sauce, French dressing and coddled egg and blend well.
3. Place the lettuce in a large salad bowl, add the pieces of toast, freshly ground black pepper to taste and the Parmesan cheese.
4. Pour the salad dressing over and toss until all the lettuce leaves are coated and no excess dressing is left at the bottom of the bowl. Serve at once.

Variation: Use croûtons (recipe 99) or herb croûtons instead of the toast.

Note:
- To make garlic oil, cut 1 clove garlic into 25 ml olive oil and leave for 2 hours. Remove garlic.
- A coddled egg is a soft-boiled egg that has been broken up with a fork.

---

200 g canned tuna, flaked
8 anchovy fillets
2 hard-boiled eggs, shelled and
quartered
4 medium tomatoes, seeded
and quartered
½ onion, thinly sliced
1 green pepper, seeded and
thinly sliced
8 radishes
2 lettuce hearts
4 stalks celery, coarsely sliced
8 black olives
Dressing:
75 ml olive oil
25 ml wine vinegar *or* lemon
juice
12 leaves fresh basil, coarsely
chopped
2 ml (½ teaspoon) salt
2 ml (½ teaspoon) pepper

382   Salad Niçoise

Serves 4;   kJ per portion 710;   Prep time 30 min.

1. Combine all the vegetables, except the olives, in a large salad bowl.
2. Place the tuna, anchovies and quartered eggs on top, and dot with the black olives.
3. Shake all the dressing ingredients together in a screw-top jar and sprinkle over the salad. Serve at once.

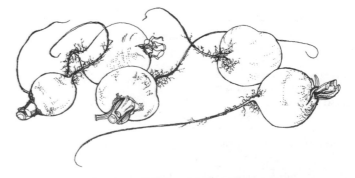

225   A winter's meal of Herbed Beef Ring (recipe 258), herbed new potatoes (recipe 352) and stewed pumpkin (recipe 356).

450 g button mushrooms
100 ml olive oil
juice of 1 lemon
5 ml (1 teaspoon) fresh chives,
finely chopped
5 ml (1 teaspoon) fresh
parsley, finely chopped
salt
black pepper

383 Marinated mushroom salad

Serves 6;   kJ per portion 410;   Prep time 15 min.

1. Remove the stems from the mushrooms. Wash and dry the caps and slice them thinly.
2. Arrange the sliced mushroom caps in a salad bowl. Sprinkle with a little salt and black pepper.
3. Combine the lemon juice and olive oil and pour over the mushrooms. Toss carefully and chill in the refrigerator for 2 hours.
4. Serve sprinkled with the chives and parsley.

---

800 g canned cream of
tomato soup
37,5 ml (3 tablespoons)
gelatine
5 ml cold water
Garnish:
lettuce leaves
sprigs of parsley

384 Tomato salad mould

Serves 6;   kJ per portion 450;   Prep time 20 min.

1. Make the soup according to the directions on the can.
2. Dissolve the gelatine in a little cold water and stir into the soup until melted. Pour the mixture into a wet ring mould.
3. Refrigerate until the mould has set.
4. Line a serving dish with the lettuce leaves and turn the mould out onto them. Serve at once, garnished with parsley sprigs.

Note: Using a non-stick spray on the inside of the mould will make it easier to turn out the salad.

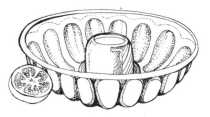

---

3 large avocado pears, peeled,
stoned and mashed
125 ml (½ cup) celery, finely
chopped
10 ml (2 teaspoons) onion,
minced
250 ml mayonnaise (p. 186) or
salad cream (recipe 412)
250 ml sour cream or yoghurt
10 ml (2 teaspoons) gelatine
65 ml cold water
125 ml boiling water
37,5 ml vinegar or lemon juice
5 ml (1 teaspoon) sugar
2 ml (½ teaspoon) onion salt
2 ml (½ teaspoon) salt
2 ml (½ teaspoon) pepper
lettuce
Garnish:
watercress or parsley sprigs

385 Avocado salad mould

Serves 6;   kJ per portion 680;   Prep time 45 min.

1. Soften the gelatine in the cold water for 5 minutes, then add the boiling water and sugar and stir until the sugar and gelatine have dissolved.
2. Combine the remaining ingredients in a large bowl and add the gelatine mixture, stirring well to blend.
3. Pour the mixture into an oiled mould and chill in the refrigerator until set.
4. Turn out on a bed of lettuce leaves, and serve garnished with watercress or sprigs of parsley.

Variation: Add 120 g cream cheese at step 2 for a richer result.

1 kg small potatoes in their
jackets, scrubbed
1 medium onion, finely
chopped
1 hard-boiled egg, shelled and
finely grated
salted water
250 ml mayonnaise (p. 186)
25 ml milk
5 ml (1 teaspoon) mixed dried
herbs
5 ml (1 teaspoon) Aromat or
Fondor
black pepper

386 Potato salad

Serves 6;   kJ per portion 820;   Prep time 30 min;   Cooking time 20 min.

1. Place the potatoes in a large saucepan with the salted water. Bring to the boil over medium heat and boil until the jackets start to split. The potatoes should be cooked but still firm.
2. Drain and allow to cool. Peel the potatoes, then cube and place them in a salad bowl.
3. Add the onion and blend carefully with a wooden spoon.
4. Shake the mayonnaise, milk, mixed herbs, Aromat or Fondor and black pepper together in a screw-topped jar. Pour over the potatoes and onions and mix carefully with a wooden spoon, making sure that all the potatoes are coated.
5. Sprinkle with a little black pepper, then top with the grated egg. Allow to stand for at least 3 hours before serving to allow the flavours to blend.

Variation: Fry 2 rashers of rindless bacon until very crisp. Allow to cool, then crumble. Mix half the crumbled bacon with the mayonnaise dressing and sprinkle the rest with the grated egg over the completed salad.

---

1 kg small new potatoes,
washed and scraped
125 ml (½ cup) onion, finely
chopped
125 ml (½ cup) parsley, finely
chopped
water
25 ml vinegar
85 ml salad oil
5 ml (1 teaspoon) salt
2 ml (½ teaspoon) pepper

387 Hot potato salad

Serves 6;   kJ per portion 840;   Prep time 20 min;   Cooking time 15 min.

1. Place the potatoes and water to cover in a saucepan. Add a little salt and boil until the potatoes are just tender. Drain well. Allow to cool, then peel and halve the potatoes.
2. Heat the oil and vinegar in a frying-pan, add the salt, pepper, onion and parsley and mix well. Sauté for 1 minute.
3. Place the potatoes in a heated serving dish, pour over the hot sauce and toss well. Serve at once.

---

225 g cooked lamb, diced
225 g salami or cervelat, skin
removed and diced
3 slices lean cooked ham, diced
225 g English cucumber,
coarsely chopped
2 large Granny Smith apples,
cored and coarsely chopped
225 g cooked macaroni
5 ml (1 teaspoon) onion, finely
chopped
50 ml (4 tablespoons) canned
butter beans, drained
125 ml mayonnaise (p. 186)
12,5 ml lemon juice
5 ml Worcester sauce
lettuce

388 Meat salad

Serves 6-8;   kJ per portion 1 200;   Prep time 25 min.

1. Combine all the ingredients except the mayonnaise, lemon juice and Worcester sauce in a salad bowl.
2. Blend the mayonnaise, lemon juice and Worcester sauce and pour over the meat mixture. Toss lightly, ensuring that all the ingredients are covered with the dressing. Serve on a bed of lettuce.

227

250 g smoked snoek, flaked and bones removed
1 small green pepper, seeded and finely chopped
1 small onion, finely chopped
4 medium mushrooms, finely sliced
50 ml (4 tablespoons) canned whole kernel corn, drained
12,5 ml vinegar or lemon juice
mayonnaise to moisten
salt and black pepper
Garnish:
thin slices of English cucumber
lemon wedges
lettuce

389 Snoek salad

Serves 2;   kJ per portion 780;   Prep time 20 min.

1. Combine the snoek, green pepper, onion, mushrooms and corn in a bowl.
2. Pour over the vinegar or lemon juice and mix well. Add sufficient mayonnaise to bind, then season to taste with salt and pepper. Allow to stand, covered, for 1 hour before serving.
3. Line a salad bowl with lettuce leaves, spoon the salad into the centre and arrange slices of English cucumber around it. Serve with wedges of lemon.

Variation: Canned peas may be used instead of the corn.

---

500 g pickling onions
2 eggs, well-beaten
water
50 ml vinegar
125 ml (½ cup) sugar
salt and pepper to taste

390 Onion salad

Serves 6;   kJ per portion 280;   Prep time 45 min;   Cooking time 30 min.

1. Place the onions in a saucepan, cover with water and boil until the onions are slightly softened, but still firm to the touch. Drain.
2. Add the beaten egg, vinegar, sugar, and salt and pepper to taste. Bring to the boil and continue boiling until the egg curdles.
3. Remove from stove, transfer to a bowl and cool before serving.

Note: Keeps up to 1 week in the refrigerator.

---

500 g sugar beans
water
50 ml vinegar
125 ml (½ cup) sugar
salt and pepper to taste

391 Sousboontjies

Serves 6;   kJ per portion 680;   Prep time 15 min;   Cooking time 1 ½ hours

1. Soak the beans overnight in water to cover. Drain.
2. Add fresh water, bring to the boil, then reduce the heat and simmer until the beans are soft and the skins loose, about 1½ hours. Drain and remove the skins.
3. Add the vinegar, sugar, and salt and pepper to taste and bring to the boil again. Boil for 5 minutes and remove from the stove.
4. Transfer to a bowl and allow to cool before serving.

Note: Sousboontjies keep well in the refrigerator.

---

750 g onions, finely chopped
1 kg canned sliced peaches in syrup
125 ml white wine vinegar
12,5 ml (1 tablespoon) curry powder
12,5 ml (1 tablespoon) turmeric
1 ml (¼ teaspoon) salt
oil for frying

392 Curried peach salad

Serves 6-8;   kJ per portion 420;   Prep time 30 min;   Cooking time 5 min.

1. Heat the oil in a large frying-pan and brown the onions in it.
2. Add the vinegar and simmer for 1 minute.
3. Stir in the curry powder, turmeric and salt and simmer a further 2 minutes.
4. Add the sliced peaches and as much syrup as the mixture will hold. Mix well.
5. Transfer to a bowl and cool. Serve with meat or fish.

375 ml (1½ cups) cooked rice
1 green pepper, seeded and coarsely chopped
1 onion, finely chopped
2 canned peach halves, finely chopped
12,5 ml chutney
12,5 ml mayonnaise
5 ml (1 teaspoon) curry powder dissolved in 65 ml vinegar
sugar to taste

393   Rice salad

Serves 4;   kJ per portion 610;   Prep time 15 min.

1. Combine all the ingredients in a large bowl.
2. Chill before serving.

---

2 kg string beans, sliced
1 kg onions, sliced
salted water
750 ml brown vinegar
500 ml (2 cups) sugar
25 ml (2 tablespoons) curry powder
50 ml (4 tablespoons) cornflour mixed with a little water
10 ml (2 teaspoons) salt

394   Curried green bean salad   (F)

Serves 8-10;   kJ per portion 210;   Prep time 25 min;   Cooking time 20 min.

1. In a large saucepan, boil the beans and onions in salted water until just tender. Drain.
2. Meanwhile, boil the vinegar and sugar in another saucepan, stirring often, until all the sugar has dissolved.
3. Add the salt, curry powder and cornflour to the vinegar and sugar. Mix well.
4. Add the sauce to the beans and onions and bring to the boil again. Cool before serving (f).

---

1 large head lettuce, shredded
1 bunch watercress
50 g small onions, quartered
125 ml (½ cup) pitted black olives
250 ml (1 cup) Feta cheese, cubed
8 anchovy fillets
25 ml (2 tablespoons) capers
1 clove garlic, finely chopped
250 ml (1 cup) croûtons (recipe 99)
75 ml olive oil
37,5 ml lemon juice
2 ml (½ teaspoon) salt
1 ml (¼ teaspoon) pepper

395   Greek salad

Serves 6-8;   kJ per portion 470;   Prep time 30 min.

1. Soak the garlic in half the olive oil overnight. Fry the croûtons in this mixture.
2. Wash and dry the greens and chill for 1 hour.
3. Place the salad greens in a large salad bowl.
4. Add the onions, olives, capers, cheese, the rest of the olive oil, salt, pepper, lemon juice and anchovies and toss well.
5. Add the croûtons just before serving and toss again.

Variation: Leave out the anchovies and add 4 quartered tomatoes and ½ sliced cucumber.

---

5 large cooked beetroot, skinned and thinly sliced
2 medium onions, thinly sliced
60 ml vinegar
sugar
salt and pepper

396   Beetroot and onion salad

Serves 6;   kJ per portion 210;   Prep time 15 min.

1. Combine the beetroot and onion in a bowl.
2. Sprinkle with a little salt, pepper and sugar and pour the vinegar over. Allow to stand for about 30 minutes before serving. Keeps well.

1 small head white cabbage, finely shredded
125 ml mayonnaise (p. 186)
2 ml (½ teaspoon) salt

397 Coleslaw

Serves 6; kJ per portion 320; Prep time 15 min.

1. Combine all ingredients thoroughly in a bowl.
2. Chill before serving.

Variations:
1. Add 3 grated carrots, 1 seeded and coarsely chopped green pepper and 50 g chopped walnuts.
2. Add 37,5 ml tomato sauce, 5 ml lemon juice, 5 ml (1 teaspoon) sugar, 170 g flaked tuna and 62,5 ml (¼ cup) coarsely chopped radishes.
3. Add 62,5 ml (5 tablespoons) smooth or chunky cottage cheese, 1 ml (¼ teaspoon) celery seed, 125 ml (½ cup) shredded carrot and 62,5 ml (¼ cup) seeded and coarsely chopped green pepper.
4. Add 62,5 ml (5 tablespoons) shredded smoked snoek, 2 grated carrots and 12,5 ml (1 tablespoon) sunflower seeds.
5. Add 62,5 ml (5 tablespoons) chopped cooked chicken, 2 grated carrots and 37,5 ml (3 tablespoons) washed raisins.
6. Add shredded pineapple, 25 ml (2 tablespoons) plumped sultanas and 3 grated carrots.
7. Add 125 ml (½ cup) shredded pineapple, 25 ml (2 tablespoons) desiccated coconut and 2 chopped celery stalks.
8. Add 2 chopped red eating apples sprinkled with a little lemon juice, 2 chopped celery stalks and 62,5 ml (5 tablespoons) shredded salami.
9. Add 2 chopped red-skinned apples sprinkled with a little lemon juice, 170 g cubed Cheddar cheese, 1 large grated carrot and 50 g chopped walnuts.

Note:
- Savoy cabbage may also be used.
- If the dressing is too thick, use 65 ml mayonnaise and 65 ml milk shaken together in a screw-topped jar instead of mayonnaise only.

2 large, firm, ripe tomatoes, thinly sliced
1 large onion, thinly sliced
50 ml vinegar
sugar
salt and pepper

398 Tomato and onion sambal

Serves 4; kJ per portion 200; Prep time 15 min.

1. Combine the onion and tomatoes in a salad bowl.
2. Sprinkle with sugar, salt and pepper and pour over the vinegar.
3. Allow to stand for about 30 minutes before serving.

1 large cucumber, skinned and coarsely grated
25 ml vinegar
5 ml (1 teaspoon) dill, finely chopped
5 ml (1 teaspoon) Aromat

399 Cucumber sambal

Serves 4; kJ per portion 20; Prep time 15 min.

1. Combine all the ingredients in a bowl.
2. Allow to stand for 15 minutes before use, then serve with green bean bredie.

4 large beetroot, cooked, skinned and thinly sliced
300 ml plain yoghurt
2 cloves garlic, crushed
caraway seeds
paprika
salt and pepper

400   Polish beetroot salad

Serves 6;   kJ per portion 350;   Prep time 15 min.

1. Place the beetroot slices in a bowl and sprinkle with salt and pepper.
2. In a separate bowl, beat the yoghurt with the garlic, a little salt and the caraway seeds.
3. Pour the dressing over the beets and sprinkle with paprika.

---

24 medium radishes, thinly sliced
1 small red onion, cut into thin rings
300 ml sour cream
12,5 ml wine vinegar
5 ml (1 teaspoon) sugar
5 ml (1 teaspoon) salt
black pepper

401   Radish and sour cream salad

Serves 6;   kJ per portion 290;   Prep time 15 min.

1. Place the vinegar, sugar, salt and a little pepper in a salad bowl and stir thoroughly.
2. Beat in the sour cream, a few spoonfuls at a time, then fold in the radishes and onion rings. Add more salt and pepper if necessary.
3. Chill in the refrigerator for at least 1 hour before serving.

Variation: Add ½ green pepper, seeded and finely chopped and 3 celery stalks, finely chopped.

---

225 g fine crushed wheat
3 medium tomatoes, coarsely chopped
225 g onions, finely chopped
cold water to cover
50 ml lemon juice
50 ml olive oil
12,5 ml (1 tablespoon) dried mint
25 ml (2 tablespoons) parsley, finely chopped
7 ml (1½ teaspoons) salt
lettuce

402   Tabbouleh

Serves 4;   kJ per portion 400;   Prep time 20 min.

1. In a large bowl, soak the crushed wheat for 10 minutes in enough cold water to cover completely. Drain in a fine sieve and allow to dry.
2. When dry, place the wheat in a deep bowl, add the tomatoes, parsley, onions, lemon juice and salt and toss gently with a fork.
3. Just before serving, stir in the olive oil and mint and add more salt if necessary. Serve at once on a bed of lettuce leaves.

SALAD DRESSINGS

---

25 ml (2 tablespoons) butter
25 ml (2 tablespoons) flour
1 whole egg or 2 egg yolks
200 ml milk
50 ml vinegar
5 ml (1 teaspoon) mustard powder
12,5 ml (1 tablespoon) sugar
5 ml (1 teaspoon) salt
1 ml (¼ teaspoon) cayenne pepper

403   Boiled salad dressing

Makes 300 ml; kJ per portion 300; Prep time 20 min; Cooking time 10 min.

1. Combine the dry ingredients in a bowl.
2. Melt the butter in a saucepan, remove from the stove and stir in the combined dry ingredients to make a roux.
3. Add the milk gradually, stirring all the time. Return to the stove and heat, stirring constantly, until the mixture thickens. Boil gently for 2 minutes.
4. Beat the eggs in the bowl in which the dry ingredients were mixed. Pour a little of the hot mixture onto the eggs, stirring all the time.
5. Gradually add the resulting mixture to the hot sauce, stirring, and heat but do not allow to boil.
6. Remove from the stove and beat in the vinegar, a little at a time.

Note: This dressing may be stored in an airtight jar in the refrigerator for up to 3 weeks.

404 Sour cream dressing

2 eggs
250 ml sour cream
12,5 ml lemon juice
2 ml (½ teaspoon) salt

Makes 300 ml; kJ per portion 450; Prep time 15 min; Cooking time 10 min.

1. Beat the eggs well in the top of a double-boiler.
2. Heat over boiling water in the bottom half of the double-boiler.
3. Add the sour cream, lemon juice and salt, beating all the time, until the sauce is thick and smooth. Do not allow to boil.
4. Remove from the stove and serve either hot or cold with vegetables or salad.

Variations:

1. Add 2 ml (½ teaspoon) mustard powder at step 3.
2. Substitute 125 ml plain yoghurt and 125 ml fresh cream for the sour cream.

405 Sour cream and herb dressing

150 ml sour cream
juice of 1 lemon
1 small clove garlic, crushed
5 ml (1 teaspoon) each fresh dill, basil and marjoram, finely chopped
5 ml (1 teaspoon) sugar
1 ml (¼ teaspoon) salt
freshly ground black pepper

Makes 200 ml; kJ per portion 320; Prep time 15 min.

1. Combine the lemon juice, sugar, salt, pepper and crushed garlic in a small bowl.
2. Stir in the sour cream and fresh herbs, blending well. Use immediately.

406 Condensed milk salad dressing

1 tin sweetened condensed milk
1 egg yolk
5 ml (1 teaspoon) mustard powder
50 ml vinegar
50 ml oil
2 ml (½ teaspoon) salt
1 ml (¼ teaspoon) pepper

Makes 300 ml; kJ per portion 480; Prep time 10 min.

1. Mix the dry ingredients in a bowl.
2. Beat the egg yolk well and add the dry ingredients to it, beating all the time.
3. Add the condensed milk to the egg mixture and beat well.
4. Beat in the oil and lastly the vinegar.

Variation: Add 5 ml lemon juice for a tart flavour.

Note:

• The oil may be omitted, if a crumbly texture is desired.
• Serve with small boiled onions.

407 Thousand island dressing

250 ml mayonnaise (p. 186)
125 ml tomato sauce
5 ml Worcester sauce
5 ml vinegar
2 ml (½ teaspoon) sugar
1 ml (¼ teaspoon) cayenne pepper
2 ml (½ teaspoon) salt
2 ml (½ teaspoon) pepper

Makes 400 ml; kJ per portion 320; Prep time 15 min.

1. Combine the ingredients thoroughly in a bowl and use immediately.

232

100 ml salad or olive oil
25 ml lemon juice
12,5 ml vinegar
5 ml (1 teaspoon) salt
sprinkling freshly ground
black pepper

408   French salad dressing (Vinaigrette)

Makes 135 ml;   kJ per portion 280;   Prep time 5 min.

1. Place all the ingredients in a glass jar or dressing jar with a tight-fitting lid.
2. Shake well and use.

Variations:
1. Add 12,5 ml (1 tablespoon) finely chopped chives, capers or gherkins.
2. Add 25 ml (2 tablespoons) crumbled Blaauwkrantz cheese.
3. Add 1 finely chopped hard-boiled egg and 12,5 ml (1 tablespoon) finely chopped chives.
4. Add 1 clove garlic, crushed.
5. Add 1 ml (¼ teaspoon) tabasco sauce.
6. Add 10 ml (2 teaspoons) grated horseradish.
7. Add 5 ml (1 teaspoon) finely chopped tarragon and 5 ml (1 teaspoon) minced onion.

Note:
- May be stored in the refrigerator for up to 2 weeks.
- Store in a container with a tight-fitting – but not metal – lid. (Metal may be corroded by the vinegar and lemon juice.)

---

25 ml (2 tablespoons) spring
onions, finely chopped
25 ml (2 tablespoons) anchovy
paste
250 ml mayonnaise (p. 186)
125 ml sour cream
37,5 ml tarragon vinegar
5 ml Worcester sauce
1 clove garlic, crushed
1 ml (¼ teaspoon) mustard
powder
62,5 ml (5 tablespoons)
parsley, finely chopped
1 ml (¼ teaspoon) pepper

409   Green goddess salad dressing

Makes 400 ml;   kJ per portion 450;   Prep time 15 min.

1. Combine all the ingredients thoroughly in a bowl.
2. Chill in the refrigerator for 2 hours to allow the flavours to blend and the dressing to thicken.

Note: This dressing will keep for about 2 weeks in the refrigerator.

---

120 g cottage cheese
60 g blue cheese, mashed finely
65 ml buttermilk
25 ml wine vinegar
freshly ground black pepper

410   Blue cheese dressing

Makes 250 ml;   kJ per portion 380;   Prep time 20 min.

1. With the back of a wooden spoon, press the cottage cheese through a fine sieve to remove lumps.
2. Add the buttermilk, stirring all the time.
3. Stir in the vinegar.
4. Add the mashed blue cheese, stirring to blend well.
5. Season lightly with black pepper and serve with green salads.

Variations:
1. Use plain yoghurt instead of the buttermilk.
2. Add 2 ml (½ teaspoon) caraway seeds.

411 Yoghurt and honey dressing

5 ml clear honey
150 ml plain yoghurt
juice of ½ lemon
1 clove garlic, crushed
12,5 ml (1 tablespoon) mint,
finely chopped
2 ml (½ teaspoon) salt
2 ml (½ teaspoon) pepper

Makes 160 ml;   kJ per portion 340;   Prep time 15 min.

1. Combine the honey and lemon juice in a small bowl.
2. Gradually add the yoghurt, stirring all the time to blend well.
3. Stir in the garlic and season with the salt and pepper.
4. Add the chopped mint. Serve with cucumber or tomato salads.

412 Salad cream

yolks of 2 hard-boiled eggs,
rubbed through a sieve
25 ml white wine vinegar
150 ml double cream
5 ml prepared English
mustard
5 ml (1 teaspoon) castor sugar
1 ml (¼ teaspoon) salt
1 ml (¼ teaspoon) cayenne
pepper

Makes 200 ml;   kJ per portion 320;   Prep time 15 min.

1. Rub the salt, cayenne pepper, mustard and sugar into the sieved egg yolks, using a wooden spoon.
2. Add 5 ml of the vinegar and mix well.
3. Gradually add the cream, stirring all the time to blend well.
4. Blend in the remaining vinegar, stirring all the time.

413 Italian dressing

4 anchovy fillets, finely
chopped
140 ml olive oil
juice of 1 lemon
salt and freshly ground black
pepper

Makes 150 ml;   kJ per portion 320;   Prep time 10 min.

1. Combine the anchovies with the olive oil and lemon juice in a small bowl.
2. Season to taste with salt and black pepper.

EGG AND CHEESE DISHES, SANDWICHES, DIPS AND SNACKS

Eggs are essential in the diet because, if fresh, they are nutritionally speaking an almost complete food. They contain proteins of a high quality, fats, vitamins, iron and several other essential elements. Although other kinds of eggs – duck, muscovy duck, ostrich – are available, the most common are those of hens and the best and freshest come from free-range ones.

To test for freshness

A fresh egg is heavy and loses a fraction of weight every day. Gauge the freshness of an egg by plunging it into lightly salted water. If the egg sinks to the bottom it is fresh; if it floats it is a few days old; and if it floats on top it is bad.

Soufflés

A delectable soufflé – light, fluffy and melt-in-the-mouth – looks impressive, tastes better and is *not* very difficult to make.

Important

- The basis of every soufflé is a sauce or a purée. Use a medium purée or sauce for a light soufflé; if it is too thick the soufflé may not rise sufficiently. Any other ingredients, such as fish or ham, must be flaked or cut up in such a way that they are not too heavy.
- Use a proper soufflé dish; the soufflé must rise 2 cm to 4 cm above the rim. Use more egg whites than yolks to obtain a lighter soufflé. Beat the whites until just stiff but not dry, then fold carefully into the sauce or purée but *do not stir or beat the mixture*.
- Bake the soufflé immediately at the given temperature. *Do not open the oven while it is rising or it will collapse.* Serve the soufflé immediately after taking it out of the oven. To serve at a party, have the sauce or purée ready and beat the egg whites, fold them in and bake at the last moment.
- When making a cold soufflé, allow the gelatine mixture to set slightly before folding the egg whites into. it.

4 eggs
cold water

414   Boiled eggs

Serves 4;   kJ per portion 300;   Prep time 5 min;   Cooking time 3½-10 min.

1. Place the eggs and cold water in a saucepan and bring to the boil. Boil for 3½ minutes for a soft-boiled egg, and 8 to 10 minutes for a hard-boiled egg.
2. Place in a container of cold water to cool down the shells, and serve.

Note: This method is best if you want a light textured egg white. If a 'heavier' egg white is desired, place the eggs in boiling water for 4 minutes for a soft-boiled egg and 10 minutes for a hard-boiled one.

4 eggs
butter or margarine

415   Fried eggs

Serves 4;   kJ per portion 515;   Prep time 10 min;   Cooking time 5 min.

1. Melt the butter or margarine in a frying-pan so that it coats the surface lightly.
2. Break each egg into a saucer and slide it carefully into the hot butter or margarine.
3. If a crisp finish under the egg is desired, heat the butter or margarine so that it bubbles as the egg is added. If you do not want a crisp finish, the fat should be just hot enough to set the egg white.
4. Remove from the frying-pan with a fish slice and serve at once.

4 eggs
butter or margarine
salt

416   Poached eggs

Serves 4;   kJ per portion 400;   Prep time 10 min;   Cooking time 4 min.

1. Melt a little butter or margarine in the cups of an egg poacher half-filled with gently simmering water.
2. Crack each egg shell in turn, pour the egg into a saucer and then slide it into one of the cups of the poacher.
3. Sprinkle with salt, cover the pan and poach over the steadily boiling water for 3 to 4 minutes.
4. Slide the egg onto buttered toast and serve at once with Worcester sauce.

Note: If you do not have a poaching pan, use the following method:
Bring 300 ml water to the boil in a saucepan and stir in 10 ml vinegar and a pinch of salt. Break the eggs one by one into a saucer, and slide each one into the boiling water and leave until the whites have set, about 3 minutes. Drain carefully with a fish slice or slotted spoon and place on the buttered toast.

4 large or 6 small eggs
25 ml milk *or* water
5 ml (1 teaspoon) parsley,
finely chopped
5 ml (1 teaspoon) salt
1 ml (¼ teaspoon) pepper
oil or butter for frying

417   Scrambled eggs

Serves 4;   kJ per portion 550;   Prep time 20 min;   Cooking time 10 min.

1. Beat all the ingredients, except the oil or butter, together in a bowl.
2. Heat a little butter or oil in a frying-pan and pour in the eggs.
3. Allow the base to set, then reduce the heat to medium and scramble the eggs with a spatula until the egg is cooked through, but taking care not to let it dry out. Serve at once.

Variations:

1. Add 1 medium onion, finely chopped and 85 g mushrooms, finely sliced. Sauté in the oil or butter before adding the eggs.
2. Add 1 medium onion, finely chopped; ½ green pepper, seeded and finely chopped and 3 tomatoes, skinned and coarsely chopped. Sauté in the oil or butter before adding the eggs.
3. Add 2 smoked frankfurters, thinly sliced; 1 medium onion, finely chopped and ½ green pepper, finely chopped. Sauté in the oil or butter before adding the eggs.
4. Add 85 g cooked ham, diced; 85 g asparagus salad cuts and 1 medium onion, finely chopped. Sauté the ham and onion in the oil or butter, add the eggs and stir in the asparagus.
5. Add 4 rashers rindless bacon, diced; 85 g mushrooms, thinly sliced and 60 g whole kernel corn. Fry the bacon until crisp, then add the mushrooms and sauté until tender. Pour in the eggs and stir in the corn.
6. Add 85 g canned tuna, flaked; 2 stalks celery, coarsely chopped and ½ green pepper, seeded and finely chopped.
7. Add 1 medium onion, finely chopped; 3 tomatoes, skinned and coarsely chopped and 2 ml (½ teaspoon) curry powder. Sauté in the oil or butter before adding the eggs.
8. Add 1 medium onion, finely chopped; 85 g mushrooms, finely sliced and 85 g mature Cheddar or blue cheese, grated. Sauté the onion and mushrooms in the oil or butter, add the eggs and stir in the grated cheese.

Scrambled eggs should have a moist, glossy look. To ensure this, keep the heat low and turn the mixture carefully; overstirring at too high a temperature makes it watery and tough.

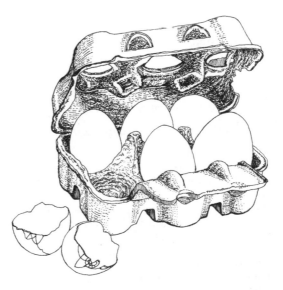

Heat the knife before cutting hard-boiled eggs.

**2 eggs
12,5 ml (1 tablespoon) butter
or margarine
12,5 ml milk or water
salt and pepper to taste**

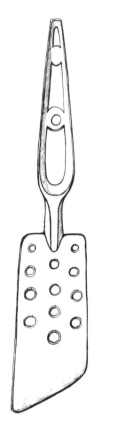

418 Basic omelette

Serves 1; kJ per portion 750; Prep time 10 min; Cooking time 5 min.

1. Combine the eggs in a bowl with the water or milk and add salt and pepper to taste. Beat well.
2. Melt the butter or margarine in a small frying-pan. When the butter or margarine begins to bubble, the temperature is right to add the eggs.
3. Pour in the beaten eggs, reduce the heat to low and leave for approximately 1 minute to allow the base to set.
4. Loosening the egg from the sides of the pan, tilt the pan from side to side so that the still-liquid egg in the centre flows to the edge and from there to the bottom.
5. When the egg is set to the desired consistency, with a spatula or fish slice fold it over away from the handle and tip onto a heated plate. Serve at once, garnished as desired.

Variations:

1. Add 12,5 ml (1 tablespoon) chopped fresh herbs or 5 ml (1 teaspoon) mixed dried herbs to the beaten eggs.
2. Add 37,5 ml (3 tablespoons) grated Cheddar or Roquefort cheese, either mixed with the beaten eggs or sprinkled over the omelette just before it is folded.
3. Add 37,5 ml (3 tablespoons) minced cooked ham in 125 ml white sauce (p. 178) just before folding the omelette.
4. Spoon 37,5 ml (3 tablespoons) minced cooked chicken in 125 ml white sauce onto the omelette just before folding.
5. Add 1 small can creamed mushrooms, heated, as a filling to the omelette.
6. Add 1 large tomato, skinned, coarsely chopped and sautéed in a little butter or margarine just before folding the omelette.
7. Make an omelette filling of 1 small can mixed vegetables in 50 ml white sauce (p. 178). Add just before folding the omelette.
8. Add 1 small can mussels, washed thoroughly and drained, in 50 ml white sauce (p. 178) as a filling just before folding the omelette.

Note:

- If you use water instead of milk the omelette will be lighter.
- Omelettes must be eaten as soon as they come off the pan.

**3 eggs
60 g streaky bacon, finely
chopped
110 g mature Cheddar cheese,
grated
1 small onion, finely chopped
½ small green pepper, finely
chopped
60 g mushrooms, thinly sliced
110 g mixed cooked vegetables,
diced
2 tomatoes, skinned and
coarsely chopped
25 ml (2 tablespoons) butter or
margarine
75 ml milk
5 ml (1 teaspoon) mixed dried
herbs
5 ml (1 teaspoon) salt
2 ml (½ teaspoon) pepper**

419 Farmhouse omelette

Serves 4; kJ per portion 950; Prep time 20 min; Cooking time 10 min.

1. Melt the butter or margarine in a large frying-pan and sauté the onion, green pepper, mushrooms and bacon in it until soft.
2. Meanwhile, beat the eggs, milk, herbs, salt and pepper together thoroughly in a bowl.
3. Add the egg mixture to the pan and sprinkle with the cooked vegetables, chopped tomatoes and grated cheese.
4. Fry over medium heat until the base is firm and the egg lightly set. Serve immediately with a green salad.

Note: To skin tomatoes, dip them in boiling water for 30 seconds and the skins will slip away from the flesh.

4 eggs
85 g Parmesan cheese, grated
680 g spinach, washed and drained
37,5 ml olive oil
grated nutmeg
salt and pepper

420 Eggs Florentine

Serves 4;   kJ per portion 500;   Prep time 20 min;   Cooking time 15 min.

1. Heat the olive oil in a large frying-pan. Add the spinach and simmer, covered, until tender.
2. Season the spinach to taste with salt, pepper and nutmeg, drain well and place in 4 ramekins.
3. Break 1 egg into each ramekin and sprinkle the Parmesan cheese on top.
4. Bake in the oven at 180 °C (350 °F) until the egg is set and the cheese starts to melt, about 15 minutes. Serve hot.

4 hard-boiled eggs, shelled and finely chopped
1 egg, lightly beaten
4 rashers rindless bacon, chopped
1 large onion, finely chopped
25 ml (2 tablespoons) butter or margarine
280 ml Béchamel sauce (p. 179)
lemon juice
12,5 ml (1 tablespoon) parsley, finely chopped
fine dry breadcrumbs
oil for frying

421 Egg croquettes

Serves 5;   kJ per portion 950;   Prep time 20 min;   Cooking time 5 min.

1. Make a thick Béchamel sauce (p. 179) and let it cool completely.
2. Heat the butter or margarine in a frying-pan and sauté the onion and bacon until the onion is golden brown.
3. Combine the onion mixture, hard-boiled eggs, parsley and the cold Béchamel sauce and form into small ovals or croquettes.
4. Dip the croquettes first in the beaten egg and then in the breadcrumbs.
5. Deep-fry the croquettes in hot oil until golden brown.
6. Drain on absorbent paper, sprinkle with lemon juice and serve at once.

4 hard-boiled eggs
225 g sausage meat
25 ml (2 tablespoons) flour
breadcrumbs for coating
1 beaten egg for coating
125 ml milk for coating
deep fat for frying

422 Scotch eggs

Serves 4;   kJ per portion 800;   Prep time 30 min;   Cooking time 5 min.

1. Roll the cooled hard-boiled eggs in a little flour.
2. Divide the sausage meat into four and fold evenly and smoothly around each of the floured eggs.
3. Combine the beaten egg and milk in a bowl.
4. Coat the sausage-covered eggs in the egg and milk mixture, then coat completely in the breadcrumbs.
5. Heat the fat or oil in a deep-fryer and fry the Scotch eggs in it until cooked through and browned all over. Drain well. Serve cold.

Note: Do not rush the frying process, because the sausage meat has to cook through; it should take about 5 minutes before it is ready.

Cheese contains a large percentage of the essential nutrients and is an excellent protein supplement to any dish or meal. It also contains calcium and the other nutrients found in milk. Cheese can be eaten as it is without any further preparation, or it can be used to flavour a wide variety of dishes from pasta to meat, fish and sauces to soups.

There are a great many varieties of cheese, many of which have taken the name of the town or city where they originated; for instance, Gouda and Cheddar. Most of those we know are made from cows' milk, but in some European and Middle Eastern countries, sheep or goats' milk is often used.

Cheeses may be divided into the following groups:

1. Soft cheeses which require no ripening
These cheeses have a high moisture content and will only keep for 1 to 2 weeks. *Cream cheese* is the best example of this type and is made from milk with a high fat content or from thin cream. The texture is soft and smooth, and it has a delicate, slightly sour taste.
Cottage cheese is very similar to cream cheese in appearance, but is made from skimmed milk with a low fat content. To both cream and cottage cheese various other ingredients – such as fruit, paprika, onion or chives – may be added.

2. Soft cheeses which are ripened
How much moisture there is in the air and at what temperature the cheese is stored determine the ripening process and thus the characteristics. Examples are Camembert, Brie, Limburger and Pont l'Evêque. These cheeses sometimes have a mould on the surface. Always check the date on which ripening commenced (given on the wrapper) and eat within 1 week of this date.

3. Semi-soft, ripened cheeses
Tilsiter and Bel Paese are ripened for a longer period than the soft cheeses above, and this makes them softer and creamier.

4. Firm or hard ripened cheeses
These cheeses keep well and are freely available. Examples are Cheddar, Gouda, Cheshire, Emmenthal and Cheddar or Gouda-type cheeses with cumin seeds or black pepper.

5. Very hard cheeses

These cheeses mature in anything from 5 months to two years. They keep exceptionally well and are generally used as flavouring in meat and pasta dishes. Parmesan is a good example.

6. The blue mould cheeses

A bacteria assisted by *Penicillium roqueforti,* a blue-green mould, is used to ripen this type of cheese. The mature cheese is soft and crumbly, with a typically marbled appearance. Traditionally, Roquefort cheese is made from sheep's milk. The local version of this type of cheese is sold under the name Blaauwkrantz. Blue cheeses can be kept for up to 2 weeks, if well-wrapped.

7. Processed and smoked cheeses

There is also a great variety of pasteurized and smoked cheeses. The cheese is processed, melted and then poured into moulds to set. Various ingredients – such as tomato juice, pimento, ham, fish, onion – may be added. Pasteurized cheeses need no further ripening and will keep for up to 1 month.

Cooking with cheese

1. Choose the right kind of cheese for the specific dish. Cheddar and Parmesan are best for cooking because they melt easily and impart a distinctive flavour. Crumbled Roquefort can add a piquant taste to a sauce, or salad. Use cream or cottage cheese instead of Béchamel sauce when making Lasagna (recipe 261) a really unusual mixture of flavours and textures.
2. Do not overcook cheese, as it turns hard and tough. If a dish must be cooked for a long time over a high temperature, add the cheese towards the end of the cooking period, when just enough time remains for it to melt.
3. When making a cheese sauce, add the cheese right at the end – after the sauce has been removed from the stove.

Homemade Cottage cheese

Either fresh or sour whole milk may be used to make cottage cheese.

1. Place milk in a bowl and allow to thicken, then skim it.
2. Stand the bowl in a basin or saucepan containing fairly warm water and, using a spatula, cut the milk to separate the curd from the whey.
3. Line a sieve with a double layer of cheesecloth and strain the milk through it. Leave to stand for 30 to 45 minutes to allow all the whey to drain out of the curd.
4. Turn the curd into a mixing bowl and add a little salt.

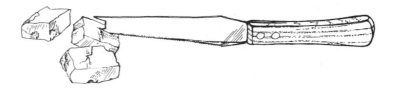

423 Welsh rarebit

500 ml (2 cups) Cheddar cheese, grated
25 ml (2 tablespoons) butter or margarine
50 ml (4 tablespoons) flour
125 ml milk
12,5 ml Worcester sauce
5 ml prepared French mustard
salt and pepper to taste
buttered toast

Serves 4; kJ per portion 950; Prep time 20 min; Cooking time 10 min.

1. Melt the butter or margarine in a saucepan over low heat.
2. Add the flour and cook, stirring all the time, for 2 to 3 minutes.
3. Gradually add the milk, stirring continuously until the sauce is smooth and thick.
4. Add most of the cheese, the mustard, Worcester sauce, salt and pepper and simmer, stirring all the time, until the cheese has melted.
5. Spread the mixture on toast, sprinkle with the remaining grated cheese and place under the grill until golden brown. Serve at once.

Variations:

1. Cover the slices of toast with hot celery or asparagus then continue with step 5.
2. Use 135 ml canned condensed tomato soup instead of the milk and Worcester sauce.
3. Place a slice of tomato on top of the rarebit-topped toast and place under the grill.
4. Place a poached egg on top of the toast after grilling.

Note: The rarebit may be kept in the refrigerator for up to 1 week.

424 Cheese fondue

500 g Gruyère or Gouda cheese, grated
300 ml dry white wine
salt and pepper to taste

Serves 4-6; kJ per portion 750; Prep time 5 min; Cooking time 15 min.

1. Grease the bottom and sides of the fondue pot or an earthenware pot with butter.
2. Add the grated cheese, salt and pepper and stir in the wine. Heat over the flame, stirring all the time to form a smooth sauce. Keep warm over gentle heat, stirring occasionally.
3. Serve with toasted cubes of bread, crisply fried bacon, thickly sliced smoked frankfurters or garlic bread cubes to dip on fondue forks into the cheese.

Variation: Add 12,5 ml brandy, Kirsch or van der Hum at step 2.

Note:
- Do not let the mixture boil as this will make it tough and tasteless.
- Using Gouda cheese will give the fondue a milder flavour.

425 Cheddar fondue

500 g Cheddar cheese, grated
12,5 ml (1 tablespoon) cornflour
1 clove garlic (optional)
300 ml cider or beer
1 ml (¼ teaspoon) nutmeg, grated
1 ml (¼ teaspoon) salt
1 ml (¼ teaspoon) cayenne pepper

Serves 4-6; kJ per portion 780; Prep time 10 min; Cooking time 15 min.

1. Grease the bottom and sides of the fondue pot or an earthenware pot with butter and rub it lightly with a cut clove of garlic.
2. Add the grated cheese and most of the cider or beer, reserving a little for blending with the cornflour.
3. Stir over a low flame until the cheese melts, then season with salt, cayenne pepper and nutmeg.
4. Blend the cornflour with the remaining cider or beer to form a smooth paste and stir into the melted cheese. Keep the mixture warm over a gentle heat, stirring from time to time.

5. Serve with toasted cubes of bread, crisply fried bacon, thickly sliced smoked frankfurters or garlic bread cubes to dip into the fondue with the fondue forks.

Note: Blending in the cornflour ensures that the mixture will not curdle.

---

170 g Blaauwkrantz cheese, crumbled
225 g cream cheese
25 ml (2 tablespoons) spring onions, finely chopped (green part only)
5 ml anchovy essence
10 ml oil
180 ml mayonnaise (p. 186)
180 ml double cream
18,5 ml (1½ tablespoons) gelatine, dissolved in 65 ml hot water
1 ml (¼ teaspoon) cayenne pepper
Garnish:
8 lettuce leaves
12 tomato slices
8 stuffed olives, halved

426 Blaauwkrantz ring

Serves 6-8; kJ per portion 520; Prep time 30 min + setting time.

1. Grease a 1 litre ring mould with the oil and drain, upside down, on absorbent paper.
2. With the back of a wooden spoon, rub the Blaauwkrantz cheese through a fine sieve into a mixing bowl.
3. Beat the cream cheese, cayenne pepper, anchovy essence and spring onions into the Blaauwkrantz.
4. Stir the dissolved gelatine into the cheese mixture and continue stirring until thoroughly blended.
5. With a metal spoon, fold the mayonnaise into the mixture, then fold in the double cream.
6. Place the mould in the refrigerator and chill until set, about 1 hour.
7. Remove from the refrigerator, dip the bottom of the mould into hot water and invert a plate over the mould. Reverse the two and the ring will slip onto the plate.
8. Serve garnished with lettuce leaves, tomato slices and olives.

To store cheese for a long time without mould forming, grate the cheese and store it in an airtight container in the freezer.

---

3 eggs, separated
85 g mature Cheddar cheese, grated
140 ml milk
25 ml (2 tablespoons) butter or margarine
25 ml (2 tablespoons) flour
2 ml (½ teaspoon) salt
2 ml (½ teaspoon) pepper

427 Cheese soufflé

Serves 4; kJ per portion 620; Prep time 30 min; Cooking time 40 min.

1. Melt the butter or margarine in a saucepan and stir in the flour, mixing to a smooth paste.
2. Gradually stir in the milk then bring to the boil, stirring all the time. Remove from the stove and cool slightly.
3. Add the cheese, salt and pepper and egg yolks one by one, beating well.
4. Beat the egg whites stiffly and fold into the cheese mixture. Pour into a soufflé dish, which has a doubled band of waxproof paper tied around it and extending above the rim.
5. Bake in the centre of the oven at 200 °C (400 °F) until well risen and brown, about 30 minutes. Remove the paper and serve immediately.

Note: Successful soufflés are achieved if two points are observed.
● The eggs should be beaten until they are stiff but still moist.
● If a soufflé is left in the oven for too long it will become tough and leathery. Ideally, the soufflé should still be slightly moist and frothy at its centre.

250 g cream cheese
3 egg yolks
3 egg whites
5 ml (1 teaspoon) butter or margarine
10 ml (2 teaspoons) flour
25 ml (2 tablespoons) dry breadcrumbs
90 ml sour cream
90 ml milk
2 ml (½ teaspoon) salt

428 Cheese and sour cream soufflé

Serves 4;   kJ per portion 700;   Prep time 30 min;   Cooking time 35 min.

1. Grease a 1 litre soufflé dish with the butter or margarine and sprinkle the breadcrumbs over it, pressing them with the fingertips to the bottom and sides. Set aside.
2. Beat the cream cheese until soft in a bowl, using a wooden spoon, then gradually beat in the sour cream. Continue beating until the mixture is smooth.
3. Add the egg yolks one at a time, beating well after each addition, then beat in the milk, salt and flour.
4. In a separate bowl, beat the egg whites until stiff but not dry and fold carefully with a metal spoon into the cheese mixture.
5. Spoon the mixture into the soufflé dish and bake in the oven at 180°C (350°F) until it is puffed up and lightly browned, about 35 minutes. Serve immediately.

Note: This soufflé may also be served as a dessert. Sprinkle the top with confectioner's sugar and serve with a hot fruit sauce.

---

450 g mashed potatoes
110 g mature Cheddar cheese, grated
1 egg yolk
flour
5 ml (1 teaspoon) chives, finely chopped
oil for shallow frying
salt and pepper

429 Cheese and potato rissoles

Serves 6;   kJ per portion 710;   Prep time 20 min;   Cooking time 5 min.

1. Combine the mashed potatoes and 85 g of the grated cheese thoroughly in a bowl.
2. Stir in the egg yolk, chives and salt and pepper to taste and mix well. With floured hands form into balls and coat the rissoles in flour.
3. Heat the oil in a frying-pan and fry the rissoles in it on both sides until golden brown. Serve hot with tomato sauce poured over them and garnished with the remaining grated cheese.

---

170 g raw elbow macaroni
120 g onion, finely chopped
170 g mature Cheddar cheese, grated
62,5 ml (5 tablespoons) butter or margarine
40 g flour
425 ml milk
1 clove garlic, crushed
salt and pepper
Garnish:
slices of green or red pepper

430 Macaroni cheese   (F)

Serves 4;   kJ per portion 2 000;   Prep time 45 min;   Cooking time 20 min.

1. In a small saucepan, boil the macaroni in salted water until tender, about 10 minutes. Drain well.
2. Meanwhile, melt the butter or margarine in a frying-pan and sauté the onion and garlic in it until soft.
3. Stir in the flour, cook for 1 minute, then gradually blend in the milk. Bring to the boil, stirring all the time, for 3 minutes.
4. Stir in 150 g of the cheese and simmer for 3 minutes, then add salt and pepper to taste.
5. Add the macaroni to the cheese sauce, blending well.
6. Transfer to an ovenproof dish and sprinkle with the remaining cheese.
7. Place under the grill until the topping is brown and bubbly (f). Serve at once, garnished with slices of red or green pepper.

Variation: Add 250 g diced corned beef and 60 g slivered almonds at step 4.

244

480 g canned asparagus spears, drained and the liquid reserved
250 ml (1 cup) Cheddar cheese, grated
37,5 ml (3 tablespoons) butter or margarine
37,5 ml (3 tablespoons) flour
125 ml cream
salt and pepper
Garnish:
small packet potato crisps, crumbled

431 Hot asparagus crisp (F)

Serves 8; kJ per portion 1 400; Prep time 30 min; Cooking time 20 min.

1. Place the asparagus spears in a greased ovenproof dish.
2. Melt the butter or margarine in a saucepan and stir in the flour gradually when it bubbles.
3. Remove the pan from the stove and gradually stir in the asparagus liquid.
4. Return to the stove and stir continuously until thickened.
5. Stir in the cream and salt and pepper to taste.
6. Pour the mixture over the asparagus, then sprinkle with grated cheese and the crushed crisps.
7. Bake in the oven at 200 °C (400 °F) for 15 minutes (f) and serve at once.

SANDWICH FILLINGS AND TOPPINGS

Sandwiches and toasts are thought of as the traditional 'packed lunches' of school-going children, office workers and others, but in reality they are much more than this: they can make tasty snacks, elegant hors d'oeuvres and substantial meals in themselves. With a little imagination, delicious and unusual combinations of flavours and textures can make every sandwich a gastronomical adventure.

SANDWICH FILLINGS

Cheese:
1. Grated Cheddar or sweetmilk cheese topped with slices of tomato and onion rings.
2. Processed cheese slices topped with thinly sliced cucumber and sprinkled with parsley.
3. Cottage cheese topped with thinly sliced salami.
   Note: Do not keep overnight as the salami will colour the cheese.
4. Thinly sliced Cheddar cheese topped with sliced radishes and a thin layer of salad cream or mayonnaise.

245

5. Grated Blaauwkrantz cheese topped with chopped fresh parsley, tomato slices and crumbled crisp bacon.
6. Slices of Gruyère cheese topped with tomato slices, salami slices, red pepper slices, sliced stuffed olives and anchovy fillets.
7. Cream or skimmed milk cheese mixed with chopped shrimps, slivered almonds and lemon juice and topped with sliced stuffed olives and drained crushed pineapple.
8. Cottage cheese mixed with minced onion, finely chopped green pepper and mayonnaise.
9. Cream cheese or skimmed milk cheese mixed with grated carrot and raisins on a bed of lettuce.
10. Cream or cottage cheese mixed with finely chopped onion and green pepper, a little hot pepper sauce, chopped nuts and finely chopped hard-boiled eggs.
11. Cream or cottage cheese topped with sliced pickled beetroot on a bed of lettuce.
12. Cottage cheese mixed with chopped gherkins, chopped stuffed olives and mayonnaise and topped with crumbled crisp bacon.
13. Cottage cheese mixed with chopped gherkins, chopped stuffed olives, finely chopped walnuts and salad dressing on a bed of lettuce.
14. Cream cheese or skimmed milk cheese mixed with horseradish, minced onion, finely shredded biltong and a little cream.
15. Gouda cheese slices on rye bread with lettuce and a dab of prepared German mustard.
16. Cream cheese or skimmed milk cheese mixed with chopped preserved ginger and a little milk.
17. Cream cheese or skimmed milk cheese mixed with finely chopped dates and a little lemon juice.

Eggs:
1. Scrambled eggs topped with slices of tomato.
2. Sliced hard-boiled egg and sliced liver sausage on a bed of lettuce, topped with watercress.
3. Chopped hard-boiled eggs topped with mayonnaise mixed with a little curry powder and a few chopped stuffed olives.
4. Sliced hard-boiled egg topped with sliced tomato and a dab of mayonnaise.
5. Finely chopped hard-boiled egg topped with sardines and a dab of mayonnaise mixed with spicy German mustard.

Meat:
1. Thinly sliced cooked ham on a bed of lettuce and topped with a little piccalilli or mustard pickles.
2. Thinly sliced cooked beef topped with a little coleslaw.
3. Shredded corned beef topped with grated Starking apple, a dab of chutney and watercress.
4. Ham on a bed of lettuce and topped with French mustard.
5. Slices of ham topped with cream or cottage cheese mixed with grated orange or lemon rind and prepared mustard.
6. Thick slices of corned beef topped with a slice of processed cheese, green pepper rings and a little prepared mustard.
7. Minced cooked ham topped with grated Cheddar cheese, chopped gherkin, mayonnaise and chopped stewed prunes, drained.
8. Minced cooked beef topped with a sprinkling of Worcester sauce and crushed pineapple.
9. Sliced frankfurters topped with sliced tomato and a dab of mayonnaise on a bed of lettuce.

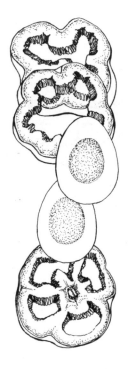

246

Chicken:

1. Sliced cooked turkey or chicken topped with blue cheese mixed with mayonnaise on a bed of lettuce.
2. Sliced cooked chicken topped with grated onion and a dab of chutney.
3. Sliced cooked chicken topped with sliced tomato, sliced raw mushrooms, a dab of mayonnaise and crumbled crisp bacon.
4. Minced chicken mixed with ground almonds and mayonnaise.

Fish:

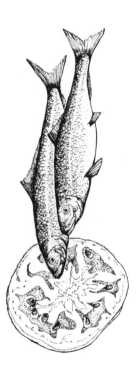

1. Flaked pink salmon or tuna mixed with tomato sauce and topped with chopped spring onions on a bed of lettuce.
2. Mashed sardines topped with tomato slices and processed cheese slices.
3. Chopped shrimps mixed with chopped raw mushrooms, prepared mustard and cream cheese.
4. Flaked middlecut topped with minced celery and mayonnaise mixed with a little curry powder.

Vegetables and fruit:

1. Sour cream mixed with finely chopped walnuts and finely chopped dried apricots.
2. Mashed banana mixed with French dressing (recipe 408).
3. Sliced tomato topped with chopped green onion, on a bed of lettuce.
4. Chopped celery mixed with chopped stuffed olives on wholewheat or rye bread.
5. Crisp bacon mixed with mashed banana and topped with mayonnaise mixed with a little curry powder.
6. Cucumber and green pepper slices on bread spread with sour cream on one side and prepared German mustard on the other.
7. Chopped pecan or walnuts mixed with minced celery, mayonnaise and a little curry powder.
8. Chopped raisins, dates, dried figs and nuts mixed with mayonnaise.
9. Mashed avocado pear mixed with a little lemon juice (to prevent discolouring) and sprinkled with salt and pepper.

Peanut butter:

1. Peanut butter topped with apricot or grape jam.
2. Peanut butter topped with chopped dates moistened with orange juice.

---

432   Swiss open-faced sandwiches

Spread squares or rounds of rye bread or pumpernickel with seasoned butter (suggestions below) and top with one of the suggested toppings.

Butters: Cream 125 g soft butter with one of the following:
1. *Mustard:* 10 ml (2 teaspoons) mustard powder and 5 ml prepared mustard.
2. *Pickle:* 5 ml (1 teaspoon) finely chopped sweet or sour pickle.
3. *Anchovy:* 10 ml (2 teaspoons) anchovy paste or finely chopped anchovies.
4. *Pepper:* 10 ml (2 teaspoons) finely chopped onion, 10 ml (2 teaspoons) finely chopped green pepper.
5. *Tomato:* 10 ml (2 teaspoons) finely chopped skinned and seeded tomato, 2 ml (½ teaspoon) dried basil.

6. *Garlic:* 1 finely chopped garlic clove, 10 ml (2 teaspoons) minced parsley.
7. *Onion:* 10 ml (2 teaspoons) minced onion, 2 ml (½ teaspoon) dried rosemary.
8. *Shrimp:* 25 ml (2 tablespoons) finely chopped cooked shrimp, 12,5 ml (1 tablespoon) finely chopped parsley, 5 ml lemon juice.

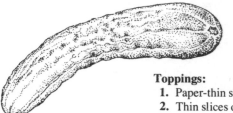

Toppings:
1. Paper-thin slices prosciutto or baked ham with green olive garnish.
2. Thin slices of baked ham with a garnish of 2 tiny asparagus tips.
3. Slices of thinly cut salami or cervelat garnished with a tiny gherkin or pickled onion.
4. Slices of white meat of chicken garnished with a tiny wedge of tomato or a green pepper ring centred with a slice of stuffed olive.
5. Small shrimp arranged on a thin spread of mayonnaise and topped with a rosette of mayonnaise and a tiny sprig of parsley.
6. Thin slice of rare roast beef with a thin sliver of pimento and a slice of gherkin.
7. Anchovy fillets with a slice of hard-boiled egg and a caper.
8. Thin slices of smoked salmon with an onion ring and capers.
9. Rolls of thinly sliced French polony with black and green olives secured by a toothpick.
10. Thin slices of chicken liver pâté topped with a small pickle.
11. Whole sardines with a slice of lemon and a slice of hard-boiled egg.
12. Thin fillets of herring with a thin slice of gherkin.
13. Alternating slices of cold tongue and Swiss cheese with mustard and a thin slice of tomato.
14. Fillets of smoked eel, a little finely chopped onion, parsley and capers.
15. Thin slices of crayfish with a green pepper ring and a slice of hard-boiled egg.
16. Rare roast beef on a spread of mustard butter and topped with a rosette of mustard butter.
17. Lettuce topped with potato salad and sliced gherkin.
18. Lettuce topped with sliced tomato and sliced stuffed olives.
19. Watercress topped with sliced pickled beetroot, apple rings, mayonnaise and ground nuts.
20. Fried sliced mushrooms topped with crisp crumbled bacon and fried tomato slices.
21. Fried sliced mushrooms topped with fried new potatoes and chopped fresh chives.
22. Lettuce topped with sliced hard-boiled eggs and rolls of thinly sliced cheese.
23. Cream or cottage cheese topped with pineapple rings.
24. Watercress topped with scrambled egg mixed with grated cheese, mayonnaise and cucumber twists.
25. Sliced tomatoes and cheese curls.
26. Sliced hard-boiled eggs topped with prawns, mayonnaise and parsley.
27. Lettuce topped with smoked snoek and scrambled egg.
28. Cooked hake, flaked and combined with flaked canned tuna, mayonnaise, paprika, cucumber twists and parsley.
29. Sardines topped with tomato slices.

30. Salami slices topped with raw onion rings.
31. Liver sausage topped with scrambled egg and crisp bacon curls.
32. Watercress topped with thin slices of ham and cream or cottage cheese and a sprinkling of paprika.
33. Slices of cold tongue topped with scrambled egg and chopped gherkins.
34. Lettuce topped with sliced cooked beef, sliced pickled beetroot and potato salad.
35. Lettuce topped with sliced cooked pork, chopped prunes and shredded red cabbage or thick apple sauce.
36. Wafer-thin slices of steak topped with raw onion rings.

Heat the knife before cutting very fresh bread.

433 Savoury toppings for toast

1. Combine 115 g soft butter or margarine, 125 ml (½ cup) grated Jarlsberg cheese, 125 ml (½ cup) grated Parmesan cheese, 25 ml cream and 1 ml (¼ teaspoon) each salt and cayenne pepper thoroughly in a bowl. Spread thickly on slices of toast and top with thin slices of cervelat or salami.
2. Combine 115 g soft butter or margarine, 12,5 ml (1 tablespoon) minced parsley, 5 ml (1 teaspoon) each of minced fresh chives, chervil and tarragon and 2 ml (½ teaspoon) minced fresh basil thoroughly in a bowl. If dried herbs are used, use half the quantities given for fresh herbs, soak in white wine or water for 10 minutes and squeeze out the excess moisture before mixing with the butter or margarine. Spread generously on thick slices of French bread and bake in the oven at 230 °C (450 °F) for 10 minutes.
3. Spread scrambled egg on buttered toast and top with crumbled crisply fried bacon and pineapple rings.
4. Spread mustard butter (recipe 432) on slices of toast and top each with cooked spinach, one poached egg and a sprinkling of paprika.
5. Spread anchovy butter (recipe 432) on thick slices of French bread, top each with a slice of Gruyère or Cheshire cheese and two canned anchovies. Place under the grill until the cheese melts.
6. Top buttered toast with a thin slice of boiled ham, a slice of mature Cheddar cheese and a slice of tomato. Sprinkle with salt and pepper and place under the grill until the cheese melts.
7. Combine 25 ml (2 tablespoons) butter or margarine, 2 ml (½ teaspoon) cayenne pepper, 5 ml prepared mustard and 5 ml piccalilli thoroughly in a bowl. Spread on rounds of toast and top with grilled chopped kidneys.
8. Toast slices of bread on one side and spread with butter or margarine and tomato sauce on the untoasted side. Top with a thick slice of processed cheese and crisply fried bacon rashers and place under the grill until the cheese melts.
9. Combine diced roast chicken, 5 ml (1 teaspoon) finely chopped green pepper and enough mayonnaise to bind in a bowl. Spread thickly on buttered toast and place under the grill until the mayonnaise starts to bubble.

Note: These suggestions are all meant for open toasts, but they can also be used for closed toasted sandwiches. Grill the closed toasts in a waffle iron until the filling is hot.

434 Fillings for toasted sandwiches

1. Welsh rarebit (recipe 423) topped with raw onion rings.
2. Fried bacon topped with fried egg and grilled tomato slices.
3. Fried bacon topped with grated cheese.
4. Thinly sliced ham topped with grated cheese.
5. Scrambled egg topped with anchovy fillets and thin slices of cucumber.

---

thinly sliced white bread

435 Melba toast

1. Remove the crusts from the bread.
2. Place the slices of bread in the oven at 75 °C (150 °F) until crisp and lightly browned.
3. Cool and store in a tightly closed container in a cool place or in the refrigerator.

Note: Melba toast is delicious served with creamy dips or omelettes.

DIPS

Ever more popular at parties are *dips* and their accompaniments or the appetizing *snacks* nibbled with drinks.

---

220 g canned salmon, drained and mashed
125 g skimmed milk cheese
5 ml (1 teaspoon) minced onion
25 ml double cream
5 ml tomato sauce
5 ml brandy
1 ml (¼ teaspoon) salt
1 ml (¼ teaspoon) black pepper
1 ml (¼ teaspoon) sugar
single cream

436 Salmon dip

Makes 300 ml; kJ per portion 450; Prep time 5 min + chilling time

1. Combine all ingredients in a blender with just enough single cream to blend easily.
2. Transfer to a serving bowl and chill for 2 to 3 hours before serving.

Variation: Use canned tuna or middlecut instead of the salmon.

---

680 g cooked shrimp, shelled and finely chopped
250 ml mayonnaise (p. 186)
5 ml lemon juice
25 ml (2 tablespoons) dried parsley
25 ml (2 tablespoons) chives, finely chopped
25 ml (2 tablespoons) horseradish or mustard
2 ml (½ teaspoon) onion salt

437 Shrimp remoulade

Makes 750 ml; kJ per portion 500; Prep time 10 min + chilling time

1. Chill the chopped shrimps for at least 45 minutes before use.
2. Combine the remaining ingredients and chill until required.
3. Just before serving, combine the mayonnaise mixture with the shrimps. Serve with melba toast (recipe 435) or crisp rye crackers.

125 g cream cheese, softened at
room temperature
200 g apricot yoghurt
5 ml (1 teaspoon) curry
powder
125 ml (½ cup) desiccated
coconut
2 ml (½ teaspoon) salt

438 Spicy yoghurt dip

Makes 500 ml;   kJ per portion 500;   Prep time 5 min + standing time

1. Beat the cream cheese in a bowl until smooth.
2. Gradually add the yoghurt, beating lightly.
3. Stir in the curry powder, coconut and salt and let stand for 2 to 3 hours at
   room temperature to thicken.
4. Spoon into a serving bowl and sprinkle with a little curry powder. Serve with
   bite-sized pieces of apple, melon, pawpaw, fresh pineapple, mandarin
   oranges or peaches.

---

120 g Blaauwkrantz cheese,
softened
85 g smooth cottage cheese
25 ml mayonnaise (p. 186)
25 ml milk

439 Blaauwkrantz dip

Makes 200 ml;   kJ per portion 580;   Prep time 15 min + chilling time

1. Combine all the ingredients thoroughly in a small bowl. Chill for at least 1
   hour.
2. Serve with potato chips, salty biscuits or fingers of toast.

Note: Any blue cheese may be used for this dip.

---

500 ml (2 cups) Cheddar
cheese, grated
85 g cream cheese, softened
85 ml beer
1 small clove garlic, crushed
(optional)
25 ml (2 tablespoons) parsley,
minced
1 ml (¼ teaspoon) salt
2 drops hot pepper sauce

440 Beer-cheese dip

Makes 375 ml;   kJ per portion 530;   Prep time 5 min + chilling time

1. Combine the cheeses, parsley, garlic, salt and pepper sauce thoroughly in a
   bowl.
2. Beat in enough beer to make a creamy spreading consistency, then chill
   overnight, covered, in the refrigerator.
3. Remove from the refrigerator 1 hour before use. Serve with salted biscuits,
   cheese straws or toast fingers.

---

2 ripe avocado pears, peeled
and mashed
12,5 ml (1 tablespoon) onion,
minced
6 rashers fried, crumbled
bacon
80 ml mayonnaise (p. 186)
1 clove garlic, minced
1 ml (¼ teaspoon) chilli
powder *or* cayenne pepper
1 ml (¼ teaspoon) salt
pepper

441 Avocado dip (Guacamole)

Makes 500 ml;   kJ per portion 650;   Prep time 15 min + chilling time

1. Combine the avocado, onion, garlic, salt, a little pepper and chilli powder or
   cayenne pepper in a small bowl.
2. Spread the mayonnaise over the top, sealing to the edges of the bowl. Chill
   in the refrigerator for at least 1½ hours.
3. Just before serving, stir in the mayonnaise and most of the bacon.
4. Top with the rest of the bacon and serve at once.

---

250 ml (1 cup) creamed
cottage cheese
½ small green pepper, seeded
and finely chopped
125 ml sour cream
25 ml prepared spicy German
mustard
2 ml (½ teaspoon) salt
freshly ground black pepper

442 Mustard dip

Makes 400 ml;   kJ per portion 590;   Prep time 5 min.

1. Combine all the ingredients thoroughly in a bowl.
2. Serve as a dip with baby marrows and celery sticks, thin slices of green
   pepper, carrot sticks, or other raw vegetables.

blanched almonds
butter or margarine
salt
cayenne pepper
paprika

443 Devilled almonds

kJ per portion 450; Prep time 20 min; Cooking time 10 min.

1. Heat a little butter or margarine in a frying-pan.
2. Add the almonds and toss to coat completely. Remove from pan.
3. Sprinkle liberally with salt and a sprinkling of cayenne pepper.
4. Sprinkle with a little paprika and store in an airtight container. Serve with cocktails.

250 g whole almonds, blanched
120 g butter or margarine
50 ml oil
salt

444 Salted almonds

Makes 250 ml; kJ per portion 500; Prep time 20 min; Cooking time 15 min.

1. Heat the butter or margarine and oil in a large frying-pan. Sauté the almonds in it over medium heat, turning frequently with a slotted spoon, until golden brown.
2. Remove with the spoon and spread on absorbent paper. Sprinkle liberally with salt while still warm, making sure that all are coated. Store in an airtight container.

110 g flour
62,5 ml (5 tablespoons) butter or margarine
60 g Cheddar cheese, grated
1 egg yolk
water to mix
1 ml (¼ teaspoon) cayenne pepper (optional)
1 ml (¼ teaspoon) celery salt (optional)
salt and pepper to taste
milk or beaten egg to glaze

445 Cheese straws

Makes 40 to 48; kJ per portion 450; Prep time 20 min; Cooking time 12 min.

1. Sift the flour, salt, pepper, cayenne and celery salt into a bowl. Rub in the butter or margarine until the mixture has the consistency of fine breadcrumbs.
2. Add the cheese and mix well.
3. Stir in the egg yolk to bind, adding a little water if the dough is too stiff.
4. Roll out the pastry to 5 mm thick on a floured surface, and cut into narrow fingers 7,5 cm long.
5. Place the fingers on a greased baking sheet and brush lightly with the milk or egg.
6. Bake in the oven at 230 °C (450 °F) for 12 minutes, then remove from the oven and cool on the baking sheet for 3 minutes.
7. Lift onto a cooling rack with a spatula and cool thoroughly.

187,5 ml (¾ cup) mature Cheddar cheese, finely grated
50 ml (4 tablespoons) sesame seeds
salt and pepper to taste

446 Sesame crisps

Makes 24; kJ per portion 510; Prep time 10 min; Cooking time 5 min.

1. Combine the cheese and sesame seeds in a bowl, pressing firmly together, and form into 24 balls, 2 cm in diameter.
2. Grease a piece of tin foil lightly with butter or oil, place it in an oven tray and arrange the sesame balls on it.
3. Press each ball lightly with the fingers until it spreads to 4 cm diameter.
4. Bake in the oven at 240 °C (475 °F) until just golden, about 5 minutes.
5. Remove from the oven and invert the foil and crisps onto a wire rack to cool. When cool enough, gently peel off the tin foil.
6. When cold, sprinkle with a little salt and store in an airtight container until needed.

250 ml (1 cup) flour
250 ml (1 cup) Cheddar
cheese, grated
1 egg, beaten
62,5 ml (5 tablespoons) butter
or margarine, melted
10 ml (2 teaspoons) baking
powder
milk
pinch salt
pinch cayenne pepper

447 Cheese puffs (F)

Makes ± 60;   kJ per portion 110;   Prep time 45 min;   Cooking time 10 min.

1. Combine the flour, salt, baking powder, cheese and cayenne pepper thoroughly in a bowl.
2. Combine the beaten egg with enough milk to make up 250 ml and stir the liquid into the dry ingredients. Mix well.
3. Stir in the melted butter or margarine and blend thoroughly.
4. Place teaspoonfuls of the batter on a greased baking sheet and bake in the oven at 200 °C (400 °F) until golden, about 10 minutes. Remove from the oven.
5. Allow to cool on the sheet for a few minutes, then remove and cool thoroughly on a wire rack (f).

Note: Pre-heat the oven and switch it off as soon as the cheese puffs go in.

---

340 g flour
170 g butter or margarine
3 eggs
170 g Cheddar cheese, grated
5 ml (1 teaspoon) mustard
powder
2 ml (½ teaspoon) salt
pinch pepper

448 Cheese biscuits (F)

*Makes ± 100 small biscuits;   kJ per portion 100;   Prep time 30 min;
Cooking time 10 min.*

1. Sift the flour, mustard, salt and pepper into a mixing bowl.
2. Rub the butter or margarine into the flour, then stir in the grated cheese.
3. Add the eggs and mix thoroughly to form a soft, but not sticky, dough.
4. Roll the dough out to 5 mm thick on a floured surface and cut into fingers 7 cm × 3 cm.
5. Place the fingers on lightly greased baking sheets and bake in the oven at 200 °C (400 °F) until lightly golden in colour, about 10 minutes.
6. Remove from the oven and place on wire racks to cool (f).

Note: Other recipes for snacks may be found in the chapter on hors d' oeuvres.

DESSERTS

Desserts, the finishing touch to a meal, may be as simple as chilled fresh fruit, as elaborate as iced confections.

Just as important as the choice of dessert is its presentation: it should complement the meal and look attractive, for it is the eye that is tempted before the taste buds. Make sure that the dessert balances what has gone before – after a filling meal, for example, the best dessert would be a simple one like chilled fresh fruit or a light-as-air soufflé. Perhaps serve a pudding in clear glass (particularly layered puddings such as trifle, where half the enjoyment lies in anticipating what the various layers will taste like) or in dishes that complement the colour and texture of a dessert.

COLD DESSERTS

Gelatine desserts require careful preparation: the proportion of gelatine to liquid must be correct, otherwise the result will either be runny (too much liquid) or too solid (too much gelatine). Specific instructions are given with the various recipes, but bear the following general points in mind:

● Either unflavoured gelatine powder or flavoured crystals can be used for gelatine desserts.

● Unflavoured gelatine must first be soaked in cold water. Sprinkle the required amount of gelatine onto cold water – 125 ml to 250 ml, depending on the consistency required – and leave for 10 minutes. Then melt the soaked gelatine in hot, but not boiling, liquid. Cool slightly and add to the other ingredients.

● If a jelly will not set, this could be because there is too much liquid, or because it was left in too warm a place to set.

● Raw pineapple and pawpaw cannot be used in gelatine desserts because they contain enzymes which prevent gelatine from setting. Always cook pineapple and pawpaw first, or use the canned fruit.

● To shorten the time needed for a jelly to set, melt the gelatine in a little hot water, then add ice cold water or fruit juice and place the bowl in a larger bowl filled with ice cubes.

Snows are made from two basic ingredients: fruit purée and beaten egg whites, although some recipes call for the addition of gelatine to make them hold better.

To make a snow

Use 250 ml (1 cup) thick fruit purée (made from 450 g fruit) to 2 egg whites.

1. Whisk the egg whites until stiff.
2. Fold in the purée.
3. Set aside to cool and serve within 1 hour.

Variations:
1. Use 150 ml cream and 250 ml (1 cup) purée to 2 egg whites for a richer snow.
2. Use 150 ml chilled evaporated milk, whipped, and 250 ml (1 cup) purée to 2 egg whites.
3. Add a little liqueur to the mixture.

Note:
- The fruit purée must have a distinctive flavour because egg whites tend to tone down flavour.
- Use a fairly thick purée to achieve the right consistency. If the purée is too moist, the snow might separate into purée and egg white.
- Add a little unflavoured gelatine powder to the fruit if it is too moist. Allow to cool completely – but not to set – then fold into the egg whites.

---

110 g raw rice
6 egg yolks
110 g castor sugar
850 ml milk
5 ml oil
5 ml vanilla essence
18,75 ml (1½ tablespoons)
butter or margarine
1 ml (¼ teaspoon) salt
Sauce:
450 g fresh apricots, peeled,
halved and stoned
170 g granulated sugar
500 ml water
25 ml Kirsch

449 Apricot condé

Serves 6;   kJ per portion 1 300;   Prep time 1 hour;   Cooking time 30 min.

1. Wash the rice under running water until the water runs clear. Drain well through a fine sieve.
2. Place in a flameproof dish with the milk, castor sugar, butter or margarine, salt and vanilla essence and bring to the boil over high heat. Stir until the sugar has dissolved and the ingredients are well mixed.
3. Bake in the oven at 190 °C (375 °F), covered, until the rice is tender, about 30 minutes. Remove and allow to cool slightly.
4. Lightly beat the egg yolks in a bowl and mix into the rice.
5. Place the rice mixture in a 200 mm soufflé dish that has been greased with the oil and cool completely, then cover and place in the refrigerator until cold.
6. For the sauce, dissolve the granulated sugar in the water in a saucepan over low heat, stirring all the time.
7. Increase the heat to high and bring the syrup to the boil.
8. Add the apricots, lower the heat and simmer until they are tender. Remove 12 apricot halves and set them aside in a bowl to cool. When cool, cover the bowl and place it in the refrigerator.
9. Pass the remaining apricots through a fine sieve or liquidise them in a blender to form a purée. Return the purée to the saucepan. Simmer over low heat until thick, then remove from the stove and stir in the Kirsch. Cool, cover and refrigerate.
10. Remove the rice mixture from the refrigerator 10 minutes before serving. Run a knife around the edge of the soufflé dish and turn the pudding out onto a serving dish. Arrange the reserved apricots on top, pour the sauce over the fruit and serve at once.

Note: This may also be served hot. Do not refrigerate the pudding or the sauce. After step 4 arrange the apricot halves on top of the rice in an ovenproof dish and heat in the oven at 160 °C (325 °F) until heated through. Serve the sauce separately.

450 Caramel cream pudding

4 egg yolks
2 egg whites
30 ml (6 teaspoons) castor sugar
75 ml (6 tablespoons) granulated sugar
100 ml (^{2}/$_5$ cup) blanched almonds, finely chopped
12,5 ml (1 tablespoon) butter or margarine
25 ml water
570 ml milk
Decoration:
145 ml double cream
12,5 ml (1 tablespoon) castor sugar
100 ml (^{2}/$_5$ cup) blanched almonds, split

Serves 4;   kJ per portion 910;   Prep time 45 min;   Cooking time 2 hours

1. In a heavy-bottomed saucepan, dissolve the granulated sugar in the water over low heat. Increase the heat to medium and boil steadily until the mixture is golden brown (caramel).
2. Remove from the stove and allow to cool, then add the milk and butter or margarine. Return to the stove and stir gently over low heat until the butter has melted and the milk has absorbed the caramel.
3. Beat first the egg yolks and then the egg whites with the castor sugar in a large bowl.
4. Stir in the caramel milk and the almonds, blending well, and pour into a greased pudding basin. Cover with a double layer of waxproof paper or a clean muslin cloth, tie securely with string and steam over a saucepan half-filled with hot but not boiling water for 2 hours.
5. Allow to cool, then turn out onto a serving dish and decorate with the cream whipped with the 12,5 ml (1 tablespoon) castor sugar and the halved almonds.

Note: Do not heat the milk too quickly as this will make the mixture curdle.

---

451 Peach mousse

6 ripe peaches, skinned and stoned
½ packet lemon or apricot jelly
145 ml double cream
Decoration:
whipped cream
pieces of angelica
halved glacé cherries

Serves 4;   kJ per portion 910;   Prep time 30 min.

1. Set 2 of the peaches aside. Press the remaining peaches through a fine sieve or liquidise in a blender to form a thick purée.
2. Make up the jelly with 145 ml boiling water and chill in the refrigerator until thick, but not completely set.
3. Whisk the jelly well with a rotary beater.
4. In a separate bowl, whisk the cream until firm enough to hold its shape. Whisk into the jelly, then fold in the peach purée.
5. Transfer to a serving bowl and leave to set.
6. Just before serving, slice the 2 whole peaches and arrange them on top of the mousse. Pipe a little whipped cream in the centre and decorate with angelica and glacé cherries.

Variations:
1. Use 12 ripe apricots instead of the peaches.
2. Use 36 large ripe strawberries and strawberry jelly instead of the peaches and apricot or lemon jelly.
3. Use a small pawpaw, skinned, seeded and stewed, instead of the peaches.
4. Use 250 g canned loganberries and portwine jelly instead of the peaches and apricot or lemon jelly.

---

452 Chocolate snow

2 egg whites
110 g plain milk chocolate or dark chocolate
25 ml milk

Serves 4;   kJ per portion 1 100;   Prep time 15 min;   Cooking time 5 min.

1. Melt the chocolate in the milk in a saucepan over low heat. Remove from stove and allow to cool.
2. Beat the egg whites stiffly, then fold into the chocolate mixture.
3. Pour into a serving bowl and chill until set. Serve with whipped cream.

Variation: Use orange juice instead of the milk.

Caramelised oranges make a cool and elegant dessert (recipe 456).

10 slices sponge cake or 1
packet sponge fingers
450 g canned loganberries,
drained
125 ml (½ cup) canned
gooseberries, drained
12,5 ml (1 tablespoon) ginger
preserve, finely chopped
12,5 ml (1 tablespoon)
watermelon preserve, finely
chopped
125 ml (½ cup) glacé cherries,
finely chopped
100 g walnuts, finely chopped
2 packets portwine jelly,
prepared according to packet
directions
250 ml prepared custard
(recipe 502)
125 ml sweet wine or sherry
Decoration:
whipped cream
10 glacé cherries, halved
chocolate vermicelli

453 Trifle

Serves 6; kJ per portion 1 800; Prep time 45 min + chilling time

1. Line the bottom of a large glass bowl with the slices of sponge cake or sponge fingers. Pour the wine over the cake, making sure that all the pieces are moistened.
2. Layer half the nuts and half the cherries on top of the sponge cake and pour the prepared jelly over them. Chill in the refrigerator until the jelly has set.
3. Place a layer of loganberries on top of the jelly and top with a layer of ginger and watermelon preserve.
4. Layer the rest of the nuts and cherries on top of the preserves and top with the gooseberries.
5. Pour the prepared custard over the gooseberries and chill in the refrigerator until set.
6. Just before serving, top with whipped cream and decorate with halved glacé cherries and chocolate vermicelli.

Variation: Almost any combination of fruit and jelly may be used, e.g. apricot jelly, puréed stewed dried apricots and canned mandarin orange segments or grenadilla pulp.

---

250 ml (1 cup) dates, finely
chopped
3 eggs, separated
37,5 ml (3 tablespoons)
cornflour
125 ml (½ cup) sugar
12,5 ml apricot jam
500 ml milk
5 ml vanilla essence
Sauce:
250 ml (1 cup) sugar
10 ml (2 teaspoons) butter or
margarine
750 ml water
6 cloves
2 ml (½ teaspoon) ground
cinnamon

454 Cold date pudding

Serves 6; kJ per portion 1 000; Prep time 40 min; Cooking time 20 min.

1. Boil the milk, dates and sugar together in a saucepan until the sugar dissolves. Remove from the stove and allow to cool slightly.
2. Stir the egg yolks and cornflour into the mixture, blending well.
3. Stir in the vanilla essence.
4. Beat the egg whites stiffly in a bowl, and fold them into the date mixture together with the apricot jam. Allow to cool.
5. Meanwhile, prepare the sauce: boil the water, sugar, cloves, butter or margarine and cinnamon together in a small saucepan until the sugar dissolves and the sauce thickens slightly.
6. Transfer the sauce to a heated sauceboat and serve immediately with the cold pudding.

Note: Thicken the sauce with a little cornflour if it is too thin.

---

600 g canned crushed
pineapple, drained
3 eggs, separated
1 envelope gelatine powder
25 ml cold water
125 ml (½ cup) sugar
250 ml double cream
1 ml (¼ teaspoon) salt
Decoration:
whipped cream
Maraschino cherries

455 Pineapple Bavarian cream

Serves 6; kJ per portion 910; Prep time 45 min; Cooking time 10 min.

1. Soften the gelatine in the cold water.
2. Combine the pineapple, egg yolks, sugar and salt in the top of a double-boiler and heat, stirring all the time, until the mixture thickens.
3. Remove from the stove and stir in the gelatine. Set aside to cool.
4. Whip the egg whites until stiff. In another bowl, whip the cream until it, too, is stiff. Fold the egg whites and cream into the pineapple mixture.
5. Pour the mixture carefully into a greased soufflé dish or mould and chill in the refrigerator until firm. Serve decorated with additional whipped cream and Maraschino cherries.

4 firm oranges, peeled and all
the pith removed
100 ml (²/₅ cup) sugar
75 ml water
Decoration:
chopped nuts
whipped cream

456   Caramelised oranges

Serves 4;   kJ per portion 690;   Prep time 45 min;   Cooking time 30 min.

1. Place the peeled oranges on a serving dish.
2. In a small saucepan, warm the sugar with half the water, stirring constantly until the sugar has dissolved.
3. Add the remaining water and bring to the boil over medium heat.
4. Boil steadily, without stirring, until a golden brown caramel is obtained.
5. Pour the caramel over the oranges and serve at once, decorated with nuts and whipped cream.

Variations:
1. Use firm, ripe pears instead of the oranges.
2. If desired the oranges may be segmented.

---

2 egg whites, stiffly beaten
25 ml (2 tablespoons) sugar
25 ml (2 tablespoons) custard
powder
375 ml water
juice of 4 oranges

457   Orange cream

Serves 4;   kJ per portion 780;   Prep time 20 min;   Cooking time 10 min.

1. Combine the orange juice and sugar in a saucepan and bring to the boil over high heat.
2. Dissolve the custard powder in the water and mix into the orange mixture. Boil, stirring, until the custard thickens.
3. Remove from the stove, transfer the mixture to a serving bowl and fold in the beaten egg whites carefully. Chill in the refrigerator until set, then serve with sweet biscuits or sponge fingers.

Variations:
1. Use 250 ml pineapple juice instead of orange juice, and add 25 ml (2 tablespoons) desiccated coconut before folding in the egg whites.
2. Use 250 ml grape juice instead of the orange juice and add 25 ml (2 tablespoons) finely chopped raisins before folding in the egg whites.

---

2 egg whites, stiffly beaten
grated rind of ½ lemon
250 ml (1 cup) sugar
12,5 ml (1 tablespoon) gelatine
powder
65 ml cold water
250 ml hot water
65 ml lemon juice

458   Lemon snow

Serves 4;   kJ per portion 580;   Prep time 20 min.

1. Soak the gelatine in the cold water, then dissolve it in the hot water.
2. Stir in the sugar, lemon juice and grated lemon rind and strain into a bowl through a fine sieve.
3. Chill in the refrigerator until the mixture begins to set, then beat until light and foamy with an egg whisk.
4. Fold the egg whites into the mixture and pour into a wet mould to set. Serve with a thin custard.

Variation: Use orange juice and rind instead of that of the lemon.

4 egg yolks
375 ml (1½ cups) castor sugar
25 ml Crème de Cacao

459 Coffee crème

Serves 4;   kJ per portion 590;   Prep time 10 min.

1. Place the egg yolks in a mixing bowl and whisk until pale and thick.
2. Add the sugar and continue beating until the mixture is very thick and smooth, about 5 minutes.
3. Spoon equal amounts of the mixture into individual ramekins and spoon a little Crème de Cacao over each one.
4. Chill in the refrigerator for 20 minutes before serving.

---

4 large Granny Smith apples, peeled, cored and coarsely chopped
2 egg whites, stiffly beaten
12,5 ml dry white wine, rum or brandy
250 ml water
12,5 ml (1 tablespoon) sugar
sprinkling cinnamon

460 Apple snow

Serves 4;   kJ per portion 700;   Prep time 45 min;   Cooking time 15 min.

1. Place the apples, water and sugar in a saucepan and bring to the boil briskly.
2. Reduce the heat to medium and simmer, covered, until the apples are soft.
3. Rub the apples through a fine sieve or liquidise in a blender to form a purée, and transfer to a deep bowl.
4. Stir in the wine, rum or brandy, mixing well.
5. Fold in the stiffly beaten egg whites and transfer to individual glasses. Chill in the refrigerator for at least 1 hour before use. Sprinkle each with cinnamon and serve, with whipped cream if desired.

Variations:

1. Use 12 fresh or 24 dried apricots, puréed, instead of the apples. Omit the cinnamon and liquor, and use orange wine or liqueur instead.
2. Use 12 stewed and puréed guavas instead of the apple. Omit the cinnamon.
3. Use 12 ripe Satsuma plums, puréed, instead of the apples. Omit the cinnamon.
4. Use 24 large stewed and puréed prunes instead of the apples. Omit the cinnamon.
5. Use 250 ml (1 cup) puréed fresh strawberries, loganberries, gooseberries or Hanepoot grapes instead of the apples. Omit the liquor and use sherry instead.

---

250 ml (1 cup) canned gooseberries, drained, or fresh gooseberries
500 ml double cream or plain yoghurt
25 ml rum or brandy
12,5 ml (1 tablespoon) castor sugar
sprinkling nutmeg

461 Gooseberry fool

Serves 4;   kJ per portion 700;   Prep time 20 min.

1. Whip the cream or yoghurt, castor sugar and rum or brandy together until thick and smooth.
2. Fold in the gooseberries and spoon the mixture into 4 serving glasses. Chill for 30 minutes.
3. Sprinkle with a little nutmeg and serve.

Variations:

1. Any fresh fruit may be used in place of the gooseberries, e.g. 250 ml (1 cup) bananas, finely mashed and whisked together with the cream or yoghurt, sugar and rum or brandy.
2. Kirsch, Calvados or van der Hum are excellent in place of rum or brandy.

259

75 ml (6 tablespoons) cornflour
1 egg, beaten
750 ml milk
62,5 ml (5 tablespoons) sugar
5 ml vanilla essence
1 ml (¼ teaspoon) salt

462   Blancmange

Serves 4;   kJ per portion 600;   Prep time 30 min;   Cooking time 20 min.

1. Combine the cornflour, sugar and salt in a bowl and mix in 65 ml of the cold milk to form a smooth paste.
2. Place the remaining milk in a saucepan and heat over low heat until it is lukewarm. Transfer to the top half of a double-boiler.
3. Gradually stir in the cornflour mixture and continue stirring until the mixture thickens.
4. Simmer for 15 minutes, stirring occasionally.
5. Stir the egg into the mixture, then stir in the essence. Pour into a mould to set.
6. Unmould and serve with a sweet sauce (recipes 497 to 506).

Variations:

1. Combine 18,75 ml (1½ tablespoons) cocoa with the sugar and cornflour for a chocolate blancmange.
2. Add 187,5 ml (¾ cup) desiccated coconut to the milk when heating it.

85 g castor sugar
4 egg yolks
25 ml (2 tablespoons)
granulated sugar
550 ml milk, scalded
5 ml lemon juice
37,5 ml water

463   Crème caramel

Serves 6;   kJ per portion 600;   Prep time 45 min;   Cooking time 1 hour

1. First make the caramel sauce. Place the castor sugar, water and lemon juice in a small heavy-bottomed saucepan and stir over low heat until the sugar has dissolved. Take care not to let the mixture boil before the sugar has melted.
2. Increase the heat to medium and continue simmering until the sauce caramelises and is a deep gold. Remove from the stove and pour into a heated, greased soufflé dish, turning the dish to ensure that the bottom and sides are evenly coated with the caramel.
3. Beat the egg yolks and granulated sugar together in a bowl, then add the scalded milk and beat well.
4. Strain the milk mixture through a fine sieve into the caramel-coated soufflé dish and cover with a piece of greased waxproof paper or foil tied with string.
5. Stand in a baking dish with sufficient water to come halfway up the sides of the soufflé dish and bake in the oven at 150 °C (300 °F) until set, about 1 hour.
6. Allow to cool, then turn out. Serve at once.

Note: Choose a soufflé dish that is just large enough to be nearly full when the custard is poured into it, otherwise the custard may break when it is turned out.

250 g soft dried prunes
125 g dried figs
125 g dried apricots
1 slice lemon
125 ml (½ cup) raisins
2 small ripe, firm pears,
peeled, cored and sliced
sugar
port
water
4 whole cloves
1 stick cinnamon
Decoration:
62,5 ml (5 tablespoons)
slivered almonds

464 Mixed fruit compôte

Serves 6; kJ per portion 500; Prep time 20 min + marinating time; Cooking time 15 min.

1. Place the figs and prunes in a jar, cover with port and marinate, covered, for 2 days.
2. Soak the apricots in water until softened and plump, then place them in a saucepan with the lemon slice, cloves, cinnamon, prunes, figs and any port that may be left over.
3. Add enough water to cover and a sprinkling of sugar and simmer, covered, until the fruit is soft, adding the raisins when half-cooked.
4. Remove the fruit and place in a serving bowl.
5. Increase the heat and boil the sauce, uncovered, until the liquid is reduced to half. Pour over the fruit, through a strainer.
6. In a saucepan, simmer the sliced pears in water to cover, with a sprinkling of sugar, until they are soft but not broken.
7. Drain, then mix the pears into the fruit and chill, covered, for 1 to 2 hours.
8. Scatter with the almonds and serve with whipped cream.

500 g fresh strawberries
3 eggs, separated
125 ml (½ cup) sugar
12,5 ml lemon juice
125 ml double cream
65 ml cold water
1 envelope gelatine powder
5 ml rum essence
1 ml (¼ teaspoon) salt

465 Cold strawberry soufflé

Serves 6; kJ per portion 710; Prep time 45 min; Cooking time 5 min.

1. Reserving a few whole strawberries for decoration, mash the remaining strawberries finely or liquidise them in a blender.
2. Soften the gelatine in the cold water.
3. Beat the egg yolks lightly in a bowl and combine with the salt, lemon juice and rum essence in the top of a double-boiler.
4. Heat over water, stirring all the time, until slightly thickened, then stir in the gelatine. Mix well and remove from the stove to cool.
5. When cool, stir the strawberries into the gelatine mixture and blend well.
6. Beat the egg whites until stiff, gradually adding the sugar, until the mixture holds a soft peak.
7. Whip the cream until stiff, then fold with the egg whites into the strawberry mixture, combining carefully until well-blended.
8. Rub a little oil over the inside surfaces of a 200 mm soufflé dish and pour the mixture in carefully.
9. Chill until firm, about 2 hours, then serve decorated with a few whole strawberries.

Variations:
1. This cold soufflé is excellent made with fresh apricots or peaches instead of the strawberries.
2. Sour cream makes a delicious alternative to the cream.

Home-made *ice-cream* is delicious and surprisingly easy to make, provided that you adhere to a few basic principles. *Fruit ices* and some *sherbets* are less rich than ice-cream, but are especially refreshing on hot days or after a heavy meal.

Remember

● To ensure rapid freezing, set the refrigerator or freezer in advance at the coldest possible temperature.

● Ice-cream should have a velvety texture and be free from large ice crystals. To prevent their formation, add 5 ml (1 teaspoon) unflavoured gelatine for every 250 ml liquid or any one of: 1 egg white, 5 ml (1 teaspoon) cornflour, 5 ml (1 teaspoon) flour or 1 to 2 marshmallows to approximately 2 litres of ice-cream.

● More flavouring should be added to a frozen dessert than to a dessert eaten at room temperature because freezing tends to diminish flavour.

● Chill all ingredients well before adding to the ice-cream mixture. Very fresh cream will not whip, so keep it for at least 24 hours and chill overnight before use. Evaporated and condensed milk must also be chilled before use.

● Allow the ice-cream or fruit ice to freeze partially, then remove from the freezer or refrigerator and mash the half-frozen dessert with a fork. Beat well with an egg-beater to incorporate air, and to break up the ice crystals.

● Fruit ices and sherbets taste better when not frozen rock hard. Remove from the freezer 15 minutes before serving time and place in the refrigerator.

● Never thaw ice-cream or sherbets and then freeze them again, as large ice crystals will form and bacterial contamination may occur.

Making ice-cream with an ice-cream maker

An electrically driven ice-cream maker will effectively prevent ice crystals forming. It has a constantly moving paddle which stirs the ice while it is freezing.

1. Pack the mixture into the machine.
2. Place the machine in the freezer or freezing compartment of the refrigerator and plug the thin cord in at the nearest socket. Close the refrigerator door securely.
3. When the mixture is thick, scoop it into a plastic container and store in the freezer immediately.

500 ml milk
190 ml (¾ cup) sugar mixed
with 12,5 ml (1 tablespoon)
cornflour
1 egg, lightly beaten
500 ml double cream
5 ml vanilla essence
2 ml (½ teaspoon) salt

466   Basic ice-cream   (F)

Serves 8;   kJ per portion 710;   Prep time 20 min;   Cooking time 10 min.

1. Heat the milk in a saucepan and add the sugar and cornflour mixture, stirring all the time.
2. Boil, uncovered, for 5 minutes, stirring constantly.
3. Remove the saucepan from the stove and cool slightly. Carefully add the egg, whisking all the time with an egg-beater. Stir in the salt.
4. Cool the mixture completely and stir in the cream and vanilla essence.
5. Place the ice-cream in the freezer and leave for 30 minutes. Mash with a fork to break up the ice crystals and freeze for a further 30 minutes. Beat again with a fork and freeze (f).

Variations: Instead of the vanilla essence, add any of the following:
1. *Chocolate:* Add 2 squares of melted chocolate to the hot mixture (step 3).
2. *Tutti-frutti:* Add 125 ml (½ cup) each of finely chopped walnuts, raisins, glacé cherries, orange peel and 25 ml port, rum or brandy. Add the fruit just as the mixture starts to thicken (step 5).
3. *Coffee:* Add 25 ml coffee essence to the warm mixture (step 3).
4. *Orange:* Use 250 ml instead of 500 ml milk. Add 250 ml orange juice to the cooled mixture (step 4).

Note: If you have an ice-cream machine, place the mixture in the machine and freeze for 3 hours, until the mixture is thick and creamy. Turn into a plastic container and leave in the freezer.

---

150 g strawberries or any
other fruit
220 g castor sugar
100 ml orange juice
100 ml lemon juice
250 ml double cream

467   Basic fruit ice-cream   (F)

Serves 6;   kJ per portion 660;   Prep time 20 min.

1. Turn the refrigerator or freezer to its coldest setting at least 2 hours before starting.
2. Clean the fruit and purée in a liquidizer with the sugar, or press through a sieve and stir in the sugar. There should be 250 ml of purée.
3. Add the lemon and orange juice to the purée.
4. Whip the cream to the soft peak stage, then fold it into the purée.
5. Pour into the freezer tray. Cover the tray with foil and place in the freezer until half frozen, 45 minutes to 1 hour.
6. Remove from the freezer, turn into a bowl and beat with an egg-beater or whisk for 30 seconds.
7. Return to the freezer for a further 45 minutes. Whisk again as in step 6.
8. Freeze once more (f) and serve when completely frozen.

---

110 g marshmallows, finely
chopped
60 g glacé cherries
60 g pineapple, finely chopped
37,5 ml (3 tablespoons)
walnuts, finely chopped
10 ml (2 teaspoons) sugar
145 ml milk
145 ml double cream, whipped
stiffly

468   Marshmallow ice-cream   (F)

Serves 4;   kJ per portion 950;   Prep time 30 min;   Cooking time 5 min.

1. Place three-quarters of the marshmallows and all the milk in a saucepan and heat until the marshmallows melt. Remove from the stove and allow to cool.
2. Stir in the rest of the ingredients and transfer to an ice-tray. Freeze, with the freezer at its coldest setting (f). Serve decorated with chopped glacé cherries.

469 Liqueur ice-cream (F)

500 ml double whipping cream
Maraschino liqueur
100 g castor sugar

Serves 4; kJ per portion 900; Prep time 15 min.

1. Whip the cream stiffly in a bowl, then fold in the sugar.
2. Add Maraschino liqueur to taste and mix well.
3. Transfer to ice-trays and freeze (f).

Variation: Use any liqueur you desire in place of the Maraschino.

470 Praline ice-cream (F)

600 ml vanilla ice-cream
(recipe 466)
300 ml double cream
120 g blanched almonds,
coarsely chopped
120 g sugar
lemon juice to taste
oil
liqueur or brandy to taste

Serves 4; kJ per portion 1 290; Prep time 20 min; Cooking time 5 min.

1. Combine the sugar with the lemon juice in a small saucepan and heat gently until the mixture is a rich caramel colour.
2. Add the almonds and stir until they are browned. Pour the mixture onto a baking sheet greased with the oil and allow to cool.
3. When cold and brittle, reduce the mixture to a powder with a mortar and pestle or in a grinder and add it to the warm vanilla ice-cream mixture (step 3 of recipe 466).
4. Cool the mixture and half-freeze in the freezer.
5. Whip the cream stiffly and fold it into the ice-cream with a little liqueur or brandy. Freeze again until stiff (f).

471 Buttermilk sherbert (F)

250 ml (1 cup) canned crushed
pineapple, drained
1 egg white, lightly beaten
125 ml (½ cup) sugar
500 ml buttermilk
7 ml vanilla essence

Serves 6; kJ per portion 850; Prep time 20 min.

1. Combine the buttermilk, sugar and pineapple thoroughly in a bowl. Pour the mixture into ice-trays and freeze until the ice-cream is frozen hard 5 cm around the edges of the trays, but is only partially frozen in the centre, then turn out into a chilled bowl.
2. Add the beaten egg white and the vanilla essence and beat until light and fluffy.
3. Replace in ice-trays and freeze once more, covered with foil (f).

472 Baked Alaska

1 round sponge cake
1 litre block ice-cream, very
firmly frozen
170 g canned fruit, drained
and the juice reserved
5 egg whites
165 ml (²/₃ cup) castor sugar

Serves 6; kJ per portion 2 100; Prep time 20 min; Cooking time 3 min.

1. Place the sponge cake in a shallow ovenproof dish and sprinkle a little of the syrup from the canned fruit over it.
2. Now place the ice-cream block topped with the canned fruit over the sponge.
3. Whisk the egg whites in a bowl until very stiff, then gradually fold in the castor sugar. Pile the mixture (meringue) over the whole of the sponge cake and the ice-cream and canned fruit.
4. Bake in the oven at 240 °C (475 °F) until golden brown, about 3 minutes. Serve at once.

Variation: Use 50 ml (4 tablespoons) fruit mincemeat instead of the canned fruit and sprinkle 37,5 ml brandy, sherry or rum over the sponge instead of syrup.

Note: Make sure that the meringue covers the ice-cream completely, otherwise it will melt when the Alaska is put in the oven.

500 ml (2 cups) sugar
1 litre water
125 ml fresh orange juice
125 ml fresh grapefruit juice

473   Citrus sherbet   (F)

Serves 6;   kJ per portion 600;   Prep time 30 min;   Cooking time 10 min.

1. Heat the sugar and water in a saucepan over low heat, stirring all the time, until the sugar dissolves.
2. Bring to the boil and boil for 6 minutes, then remove from the stove and allow to cool.
3. Stir in the fruit juices, mixing well, and pour into ice-trays. Freeze until mushy.
4. Empty the sherbet into a bowl and beat vigorously until the ice crystals are broken up. Return to the ice-trays and freeze through (f).

HOT PUDDINGS

Like snows, *whips* are made from fruit purée and whisked egg whites, but *whips* are then baked in the oven.

To make a whip

Use 250 ml (1 cup) thick fruit purée to 4 egg whites.

1. Prepare the purée.
2. Whisk the egg whites stiffly.
3. Fold the purée into the egg whites and transfer the mixture to an ovenproof dish.
4. Bake in the oven at 180 °C (350°F) for 30 minutes. Serve immediately.

Note: As a whip is a simple kind of soufflé, do not open the oven door before the end of the baking time or it will collapse.

Steamed puddings, a favourite for winter, are both easy to make and delicious. Served with one of the sweet sauces (recipes 497 to 506) they make a filling and satisfying end to a meal.

To steam a pudding

1. Grease a pudding basin or mould very well.
2. Pour in the pudding until the container is two-thirds full – the pudding must have space in which to rise. Close securely (see note below).
3. Pour sufficient water to reach halfway up the sides of the basin or mould into a large, deep saucepan, with a false bottom. If using a pressure cooker, pour in only 250 ml to 300 ml water.

265

4. Bring the water to the boil, then place the basin or mould in the water, cover the saucepan and allow the water to bubble gently for as long as required (see individual recipes).
5. If the water should boil away, carefully add more hot water.
6. When the pudding has steamed for as long as required, take the basin or mould out of the saucepan and place it in cold water for 5 minutes. Remove the lid or covering and unmould the pudding. Serve hot with a sweet sauce.

Note:

- Use either a watertight mould with a tight-fitting lid or a pudding basin with a double layer of waxproof paper over the top, securely fastened with string (see recipe 474).
- The flavour of a dark fruit pudding improves if left to mature for 2 to 3 weeks. To serve, pour 50 ml brandy over the pudding, wrap it in foil and heat in the oven at 160°C (325°F) for 45 minutes to 1 hour.
- To serve a pudding flambé, heat 50 ml brandy, pour it over the hot pudding and ignite.

The skins of apples will not crack during baking if you make a shallow cut around the apple about 2,5 cm from the stalk.

2 eggs, lightly beaten
110 g self-raising flour
85 g butter or margarine
12,5 ml milk
100 ml (²/₅ cup) castor sugar

474   Steamed sponge pudding   (F)

Serves 4;   kJ per portion 910;   Prep time 45 min;   Cooking time 1 ½ hours

1. Cream the sugar and butter or margarine in a bowl until soft and light.
2. Add the beaten eggs gradually, stirring all the time.
3. Sift the flour into the bowl and stir to mix thoroughly.
4. Stir in the milk and pour the pudding into a greased pudding basin.
5. Cover the basin with a double layer of waxproof paper or clean muslin tied on with string and steam in a saucepan half-filled with boiling water for 1 ½ hours (f).
6. Turn out onto a heated serving dish and serve at once with a sweet sauce (recipes 497 to 506).

Variations:

1. Place 37,5 ml (3 tablespoons) apricot, fig or youngberry jam at the bottom of the basin.
2. Sift 5 ml (1 teaspoon) ground ginger with the flour into the creamed mixture and add 60 g diced glacé ginger before adding the milk.
3. Place 37,5 ml golden syrup at the bottom of the pudding basin and serve with ginger sauce (recipe 498).
4. Add the grated rind of 1 lemon to the butter and sugar mix with 12,5 ml lemon juice instead of milk. Place 37,5 ml lemon curd (recipe 590) at the bottom of the basin and serve with lemon sauce (recipe 503).

500 ml (2 cups) flour
2 eggs, beaten
90 g butter or margarine
250 ml (1 cup) sugar
450 g fruit cake mixture
125 ml (½ cup) glacé cherries,
finely chopped
125 ml (½ cup) glacé ginger,
finely chopped
250 ml (1 cup) mixed nuts,
finely chopped
250 ml water
5 ml (1 teaspoon) baking
powder
5 ml (1 teaspoon) bicarbonate
of soda
5 ml (1 teaspoon) mixed spice
5 ml (1 teaspoon) salt

475   Christmas pudding   (F)

Serves 10; kJ per portion 980; Prep time 45 min; Cooking time 1 ¼ hours

1. Combine the fruit cake mixture, sugar, water, butter or margarine, salt, mixed spice, glacé cherries and ginger in a saucepan.
2. Bring to the boil and boil for 5 minutes, then allow to cool.
3. When cooled, stir in the bicarbonate of soda.
4. Sift the flour and baking powder together into a bowl, then stir into the cooled fruit mixture. Add the nuts.
5. Stir in the beaten eggs and mix well.
6. Pour the batter into a greased pudding basin. Cover with a double thickness of waxproof paper and tie securely with string.
7. Place in a large saucepan half-filled with water and steam covered, for 1 ¼ hours (f). Serve hot with brandy or wine sauce (recipes 500 and 501).

---

250 ml (1 cup) flour
125 ml (½ cup) sugar
1 egg, beaten
12,5 ml (1 tablespoon) butter
or margarine, melted
12,5 ml apricot jam
250 ml milk
5 ml (1 teaspoon) bicarbonate
of soda dissolved in 5 ml
vinegar
2 ml (½ teaspoon) salt
Sauce:
230 g butter or margarine
187,5 ml (¾ cup) sugar
250 ml single cream
250 ml milk
5 ml vanilla essence

476   Marshmallow pudding

Serves 6; kJ per portion 980; Prep time 30 min; Cooking time 15 min.

1. Combine the flour and sugar in a mixing bowl, then stir in the milk, mixing well to blend.
2. Stir in the apricot jam and the butter or margarine, mixing well.
3. Add the dissolved bicarbonate of soda, mix well, then blend in the beaten egg and salt to form a soft batter.
4. Transfer to an ovenproof dish and bake in the oven at 180 °C (350 °F) until the top is browned and a knife inserted in the pudding comes out clean.
5. Meanwhile, combine the sauce ingredients in a small saucepan and heat over medium heat, stirring all the time to blend well. Do not allow to boil.
6. As soon as the pudding comes out of the oven, pour the sauce over it and allow to cool for a few minutes before serving.

Note: The pudding is also very good served cold. Allow to cool completely at room temperature before serving.

---

4 large cooking apples
yellow sugar
butter or margarine
water

477   Baked apples

Serves 4; kJ per portion 500; Prep time 10 min; Cooking time 30 min.

1. Wash the apples well and core them. Peel about 2,5 cm of the skin from the tops of the apples.
2. Arrange the apples in a baking dish and fill the centres with yellow sugar. Place a little butter or margarine on top of each.
3. Pour in enough water to reach a depth of 1 cm in the dish and bake the apples in the oven at 180 °C (350 °F), basting frequently, until they are soft, about 30 minutes. Serve hot or cold.

Variation: Fill the apples with fruit mincemeat instead of the sugar and butter or margarine.

225 g flour
2 egg yolks, lightly beaten
50 to 75 ml (4 to 6 tablespoons) butter or margarine
25 ml (2 tablespoons) sugar
150 ml milk
15 ml (3 teaspoons) baking powder
2 ml (½ teaspoon) salt
Filling:
fresh strawberries, halved
sugar
juice of ½ lemon
softened butter

478 Strawberry shortcake (F)

Serves 6; kJ per portion 1 600; Prep time 45 min; Cooking time 15 min.

1. Sift the flour, baking powder, salt and sugar into a mixing bowl.
2. Work in the butter or margarine with a fork or the fingers, then add the milk and eggs, a little at a time, until the mixture holds its shape but is still soft. Stir continuously with the fork.
3. Turn the dough out onto a floured surface and roll out into 4 rounds.
4. Place the rounds on greased baking sheets and bake in the oven at 220 °C (425 °F) until lightly golden, 10 to 15 minutes. Allow to cool slightly (f).
5. Combine the fresh strawberries with a little sugar and the lemon juice in a bowl.
6. Split each shortcake round in half carefully with a knife and spread each half on one side with softened butter.
7. Place one round, buttered side up, on a plate, spoon some of the strawberry mixture on top. Repeat until all the filling and all the shortcake rounds have been used up, ending with a layer of strawberries. Serve warm with whipped cream.

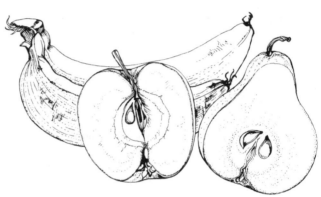

1 kg apples, cored, peeled and thinly sliced
110 g raisins
grated rind of ½ lemon
62,5 ml (5 tablespoons) butter or margarine
500 ml (2 cups) fresh breadcrumbs
25 ml lemon juice
100 ml sherry
110 g brown sugar
1 ml (¼ teaspoon) grated nutmeg

479 Apple brown betty (F)

Serves 4; kJ per portion 1 030; Prep time 30 min; Cooking time 45 min.

1. Grease an ovenproof dish with 12,5 ml (1 tablespoon) of the butter or margarine.
2. Layer a third of the breadcrumbs on the bottom of the dish and dot with some of the butter or margarine.
3. Place half the apples on top, sprinkle with half the sugar, nutmeg, grated lemon rind and raisins. Sprinkle 12,5 ml lemon juice on top.
4. Layer another third of the breadcrumbs on top, dot with butter or margarine and repeat step 3.
5. Cover with the remaining breadcrumbs, dot with butter or margarine and bake in the oven at 190 °C (375 °F) until the apples are tender and the top is golden brown, about 40 minutes.
6. Pour the sherry over the pudding and bake a further 5 minutes (f). Serve hot with whipped cream or custard.

Variations:
1. Use chopped fresh apricots or stewed and drained dried apricots instead of apples.
2. Use canned gooseberries, drained, instead of apples.
3. Use canned loganberries instead of apples.

310 g canned mandarin
oranges, drained
110 g cottage cheese
grated rind of 1 orange
Topping:
85 g oats
62,5 ml (5 tablespoons) butter
or margarine
75 ml (6 tablespoons)
yellow sugar

480 Citrus crisp

Serves 4;   kJ per portion 800;   Prep time 30 min;   Cooking time 10 min.

1. Combine the cottage cheese, mandarin oranges and orange rind in a bowl
   and transfer to an ovenproof dish.
2. Melt the butter or margarine and sugar together in a saucepan, then stir in the
   oats and mix well. Remove from the stove.
3. Layer the oats mixture over the cottage cheese mixture in the casserole and
   smooth the surface.
4. Place under the grill until the topping browns, then serve with melted honey.

Variation: Fresh orange segments, lightly sautéed, are a tasty alternative to the
mandarin oranges.

---

6 ripe bananas, peeled and
halved lengthwise
62,5 ml (5 tablespoons) butter
or margarine
62,5 ml (5 tablespoons) soft
brown sugar
50 ml rum
sprinkling cinnamon

481 Bananas in rum

Serves 4;   kJ per portion 900;   Prep time 15 min;   Cooking time 5 min.

1. Melt the butter or margarine in a large frying-pan.
2. Add the bananas and sprinkle them with half the sugar and a little cinnamon.
   Sauté until the bananas are lightly browned on one side, then turn them over.
3. Sprinkle with the rest of the sugar and a little cinnamon.
4. Add the rum and set it alight. Serve with the liquid poured over the bananas
   when the flames subside.

Variations:
1. Serve with whipped cream flavoured with rum essence and a little sugar.
2. Bananas in rum go well with ice-cream.

---

6 ripe pears, peeled, cored and
halved lengthwise
grated rind of ½ lemon
12,5 ml lemon juice
125 ml dry red wine
250 ml clear honey
1 stick cinnamon

482 Baked pears with wine

Serves 6;   kJ per portion 580;   Prep time 20 min;   Cooking time 20 min.

1. Place the pears, cut side down, in a large shallow baking dish and sprinkle
   with the lemon juice.
2. Combine the wine, honey, cinnamon and lemon rind in a saucepan over
   medium heat and bring to the boil, stirring now and then.
3. Pour the boiling syrup over the pears and cover the dish.
4. Bake in the oven at 190 °C (375 °F), basting occasionally, until the pears are
   tender when pricked with a sharp knife, about 20 minutes.
5. Cool the pears at room temperature, then chill in the refrigerator for
   30 minutes. Remove the cinnamon stick before serving.

Variations:
1. Fresh peaches may be used instead of pears.
2. Stuff the pears or peaches with a mixture of almonds, soft brown sugar or
   honey and finely chopped candied peel, moistened with a little medium
   cream sherry to form a paste. However, place the pears or peaches cut side
   up in the dish and use only 125 ml clear honey instead of 250 ml, before
   continuing with step 2.

400 g canned black cherries,
drained and stoned
250 ml canning juice
10 ml (2 teaspoons) cornflour
12,5 ml (1 tablespoon) sugar
65 ml brandy
1 ml (¼ teaspoon) ground
cinnamon
vanilla ice-cream

483   Flambé cherries

Serves 6;   kJ per portion 1 500;   Prep time 15 min;   Cooking time 5 min.

1. Heat the reserved can juice, cinnamon, sugar and cornflour in a saucepan over very low heat, stirring all the time with a wooden spoon.
2. Heat until the ingredients are well-blended and the juice is just warm, about 4 minutes.
3. Add the cherries and heat a further 2 minutes, then pour the cherries and juice into a serving bowl and set aside.
4. Warm the brandy in a small saucepan over low heat, then pour over the cherries and ignite it. Serve with vanilla ice-cream as soon as the flames have died down.

Variation: Use canned litchis instead of cherries.

---

5 egg yolks
75 ml (6 tablespoons) sugar
170 g brown sugar
500 ml double cream, scalded
5 ml vanilla essence

484   Crème brulée

*Serves 4;   kJ per portion 680;   Prep time 1 hour + chilling time;
Cooking time 10 min.*

1. Beat the 75 ml (6 tablespoons) sugar and egg yolks together in a large mixing bowl until pale and smooth and the mixture forms a ribbon trail when the whisk is lifted.
2. Gradually beat in the scalded cream and pour the mixture into a large, heavy-bottomed saucepan.
3. Heat gently, stirring all the time with a wooden spoon, until the mixture is thick enough to coat the spoon.
4. Remove from the stove and continue beating the mixture for a further 2 minutes, then stir in the vanilla essence.
5. Strain the mixture through a fine sieve into a deep ovenproof serving dish and allow it to cool.
6. Chill in the refrigerator for 2 hours.
7. Sprinkle the surface of the crème with a 5 mm thick layer of brown sugar.
8. Place the dish on a baking sheet and place it under a preheated grill until the sugar melts and caramalises, about 4 minutes, taking care to remove it before it burns. Serve immediately.

Note: When heating the cream, do not allow it to boil, as it will curdle.

---

375 ml (1½ cups) flour
2 eggs, beaten
125 ml (½ cup) sugar
18,75 ml (1½ tablespoons)
butter or margarine
25 ml apricot jam
5 ml (1 teaspoon) bicarbonate
of soda
10 ml (2 teaspoons) ground
ginger
2 ml (½ teaspoon) grated
nutmeg
Syrup:
500 ml (2 cups) sugar
500 ml water
125 ml vinegar

485   Vinegar pudding   (F)

Serves 4;   kJ per portion 890;   Prep time 30 min;   Cooking time 40 min.

1. Cream the butter or margarine and sugar together in a mixing bowl.
2. Gradually add the beaten eggs to the mixture, beating all the time.
3. Sift the flour, bicarbonate of soda, ground ginger and grated nutmeg into the butter mixture, mixing well.
4. Stir in the apricot jam, blending well. The dough should be fairly soft.
5. Boil the syrup ingredients together in a saucepan for 5 minutes, stirring occasionally, and allow to cool.
6. Transfer the syrup to a large ovenproof dish and pour the dough into it.
7. Bake in the oven at 180 °C (350 °F) until browned, about 40 minutes (f). Serve hot with custard or cream.

250 g dates, stoned and finely chopped
500 ml (2 cups) flour
2 eggs, beaten
250 ml (1 cup) walnuts or pecan nuts, finely chopped
115 g butter or margarine
250 ml (1 cup) sugar
250 ml boiling water
5 ml (1 teaspoon) bicarbonate of soda
5 ml (1 teaspoon) baking powder
2 ml (½ teaspoon) salt
Sauce:
12,5 ml (1 tablespoon) butter or margarine
312,5 ml (1¼ cups) sugar
185 ml water
125 ml brandy
5 ml vanilla essence
1 ml (¼ teaspoon) salt

486 Cape brandy pudding (F)

Serves 6; kJ per portion 1 200; Prep time 45 min; Cooking time 40 min.

1. Divide the dates into two equal portions and place them in separate bowls.
2. Add bicarbonate of soda to one portion and pour the boiling water over it. Mix well and leave to cool.
3. Cream the butter or margarine and sugar in a mixing bowl and beat in the eggs. Mix well.
4. Sift the flour, baking powder and salt through a fine sieve into the mixing bowl and fold into the creamed mixture.
5. Add the dry portion of dates and the nuts, mixing well to blend.
6. Stir in the bicarbonate of soda and date mixture and mix thoroughly, then turn the batter into a large baking dish and bake in the oven at 180°C (350°F) until done, about 40 minutes.
7. Meanwhile, prepare the sauce. Heat the sugar, butter or margarine and water together in a saucepan for 5 minutes. Remove from the stove and stir in the vanilla essence, salt and brandy.
8. Pour the sauce over the pudding as soon as it comes out of the oven (f) and serve hot or cold with whipped cream.

Baked custard can be prevented from turning watery by warming the milk before adding the eggs.

Skin can be prevented from forming on the custard by dusting the top with sugar.

Curdled custard can be saved by putting it in the blender and whirling for a few seconds.

---

4 eggs
62,5 ml (5 tablespoons) sugar
1,25 litres milk
5 ml vanilla essence
grated nutmeg
1 ml (¼ teaspoon) salt

487 Baked custard

Serves 4; kJ per portion 880; Prep time 30 min; Cooking time 45 min.

1. Beat the eggs, sugar and salt together in a bowl.
2. Heat the milk to lukewarm and add to the beaten egg mixture. Stir in the vanilla essence, mixing well.
3. Pour the mixture into a greased fireproof baking dish and sprinkle with nutmeg.
4. Stand the baking dish in a pan quarter-filled with warm water and bake in the oven at 180°C (350°F) until the custard is set, about 45 minutes. Serve hot or cold.

Variations:
1. Add 125 ml desiccated coconut to the milk and egg mixture.
2. Melt 1½ squares of plain milk chocolate in the milk.

Note:
• The custard is done if a knife inserted in the centre comes out clean.
• This custard is not firm enough to turn out.

250 ml (1 cup) cooked long-grained rice
2 eggs, separated
500 ml milk
2 ml vanilla essence
125 ml (½ cup) sugar
1 ml (¼ teaspoon) salt

488   Baked rice pudding   (F)

Serves 4;   kJ per portion 780;   Prep time 25 min;   Cooking time 40 min.

1. Heat the milk to lukewarm in a saucepan and stir in the rice. Remove from the stove.
2. Beat the egg yolks with the sugar and salt in a bowl. Gradually add the milk mixture, beating all the time.
3. Beat the egg whites until stiff and fold into the milk and rice mixture. Stir in the vanilla essence and pour into a greased, ovenproof baking dish.
4. Bake in the oven at 180°C (350°F) until set, about 40 minutes (f).
5. Serve hot with golden syrup, honey, the syrup from green fig preserve or watermelon preserve.

---

250 ml (1 cup) soaked sago or tapioca
2 eggs, separated
500 ml milk
2 ml vanilla essence
125 ml (½ cup) sugar
1 ml (¼ teaspoon) salt

489   Baked sago or tapioca pudding   (F)

Serves 4;   kJ per portion 780;   Prep time 25 min + soaking time;
Cooking time 40 min.

1. Soak the sago or tapioca overnight. Do not drain as the cereals will absorb almost all the water in which they have been soaked.
2. Heat the milk to lukewarm in a saucepan and stir in the sago or tapioca. Remove from the stove.
3. Beat the egg yolks with the sugar and salt in a bowl. Gradually add the milk mixture, beating all the time.
4. Beat the egg whites until stiff and fold into the milk and sago or tapioca mixture. Stir in the vanilla essence and pour into a greased ovenproof baking dish.
5. Bake in the oven at 180°C (350°F) until set, about 40 minutes (f).
6. Serve hot with golden syrup, honey, the syrup from green fig preserve or watermelon preserve.

---

1 kg canned pie apples
grated rind of 1 lemon
125 ml (½ cup) seedless raisins, soaked in water for 30 minutes
25 ml (2 tablespoons) brown sugar (optional)
5 ml (1 teaspoon) ground cinnamon
Topping:
62,5 ml (5 tablespoons) butter or margarine
110 g flour
110 g sugar

490   Apple crumble   (F)

Serves 6;   kJ per portion 1 100;   Prep time 30 min;   Cooking time 45 min.

1. Combine the apples, lemon rind, raisins, sugar and ground cinnamon in a bowl, then transfer to a lightly greased pie dish.
2. Cream the butter or margarine and sugar in a bowl.
3. Work the flour into the butter and sugar with the fingertips until the mixture resembles fine breadcrumbs.
4. Sprinkle the crumbs over the apple mixture.
5. Bake in the oven at 180°C (350°F) until the topping is lightly browned, about 45 minutes (f). Serve hot or cold with cream or custard.

Variations:

1. Use canned loganberries, gooseberries or youngberries or a mixture of one of these and canned pie apples instead of the apples.
2. Stewed dried peaches, apricots or mixed fruits may be substituted for the apples.
3. 10 ml (2 teaspoons) ground coriander may be added to the topping.
4. Use fruit mincemeat or rhubarb instead of the apples and omit the raisins.
5. Use stewed Satsuma plums instead of the apples and chopped preserved ginger instead of the raisins.

4 slices stale white bread, 2 cm thick, thickly buttered
2 eggs
190 ml (¾ cup) seedless raisins
750 ml milk
125 ml (½ cup) sugar
1 ml (¼ teaspoon) salt

491 Bread-and-butter pudding (F)

Serves 4; kJ per portion 1 100; Prep time 20 min + soaking time; Cooking time 30 min.

1. Arrange the slices of bread in a greased ovenproof baking dish, buttered sides down. Sprinkle with the raisins.
2. Beat the eggs in a bowl, then stir in the sugar, salt and milk.
3. Pour the milk mixture over the bread and raisins and leave for 30 minutes to soak through.
4. Bake in the oven at 160°C (325°F), covered, for 30 minutes. Uncover and bake until the top is golden brown (f). Serve hot with golden syrup, honey or moskonfyt.

---

250 ml (1 cup) raw rice
2 eggs, beaten
50 ml (4 tablespoons) flour
25 ml (2 tablespoons) butter or margarine, melted
5 ml (1 teaspoon) baking powder
water for boiling
1 ml (¼ teaspoon) salt
125 ml (½ cup) sugar and ground cinnamon, mixed

492 Sweet rice dumplings (Souskluitjies) (F)

Serves 4; kJ per portion 950; Prep time 30 min; Cooking time 35 min.

1. Place the rice and 1 litre of salted water in a large saucepan. Bring to the boil and boil for 20 minutes. Drain well and allow the rice to cool.
2. Combine the flour, baking powder and salt in a bowl and stir into the rice, mixing well to blend.
3. Stir in the eggs and mix thoroughly.
4. Form the mixture into small balls (dumplings) and dust each with a little flour.
5. Half-fill a saucepan with water and bring to the boil. Drop the dumplings into the boiling water and boil, covered, until the dumplings rise to the top, about 15 minutes. Drain (f) and place on a heated serving dish.
6. Pour the melted butter or margarine over the dumplings and sprinkle with the cinnamon and sugar mixture. Serve hot.

---

10 ml (2 teaspoons) powdered or granulated yeast
2 eggs
225 g flour
62,5 ml (5 tablespoons) butter or margarine, softened
75 ml (6 tablespoons) sugar
50 ml warm water
50 ml warm milk
2 ml vanilla essence
1 ml (¼ teaspoon) salt
25 ml (2 tablespoons) currants
12,5 ml (1 tablespoon) sultanas
Syrup:
75 ml rum
225 g sugar
285 ml water

493 Rum baba (F)

Serves 6; kJ per portion 1 200; Prep time 45 min + proving time; Cooking time 30 min.

1. Mix the yeast with the warm water and warm milk in a mixing bowl and set aside for 5 minutes.
2. Rinse a mixing bowl in boiling water and dry thoroughly, then sift the flour, sugar and salt into it.
3. In a separate bowl, beat the eggs with the vanilla essence.
4. Make a well in the centre of the flour and add the yeast mixture, little by little, mixing lightly with the hands.
5. Add the beaten egg a little at a time, still using your hands. The resulting dough should be soft and sticky.
6. Cut the butter or margarine into small pieces and distribute it over the dough. Cover and set aside until the dough has doubled in size, about 1 hour.
7. Knead the dough down and beat, preferably with an electric mixer, until the dough leaves the side of the bowl, about 5 minutes.
8. Add the currants and sultanas and mix well.
9. Transfer the dough to a large greased ring mould. Cover with a towel and place in a warm place until the dough rises to the top of the mould.

273

10. Bake in a preheated oven at 230 °C (450 °F) for 10 minutes, reduce the heat to 190 °C (375 °F) and bake until the cake is golden brown.
11. Remove from the oven and set aside to cool before turning out onto a wire rack.
12. Meanwhile, make the syrup. Combine the sugar and water in a saucepan and simmer over low heat until the syrup thickens.
13. Stir in the rum and blend well.
14. Prick the cake all over with a fork and spoon the syrup over it. Allow it to soak in completely (f).
15. Just before serving, sprinkle the cake with a little more rum and serve with fresh fruit and whipped cream, or on its own.

Variations:

1. Follow this recipe up to step 11. Place the syrup from a large can of pineapple rings in a saucepan with 37,5 ml (3 tablespoons) sugar and simmer over low heat until it thickens. Stir in 75 ml Kirsch and pour half the mixture over the pricked cake. Increase the heat to high and boil until the rest of the syrup is reduced to half. Arrange the chopped pineapple rings on top of the cake and add a few halved glacé cherries. Just before serving, pour over the thickened sauce.
2. Use chopped black cherries instead of the currants and sultanas.

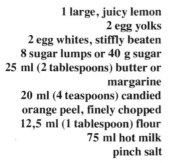

---

1 large, juicy lemon
2 egg yolks
2 egg whites, stiffly beaten
8 sugar lumps or 40 g sugar
25 ml (2 tablespoons) butter or margarine
20 ml (4 teaspoons) candied orange peel, finely chopped
12,5 ml (1 tablespoon) flour
75 ml hot milk
pinch salt

494   Lemon soufflé

Serves 4;   kJ per portion 900;   Prep time 40 min;   Cooking time 30 min.

1. Rub the sugar lumps hard against the skin of the lemon to allow them to absorb the essence (optional).
2. Combine the hot milk and the sugar in a bowl, stirring until the sugar dissolves.
3. Peel the lemon thinly and chop the rind very finely. Squeeze out the juice, reserving 50 ml for the soufflé.
4. Place the flour in a small saucepan and add the milk, stirring with a wooden spoon until smooth.
5. Add the butter or margarine and heat gently, stirring constantly, until the sauce is thick and smooth. Add the salt, stir well and remove from the stove.
6. Beat in the egg yolks, one at a time, and pour in the lemon juice in a thin steady stream at the same time to prevent curdling. Stir in the lemon rind and candied orange peel.
7. Fold in the stiffly beaten egg whites and pour the mixture into a well-greased soufflé dish.
8. Bake in the oven at 180 °C (350 °F) for 30 minutes. Serve immediately.

Note:
- Prepare the soufflé dish before starting to make the soufflé.
- The egg whites should be stiff and shiny but not dry for the best results.
- Eat the soufflé immediately, otherwise it will collapse.

140 g flour
2 eggs
2 egg yolks
2 large oranges
225 g butter
140 g castor sugar
285 ml milk
50 ml Grand Marnier or Cointreau
25 ml oil
37,5 ml brandy
1 ml (¼ teaspoon) salt

495 Crêpes Suzettes

Serves 6; kJ per portion 800; Prep time 45 min + chilling time; Cooking time 10 min.

1. Sift the flour and salt into a mixing bowl.
2. Add the eggs, egg yolks and 100 ml of the milk and whisk until smooth.
3. Beat in the rest of the milk and chill the batter in the refrigerator for 1 to 2 hours.
4. Grate the rind of both oranges finely and set aside.
5. Melt the butter in a small frying-pan, then add 60 g of the castor sugar, half the orange rind and the juice of 1 orange. Simmer for 10 minutes, then add the segments (membranes removed) of the other orange and 25 ml of the Grand Marnier or Cointreau. Set aside.
6. Brush a small frying-pan with a little of the oil and coat the base evenly with the crêpe batter. Fry until lightly browned, then turn and brown the other side lightly. Repeat until all the batter is used up. Stack each crêpe between oiled sheets of greaseproof paper.
7. Beat the remaining butter, sugar, liqueur and orange rind together until light and fluffy and spread the mixture over each of the crêpes. Fold the crêpes in half and then in half again and arrange in the pan of sauce. Heat until the crêpes are heated through and the sauce is hot.
8. Place the brandy in a metal ladle and heat it over a pan of boiling water or an open flame. Set the brandy alight and pour over the crêpes. Serve when the flames die down.

Note: The crêpes must be wafer-thin.

496 Filling for sweet pancakes

Batter (recipe 547)

Prepare the pancakes as directed, and fill them with one of the following:

- Sprinkle with sugar and lemon juice when done, then roll them up and serve dredged with castor sugar and pieces of lemon or castor sugar mixed with cinnamon.
- Add grated lemon rind to the batter and fill the pancakes with apple purée mixed with seedless raisins and a little lemon juice.
- Spread with apricot jam or moskonfyt before rolling up.
- Sprinkle the pancakes with orange juice and serve with wedges of orange.
- Add grated naartjie rind to the batter and sprinkle with naartjie juice before rolling up.
- Cream together 62,5 ml (5 tablespoons) butter or margarine and 31,25 ml (2½ tablespoons) castor sugar until soft. Work in 12,5 ml brandy and 5 ml lemon juice, spread the pancakes with this mixture and roll up.
- Fill with fruit purées such as apricot, pear, fig.

275

5 ml (1 teaspoon) cornflour
12,5 ml (1 tablespoon) butter
or margarine
500 ml (2 cups) brown sugar
100 ml cold water
65 ml boiling water
190 ml warm milk
5 ml vanilla essence
1 ml (¼ teaspoon) salt

497   Caramel sauce

Makes 300 ml;   Prep time 10 min;   Cooking time 10 min.

1. Place the sugar, cold water and butter or margarine in a frying-pan and heat over medium heat, stirring continuously, until the syrup is a light, clear brown.
2. Add the boiling water and stir until smooth, then stir in the milk.
3. Mix the cornflour and salt to a smooth paste with a little cold milk and stir gradually into the sauce.
4. Bring to the boil and boil for 3 minutes, then remove from the stove.
5. Stir in the vanilla essence and serve hot over ice-cream.

37,5 ml (3 tablespoons) ginger
preserve, finely chopped
250 ml (1 cup) sugar
125 ml water
1 ml (¼ teaspoon) ground
ginger

498   Ginger sauce   (F)

Makes 150 ml; kJ per portion 550; Prep time 15 min; Cooking time 10 min.

1. Combine all the ingredients in a saucepan.
2. Bring to the boil and boil for 10 minutes.
3. Remove from the stove and allow to cool before use. Serve with steamed puddings (f).

---

75 ml (6 tablespoons) apricot
purée or canned apricot nectar
12,5 ml (1 tablespoon) butter
or margarine
65 ml hot water
125 ml sweet sherry

499   Apricot sauce   (F)

Makes 225 ml; kJ per portion 550; Prep time 15 min; Cooking time 10 min.

1. Place the apricot purée and hot water in a saucepan and blend, stirring often, over medium heat.
2. Stir in the wine and continue heating, stirring all the time, until the mixture is smooth.
3. Strain the sauce through a fine sieve and return the strained liquid to the saucepan.
4. Add the butter or margarine and stir until it has melted (f). Serve hot with steamed puddings.

Variation: Use jams such as ripe fig jam, strawberry jam or youngberry jam instead of the apricot purée.

Note: This sauce may also be used as a glaze for baked ham. If a thicker consistency is required, the sauce may be thickened with 10 ml (2 teaspoons) cornflour.

12,5 ml (1 tablespoon)
cornflour
12,5 ml (1 tablespoon) butter
or margarine
125 ml sweet sherry
125 ml boiling water
25 ml lemon juice
125 ml (½ cup) sugar
1 ml (¼ teaspoon) salt
1 stick cinnamon

500   Wine sauce   (F)

Makes 275 ml; kJ per portion 650; Prep time 15 min; Cooking time 10 min.

1. Combine the sugar and cornflour in a small saucepan.
2. Gradually add the sweet sherry and water, to which the stick of cinnamon has been added, stirring all the time over medium heat.
3. Bring to the boil and boil for 3 minutes, then remove from the stove.
4. Add the butter or margarine, lemon juice and salt and stir until the butter or margarine has melted (f). Serve hot, with steamed puddings.

12,5 ml (1 tablespoon)
cornflour
12,5 ml (1 tablespoon) butter
or margarine
250 ml boiling water
37,5 ml brandy
125 ml (½ cup) sugar
1 ml (¼ teaspoon) salt

501   Brandy sauce   (F)

Makes 300 ml; kJ per portion 600; Prep time 15 min; Cooking time 10 min.

1. Combine the sugar and cornflour in a small saucepan.
2. Gradually add the water, stirring all the time over medium heat.
3. Bring to the boil and boil for 3 minutes, then remove from the stove.
4. Add the butter or margarine, brandy and salt and stir until the butter or margarine has melted (f). Serve hot, with steamed puddings.

---

4 egg yolks
375 ml milk
2 ml vanilla essence
37,5 ml (3 tablespoons) sugar
1 ml (¼ teaspoon) salt

502 Egg custard

Makes 400 ml; kJ per portion 450; Prep time 20 min; Cooking time 15 min.

1. Bring the milk to the boil in a saucepan.
2. Meanwhile, beat the egg yolks, sugar and salt together in a bowl.
3. Pour the hot milk into the egg mixture, stirring well to blend, and return the mixture to the saucepan.
4. Cook over low heat, stirring all the time, until the mixture coats the spoon. Be sure not to let the mixture boil.
5. Remove from the stove and cool slightly, then stir in the vanilla essence. Serve hot or cold.

Variation: Substitute almond or rum essence for the vanilla essence.

Note:
- Using 2 eggs instead of 4 egg yolks will make a lighter custard.
- If the custard is allowed to boil, it will curdle. If cooked in the top of a double-boiler over hot water, the risk of curdling and lumpiness is lessened.

---

grated rind and juice of 1 large
lemon
5 ml (1 teaspoon) cornflour
140 ml water
12,5 ml to 25 ml golden syrup

503   Lemon sauce

Makes 200 ml; kJ per portion 570; Prep time 15 min; Cooking time 10 min.

1. Blend the lemon juice, rind and cornflour in a saucepan.
2. Add the water and golden syrup and heat over low heat, stirring all the time, until the sauce is smooth and thick.
3. Serve either hot or cold with ice-cream or steamed puddings.

---

85 g butter or margarine
25 ml (2 tablespoons) brown
sugar
37,5 ml golden syrup
37,5 ml single cream
2 ml vanilla essence

504   Butterscotch sauce

Makes 125 ml;   kJ per portion 570;   Prep time 10 min;   Cooking time 5 min.

1. Heat the butter or margarine, sugar and golden syrup together in a saucepan, stirring all the time, until the sugar and butter melt.
2. Add the cream and vanilla essence and mix well.
3. Bring to the boil and boil for 3 minutes, stirring now and then. Serve either hot or cold with ice-cream or steamed puddings.

Note: Do not let the sauce boil for too long, as this will make it stiff and sticky.

277

62,5 ml (5 tablespoons) butter
or margarine
60 g cocoa powder
37,5 ml (3 tablespoons) sugar
37,5 ml golden syrup or treacle
5 ml vanilla essence
50 ml water

505 Chocolate sauce (F)

Makes 175 ml; kJ per portion 750; Prep time 15 min; Cooking time 10 min.

1. Blend all the ingredients thoroughly in a saucepan and heat gently until the cocoa melts.
2. Continue heating until hot enough to serve (f). Serve with ice-cream or steamed puddings.

Variations:
1. Use milk instead of the water to obtain a milk chocolate sauce.
2. Use strong black coffee instead of water, and treacle instead of golden syrup to make a rich coffee-flavoured sauce.

Note: Chocolate sauce keeps very well in the refrigerator. Store in a screw-topped jar.

---

250 ml (1 cup) seedless raisins
62,5 ml (5 tablespoons)
walnuts, coarsely chopped
190 ml honey, melted
65 ml rum

506 Rum and raisin sauce (F)

Makes 250 ml; kJ per portion 660; Prep time 20 min.

1. Combine all the ingredients thoroughly in a bowl.
2. Leave, covered, at room temperature for 2 to 3 hours (f). Serve with chocolate, coffee or vanilla ice-cream.

BAKING

CAKES

Although the number of cake recipes may confuse the beginner, all cakes are really variations of a few basic mixing methods. Knowing how to use these, and having the correct utensils at hand go a long way towards making successful cakes.

You will need the following:
- To make blending and creaming easier, use *mixing bowls* with a round bottom that are not too small.
- Use firm, easy to handle *wooden* or *plastic spoons* for creaming or mixing.
- Use a *spatula* or a fairly large, flat *wooden spoon* to fold in the flour mixtures.
- A *whisk* is essential to beat together eggs and sugar, or egg whites.
- Your oven should have an efficient *thermostat*. As no two ovens are exactly alike, if you find that the given temperature in the recipe is too high or too low, adjust it slightly to suit your oven.
- *Sieves:* It is important to sift the dry ingredients together to incorporate air into the flour mixture.
- *Electric mixers* are a boon to the cake maker. Use a medium speed for creaming butter and sugar, and a higher speed for beating and whisking. It is better, however, to fold in flour by hand, because the mixer may disturb the small air bubbles, with the result that the cake will not rise well.
- Good quality *baking tins*. Calculate a longer baking time if the cake tin is smaller than specified in the recipe, and use a slightly lower heat as the cake may brown on top but still be raw inside. If you use a larger cake tin than stated, the mixture will be shallower and will need about 10 minutes less baking time. Tins with non-stick finishes produce very good results. If you do not have one, spray an ordinary tin with a non-stick spray or grease and line it with greaseproof paper. Light sponge cakes may be baked in tins which are lightly greased and dusted with flour; richer cakes should be baked in a lined tin. Remember never to scour a tin with a non-stick finish — wipe or wash it carefully.

Do's and dont's when making a cake

1. Use only the best and freshest ingredients:

   Flour. Cake flour has a low gluten content, which makes the best texture for cakes. Always use a good quality flour, and store all kinds of flour – but especially the self-raising kind – in airtight containers and in a cool, dry place.

   Eggs. Use large, fresh eggs, which should be at room temperature and not straight from the fridge.

   Shortening (Butter, margarine, lard, oil). Shortening should be at room temperature. Never melt shortening if it is to be creamed with sugar, but if a recipe *does* call for melting, melt over low heat and take care not to let it boil. When creaming butter or sugar together, wash the bowl out beforehand with hot water and dry thoroughly.

   Sugar. Use fine granulated sugar, unless the recipe calls for castor sugar, brown sugar or honey.

2. Never open the oven door during the early baking stages while the cake is still rising. Remember, too, that the oven must reach the correct temperature *before* the cake is placed in it and that the door should be closed immediately, so that there is not too great a temperature drop.

3. Always weigh and measure ingredients *meticulously* and use the right measuring equipment: a slight difference from the quantities specified in the recipe can make a big difference to your cake. Remember that flour should not be pressed tightly into measuring cups; scoop it up with the cup and level the top with a spatula.

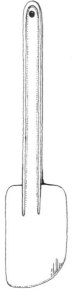

4. To test if a cake is done: towards the end of the baking time, press lightly with the fingertips – the cake should feel spongy; or insert a thin testing skewer into the cake – if done, the skewer should come out clean. The edges should have shrunk away from the sides of the cake tin.

5. To remove cakes from tins, invert onto a cooling rack, leave to cool for a while and then remove the tin. Do not be in too much of a hurry to do so. If a cake is really stuck, place a wet dish towel over the bottom of the tin for a minute – the steam will loosen the cake.

In general, cakes may be classified into two categories:

• Cakes which contain shortening or oil and a chemical leavening agent such as baking powder; for example, butter cakes.

• Cakes which do not contain shortening or a chemical leavening agent. The egg is separated and the beaten egg white folded in to incorporate air.

1. Cakes which contain shortening and a chemical leavening agent

There are numerous mixing methods, and the texture and taste of the cake will depend on which of these you use, as well as on the basic ingredients.

Basic creaming method

1. Grease cake tins or spray them with a non-stick spray if you are not using a non-stick cake tin. Set the oven to the temperature required.

2. Weigh or measure all the ingredients carefully, starting with the flour, then measuring the baking powder and salt. Sift the dry ingredients together into a mixing bowl.
3. Cream the shortening thoroughly with a wooden spoon in another bowl, or use an electric mixer.
4. Add the sugar very gradually, beating all the time until the sugar has been incorporated. The mixture must be light, creamy and fluffy. This step is extremely important as it influences the texture of the final product.
5. Either add the unbeaten eggs one at a time, or beat eggs well and add them a little at a time. Beat the mixture well after each addition.
6. Add the sifted dry ingredients and the liquid to the egg-sugar-shortening mixture, alternating a third of the dry ingredients with a third of the liquid and blending well after each addition. Mix until smooth.
7. Bake in the centre of the oven at 180 °C (350 °F) for 40 to 50 minutes.
8. Test to see if the cake is done by pressing the surface lightly with the fingertips – it should be elastic and the sides should have shrunk away slightly from the sides of the tin.

Note:
- The batter must be light and creamy – neither too thick nor too thin.
- Do not mix too much when adding the flour, as this may result in uneven texture. Do beat thoroughly, however, when adding the eggs to the butter and sugar mixture.
- The shortening must not be too cold: leave the butter or margarine to soften out of the refrigerator for several hours before use. Do not melt the shortening, as this will prevent the mixture from becoming light and fluffy.
- The cake should be well-shaped and have a thin, fine, soft crust. The crumbs should be soft and fine and the texture velvety.

Quick-mix or muffin method
1. Set the temperature of the oven and prepare the baking tins.
2. Sift all the dry ingredients together into a mixing bowl.
3. Melt the shortening and cool until just lukewarm.
4. Beat the eggs and milk together thoroughly in a bowl, then add the melted shortening to the egg and milk mixture beating all the time.
5. Add the dry ingredients with the flavourings and beat until the mixture is smooth, 1 to 2 minutes.
6. Bake at 180 °C (350 °F) to 190 °C (375 °F) in layer cake tins or in a muffin tin, for the time specified in the recipe.

Note:
- Oil may be used instead of the shortening.
- The texture of a cake made by this method will be crumbly and less velvety than that of butter cakes.
- The crust will be smooth.
- Muffins will become stale sooner than a butter cake.

Melting method
1. Set the oven temperature at 200 °C (400 °F), and place the racks in the middle of the oven.

2. Melt the butter or margarine in the milk or water. Cool slightly.
3. Sift all the dry ingredients, except the sugar, into a large mixing bowl.
4. Beat the eggs until light and foamy. Add the sugar gradually, beating well after each addition. The egg mixture should become thick and creamy and all the sugar should have dissolved.
5. Fold the sifted flour mixture into the egg and sugar mixture, working with light, firm movements.
6. Add the liquid and melted butter or margarine and beat for 1 minute.
7. Pour immediately into greased, lined baking tins.
8. Place in the oven immediately and bake for 25 to 30 minutes.
9. Cool the cake in the tin before turning it out.

Note:
- The batter is thinner than that for a butter cake, so if it is left standing before baking, the solid ingredients may sink to the bottom, making a soggy layer.
- A cake made using the melting method will have a fine, soft, even texture. It will be more airy than a butter cake but less spongy than a sponge cake.

Meringue-creaming method

1. Separate the eggs and beat the whites until stiff but not dry. Add cream of tartar or lemon juice and one-third of the sugar, beating continuously.
2. Sift all the dry ingredients together into a bowl. Add the unbeaten egg yolk, the rest of the sugar, the oil, liquid and flavouring to the dry ingredients. Beat until the sugar has dissolved and the mixture is smooth: 2 minutes should be sufficient.
3. Fold this mixture very carefully into the egg white mixture, using a spatula; the air which has been beaten in must be retained.
4. Pour into ungreased and lined baking tins and bake in the oven at 180°C (350°F) for 30 minutes.

Mixing method	Type of cake
Basic creaming method	Butter cake and variations, for example, chocolate cake, coffee cake, coconut cake, Madeira cake, fruit cake
Quick-mix or muffin method	One-step cake, muffins, fruit bread
Melting method	Flans, feather cake, layer cakes and variations
Meringue-creaming method	Chiffon cakes

2. Cakes which do not contain shortening or a chemical leavening agent (sponge cakes)

In sponge cakes, air is beaten into the egg, which is then incorporated into the mixture. The cream of tartar or lemon juice added to the egg white has four functions: it serves as a stabilising agent, which means that the egg white will hold more air; it reduces shrinkage during the baking process; it gives a finer texture; and it produces a whiter Angel cake (white sponge cake).

Note: Do not add salt to the egg or egg whites before beating.

Mixing methods for sponge cakes

Meringue method
1. Separate the eggs. Beat the whites until stiff but not dry. Add cream of tartar dissolved in water or lemon juice, beating all the time. Add two-thirds of the sugar and beat well.
2. Beat the egg yolks until light and thick. Add the remainder of the sugar to the yolks and beat until it has dissolved.
3. Fold the yolks into the whites.
4. Sift a layer of flour and salt mixture over the egg and fold in carefully. Repeat until all the flour and salt has been used. Pour into an ungreased but lined tin.
5. Bake in the oven at 160°C (325°F) for 50 to 60 minutes.

Quick method
1. Beat the whole eggs until light and foamy.
2. Add the sugar very gradually, beating constantly.
3. Sift a layer of flour and salt mixture over the eggs and fold in carefully. Repeat until all the flour and salt has been used, then bake in the oven at 160°C (325°F) for 50 to 60 minutes.

Note: The meringue method is also used for Angel cake (white sponge cake), but egg whites *only* are used (recipe 511).

What went wrong?
Some common faults and their causes:

Type	Appearance and texture	Fault
Sponge cakes	close, firm, heavy	air lost during mixing process
	close-textured layer at the bottom	egg yolk not beaten until foamy before adding the sugar
	dry	wrong proportion of ingredients; baked for too long; temperature incorrect; too much flour
	cracked upper crust and hard crust	mixture too stiff; eggs beaten too much; oven temperature too high
	smooth shiny crust at the sides	pan greased (should be ungreased)
	white specks on upper crust	sugar not completely dissolved

Type	Appearance and texture	Fault
Butter cakes	close, firm, heavy	overmixed; too little leavening agent; incorrect oven temperature and baking time; too much sugar or shortening
	dry texture	too much baking powder; overmixed; baking times and temperature wrong
	tunnels and holes	poor mixing; overmixing; oven temperature too high
	unpleasant taste	poor quality ingredients or incorrect quantities of ingredients
	cracked upper crust	same as sponge cake
	speckled crust	same as sponge cake
	cake fallen in the middle	oven opened while baking; temperature too low; baking time too short; too much leavening agent; batter too thin

CAKES

240 g cake flour
100 g butter or margarine
160 g fine granulated sugar
2 large eggs, at room temperature
10 ml (2 teaspoons) baking powder
125 ml milk
5 ml vanilla essence
1 ml (¼ teaspoon) salt

507 Basic butter cake (F)

Serves 6-8;   kJ per portion 600;   Prep time 45 min;   Cooking time 30 min.

1. Using the creaming method (p. 280), cream the butter, gradually adding the sugar. Beat until light and creamy and all the sugar has dissolved.
2. Beat in the vanilla essence.
3. Beat the eggs until light and foamy, then fold into the creamed mixture; it should be smooth.
4. Sift together all the dry ingredients. Add the dry ingredients to the egg mixture, a third at a time, alternating with milk. Beat well after each addition.
5. Grease two layer tins, 200 to 220 mm in diameter, and turn the batter into them. Bake immediately in the oven at 190 °C (375 °F) for 25 to 30 minutes.
6. Invert the tins on a cooling rack and leave for 5 to 10 minutes before removing the tins (f).

Variations:

1. *Chocolate cake:* Mix 50 ml (4 tablespoons) cocoa with 30 ml water. Heat the milk and stir into the cocoa mixture. Allow to cool before adding to the batter.
2. *Coconut cake:* Fold 125 ml (½ cup) desiccated coconut into the batter just before baking.
3. *Coffee cake:* Heat the milk and add 25 ml coffee extract or instant coffee. Cool, then continue with step 4.
4. *Nut cake:* Fold 125 ml (½ cup) chopped nuts into the batter just before baking.
5. *Orange cake:* Omit the vanilla essence and substitute 5 ml (1 teaspoon) grated orange rind. Substitute 30 ml orange juice for 30 ml of the milk when mixing the batter.

6. *Spice cake:* Sift 5 ml (1 teaspoon) ground ginger, 5 ml (1 teaspoon) ground cinnamon and 2 ml (½ teaspoon) ground cloves together with the dry ingredients.
7. *Upside-down cake:* Grease the bottom of a deep cake or tube tin very well. Sprinkle with 50 ml (4 tablespoons) brown sugar. Arrange pineapple rings, glacé cherries, banana slices and chopped nuts on the sugar. Spoon the batter onto the fruit and bake at 180 °C (350 °F) for 35 to 45 minutes.

---

240 g cake flour
250 g sugar
3 eggs, separated
125 ml oil
125 ml water
5 ml vanilla essence or other flavouring
15 ml (3 teaspoons) baking powder
2 ml (½ teaspoon) salt

508   Basic cake with oil   (F)

Serves 6-8;   kJ per portion 610;   Prep time 45 min;   Cooking time 30 min.

1. Sift the flour, sugar, baking powder and salt together in a mixing bowl.
2. Beat the egg yolks, oil and water together well in a bowl, then stir in the vanilla essence.
3. Add the egg mixture to the dry ingredients and mix thoroughly.
4. Beat the egg whites in another bowl until stiff but not dry, and fold into the batter.
5. Turn the batter into two greased layer cake pans, 220 mm in diameter, and bake in the oven at 190 °C (375 °F) for 30 minutes.
6. Turn out onto a wire cooling rack (f).

Variations:

1. *Chocolate cake:* Sift 25 ml (2 tablespoons) cocoa with the dry ingredients.
2. *Spice cake:* Sift 5 ml (1 teaspoon) each of ground cinnamon, ground ginger and ground allspice together with the dry ingredients.
3. *Coconut cake:* Stir 50 ml (4 tablespoons) desiccated coconut into the batter before adding the egg whites.

---

240 g cake flour
250 g castor sugar
5 eggs, separated
180 ml water
125 ml oil
5 ml lemon juice
15 ml (3 teaspoons) baking powder
5 ml (1 teaspoon) grated lemon rind
2 ml (½ teaspoon) cream of tartar
2 ml (½ teaspoon) salt

509   Chiffon cake   (F)

Serves 8-10;   kJ per portion 530;   Prep time 50 min;   Cooking time 1 hour

1. Sift the flour, baking powder, salt and castor sugar together into a large mixing bowl.
2. Add the cream of tartar to the egg whites in a large bowl and beat until stiff but not dry.
3. Make a well in the centre of the dry ingredients and add the oil, unbeaten egg yolks, lemon rind and juice, and water. Beat with a wooden spoon or an electric beater until the mixture is smooth.
4. With a spatula, fold the yolk and flour mixture lightly into the beaten egg whites.
5. Line two layer cake tins, 220 mm in diameter, or a tube tin with ungreased butter paper, and turn the batter into the tin(s). Bake in the oven at 180 °C (350 °F), allowing 50 to 60 minutes for a tube cake and 35 to 40 minutes for layer cakes.
6. Test by pressing lightly with the fingertips to see if cake is done. If the top of the cake is springy to the touch, it is ready.
7. Allow the cake to cool slightly, then loosen the sides of the cake gently with a knife and turn out onto a wire cooling rack (f).

Variation: *Walnut chiffon cake:* Add 100 g finely chopped walnuts to the batter before folding in the egg whites.

510 Basic sponge cake (F)

120 g cake flour
5 large eggs, separated
160 g fine granulated sugar
5 ml (1 teaspoon) cream of
tartar dissolved in 10 ml water
or 12,5 ml lemon juice
2 ml (½ teaspoon) salt

Serves 8-10;   kJ per portion 610;   Prep time 45 min;   Cooking time 1 hour

1. Sift the flour and salt together into a bowl.
2. In a large mixing bowl, beat the egg whites until stiff but not dry. Gradually beat in 100 g of the sugar and the cream of tartar mixture or lemon juice.
3. Beat the egg yolks in a small bowl until pale yellow and thick. Add the rest of the sugar gradually to this, beating until all the sugar has dissolved.
4. Fold the beaten egg yolks into the egg whites, working with a spatula or a wooden spoon; do not stir.
5. Sift the flour and salt mixture onto the eggs in thin layers, folding in each layer of flour lightly to ensure that the air in the egg mixture is not disturbed.
6. Line the bottom of an ungreased tube tin or 2 layer tins with butter paper. Turn the batter into the tin(s) and tap it/them lightly on the table to break the bigger air bubbles.
7. Bake in the oven at 160°C (325°F) until the crust is a light golden brown and the cake has shrunk from the sides of the tin, 50 to 60 minutes. The cake should spring back if lightly touched with the fingertips.
8. Invert the tin(s) onto a cooling rack and leave until the cake is almost cold before carefully removing the tin(s) (f).

Note: Use a very sharp, serrated-edge knife to cut sponge cake.

511 Angel cake (F)

120 g cake flour
250 g fine granulated sugar
10 egg whites
5 ml (1 teaspoon) cream of
tartar
1 ml almond essence or 2 ml
vanilla essence
2 ml (½ teaspoon) salt

Serves 8-10;   kJ per portion 610;   Prep time 45 min;   Cooking time 1 hour

1. Sift the flour and half the sugar together several times to incorporate as much air as possible.
2. In a separate bowl, beat the egg whites until foamy, then add the cream of tartar and salt and continue beating until the egg whites are stiff but not dry.
3. Add 25 ml (2 tablespoons) of the remaining sugar to the egg whites and beat well. Continue adding the sugar, 25 ml at a time, beating after each addition until all the sugar has been incorporated.
4. Sift the flour and sugar mixture in thin layers over the egg whites and fold in each layer carefully.
5. Fold in the vanilla or almond essence.
6. Spoon the mixture carefully into an ungreased tube tin, 240 mm in diameter, and bake in the oven at 160°C (325°F) for 1 hour.
7. Invert the tin onto a cooling rack and cool the cake in the tin for approximately 1 hour. Loosen the cake carefully from the sides of the tin and remove the tin (f).

Note: Tap the tin lightly on a flat surface before baking to remove any big air bubbles.

512 Swiss roll (F)

60 g cake flour
100 g fine granulated sugar
3 eggs, separated
7 ml lemon juice
1 ml (¼ teaspoon) salt
smooth apricot jam or other
filling (see below)

Serves 10;   kJ per portion 810;   Prep time 45 min;   Cooking time 10 min.

1. Sift the flour and salt together into a mixing bowl.
2. Beat the egg whites in a large mixing bowl until stiff but not dry.
3. Fold in the egg yolks and beat the yolks and whites until thick and pale yellow.

4. Gradually add the sugar and lemon juice, beating all the time.
5. Fold in the sifted flour mixture.
6. Spoon or pour the batter into a 220 mm x 350 mm tin lined with greased butter paper, tilting the tin to spread the batter evenly.
7. Bake in the oven at 200 °C (400 °F) for 10 minutes.
8. Spread a damp cloth over a cooling rack and turn the cake out onto this. Carefully remove the butter paper.
9. Spread the cake carefully with apricot jam or other filling of your choice and roll it up, using the cloth to turn the roll and keep the cake from breaking.
10. Remove the cloth and leave the cake on a cooling rack to cool completely (f).

Variation: Add 37,5 ml (3 tablespoons) cocoa to the flour and sift together with the sugar. Add 50 ml water to the batter after step 5.

Fillings:
1. *Cottage cheese and apricot:* Roll the cake up without adding any filling and allow to cool. When cool, unroll gently and spread with a mixture of smooth cottage cheese mixed with crushed canned apricots. Roll up again and serve cold.
2. *Ice-cream Swiss roll:* Roll the cake up without filling and allow to cool. Unroll carefully and spread with slightly softened ice-cream. Roll up again and place in the freezer for 1 hour before serving. Serve with chocolate sauce.
3. *Ice-cream youngberry Swiss roll:* Spread hot cake with youngberry or strawberry jam. Roll up and leave to cool. When cold, unroll the cake carefully and spread with softened ice-cream. Continue as for 2.
4. Any cream and fruit mixture, for example, apple or stewed dried fruit, makes a delicious filling.

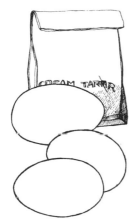

225 g self-raising flour **170 g castor sugar or fine granulated sugar** **110 g butter or margarine, softened** **3 eggs** **45 ml lukewarm milk** **5 ml vanilla essence** **5 ml (1 teaspoon) baking powder** **2 ml (½ teaspoon) salt**	**513 Quick mix cake** (F) *Serves 6-8; kJ per portion 710; Prep time 45 min; Cooking time 20 min.* 1. Sift the flour, salt and baking powder together into a large mixing bowl. 2. Stir in the remaining ingredients and mix thoroughly with a wooden spoon or beat for 1 minute with an electric mixer. Add an additional 10 to 20 ml milk if the batter is too stiff. 3. Line two 200 mm layer tins with greased butter paper and pour the batter into them. Bake in the oven at 180 °C (350 °F) for 20 minutes. 4. Turn out onto a cooling rack (f). **Variation:** *Chocolate cake:* Mix 50 ml (4 tablespoons) cocoa with 25 ml water. Heat the milk, stir in the cocoa mixture and allow to cool before continuing with step 1. **Note:** All the ingredients must be at room temperature.

250 g cake flour
250 g castor sugar or fine granulated sugar
250 g butter or margarine
5 large eggs
15 ml milk, if necessary
3 ml almond essence
5 ml (1 teaspoon) baking powder
1 ml (¼ teaspoon) salt

514 Madeira cake (F)

Serves 8-10; kJ per portion 710; Prep time 50 min; Cooking time 45 min.

1. Sift the flour, salt and baking powder together into a mixing bowl.
2. In a separate bowl, cream the butter or margarine and sugar together.
3. Add the unbeaten eggs one by one to the butter and sugar mixture, beating well after each addition. Stir in the almond essence.
4. Fold the sifted ingredients, a little at a time, into the creamed mixture. The batter should be fairly stiff, but if it is too stiff, stir in the milk.
5. Turn into a lined, greased cake or bread tin and bake in the oven at 180 °C (350 °F) for 35 to 45 minutes.
6. Allow to cool slightly in the tin and turn out onto a cooling rack (f).

Variations:

1. *Madeira cherry cake:* Stir 125 g glacé cherries into the batter before baking and bake at 160 °C (325 °F) for 1 hour.
2. *Walnut or pecan cake:* Stir 125 g finely chopped nuts into the batter before baking and bake at 160 °C (325 °F) for 1 hour.
3. *Ginger cake:* Add 125 g finely chopped preserved ginger to the batter before baking.
4. *Fruit cake:* Mix glacé cherries, walnuts or pecans and finely chopped preserved ginger to make 125 g in all and stir into the batter before baking.

---

500 ml (2 cups) cake flour
25 ml (2 tablespoons) butter
375 ml (1½ cups) sugar
4 eggs
20 ml (4 teaspoons) baking powder
250 ml hot milk
25 ml (2 tablespoons) cocoa
2 ml (½ teaspoon) salt

515 Hot milk chocolate cake (F)

Serves 6-8; kJ per portion 780; Prep time 20 min; Cooking time 20 min.

1. Beat the eggs well, then add the sugar and beat until light and fluffy.
2. Add the butter to the milk and heat to boiling point.
3. Sift the dry ingredients together in a large mixing bowl.
4. Add the egg mixture to the dry ingredients and fold in.
5. Add the hot milk and butter, mixing well.
6. Pour the batter into 2 greased, waxpaper-lined cake tins, 200 mm in diameter. Tap tins lightly on a flat surface to expel air bubbles.
7. Bake in the oven at 180 °C (350 °F) for 20 minutes (f).

---

225 g cake flour
3 eggs, beaten
170 g butter or margarine
170 g sugar
450 g dried fruit cake mixture
60 g almonds, chopped
60 g almonds, split
60 g glacé cherries, coated in flour
25 ml milk
7 ml (1½ teaspoons) baking powder
5 ml (1 teaspoon) mixed spice

516 Dundee cake (F)

Serves 10; kJ per portion 810; Prep time 45 min; Cooking time 2½ hours

1. In a mixing bowl, cream the butter or margarine and sugar together until soft and light.
2. Stir in the beaten eggs with a wooden spoon, blending well.
3. Sift the flour, baking powder and mixed spice together and stir into the creamed mixture with enough milk to make a 'slow dropping' consistency.
4. Combine the cake mixture, chopped almonds and cherries in a bowl and stir into the batter. Pour into a greased and lined 200 mm cake tin and cover with the split almonds. Brush with a little beaten egg white.
5. Bake in the centre of the oven at 180 °C (350 °F) until done, 2 to 2½ hours. Cool in the tin for about 10 minutes, then turn out onto a wire rack to cool completely (f).

517 Cheesecake (F)

Pastry:
250 g cake flour
125 g butter or margarine
37,5 ml (3 tablespoons) sugar
1 egg yolk beaten with
25 ml water
pinch salt
Filling:
250 g cottage cheese
12,5 ml (1 tablespoon) cake flour
4 eggs
50 ml (4 tablespoons) sugar
100 g sultanas
finely grated rind and juice of
1 lemon
250 ml sour cream

*Serves 6-8;   kJ per portion 2 165;   Prep time 45 min;
Cooking time 1 hour 10 min.*

1. First make the pastry. Sift the flour into a bowl.
2. Rub the butter or margarine into the flour, then stir in the salt and sugar.
3. Add the egg yolk and water mixture and mix to a stiff dough.
4. Line a greased 200 mm loose-bottomed cake tin with the pastry.
5. Beat together until thick and creamy the eggs and sugar for the filling. Fold in the cottage cheese, cake flour, sultanas, grated rind and juice of lemon and the sour cream.
6. Pour the filling into the case and bake in the oven at 180 °C (350 °F) for 45 to 60 minutes.
7. Turn off the oven and leave the cake to cool in it (f).

Note: After freezing, thaw in the refrigerator and heat gently in a warm oven before serving.

Add a little cooking oil to the saucepan to melt butter or margarine without burning.

---

518 Health date loaf (F)

450 g stoneless dates, finely chopped
500 ml (2 cups) shelled peanuts, crushed
800 g unsifted flour
250 ml (1 cup) brown sugar
37,5 ml (3 tablespoons) margarine
3 eggs
315 ml boiling water
10 ml vanilla essence
10 ml (2 teaspoons) baking powder
5 ml (1 teaspoon) bicarbonate of soda
2 ml (½ teaspoon) salt

*Serves 8-10;   kJ per portion 860;   Prep time 35 min;
Cooking time 1 hour 10 min.*

1. Pour the water into a large mixing bowl and stir in the margarine and bicarbonate of soda.
2. Stir in the dates, eggs and sugar and mix well.
3. Stir in the flour, baking powder, brown sugar and salt and mix well. Stir in the vanilla essence and the crushed nuts, blending thoroughly.
4. Pour the mixture into 2 large greased loaf tins.
5. Bake on the middle shelf of the oven at 180 °C (350 °F) for 1 hour and 10 minutes. Leave to cool in the tins, then turn out onto a wire rack (f). Serve sliced and spread with butter.

Variations:

1. Use chopped walnuts or pecan nuts instead of the peanuts.
2. Add 62,5 ml (5 tablespoons) seedless raisins with the nuts.

---

519 Light fruit cake (F)

750 ml (3 cups) cake flour
250 g butter or margarine
250 g castor sugar
450 g fruit cake mixture, rinsed thoroughly
250 g glacé cherries, finely chopped
100 ml (²/₅ cup) mixed nuts, finely chopped
6 eggs
50 ml brandy
5 ml lemon essence
2 ml (½ teaspoon) baking powder
2 ml (½ teaspoon) salt

*Serves 8-10;   kJ per portion 880;   Prep time 45 min;
Cooking time 2 ½ hours*

1. Cream the butter or margarine and castor sugar together in a bowl until light and creamy.
2. Add the eggs, one at a time, beating well after each addition.
3. Stir in the fruit cake mixture, cherries and mixed nuts, mixing well.
4. Sift the flour, baking powder and salt together and fold into the batter.
5. Stir in the lemon essence and brandy and blend thoroughly.
6. Turn the batter into a greased and lined cake tin and bake in the oven at 150 °C (300 °F) for 2 to 2½ hours (f).

500 ml (2 cups) cake flour
2 eggs, beaten
90 g butter or margarine
250 ml (1 cup) sugar
450 g fruit cake mixture
125 ml (½ cup) glacé cherries, finely chopped
125 ml (½ cup) glacé ginger, finely chopped
250 ml (1 cup) mixed nuts, finely chopped
250 ml water
5 ml (1 teaspoon) baking powder
5 ml (1 teaspoon) bicarbonate of soda
5 ml (1 teaspoon) mixed spice
1 ml (¼ teaspoon) salt

520 Boiled fruit cake (F)

Serves 8-10; kJ per portion 960; Prep time 45 min; Cooking time 45 min.

1. Combine the fruit cake mixture, sugar, water, butter or margarine, salt, mixed spice, glacé cherries and ginger in a saucepan.
2. Bring to the boil and boil for 5 minutes, then allow to cool.
3. When cooled, stir in the bicarbonate of soda.
4. Sift the flour and the baking powder together in a bowl, then stir into the cooled fruit mixture. Stir in the nuts.
5. Stir in the beaten eggs and mix well.
6. Pour the batter into a greased and lined round cake tin and bake in the oven at 180°C (350°F) for 45 minutes (f).

Note:

● The cake should be allowed to mature in a tightly closed tin for at least a month to obtain the best flavour.
● If desired, 65 ml brandy, or more, may be sprinkled over the cake before placing it in the tin.
● The batter should have a dropping consistency. If it is too runny, the fruit will sink to the bottom; if it is too stiff the top of the cake will split when it is baked.

---

170 g cake flour
125 g butter or margarine
200 g castor sugar
2 small eggs, separated
65 ml milk
125 ml sour cream
7 ml (1½ teaspoons) baking powder
pinch ground nutmeg
1 ml (¼ teaspoon) ground cinnamon
pinch mixed spice
7 ml (1½ teaspoons) castor sugar

521 Rich crumb cake (F)

Serves 10; kJ per portion 710; Prep time 1 hour; Cooking time 50 min.

1. Sift the flour and baking powder into a large mixing bowl.
2. Cut the butter or margarine into it with a knife and rub into the flour until the mixture resembles breadcrumbs.
3. Stir in the 200 g castor sugar, mixing well.
4. Place a quarter of the mixture in a small bowl and set aside.
5. Beat the egg yolks, sour cream and milk together in another bowl and pour into the flour mixture in the large mixing bowl. Beat well with a wooden spoon until the mixture is smooth.
6. Beat the egg whites in a bowl until they form stiff peaks. With a spatula fold them gently into the batter.
7. Spoon the batter into a greased 160 mm sandwich tin, smoothing the top with the back of the spoon.
8. Sprinkle the reserved flour and butter or margarine mixture over the top of the batter and bake in the oven at 190°C (375°F) until the cake is golden brown on top and a skewer inserted into the centre comes out clean, about 50 minutes.
9. Allow the cake to cool in the tin for 10 minutes, then turn out onto a wire rack.
10. Combine the 7 ml castor sugar, the nutmeg, cinnamon and mixed spice in a small bowl and sprinkle over the top of the cake (f). Allow to cool completely before cutting.

522 Banana loaf (F)

500 ml (2 cups) flour
250 ml (1 cup) sugar
120 g butter or margarine
2 eggs
3 large, ripe bananas, peeled and mashed
65 ml water
7 ml (1½ teaspoons) baking powder
5 ml (1 teaspoon) bicarbonate of soda
pinch salt

Serves 10;   kJ per portion 680;   Prep time 45 min;   Cooking time 45 min.

1. Cream the butter or margarine and sugar in a bowl until light and creamy in texture.
2. Stir in the mashed bananas and beat to combine thoroughly.
3. Beat in the eggs, one at a time, blending well.
4. Sift the flour and salt into the mixture and stir to blend well.
5. Dissolve the bicarbonate of soda in the water and stir into the mixture, then stir in the baking powder.
6. Pour the batter into a greased loaf tin and bake in the oven at 180 °C (350 °F) until done, about 45 minutes.
7. Let cool in the tin for a few minutes, then turn out onto a wire rack to cool completely (f).

523 Petit fours

Use the basic Angel cake recipe (recipe 511)

Makes 12;   kJ per portion 510;   Prep time 1 hour;   Cooking time 20 min.

1. Pour the batter into a greased muffin tin or a square or rectangular 200 mm cake tin.
2. Bake in the oven at 180 °C (350 °F) for 20 minutes.
3. Turn the small cakes out of the muffin tin onto a cooling rack, or cut the large cake into smaller squares, 3 cm by 3 cm.
4. Pour petit four icing (see below) over the cakes. Allow to harden and decorate with cherries or butter icing(recipe 529), coconut or chocolate vermicelli.

Icing

500 ml (2 cups) sugar
1 ml (¼ teaspoon) cream of tartar
250 ml water
flavouring

1. Heat the sugar, cream of tartar and water in a small saucepan, stirring to dissolve the sugar. With a brush, wash the sugar crystals from the sides of the saucepan and cover the saucepan as soon as the water starts to boil.
2. Boil to the soft-ball stage (see p. 333); do not stir.
3. Remove from the stove and allow to cool until lukewarm (38 °C/97 °F) Add the flavouring. Beat with a wooden spoon until the mixture starts to thicken, then pour over the cakes before it becomes too stiff.

Note: Stir in a little hot water if the icing becomes too stiff to pour over the cakes.

524 Carrot cake (F)

340 g cooked carrots, puréed
500 ml (2 cups) ground almonds
6 eggs, separated
250 g sugar
5 ml (1 teaspoon) butter or margarine
12,5 ml (1 tablespoon) grated orange rind
12,5 ml brandy

Serves 10;   kJ per portion 690;   Prep time 45 min;   Cooking time 50 min.

1. Grease a 220 mm loose-bottomed cake tin with the butter or margarine and set aside.
2. Beat the egg yolks in a bowl until pale and frothy, then add the sugar gradually, beating all the time, until the mixture is thick and creamy and makes a ribbon trail if the whisk is lifted.
3. Stir in the carrot purée, orange rind, brandy and almonds and blend well.
4. Beat the egg whites until stiff and fold into the carrot mixture with a spatula. Spoon into the prepared cake tin.
5. Bake in the centre of the oven at 160 °C (325 °F) until a skewer inserted into the centre comes out clean, about 50 minutes.
6. Remove from the oven and leave to cool in the tin for 15 minutes. Turn out carefully onto a wire rack to cool completely (f).

125 ml (½ cup) cream cheese
375 ml (1½ cups) icing sugar
1½ squares unsweetened
chocolate, melted
25 ml (2 tablespoons) butter or
margarine
65 ml single cream
2 ml vanilla essence
1 ml (¼ teaspoon) salt

525   Chocolate cream frosting

Prep time 15 min.

1. Cream the butter or margarine and the cream cheese in a mixing bowl until light and fluffy.
2. Stir in the other ingredients and mix well.

Note: Use for chocolate or spice cakes.

---

250 g icing sugar, sieved
120 g butter or margarine
12,5 ml milk
3 drops peppermint essence
green colouring

526   Peppermint frosting

Prep time 10 min.

1. Beat the butter or margarine thoroughly in a bowl with the icing sugar. The mixture should be light and fluffly.
2. Beat in the milk and the peppermint essence, then add a few drops of green colouring.

Note: This quantity is sufficient to sandwich two layer cakes together and also provide a topping.

---

520 g icing sugar, sifted
200 g butter
20 ml van der Hum liqueur
single cream to moisten
10 ml (2 teaspoons) mixed
spice

527   Van der Hum icing

Prep time 15 min.

1. Cream the butter and icing sugar together in a bowl until smooth and creamy.
2. Stir in the mixed spice, van der Hum and enough of the cream to give a spreading consistency. Use for spice or nut cakes.

Variation: Use orange liqueur and finely grated orange rind instead of van der Hum and mixed spice. Use for orange or lemon cakes.

---

120 g ground almonds
75 ml (6 tablespoons) icing
sugar
75 ml (6 tablespoons) castor
sugar
egg yolk to mix
3 drops almond essence

528   Marzipan (Almond paste)

Prep time 10 min.

1. Combine all the ingredients in a bowl, adding just enough egg yolk to make a firm mixture. Knead thoroughly.
2. Roll out and use for the top of a 20 cm cake.

Note: If the sides as well as the top are to be covered, make three times the quantities given here.

85 to 110 g icing sugar, sieved
62,5 ml (5 tablespoons) butter
flavouring

529   Butter icing

Prep time 15 min.

1. Cream the butter in a bowl until very soft and white.
2. Beat in the icing sugar and flavouring and use to ice the cake.

Variations:
1. *Chocolate:* Add 10 ml (2 teaspoons) drinking chocolate or cocoa and 3 drops vanilla essence.
2. *Coffee:* Add 10 ml coffee essence.
3. *Lemon:* Add 10 ml (2 teaspoons) grated lemon rind and beat in 10 ml lemon juice.
4. *Orange:* Add 15 ml (3 teaspoons) grated orange rind and beat in 10 ml orange juice.
5. *Vanilla:* Add 2 ml vanilla essence.
6. *Grenadilla.* Add 30 ml grenadilla pulp.

Note: Use more icing sugar if a firmer consistency is required.

---

250 g icing sugar, sieved
1 egg white, lightly beaten
15 ml lemon juice

530   Royal icing

Prep time 30 min.

1. Combine the egg white, lemon juice and icing sugar in a bowl.
2. Beat vigorously until the mixture is very white and firm enough to stand up in points.

Note:
- Royal icing must be firm. If the icing is too soft it has not been beaten sufficiently. Beat until very smooth.
- If a less firm result is desired, beat in a few drops of glycerine once the mixture is smooth.

---

500 g icing sugar, sieved
200 g icing sugar for
thickening and kneading
62,5 ml (5 tablespoons)
margarine
50 ml lemon juice

531   Satin icing

Prep time 20 min;   Cooking time 5 min.

1. Place the lemon juice and margarine in a saucepan and stir over low heat until the margarine has melted.
2. Add 250 g of the sifted icing sugar and stir until dissolved. Do not cook for longer than 2 minutes, however, as the icing will be difficult to use if it is boiled for longer. Remove from stove.
3. Add the other 250 g icing sugar and beat very hard to blend well. Allow to cool.
4. Work in enough of the unsifted icing sugar to enable the icing to be kneaded and make a pliable dough. Roll out and use like almond paste to coat cakes; or use to make petit fours.

Note: Satin icing keeps very well in the refrigerator or freezer if wrapped in foil or waxproof paper.

250 g icing sugar, sieved
20 ml warm water

532 Water icing (Glacé icing)

Prep time 15 min.

Combine the icing sugar and warm water thoroughly, adding the water very gradually. The mixture should be very smooth.

Variations:
1. Add 10 ml (2 teaspoons) cocoa powder to the icing sugar and beat in a knob of butter or margarine before adding the water.
2. Use strong black coffee instead of the water.
3. Use lemon juice instead of the water.
4. Use orange juice instead of the water.
5. Add 5 drops vanilla essence before adding the water.

Note: This quantity is sufficient to ice the top of a 21 cm cake. If the sides are also to be iced, make double quantities.

---

250 g icing sugar, sieved
62,5 ml (5 tablespoons) butter
or margarine
35 ml milk or water
colouring
flavouring

533 Glacé fudge icing

Prep time 20 min;   Cooking time 10 min.

1. Place the butter or margarine, milk or water and flavouring in a saucepan and stir over low heat until the butter or margarine has melted.
2. Remove from the stove and stir in the icing sugar and the colouring.

Variations:
1. Use orange or lemon squash instead of the milk or water.
2. Use strong black coffee instead of the milk or water.
3. Use 200 g icing sugar and 30 g cocoa instead of 250 g icing sugar.

Note:
● This icing will pipe and can be moulded into flowers and other shapes.
● This quantity is sufficient to ice the top of a 21 cm cake. If the sides are also to be iced, make double quantities.

---

500 g desiccated coconut
250 ml (1 cup) sugar
yolks of 3 eggs
200 ml milk
5 ml vanilla essence

534 Coconut filling

Prep time 20 min;   Cooking time 10 min.

1. Combine the coconut, sugar, milk and egg yolks thoroughly in a saucepan and simmer over medium heat until the mixture thickens.
2. Remove from the stove and stir in the vanilla essence, blending well.

Note: Use as a filling for layer cakes.

294

125 ml (½ cup) dates, finely chopped
125 ml (½ cup) sugar
125 ml (½ cup) pecan nuts, finely chopped
12,5 ml (1 tablespoon) butter
125 ml water
18,75 ml (1½ tablespoons) cocoa

535   Date filling

Prep time 20 min;   Cooking time 10 min.

1. Combine the cocoa, sugar and water in a saucepan, mixing well.
2. Stir in the butter and dates and simmer over medium heat until thick and smooth, stirring now and then.
3. Remove from the stove and cool for 2 minutes, then stir in the nuts, blending well.

Note: Delicious as a filling for spice or chocolate cakes.

QUICK FLOUR MIXTURES

The leavening agent used in quick flour mixtures acts rapidly, which means that quick mixing methods must be used, and the products cooked at a fairly high temperature for the best results.

The *main ingredients* in basic recipes for batters and doughs are flour, liquid, fat, egg, sugar (optional), leavening agent and salt. Different kinds of *flour* vary the appearance and taste. The grading of wheat flour depends on how much bran and wheat germ have been removed: a product may include the whole wheat grain or only a part of it. Any one or a mixture of the various wheat flours may be used and mealiemeal, buckwheat, rice flour, rye or potato flour are also alternatives.

Note: The kind of flour used will to a large degree determine the texture and consistency of the final product.

Dough and batter consistencies

Mixture	Liquid	Flour	Product	Mixing method	Cooking method
Batter (thin)	250 ml	125 g	crumpets	beating	frying on griddle or in pan
			pancakes	beating	baking in pan
			waffles	beating	baking in waffle iron
			coating batter	beating	deep-fat frying
			pop-overs	beating	baking
			timbales	beating	baking

Mixture	Liquid	Flour	Product	Mixing method	Cooking method
Batter (drop)	250 ml	180-200 g	dumplings	muffin or combined scone and muffin method	steaming in hot liquid
			fritters	muffin or combined scone and muffin method	deep-fat frying
			vetkoek	muffin or combined scone and muffin method	deep or shallow fat frying
			upside-down cake	combined scone and muffin method	baking
			coffee cakes	combined scone and muffin method	baking
			fruit loaves	combined scone and muffin method	baking or steaming
			muffins	muffin method	baking
Soft dough	180 ml	240 g	scones	scone method	baking
			shortcake	scone method	baking
			doughnuts made with baking powder	scone or muffin method	deep-fat frying
			koeksisters made with baking powder	scone or muffin method	deep-fat frying

Mixing methods

Beating method
1. Sift the dry ingredients together into a mixing bowl.
2. Beat the egg and liquid together, but note that some recipes will require separating the yolk and the white. If so, the whites are stiffly beaten and then folded into the mixture right at the end.
3. Add the sifted dry ingredients gradually to the beaten egg mixture and mix until the mixture is smooth.

Note:
- Do not beat for too long or too vigorously.
- Use the batter immediately; do not allow it to stand.
- Sifting the dry ingredients incorporates air into the flour mixture and gives a lighter result.

Scone method
1. Sift the dry ingredients into a mixing bowl.
2. Grate the shortening or soften it at room temperature.
3. With the fingertips rub the shortening into the dry ingredients until the mixture resembles coarse crumbs.
4. Cut in the liquid with a spatula to form a soft dough.
5. Pat together lightly with floured hands and turn out onto a floured board.

296

Note:
- Do not stir or knead too much as this will make the dough tough and result in a coarse texture and dry crust.
- Never use the palm of the hand to rub the shortening into the dry ingredients, as the ingredients should remain cool.

Quick or muffin method
1. Sift the dry ingredients together into a mixing bowl.
2. Melt the shortening – or use oil – and mix with the warm or cold liquid (milk, water or a combination of the two).
3. Beat the egg slightly and stir into the liquid mixture.
4. Add all the mixture to the dry ingredients and mix lightly until the liquid is fully incorporated. Note, however, that the mixture must still be slightly lumpy, not smooth.

Note:
- The mixture should rise evenly and the finished product should have a smooth upper crust with a light delicate texture.
- When a mixture is overmixed it 'peaks' after cooking, has a close texture and tunnels running in the same direction as the peak.

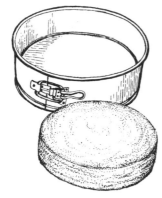

Scone and muffin method
1. Sift the dry ingredients together into a mixing bowl.
2. With the fingertips rub the shortening into the dry ingredients.
3. Beat together the milk and/or water, egg and sugar (if desired).
4. Add the liquid mixture to the dry ingredients and mix lightly to form a firm but light dough.

Baking and cooking methods
Baking
Quick flour mixtures should be baked in the oven at 200 °C (400 °F) to 240 °C (450 °F) to obtain a light, delicate texture: the product must rise quickly and then bake through. If the dough contains dried or fresh fruit, however, bake at 180 °C (350 °F) to 190 °C (375 °F) and for a longer period.

Frying
Deep or shallow fat fry as described on p. 199 for waffles, fritters and koeksisters.

Frying on a griddle or in a hot frying-pan
A frying-pan or griddle may be greased lightly with oil to bake pancakes or crumpets. Some batters include oil in the ingredients in which case greasing is unnecessary, except for the very first pancake or crumpet. Non-stick pans are also used without greasing.

Steaming

Bring the liquid to the boil in a saucepan and drop spoonfuls of batter into it. Cover tightly and steam for as long as is required. The batter for fruit loaves may be poured into a container, covered tightly and then placed in a large saucepan half-filled with boiling water. Cover with a lid and steam.

---

500 ml (2 cups) cake flour
20 ml (4 teaspoons) baking
powder
25 ml (2 tablespoons) sugar
50 ml (4 tablespoons) melted
butter or margarine
250 ml milk
1 egg
2 ml (½ teaspoon) salt

536   Muffins   (F)

Makes 12 muffins;   kJ per portion 280;   Prep time 10 min;
Cooking time 20 min.

1. Sift together the dry ingredients.
2. Mix the melted butter or margarine with the milk and egg. Beat and add to the dry ingredients. Mix lightly and spoon into a muffin pan.
3. Bake in the oven at 220 °C (425 °F) for 15 to 20 minutes (f).

Variations:

1. Use 250 ml (1 cup) unsifted flour and 250 ml (1 cup) cake flour instead of 500 ml (2 cups) cake flour. Do not sift the unsifted flour; add after step 1.
2. Omit the sugar and add 250 ml (1 cup) grated Cheddar cheese and 3 rashers of bacon, finely chopped, to the dough.
3. Add 125 ml (½ cup) raisins to the dough.
4. Add 250 ml (1 cup) chopped dates to the dough.
5. Substitute 250 ml (1 cup) mealiemeal and 250 ml (1 cup) cake flour for 500 ml (2 cups) cake flour.

---

500 ml (2 cups) cake flour
50 ml (4 tablespoons) butter
25 ml (2 tablespoons) sugar
(optional)
200 ml milk *or* **1 egg and**
150 ml milk mixed together
20 ml (4 teaspoons) baking
powder
2 ml (½ teaspoon) salt

537   Scones   (F)

Makes 12 scones;   kJ per portion 300;   Prep time 20 min;
Cooking time 10 min.

1. Sift the dry ingredients together.
2. Cut the butter into the dry ingredients and rub lightly with the fingertips until the mixture resembles coarse crumbs.
3. Add the liquid and mix lightly with a knife or with the fingertips. Do not knead the dough.
4. Turn the dough out onto a lightly floured board and press into an oblong shape, 20 mm thick.
5. Cut into squares or press out scones with a cutter.
6. Place on a greased baking sheet. Brush the top of the scones with a little milk and bake in the oven at 240 °C (475 °F) until done, about 10 minutes (f).
7. Serve warm with cheese or jam and cream.

Variations:

1. Use 125 ml sour cream instead of the butter and the milk or milk and egg.
2. Substitute 250 ml (1 cup) unsifted flour and 250 ml (1 cup) cake flour for 500 ml (2 cups) cake flour and omit the sugar. Do not sift the unsifted flour; add after step 1.

3. Substitute 250 ml (1 cup) unsifted flour and 250 ml (1 cup) cake flour for 500 ml (2 cups) cake flour, omit the sugar and add 125 ml (½ cup) finely grated Cheddar cheese. Add the unsifted flour after step 1.
4. Add 125 ml (½ cup) raisins to the dough.

Note: Scones may be baked on a heated, greased griddle instead of in the oven. Turn once.

To freshen scones, brush with a little milk and pop into a hot oven for 5 to 10 minutes.

500 ml (2 cups) cake flour
1 medium-sized egg
100 ml oil
125 ml milk
20 ml (4 teaspoons) baking powder
2 ml (½ teaspoon) salt

538 Scones with oil (F)

Makes 12 scones; kJ per portion 300; Prep time 15 min; Cooking time 10 min.

1. Sift the dry ingredients together.
2. Combine the oil, egg and milk in a bowl.
3. Add to the dry ingredients and cut into the flour mixture. Do not knead.
4. Mix lightly, then drop tablespoonfuls onto a greased baking sheet.
5. Bake in the oven at 240 °C (475 °F) for 10 minutes (f).

Variations:
1. Substitute 250 ml (1 cup) unsifted flour and 250 ml (1 cup) cake flour for 500 ml (2 cups) cake flour. Do not sift the unsifted flour; add after step 1.
2. Add 20 ml (4 teaspoons) sugar or honey to the mixture.
3. Add 125 ml (½ cup) grated Cheddar cheese to the dry ingredients.

500 ml (2 cups) cake flour
10 ml (2 teaspoons) sugar
50 ml (4 tablespoons) butter, melted
2 eggs, separated
250 ml milk
20 ml (4 teaspoons) baking powder
2 ml (½ teaspoon) salt

539 Waffles (F)

Makes 10; kJ per portion 300; Prep time 20 min; Cooking time 5 min.

1. Sift the dry ingredients together into a mixing bowl.
2. Gradually add the milk and mix well.
3. Beat the egg yolks and add to the batter. Fold in the melted butter.
4. Beat the egg whites until stiff but not dry. Fold into the batter.
5. Bake in a waffle iron (f).

Note: To serve after freezing, place frozen waffles either in a toaster for 1 minute or heat under the grill for 2 minutes.

250 ml (1 cup) cake flour
1 egg
125 ml milk
5 ml (1 teaspoon) baking powder
2 ml (½ teaspoon) salt
125 ml oil for frying

540 Vetkoek

Makes 8-10; kJ per portion 550; Prep time 15 min; Cooking time 10 min.

1. Sift the dry ingredients together into a bowl.
2. In a separate bowl, beat the egg lightly and add to the dry ingredients. Add the milk and mix the batter until smooth.
3. Heat the oil in a frying-pan and drop tablespoonfuls of batter into the hot oil. Fry for 2 to 3 minutes on one side, then turn and fry for another minute on the other side. Serve hot with butter and jam.

299

500 ml (2 cups) cake flour
50 ml (4 tablespoons) sugar
2 eggs
20 ml (4 teaspoons) butter, melted
250 ml milk
20 ml (4 teaspoons) baking powder
2 ml (½ teaspoon) salt

541　Crumpets　(F)

Makes 25 to 30;　kJ per portion 280;　Prep time 20 min;
Cooking time 5 min.

1. Sift the flour, baking powder and salt together into a bowl.
2. Beat the eggs and sugar in another bowl, and add the milk and butter.
3. Fold the dry ingredients into this mixture and stir well to form a smooth batter.
4. Bake on a hot griddle or in a heavy-based frying-pan. Turn once (f).
5. Serve with honey, butter, jam and cream.

---

1 kg self-raising flour
2 eggs
200 ml (⁴/₅ cup) sugar
190 g butter, melted
500 ml buttermilk
5 ml (1 teaspoon) baking powder
10 ml (2 teaspoons) salt

542　Buttermilk rusks

Makes ± 30;　kJ per portion 310;　Prep time 45 min;　Cooking time 30 min.

1. Sift the flour, baking powder and salt into a bowl.
2. Beat the eggs, sugar and buttermilk together.
3. Cut this mixture into the dry ingredients with a knife.
4. Knead the dough lightly, gradually adding the butter while kneading. This will take about 7 minutes.
5. Place balls of the dough next to each other in bread tins. The balls should reach to about ²/₃ the height of the tin.
6. Place in the oven immediately and bake at 180 °C (350 °F) for 30 minutes.
7. Turn out onto a cooling rack and break into individual rusks.
8. Lower the heat of the oven to 100 °C (200 °F) or less and dry the rusks in the oven. Turn them every 30 minutes.

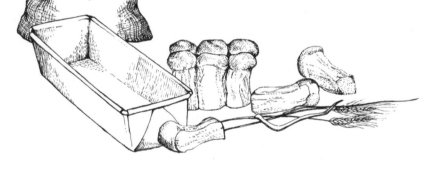

---

780 g unsifted wholewheat flour
420 g bread flour
500 g butter or margarine
250 ml (1 cup) sugar
575 ml milk
20 ml (4 teaspoons) baking powder
5 ml (1 teaspoon) salt

543　Wholewheat rusks

Makes ± 40 rusks;　kJ per portion 210;　Prep time 45 min;
Cooking time 45 min.

1. Place the milk, margarine or butter and sugar in a saucepan and bring to the boil over medium heat, stirring all the time. Remove from the stove.
2. Combine the wholewheat flour, bread flour, baking powder and salt in a bowl. Stir in the milk mixture and mix well.
3. Shape tablespoons of the mixture into buns and place them on lightly greased baking sheets.
4. Bake in the oven at 180 °C (350 °F) for 45 minutes.
5. Allow to cool on a wire rack, then pack in airtight containers and allow to dry out for 2 to 3 days before use.

1 kg unsifted wholewheat flour
240 g cake flour
375 ml (1½ cups) sugar
250 g margarine
2 eggs
250 ml oil
500 ml buttermilk
10 ml (2 teaspoons) baking powder
10 ml (2 teaspoons) bicarbonate of soda
10 ml (2 teaspoons) cream of tartar
125 ml (½ cup) raisins
10 ml (2 teaspoons) salt

544   Wholewheat buttermilk rusks

*Makes ± 50 rusks;   kJ per portion 310;   Prep time 45 min;
Cooking time 45 min.*

1. Combine all the dry ingredients except the sugar in a large mixing bowl.
2. Cut the margarine into small pieces and rub it into the dry ingredients until the mixture resembles fine breadcrumbs. Add the raisins.
3. Beat the eggs, sugar, buttermilk and oil together.
4. Combine the egg mixture and the dry ingredients to form a stiff dough.
5. Shape into balls and pack tightly against one another in a greased bread tin.
6. Bake in the oven at 190°C (375°F) for 45 minutes.
7. Turn out of the bread tin, allow to cool for 30 minutes and break into individual rusks.
8. Dry out in the oven at 100°C (200°F) for 4 to 5 hours, or overnight in the warming drawer of the stove. Allow to cool completely and store in airtight containers.

---

480 g cake flour
50 ml (4 tablespoons) butter or margarine
2 eggs
250 ml milk
30 ml (6 teaspoons) baking powder
2 ml (½ teaspoon) salt
oil for baking
Syrup:
800 g sugar
375 ml water
2 ml (½ teaspoon) cream of tartar
2 ml (½ teaspoon) ground ginger
3 sticks cinnamon

545   Koeksisters   (F)

*Makes ± 24;   kJ per portion 510;   Prep time 1 hour + proving time;
Total cooking time 1 hour*

1. First make the syrup. Heat the water in a saucepan, add the sugar and stir until all the sugar has dissolved. Wash down all the sugar crystals adhering to the sides of the saucepan.
2. Add the cream of tartar, ginger and cinnamon to the syrup. Boil, uncovered, for 5 minutes. Do not stir.
3. Remove from the stove and chill in the refrigerator.
4. Make the koeksisters. Sift the dry ingredients together in a mixing bowl. Add the butter or margarine and rub in with the fingertips until the mixture resembles fine crumbs.
5. Beat the eggs and milk together and add to the dry ingredients. Mix the dough well, then knead lightly for 2 minutes to make it pliable. Cover the basin with wax paper and leave for 1 hour.
6. Roll the dough out to a thickness of 7,5 to 10 mm with a rolling pin. Cut oblongs 80 mm by 40 mm. Starting 1 cm from one end, make 2 vertical cuts in the oblongs so that there are 3 strips joined at the end. Plait these strips loosely, and secure at the loose end.
7. Heat the oil to 190°C (375°F) and deep-fry the koeksisters for 1 minute.
8. Remove from the oil, drain on brown paper for 1 minute and dip in the cold syrup for 30 seconds. Remove from the syrup and place on a dish to dry (f).

Note:
● Handle the dough lightly and fry the koeksisters soon after plaiting.
● The syrup must remain cold so use only small quantities at a time, and leave the remainder in the refrigerator. Top up the syrup from that in the refrigerator when necessary.
● Do not cook too many koeksisters at a time.

546 Doughnuts

Makes ± 36;   kJ per portion 510;   Prep time 1 hour;   Cooking time 1 hour

Use the same recipe as koeksisters (recipe 545), but instead of plaiting the dough, roll each oblong into a ball and flatten slightly to form circles. Bake in the same way as koeksisters, but instead of dipping in syrup, allow the doughnuts to cool and dust them with icing sugar.

---

500 ml (2 cups) cake flour
2 eggs
30 ml (6 teaspoons) melted butter or oil
600 ml milk
60 ml single cream
12,5 ml brandy
2 ml (½ teaspoon) baking powder
2 ml (½ teaspoon) salt
oil for baking

547 Pancakes   (F)

Makes ± 25 small;   kJ per portion 280;   Prep time 15 min; Cooking time 30 min.

1. Combine the cake flour, salt and baking powder in a bowl.
2. Beat the eggs and milk together in a separate bowl.
3. Gradually add the dry ingredients, beating all the time. Beat in first the cream, then the melted butter or oil and the brandy.
4. Pre-heat a heavy-based frying-pan and grease lightly with oil.
5. Pour a thin layer of the batter into the pan, tilting it to distribute the batter evenly.
6. Bake on one side until lightly browned, about 2 minutes, then turn the pancake over with a fish slice or spatula and bake for another minute (f).
7. Turn the pancake onto a plate and keep warm over a saucepan of boiling water or, covered, in the oven at 100 °C (200 °F).
8. Continue until all the batter has been used.

Note:
- Leave the batter to stand for 1 hour before making the pancakes.
- The pan need only be greased once.
- Freeze pancakes with waxed paper or plastic in between each one. Wrap securely in foil or plastic.
- To serve after freezing, remove the wrap and interleaving sheets. Heat for 30 seconds on either side in a warm frying-pan or heat in the oven at 100 °C (200 °F) for 30 minutes or on a plate over boiling water for at least 30 minutes.

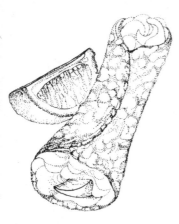

---

750 ml (3 cups) yellow unsifted mealiemeal
50 ml (4 tablespoons) sugar
250 ml (1 cup) onion, finely chopped
250 ml (1 cup) sweet red pepper, finely chopped
250 g canned creamed sweetcorn
500 ml (2 cups) Cheddar cheese, grated
6 eggs
500 ml sour cream or plain yoghurt
320 ml oil
30 ml (6 teaspoons) baking powder
20 ml (4 teaspoons) salt

548 Mexican mealiemeal bread   (F)

Serves 12;   kJ per portion 410;   Prep time 40 min;   Cooking time 1 hour

1. Combine all the dry ingredients in a large mixing bowl.
2. Beat the eggs, oil and sour cream in another bowl, and stir in the sweetcorn.
3. Stir the dry ingredients into the beaten egg mixture. Mix well, then add the onion and red pepper.
4. Turn half the batter into a greased pie dish or cake tin.
5. Sprinkle the grated cheese over the top.
6. Spread the rest of the batter over the cheese.
7. Bake in the oven at 180 °C (350 °F) for 1 hour (f).

Note: The batter may also be baked in a muffin tin. Bake for 30 minutes at 180 °C (350 °F).

250 ml (1 cup) cake flour
125 ml (½ cup) sugar
1 egg
50 ml (4 tablespoons) butter, melted
125 ml milk
20 ml (4 teaspoons) baking powder
2 ml (½ teaspoon) salt
Syrup:
50 ml (4 tablespoons) butter
20 ml honey

549   Honey cake   (F)

Serves 6;   kJ per portion 810;   Prep time 15 min;   Cooking time 15 min.

1. Sift the dry ingredients together in a mixing bowl.
2. Heat the milk with the butter until lukewarm and remove from the stove.
3. Beat the egg and add to the milk mixture.
4. Add the milk mixture to the dry ingredients and mix well.
5. Spoon the batter into a greased pie dish and bake for 15 minutes in the oven at 180 °C (350 °F).
6. Make the syrup. Melt the honey with the butter and pour the syrup over the cake when it comes out of the oven (f). Serve warm.

Variations:

1. For a savoury tart, omit the sugar and sprinkle 250 ml (1 cup) grated cheese over the cake when done. Instead of honey, melt 10 ml (2 teaspoons) Marmite with the butter and pour over the cake.
2. Substitute 125 ml (½ cup) unsifted flour for half the cake flour. Add the unsifted flour after sifting the other dry ingredients.
3. Pack 250 ml (1 cup) canned apples, peaches or apricots on the bottom of the greased pie dish, cover with the batter and continue with steps 5 and 6.

250 ml (1 cup) bread flour
250 ml (1 cup) wholewheat flour
12,5 ml (1 tablespoon) sugar
125 ml (½ cup) seedless raisins
1 egg
25 ml (2 tablespoons) butter or margarine, melted
12,5 ml (1 tablespoon) mixed nuts, finely chopped
250 ml buttermilk or yoghurt
65 ml molasses
5 ml (1 teaspoon) bicarbonate of soda
2 ml (½ teaspoon) salt

550   Raisin wholewheat bread   (F)

Serves 6-8;   kJ per portion 350;   Prep time 45 min;   Cooking time 50 min.

1. Combine the bread flour, wholewheat flour, sugar, bicarbonate of soda and salt in a mixing bowl.
2. Stir in the raisins, coating well.
3. Add the buttermilk or yoghurt, egg and molasses and mix until the dry ingredients are moistened.
4. Stir in the melted butter or margarine, mixing well.
5. Turn the mixture into a well-greased ovenproof dish or small bread tin and sprinkle with the chopped nuts.
6. Bake in the oven at 180 °C (350 °F) until a skewer inserted in the centre of the loaf comes out clean, about 50 minutes.
7. Cool in the ovenproof dish or bread tin for 10 minutes, then turn out and cool on a wire rack (f).

Note:

• The loaf might crack on top while baking, and does not rise very much.
• The loaf will keep for about 1 week in the refrigerator.

BAKING WITH YEAST

Cakes and breads containing yeast are usually popular because they look and smell so good – especially when newly-baked. Yeast is a leavening agent which is first soaked in the right amount of liquid and left at the right temperature, before being added to flour and other ingredients to make a dough. It then ferments and it is this process that makes the dough rise.

There are many kinds of yeast:

Dry yeast can be:

- *active dry yeast*, which must be soaked for 10 to 15 minutes in liquid at 40 °C to 45 °C (80 °F to 90 °F), but not hotter than this;
- *dry yeast cakes*, which must be soaked for at least 30 minutes in liquid; or
- *dried, fully-risen dough or sour-dough*. A piece of dough is allowed to rise and then dry out. It must be soaked in liquid for at least 30 minutes to 1 hour, but preferably overnight, before use.

Note: These kinds of yeast will remain active longer if stored in a cool, dry place.

Compressed yeast should be used within 3 to 4 days if stored in the refrigerator. If it is to be kept longer, freeze it. It is active and ready to use within 10 to 15 minutes if mixed with lukewarm water and flour.

Yeast plants must be kept alive continuously. Start the plant with a little active dry yeast or a cake of compressed yeast. Grated or cooked potato, a little bread flour and/or sugar, salt and lukewarm water must be added. Leave in a warm place, preferably overnight, but for at least 6 to 8 hours. The yeast will then be ready for mixing and kneading. Keep 125 ml to 250 ml of the yeast and use to prepare a fresh batch.

Raisin yeast or 'must' is the product of the natural fermentation of grapes or raisins. *Mosbeskuit* is typical of the sort of product made with this kind of yeast. Once the yeast is active, prepare a sponge (see p. 305) which should be ready for use after 6 to 8 hours. Rusks made with this kind of yeast will have a feathery texture and a distinct taste of the must.

Bread may also be baked with *salt-rising yeast* (recipe 552), which causes the dough to rise through the action of bacteria.

Often products baked with yeast taste strongly of the yeast. This is not necessarily because too much yeast was used, but rather because the fermentation period was too long.

Use the following proportions:

Water/Liquid	Flour	Yeast
500 ml	1 kg	½ cake compressed yeast and 100 ml lukewarm water to soak it in
500 ml	1 kg	5 ml (1 teaspoon) active dry yeast and 100 ml lukewarm water to soak it in
500 ml	1 kg	125 ml to 250 ml already liquid yeast, for example, potato yeast (recipe 551)

Use only good quality *flour* containing gluten, the protein in cereals, which forms the framework of fully-risen dough. When using rye, buckwheat or oats, add some wheat flour to raise the gluten content.

304

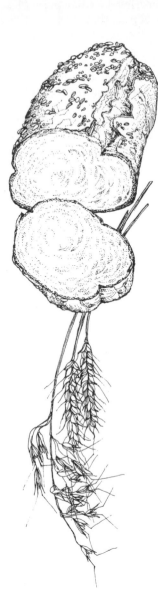

The *liquid* used may be water, milk or a mixture of the two. Water promotes fermentation, and will yield increased bulk with a dry crumb texture and crisp crust. The finished product will not last very long, however. Potato water is excellent for fermentation, and the finished product will not dry out quickly. Using fresh, evaporated, powdered, sour or buttermilk will increase the nutritional value considerably. Scald the milk, then cool to the desired temperature before using it to inhibit the growth of bacteria. Using milk in one of these forms will yield a product that tastes good and keeps well.

Although *salt* enhances the taste of the product and controls the fermentation process, using too much may retard fermentation.

Using moderate amounts of *shortening* will improve the texture and increase the length of time the finished product will keep. Use butter, margarine, lard, oil or soft mutton fat.

Eggs will improve the texture and colour, as well as the nutritional value, but a mixture containing eggs will take longer to rise.

Mixing methods

How the dough is mixed and kneaded is extremely important as it may affect the consistency of the finished product greatly. Use one of the following methods to make the dough:

● Prepare a *sponge* as follows: use active yeast, lukewarm liquid and enough flour to form a thin batter. If sugar is added, it will speed up the fermentation. Cover the basin with an old blanket and leave in a warm spot to ferment. When ready, it should be light, full of bubbles and have a warm yeasty smell. Do not leave the yeast to ferment for too long: calculate 1 hour for compressed yeast and 8 to 10 hours for sourdough yeast. Mix with the other ingredients, knead and leave in a warm place to rise.

● The *straight dough* method: Mix active yeast with the given amount of lukewarm liquid, add the other ingredients and knead well. Leave the dough to rise in a warm place. It will probably take 4 to 6 hours.

● The *batter* method: Place all the ingredients in a bowl and stir well with a spoon. Leave to rise in a warm place.

How to knead dough

1. Dust your hands with a little flour or cover them with butter or oil to prevent the dough from sticking to them, then mix the ingredients well. Work the dough with your hands and fists to develop the gluten and form the dough into a shiny smooth mass. Work in all the dry flour and mix evenly with the yeast. *Do not let the dough become cold.* Knead the dough thoroughly, turning it around from time to time.
2. After about 10 minutes, cover the dough in the basin with a blanket and leave to rise until twice its original size.

Note: Spread a little butter over the dough before leaving it to rise.

3. Knead the risen dough very lightly and form into loaves or buns. Place in greased pans or on baking sheets. Bread pans should be half-filled with dough. Cover lightly and leave to rise in a warm place until double in size.
4. Bake at 190°C (375°F) to 220°C (425°F) for 40 to 60 minutes. The dough will continue to rise for the first 10 minutes of the baking time, then start turning brown. To test if it is done, tap lightly with the knuckles; it should sound hollow.
5. Turn onto a cooling rack immediately and wrap in a dish towel or blanket to obtain a soft crust or, if a crisp crust is desired, leave to cool uncovered.

---

2 medium potatoes
500 ml boiling water
3 ml active dry yeast soaked in
125 ml lukewarm water
25 ml (2 tablespoons) sugar
10 ml (2 teaspoons) salt

551 Potato yeast

Prep time 15 min.

1. Peel and grate the potatoes. Place them in a glass jar with a screw top and pour the boiling water into the jar. Set aside to cool.
2. Mix the sugar, salt and active yeast soaked in lukewarm water and add to the potatoes.
3. Screw the top firmly on the jar then give one twist backwards to allow some air to get into the jar.
4. Cover and leave in a warm place for 6 to 8 hours.
5. Strain all but 250 ml of the yeast and use.

Note: Keep the reserved 250 ml yeast as a starter for a new batch. Keep for 8 to 10 days, then repeat as above, omitting the yeast.

---

850 ml boiling water + 250 ml boiling water
5 ml (1 teaspoon) sugar
10 ml (2 teaspoons) salt
480 g wholewheat flour

552 Salt-raising dough yeast

Prep time 10 min.

1. Place 850 ml boiling water in a small bucket with a tight-fitting lid or a glass jar with a lid, then add the sugar and salt.
2. Carefully sprinkle the flour on top of the water.
3. Close the bucket or jar and leave in a warm place overnight.
4. Stir 250 ml boiling water into the mixture and leave for 1 hour, or until foamy.

Note:
- This amount of yeast should be sufficient for 3 kg flour (3 to 4 loaves).
- The container should be large enough to hold about 2 litres of liquid.
- This yeast must be used immediately.

306

553 Sourdough yeast

Prep time 10 min.

1. Sprinkle a piece of dough from a previous batch with 250 ml (1 cup) of flour.
2. Set aside to dry. Place the dried yeast in a jar, close securely and store in a cool place.
3. To use, soak the dried dough in 500 ml warm water. Add 250 ml (1 cup) flour and stir to a slack dough.
4. Leave overnight in a warm place. Use when it is foamy, with lots of bubbles.

Note: The yeast will keep for 1 month.

554 Basic rich yeast dough

5 ml (1 teaspoon) active dry yeast
12,5 ml (1 tablespoon) sugar
250 ml warm scalded milk
250 ml (1 cup) cake flour
50 ml (4 tablespoons) butter or margarine melted in 250 ml lukewarm scalded milk
3 eggs, beaten
1 kg cake flour
5 ml (1 teaspoon) salt

Prep time 30 min + proving time;   Cooking time 1 hour

1. Mix the yeast and sugar with the warm scalded milk in a large mixing bowl.
2. Add the 250 ml (1 cup) cake flour to the yeast mixture and beat well. Cover and leave for about 45 minutes to an hour in a warm place until foamy and light.
3. Add the butter and lukewarm milk mixture to the yeast. Add the eggs, flour and salt and mix very well.
4. Knead the dough until smooth, 4 to 5 minutes.
5. Cover dough and allow to rise in a warm place until doubled in size, about 1 hour.

555 Doughnuts with yeast

Makes 40-50;   kJ per portion 520;   Prep time 1 hour;   Total cooking time 1 hour

Use the basic yeast dough (recipe 554). Punch down and roll dough out to a rectangle 5 mm thick. Cut into 15 cm long strips and join the ends to form circles. Set aside until doubled in size and then prepare in the same way as koeksisters (recipe 545), but instead of dipping in syrup, allow the doughnuts to cool and then dust them with icing sugar.

556 Koeksisters with yeast   (F)

Makes 40-50;   kJ per portion 510;   Prep time 45 min;   Total cooking time 1 hour

Use the basic yeast dough (recipe 554). Punch down and roll dough into a rectangle about 5 mm thick. Cut into 5 to 7 mm wide strips. Press the ends of 3 strips together and plait loosely into a long plait. Cut plait into 50 mm lengths and press ends together. Leave plaits in a warm place for 15 minutes to rise. Prepare as for koeksisters (recipe 545), using the same syrup and cooking method (f).

557 Luncheon rolls   (F)

Makes 40-50;   kJ per portion 250;   Prep time 45 min;   Cooking time 15 min.

Use the basic yeast dough (recipe 554). Punch down dough and shape into rolls. Set aside until the rolls have doubled in size, then bake on a greased baking sheet at 200 °C (400 °F) for 15 to 20 minutes (f).

307

558 Bread sticks (F)

Makes ± 50; kJ per portion 200; Prep time 45 min + proving time; Cooking time 15-20 min.

Use the basic yeast dough (recipe 554). Roll out the risen dough to 10 mm thickness. Cut into strips 10 mm wide and 80 mm long. Place on a greased baking sheet and allow to rise to double the size. Brush with a mixture of milk and egg yolk and sprinkle with coarse salt. Bake in the oven at 200 °C (400 °F) for 15 to 20 minutes (f).

559 Hot cross buns (F)

Makes ± 36; kJ per portion 290; Prep time 45 min + proving time; Cooking time 15-20 min.

Use the basic yeast dough (recipe 554). Knead 10 ml (2 teaspoons) ground cinnamon, 60 g mixed peel, 60 g seedless raisins into the risen dough. Shape into buns, place on a greased baking sheet and with a very sharp knife cut a deep cross into the top of every bun. Cover closely and set aside in a warm place until risen to double the size, about 30 minutes. Brush with egg yolk beaten with milk and bake in the oven at 200 °C (400 °F) for 15 to 20 minutes (f).

560 Danish pastry (F)

Makes ± 36; kJ per portion 500; Prep time 45 min + proving time; Cooking time 25 min.

Use the basic yeast dough (recipe 554). Knead 5 ml vanilla essence and 5 ml (1 teaspoon) ground mace into the risen dough. Knead until bubbles form under the surface of the dough. Grate 500 g chilled butter and divide into three portions. Roll dough out to a rectangular shape. Cover half of the dough with one portion of the butter. Fold over and roll out again. Repeat twice with the remaining butter. Cover the dough and allow to rise for 20 minutes. Roll the dough out to 15 mm thick then cut, shape and flavour as desired. Set aside until doubled in size and bake in the oven at 190 °C (375 °F) for 25 minutes (f).

561 Croissants (F)

Makes ± 36; kJ per portion 480; Prep time 45 min + proving time; Cooking time 25 min.

Use basic yeast dough and prepare as for Danish pastry (recipe 560), forming the dough into crescents before baking. Leave out the flavouring (f).

562 Wholewheat loaf (F)

480 g unsifted wholewheat flour
120 g bread or cake flour
125 ml milk
500 ml plain yoghurt
10 ml (2 teaspoons) bicarbonate of soda
12,5 ml honey
12,5 ml oil
5 ml (1 teaspoon) salt

Serves 8; kJ per portion 200; Prep time 15 min; Cooking time 1 hour

1. Combine the flours, bicarbonate of soda and salt in a mixing bowl.
2. Warm the milk and honey in a saucepan over medium heat, stirring until the honey melts.
3. Remove from the stove and stir in the yoghurt and oil.
4. Add this mixture to the flour and stir well.
5. Pour into a greased bread tin and bake in the oven at 180 °C (350 °F) for 1 hour. Allow to cool in the tin for a few minutes, then turn out onto a wire rack to cool completely (f).

Note: This bread does not rise very much, and has a moist consistency.

500 g bread flour
50 ml (4 tablespoons)
margarine or oil
1 egg (optional)
5 ml (1 teaspoon) active dry
yeast
25 ml (2 tablespoons) sugar
60 ml warm water
250 ml milk or water
10 ml (2 teaspoons) salt

563   Basic white bread   (F)

Serves 10;   kJ per portion 280;   Prep time 1 hour;   Cooking time 45 min.

1. Heat the 250 ml milk or water to boiling point.
2. Add the salt, sugar and margarine or oil. Set aside and cool until lukewarm.
3. Add the yeast to the 60 ml warm water.
4. Place half the flour in a bowl and add the yeast mixture. Mix well.
5. Add the egg to the dough, if desired. Mix the rest of the flour into the dough.
6. Leave for 10 to 15 minutes.
7. Knead well for 3 to 5 minutes, until the dough is smooth and pliable. Place it in a well-greased bowl, cover and leave in a warm place until doubled in size.
8. Knead lightly and shape into a loaf. Place in a greased bread tin, cover and leave in a warm place until doubled in size.
9. Bake in the oven at 200 °C (400 °F) for 40 to 45 minutes (f).

Variations:
1. Shape into rolls instead of a loaf and bake in the oven at 200 °C (400 °F) for 12 to 20 minutes.
2. *Raisin Bread.* Add 120 g pitted raisins at step 5.

---

625 ml (2½ cups) cake flour
5 ml (1 teaspoon) active dried
yeast
250 ml warm milk
15 ml (3 teaspoons) butter
12,5 ml (1 tablespoon) sugar
2 eggs
5 ml (1 teaspoon) salt

564   South American pizza   (F)

Serves 8;   kJ per portion 210;   Prep time 20 min + proving time; Cooking time 15 min.

1. Dissolve the yeast in the milk.
2. Mix all the dry ingredients.
3. Beat the eggs and add to the milk/yeast mixture.
4. Add the egg mixture to the dry ingredients. Mix well then knead till smooth, about 1 minute. Add the butter and knead it into the dough for another minute.
5. Cover dough and leave to rise in a warm place until doubled in size, about 1 hour.
6. Punch down (f) and stretch dough with the hands to fit a greased shallow 400 mm x 300 mm tin, or a large pizza plate. Press onto plate or tin.
7. Cover the dough with all or a mixture of the following: tomato purée seasoned with 5 ml (1 teaspoon) oreganum, onion, 1 crushed clove garlic, freshly ground black pepper; olives, salami slices, tomato slices, grated Cheddar or Pizzarella cheese slices.
8. Trickle 25 ml oil over the pizza and bake in the oven at 230 °C (450 °F) for 25 minutes (f). Serve immediately.

Variations:
Spread the pizza dough with tomato purée and one of the following fillings, then sprinkle grated cheese thickly over the top and continue with step 8.
1. Strips of green pepper and capers.
2. 60 g shelled prawns and 12,5 ml (1 tablespoon) black olives.
3. 60 g sliced mushrooms and chopped bacon.
4. Sliced salami and anchovy fillets.
5. Thin slivers of sliced ham, green pepper sliced in thin rings and chunks of tinned pineapple.
6. Artichoke hearts, capers, anchovies and mushrooms.

Note: Do not allow the dough to brown, as this will make it tough. As soon as the dough is puffed up and the cheese is sizzling the pizza is ready to be served.

Anyone who has ever done any baking cherishes the desire to make perfect pastry. This is easier to achieve than is generally thought, if the instructions are followed carefully. Some of the many kinds of pastry require more effort than others, but the results are well worth it.

The main varieties of pastry are puff pastry, flaky pastry, hot water pastry, short pastry and pastry made with baking powder. Whichever kind you are making, remember *always* to use the best quality ingredients.

Basic methods for making pastry
- *Rubbing in* (shortcrust, cheese pastry). Use cake flour or wholewheat meal. With the fingertips rub the shortening into the dry ingredients until the mixture resembles fine crumbs. Never allow the mixture to become warm. Baking powder and sugar may or may not be used, depending on the individual recipe.
- *Heating fat with liquid* (choux and hot water crust pastry).
- *Folding and rolling* (flaky and puff pastry).
- *Fat added to flour* (suet pastry).

Important

- Weigh all ingredients and measure the liquid *carefully*.
- Bake at the correct temperature for as long as required by the recipe.
- When making flaky or shortcrust-type pastry, keep both your hands and the ingredients cool.
- Do not manipulate pastry too much – mix with the fingertips only and roll lightly with a rolling pin.

---

500 g cake flour
350 g shortening (butter, margarine or a combination of butter and lard)
175 ml iced water
25 ml lemon juice
5 ml (1 teaspoon) salt

565 Basic shortcrust pastry (F)

Makes 4 shells (± 1 kg); Prep time 20 min; Cooking time 15 min.

1. Sift the dry ingredients together in a bowl.
2. Cut or rub the shortening into the flour mixture until it resembles coarse crumbs.
3. Sprinkle the water and lemon juice onto the crumbs.
4. Press lightly together – do not knead. Wrap in waxed paper and chill until needed (f).

Variations:

1. *Sweet pastry:* For a sweet tart add 40 g sugar to the dry ingredients and bake at 190 °C (375 °F).
2. *Cheese pastry:* Rub 60 g finely grated Cheddar cheese into the dry ingredients together with the shortening.
3. *Wholemeal pastry:* Substitute unsifted flour for half of the cake flour and add after sifting the other dry ingredients. Use for a savoury tart.
4. For a lighter pastry add 5 ml (1 teaspoon) baking powder to the dry ingredients.
5. For a richer pastry use 1 egg yolk with 150 ml water for mixing instead of 175 ml iced water.

6. For a richer pastry add 150 ml heavy sour cream to 75 ml ice water and use instead of 175 ml iced water.
7. *Cinnamon pastry:* Add 5 ml (1 teaspoon) ground cinnamon to the dry ingredients. Use for apple tart.
8. *Lemon pastry:* Add 10 ml (2 teaspoons) grated lemon peel to dry ingredients. Use for lemon or citrus tarts.

Note: Shortcrust pastry must be baked at 200 °C to 230 °C (400 °F to 450 °F).

---

250 g cake flour
12,5 ml (1 tablespoon) lard
250 g butter, grated and chilled
125 ml iced water mixed with
10 ml brandy or 10 ml lemon juice or 1 egg yolk
2 ml (½ teaspoon) salt

566   Basic puff pastry   (F)

Makes 2 shells (± 500 g);   Prep time 20 min;   Cooking time 10 min.

1. Sift the flour and salt together twice.
2. With the fingertips rub the lard into the flour and salt.
3. With a knife cut the iced water mixed with brandy, lemon juice or egg yolk into the flour.
4. Knead the dough lightly on a floured surface until it is smooth and elastic and small bubbles form on the surface. Work lightly and quickly to keep the dough cool.
5. Roll the dough out to a thickness of 5 to 10 mm.
6. Sprinkle one-third of the grated butter over the whole of the rolled dough. Fold the dough over, envelope-fashion, until you have a parcel 6 cm x 4 cm.
7. Repeat steps 5 and 6 twice.
8. Wrap the dough in waxed paper and cool in the refrigerator before use (f).

Note:
- All the ingredients must be kept as cold as possible.
- Work lightly; roll lightly and evenly, do not press the dough with the rolling pin.
- Use very little flour to dust the rolling pin and the working surface.
- If the dough becomes too sticky to handle, place it in the refrigerator for a few minutes.
- Puff pastry should be thoroughly chilled before use. Never pull or stretch it when rolling out.
- After rolling, bake immediately at 230 °C to 260 °C (450 °F to 500 °F). Reduce the temperature to 200 °C (400 °F) after 5 to 10 minutes.
- Be careful not to scorch pastry – if it is scorched it tastes bitter.
- Cut the dough at least 10 to 15 mm larger than the pie plate, because it will shrink during baking.
- To obtain a raised edge, cut a strip of dough as wide as the pie plate's edge, brush the plate's edge with cold water and arrange the strip on this.

To bake blind:
Line a pie or tart plate with pastry, prick base with a fork. Cover pastry with a piece of greaseproof paper, just bigger than the plate. Spoon in dried beans or rice. Bake at 200 °C (400 °F) for 15 minutes. Remove the paper and the rice or beans.

Glaze pastry with a whole beaten egg for a shiny finish and a beaten egg mixed with 12,5 ml milk for a high gloss finish. To glaze pastry, brush the beaten egg over the top but NOT on the edges, as this prevents the pastry from rising.

250 g flour mixed with
2 ml (½ teaspoon) salt
250 g butter
1 egg
5 ml (1 teaspoon) cream of
tartar
90 g flour
juice of half a lemon
90 ml water (approximately)

567 Quick puff pastry (F)

Makes 2 shells (±500 g);   Prep time 20 min;   Cooking time 10 min.

1. Freeze the butter, and cool the flour and salt mixture in the refrigerator.
2. Sift the flour, grate half the butter and rub into the flour with the fingertips.
3. Beat the egg, water and lemon juice together. Stir into the flour and butter mixture, and with the fingers work into a stiff dough.
4. Turn the dough out onto a board. Sift the 90 g flour and cream of tartar together and grate the remaining butter. Sift a little flour and cream of tartar mixture onto the butter.
5. Roll the pastry into a rectangle on a lightly floured surface.
6. Sprinkle the grated butter over two-thirds of the pastry, fold the remaining third of pastry back to cover the butter. Sprinkle liberally with flour and cream of tartar.
7. Roll out again, to ensure that all the butter is incorporated. Sprinkle with a little of the flour mixture and fold in half.
8. Repeat step 7 a few more times, folding into three and sprinkling with a little of the flour mixture after each rolling.
9. Wrap in foil and place in the refrigerator for 1 hour (f).

Note: Bake at 230 °C to 260 °C (450 °F to 500 °F). Reduce the temperature to 200 °C (400 °F) after 5 to 10 minutes.

---

500 g cake flour
300 g butter, chilled
12,5 ml lemon juice or brandy
250 ml ice water
5 ml (1 teaspoon) salt

568 Flaky pastry (F)

Makes 4 shells (±1 kg);   Prep time 30 min;   Cooking time 15 min.

1. Sift the flour and salt together into a bowl.
2. Cut the butter into small cubes about the size of a pea and add to the flour. Coat the butter completely with flour, but do not stir.
3. Combine the lemon juice or brandy and the water and cut into the flour mixture.
4. Knead lightly into a ball, using your hands.
5. Place the dough in the refrigerator for 15 minutes.
6. Roll the dough out thinly, fold as directed for puff pastry (recipe 566) and roll out again. Repeat twice.
7. Chill, roll out and use or freeze for later use (f).

Note:

- Flaky pastry must be baked in a hot oven, 240 °C (475 °F), for 10 to 15 minutes. For flaky pastry tarts with a filling, bake at 240 °C (475 °F) for 10 minutes, lower heat to 190 °C (375 °F) and bake till the filling is done.
- To freeze, divide pastry into 4 portions. Wrap each portion well and freeze. The pastry can also be rolled out into a rectangle. Cut a piece of plastic wrap the size of the pastry, place over the pastry, roll up, wrap well and freeze. To use after freezing, thaw in the refrigerator for 8 hours and prepare as desired.

---

500 g butter, chilled
500 g flour
150 ml iced water
7 ml (1½ teaspoons) cream of
tartar
2 ml (½ teaspoon) salt

569 Quick flaky pastry (F)

Makes 4 shells (± 1 kg);   Prep time 20 min;   Cooking time 10 min.

1. Grate the butter coarsely and place in the refrigerator.
2. Sift the flour, salt and cream of tartar together into a bowl.
3. Add the butter to this mixture and rub in lightly with the fingertips.
4. Cut in the iced water with a knife. Place in the refrigerator for at least 1 hour.
5. Roll the dough out on a floured surface, fold into a parcel as directed in the recipe for puff pastry (recipe 566), and roll again. Repeat twice. Use immediately or freeze for later use (f).

Note: Bake at 240 °C (475 °F) for 10 to 15 minutes. For tarts with a filling, bake at 240 °C (475 °F) for 10 minutes, lower heat to 190 °C (375 °F) and bake until the filling is done.

---

500 g cake flour
500 g butter, chilled
12,5 ml brandy
250 ml soda water
5 ml (1 teaspoon) salt

570 Soda water pastry   (F)

Makes 4 shells (± 1 kg);   Prep time 20 min;   Cooking time 10 min.

1. Sift the flour and salt together.
2. Cut in 125 g of the butter. Grate the rest of the butter coarsely and store in the refrigerator.
3. Moisten the flour mixture with the brandy and soda water to form a stiff but pliable dough.
4. Roll the dough out to 5 mm thickness. Cover two-thirds of the dough with one-third of the grated butter. Fold and roll out again.
5. Repeat twice.
6. Wrap the dough in waxed paper or aluminium foil and chill or freeze (f).

Note: Soda water pastry should be baked at 230 °C to 260 °C (450 °F to 500 °F) for the first 5 to 10 minutes, and the heat then reduced to 200 °C (400 °F) for the rest of the baking time.

---

500 ml (2 cups) cake flour
100 ml cooking oil
50 ml milk or cold water
5 ml (1 teaspoon) baking
powder
2 ml (½ teaspoon) salt

571 Pastry with oil   (F)

Makes 4 shells (± 750 g);   Prep time 20 min;   Cooking time 10 min.

1. Sift the dry ingredients together.
2. Mix the oil with the milk or water, add to the dry ingredients and mix lightly.
3. Wrap in waxed paper until ready to use, or freeze (f).

Variations:
1. Add 10 ml (1 teaspoon) sugar for a sweet tart.
2. For a less rich pastry, use 50 ml oil and 100 ml milk or water. Such pastry will have a coarser texture.

Note: This kind of pastry should be baked at 220 °C (425 °F) for 10 to 15 minutes.

---

2 egg whites
50 ml (4 tablespoons) sugar
1 ml vanilla essence
pinch salt

572 Soft meringue topping

Prep time 20 min;   Cooking time 15 min.

1. Beat the egg whites until foamy (approximately 50 turns with an egg-beater). Add the salt and vanilla essence and beat a further 50 turns.
2. Add the sugar, 10 ml (2 teaspoons) at a time, beating to dissolve all the sugar before adding more.
3. When all the sugar has dissolved, beat the meringue until it is stiff but not dry.
4. Spoon onto the tart or cake.
5. Bake at 180 °C (350 °F) for 10 to 15 minutes.

Note: Sufficient to cover four 15 cm tarts.

To store meringues, keep in an airtight tin between layers of greaseproof paper. They will keep for up to 2 months.

1 packet tennis, digestive or other biscuits
150 g butter, melted

573 Basic biscuit crumb base

Makes 2 pies or tarts;   Prep time 10 min.

1. Place the biscuits between 2 sheets of waxproof paper. Crush finely with a rolling pin and place the crumbs in a dish.
2. Add the melted butter and mix well.
3. With the back of a metal spoon, press the mixture into a greased pie dish, then work the mixture smoothly over the base and sides with a smooth-sided glass. Chill.

---

8 egg whites
250 ml (1 cup) fine granulated sugar
250 ml (1 cup) castor sugar
5 ml (1 teaspoon) cream of tartar
10 ml vanilla essence *or* peppermint essence with
5 ml green colouring
2 ml (½ teaspoon) salt

574 Meringues

Makes 120 small meringues;   kJ per portion 250;   Prep time 40 min; Cooking time 1 hour

1. Beat the egg whites until foamy.
2. Add the salt and cream of tartar and beat again until just stiff but not dry.
3. Add the sugar gradually, about 25 ml (2 tablespoons) at a time, and beat to dissolve the sugar.
4. Add the castor sugar gradually and fold in the last 25 ml (2 tablespoons) with the essence and colouring. Add the essence and colouring drop by drop.
5. Line a baking sheet with foil, dull side up, and grease well. Dust with a thin layer of cornflour.
6. Shape the meringues neatly with two spoons or a large icing tube.
7. Bake for 1 hour at 120 °C (250 °F). Switch off the oven, and leave the meringues in it for about 2 hours to dry out. Store in a tightly closed container.

Variations:
1. *Chocolate meringues:* Mix 25 ml (2 tablespoons) cocoa with the last 25 ml (2 tablespoons) castor sugar and fold into the stiffly beaten mixture. Omit vanilla essence or peppermint essence and colouring.
2. *Coffee meringues:* Add 25 ml coffee essence to the meringue mixture. Omit vanilla essence or peppermint essence and colouring.
3. *Nut meringues:* Mix 85 g finely chopped nuts with the last 25 ml (2 tablespoons) castor sugar and fold into the stiffly beaten mixture. Omit vanilla essence or peppermint essence and colouring.

Note: To make a meringue case, pencil a round shape onto unwaxed butter paper then spread a 2 cm thick layer of meringue evenly onto this shape. Pipe small meringues around the outer edge of the base and continue with step 7.

---

250 g of any basic flaky or puff pastry (recipes 566 to 569)

575 Vol-au-vent cases   (F)

Makes 12;   Prep time 15 min;   Cooking time 10 min.

1. Roll the dough out to a thickness of 3 mm.
2. Press out rounds 50 to 60 mm in diameter.
3. Press a hole 10 mm in diameter in the centre of half the rounds, using a small biscuit cutter.
4. Moisten the whole rounds with water and place a round with a hole on top of each one. Arrange neatly on an ungreased baking sheet. Bake in the oven at 230 °C to 260 °C (450 °F to 500 °F) for 8 minutes (f).

Note: The dough pressed out in step 3 can either be used as lids for the cases or rolled out again to make additional cases.

576 Jam tarts

Makes 12;   kJ per portion 450;   Prep time 15 min;   Cooking time 10 min.

Prepare as vol-au-vents (recipe 575) but spoon smooth apricot jam into the cases before baking. Bake in the oven at 230 °C to 260 °C (450 °F to 500 °F) for 10 minutes.

To prevent jam from running over when making jam tarts, brush the pastry with beaten egg white before adding the jam OR add desiccated coconut to the jam.

450 g flaky pastry (recipe 568)
100 ml (²/₅ cup) sugar
250 g currants

577 Palmiers

Makes 15;   kJ per portion 390;   Prep time 30 min;   Cooking time 20 min.

1. Roll the pastry out thinly on a lightly floured surface and cut into long strips 1 cm wide.
2. Sprinkle the pastry strips with half the sugar.
3. Place a few currants on one strip of pastry, then roll the strip up from both ends towards the middle, swiss roll fashion. Repeat until all the pastry strips have been rolled.
4. Place the palmiers on a greased baking sheet and sprinkle with the remaining sugar.
5. Bake in the oven at 230 °C (450 °F) for 10 minutes, then lower the heat to 180 °C (350 °F) and continue baking for a further 10 minutes. Serve hot or cold.

Note: Palmiers can also be made without the currants.

250 g puff pastry (recipe 566)
strawberry jam
water icing (recipe 532)
sweetened whipped cream
chopped mixed nuts

578 Mille feuilles

Serves 8;   kJ per portion 510;   Prep time 30 min;   Cooking time 15 min.

1. Divide the pastry into two and cut into rounds about 1 cm thick, with a diameter of 22 cm.
2. Bake in the centre of the oven at 240 °C (475 °F) for 10 minutes, then lower the heat to 180 °C (350 °F) and bake until the pastry is done, about 5 minutes. Remove from the oven and allow to cool thoroughly.
3. Sandwich the two layers with jam and sweetened cream. Coat the outside with more cream and nuts and the top with icing and nuts. Serve cold.

Variation: Use fresh strawberries or canned fruits such as gooseberries or loganberries instead of the jam.

Note: These can also be served as fingers. Cut the pastry into fingers 3 to 4 cm wide and bake on a baking tray for approximately 13 minutes. Fill and decorate as for large cake.

castor sugar
250 g flaky pastry (recipe 568)
Filling:
450 g cooking apples, peeled,
cored and thinly sliced
100 ml (^{2}/$_5$ cup) sultanas
100 ml (^{2}/$_5$ cup) currants
grated rind of 1 lemon
75 ml (6 tablespoons) brown
sugar
12,5 ml (1 tablespoon) butter
or margarine

579   Apple turnovers

Makes 12;   kJ per portion 680;   Prep time 45 min;   Cooking time 30 min.

1. Prepare the filling. Melt the butter or margarine in a saucepan over medium heat.
2. Add the apples, sultanas, sugar and lemon rind and simmer, covered, for 10 minutes, stirring often to prevent sticking. Set aside.
3. Remove the pastry from the refrigerator and roll it out into a large square on a floured surface. Cut into 12 squares, 10 cm x 10 cm in size.
4. Place a teaspoonful of the apple mixture on one triangle half of each square and fold the other half over. Dampen the edges with water and press down to seal.
5. Place the turnovers on a greased baking sheet and bake in the oven at 180 °C (350 °F) for 30 minutes.
6. Remove from the oven, sprinkle with castor sugar and serve. Turnovers are also good served cold (f).

Variation: Substitute canned gooseberries or loganberries for the apple mixture.

SWEET PIES AND TARTS

250 g puff or flaky pastry
(recipes 566, 568)
Filling:
1,5 litres milk
50 ml cold milk
20 ml (4 teaspoons) custard
powder
20 ml (4 teaspoons) cornflour
30 ml (6 teaspoons) cake flour
15 ml (3 teaspoons) butter
250 ml (1 cup) sugar
7 eggs, separated
5 ml almond essence
2 ml (½ teaspoon) salt

580   Melktert

Makes 4 tarts; kJ per portion 810; Prep time 1 hour; Cooking time 25 min.

1. Line 4 pie plates with the puff or flaky pastry. Cut an extra strip for each and decorate the edge of each case.
2. Heat the 1,5 litres milk to boiling point in a heavy-based saucepan and add the butter and salt.
3. In a bowl, mix the custard powder, cornflour and cake flour with the cold milk to form a paste. Add a little of the hot milk mixture to the paste, stirring all the time. Add this mixture to the rest of the hot milk, stirring.
4. Add 125 ml (½ cup) of the sugar and bring back to the boil, stirring all the time. Remove from the stove as soon as the mixture thickens.
5. Lightly beat the egg yolks. Beat the egg whites in a separate bowl until stiff but not dry. Gradually beat the rest of the sugar into the egg whites.
6. Cool the milk and custard mixture slightly, and add a little to the egg yolks, stirring all the time. Stir the egg yolks into the milk mixture, then stir in the almond essence.
7. Fold the egg whites into the milk and egg mixture.
8. Pour into the pastry cases and bake immediately at 200 °C (400 °F) for 10 minutes. Lower the heat to 180 °C (350 °F) and bake a further 10 to 15 minutes.

baked rich shortcrust pastry
shell (recipe 565)
Filling:
3 eggs, separated
250 g sweetened condensed
milk
grated rind and juice of
3 lemons
62,5 ml (5 tablespoons) castor
sugar

581   Lemon meringue pie   (F)

Serves 6;   kJ per portion 1 010;   Prep time 20 min;   Cooking time 25 min.

1. Beat the egg yolks, lemon rind and juice together until thick and creamy.
2. Beat in the condensed milk and pour into the baked pastry shell.
3. In a separate bowl, beat together the egg whites and the castor sugar until stiff but not too dry. Spoon the mixture over the lemon filling.
4. Bake in the oven at 180 °C (350 °F) for 25 minutes. Serve cold (f).

300 g rich shortcrust pastry
(recipe 565)
Filling:
1 kg Granny Smith apples,
peeled, cored and cut into thin
slices
170 g sugar
12,5 ml (1 tablespoon)
cornflour
25 ml (2 tablespoons) butter or
margarine, cut into small
pieces
12,5 ml lemon juice
5 ml (1 teaspoon) ground
cinnamon
1 ml (¼ teaspoon) ground
allspice
1 ml (¼ teaspoon) ground
nutmeg

582 Apple tart (F)

Serves 6;   kJ per portion 1 100;   Prep time 1 hour;   Cooking time 40 min.

1. Roll out half the pastry thinly, on a floured surface, into a circle large enough to line the pie dish. Line the pie dish, easing the pastry into the dish without pulling it.
2. Blend the sugar, ground cinnamon, allspice, nutmeg and cornflour in a large bowl.
3. Add the apples and lemon juice and toss with a wooden spoon. Fill the pie shell with the mixture, piling it higher in the centre. Dot with the butter or margarine.
4. Roll out the remaining half of the pastry into a circle 5 mm thick and 30 cm in diameter. Lift it up carefully and place over the filling. Trim around the edges with a sharp knife and pinch the two crusts attractively together to seal well.
5. Brush the pastry with a little milk or beaten egg white and cut two small gashes in the centre of the top to allow the steam to escape.
6. Bake in the centre of the oven at 190 °C (375 °F) until the crust is golden brown, about 40 minutes (f). Serve hot or cold with cream or ice-cream.

---

250 g shortcrust pastry
(recipe 565)
Filling:
500 ml (2 cups) desiccated
coconut
110 g butter or margarine
125 ml (½ cup) sugar
2 eggs, beaten with
1 ml (¼ teaspoon) salt
apricot jam
1 ml almond essence

583 Coconut tart

*Makes 2 tarts;   kJ per portion 1 200;   Prep time 45 min;
Cooking time 30 min.*

1. Line two 220 mm pie plates with the pastry.
2. Spread a layer of apricot jam in the base of each lined plate.
3. Beat the butter or margarine and sugar together in a bowl until light and creamy.
4. Gradually add the beaten eggs, beating all the time.
5. Stir in the coconut and almond essence and mix well.
6. Divide the mixture and spread evenly over the jam in each of the two cases. Bake in the oven at 200 °C (400 °F) for 30 minutes. Serve either hot or cold.

---

1 biscuit crumb crust
(recipe 573)
250 ml double cream
250 ml sweetened condensed
milk
125 ml lemon juice
250 g homogenised cottage
cheese
Glazing:
500 ml (2 cups) fresh
strawberries, cleaned
50 ml strawberry jam
12,5 ml lemon juice

584 Quick strawberry cheese tart

Serves 10-12;   kJ per portion 810;   Prep time 20 min.

1. Line a 220 mm pie dish with the biscuit crumb crust.
2. In a mixing bowl, mix the condensed milk with the lemon juice, and fold in the cottage cheese.
3. Whip the cream and fold into the condensed milk mixture. Spoon into the crust.
4. In a small saucepan, heat the strawberry jam and the lemon juice. Cool slightly.
5. Arrange the strawberries on top of the condensed milk mixture. Pour the glazing over the strawberries and chill before serving.

317

250 g biscuit crust (recipe 573)
Filling:
315 ml (1¼ cups) cooked
pumpkin
62,5 ml (5 tablespoons) pecan
nuts, finely chopped
3 eggs, separated
1 envelope unflavoured
gelatine powder
sugar
65 ml cold water
125 ml sour cream
250 ml whipped cream
7 ml (1½ teaspoons) mixed
spice
1 ml (¼ teaspoon) ground
ginger
2 ml (½ teaspoon) salt

585   Pumpkin pie

Serves 8;   kJ per portion 980;   Prep time 1 hour;   Cooking time 15 min.

1. Line a 220 mm pie plate with the crust.
2. Soften the gelatine in the cold water.
3. Beat the egg yolks and 85 ml (⅓ cup) sugar together in a saucepan, then stir in the pumpkin, sour cream, salt, ginger and mixed spice.
4. Simmer over medium heat until the mixture comes to the boil, then reduce heat to low and simmer for 2 minutes, stirring all the time.
5. Remove from the stove and stir in the softened gelatine until it is completely dissolved.
6. Cool and stir in the pecans.
7. Beat the egg whites in a bowl until fluffy, then gradually beat in 62,5 ml (5 tablespoons) sugar and continue beating until stiff peaks form. With a spatula fold gently into the pumpkin mixture.
8. Spoon half the mixture into the crust and chill in the refrigerator until almost set, then spread half the whipped cream over the pumpkin filling and top with the remaining pumpkin. Chill in the refrigerator until set.
9. Garnish with the remaining whipped cream and serve cold.

---

2 packets Marie or Tennis
biscuits, broken into small bits
2 eggs, beaten
250 g sugar
250 g butter or margarine,
melted
250 ml (1 cup) dates, finely
chopped
250 ml (1 cup) desiccated
coconut
250 ml (1 cup) glacé cherries,
halved
125 ml (½ cup) walnuts or
pecan nuts, finely chopped
25 ml brandy
5 ml vanilla essence
10 ml (2 teaspoons) cocoa
pinch salt

586   Date fridge tart

Serves 6-8;   kJ per portion 1 200;   Prep time 30 min;   Cooking time 10 min.

1. Combine the dates, cherries, cocoa and salt in a bowl.
2. Dissolve the sugar in the melted butter or margarine in a saucepan over medium heat, stirring often, and add a little to the beaten eggs. Beat well and return to the saucepan with all the other ingredients except the biscuits.
3. Bring to the boil, stirring all the time, then reduce the heat to low and simmer a further 5 minutes. Remove from the stove.
4. Stir in the broken biscuits and mix well, then press into a greased and lined shallow baking tin and chill in the refrigerator overnight. Cut into slices and serve.

Use heated scissors to cut dates.

318

biscuit crust made with 250 g digestive biscuits (recipe 573)
Filling:
500 g fresh apricots, blanched, peeled, stoned and finely chopped
15 g gelatine, dissolved in 50 ml hot water
75 ml (6 tablespoons) castor sugar
315 ml plain yoghurt
500 ml double cream
12,5 ml lemon juice
Topping:
60 g chocolate flake
100 ml (²/₅ cup) toasted slivered almonds

587 Yoghurt cream cake

Serves 6; kJ per portion 890; Prep time 1 hour

1. Line a lightly greased loose-bottomed 220 mm cake tin with the biscuit crust, with the fingertips pressing it firmly against the bottom of the tin. Set aside.
2. Using a wooden spoon, beat the yoghurt, half the cream, the lemon juice and the sugar together in a bowl, until the mixture is smooth and creamy.
3. Stir in the apricots, blending well, then beat in the dissolved gelatine mixture. Set aside in a cool place until just about to set, about 20 minutes.
4. With a spatula, spoon the yoghurt mixture onto the biscuit crust and chill until set, about 30 minutes. Remove cake from tin.
5. Beat the remaining cream in a bowl until it forms stiff peaks and spoon over the top of the cake. Sprinkle with the chocolate flake and toasted almonds and serve immediately.

Variation: Dried apricots, soaked overnight in a little wine or water, can be used instead of fresh apricots.

---

2 packets tennis biscuits
1 packet lemon jelly
125 ml (½ cup) sugar
125 ml grenadilla pulp
500 ml sweetened evaporated milk, chilled and well-beaten
250 ml boiling water

588 Grenadilla fridge cake

Serves 6; kJ per portion 800; Prep time 40 min.

1. Make the lemon jelly with the boiling water and set aside to cool slightly.
2. Gradually add the sugar to the beaten evaporated milk and mix well.
3. Stir in the grenadilla pulp and the cooled jelly, combining thoroughly.
4. Place a layer of tennis biscuits in the bottom of a 200 mm x 300 mm dish and cover with some of the grenadilla mixture. Top with another layer of biscuits and another of grenadilla mixture. Continue with the layers, ending with a layer of grenadilla mixture and reserving one or two tennis biscuits.
5. Crumb the remaining tennis biscuits and sprinkle over the filling. Chill in the refrigerator until set. Serve cold.

Variations:
1. Use canned crushed pineapple, drained, and pineapple jelly instead of grenadilla pulp and lemon jelly.
2. Use puréed stewed dried apricots or figs instead of the grenadilla pulp.
3. Use finely chopped dates and portwine jelly instead of grenadilla pulp and lemon jelly.

---

biscuit crust, using 1 packet digestive biscuits (recipe 573)
Filling:
1 packet vanilla instant pudding mix
3 ripe bananas, peeled and thinly sliced or mashed
12,5 ml lemon juice
375 ml sour cream

589 Banana sour cream pie

Serves 6; kJ per portion 850; Prep time 30 min; Cooking time 10 min.

1. Line a 220 mm pie plate with the biscuit crust and refrigerate until needed.
2. Make the filling. Combine the vanilla instant pudding mix and the sour cream in a saucepan over medium heat.
3. Bring to the boil, stirring all the time, then remove from the stove and allow to cool for 20 minutes, stirring occasionally.
4. Turn half the pudding into the pie shell, then top with the sliced bananas. Sprinkle the lemon juice over the bananas and cover with the remaining pudding. Refrigerate for at least 2 hours before serving, either plain or garnished with whipped cream.

Variation: Use caramel or butterscotch instant pudding mix instead of vanilla and add 25 ml (2 tablespoons) seedless raisins soaked in red wine for 30 minutes and drained.
Note: This filling may also be used for flans.

319

grated rind of 3 lemons
juice of 2 large lemons
250 g sugar
120 g butter
2 eggs, beaten

590   Lemon curd

Makes 300 ml;   kJ per portion 200;   Prep time 30 min;
Cooking time 15 min.

1. Place all the ingredients except the eggs into the top of a double-boiler over hot water.
2. Simmer, stirring occasionally, until the butter and sugar have melted.
3. Add the eggs and continue simmering, stirring now and then, until the mixture coats the back of a wooden spoon.
4. Pour into sterilized jars and seal.

Variation: Use the rind of 3 oranges and juice of 2 large oranges instead of the lemon rind and lemon juice.

---

500 g mixed dried fruit, finely
chopped
120 g apple, peeled, cored and
grated
120 g mixed peel, finely
chopped
120 g shredded suet or
margarine, melted
120 g sugar
120 g blanched almonds, finely
chopped
finely grated rind and juice of
1 large lemon
50 ml brandy or rum
5 ml (1 teaspoon) mixed spice
2 ml (½ teaspoon) ground
cinnamon
2 ml (½ teaspoon) grated
nutmeg

591   Fruit mincemeat filling   (F)

Makes ± 1 kg;   Prep time 20 min.

1. Combine all the ingredients thoroughly in a large bowl (f).
2. Place in dry jars, seal and store in a cool, dry place. Use for mince tarts or as pie fillings.

Note:

● Make sure that the fruit is completely dry before starting.
● These proportions of ingredients ensure that the mincemeat keeps well.
● Freeze in small quantities for easier use.

To make your own castor sugar, put ordinary granulated sugar into a blender, a cupful at a time, and switch on for a few seconds OR iron between 2 sheets of brown paper.

Add nuts and fruit to this basic Madeira cake (recipe 514) for endless variety.

170 g flaky pastry, rolled out
to fit pie plate (recipe 568)
Filling:
1 pheasant, cut into pieces
2 rashers bacon, cut in thin
strips
1 small onion, finely chopped
110 g mushrooms, finely
chopped
2 hard-boiled eggs, sliced
62,5 ml (5 tablespoons) flour
280 ml chicken stock
5 ml (1 teaspoon) salt
2 ml (½ teaspoon) pepper

592 Game pie (F)

Serves 4; kJ per portion 1 750; Prep time 20 min;
Cooking time 1 ½ hours

1. Coat the pieces of pheasant in flour and arrange, together with the egg, bacon, onion and mushrooms, in a deep pie plate.
2. Season with salt and pepper and pour over the stock, then place the pastry on top and brush with a little milk or egg to glaze.
3. Bake in the oven at 230°C (450°F) for 15 minutes, then cover the pastry with a piece of paper foil, lower the heat to 190°C (375°F) and bake for a further 1¼ hours (f). Serve hot.

Note: To serve after freezing, thaw completely and heat in the oven at 160°C (325°F) for 15 minutes.

200 g shortcrust or puff pastry
(recipes 565, 566)
500 g cooked chicken, jointed
4 rashers rindless bacon, diced
6 slices salami, quartered
2 bananas, thickly sliced
250 ml (1 cup) canned peach
slices, drained
1 green pepper, seeded and
thinly sliced

593 Hawaiian chicken pie (F)

Serves 6; kJ per portion 1 800; Prep time 30 min; Cooking time 35 min.

1. Sauté the bacon in a frying-pan for 2 to 3 minutes. Add the green pepper and sauté for 2 minutes.
2. Add the chicken and heat for 3 minutes.
3. Place the filling in a 220 mm pie plate. Layer the salami, bananas and peaches on top of the chicken.
4. Roll the pastry out to a round that will fit the plate and place on top of the filling.
5. Bake in the oven at 220°C (450°F) for 15 minutes. Lower the heat to 180°C (350°F) and bake for a further 10 minutes (f).

170 g short crust or puff pastry
(recipes 565, 566)
Filling:
500 g cooked chicken, cubed
4 rashers bacon, diced
120 g button mushrooms
62,5 ml (5 tablespoons) flour
62,5 ml (5 tablespoons) butter
or margarine
300 ml milk
salt and pepper

594 Chicken and bacon pie (F)

Serves 6; kJ per portion 1 890; Prep time 20 min; Cooking time 45 min.

1. Heat half the butter in a frying-pan and sauté the bacon and mushrooms in it for 2 to 3 minutes. Remove and set aside.
2. Heat the remaining butter in the frying-pan, stir in the flour to blend smoothly and cook for 2 to 3 minutes, stirring constantly.
3. Stir in the milk and season to taste, then bring to the boil and cook until thickened.
4. Add the chicken pieces, bacon and mushrooms and blend well. Allow to cool slightly.
5. Place the filling in a 200 mm pie plate.
6. Roll the pastry out to a round to fit the plate and place on top of the filling (f).
7. Brush the crust with the milk and bake in the oven at 200°C (400°F) for 30 to 35 minutes (f). Serve hot.

Note: The pie can be frozen baked or unbaked.

**500 g short crust pastry
(recipe 565)**
Filling:
**700 g rump steak, cubed
2 medium potatoes, cubed
2 medium onions, cubed
25 ml water
5 ml (1 teaspoon) salt
2 ml (½ teaspoon) pepper**

595   Cornish pasty   (F)

Makes 4;   kJ per portion 1 780;   Prep time 30 min;   Cooking time 50 min.

1. Roll the pastry out into 4 rounds the size of a large side plate.
2. Combine the meat, potatoes, onions, salt and pepper in a bowl, then place a quarter of the mixture into the centre of each round of pastry. Add a little water to the mixture in each round.
3. Brush the edges of each round of pastry lightly with water and press together firmly to form a half-moon shape.
4. Lift each pasty carefully onto a lightly greased baking sheet, using a fish slice, and brush each one with a little beaten egg (f).
5. Bake in the oven at 220 °C (425 °F) for 25 minutes, then lower the heat to 180 °C (350 °F) and bake a further 25 minutes (f). Serve hot or cold.

Note: Freeze either after step 4 or 5. If frozen after step 4, the pasties can be baked without thawing, at the temperatures given in step 5. If frozen after step 5, thaw and reheat in the oven at 160 °C (325 °F) for 15 to 20 minutes.

**250 g shortcrust pastry
(recipe 565)**
Filling:
**250 g minced beef
110 g mushrooms, finely
chopped
1 medium onion, grated
5 ml (1 teaspoon) salt
2 ml (½ teaspoon) pepper**

596   Beef and mushroom pasties   (F)

Makes 6;   kJ per portion 1 690;   Prep time 30 min;   Cooking time 1 hour

1. Combine the minced beef, onion, mushrooms, salt and pepper in a large bowl.
2. Roll the pastry out to 4 mm thickness on a lightly floured surface and cut out four rounds, using a 10 cm saucer as a guide. Gather the scraps together and roll out again to the same thickness, then cut out a further two rounds.
3. Divide the filling between the rounds. Moisten the edges of the pastry with a little water and fold the rounds in half, enclosing the filling and pressing the edges firmly together.
4. Mark the edge of the rounds with a fork. Place them on a greased baking sheet and brush with milk.
5. Bake in the oven at 200 °C (400 °F) for 15 minutes, then reduce the heat to 180 °C (350 °F) and bake until the pasties are golden brown and the meat filling is thoroughly cooked, about 45 minutes (f). Serve hot or cold.

Note: The pasties will keep for up to 6 months in a freezer.

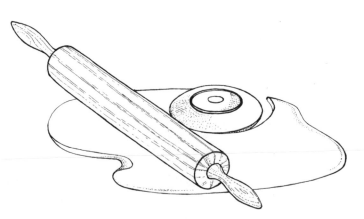

200 g flaky pastry (recipe 568)
700 g stewing steak, cubed
2 lamb's kidneys, diced
12,5 ml (1 tablespoon) flour
125 ml meat stock
salt and pepper
fat or oil for frying

597 Steak and kidney pie (F)

Serves 6; kJ per portion 1 780; Prep time 30 min; Cooking time 2 hours

1. Heat the fat or oil in a saucepan and fry the meat in it for 2 to 3 minutes, until lightly browned.
2. Pour the stock into the saucepan, reserving 50 ml, and bring to the boil.
3. Season to taste with salt and pepper then simmer, covered, until the meat is tender, about 1½ hours.
4. Blend the flour with the remaining stock in a small bowl then stir with a wooden spoon into the steak and kidney mixture and continue stirring until the sauce thickens.
5. Stand a pie support or egg-cup in the centre of a pie plate to support the pastry, then place the meat in the pie plate and allow to cool.
6. Roll out the pastry and cover the pie, brushing it with 12,5 ml milk (f).
7. Place the pie plate in the oven at 220 °C (425 °F) and bake for 25 minutes. Lower the heat to 180 °C (350 °F) and bake a further 10 minutes (f). Serve at once.

Note: Freeze either baked or unbaked. To serve after freezing, continue with step 7 for an unbaked pie or, if baked, reheat in the oven at 160 °C (325 °F), uncovered, for approximately 25 minutes.

400 g shortcrust pastry (recipe 565)
Filling:
3 rashers bacon, finely chopped and sautéed until crisp
110 g ham, cubed
4 Vienna sausages, diced
250 ml (1 cup) mature Cheddar cheese, grated
4 eggs, beaten
25 ml (2 tablespoons) onion, grated
25 ml (2 tablespoons) cornflour
25 ml (2 tablespoons) butter or margarine, melted
500 ml milk
25 ml (2 tablespoons) parsley, finely chopped
pinch cayenne pepper
1 ml (¼ teaspoon) salt

598 Savoury tart (F)

Serves 6-8; kJ per portion 1 310; Prep time 30 min; Cooking time 25 min.

1. Line one large or two smaller pie plates with the pastry.
2. Mix the cornflour with a little milk to form a smooth paste, then stir in the rest of the milk, the butter or margarine, diced bacon and cubed ham.
3. Stir in the grated cheese, onion, Vienna sausages, parsley, salt and cayenne pepper and mix well. Fold in the beaten eggs.
4. Pour the mixture into the prepared pastry shell(s) and bake in the oven at 190 °C (375 °F) until the filling has set, about 25 minutes. Serve, sliced, hot or cold (f).

Variation: Substitute 100 g sliced sautéed mushrooms for the Vienna sausages.

250 g shortcrust pastry (recipe 565)
Filling:
6 large ripe tomatoes, peeled, seeded and chopped
3 large onions, thinly sliced
25 ml (2 tablespoons) Parmesan cheese, grated
75 g anchovy fillets
black olives
1 egg yolk, beaten
25 ml tomato paste
25 ml (2 tablespoons) butter or margarine
olive oil
25 ml (2 tablespoons) fresh rosemary, finely chopped
2 ml (½ teaspoon) freshly ground black pepper

599 Tomato and onion tart

Serves 8; kJ per portion 1 500; Prep time 1 hour + chilling time; Cooking time 40 min.

1. Line the pie plate with the pastry and chill for 1 hour. Brush with a little beaten egg yolk and bake in the oven at 230 °C (450 °F) until set but not brown. Remove and allow to cool.
2. Heat 50 ml olive oil in a frying-pan. Add the tomatoes, tomato concentrate and black pepper and simmer over low heat until the excess moisture has cooked away, mashing occasionally with a wooden spoon.
3. In a separate frying-pan, melt the butter or margarine and sauté the onions and rosemary until the onions are soft and transparent but not brown.
4. Sprinkle the bottom of the pastry case with the Parmesan cheese, top with the onions and then with the tomato mixture.
5. Arrange the anchovies in a lattice pattern on top of the tomatoes and place a black olive in the centre of each square. Brush the olives and anchovies with a little olive oil and bake in the oven at 180 °C (350 °F) for 30 minutes. Serve hot.

---

250 g cheese shortcrust pastry (recipe 565)
Filling:
300 g canned asparagus spears, drained
125 ml (½ cup) Cheddar cheese, grated
2 eggs
250 ml evaporated milk
1 ml (¼ teaspoon) salt
1 ml (¼ teaspoon) pepper

600 Asparagus and cheese flan (F)

Serves 8; kJ per portion 1 010; Prep time 40 min; Cooking time 30 min.

1. Line a 200 mm flan case with the pastry and brush with a little egg white or milk.
2. Beat the eggs, evaporated milk, salt and pepper together in a bowl, then stir in the cheese.
3. Arrange the asparagus spears in the pastry shell and pour over the egg and milk mixture.
4. Bake in the oven at 180 °C (350 °F) until the filling has set, about 30 minutes (f). Serve hot.

Crust:
500 ml (2 cups) cake flour
250 ml (1 cup) homogenised cottage cheese
250 g butter, grated
Filling:
500 g frozen chopped spinach
3 eggs, beaten
250 g homogenised cottage cheese
40 ml cream
2 cloves garlic, crushed
5 ml (1 teaspoon) salt

601 Spinach-cottage cheese pie

Serves 10-12; kJ per portion 1 410; Prep time 45 min; Cooking time 45 min.

1. First make the pastry. Combine the cottage cheese and the flour in a bowl. Add the butter and mix to form a smooth dough. Cover with wax paper and chill in the refrigerator until ready to use.
2. Steam the spinach in a saucepan without water. Cool slightly when cooked.
3. Add the salt and garlic, then stir in the beaten eggs.
4. Fold the cottage cheese and cream into this mixture.
5. Roll half the dough out to 5 mm thickness on a lightly floured surface. It should fit a pie dish 300 mm x 200 mm. Roll out the other piece of dough for the crust and set aside.
6. Pour the filling into the lined pie dish and place the other piece of pastry on top of it. Brush the surface with a little egg and milk.
7. Bake in the oven at 200 °C (400 °F) for 10 minutes. Reduce the heat to 180 °C (350 °F) and bake a further 30 minutes.

1 kg cake flour
500 g margarine
500 g sugar
5 eggs
25 ml (2 tablespoons) baking powder
10 ml (2 teaspoons) salt

602   Basic biscuit recipe   (F)

Makes ± 240 biscuits;   kJ per portion 410;   Prep time 20 min;
Cooking time 10 min.

1. Sift the dry ingredients, except the sugar, together into a mixing bowl.
2. Cream the margarine and sugar in another bowl until light and fluffy.
3. Add the eggs to the creamed mixture, one by one, beating well after each addition.
4. Fold in the dry ingredients and mix well (f).
5. Roll the dough out to a thickness of 5 mm on a lightly floured surface and press out biscuits with a cutter. Place on a greased baking sheet and bake in the oven at 180 °C (350 °F) for 10 minutes.

Variations:

1. *Spice biscuits:* Add 5 ml (1 teaspoon) each of ground ginger, ground cinnamon and mixed spice to the dry ingredients.
2. *Coconut biscuits:* Add 120 g desiccated coconut to the dry ingredients.
3. *Coffee biscuits:* Add 50 ml coffee essence to the dough.

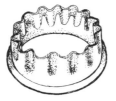

Note: To freeze, shape dough into long rolls 4 to 5 cm in diameter, wrap well and freeze. To bake, cut the rolls into 5 to 7 mm slices and bake on a greased baking sheet in the oven at 180 °C (350 °F) for 7 to 10 minutes.

250 ml (1 cup) cake flour
125 ml (½ cup) butter
4 eggs
250 ml water
1 ml (¼ teaspoon) salt

603   Basic choux pastry   (F)

Prep time 30 min;   Cooking time 15 min.

1. Boil the water in a small saucepan. Add the butter and stir until it has melted.
2. Add the flour and salt to the water and butter, all at once, and stir vigorously with a wooden spoon until the mixture forms a ball.
3. Remove from the stove and cool slightly.
4. Add the eggs one by one, beating well after every addition; the pastry should have a stiff consistency (f).
5. See following recipes for baking instructions, fillings and decoration.

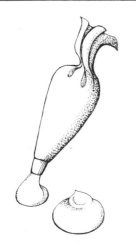

604   Cream puffs   (F)

Makes ± 50 small;   kJ per portion 210;   Prep time 30 min;
Cooking time 15 min.

Using the basic choux pastry (recipe 603), fill an icing bag with the mixture and press out small puffs onto a greased baking sheet. Bake in the oven at 200 °C (400 °F) for 15 minutes, then reduce the heat to 160 °C (325 °F) and bake a further 10 minutes (f). Just before serving, fill with whipped cream and glaze with melted chocolate. Alternatively, serve filled with a savoury cream cheese and diced ham mixture as an hors d'oeuvre.

Note: To serve after freezing, place in the oven at 180 °C (350 °F) for approximately 15 minutes. Allow to cool and then fill.

605 Éclairs (F)

Makes ± 36; kJ per portion 500; Prep time 45 min; Cooking time 15 min.

Using the basic choux pastry (recipe 603), fill an icing bag with the mixture and press out long tubes 3 cm x 10 cm onto a greased baking sheet. Bake in the oven at 200°C (400°F) for 15 minutes then reduce the heat to 160°C (325°F) and bake a further 10 minutes (f). If served as an hors d'oeuvre, fill with a delicate-flavoured cream cheese mixture and diced ham. For dessert or tea, fill with whipped cream and glaze with melted chocolate.

Note: To serve after freezing, place in the oven at 180°C (350°F) for approximately 15 minutes. Allow to cool and then fill.

---

225 g cake flour
110 g custard powder
110 g icing sugar
225 g butter or margarine
1 ml (¼ teaspoon) salt
Decoration:
halved glacé cherries

606 Custard powder biscuits (F)

Makes ± 40 biscuits; kJ per portion 300; Prep time 30 min; Cooking time 20 min.

1. Combine the flour, custard powder, icing sugar and salt in a bowl.
2. Rub in the butter or margarine, blending to a smooth dough.
3. Roll little bits of the dough between the palms to form balls the size of walnuts.
4. Place the balls on lightly greased baking sheets and flatten them slightly with a fork. Place a halved cherry on each.
5. Bake in the oven at 180°C (350°F) for 20 minutes. Remove from the oven and cool on a wire rack (f).

87,5 ml (7 tablespoons) cornflakes or rice crispies
62,5 ml (5 tablespoons) drinking chocolate
25 ml (2 tablespoons) butter or margarine
60 g golden syrup

607 Chocolate crisps (F)

Makes 10; kJ per portion 310; Prep time 30 min; Cooking time 10 min.

1. Place the butter or margarine and syrup in a saucepan and melt over low heat.
2. When melted, add the drinking chocolate and stir well to blend. Heat thoroughly.
3. Remove from the stove and with a metal spoon, fold in the cereal, ensuring that the cereal is completely coated.
4. Spoon the mixture into 10 paper cupcakes and allow to set (f).

---

85 g icing sugar
62,5 ml (5 tablespoons) flour
85 g cornflour
85 g butter
melted chocolate
butter icing (recipe 529)

608 Melting moments (F)

Makes ± 40; kJ per portion 330; Prep time 45 min; Cooking time 15 min.

1. Cream the butter and sugar together in a bowl until very soft and light.
2. Sift the flour and cornflour together, then work into the butter and sugar mixture with a wooden spoon.
3. Place the mixture into a forcing bag and, using a large piping rose, pipe into fingers on a greased baking sheet.
4. Bake in the centre of the oven at 180°C (350°F) for 15 minutes, then cool in the tin.
5. When cool, sandwich two together with butter icing, or coat the ends of each finger with melted chocolate (f).

Variation: Substitute 62,5 ml (5 tablespoons) cocoa for the flour.

250 ml (1 cup) cake flour
500 ml (2 cups) wholewheat flour
85 ml (¹/₃ cup) castor sugar
1 egg
100 g butter or margarine
100 g lard
50 ml water
2 ml (½ teaspoon) salt

609   Digestive biscuits   (F)

Makes 60-70;   kJ per portion 300;   Prep time 45 min;   Cooking time 15 min.

1. Sift the cake flour and salt into a mixing bowl and mix in the wholewheat flour.
2. Cut the butter or margarine and lard into the flour and rub with the fingertips until the mixture resembles coarse breadcrumbs.
3. Stir in the sugar, mixing well, and make a well in the centre.
4. Whisk the egg and water together lightly and pour into the well. Mix with a fork, drawing in all the ingredients until the mixture sticks together. Knead to form a ball.
5. Turn the dough out onto a floured surface and roll out to 6 mm thick with a floured rolling pin. Cut into 5 cm rounds with a pastry cutter. Place on greased baking sheets.
6. Bake just above the centre of the oven at 200 °C (400 °F) until golden brown, about 15 minutes. Remove from oven and cool on the sheets for 5 minutes, then transfer to a wire rack to cool (f).

1 kg cake flour
1 kg desiccated coconut
1 kg oatmeal
1 kg sugar
500 g butter or margarine
25 ml golden syrup
5 ml (1 teaspoon) baking powder
2 ml (½ teaspoon) salt

610   Oatmeal and coconut biscuits   (F)

Makes ± 200;   kJ per portion 380;   Prep time 45 min;
Cooking time 15 min.

1. Combine the oatmeal, salt, sugar and coconut in a bowl.
2. Melt the butter or margarine together with the syrup in a saucepan over medium heat.
3. Sift the flour and baking powder into a mixing bowl and stir in all the other ingredients except the butter and syrup mixture.
4. Make a well in the centre of the flour mixture, pour in the butter and syrup mixture and mix well with a wooden spoon.
5. Press into a greased shallow baking tin and bake in the oven at 180 °C (350 °F) until done, about 15 minutes. Cut in blocks and allow to cool completely before serving (f).

750 ml (3 cups) flour, sifted
25 ml (2 tablespoons) cornflour
50 ml (4 tablespoons) castor sugar
120 g margarine
120 g butter

611   Shortbread   (F)

Makes 24;   kJ per portion 390;   Prep time 40 min;   Cooking time 1 hour

1. Cream the butter, margarine and sugar in a mixing bowl until light and creamy.
2. Stir in the cornflour and flour gradually, mixing with the fingertips to form a stiff dough. The mixture must not be crumbly.
3. Press the mixture into greased baking tins. Mark into fingers or squares with a knife and prick the shortbread with a fork.
4. Bake in the oven at 150 °C (300 °F) until slightly browned and shrunk from the sides of the tins, about 1 hour.
5. Remove from the oven and sprinkle with a little castor sugar. Allow to cool slightly in the tin, then remove and cool completely on a wire rack (f). Store in an airtight tin.

375 ml (1½ cups) flour
250 ml (1 cup) sugar
125 ml (½ cup) peanut butter
1 egg, beaten
85 g butter or margarine
5 ml vanilla essence
4 ml (¾ teaspoon) baking powder
1 ml (¼ teaspoon) salt

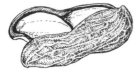

612   Peanut butter biscuits   (F)

Makes ± 30;   kJ per portion 390;   Prep time 45 min;   Cooking time 15 min.

1. Cream the butter or margarine and sugar together in a mixing bowl until light and creamy.
2. Stir in the beaten egg, mixing well to blend, then stir in the peanut butter.
3. Sift in the dry ingredients, mixing well.
4. Stir in the vanilla essence.
5. Knead the mixture slightly to form a smooth, stiff dough, then roll small pieces of the dough into balls. Place the balls on a greased baking sheet and press them flat with a fork.
6. Bake in the oven at 180 °C (350 °F) until firm, about 15 minutes.
7. Allow to cool slightly in the pan, then transfer to a wire rack to cool completely (f). Store in airtight containers.

Note: Place the biscuits well apart on the baking sheet to allow for expansion during baking.

---

500 g self-raising flour
50 ml (4 tablespoons) sugar
25 ml (2 tablespoons) margarine
3 egg yolks
milk or water
5 ml vanilla essence
1 ml (¼ teaspoon) salt
Filling:
apricot jam
3 egg whites, stiffly beaten
250 ml (1 cup) sugar
500 ml (2 cups) desiccated coconut

613   Hertzog cookies   (F)

Makes ± 60;   kJ per portion 380;   Prep time 50 min;   Cooking time 15 min.

1. Cream the margarine and sugar in a bowl until light and creamy.
2. Stir in the egg yolks and vanilla essence, blending well.
3. Sift the flour and salt into the mixture, blending well, then stir in a little milk or water to form a fairly stiff dough.
4. Roll the dough out to 5 mm thick on a floured surface and cut into rounds with a pastry cutter. Line greased patty tins with the rounds of pastry.
5. Make the filling. Gradually add the sugar to the beaten egg whites, beating well to blend.
6. Fold in the coconut and mix well.
7. Place a little apricot jam in the centre of the rounds in the patty tins and spoon some of the coconut mixture over the jam.
8. Bake in the oven at 200 °C (400 °F) until the pastry is lightly golden, about 15 minutes. Cool slightly in the patty tin, then cool completely on a wire rack (f).

---

110 g self-raising flour
170 g sugar
4 eggs
110 g butter or margarine
110 g plain chocolate
110 g ground almonds

614   Brownies

Makes 12-16;   kJ per portion 310;   Prep time 30 min;   Cooking time 40 min.

1. Place the butter or margarine and chocolate in the top half of a double-boiler over hot water, or in a basin over a saucepan of hot water, and heat gently until the chocolate has melted.
2. Meanwhile, beat the eggs and sugar together in a bowl until light and thick.
3. Fold the chocolate mixture into the egg mixture, then fold in the flour and nuts.
4. Pour the mixture into a greased and lined shallow tin, 250 x 200 mm and bake in the oven at 180 °C (350 °F) until firm, about 40 minutes.
5. Turn out onto a wire rack and cut into fingers.

Note: Brownies should be sticky in the middle, so do not bake too long.

500 ml (2 cups) oatmeal
125 ml (½ cup) wheatgerm, toasted
125 ml (½ cup) desiccated coconut
125 ml (½ cup) skimmed milk powder
250 ml (1 cup) packed brown sugar
100 ml (²/₅ cup) chocolate vermicelli
25 ml (2 tablespoons) sprinkle nuts
25 ml (2 tablespoons) cocoa
150 g soft butter or margarine
5 ml vanilla essence

615   Crunchy chocolate biscuits

Makes 30;   kJ per portion 300;   Prep time 45 min.

1. Cream the butter or margarine and sugar together in a bowl until light and fluffy.
2. Beat in the oatmeal, cocoa, wheatgerm, coconut, skimmed milk powder, chocolate vermicelli and sprinkle nuts, in that order, then stir in the vanilla essence.
3. Form the dough into a ball with the hands, then press it evenly into a shallow buttered dish or baking sheet.
4. Mark into squares with a wet knife and chill in the refrigerator for at least 1 hour before use. These biscuits should be stored in the refrigerator.

---

500 ml (2 cups) self-raising flour
125 ml (½ cup) castor sugar
1 large egg
120 g butter
2 ml vanilla essence
1 ml (¼ teaspoon) salt

616   Butter cookies   (F)

Makes 50;   kJ per portion 390;   Prep time 30 min;   Cooking time 15 min.

1. Sift the flour and salt together into a bowl.
2. Beat the butter and sugar together in a bowl until smooth and creamy.
3. Beat in the egg, to form a smooth mixture.
4. Mix in the sifted flour and salt, then stir in the vanilla essence, blending well. Chill in the refrigerator for 15 minutes.
5. Take small portions of the dough and shape them into balls. Place them, 5 cm apart, on a greased baking sheet.
6. Bake in the oven at 180 °C (350 °F) for 10 to 15 minutes, then lift onto a wire rack and allow to cool (f).

---

1 kg flour
1,2 kg sugar
8 eggs
450 g butter or margarine
dried naartjie peel, finely chopped
125 ml milk
12,5 ml (1 tablespoon) baking powder
12,5 ml (1 tablespoon) bicarbonate of soda
12,5 ml (1 tablespoon) ground cinnamon
12,5 ml (1 tablespoon) grated nutmeg
12,5 ml (1 tablespoon) ground cloves
12,5 ml (1 tablespoon) ground ginger
12,5 ml (1 tablespoon) aniseed
2 ml (½ teaspoon) salt

617   Ouma's spice biscuits   (F)

Makes ± 120 biscuits;   kJ per portion 300;   Prep time 1 hour; Cooking time 15 min.

1. Cream the butter or margarine and sugar together in a bowl until light and creamy.
2. Sift the dry ingedients into a bowl and stir in the naartjie peel and aniseed.
3. Fold the dry ingredients into the creamed mixture, blending well.
4. Fold in the eggs, one at a time, and then add the milk. Blend to a fairly stiff dough.
5. Roll the dough out to 5 mm thickness on a floured surface and cut out rounds with a pastry cutter.
6. Bake the biscuits on greased baking sheets in the oven at 200 °C (400 °F) for 15 minutes. Cool on a wire rack and store in a tightly closed cake tin in a cool, dry place (f).

75 ml (6 tablespoons) castor
sugar
60 g black treacle
62,5 ml (5 tablespoons) butter
or margarine
125 ml (½ cup) flour, sifted
5 ml lemon juice
5 ml (1 teaspoon) ground
ginger
2 ml (½ teaspoon) salt

618 Brandy snaps

Makes 18; kJ per portion 510; Prep time 15 min; Cooking time 5 min.

1. Combine the butter or margarine, sugar, treacle and lemon juice in a saucepan and simmer over low heat until melted, stirring occasionally. Remove from the stove.
2. Add the flour, salt and ground ginger and mix well to blend.
3. Place teaspoonfuls of the batter 12 cm apart on well-greased baking sheets and bake in the oven at 190°C (375°F) until rich brown and well spread out, about 5 minutes.
4. Remove the sheet from the oven and allow to cool until the biscuits can be lifted easily, about 1 minute.
5. While still warm, wrap each biscuit around a wooden handle. Allow to become firm before removing the wooden handle and lifting onto a wire tray.
6. Cool thoroughly then store in an airtight container until needed. Serve filled with whipped cream.

Note:
- Put one tray in the oven at a time to allow you time to roll the brandy snaps.
- Work quickly when you roll the brandy snaps, so that the others on the sheet do not become too firm before you start to roll them.

450 g cake flour
110 g sugar
110 g treacle
170 g butter or margarine
2 eggs, beaten
10 ml (2 teaspoons) ground
ginger
5 ml (1 teaspoon) bicarbonate
of soda dissolved in 50 ml hot
water
2 ml (½ teaspoon) salt
Decoration:
blanched, split almonds

619 Gingerbread (F)

Serves 10; kJ per portion 810; Prep time 30 min; Cooking time 1 hour

1. Heat the butter or margarine, sugar and treacle in a saucepan over medium heat until the sugar dissolves. Remove from the stove and allow to cool.
2. Meanwhile, combine the flour, salt and ginger in a mixing bowl.
3. Stir the sugar mixture into the flour, mixing well, then stir in the beaten eggs and blend thoroughly.
4. Stir in the dissolved bicarbonate of soda and pour the mixture into a greased and lined 220 mm square baking tin.
5. Arrange almonds on top and bake in the centre of the oven at 180°C (350°F) until firm, about 1 hour.
6. Remove from oven, allow to cool slightly in the tin, then cut into squares, remove from the tin and cool thoroughly on a wire rack (f).

900 g flour
250 ml (1 cup) sugar
1 egg
250 g butter or margarine
450 g golden syrup
125 ml milk
20 ml (4 teaspoons) ground ginger
10 ml (2 teaspoons) bicarbonate of soda
2 ml (½ teaspoon) salt

620 Ginger biscuits (F)

Makes ± 120 biscuits;   kJ per portion 310;   Prep time 40 min; Cooking time 10 min.

1. Cream the butter or margarine and sugar in a bowl until light and creamy.
2. Add the egg and mix well.
3. Stir in the golden syrup and salt, mixing well.
4. Sift the flour, bicarbonate of soda, ginger and salt together in a bowl, then add to the creamed mixture alternately with the milk, mixing well after each addition.
5. Blend thoroughly, using the hands, and knead to a stiff, smooth dough.
6. Shape the dough into nut-sized balls. Place them on greased baking sheets and press down lightly with a fork.
7. Bake in the oven at 180 °C (350 °F) for 10 minutes. Remove from the tin and cool on wire racks (f).

Note: These biscuits keep extremely well if stored in an airtight container in a dark, cool place.

FREEZING

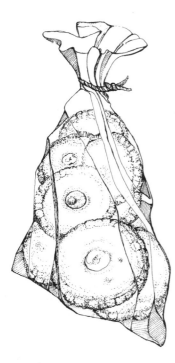

In general, baked products freeze very well indeed.
1. Cool completely, then wrap in aluminium foil or place in plastic bags, expelling all the air.
2. Label with all the relevant information – type, and date of freezing – and freeze.
3. Store for 4 to 5 months only.

Note:
- Take care not to place heavy objects on top of soft cakes in the freezer before they have frozen hard.
- Pancakes, crumpets and waffles should be frozen with greaseproof paper in between them.
- Any yeast product may be frozen either baked or unbaked. Treat baked products as outlined above. Unrisen dough should be frozen in a tightly sealed bag, and risen dough can be frozen in one piece or first shaped into buns or loaves. It should be kneaded after the first rising, then placed in a polythene bag and frozen.

To use after freezing
1. Remove from the freezer and thaw either at room temperature or in the refrigerator.
2. Cakes may also be placed in a pre-heated oven at 200 °C (400 °F) for 5 minutes after thawing or at 180 °C (350 °F) for 10 to 15 minutes if still frozen.
3. Frozen scones and muffins should always be reheated before serving.
4. Layer cakes are sometimes slightly dry after being frozen – cover with canned fruit and a honey-butter sauce to serve as a dessert.

331

5. Wrap baked frozen yeast products in aluminium foil and bake in the oven at 180 °C (350 °F) for 30 to 45 minutes. Open the foil for the last 5 minutes. These products may also be thawed and heated for 5 minutes in the oven at 200 °C (400 °F).
6. Thaw unrisen dough for 5 to 6 hours at room temperature, knead slightly and leave to rise in the warming drawer of the stove or in a warm place.
7. Thaw risen dough at room temperature, allow to rise for 30 to 40 minutes and continue with the recipe.

SWEET-MAKING

Homemade *sweets* are firm favourites at bazaars and with the family, and are simple to make if the basic rules are followed. Some sweets – for instance, fondant and fudge – contain small sugar crystals (crystalline sweets). The texture of these sweets must be so smooth, however, that the crystals are not felt on the tongue. Other sweets, for example caramels, marshmallows and nougat, do not contain crystals (non-crystalline sweets).

When making sweets
1. Use a medium-sized heavy-based saucepan unless the sweets contain a great deal of milk or cream. For such sweets use a larger saucepan as the mixture tends to boil up high.
2. Invest in a good sugar thermometer – registering up to 180 °C (350 °F) – for controlled and error-free sweet-making. Test the accuracy of the thermometer. Place it in a saucepan of water reaching halfway up the thermometer: the boiling point of water should be 100 °C (212 °F) at sea-level. The boiling point of water decreases by 1 °C (±2 °F) for

approximately every 300 metres above sea-level – adjust your recipes to the height above sea-level where you live.

As sudden heating or cooling will cause the glass of a thermometer to crack, place the thermometer in lukewarm water and heat it to boiling point before placing it in the boiling syrup. The thermometer must be placed in boiling or very hot water after removing it from the syrup and left to cool gradually.

3. Use only the best quality sugar – the main ingredient in sweets.
4. Mix all ingredients very well before boiling.
5. Dissolve the sugar completely before the mixture begins to boil to ensure that crystalline sweets have a velvety texture: the presence of even a few crystals can cause the whole mixture to become granular. A further safeguard is to wash down the sugar crystals adhering to the sides of the saucepan with a small brush dipped in hot water, or to cover the saucepan for a few moments to let the steam melt the crystals.
6. Do not stir sugar mixtures while they are boiling, except when the recipe uses a great deal of milk or cream. Even then, stir only when necessary.
7. For crystalline sweets allow the mixture to cool until lukewarm, (40 °C/80 °F), then beat briskly until creamy.
8. Plunge the bottom of the saucepan into cold water for a few seconds as soon as the mixture reaches the correct temperature to prevent the heat of the saucepan from raising the temperature of the mixture still further.
9. Do not add too much colouring or flavouring – sweets should have a delicate colour and taste.

Use the following table to ensure good results:

Name of Sweet	Temperature		Stage	Cold Water Test
	°C	°F		
Syrup	110-112	230-234	Thread	The syrup will spin a thread of approximately 50 mm if dropped from a spoon, or if tested between thumb and forefinger.
Fondant, fudge, coconut ice, marshmallows	115-116	237-240	Soft-ball	A very soft ball forms when a little of the syrup is dropped into cold water.
Caramel	118-120	240-248	Firm-ball	A firm ball forms when a little of the syrup is dropped into cold water.
Nougat, Divinity fudge	126-130	260-266	Hard-ball	A hard ball, which is still pliable, forms when a little of the syrup is dropped into cold water.
Toffee, Bulls' Eyes, brittle sweets, toffee apples	132-143	270-289	Light-crack	The syrup separates into firm, slightly brittle threads when a little is dropped into cold water.
Butterscotch	149-154	300-310	Hard-crack	The syrup separates into hard, brittle threads which snap like ice when a little is dropped into cold water.
Caramel syrup	154-170	310-338	Brown syrup	Syrup becomes brown.

What went wrong:

Fault: Granular texture	Cause:	• Stirred too much while boiling.
		• Mixture beaten while still hot.
		• Sugar crystals remained on the sides of the saucepan.
		• Mixture boiled before all the sugar crystals have dissolved.
Sweet does not set		• Sugar mixture not boiled long enough.
		• Too much acid or glucose added.
		• The atmosphere is too humid.

250 ml (1 cup) peanuts, coarsely chopped
250 ml (1 cup) sugar

621 Peanut brittle

Makes 500 g;   kJ per portion 450;   Prep time 45 min;   Cooking time 25 min.

1. Grease the *outside* base of a square 200 mm pan and sprinkle evenly with the chopped nuts.
2. Heat the sugar in a frying-pan over medium heat, stirring all the time, until golden brown and syrupy.
3. Pour evenly over the nuts and allow to cool slightly.
4. Remove in one piece to a board and cut into 2 cm squares.

250 g marzipan (recipe 528)
120 g fresh cherries, soaked in Kirsch
apricot glaze (recipe 499) *or* **smooth apricot jam**
desiccated coconut
glacé icing (recipe 532)

622 Bonbons

Makes 14 bonbons;   kJ per portion 380;   Prep time 20 min.

1. Mould a little marzipan around each cherry and dip it in apricot glaze or smooth apricot jam.
2. Toss in coconut or dip in thick glacé icing.

800 g sugar
300 ml water
1 ml (¼ teaspoon) cream of tartar
1 ml (¼ teaspoon) salt
vegetable colouring

623 Fondant

Makes 10;   kJ per portion 300;   Prep time 45 min + setting time;   Cooking time 30 min.

1. Combine the sugar, salt and water in a saucepan. Stir well over low heat until all the sugar has dissolved. Wash down the sugar crystals on the sides of the saucepan and cover for 30 seconds.
2. Stir in the cream of tartar and place the sugar thermometer in the saucepan. Boil rapidly, uncovered, to the soft ball stage (see chart p. 333). Remove from the stove.
3. Stir in a little vegetable colouring, mixing well, then pour the fondant onto a slightly dampened, cold, flat surface. Leave until lukewarm.
4. Now beat the mixture with a wooden spoon until light and creamy and knead with the hands until smooth.
5. Roll out to the thickness of 10 mm. Dampen a cloth and use to cover the fondant. Leave for 1 hour, then cut into blocks and store in an airtight container.

Variations:
1. *Fruit:* Add 1 ml almond essence while kneading the fondant. Add 125 ml (½ cup) chopped glacé cherries. Cut or mould into shapes.
2. *Chocolate:* Dip fondants in melted chocolate and leave to dry.

450 g sugar
450 g whole almonds
100 ml water
5 ml (1 teaspoon) ground cinnamon

624   Sugared almonds

Makes 450 g;   kJ per portion 560;   Prep time 30 min;   Cooking time 30 min.

1. Place the sugar and water in a saucepan and heat over low heat, stirring constantly, until the sugar dissolves.
2. Stir in the cinnamon, then increase the heat to high and bring to the boil. Boil the syrup briskly until it falls from the spoon in big heavy drops.
3. Add the almonds and stir until they are well-coated.
4. Remove the pan from the stove and continue stirring until the syrup dries into sugar.
5. Place the almonds in a sieve and shake to dislodge the excess sugar.
6. Replace the excess sugar in the pan, add a little water and dissolve the sugar over low heat. Increase the heat to high and boil until the syrup clears.
7. Add the almonds, stir again until the almonds are coated. Turn out onto a board and leave to cool and dry.

---

170 g icing sugar, sifted
110 g plain chocolate
2 egg yolks
1 egg white, lightly beaten
62,5 ml (5 tablespoons) butter or margarine
100 ml ($^2/_5$ cup) ground almonds
25 ml coffee essence
cocoa
desiccated coconut

625   Coffee truffles

Makes 30;   kJ per portion 400;   Prep time 45 min + setting time;   Cooking time 15 min.

1. Place the butter or margarine and chocolate in the top of a double-boiler over hot water, or in a basin over a saucepan of hot water, and simmer gently until the chocolate melts.
2. Remove from the stove and stir in the coffee essence and egg yolks.
3. Work the ground almonds and icing sugar into the mixture with a wooden spoon, then spread out on a flat plate and leave to set in the refrigerator or in a cold place, about 1 ½ hours.
4. When set, divide into 30 balls. Toss 15 of the balls in cocoa and roll the others first in the egg white and then in the coconut. Place in paper cases.

Variation: Use 25 ml rum essence instead of the coffee essence.

---

225 g sugar
225 g golden syrup
110 g butter or margarine

626   Toffee

Makes 500 g;   kJ per portion 300;   Prep time 30 min + setting time; Cooking time 20-25 min.

1. Melt the butter or margarine in a heavy-bottomed saucepan over high heat.
2. Stir in the sugar and syrup and boil steadily, without stirring, until the mixture reaches the hard-crack stage when tested in water (it will break easily between the fingers: see chart p. 333).
3. Pour the mixture into a well-greased tin and allow to set. When set, cut into squares.

Variations:
1. Add 60 g desiccated coconut to the toffee just before it reaches the hard-crack stage.
2. Add 170 g chopped walnuts to the toffee just before it reaches the hard-crack stage.
3. Use black treacle instead of the golden syrup.
4. Add 7 ml vanilla essence when the sugar has dissolved.

Note: This kind of toffee should be wrapped in waxed paper.

627 Toffee apples

50 firm red apples, stalks removed
50 ice-cream sticks
800 g sugar
250 ml water
20 ml vinegar
200 g golden syrup
25 ml (2 tablespoons) butter
2 ml (½ teaspoon) salt

Makes 50; kJ per portion 500; Prep time 45 min; Cooking time 30 min.

1. Insert an ice-cream stick into the stem end of each apple.
2. Place buttered wax paper onto trays.
3. Heat the sugar, water, vinegar, golden syrup, butter and salt together over low heat, stirring well to dissolve the sugar.
4. Boil the syrup to the light-crack stage.
5. Remove the saucepan from the stove and place in warm water. Dip the apples into the syrup, holding them by the stick. Place each apple on the paper-covered trays and leave to dry.

Note: Do not stir the syrup once it has begun to boil.

628 Butterscotch

500 ml (2 cups) sugar
165 ml dark corn syrup
65 ml water
65 ml single cream
62,5 ml (5 tablespoons) butter

Makes 500 g; kJ per portion 300; Prep time 30 min; Cooking time 20 min.

1. Combine all the ingredients, except the butter, in a saucepan and bring to the boil, stirring, over medium heat.
2. Boil, stirring often, to the hard-ball stage (see chart p. 333).
3. Stir in the butter and boil, stirring all the time, until a small amount of the mixture separates into threads which are hard but not brittle when dropped in very cold water.
4. Pour the mixture into a greased 200 mm square pan to set.
5. When almost set, cut into squares and when cold, break into squares along the cuts.

629 Nougat

250 ml (1 cup) hazel nuts, coarsely chopped
500 ml (2 cups) sugar
62,5 ml (5 tablespoons) glacé cherries, coarsely chopped
2 egg whites
375 ml light corn syrup
65 ml water
5 ml vanilla essence
62,5 ml (5 tablespoons) butter or margarine
1 ml (¼ teaspoon) salt

Makes 1 kg; kJ per portion 350; Prep time 30 min; Cooking time 30 min.

1. Combine the corn syrup, sugar, salt and water in a heavy-bottomed saucepan and simmer, stirring, until the sugar dissolves. Bring to the boil and boil, without stirring, until a small amount dropped in very cold water forms a hard ball.
2. Beat the egg whites in a large mixing bowl until stiff but not dry, then gradually beat in ¼ of the corn syrup mixture and continue beating until the mixture holds its shape.
3. Boil the remaining syrup until the mixture reaches the hard-crack stage, then beat gradually into the first mixture. Continue beating until the mixture begins to hold its shape.
4. Stir in the vanilla essence and the butter or margarine and beat until very thick and creamy.
5. Stir in the nuts and cherries and pour into a buttered square 200 mm pan, smoothing the top, and let stand until firm.
6. Turn out of pan and cut into 2 cm pieces.

Note: For best flavour, store for several days in a cool place before serving.

630 Turkish delight

37,5 ml (3 tablespoons) powdered gelatine
450 g sugar
280 ml water
juice of 2 lemons or 2 ml rose water
2 ml (½ teaspoon) tartaric acid
cochineal
sifted icing sugar

Makes 500 g; kJ per portion 300; Prep time 45 min; Cooking time 15 min.

1. Sprinkle the gelatine on the cold water in a saucepan and heat gently until the gelatine dissolves.
2. Add the sugar and heat until the sugar dissolves, stirring all the time.
3. Bring to the boil and boil for 8 minutes, stirring all the time, then stir in the lemon juice and tartaric acid. Remove from the stove.
4. Pour half the mixture into a wet pan.
5. Colour the rest of the mixture with a few drops of cochineal and pour into another wet pan. Allow to set.
6. When set, with a wet knife cut into squares and roll in the icing sugar.

Variation: Add 50 ml Crème de menthe liqueur or a few drops peppermint essence to the water and sugar and proceed as above, omitting the cochineal.

631 Marshmallows

12,5 ml (1 tablespoon) gelatine powder
125 ml (½ cup) sugar
80 ml cold water
160 ml golden syrup
5 ml vanilla essence
2 ml (½ teaspoon) salt
toasted coconut

Makes 400 g; kJ per portion 350; Prep time 45 min; Cooking time 10 min.

1. Combine the gelatine and water in the top of a double-boiler and allow to stand for 5 minutes to soften.
2. Place over boiling water in the bottom of the double-boiler and heat over medium heat until the gelatine dissolves, then add the sugar. Stir until the sugar dissolves.
3. In a separate bowl, combine the golden syrup, vanilla essence and salt.
4. Stir in the gelatine mixture and beat briskly until light and fluffy, about 15 minutes.
5. Pour the mixture into a lightly greased square 220 mm pan and allow it to stand in a cool place until set.
6. Cut in squares and roll in toasted coconut.

632 After-dinner mints (F)

450 g icing sugar
1 egg white
5 ml (1 teaspoon) butter or margarine, softened
12,5 ml single cream
5 ml vanilla essence
3 drops peppermint essence
pastel vegetable colouring

Makes 500 g; kJ per portion 250; Prep time 20 min.

1. Combine thoroughly the egg white, cream, vanilla essence, peppermint essence and colouring in a bowl.
2. Add the icing sugar and butter or margarine and mix well. Add more butter or margarine, cream and sugar if necessary to form a smooth, firm consistency.
3. Form into small balls and arrange them on wax paper, then press them flat with the prongs of a fork dipped in icing sugar.
4. Stand overnight to allow the outer surface to harden, then store in tins with wax paper between each layer (f).

Note: These mints may be stored, frozen, for several months.

1 packet butterscotch instant pudding
250 ml (1 cup) brown sugar
250 ml (1 cup) sugar
12,5 ml (1 tablespoon) butter or margarine
125 ml (½ cup) pecan nuts
125 ml evaporated milk

633 Pecan pralines

Makes 500 g; kJ per portion 350; Prep time 45 min; Cooking time 20 min.

1. Combine all the ingredients except the pecans in a saucepan and simmer gently until the sugar has dissolved.
2. Increase the heat and boil until the soft-ball stage is reached (see chart p. 333), then add the pecans and stir until the mixture just begins to thicken.
3. Drop by teaspoonfuls onto waxpaper and let stand until firm.

Note: Make the sweets immediately the mixture starts to thicken as the hardening process is extremely rapid.

---

125 ml (½ cup) brown sugar
125 ml (½ cup) sugar
125 ml (½ cup) toasted almonds, finely chopped
25 ml (2 tablespoons) butter or margarine
250 ml cream mixed with 125 ml milk
190 ml golden syrup
5 ml vanilla essence
1 ml (¼ teaspoon) salt

634 Nutty caramels

Makes 1 kg; kJ per portion 350; Prep time 30 min; Cooking time 20 min.

1. Combine three-quarters of the cream and milk mixture, the sugars, syrup and salt in a heavy-bottomed saucepan and bring to the boil over medium heat, stirring all the time until the sugar dissolves. Boil, stirring occasionally, to the soft-ball stage (see chart p. 333).
2. Gradually stir in the remaining cream and milk mixture, ensuring that the syrup does not come off the boil while you do so. Boil, stirring occasionally, to the firm-ball stage.
3. Remove from the stove and stir in the vanilla essence, almonds and butter or margarine, combining well.
4. Pour the mixture into a greased 220 x 70 x 120 mm loaf tin and cool completely at room temperature. Turn out of tin and cut into pieces with a knife dipped in hot water. Store in an airtight container in a cool place.

800 g sugar
250 g butter or margarine
250 ml milk
250 ml condensed milk
10 ml vanilla essence

635 Fudge

Makes 1 kg; kJ per portion 400; Prep time 45 min; Cooking time 45-50 min.

1. Boil the sugar, butter or margarine and milk together in a saucepan over medium heat, stirring all the time until the sugar dissolves.
2. Stir in the condensed milk and boil for 40 minutes, stirring all the time.
3. Remove from the stove and beat in the vanilla essence. Continue beating until the mixture is thick and foamy.
4. Pour the fudge into a shallow greased dish and cut into squares. Allow to set.

400 g sugar
12,5 ml (1 tablespoon) butter
or margarine
600 to 700 g desiccated or
baking coconut
375 ml milk
1 ml (¼ teaspoon) salt
1 ml (¼ teaspoon) cream of
tartar
few drops cochineal

636 Coconut ice

Makes 1,5 kg;   kJ per portion 300;   Prep time 20 min;   Cooking time 15 min.

1. Place the sugar, butter or margarine, milk and salt in a saucepan. Bring to the boil and boil for 7 minutes.
2. Remove the saucepan from the stove and stir in the coconut and cream of tartar, mixing well.
3. Pour half the mixture into a greased dish or pan. Colour the remainder with a few drops of cochineal, beating well to distribute the colour evenly, and pour either on top of the white coconut ice or into a separate greased dish.
4. Allow to set for a while, then mark into squares. When completely set, remove from the dish, break into squares along the marked lines, and dry on a wire rack.

Note:
- This coconut ice is not as sweet as usual; it contains less sugar and more coconut and this makes for a fluffier result. The amount of coconut used, however, depends on taste.
- If the greased dish is lined with waxproof paper, it is easier to remove the coconut ice when it has set.

CANNING AND PRESERVING FRUIT AND VEGETABLES

Many people shy away from attempting to can fruit and vegetables or make preserves, jam, pickles or chutney because they think it is too difficult. This is not strictly true: some of the processes may be complicated, but if the instructions are followed carefully there should be a good result.

Choosing and sterilizing jars
1. Choose jars which can be cleaned easily and thoroughly. Jars with wide necks and straight sides are best.
2. Do not use jars that are cracked or chipped.
3. Metal lids should not be bent or rusted and should fit the jars securely.
4. Metal lids have a rubber ring attached, which helps to seal the jar so that it is airtight. Leave the lids in boiling water for 1 to 2 minutes to sterilize them.
5. Glass lids need a separate rubber ring. Use new rings every time you use the jars: wash the rings well and sterilize them in boiling water for 1 to 2 minutes.
6. There are two ways to sterilize jars:
   ● fill the *clean* jars with lukewarm water, leaving 1 cm headspace, and screw on the lids. Use a special waterbath or put a false bottom or a clean dish towel in the bottom of a large, deep saucepan. Place the jars in the saucepan and fill it with warm water. Bring to the boil and continue boiling for 10 minutes. Use tongs to lift the jars out and pour out the water. Fill with fruit or vegetables.
   ● Fill clean jars with warm water and screw on the lids. Place on an asbestos mat in the oven at 100 °C to 120 °C (200 °F to 240 °F) for 20 minutes. Remove from the oven and pour out the water. Fill with fruit or vegetables.

Note:
● Clean *dry* sterilized jars are needed for jams, jellies and pickles. Place the jars and the glass lids on an asbestos mat in the oven at 100 °C to 120 °C (200 °F to 240 °F) and leave for 15 to 20 minutes. Remove from the oven when ready to fill. Metal lids should be sterilized in boiling water.

- Instead of sterilizing the jars beforehand, the fruit may be packed into clean jars and the filled jars sterilized in a waterbath (method p. 342) or in a pressure cooker (method p. 343).

Canning fruit

When canning fruit it is imperative that only the best quality is used: green or over-ripe fruit will have an inferior flavour and texture, and bruised fruit may lead to decay. Fruit may be preserved whole, halved or quartered.

Note: Use 250 ml to 375 ml liquid (syrup, water or fruit juice) for every 1 litre jar.

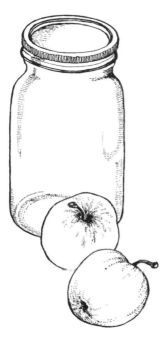

1. Sterilize or wash jars and lids beforehand.
2. Wash fruit well. Peel thinly and neatly. Cling peaches, however, should first be halved, the two halves then twisted to divide them and the pip removed before they are peeled.
3. To prevent discolouring, place each fruit in a solution of 30 ml (6 teaspoons) of either salt, vinegar or lemon juice to every 5 litres of water after it has been peeled.
4. Skins of peaches or pears can be removed by using a solution of 25 ml caustic soda dissolved in 3,5 litres water. Heat the solution to boiling point. Place the fruit in a piece of cheesecloth, tie the ends loosely and dip the cloth into the solution for 15 to 20 seconds. Remove and rinse very well in cold water. Discard the water and rinse again twice. Make a solution of 75 ml vinegar in 3,5 litres water. Remove the fruit from the cloth and rinse thoroughly in the vinegar solution to neutralize any remaining caustic soda. Rub the skins off with the cheesecloth. Place each fruit in a solution of 50 ml (4 tablespoons) salt to 5 litres water after the skin has been rubbed off to prevent discolouring. Halve the fruit and remove the pip.

Note:
- Always add the soda to the water.
- Only unblemished fruit should be used for this method.

5. Make the syrup. Use the following table as a guide:

Thickness of Syrup	Sugar	Water	Use for
Thin (Light)	200 g (250 ml: 1 cup)	750 ml	very sweet fruit
Medium	200 g (250 ml: 1 cup)	500 ml	peaches, pears, apples, guavas, pineapples, grapes, berries
Thick (Heavy)	200 g (250 ml: 1 cup)	250 ml	apricots, quinces, rhubarb, plums

Boil the water, add to the sugar and stir until the sugar has dissolved. For a clear syrup, strain through a double layer of cheesecloth.

Note:
- While the syrup does not influence how long the fruit will keep, it will influence the taste.
- Use boiling water or boiling fruit juice instead of the syrup for unsweetened fruit.

Canning methods

There are 3 basic *methods* of canning:

The *boiling* method is used for firm fruits like cling peaches, pears, apples, guavas and quinces.

1. Heat the syrup to boiling point in a saucepan. Add the raw, peeled fruit – only enough to fill two jars – and boil until the fruit is just tender when tested with a skewer. Very firm fruit should first be boiled in water until just tender, then added to the syrup for 3 to 4 minutes – if the fruit is too firm or hard it will not become tender if boiled in the syrup only.
2. Pack the fruit into warm sterilized jars, cut side down. Fill with the boiling syrup, making sure that there are no air bubbles.
3. Wipe the rim with a clean, damp cloth and *immediately* screw the lids on firmly: the steam that forms will make the jar airtight.
4. To make sure that the jars are airtight, allow to cool then turn them upside down and leave overnight. If the syrup leaks out, do not store but use immediately.

The *sterilizing* or *waterbath* method: Use a special waterbath or a large saucepan, with a tight-fitting lid, which is deep enough to ensure that all the jars will be completely covered with water while sterilizing.

Note: Use a false bottom in the saucepan, otherwise the jars may become too hot and crack.

1. Clean the jars thoroughly but *do not sterilize*. Fill them with hot water until required.
2. The fruit may either be boiled in the syrup for a few minutes or wrapped in cheesecloth and submerged in boiling water for 1 minute to minimize shrinkage of the fruit in the jars. Plunge into cold water immediately. Soft fruit such as berries or grapes may be preshrunk by steaming them over boiling water for 5 to 7 minutes. *Do not bring the fruit into direct contact with the boiling water*.
3. Pack the fruit firmly into the jars with the cut sides down. Fill with hot syrup, making sure that there are no air bubbles. Leave 20 mm headspace, otherwise the syrup will boil over during sterilization.
4. Wipe each jar with a damp cloth.
5. Screw on the lid until it locks, then give it a half turn back again – if the jars are too tightly closed they may crack while heating.
6. Place the jars on the false bottom of the saucepan or waterbath in an upright position, without touching each other.
7. Fill the saucepan or waterbath with hot water until all the jars are at least 50 mm under water.
8. Cover, bring to boiling point and *boil for the total time* given in the specific recipe.

9. Lift the jars out of the saucepan with tongs. Close the lids tightly with a cloth and leave to cool.
10. Test whether the jars are airtight by inverting them and leaving them overnight.

Note:
- Once it has been sterilized, do not open a jar to add more fruit.
- Strawberries, grapes or apricots will retain their colour better if sterilized at just below boiling point.
- If a jar leaks, use the fruit immediately. Do not store.

The *steam pressure* method: Use a pressure cooker with a well-fitting lid and a reliable steam gauge. This method is particularly suited to canning vegetables, meat and fish as the temperatures required are at least 15°C to 20°C (30°F to 40°F) higher than boiling point: these foodstuffs spoil easily unless all the bacteria are destroyed.
1. Prepare the fruit and jars in the same way as for the waterbath method.
2. Place the bottles on the false bottom in the pressure cooker and add water to a level of 50 mm to 70 mm from the bottom.
3. Close the pressure cooker, let the steam escape for 10 minutes and close the valve.
4. When the desired pressure has been reached, steam for the time required. *Remember to keep the pressure constant throughout.*
5. Turn off the stove and remove the cooker. Leave to cool for at least 10 minutes before opening.
6. Open the cooker, lift the jars out with tongs and screw the lids on tightly. Leave to cool, then test whether the bottles are airtight.

Note:
- For every 500 metres above sea-level, increase the sterilizing time needed for cut fruit by 2 minutes and for whole fruit by 3 minutes.
- Do not cool too rapidly, as the syrup may be drawn out of the jars.

Fruit	Method	Preparation	Syrup	Sterilizing
Peaches	boiling	boil 20 to 30 minutes	medium	pack in sterilized jars
	waterbath	boil in syrup for 3 minutes	medium	20 minutes at 100°C (212°F) or 10 minutes at 50 kPa in a pressure cooker
Pears	boiling	boil in syrup for 15 to 20 minutes	medium	pack in sterilized jars
	waterbath	boil in syrup for 5 minutes	medium	20 minutes at 100°C (212°F) or 10 minutes at 50 kPa in a pressure cooker
Apples	boiling	boil in syrup for 20 minutes	thin (light)	pack in sterilized jars
	waterbath	boil in water for 2 to 3 minutes	medium	20 minutes at 100°C (212°F) or 5 minutes at 50 kPa in a pressure cooker

Fruit	Method	Preparation	Syrup	Sterilizing
Apricots	boiling	boil in syrup for 10 minutes	thick (heavy)	pack in sterilized jars
	waterbath	immerse in boiling water for 1 minute	thick (heavy)	20 minutes at 90°C (180°F) or 15 minutes at 100°C (212°F) or 5 minutes at 50 kPa in a pressure cooker
Guavas	boiling	boil in syrup for 15 minutes	medium	pack in sterilized jars
	waterbath	immerse in boiling water for 1 minute	medium	20 minutes at 90°C (180°F) or 15 minutes at 100°C (212°F), or 5 minutes at 50 kPa in a pressure cooker
Quinces	boiling	boil whole, peeled fruit in water for 20 minutes, then slice	medium	pack in sterilized jars
	waterbath	boil whole, peeled fruit in water for 15 minutes, then slice	medium	20 minutes at 100°C (212°F) or 10 minutes at 50 kPa in a pressure cooker
Strawberries	waterbath	steam for 5 minutes or use fresh	thick (heavy)	20 minutes at 100°C (212°F)
Grapes	waterbath		thin or medium	20 minutes at 100°C (212°F)
Youngberries	waterbath		thick (heavy)	20 minutes at 100°C (212°F)
Gooseberries	waterbath		medium	20 minutes at 100°C (212°F)
Oranges, Lemons or Grapefruit	waterbath	peel, cut into segments, removing all the pith	medium	20 minutes at 90°C (180°F)
Ripe figs	waterbath		medium	20 minutes at 100°C (212°F)

Canning vegetables

Only young, fresh vegetables should be used.

1. Wash vegetables well and cut as desired.
2. Immerse the vegetables in boiling water for a few minutes: peas, beans and asparagus for 3 minutes, harder vegetables for 5 to 7 minutes. Immerse in ice-cold water until chilled, about 2 minutes.
3. Fill the clean, warm jars with the vegetables but do not pack too tightly – except for tomatoes.
4. Add 5 ml (1 teaspoon) salt and 5 ml vinegar or lemon juice to every 1 litre jar. 2 ml to 5 ml (½ to 1 teaspoon) sugar may be added to tomatoes, green peas and green mealies.
5. Fill the jar with hot water to within 5 mm of the top. Make sure no air bubbles remain in the jars.
6. Screw the lids on and loosen again slightly.
7. Sterilize as for fruit. It is preferable, however, to use the pressure cooker method.

Note: *Never* use a jar of preserved fruit or vegetables if there is any leakage or fermentation.

344

Vegetable	Preparation	Steam Pressure (50 kPa)	Waterbath method 100°C (212°F)
Asparagus	Wash, tie in bunches and place in boiling water for 2 to 3 minutes. Pack in jars, adding 5 ml (1 teaspoon) salt for 1 litre vegetables. Fill with boiling liquid to 25 mm from top.	45 minutes	4½ hours
Beetroot	Wash, boil beetroot until almost tender. Remove skin. Cut in slices or, if small, leave whole. Pack into jars, adding 5 ml (1 teaspoon) each of salt, sugar and vinegar for a 500 ml jar. Fill with boiling water, seal and sterilize.	40 minutes	4½ hours
Cauliflower	Wash and break into flowerets. Soak for 30 minutes in salted water. Drain and immerse in boiling water for 1 minute. Pack into jars, adding 5 ml (1 teaspoon) each salt and vinegar for 1 litre vegetables. Fill with boiling water, seal and sterilize.	45 minutes	4 hours
Green beans	Wash and cut beans. Boil for 5 minutes. Pack into clean jars. Fill to within 5 mm of the top with boiling water and add 5 ml (1 teaspoon) each of salt and vinegar. Seal and sterilize.	45 minutes	4 hours
Green peas	Shell, wash and prepare as for green beans.	45 minutes	4 hours
Tomatoes	Wash the tomatoes. Immerse in boiling water for 1 minute and then in cold water. Skin. Pack tightly into clean jars, *but do not add liquid.* Add 5 ml (1 teaspoon) each of salt, sugar and vinegar or lemon juice. Seal and sterilize.	15 minutes	20 minutes
Tomato purée	Skin tomatoes as described above. Place in a saucepan and simmer, uncovered, until half the original volume. Using *sterilized* jars, fill immediately with the hot purée, add 5 ml (1 teaspoon) each of salt, sugar and vinegar to each jar and seal immediately.		

PRESERVES

Preserves are whole or large pieces of fruit in a thick, clear syrup; for example green fig preserve or melon preserve.

1. Peel the fruit thinly, using a sharp knife, or scrape the skin – for instance oranges are prepared in this way. Some fruits are cooked without peeling; for example apricots, figs, tomatoes and berry fruits.
2. Immerse peeled fruit in salt water for a few seconds to prevent discolouring.
3. Measure or weigh the fruit after peeling, or after the pips have been removed.
4. Prick the fruit all over with a thick darning needle to make sure that all the syrup will be absorbed. Make a shallow incision in the form of a cross at the flower end of figs and kumquats.

To prevent boiling over when cooking jams and preserves, rub the inside rim of the saucepan about 2 cm from the top with butter or margarine.

5. As green figs, melon peel and gherkins (agurkies) should have a crisp texture, soak them for 12 to 36 hours in a solution of one of the following:
   ● 25 ml (2 tablespoons) slaked lime mixed with 5 litres water. Leave the mixture to settle for a few minutes and use the clear liquid to cover the pricked fruit, discarding the sediment.
   ● 50 ml (4 tablespoons) bicarbonate of soda mixed with 5 litres water.
   Rinse the fruit well and soak for 30 minutes in fresh cold water.
6. Boil the fruit in water until just tender before boiling in the syrup. Pierce the flesh with a matchstick – if the matchstick goes in easily, the fruit is ready.
7. Grease a large saucepan lightly with oil or butter to prevent burning, and use to make the syrup.
8. For sweet fruits such as peaches and pears use 700 g sugar per 1 kg fruit; for all other fruit use 1 kg sugar per 1 kg of fruit. Use 2 litres water per 500 g sugar for fruit that takes a long time to boil, such as quinces and 1 litre water per 500 g sugar for all other fruit. Add 50 ml lemon juice or 5 ml (1 teaspoon) cream of tartar for every 3 kg of fruit that contains too little acid; for example, any ripe fruits. Boil the water and dissolve the sugar in it. Bring to the boil again and continue boiling for 2 minutes. Strain the syrup through a double layer of cheesecloth and boil again for 1 minute.
9. Place the fruit in the syrup bit by bit so that the temperature is not lowered too much.
10. Boil rapidly, uncovered, until the fruit is tender and shiny and the syrup has the right consistency.

Note:
● To test whether the syrup is thick enough, either spoon a few drops onto a plate – it should be thick and sticky with a consistency like honey – or place a sugar thermometer in the syrup: if it is 5 °C (9 °F) higher than the boiling point of water, the syrup is ready.
● If the fruit is tender and translucent but the syrup is not thick enough, remove the fruit and boil the syrup until it reaches the desired thickness.
● If the syrup is thick enough but the fruit needs to boil longer, prepare 500 ml or more thin (light) syrup and add to the mixture, then continue boiling.

11. Towards the end of the boiling time, use a slotted spoon to skim the foam from the surface.
12. Sterilize the jars and keep them warm.
13. Fill the jars with the fruit and syrup, seal immediately and allow to cool.

Note:
● Green figs or melon pieces may be left in the saucepan overnight to cool. Pack in clean jars, then sterilize for 10 minutes in a waterbath (see p. 342).
● The fruit should be shiny but not too dark, with a firm texture.
● The syrup should be clear, without sugar crystals.

346

2 kg firm, ripe peaches or pears
500 g sugar
brandy

637   Brandied fruits

Makes 2 litres;   kJ per portion 300;   Prep time 20 min.

1. Wash and peel the fruit and prick all over with a fork as deep as the pit or core.
2. Pack in clean, dry jars with a layer of sugar in between each layer of fruit.
3. Pour in enough brandy to cover the fruit.
4. Seal the jars and store in a cool dry place: at least 3 months for peaches and 1½ months for pears.
5. Serve with whipped cream or hot custard.

Variation: Use large plump prunes instead of the peaches or pears and leave in the brandy for at least 3 months before use.

---

green figs from first crop
1,25 kg sugar per 1 kg fruit
1,5 litres water per 1 kg sugar
20 ml lemon juice for every 1 kg fruit
Lime solution:
25 ml slaked lime per 5 litres water

638   Green fig preserve

1. Scrape the figs with a knife or scouring pad and make a cross at the blossom end of each fig. Determine the mass.
2. Leave overnight in the lime solution. Rinse thoroughly. Place the figs in boiling water and boil until tender, about 15 minutes.
3. Prepare the syrup from the sugar, water and lemon juice and bring to the boil. Add the figs one by one and boil rapidly until the figs are tender but still crisp and the syrup thick.
4. Turn into hot, dry sterilized bottles, fill with syrup and seal immediately.

---

kaffir watermelon, green rind and fleshy part removed, leaving the peel
1 kg sugar per 1 kg peel
2 litres water per 1 kg sugar
20 ml lemon juice per 1 kg peel
pinch salt
1 small piece bruised ginger per 1 kg peel
Lime solution:
25 ml slaked lime per 5 litres water

639   Watermelon preserve

1. Prick the peel well on both sides. Cut into squares and weigh to get the mass.
2. Leave the peel in the lime solution for 2 days, rinse thoroughly and leave in fresh water for 2 hours. Drain.
3. Drop the pieces one by one in boiling water and boil until just tender: it should be easy to pierce the peel with a blunt match-stick.
4. Prepare the syrup from the sugar, water, lemon juice, salt and ginger. Bring to the boil.
5. Place the peel in the boiling syrup and boil rapidly until the pieces are clear and transparent and the syrup thick. Pack into hot, dry sterilized bottles, fill with syrup and seal immediately.

JAMS

Jams are made from any ripe fruit which can be boiled to a pulp. Some fruits are cooked whole, while others are sliced or minced and then cooked.

How to make jam

Use only ripe – or a mixture of ripe and half-ripe – healthy fruit without any blemishes. Do not use over-ripe fruit, as the pectin (plant jelly) content will be too low (see table p. 349).

1. Wash the fruit, peel and prepare as directed for the specific type of jam; for instance, strawberries and other types of berries, figs and tomatoes may be left whole; ripe apricots are usually halved.

2. Weigh the fruit and calculate the amount of sugar needed. Use equal quantities of sugar and whole fruit. Add 50 ml lemon juice for every 2 kg of fruit.
3. Boil firm, hard fruits slowly in very little water in a large, heavy-based saucepan, covered. Berries or soft fruit may be mixed with the sugar and heated slowly – they do not need to be boiled in water first.
4. Add the sugar to the fruit and heat gently, uncovered, in the saucepan. Stir slightly to ensure that the sugar melts. Juicy fruits, such as berries, may be layered alternately with the sugar and left overnight, then boiled the following day.
5. When all the sugar has dissolved, boil fairly rapidly to ensure a light colour. Stir gently once in a while with a wooden spoon.
6. Test the jam to see if it is ready:
   - Place a little jam on a saucer – it should set if it is done; *or*
   - Use a sugar thermometer. The temperature of the jam should be 5°C (9°F) higher than that of boiling water.
7. With a slotted spoon skim the foam off the top and ladle the jam into warm sterilized jars, filling to within 8 mm of the top of the jar. Seal while hot and store in a cool, dry place.

Note:
- How much pectin there is in a fruit determines how well the jam will set.
- Boil only about 2 kg jam at a time to ensure the best results.
- The texture of jam should be soft and mushy and there should be enough syrup or jelly.
- The jam should not be so sweet that it masks the taste of the fruit.

To skin gooseberries and grapes, plunge them into boiling water and the skins will slide off.

hulled strawberries
750 g sugar per 1 kg fruit
25 to 30 ml lemon juice per
1,5 kg fruit

640   Strawberry jam

1. Determine the mass of the strawberries. Pack the fruit and sugar in alternate layers in a stainless steel or enamel saucepan and leave overnight.
2. Heat very slowly, stirring occasionally until the sugar has dissolved. Add the lemon juice.
3. Boil rapidly until the jam is ready, stirring occasionally to prevent burning.
4. Skim the surface of the jam to remove the scum and pour into hot sterilized bottles. Seal immediately.

Note: Use this method for all berry jams.

jam tomatoes, skinned
750 g sugar per 1 kg tomatoes
25 to 30 ml lemon juice per
1,5 kg tomatoes

641   Tomato jam

1. Determine the mass of the tomatoes, then chop them coarsely.
2. Pack the tomatoes and sugar in alternate layers in a stainless steel or enamel saucepan and proceed as for strawberry jam.

apricots, halved and stones removed
100 ml water per 1,5 kg fruit
750 g sugar per 1 kg fruit for sweet fruit and 1 kg for acid fruit

642 Apricot jam

1. Determine the mass of the fruit.
2. Place the fruit and the water in a saucepan and simmer, covered, until the fruit is tender.
3. Add the sugar and heat slowly, stirring occasionally, until all the sugar has dissolved.
4. Boil rapidly until ready and skim to remove the scum from the surface.
5. Pour the jam into hot sterilized bottles and seal immediately.

black or green grapes, pips removed
750 g sugar per 1 kg fruit
25 to 30 ml lemon juice per 1,5 kg fruit

643 Grape jam

Determine the mass of the fruit and continue as for apricot jam.

ripe figs, peeled
250 ml water per 1,5 kg fruit
750 g sugar per 1 kg fruit
50 to 60 ml lemon juice per 1,5 kg fruit

644 Fig jam

1. Determine the mass of the fruit and boil until tender in the water.
2. Mash or liquidise the fruit to make it smooth, then add the sugar and lemon juice and proceed as for apricot jam.

JELLY

Jelly is a clear, shiny and fairly stiff 'jam' made from fruit that is high in pectin and acid. These substances are highest in fruits just before they ripen, but not all jellies are made from green fruit: sometimes green and ripe fruits are mixed. The pectin and acid content of fruit must be measured before the jelly is boiled and, if not high enough, commercial pectin or lemon juice added. How much pectin there is will determine how much sugar will be needed.

Pectin and acid content of fruit:

High in pectin and acid	High in pectin but low in acid	High in acid but low in pectin	Low in pectin and acid
Sour apples	Sweet apples	Strawberries	Ripe pears
Quinces	Ripe quinces	Rhubarb	Peaches
Marula	Green figs	Ripe apricots	Ripe figs
Catawba grapes	Green bananas	Pineapples	All other ripe fruit
Sour grapes	Green pears	Pomegranates	
Gooseberries			
Plums			
Loganberries			
Lemons			
Grapefruit			
Oranges with pips			
Loquats			

Note: The peel and pips of oranges, quinces and apples are boiled with the fruit and the juice extracted because they are high in pectin.

There are 4 stages to making jelly: extracting the juice, the pectin test and adding the sugar, boiling the jelly and filling and sealing the jars.

Extracting the juice

1. Wash and cut the fruit in large pieces, leaving the peel or skin intact. Add water as indicated below:

Fruit	Amount of water per 500 g fruit	Time needed to extract juice
Gooseberries	65 ml	5 to 10 minutes
Sour apples	500 ml	20 to 25 minutes
Booysenberries	65 ml	5 to 10 minutes
Catawba grapes	65 ml	5 to 10 minutes
Youngberries	–	5 to 10 minutes
Crab-apples	250 ml	20 to 25 minutes
Guava	250 ml	25 minutes
Quinces	500 ml	60 minutes
Plums (Gaviota)	125 ml	15 to 20 minutes
Citrus fruits	500 ml for every 250 ml (1 cup) of shredded fruit	45 minutes
All other berries	250 ml for every 2,5 kg fruit	15 minutes

2. Boil the fruit and water rapidly, uncovered, stirring now and then.
3. Place a layer of cheesecloth in a sieve, then a layer of cottonwool and another layer of cheesecloth. Pour the juice and pulp into the sieve, a little at a time. *Do not stir or press the pulp* or the jelly may be cloudy; allow the juice to drip through at its own pace.

Note: The pulp may be placed in a saucepan, covered with water and boiled again, but this will yield an inferior jelly.

The pectin test and adding the sugar

1. Measure 10 ml methylated spirits into a glass and carefully add 10 ml boiled fruit juice. Do not stir, but rotate the glass gently to mix.
2. Leave for 5 seconds, then pour out onto a saucer. A clot of jelly will form: if it is firm, this indictes a high pectin content; if two medium-sized blobs form, this indicates a moderate pectin content; and if a number of small clots form, this indicates a low pectin content. If no clots form, commercial pectin or lemon juice should be added.
3. Add the sugar: for juice with a high pectin content, add 250 ml (1 cup) sugar for every 250 ml juice; for juice with a moderate pectin content, add 190 ml (¾ cup) sugar for every 250 ml juice.
4. Stir well and heat slowly to boiling point.
5. Strain the juice again as described above to ensure that a clear jelly is obtained.

350

Boiling the jelly
1. Place the strained juice in the saucepan and bring to the boil, uncovered.
2. Boil rapidly, without stirring.
3. Use a sugar thermometer to see if the jelly is done: the temperature should be 105 °C (221 °F); 5 °C (9 °F) higher than the boiling point of water at sea-level. Allow for a temperature drop of 0,5 °C (1 °F) for every 152 metres above sea-level. If you do not have a sugar thermometer, spoon a little jelly onto a plate, allow to cool and press lightly to test if it is firm.

Note:
- Do not boil more than 2 litres of the juice at a time.
- Use a large, heavy-based saucepan as jelly has a tendency to boil over.
- Just before the jelly reaches the desired temperature, add the acid: 12,5 ml lemon juice for 500 ml juice. This will ensure that the jelly becomes firm enough.

Bottling the jelly
1. Fill sterilized, warm jars completely with the hot jelly.
2. Leave to cool, then seal with little rounds of paper dipped in brandy or with a layer of paraffin wax, and screw on the lids.

MARMALADE

Marmalade is jelly with pieces of citrus fruit in it. Any single citrus fruit or a mixture of citrus fruits may be used: grapefruit and Seville oranges, for instance, yield a bitter marmalade; lemons, oranges and naartjies a sweet marmalade.

Note: The basic principles of jelly-making also apply to making marmalade.

Making marmalade
1. Wash the fruit well.
2. Cut the unpeeled fruit in thin strips, discarding the pips.
3. Soak for a few hours, or overnight, in 750 ml water for every 250 ml (1 cup) fruit.
4. Boil in the same water, covered, until tender. Measure the contents.
5. Test the juice for pectin as described on p. 348 and add sugar according to the pectin content.
6. Add the sugar to the hot mixture and stir well until all the sugar has dissolved.
7. Bring back to the boil and continue boiling rapidly, uncovered. Test to see if the marmalade is done and bottle in the same way as for jelly.

What went wrong:

Formation of mould
- Poor quality ingredients used
- Cold, wet jars used
- Storage place damp
- Sealing not airtight; cold air entered the jar

Crystallization
- Boiled before the sugar had dissolved completely
- Too much sugar added
- Too little acid present
- Overboiled
- Stirred too much while boiling

Fermentation
- Insufficient boiling
- Storage place too warm

Formation of air bubbles
- Poured into jars too quickly
- Poured into cold jars
- Jelly allowed to become too cool before bottling
- Boiled for too long

2 large lemons
750 ml sugar
1 litre water

645 Lemon marmalade

Makes 1 litre

1. Halve the lemons, slice them thinly and remove the pips.
2. Place the lemon slices in a bowl and pour over the boiling water. Leave overnight.
3. Transfer to a saucepan and cook gently, uncovered, until the fruit is tender and the liquid reduced by about one third.
4. Warm the sugar slightly in the oven, add it to the marmalade and stir until it dissolves.
5. Bring to the boil and boil rapidly until setting point is reached. Leave for 10 minutes, stir gently and bottle.

Note: Limes can also be used.

1 large orange, thinly peeled
1 large lemon, thinly peeled
1 grapefruit, thinly peeled
750 ml water per 250 ml fruit pulp
250 ml sugar per 250 ml fruit pulp
5 ml glycerine

646 Minced marmalade

Makes 1 litre

1. Wash the fruit, remove the pips and mince finely.
2. Place the fruit and water in a saucepan and boil for 5 minutes.
3. Add the sugar and heat gently, stirring occasionally, until the sugar has dissolved.
4. Stir in the glycerine and boil rapidly until the marmalade jells.
5. Pour into hot sterilized bottles and leave to cool. Seal the next day.

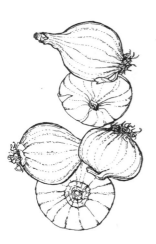

Either vegetables or fruit may be used to make *pickles,* but remember always that they must be fresh and young for the best flavour. Using green or half-ripe fruit and vegetables will ensure that the pickles are firm and crisp. White vinegar is generally used because, although its flavour is superior, brown vinegar colours the pickles – only pickled onions are steeped in brown vinegar. Pickles may also be made with curry. Most pickles should be stored for 2 to 3 months before use.

Note: Never allow metal to come into contact with the pickles while preparing or bottling, as the vinegar will corrode it.

Chutneys, served with curries or to brighten up cold meats, may be made from either ripe or dried fruit. They are very easy to make, and keep well.

Note: While it is not necessary to sterilize the jars for bottled pickles or chutney, make sure that the jars are very clean before you fill them.

---

1 kg pickling onions
1 bottle brown vinegar
5 ml (1 teaspoon) salt
10 ml (2 teaspoons) pickling spice (optional)

647   Pickled onions

Makes 4 litres

1. Peel the onions and cut a cross in the stalk end.
2. Place the onions, vinegar, pickling spice and salt in a saucepan and simmer, covered, for 20 minutes.
3. Bottle in hot sterilized bottles, seal and let stand in a cool, dry place for at least 1 week before use.

Note: If a really crisp result is desired, do not simmer the onions, but place them directly in sterilized bottles, add the other ingredients and seal.

---

500 ml (2 cups) gherkins, coarsely chopped
500 ml (2 cups) cucumber, thickly sliced
500 ml (2 cups) pickling onions
250 ml (1 cup) green beans, sliced
1 small cauliflower, broken into flowerets
6 small carrots, cut in strips
spiced vinegar
Brine solution:
500 g salt
5 litres water

648   Mixed pickles

Makes 5 litres

1. Place the vegetables in a large pottery or earthenware basin, cover with the brine and leave for 2 days.
2. Drain, and pour fresh water over. Leave for 2 hours.
3. Plunge the vegetables into boiling water, then drain.
4. Pack into clean, hot, dry bottles and fill with boiling hot spiced vinegar. Seal immediately.

Note: Hard vegetables must be brought to the boil, not just dipped in the boiling water.

4 green tomatoes, coarsely chopped
1 large cauliflower, broken into flowerets
500 g green beans, thickly sliced
2 cucumbers, coarsely chopped
500 g pickling onions
1 red chilli, coarsely chopped
salt
Sauce:
15 ml (3 teaspoons) curry powder
10 ml (2 teaspoons) turmeric
30 ml (6 teaspoons) mustard powder
50 ml (4 tablespoons) flour
50 ml (4 tablespoons) sugar
1 litre vinegar
5 ml (1 teaspoon) salt
1 ml (¼ teaspoon) cayenne pepper

649 Piccalilli

Makes 5 litres

1. Pack the vegetables in layers in an earthenware container, sprinkling each layer with a little salt. Leave for 24 hours.
2. Rinse thoroughly under running water and drain.
3. Transfer the vegetables to a large stainless steel or enamel saucepan, pour boiling water over and heat to boiling point. Remove from the stove and allow to cool. Drain.
4. Prepare the sauce. Combine the dry ingredients with a little of the vinegar to form a smooth paste.
5. Heat the rest of the vinegar to boiling point, add the paste a little at a time and bring to the boil again, stirring all the time.
6. Add the drained vegetables and boil for 5 minutes.
7. Turn into clean, dry, hot bottles and seal immediately.

---

375 ml (1½ cups) canned whole kernel corn, drained
125 ml (½ cup) celery, diced
12,5 ml (1 tablespoon) green pepper, seeded and finely chopped
1 red chilli, finely chopped
25 ml (2 tablespoons) brown sugar
37,5 ml wine vinegar
1 ml (¼ teaspoon) turmeric
2 ml (½ teaspoon) salt
1 ml (¼ teaspoon) pepper

650 Corn relish

Makes 500 ml

1. Combine all the ingredients except the chilli in a saucepan. Heat to nearly boiling, then stir in the chilli.
2. Remove from the stove and allow to cool. Transfer to clean bottles, seal and refrigerate.

Note: Use this relish within a week.

---

500 ml (2 cups) dried figs, finely chopped
1 lemon, thinly sliced
1 green apple, peeled, cored and diced
5 ml (1 teaspoon) ginger, finely chopped or 2 ml (½ teaspoon) ground ginger
125 ml (½ cup) brown sugar
125 ml molasses
125 ml cider vinegar
2 ml (½ teaspoon) ground cloves
2 ml (½ teaspoon) ground cinnamon

651 Golden State chutney

Makes 1 litre

1. Combine all the ingredients in a large saucepan. Bring to the boil and reduce the heat, then simmer, uncovered, for 30 minutes. Allow to cool.
2. Pour into clean bottles, seal and store in the refrigerator. Serve as an accompaniment to pork, lamb and chicken.

Variations:
1. Add 10 ml (2 teaspoons) sunflower seeds.
2. Use stoned Satsuma plums instead of the figs.

354

500 g dried peaches
500 g dried apricots
500 g stoned dates
500 g seedless raisins
1 clove garlic, crushed
400 g sugar
1,5 litres vinegar mixed with
500 ml water
1 ml (¼ teaspoon) ground
cinnamon
15 ml (3 teaspoons) salt
1 ml (¼ teaspoon) cayenne
pepper

652 Fruit chutney

Makes 2 litres

1. Soak the peaches and apricots overnight in water to cover. Drain.
2. Mince all the fruit together and place in a saucepan.
3. Add all the other ingredients and simmer, stirring occasionally, until the chutney thickens, about 2 hours.
4. Bottle and seal immediately.

---

2 kg ripe peaches, peeled and
stoned
500 g tart apples, peeled and
cored
500 g sultanas
1 medium onion
1 clove garlic
400 g sugar
1 litre vinegar
10 ml (2 teaspoons) ground
ginger
ml (1 teaspoon) ground
cinnamon
15 ml (3 teaspoons) salt
1 ml (¼ teaspoon) cayenne
pepper

653 Peach chutney

Makes 2 litres

1. Mince the peaches, sultanas, garlic and onion together and place in a large saucepan.
2. Add the other ingredients and boil, uncovered, until the chutney is thick, stirring occasionally.
3. Bottle and seal immediately.

---

2 tart apples, peeled and cored
1 kg tomatoes, skinned
2 medium onions, thinly sliced
200 g sultanas, minced
200 g sugar
400 ml vinegar
15 ml (3 teaspoons) mustard
powder
15 ml (3 teaspoons) ground
ginger
15 ml (3 teaspoons) salt
1 ml (¼ teaspoon) cayenne
pepper

654 Tomato chutney

Makes 2 litres

1. Combine all the ingredients except the sultanas in a large saucepan. Simmer, stirring occasionally, until the tomatoes and apples are tender.
2. Rub through a coarse sieve or liquidise in a blender to form a purée. Return to the saucepan.
3. Stir in the sultanas and bring to the boil. Boil until the desired consistency is obtained, pour the chutney into clean bottles and seal immediately.

---

3 kg green mangoes, peeled
and thinly sliced
250 g seedless raisins, minced
400 g sugar
1 litre vinegar
5 ml (1 teaspoon) ground
ginger
5 ml (1 teaspoon) salt

655 Mango chutney

Makes 4 litres

1. Sprinkle the mangoes with salt and place all the ingredients in a large saucepan.
2. Simmer, uncovered, until the chutney is thick.
3. Pour into hot bottles and seal immediately.

355

Although most raw fruit may be frozen successfully, bananas, pears, grapes and avocado pears do not freeze well because they become soft and mushy when thawed. Fruits will freeze better if blanched beforehand.

Note:
- Do not freeze either green or over-ripe fruits.
- Fruit to be frozen must be bruise and blemish-free.

1. Sort and wash the fruit, preferably in ice-water.
2. Do not soak, but prepare for freezing immediately.
3. Peel and cut the fruit ready for eating; remember not to blanch fruit that is to be eaten raw.
4. Prepare only a small quantity of fruit at a time and freeze immediately.
5. Fruits which tend to brown may be treated as follows:
   - Soak the peeled, cut fruit for 15 minutes in a brine solution of 12,5 ml (1 tablespoon) salt per 2 litres of water. Rinse and pack in syrup. OR
   - Soak for 30 seconds in a solution of 50 ml lemon juice and 2 litres of water. Drain and pack in syrup. OR
   - Crush ascorbic acid (vitamin C) tablets and mix with the syrup for packing or add to 25 ml water if a dry sugar pack is to be used. Use a 1 500 mg tablet for 1 litre of syrup or a 375 mg tablet for every 125 g sugar.

   Note: A 375 mg ascorbic acid tablet equals 0,5 ml ascorbic acid powder.

6. Use a dry sugar pack for soft, juicy fruit: 500 g sugar plus 1 ml (¼ teaspoon) crushed ascorbic acid tablet for 2 kg fruit. Mix with 25 ml water. Sprinkle a layer of the sugar mixture over the bottom of rigid containers and pack a layer of fruit on top. Continue with these layers until all the fruit and sugar has been used. Leave 20 mm headspace to allow for expansion. Seal and freeze.
   Note: Pack berry fruits on a tray, sprinkle with sugar and freeze. When hard, remove from the tray, place in rigid containers or plastic bags, seal and freeze once more.
7. A syrup pack may also be used to freeze fruit. Make the syrup according to taste:
   Thin (Light): 250 ml (1 cup) sugar to 1 litre water
   Medium: 500 ml (2 cups) sugar to 1 litre water
   Thick (Heavy): 1 litre (4 cups) sugar to 1 litre water
   Quarter-fill the containers with the syrup and add the cut fruit, leaving 25 to 30 mm headspace for expansion. Seal and freeze.
   Note:
   - The syrup must cover the fruit completely.
   - Blanched fruit should be used in tarts.

Using frozen fruit
Whether frozen fruit is only half or completely thawed depends on how it is to be used:

- if it is to be eaten raw, leave the fruit in its container and thaw in the refrigerator for 1 hour. Serve while still partially frozen: if allowed to thaw completely, frozen fruit will become soft and mushy.
- if it is to be used in pies, thaw completely before adding to the pastry shell.

Freezing fruit juices

Only ripe fruit should be used to extract juice. All fruits except citrus and berry fruits can be liquidised and then frozen. Chill *citrus fruits* in the refrigerator for 1 hour, then squeeze out the juice and pour into rigid containers, leaving 25 mm headspace for expansion. Seal and freeze. Crush *berries* and heat to just below boiling point, stirring all the time. Strain if necessary and freeze in rigid containers. *Strawberries* do not need to be heated; crush, strain and then freeze.

Note:

- Freeze juice in quantities ready for use, and treat as fresh juice after thawing.
- Lemon juice may be frozen in ice-trays. Remove when hard and pack in plastic bags for use in sauces and drinks.

INDEX

Entries in this index refer to page, not to recipe, numbers.

358

LIST OF ILLUSTRATIONS

Note: Meat charts on p. 96 to 98 adapted with the permission of the Meat Board.